Whitman's Presence

WHITMAN'S PRESENCE

Body, Voice, and Writing in
Leaves of Grass

Tenney Nathanson

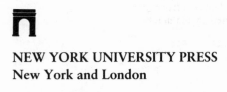

NEW YORK UNIVERSITY PRESS
New York and London

811.38
W6l5zn

New York University Press
New York and London

Copyright © 1992 by New York University

Library of Congress Cataloging-in-Publication Data
Nathanson, Tenney.
Whitman's presence : body, voice, and writing in Leaves of grass /
Tenney Nathanson.
p. cm.
Includes bibliographical references and index.
ISBN 0-8147-5770-7 (alk. paper)
1. Whitman, Walt, 1819–1892. Leaves of grass. I. Title.
PS3238.N38 1992
811'.3—dc20

92-1309
CIP

New York University Press books are printed on acid-free paper,
and their binding materials are chosen for strength and durability.

Manufactured in the United States of America

c 10 9 8 7 6 5 4 3 2 1

*For Quentin Anderson
and in memory of my father
Jerome Nathanson*

. . . let us be quite clear that the expression "use of language" can cover other matters even more diverse than the illocutionary and perlocutionary acts and obviously quite diverse from any with which we are here concerned. . . . There are aetiolations, parasitic uses, etc., various "not serious" and "not full normal" uses. The normal conditions of reference may be suspended, or no attempt made at a standard perlocutionary act, no attempt to make you do anything, as Walt Whitman does not seriously incite the eagle of liberty to soar.

—J. L. Austin, *How To Do Things with Words*

Walt Whitman inciting the Bird of Freedom to Soar.
Cartoon by Max Beerbohm. Courtesy of Mrs. Eva Reichman.

Whoever you are, now I place my hand upon you, that you be my poem,
I whisper with my lips close to your ear,
I have loved many women and men, but I love none better than you.

—"To You"

Contents

Acknowledgments

Many friends and colleagues contributed essential suggestions and encouragement to this project. I want to thank David Greenlee, Anneta Greenlee, Floyd Byars, Julie Silverman, Steve Berkowitz, and John Johnston for their support; Herbert Schneidau, Jerrold Hogle, and Susan White for their insightful comments; and Donald Pease for his reading of an earlier version of chapter 4, which proved crucial. I am especially grateful to Edgar Dryden, Patrick O'Donnell, Kenneth Gross, and Lynda Zwinger for their advice and their astute criticism of the manuscript. I also want to thank Jason Renker and Despina Gimbel of New York University Press for their help in seeing the book through to publication.

My greatest debt is to Quentin Anderson. He has supported this project since its inception with unfailing enthusiasm, generosity, and acumen.

Portions of the manuscript, now re-written and re-distributed, first appeared in *ESQ* (1985), *The Journal of Comparative Literature and Aesthetics* (1986), and *Mickle Street Review* (1986); permission to reprint this material is gratefully acknowledged. The author also gratefully acknowledges financial support from the University of Arizona Foundation and the University of Arizona Faculty of Humanities, and release time awarded by the University of Arizona Department of English. Publication of this book was made possible in part by a grant from the University of Arizona Provost's Author Support Fund.

Finally, I wish to thank the following for granting me permission to quote from copyrighted material:

Extracts from *Of Grammatology* by Jacques Derrida, English translation copyright 1976 by The Johns Hopkins University Press, are reprinted by permission of The Johns Hopkins University Press.

Abbreviations

1855	*Leaves of Grass: The First (1855) Edition* (ed. Cowley)
1856	*Leaves of Grass: Facsimile of 1856 Edition* (introd. Allen)
1860	*Leaves of Grass: Facsimile Edition of the 1860 Text* (introd. Pearce)
CORR	*The Correspondence* (ed. Miller)
CRE	*Leaves of Grass: Comprehensive Reader's Edition* (ed. Blodgett and Bradley)
CW	*The Complete Writings of Walt Whitman* (ed. Bucke et al.)
DBN	*Daybooks and Notebooks* (ed. White)
NUPM	*Notebooks and Unpublished Prose Manuscripts* (ed. Grier)
PW	*Prose Works 1892* (ed. Stovall)
UPP	*The Uncollected Poetry and Prose of Walt Whitman* (ed. Holloway)
V	*Leaves of Grass: A Textual Variorum of the Printed Poems* (ed. Bradley et al.)
WWC	*With Walt Whitman in Camden* (Traubel)

1. Declarations

GLENDOWER: I can call spirits from the vasty deep.
HOTSPUR: Why so can I, or so can any man, but will they come when you do call for them?

—*Henry IV*, Part I, III, i

In "Crossing Brooklyn Ferry," one of the major new poems Whitman composed for the 1856 edition of *Leaves of Grass,* the poet interrupts the excited but troubled account he has been offering his audience of his daily life as a denizen of Manhattan and a frequenter of Brooklyn harbor to turn directly to us, making some startling claims and posing some unnerving questions:

> Closer yet I approach you,
> What thought you have of me, I had as much of you—I laid in my stores in advance,
> I considered long and seriously of you before you were born.
>
> Who was to know what should come home to me?
> Who knows but I am enjoying this?
> Who knows but I am as good as looking at you now, for all you cannot see me? (1856 218)[1]

Whitman's attentive concern here may strike us as touching; but these lines possess an uncanny quality that makes their very solicitude unsettling. Their disconcerting effect turns on the poet's suggestion that he is hovering near us as an invisible but actual presence as we encounter his poem.

Such suggestions abound in the early editions of *Leaves of Grass,* and despite their air of being affectionate digressions from the principal business at hand they possess an imaginative urgency unsurpassed in Whitman's work.[2] In his early editions Whitman attributes preternaturally active powers both to his poems and to the figure of the poet who

I

stands at their center, and at its best his work does bear on us with an immediacy not ordinarily associated with poetry: the figure who is said to rise up and appear to us in the poet's direct addresses to his audience seems to overflow the boundaries of the very work that conveys him to us, to shuck off his status as a fictive character existing in a literary representation and impinge on us personally and directly. This unlikely sense of immediacy exerted by the poems is one of Whitman's finest accomplishments. Early readers of *Leaves of Grass* were perhaps the most extravagant, but by no means the only members of Whitman's audience to experience the transports induced by the poems' supposed active powers. Their fantasies of having undergone intense and intimate encounters with the poet himself, encounters that already initiated them into the pleasures supposedly afforded by his actual living presence, may strike us as naive.[3] But this naivete is one the poems themselves encourage and indeed depend on; our reaction registers the presence and attests to the powers of the figure *Leaves of Grass* claims to produce. Whitman's work thus demands an ingenuous reading, from the critic as well as the casual reader, though our encounter with *Leaves of Grass* ought not to be wholly shaped by such innocent suspension of disbelief. The presence our credulity sustains embodies and seems to fulfill the "omnivorous" ambitions Whitman announced more than once as motivating *Leaves of Grass.*

The world that presence implies might best be called magical: the figure Whitman's apostrophes announce seems to subdue time, space, and the identities of other persons to his own extensible identity; standing at the center of the universe the poems bring into being, the poet diffuses himself until that center is everywhere.[4] An address to us early in "Crossing Brooklyn Ferry" suggests the unlikely range of this presence, foregoing the slightly teasing, flirtatious quality of Whitman's later questions to declare explicitly that the poet flows effortlessly through time and space to impinge on us immediately and directly:

> It avails not, neither time or space—distance avails not,
> I am with you, you men and women of a generation, or ever so many generations hence,
> I project myself, also I return—I am with you, and know how it is. (1856 212–13)

The infinite domain of this emanating figure is oddly compounded with the personal relation he seems to enjoy with particular members of his audience. Claiming to diffuse himself through space and time, he also rests familiarly in particular places and moments, and incongruously approaches each of his auditors as if involved with him or her alone. Thus the panoramic outlook of the 1860 "Starting from Paumanok" narrows to the dimensions of a private communion as our poet suggests he is "coming personally to you now" (1860 19). And at its close, the poem modulates into a quiet declaration of the sort of tender, eroticized encounter this presence so frequently promises us:

O my comrade!
O you and me at last—and us two only. (1860 22)

Despite Whitman's gesture of election here, this sudden focusing of the poet's attentions may not be wholly reassuring; the figure who singles us out for this communion is himself rather hard to pin down. At once ubiquitous and local, the poet's presence also compounds the physical and the vaporous; repeatedly claiming to impinge on us as an actual, embodied presence, he nonetheless enjoys an elusiveness that suggests the immaterial. While his physical presence is most often the aspect that needs insisting on, this figure's uncanny effect typically depends on the unlikely conjunction of these two qualities:

This is the press of a bashful hand . . . . this is the float and odor of hair,
This is the touch of my lips to yours . . . . this is the murmur of yearning.
   ("Song of Myself," 1855 42)

Though an actual physical presence is announced here, the irresistible intimacy this figure seems to enjoy depends on an obverse quality that remains unstated: we are caressed, as it were, by a phantom. This labile presence is indeed, as Whitman declares in "Song of Myself," "around, tenacious, acquisitive, tireless . . . . and can never be shaken away" (1855 31).

For all his occasional wistfulness, the figure implied by such announcements can thus also impinge on us in a manner more invasive and disturbing. In "Crossing Brooklyn Ferry" the poet is said not only to approach but also to commingle with those he addresses, suffusing us by means of an unnamed force "which fuses me into you now, and pours my meaning into you" (1856 219). Flowing not only around us but also within us, he subdues our individual identities to his emanating form.

The resonance of such transactions depends in part on their ability to activate simultaneously normally divergent associations. The very strangeness of these intensely imagined encounters is crucial to their effect:

> Whoever you are, now I place my hand upon you, that you be my poem,
> I whisper with my lips close to your ear,
> I have loved many women and men, but I love none better than you. ("To You," 1856 206–207)

Difficult to gauge, the poet's idiom here might be seductive or sacramental, promising either amorous encounter or apotheosis. A tone of voice that might initiate both these prospects at once is hard to imagine—a sign that neither mystical insight nor sexual liberation, nor even some happy resolution of the two, quite encompasses what these announcements portend. The poet's advent seems to transfigure the very possibilities to which it alludes, redeeming us by means of a transaction we do not quite know how to specify. Both tangible and intangible, incarnate and ideal, this figure impinges on us as body and utterance, presence and word, folding us into a unity for which we have no single name unless it be that of the poet himself.

This focal strangeness typically disappears from accounts of *Leaves of Grass*. The poet's presence severely strains the received vocabularies commonly employed to account for him; efforts to describe Whitman's work in these familiar terms tend to slight or subdue the poet's unruly effects rather than attend to them, deflecting our attention from the unsettling urgency with which the poems bear on us. So Whitman is sometimes described as the apostle of the body, celebrating sexual liberation—or else as a visionary intent on expounding his mystical sense of the soul. In these narratives the poet's presence is characteristically regarded as a slightly quirky trope for some such stable term. Edwin Miller, for example, describes "Crossing Brooklyn Ferry" as "a hedonistic statement of faith" (200) and "a sustained hymn to joy—the joy of the sensuous body"(199); the poet's diffusing presence is regarded as the emissary of such good tidings, though it violates the very laws and limitations to which all ordinary bodies (however sensuous) are subject (205). This description can be instructively juxtaposed to James Miller's reading of "Crossing Brooklyn Ferry" as an early example of Whitman's mystical bent, an account that also runs into difficulties over the poet's claim that he projects himself directly to us. "This suggestion of the poet's physical presence," Miller remarks with some loss of composure, "perhaps meant to shock with its novelty, is surely intended to imply the immanence of spiritual union" (86).

Such wholly opposed readings indicate more than simple disagreement: they suggest that the very vocabularies employed cannot be applied to the first three editions of *Leaves of Grass* without a certain slippage. "Body" and "soul," for example, can no longer be defined through mutual opposition. Too vaporous and elusive to be thought of as an ordinary body, yet claiming to impinge on us in the here and now of our actual world with too much quirky specificity to be thought of as a soul, the poet's presence effaces the very distinction between the material and the spiritual from which those terms ordinarily take their meanings. It also elides the distinction between the transitory and the eternal: speaking from its own particular time and place, this presence seems also to transcend it, projecting itself through intervals of time, as well as space, it thereby annuls.[5] It can pronounce itself to be "here" and mean everywhere; it can say it speaks "now" and mean forever. It can also suggest that it comes "personally to you now" and be speaking at once to everyone; inaugurating an encounter supposedly intimate yet also universal, it exerts a peculiar, centripetal pressure on the individuals it reaches, disturbing the very notion of discrete identity.

The oppositions thus subverted are not of course irrelevant to *Leaves of Grass*. We can find Whitman worrying the quandaries they suggest in some of his slacker stretches: the poems abound in declarations concerning the body and soul; the material and the spiritual; the many and the one; surface appearance and underlying reality; spatial dispersion and its transcendence; time and eternity.[6] Yet elaborate efforts to read *Leaves of Grass* as the working through of some philosophical insight tend to accord Whitman's conceptual labors more intensity than the poems authenticate—they indeed typically solemnize the very vocabulary with which Whitman's early editions play fast and loose. In his announcements of the poet's presence Whitman short-circuits such polarities rather than reconciling them systematically; this peremptory subversion is one sign of the poet's power. Despite Whitman's penchant for the sweeping, doctrinaire pronouncement, the cosmic good news the poet of the early work is intent on telling us turns out to be less important than how he claims to be able to tell it: directly and personally to each of us, whoever and wherever we may be, and whenever we may live.[7] Rather than celebrating multiplicity or subduing the world to some governing principle or value, whether physical or spiritual, Whitman's work tames dispersion and difference by means of a more archaic transaction: it subsumes them within an agglomerating space defined by and indeed finally indistinguishable from the poet's own effusing presence.[8]

We can begin to trace the archaic configuration Whitman's declarations of the poet's presence evoke, and to see how this organization pre-empts the very contraries I have been detailing, by attending more closely to the linguistic features of these announcements. They do not quite seem to be statements of fact:

> It avails not, neither time or place—distance avails not,
> I am with you [. . . .] (1856 212)

This hardly strikes us as simply descriptive; to regard this utterance as a statement, the report of an already existent condition, is to subdue rather than account for the eerie feeling it provokes. The peculiar pressure of this announcement derives instead from the implication that an invisible presence is rising up to hover near us precisely *as* we hear these words. Though it might be suggested that he must have been here already—we simply didn't realize it till he told us so—it is more likely that the declaration disconcerts us by making us feel that the very words which announce the speaker's presence also produce it. The proclamation seems to be conjuring up the figure it names, to be making true what it declares. Rather than being a statement of fact, it operates as a performative utterance.

Performatives, as J. L. Austin defined them, make something true by virtue of declaring it: "I now," for example, "pronounce you man and wife." As this single instance should suggest—you haven't after all just been married as you read this—the locutions Austin isolated operate only in circumstances sanctioned by custom: the performatives he described "make something true" only within the symbolic realm of codified human institutions and practices. Whitman's performative aspirations, it should be clear, are more grand. Rather than simply altering somebody's social status, the declarations I have been considering claim to produce an actual presence by speaking. Throughout his early work, Whitman aspires to the word magic of the shaman: the sense of words the early poems seek to convey has more in common with the archaic belief in the magical power of naming than with a reflective awareness of the constitutive role language plays in shaping the symbolic space a culture shares.[9] Though Whitman was unusually attentive to the force of this sort of symbolic authority, I shall be arguing that his declarations of the poet's presence are attempts to ward off its effects by activating a power anterior to its operation and exempt from its interference.[10]

Performative declarations that suggest the magical efficacy of the word abound in Whitman's early work.[11] At their most dramatic, Whitman's performatives claim to produce actual presences, disposing creatures and objects by intoning their names as easily as the poet conjures up his own presence by declaring it. "See! steamers steaming through my poems!" he proclaims in "Starting from Paumanok,"

> See, in my poems, old and new cities, solid, vast, inland, with paved streets, with iron and stone edifices, and ceaseless vehicles, and commerce. (1860 21)

In such announcements, object and name are radically conflated: the word attests to the presence of what it names, as if the name were fused with its referent.[12] In the magical universe of *Leaves of Grass* the poet himself is the key instance of such fusion: the word that announces him to us does not simply stand for the poet's presence but apparently produces and is indeed part of it. Consubstantial with this presence, the word infuses it with its own qualities: supposedly impinging on us as a physical being, the poet seems to be an ideal entity capable of innumerable manifestations or embodiments.

What we might call Whitman's image of voice is crucial to this fusion of body and word the poems strive to suggest.[13] In *Leaves of Grass* voice is both the irrefutable sign of the poet's presence and its crucial synecdoche. Whitman's appeal to voice helps account for the fact that the poet's declarations of his own presence manage to attain an uncanny immediacy his other performative transactions often lack. His claims that real objects inhabit his poems may sometimes strike us as unintended instances of poetry making the visible a little hard to see. The poet's projected presence, of course, is itself rather difficult to glimpse. Yet the relation between Whitman's declarations and the creature they claim to conjure up is nonetheless oddly indissoluble:

> I am with you. ("Crossing Brooklyn Ferry," 1856 212)

We may not see this presence, but we do seem to hear it. Indeed, if we direct our attention for a moment to the voice Whitman works to make us think we hear, this announcement reduces itself to tautology: what is declared is the speaker's presence; but our casual sense of hearing this announcement already implies what it proclaims—someone must be present to make it. The very utterance that announces the poet's performative claim seems to be evidence of its fulfillment; in such announcements, voice itself seems to possess performative efficacy.

In these declarations, moreover, voice also defines the presence to which it attests. The presence projected by the poems is as it were a living being who possesses all the powers voice seems to exercise, while being compromised by none of the limitations attendant on the fact that we are not simply our voices. This presence projects itself as easily as a voice can emanate and project its sound. Also sharing the voice's fluidity, no longer contained within the bounding surfaces that restrict ordinary bodies, the poet acquires a magical ability to fuse himself into us, commingling his presence with our own. This presence modeled on voice already implies the peculiar world in which, as Whitman declares in "Song of Myself," "every atom belonging to me as good belongs to you" (1855 25).

Voice is a crucial mediating trope in Whitman's work: defining the figure of the poet, it melds presence and language, body and name. Seeming sometimes like a disembodied voice seeking wistfully to incarnate itself, the poet's presence can also suggest to us a numinous, still unfallen body. Produced by speech and modeled on the voice, that presence still shares the ideality of the words that name him—an ideality which the voice with its vaporous quality both figures and translates toward an incarnation the poet's performative announcements claim to complete; voice both attests to the productive, incarnating power of language and suggests that what the word incarnates still shares the ideality of its origins. The productive force voice thus implies is crucial to the poet in several respects: embodied by and as the word in an act of spontaneous self-creation, the poet seems not to occupy the sort of self-divided body that has been shaped by the history of its interactions with others or its encounters with cultural constraints and inscriptions; instead he can regenerate himself in always identical form, as the unchanging, ideal figure language names.

This vision of word magic, projected most powerfully in the direct addresses to us that engender the poet's presence, is a crucial determinant of the imaginative space of Whitman's work. In *Leaves of Grass* the productive power of voice which the poet's apostrophes suggest is balanced by the magical vocative pull seemingly activated by Whitman's notorious catalogues. The magic word, producing the poet himself as a figure immune to mediation, also recalls his objects from an adversarial space shaped by distance and difference, collapsing them into the plenum of the poet's identity.

But in *Leaves of Grass* Whitman's figure of voice also recalls a fantasmatic space anterior to that shaped by word magic, a more archaic organization than that implied by the apparent power of voice to incarnate or retrieve the things it names. The presence evoked by Whitman's apostrophes is also the crucial instance of this prior relation between body and voice. It not only suggests that a body might share the undefiled ideality of the word that generates it, a trait implied by the poet's power of punctual self-production. The presence evoked by and modeled on voice, I suggested above, is also notable for its lability: it no sooner incarnates itself than it dissolves; scudding, scooting, effusing, and flowing are all processes that characterize this presence either directly or through metonymic suggestion. In *Leaves of Grass* the voice that conjures up this elusive presence shares and perhaps defines its fluidity. The preferences concerning voice declared in section five of "Song of Myself" —"Not words, not music or rhyme I want . . . . not custom or lecture, not even the best / Only the lull I like, the hum of your valved voice" (1855 28)—turn out to be characteristic; in Whitman's work voice is repeatedly praised for echolalic qualities that certainly resemble and perhaps determine the kinesthetic traits of the body they announce. Ascribing such traits to primitive languages, Whitman evokes a superseded but supposedly retrievable relation between body and voice that can profitably be associated with psychic as well as cultural archaism: the poet's body in *Leaves of Grass* recalls an organization in which vocal and kinesthetic rhythms interact to shape a labile, diffuse sense of body and self. Both transmuted and extended by the word magic that succeeds this formation, the ties among body, voice, and word in *Leaves of Grass* work to sustain a sense of agglomerating identity that wards off threats of division and difference as immediate as the impending war that shadowed Whitman's book and as global as our subjection to cultural encoding.[14]

As tangential to lyric tradition as this archaic universe may seem, the vision of language and voice that shapes it is central to poetry: lyric apostrophe, both Paul de Man and Jonathan Culler have recently suggested, may be not an embarrassing period aberration but a crucial sign of powers to which lyric speech characteristically aspires; as Culler notes, apostrophe implies a world where "presence and absence" are "governed not by time but by poetic power" ("Apostrophe" 150).[15] Neither Culler nor de Man, however, evinces much interest in the relation between such lyric speech acts and the linguistic and social space that surrounds poetry, or in the psychic terrain lyric apostrophe implies.[16] An encounter with *Leaves of Grass* obtrudes such issues on our attention forcibly, since in Whitman's work the power of a magic speech is explicitly brought to bear on the constricting linguistic, social, and psychic structures that inhibit the poet. For all the extremity of its claims, *Leaves of Grass* thus turns out to be oddly exemplary: Whitman's work suggests that lyric apostrophe is a culturally sanctioned site in which we entertain the atavistic belief in what Freud called word magic or the omnipotence of thought.[17] The apostrophes in *Leaves of Grass* that claim to produce the poet's presence give this vision of mastery radical embodiment. If poetic apostrophe typically works to subject the external world to the power of language, overcoming spatial and temporal intervals by means of the invocatory power of address, Whitman's announcements seem to annul these manifolds altogether, re-shaping time and space as the place and occasion of the poet's utterance, the singular "here" and "now" his proclamations announce and seem to create. And the figure who wields such powers, we have just seen, has himself been re-defined by them: giving the poet's speech a body, this presence impinges on us as the magical incarnation of the word. The satisfactions afforded by this mythic personage and the speech whose powers he embodies compel a fascination we can rightly call uncanny.[18] To feel the extrinsic and contingent attributes that shape ordinary selves fall away like so many accidents as one conjures up one's own self-generating presence; to shape a magical space in which one creates or disposes objects as easily as one intones their names; to be oneself the body of this speech that weaves the world by naming it, to flow into and master other identities as easily as language weaves itself through names, as voices seem to animate the words they speak: these are the archaic satisfactions given voice for us in *Leaves of Grass*, prospects the poems name and claim to make true by virtue of that naming.

Central to *Leaves of Grass* and its imaginative appeal, such dreams are suggested by unlikely means; the poems finesse their crucial transactions with us and thus eventually provoke the skeptical response they try to preclude. Claiming to conjure up a body that is less like a body than a voice, *Leaves of Grass* seems to accomplish this feat by means of a voice that is like no voice we have ever heard. Whitman's announcements do appeal to our experience of actual voices to lend the poet's proclamations credibility: when ordinary voices announce that their owners are present, they must be in the vicinity or we wouldn't hear their words. Yet these appeals are as canny as they are effective. Given the peculiar contexts in which they are made, the poet's claims that he speaks to us "here" and "now"—already implied by what we know of voices—trope such experience rather than simply reproducing it, creating the magical, virtually omnipotent voice that seems to speak in Whitman's poems: the poet's announcements to us seem to compress all space, from the landscape of the poem to "here," and all time, from a century ago till "now," into the modest intervals ordinary voices can traverse. It is not voice but Whitman's troping of voice that achieves the crucial re-figuring of the poet's presence.

That presence maintains its magical powers only so long as the machinery which stages Whitman's image of voice is not permitted to obtrude on and disrupt the scene it shapes. A disclaimer later deleted from the eighth section of "Crossing Brooklyn Ferry" may thus manage to strike us as outrageous without quite being surprising. We can there find Whitman carefully circumscribing the sort of encounter we are to imagine as taking place between ourselves and our poet. The crucial, later-deleted line is the final one, which as it were wards off a misunderstanding that might have dangerous consequences:

We understand, then, do we not?
What I promised without mentioning it, have you not accepted?
What the study could not teach—what the preaching could not accomplish is accomplished, is it not?
What the push of reading could not start is started by me personally, is it not? (1856 219)

This is audacious, since it patently flies in the face of simple fact: we are reading this poem and indeed this declaration. For the poet of the 1850s this improbable disavowal evidently seemed worth the risk of absurdity it ran; such announcements recur throughout the poems Whitman composed for his early editions. The fervor with which Whitman repeatedly denies the role of the very text we are reading, the sheer bluff with which he sometimes declares that *Leaves of Grass* is not a book, suggest that writing and reading possess an uncomfortable relation to the imaginative universe the poems generate. Declaring that the text of *Leaves of Grass* is either non-existent or incidental, Whitman tries to consign writing to a marginal place in which it would neither compromise nor constitute the poet's powers.

The fact that writing frustrates the poet's aspirations has long been recognized. Edwin Miller, for example, notes "Whitman's desire to transcend 'cold types' " and explains that, since the poet longs for intimate communication with his audience, writing and reading and the distance they imply must be wished away (12); he also suggests that the poet's amorous announcements of his presence are one crucial means of evoking the immediacy the poet desires (11). This notion that Whitman's apostrophes seem to generate a familiarity between poet and audience not usually attained by the written word has rightly become a truism of Whitman criticism.[19] Yet we may profitably puzzle over the role of writing and reading in Whitman's poems a bit longer here, as we shall do at greater length further on. The poet's denials of their function possess an urgency that does not quite seem adequately explained by the somewhat sentimental suggestion that Whitman wishes to widen the sphere of his intimacies to include his readers as well as his actual associates. Such an account scants the uncanny qualities of the figure who rises up by circumventing his text and declaring his immediate presence; and it fails to consider the strange relation between this presence and the book it claims to by-pass. Whitman's insistence that his poems are spoken does not simply extend his affectional range; it redefines the poet himself by endowing his presence with the apparent traits and powers of the voice. Yet even this voice is no ordinary one: it traverses not only space, but also time; it conveys not only sound, but a personal presence. It is just these aberrant traits that make the poet's voice and presence seem magical; and these aberrations have a close and uncomfortable connection to the writing which should play no part in the poet's announcements.

Whitman's disavowals of his book are typically lodged in the midst of just such visionary proclamations of the poet's manifestation:

> Camerado! This is no book,
> Who touches this, touches a man. ("So Long!" V 2:452)[20]

This announcement may not exactly deny the existence of the book we are reading; suspended ambiguously between the modes of statement and performance, it may instead prophesy or seek to enact a kind of transubstantiation, in which the text that preserves the poet's word and conveys it to us would be transformed into an actual voice and presence. Such pronouncements manage an unlikely, affecting grandeur. Yet the prestidigitation on which their visionary possibility depends implies an oddly indissoluble tie among the very terms whose relation the poet denies or seeks to transfigure: between the writing we are told we are not reading and the voice that seems to speak to us directly; between Whitman's text and the living person its supposed dissolution seems to conjure up. It is of course writing that makes the poet's voice seem magical, enabling it to traverse and collapse space and time. And it is only the sort of voice a text implies, a "voice" emanating from no actual physical source, that may seem to generate the diffuse, invisible presence the poems so unnervingly evoke. The poet's magical advent depends on a carefully deployed economy, on the simultaneous employment and effacing of the volume in which the words that announce him appear. The declaration in which Whitman denies his book is no mere sentimental gesture: it is the origin of the poet who creates himself by speaking, the birth of a god and the creation of a world suffused and shaped by his presence. Whitman needs to remind us to forget writing, in order that the poet may speak, and rise up and be revealed.[21]

The supreme fiction of *Leaves of Grass* is thus perhaps the myth of the poems' own mode. Admitted openly into the universe of *Leaves of Grass,* the writing that stages Whitman's image of voice, and lends that voice the resources that make it seem magical, would undermine the very powers its surreptitious use suggests. Whitman's countless diatribes against writing indeed spell out in some detail the limitations of this mechanism and suggest the liabilities of admitting the role it plays in the poems: if writing perfects the powers of the poet's voice and person, it perfects them only as the obverse of what they are declared to be. Writing, Whitman tells us himself, neither produces nor implies an actual presence; it re-presents words spoken in another place and time and offers us only the representation of the actual presence to which speech attests. Writing thus comes to represent all that separates the poet from his divine origins: dramatically detaching his presence from his word, it consigns him clearly to an ordinary body and leaves his language plainly bereft of the productive, performative power to which Whitman aspires.[22] All Whitman's most dramatic verbal gestures, I shall argue, finally situate themselves in just this gap. The words of Whitman's book recall a magical power they cannot re-capture or re-activate: deriding the merely representational function of ordinary language and seeking to reclaim the power of the word as magical act, Whitman's poems occupy the sometimes comic, often melancholy space in which such archaic performative power is itself represented rather than enacted.[23]

Whitman's recourse to writing marks this gap in *Leaves of Grass;* but it does not quite cause it. If writing palpably fails to convey the presence the poet's voice seems to generate, that is because it manifests starkly limitations that lurk in oral language as well: while voice may attest to the presence of a speaker, it does not of course produce that presence; in Whitman's work it is not voice but the carefully orchestrated economy of voice and writing, a shell-game of presence and absence, that generates the illusion of such productive power.[24] Detailing repeatedly in his work defects supposedly confined to writing, Whitman indeed inadvertently enumerates the linguistic liabilities that trouble all the gestures at word magic central to *Leaves of Grass,* whether we think of these as spoken or written. Foremost among these faults is the gap between the sign and its referent, the word and the thing itself, a gap which writing emphasizes but does not, of course, inaugurate.[25] All Whitman's performative announcements thus turn out to be liable to the sort of fading that haunts the poet's proclamations of his own advent, though they do not all depend so dramatically on the tie between voice and presence these declarations manipulate and are thus not so starkly undermined by the lapse from speech to writing; whether written or spoken, the poet's word cannot achieve that fusion between the self and its objects to which word magic would attain.

Devoid of such archaic power, the poet is left despite himself in an exterior space subject to external definition and control. The diminished but still considerable power his word can exercise in this space is also epitomized by writing;—or by the supposedly negative traits Whitman would like to consign to it. Sign of the sign, writing clearly disposes symbolic objects rather than real things; the poet's word, whether written or spoken, takes up its place in the contested, coercive sphere of cultural action, entering the very struggle over symbolic forms from which *Leaves of Grass* often claims to free us. As we shall see, Whitman reserves some of his most vehement denunciations for the power which culture and the symbolic entities it spawns exert over us; this power provokes anxiety as sharp as any displayed in his work.[26] Yet even Whitman's magisterial declarations of the poet's own presence are symbolic rather than magical acts, producing only what any such act can produce. They situate the poet firmly in the midst of the very arena Whitman's more inflammatory pronouncements make him responsible for abolishing or redeeming; both the poet's performatives and the figure they evoke are consummate instances of the hegemony they supposedly overthrow.

The appearance of the poet's word in a book, of his voice in a text, might therefore serve to remind us of what amount to truisms: the figure of the poet is not a magical presence but an ordinary representation; the words which claim to conjure him up can name but not produce him; *Leaves of Grass* shapes a symbolic space that is part of the very cultural system it contests rather than an alternative to it. Yet it is less important to record such truisms than to acknowledge and lend adequate weight to the fact of how deeply Whitman is committed to warding them off. Not simply mystified or demystified, Whitman's poems elaborate the never completed movement of a mystification; the poems are an anxious meditation on the ritual possibilities they seek to suggest; they brood over the linguistic and psychic liabilities they claim to avert. Attending to such equivocations, we can perhaps best recover and understand the unreconciled strains of exuberance and pathos, of grandeur and poverty, whose uneasy conjunction defines Whitman's early editions. The poet's apostrophes and the figure they imply sustain a vision of identity as fragile as it is exuberant and overbearing; crucial not only to the imaginative universe of *Leaves of Grass* but to its creator as well, this imperial self is called into question by the very scenes that call him into being. It is in something like these terms that we can understand the peculiar urgency that always attends Whitman's declarations of voice and denials of writing: the person who rises up in the poems, whom we have learned to call Walt Whitman, depends for his very existence on a tenuous and barely conceivable mode of communication—a mode which would convey the poet's actual presence to us as easily as representations are disseminated by ordinary writing. The poet's presence, Whitman's grandest trope of power, is also a figure of pathos and desire, an elusive prospect evoked but not produced by gestures at word magic. We need to read Whitman not only as the grand and visionary bard he typically claims to be, but also as the reluctant comedian or elegist of the very program he propounds. Whitman is often both poets—both vatic speaker and gnomic, troubled avatar, both voice and scribe—not only in the same poem but in one and the same pronouncement; therein, perhaps, lies the troubled, self-contradictory greatness of his best work.

What follows has the rhythm of a double movement. Beginning by explicating a pattern of figures and claims central to the early editions of *Leaves of Grass,* I focus increasingly on the mechanisms Whitman simultaneously commandeers and occults in order to generate the magical space of the poems, and on the way Whitman's work thus re-inscribes the poet's presence and word as functions of the very structures they supposedly resist. For the vision *Leaves of Grass* foregrounds, the poet's presence is the crucial synecdoche; but I begin by trying to establish the contours of that imagined whole of which he would be the uncannily incarnate part. Whitman's vision of language as the mastery and transfiguration of presence pervades and structures his early editions: such diverse features of *Leaves of Grass* as Whitman's idiosyncratic catalogues, his sometimes quirky cosmological musings, and his depictions of the vigorously pneumatic figure of the poet we often glimpse huffing and puffing his way through the landscape of the poems, I argue, can all best be understood as efforts to convey this vision of speech as power. My discussion of Whitman's catalogue technique in chapter 2 focuses on the archaic vision of space, time, and identity the highly stylized syntax of these litanies projects. Even Whitman's lists have a performative dimension, and their sometimes unfortunate prolixity is thus a defect risked in the name of the linguistic values to which *Leaves of Grass* is committed: like ceremonial utterance, Whitman's distended, iterative

sentences may be intent on accumulating power over the myriad creatures and objects they name rather than rendering any particular thing
in precise detail. Whitman's cosmic myth-making, I try to show in
chapter 3, reifies and thereby serves to naturalize the linguistic powers
his verbal practice implies, also giving the imaginative space that practice
suggests hypostatized embodiment. The poet's transfigured body can be
understood in part as one such hypostatization.

In chapter 4 I turn to an extended account of the poet's presence. I
am concerned not only with how the poet seems to incarnate the word
magic that suffuses *Leaves of Grass* but also with the way the archaic
identity thus evoked alleviates anxieties also amply rendered in the
poems. Such anxieties are conspicuously provoked not only by the poet's
vulnerability to the demands of some particular social organization but
also by the fact of social shaping itself, by his enforced assumption of a
symbolically structured and culturally grounded, no longer self-contained identity. This loss of autonomy, I try to show, has more than an
incidental connection to the linguistic rift in which the powers of word
magic are foresworn and the mediated and mediating cultural powers of
the symbolic sign assumed. Fighting off this supposed linguistic debacle,
the poet would thereby fend off our psychic subjection as well.

Central to the poems, this attempt to forestall a linguistic and psychic
disaster by recovering the supposed powers of a hypothesized primordial
language is worked through in more explicit and intellectually exacting
terms in Whitman's theoretical remarks on language, to which I turn in
chapter 5. Attempts at discursive rigor, however, end up entoiling Whitman in awkward efforts to sustain unlikely distinctions. We repeatedly
encounter moments in which his enabling oppositions—between statement and performance, indication and expression, arbitrary and organic
signs—threaten to collapse. The language theory thus verges on subverting the very claims it tries to sustain. The crucial instance of Whitman's
polemical dichotomizing labors under just this sort of difficulty: what
Whitman wants to mean by voice is already imbricated in what he wants
to mean by writing; the defects epitomized by this rejected mode manage
to contaminate oral language with uncanny recurrence. The redemptive
powers voice ought to exercise thus turn out to be virtually indistinguishable from the aggressive, illicit powers writing is said to wield.
Persuasively associating these dangerous linguistic powers with coercive
cultural mechanisms, Whitman also makes writing a crucial metonymy

for the sort of psychic self-division such cultural coding enforces. Yet just as he finds it difficult to isolate an unfallen oral language not already contaminated by the linguistic defects writing is made to exemplify, so too he has trouble imagining a credible version of the sort of body from which an unfallen voice might emerge, a body not yet sullied by the cultural inscription writing represents. These complementary tasks indeed turn out to be circular: the unfallen language and unfallen body of which *Leaves of Grass* dreams each require the prior existence of the other in order to come into being. Whitman's language theory thus ends up tracing the closed circle the poems try to re-enter but often seem consigned to musing on instead, a superseded space in which an archaic body and language define each other.

A study of Whitman's language theory can thus help us specify not only the ambitions Whitman's performative declarations condense but also the linguistic liabilities by which those aspirations are undermined. In chapter 6 I accordingly return to the poems to attend more closely to the dramatic but equivocal transactions that evoke a magical idiom they cannot quite activate and an agglomerative identity they cannot sustain. Envisioning language as power, the poems sometimes seem to lament the poverty of words; imagining an imperial self generated by voice, they are haunted by its inevitable ruin. But Whitman's poems are troubled as well by an obverse recognition: lacking the magical power of which Whitman dreams, the poet's word sometimes reveals itself not as impotent, but as an instance of the coercive social force it supposedly overcomes. This ambivalent sense of the word, and of the fiction of self the word should enable, is registered in the mobile, divided tone of Whitman's most moving proclamations. A close reading of Whitman's performatives reveals a poet who is both grandiose and vulnerable, and who can be visionary, poignant, comic, and domineering—sometimes all at once. I think this is the Whitman that matters most.

Crucial to Whitman's first three editions, such ambivalence is perhaps most striking in the poems in which the vision of word magic first emerges and finally dissolves. In chapter 7, I thus turn to extended readings of the 1855 "Song of Myself" and the 1860 *Calamus* sequence and *Sea-Drift* poem "As I Ebb'd with the Ocean of Life." These pieces powerfully suggest the impediments against which word magic and the archaic identity it engenders are brought to bear and the pressures it fends off, pressures to which the poet and his word remain vulnerable and to which they ultimately succumb. Whitman's fascination with magical performative utterance is already evident in "Song of Myself"; but the incorporative vision such language sustains struggles overtly in this early poem against contrary recognitions amply registered in digressive energies and comic demurs. The universe the poem celebrates is poised explicitly between unification and dispersion; the assimilative urge that propels the piece bumps up repeatedly against the rediscovered density and opacity of individual lives and objects, as well as against the structures, both natural and cultural, that have helped make these myriad creatures and things what they are. This conflict, I try to show, is registered in the poem primarily as a tension between bodies and voices —between limited incarnate forms and a form of presence that seems to annul all such limitation.

By 1860, the project thus ambiguously inaugurated in the grand, ironic comedy of "Song of Myself" has pretty much run its course: the great *Calamus* sequence of Whitman's third edition announces an end to the poet's imperial ambitions. Celebrating particular affections rather than the agglomerative powers exercised by the generic figure of the poet, the *Calamus* poems return Whitman to a space nearly devoid of magic. Here relations between self and other are no longer susceptible to incorporative mastery; the poet is now at the mercy of contingent events and must use some delicacy in negotiating amorous encounters that are no longer brought off by imperial fiat. He must also communicate with us by means he once spurned: the poet of *Calamus* is typically said to write to us. Addressing us from a particular time and place and by ordinary means, Whitman relinquishes the performative powers of that mythic speech which had earlier seemed to produce his endless, emanating presence, entering instead into a circuit of symbolic relations; assuming his place in a cultural economy of persons, he offers up as the price of initiation the very claims to self-sufficiency that had energized the first two editions of *Leaves of Grass*. In *Calamus* the poet's own body becomes the text of this loss: the poet is haunted by a kind of hermetic writing inscribed either within his body or on it, an inscription whose meaning—which is himself—remains as elusive to the poet as to others. Entoiled in the practice of writing, the poet of *Calamus* is himself subject to those self-dividing structures for which writing comes to stand in Whitman's work: no longer self-generating and self-contained, he is at the mercy not only of others but also of the forces that structure both himself and his relations to them; figured sometimes as natural, these are also the cultural codes and prohibitions whose weight the *Calamus* poems conspicuously register.

The accommodations detailed in *Calamus* are thus not without their price: the great *Sea-Drift* poem "As I Ebb'd with the Ocean of Life" is an agonized appraisal of what feels to Whitman like a ruined and bankrupt selfhood. Yet the poem's bitterness, which is extreme, is also divided: here Whitman seems to reject the animating myth of his first two editions, the consolations of *Calamus,* and the merely human self who, torn between these antipodal visions, has failed to live up to either one. This equivocal leave-taking registers both the complexity and the strength of Whitman's investment in the powers that are the subject of this study.

Both the gigantesque claims to performative power and the anxiety which the fragility of those claims occasions, however, are virtually absent from Whitman's later work; they are replaced by tireless exposition of a cosmic vision we might best regard as a sort of congealing of the still-elusive intimations proffered by Whitman's image of voice in his earlier poems.[27] The poet of these later pieces is not the subject of my study.

The exuberant vision of language that animates the early *Leaves of Grass* is probably sharpest in the new poems Whitman composed for the 1856 edition; his evocation of the mythic poet created by apostrophe is nowhere more crucial than in "Crossing Brooklyn Ferry." In what follows, I therefore make this piece a kind of specimen text. Rather than organizing my exposition around a series of close readings of entire poems—an approach Whitman's theory and practice of poetry tend to vitiate—I trace a crucial imaginative pattern through Whitman's work, recurring to "Crossing Brooklyn Ferry" to recall the drama within which Whitman's central claims characteristically function.

Focusing on the attractions of archaic processes and the vicissitudes that befall them, as well as on the cultural mechanisms they supposedly resist, my account of *Leaves of Grass* takes up a view of Whitman's work already suggested by such sometimes divergent critics as Mark Van Doren, Richard Chase, John Kinnaird, Ivan Marki, and Quentin Anderson. Acknowledging the social agenda of *Leaves of Grass,* these critics nonetheless locate the crucial sustaining impulse for Whitman's early editions in the more private concerns with which public material in the poems persistently intertwines. In a similar way, I have chosen to attend to the uncanny energies activated by announcements of the poet's presence and to map the archaic space these scenes generate, rather than detail the political implications Whitman sometimes tries to lend such encounters or pursue the democratic social vision they can be taken to imply. Despite Whitman's quite genuine and passionate political commitments, the performative impulse in *Leaves of Grass* does not seem to me to be motivated primarily by these concerns. The overtly political passages in Whitman's early editions tend to be melodramatic or maudlin; more often than not, they feel like awkward efforts to displace to the domain of public policy visions of danger and possibility that originate elsewhere.[28] The political claims Whitman sometimes makes for the poet's presence may serve in part as a protective distancing of more intimate, less easily acknowledged material.

Having made my case for the archaic resonance of the crucial transactions in *Leaves of Grass,* in chapter 8 I thus argue that the poet's presence can be enlisted as a figure for the explicitly political vision sometimes expounded in *Leaves of Grass* only by leaving out of account a considerable residue; this remainder, I contend, is crucial to the poet's appeal. Recent accounts of Whitman's work that focus on the poet's addresses to his audience have on the whole been less interested in the peculiar features the poet himself assumes by virtue of these apostrophes than in his possible didactic effects on us; studies that regard the poet's presence primarily as a trope for some political possibility which Whitman is intent on making available to his audience have lately become the most popular version of this enterprise.[29] Yet the appeal of the poet's presence may depend less on the shared social prospect he supposedly embodies than on the exceptional status he himself enjoys. The working assumption of my own study is that we need to take a sustained look at the peculiar characteristics of this presence, and at the benefits that accrue to the poet by imaginatively assuming them, before we can say what this figure might mean to democracy, or to us. The ideological work Whitman's figure of voice performs, I argue in conclusion, is hardly exhausted by the poet's advocacy of strictly political possibilities; more crucially, it depends on the way his advent manages to confound such prospects with archaic satisfactions by no means reducible to them. This enticing confusion is bound up intimately with the tricky relation between voice and writing that organizes *Leaves of Grass.* If the poet's voice were in fact capable of the magic which writing is enlisted to suggest, then the prospects the poet's advent seems to embody might be socially sustainable. But voice, which should inaugurate a re-fashioned politics, is instead a figure in *Leaves of Grass* for desires politics cannot fulfill.

Articulated in classic accounts by Jacques Derrida, the economy of voice and writing I track through Whitman's work has more than an incidental relation to romanticism. Introducing his extended reading of the *Essay on the Origin of Languages,* Derrida argues that Rousseau's wedding of voice not simply to presence but to self-presence, to consciousness and its supposed translucence, is paradigmatic for the extended epoch Rousseau helps define (*Grammatology* 16–17). Romantic rhetoric provides ample evidence of this privileging of interiority which voice comes to imply. The characteristic romantic figures of invocation and apostrophe do not merely call to objects over a distance, nor even, conversely, simply suggest a collapse or contraction of the spatial and temporal intervals voice seems to traverse. Flowing forth from the body's interior, the voice which is its crucial synecdoche becomes its agent as well: romantic invocation and apostrophe, it might be argued, characteristically aim not only to draw objects into the human community of speech but also to internalize their powers by sheltering or subsuming them within the interior space from which voice emanates, a space whose domain voice seems ambiguously to extend. This vision of interiorization is abetted by the fusion of word and thing toward which romantic rhetoric sometimes aspires, a fusion that would collapse the external object into the word apparently given birth in the internal space of consciousness by voice. Working to transfigure the recalcitrant relation between subject and object, apostrophe and invocation bespeak a desire to dissolve presence into self-presence. This association with an archaic topology is of course not an invariant feature of romantic figures of voice, any more than writing always tropes the priority of external agents or structures that frustrate such dreamed-of completeness. But both incorporative metaphor and the related connection between voice and translucent interiority appear repeatedly in romantic texts. As the seminal work of Paul de Man on the romantic topos of the epitaph suggests, so too does the association of writing with a proleptic anteriority that threatens to foreclose the present before the self can inhabit and mold it.[30] For reasons too complex to speculate on here, images of incorporation are especially notable in American romanticism, just as claims for the power of voice and word are particularly extreme; they are marshaled against a writing whose attempts to stifle original speech are frequently given lurid embodiment.[31]

Claims for the transumptive power of the word are nowhere stronger than in *Leaves of Grass;* the relation between voice and the writing that undoes its supposed effects is correspondingly volatile. Whitman's work is therefore especially amenable to the mode of reading Derrida practices. Admittedly a kind of bricolage, Derrida's characteristic approach applies a broadly Freudian sense of overdetermination to the multiple, frequently contradictory strands of assertion that make up a text; a single assertion or figure may advance claims or condense suggestions that proceed simultaneously despite their ultimate incompatibility.[32] Derrida typically situates writers in relation to such textual systems on an ad hoc basis, dividing what might be called manifest from latent strands, consequences insisted upon from implications ignored or repudiated (*Grammatology* 157–64). Such an approach might be criticized as arbitrary or opportunistic; but it preserves a useful sense that writers, too, negotiate their way through texts, and are sometimes situated in them awkwardly. From the rigorous if cold perspective provided by de Man's notion of rhetoricity, the resultant agon may seem rather melodramatic.[33] But a tolerance for melodrama and a taste for the histrionic are perhaps not vestigial equipment for the reader of *Leaves of Grass:* much of the poetry's energy derives from its passionate and vehement claims to perform a transfiguration it can never quite bring off.

Harold Bloom, recalling everything himself but situating poetry in a realm of power where the trope succeeds by repressing what it knows— the memory of its own belatedness, and ours—takes up a stance antipodal to the de Manian position that literature is inherently demystified; he has recently suggested that deconstructing Whitman is possible but uninteresting (*Wallace Stevens* 12–13).[34] This judgment follows naturally from Bloom's vision of poetry as a struggle in which poets grapple with their precursors, and victory and defeat lead to inclusion in the canon or exclusion from it; in this formula loss of power equals oblivion. But the anxiety of influence that attends this struggle is not the only anxiety to which poetry and poets are susceptible, just as belatedness is not solely an intrapoetic phenomenon: poetry, whose magical speech supposedly came first, finds itself preceded and preempted by other discourses whose powers far exceed its own, languages that co-opt the very speakers they enfranchise. Aspiring to the unmediated power of word magic but not attaining it, poetry names but fails to perform its own earliness, and ours, suggests but cannot recover the sacred origin from which all secular speech and the alienation it instigates would be a fall, the fall. We might call the anxiety that attends this impasse a rhetorical one; it would manifest itself as apprehension or restlessness concerning poetic language—its resources and limitations, its vexed relation to the discourses that surround it.[35] Broached unwillingly but not unwittingly in *Leaves of Grass,* the topos of a mythic speech that is not our own—and, much more, not ourselves—has been the character-istic site of much American poetry. The preoccupation with Whitman among the poets who follow him may thus be only in part anxiety of influence. As Bloom suggests, we hear in Whitman an original, perennial earliness. But the self-creating power Whitman's trope of voice implies is staged by a scene of writing. Whitman's lateness is his text: undoing the very self-production it enables, it consigns the poet's word once more to time and entoils him again in a cultural space in which his utterance is neither magical nor preternaturally early. This belatedness may ad-dress our own; but it is one the poems themselves inscribe. Whitman left us himself in his book.

Notes

1. I quote here from the text of the 1856 edition, where this piece is entitled "Sun-Down Poem"; in the *Comprehensive Reader's Edition,* the last of these lines reads "Who knows, *for all the distance,* but I am as good as looking at you now, for all you cannot see me?" (emphases added). In the early editions of *Leaves of Grass* one of the poet's key attributes is the ability to erase such distance; by 1881 the immediate presence the 1856 lines declare is no longer crucial to the imaginative universe of the poems.

    Since the focus of my study is the poet of the first three editions, unless otherwise noted I cite the text of the earliest edition of *Leaves of Grass* in which the poem from which I quote appears. For the 1855 edition I use the widely accessible Viking reprint edited by Malcolm Cowley; for the 1856 edition, the Norwood Editions facsimile; for the 1860 edition, the Cornell UP facsimile. In citing from the 1860 text I omit stanza numbers, an idiosyncrasy of the 1860, 1867, and 1871 editions. Since I cite infrequently from editions later than 1860 and reprints of these volumes are hard to come by, I use the *Variorum* (V) for these passages; as this text is difficult to work with, where the lines I cite are identical to the text of the "death-bed" edition, I also give page numbers for the *Comprehensive Reader's Edition* (CRE). For ease of reference, unless otherwise noted I give poem titles and section numbers as these appear in CRE. For all quotations from Whitman's work, I enclose my own ellipses in brackets, in order to avoid confusion with Whitman's use of a similar notation in the 1855 edition.

2. The poet's addresses to his audience have elicited comment from virtually every generation of Whitman critics, but not until recently have they been accorded a central role. Analyses with which I disagree in important respects but from which I have benefited include C. Carroll Hollis, *Language and Style in Leaves of Grass;* Donald Pease, "Blake, Crane, Whitman, and Modernism" and *Visionary Compacts* 108–57; Calvin Bedient, "Orality and Power (Whitman's *Song of Myself*)"; Mitchell Breitwieser, "Who Speaks in Whitman's Poems?"; Joseph Kronick, *American Poetics of History* 90–123; Allen Grossman, "The Poetics of Union in Whitman and Lincoln: An Inquiry toward the Relationship of Art and Policy"; and Kerry C. Larson, *Whitman's Drama of Consensus,* especially 3–74; all appeared while the present study was in progress. I detail briefly below, at opportune spots in the notes that follow, some of the principal differences between these accounts and my own. Two brief articles by Régis Durand which I came across some time after they appeared, "The Anxiety of Performance" and "Whitman, le rythme, le sujet de l'écriture," are closer to the spirit of my argument; Durand's analysis of Whitman, like my own, makes use of work by Lacan and Kristeva. See also Thomas B. Byers, *What I Cannot Say: Self, Word, and World in Whitman, Stevens, and Merwin* 15–42 and 111–13. Michael Moon's valuable *Disseminating Whitman* appeared as the present study was going to press.

3. See Kaplan 329–34 for an account of some of the more spectacularly credulous early responses to *Leaves of Grass;* I return to this bizarre reception history in chapter 5, below.

4. John Kinnaird was one of the first to emphasize this notion of Whitman's "magical universe"; see "*Leaves of Grass* and the American Paradox" 29.

5. As many critics have noted, this confounding of time and eternity is especially striking in "Crossing Brooklyn Ferry"; see for example Anderson, *Imperial Self* 94.

6. Roger Asselineau's is probably the most sustained and sophisticated account of Whitman's transactions with this sort of quasi-philosophical vocabulary; see 2:3–77.

7. Larson (11–12) makes a similar assertion about the priority of the poems' imagined mode of address, though the consequences he draws are rather different.

8. As readers of *The Imperial Self* will be aware, this is a version of Quentin Anderson's argument, to which I am very much indebted; I see voice as the

crucial synecdoche of the archaic body Anderson describes. Edwin Miller (21–22 and passim) and Stephen Black (126–37 and passim) both discuss the importance of regressive features in Whitman's work. I am indebted as well to Dorothy Gregory's discussion of pre-Oedipal material in Whitman's first two editions: see especially 19–49.

9. For Austin's explanation of performatives and his emphasis on their necessary embedding in conventional procedures and institutionalized contexts see especially 1–66. Though they are problematic, Austin's brief remarks about the peculiarities of written performatives (60–61), as well as his marginalizing of the performative utterances that appear in literary works (9, 22, 104–105), shed some light on Whitman's special predicaments, helping to explain the repeated denials of writing, and of the fictive status of *Leaves of Grass,* that traverse Whitman's work. More illuminating, since they place these supposedly marginal problems at the center of speech act theory and thus suggest that Whitman's seemingly peculiar difficulties are peculiarly revelatory, are Jacques Derrida's explorations of just these "etiolations." See "Signature Event Context"; Searle, "Reiterating the Differences: A Reply to Derrida"; and Derrida, "Limited Inc." Also useful on the problem of performatives in literary works is Stanley Fish, "With the Compliments of the Author: Reflections on Austin and Derrida." For a firmly teleological account of the gradual shift between magical and conventional understandings of linguistic power, see Cassirer 44–62 and 83–99; I take up some of the problems with this teleological vision in chapter 2, below.

10. By contrast, both Pease ("Blake, Crane, Whitman, and Modernism" 77–79) and Larson (xiv–xv, 58) argue that Whitman's crucial linguistic transactions aim at a mode of authority that by-passes existing institutions but is still explicitly symbolic. They therefore view Whitman's declarations of the poet's presence as tropes for a re-fashioned politics (Pease, "Blake, Crane, Whitman, and Modernism" 78, Larson 73–80). I argue instead that, in the early editions of *Leaves of Grass,* this political dimension is a kind of secondary elaboration, and that Whitman's visionary politics is itself refashioned on the basis of an imagined encounter that is supposedly magical rather than symbolic.

11. The most sustained analysis of Whitman's poems in terms of speech act theory is Hollis 65–123.

12. On this fusion of word and thing see Cassirer 49–54. On its relation to psychic and somatic (rather than cultural) archaism, see chapter 4, below.

13. I take the notion of an "image of voice" from Geoffrey Hartman and Harold Bloom. See for example Hartman, *The Fate of Reading* 289 and *Criticism in the Wilderness* 30; and Bloom, "Whitman's Image of Voice."

14. On the tie between body and voice in Whitman, see Régis Durand, "Whitman, le rythme, le sujet de l'écriture." On the regressive implications of the performative see Durand, "The Anxiety of Performance," especially 169–70.

15. See Culler, "Apostrophe" and "Changes in the Study of the Lyric"; and de Man, "Lyrical Voice in Contemporary Theory: Riffaterre and Jauss." On temporality in the lyric see also Cameron, *Lyric Time*, especially 23 and 92.

16. Paul Fry takes up the relation between psychic and what might be called rhetorical space in *The Poet's Calling in the English Ode;* see especially 2–3 and 12–14.

17. On the related notions of word magic and the omnipotence of thought see Freud, *Totem and Taboo* 79–90, and "On Narcissism: An Introduction," *Collected Papers* 4:32.

18. I have in mind Freud's definition in "The Uncanny": the sensation of uncanniness can be provoked by either repressed infantile material or an evocation of the superseded belief in what Freud calls the omnipotence of thought. See especially *Collected Papers* 4:391–406. Freud's remarks about the special difficulties presented by literary attempts to evoke the omnipotence of thought help illuminate Whitman's repeated insistence that the poet's presence is not merely fictive; we can understand this insistence as an extreme version of the strategy in which "the writer pretends to move in the world of common reality" (4:405). Inasmuch as Whitman's gestures at word magic evoke an infantile body and thus, indirectly, an archaic relation to the mother, the rhetoric of *Leaves of Grass* possesses a connection to repressed material as well as to this superseded belief in word magic; see chapter 4, below.

19. Ivan Marki, for example, also takes up the relation between Whitman's "vocal style" and our sense of the poet's presence; see especially 26. See also Bedient, especially 80–82; Bedient mentions the paradox that writing constitutes the poet's "voice," but does not detail the attendant loss of power that shadows *Leaves of Grass*.

20. I quote here from the 1867 rather than the 1860 text. Whitman's earlier version lacks the "Camerado!"—a perhaps bombastic apostrophe which nonetheless has the advantage of making more explicit the relation between voice and presence.

21. This sort of christological discourse was first attached to the poet's person by such early commentators as Burroughs, O'Connor, and Bucke; Anderson resurrects it ironically ("Whitman's New Man" 49). See chapter 5, below.

22. On the paradoxical connections between voice and writing in Whitman's poems see especially Breitwieser. My own account differs from his in that Breitwieser sees Whitman as revelling in the play between voice and writing, and the different senses of identity they imply: according to Breitwieser voice figures a personal, individual identity, writing an abstract or representative self liberated from such limitation; the gap between these two identities supposedly figures tensions endemic to American democracy, in which claims to representative status are always made by particular interests or factions. I argue instead that Whitman surreptitiously enlists writing to constitute the image of voice to which he is committed, a reliance his

diatribes against writing serve in part to disguise; this image of voice is determined less by political exigencies than by the attraction of archaic processes. On voice and writing in Whitman's work, see also Bauerlein.

23. By contrast, Pease ("Blake, Crane, Whitman, and Modernism" 78) implies and Kronick (106–10) explicitly argues that the sort of symbolic interchange writing facilitates is precisely what Whitman wants. See also Bové (131–79), who argues that Whitman's work de-centers or displaces just the sorts of claims I regard as central to it.

24. Durand thus suggests that in Whitman's work "the individual voice is in fact already caught up in . . . the logic of writing ("The Anxiety of Performance" 168–69).

25. From the vantage of post-Saussurian linguistics, or indeed from any view inflected by nominalism, the "gap between the sign and its referent" and that between "the word and the thing itself" are not of course equivalent. But from the vantage of the word magic I am attempting to paraphrase here, they are one and the same.

26. Grossman argues similarly that the poet's presence should serve to eliminate the need for "all representational mediations" (208n28). I find it significant that Grossman judges the anti-institutional political vision this presence and the poet's catalogues supposedly embody to be necessarily unrealizable; he indeed accuses Whitmanian "open form" of " 'bad faith' " (203).

27. While the early editions already project linguistic, vocal, and somatic powers and perils onto cosmic structures, it is only in the later work that cosmic doctrine virtually obliterates attention to the processes it reifies. See chapter 3, below.

28. Thus, for example, even Larson's qualified linking of erotic and political material in "The Sleepers" is more persuasive than Whitman's own (59–72).

29. Like recent accounts of the political implications of the poet's apostrophes, Hollis's ground-breaking study of speech acts in *Leaves of Grass* focuses on their persuasive effects.

30. See de Man, "Autobiography as De-Facement," *The Rhetoric of Romanticism* 67–82. For a less severe account of romantic epitaph, see Hartman, "Wordsworth, Inscriptions, and Romantic Nature Poetry," *Beyond Formalism* 206–30; "Romantic Poetry and the Genius Loci," *Beyond Formalism* 311–36, offers a related discussion of invocation. On prolepsis, see Fry 12–14.

31. Anderson's seminal account of incorporative figures in American literature might be called psycho-political; see *Imperial Self*, especially 11–20 and 88–165. His analysis takes up some of Tocqueville's darker insights: see for example Tocqueville 2:82–83. Sharon Cameron relates incorporative imagery to geographical or phenomenological as well as political factors (*The Corporeal Self* 3ff.). So does Charles Olson, *Call Me Ishmael* 3–7, 81–85.

32. This is a rough paraphrase of Barbara Johnson's account; see her introduction to Derrida's *Dissemination,* especially xiv–xvi.

33. See de Man, "The Rhetoric of Blindness: Jacques Derrida's Reading of Rousseau," *Blindness and Insight* 102–41; and *Allegories of Reading* 3–19. Kronick's reading of Whitman is explicitly de Manian.

34. For Bloom's argument with deconstruction, see *Wallace Stevens* 1–26 and 375–406. Bedient's reading of Whitman, with its praise of voice as presence and power, is broadly Bloomian; see especially 80.

35. I am indebted here to Cynthia Chase's suggestions concerning the desirability of "an intertextual reading less eager to evoke persons and more attentive to recurrent rhetorical patterns" (" 'Viewless Wings' " 213).

2. The World in the Word

I expect him to make the songs of the nation, but he seems to be contented to make the inventories.

—Emerson, quoted in Schyberg 104[1]

1. What does it mean to name something, to bestow or utter a name? Whitman's poetry is a sustained if troubled effort to conceive of naming as an act of mastery and transfiguration, and to inherit the powers this conception implies. We will be concerned throughout with how this notion of naming shapes *Leaves of Grass;* in this chapter, I want to attend to the way Whitman's catalogues enact it. In these litanies the word seems to assume a magical power over the thing: the poet characteristically claims to control the objects whose names he pronounces, indeed often suggesting that he assimilates them. Whitman's hypnotic lists thus complement the direct addresses to us that announce the poet's advent. Diffusing his presence, the poet's apostrophes suggest the word's productive, positional force; his catalogues typically mobilize the vocative power of the word instead, retrieving things from the dispersed exterior space in which they have hitherto been isolated and immersing them in the fluid, somaticized realm these litanies suggest.

"Crossing Brooklyn Ferry" is explicit about this transformation supposedly worked by the word. It culminates with an apostrophe to the objects of the harbor scene that announces the redeemed relation the poem itself inaugurates, adverting as well to the blockage the poet has supposedly annulled:

> You have waited, you always wait, you dumb beautiful ministers! you novices!
> We receive you with free sense at last, and are insatiate henceforward,
> Not you any more shall be able to foil us, or withhold yourselves from us,
> We use you, and do not cast you aside—we plant you permanently within us. (1856 222)

While a purely ideal power of introjection may be the basis of the assimilation the poet declares here, the avidity of these lines suggests something more: here Whitman depicts the interiorizing of objects as an ingestion, a magical incorporation of the world into the body.[2] I will take up at length in chapter four the connections between Whitman's vision of the word and the sense of the body this passage records. But I can indicate quickly the scope of what this archaic mingling of linguistic and somatic processes seems to abrogate: it might be described as the realm of the Kantian categories; the world apprehended according to the demands of the reality principle or the psychological orientation Freud called the secondary processes; or the symbolic space organized by cultural codes that govern the relations between a subject and its objects. We can associate the archaic zone whose restoration is thus suggested with the Freudian primary processes or pleasure principle; we should remember that, according to Freud, this superseded organization has an intimate relation to that reification of linguistic powers he called word magic.[3]

The power ascribed to the word is thus antithetical. And as the concluding passage from "Crossing Brooklyn Ferry" adverting to the resistance hitherto exerted by objects suggests, *Leaves of Grass* amply records the competing energies against which it is brought to bear.[4] The more overt terrors of a newspaper sketch Whitman composed in 1847 for the Brooklyn *Daily Eagle* can nonetheless serve to remind us that such poems as "Crossing Brooklyn Ferry" are more like a spell than like the ecstatic chronicle of the poet's perceptions or the all-inclusive hymn to urban life they are often said to be:

Our Brooklyn ferries teach some sage lessons in philosophy, gentle reader [. . . they move] on like iron-willed destiny. Passionless and fixed, at the six-stroke the boats come in; and at the three-stroke, succeeded by a single tap, they depart again, with the steadiness of nature herself. Perhaps a man, prompted by the hell-like delirium tremens, has jumped over-board and been drowned: still the trips go on as before [. . . .] How it deadens one's sympathies, this living in a city! [. . .] This rushing and raging is not inconsistent, however, with other items of the American character. (UPP 1:168–69)

If such ominous energies are difficult to discern in "Crossing Brooklyn Ferry," that is not quite owing to their absence. Whitman's catalogues simultaneously render and subdue this urban, industrial scene. The poem's key *peripeteia* is at first hard to see for just this reason: Whitman's litanies are a kind of apotropaic ritual in which the very act of naming wards off the threats lurking in the thing named; the phrases that obliquely register the daunting aspects of the harbor scene also obliquely dispel them. In "Crossing Brooklyn Ferry" all "rushing and raging" is suspended, as objects slip into an intransitive domain Whitman identifies with the "float forever held in solution"(1856 216).[5] Briefly described in the poem's elliptical creation myth as an untroubled cosmic sphere from which all things are precipitated into separate incarnate forms, this enchanted realm is also both the space of the poet's own body and a reified version of Whitman's syntax, a zone defined by language.

The long catalogue that makes up most of poem's third section renders a universe teeming with objects and actions, and might seem simply to celebrate the world full of being and doing it depicts. But the anxieties provoked by such activity are still discernible in the language that is busy annulling its force. Despite its celebratory air, this catalogue registers Whitman's misgivings concerning not only the hectic energies that traverse the harbor scene but also the very power of independent action that finds concentrated expression in this urban setting:[6]

> I too saw the reflection of the summer-sky in the water.
> [. . . .]
> Looked toward the lower bay to notice the arriving ships,
> Saw their approach, saw aboard those that were near me,
> Saw the white sails of schooners and sloops, saw the ships at anchor,
> The sailors at work in the rigging or out astride the spars,
> The round masts, the swinging motion of the hulls, the slender serpentine pennants,
> The large and small steamers in motion, the pilots in their pilot-houses,
> The white wake left by the passage, the quick tremulous whirl of the wheels.
>   (1856 213–14)

This apparent panegyric is less sanguine than we tend to assume. I quote here only a brief portion of this typically distended catalogue, virtually all of whose lines present additional objects for the observer to register; the poet's attention is drawn into a densely populated space that recedes from him and escapes his control. The sense of continuous proliferation here is rather vertiginous; the scene is an unsettling version of what can be praised as plenitude only when such burgeoning has been safely contained and mastered. Here objects "withhold" themselves, resisting the poet's attempts to "receive" them "with free sense," in part through their very multiplicity.

In contrast to the sort of space which can be planted "permanently" within the poet, everything here is also in constant flux: hulls swing, wheels whirl, steamers move and presumably disappear from the speaker's field of vision; a no-longer-visible boat leaves a wake, the trace of its own disappearance. While recorded in the passage, such unruly activities are already partially subdued by the very tense in which they are rendered: recollection is a sign here of the power to dispose. The scene's centrifugal energies become more striking if we re-cast the passage as a present-tense description:

> [I see] the white sails of schooners and sloops, [see] the ships at anchor,
> The sailors at work in the rigging or out astride the spars,
> The round masts, the swinging motion of the hulls, the slender serpentine pennants.

In this version multiple energies continually re-shape what the observer sees. "Crossing Brooklyn Ferry" accordingly not only attempts to collapse the dispersed object world into the self and to elide autonomous acts; it also effaces the immediate present that is the site of such independence.

2. My contention that the poet is ill-at-ease not only with the turbulence of the harbor scene but also with the present moment that is the domain of such activity may seem unlikely: it appears to be contradicted by the end of the catalogue I have been discussing, as well as by some overt declarations elsewhere in the poem. "Crossing Brooklyn Ferry" is indeed often regarded as a hymn to the splendors of the immediate and the given.[7] The catalogue in section three does seem increasingly haunted by the evanescence of the spectacle it records, dwelling on it with a kind of rapt intensity. As Whitman's litany progresses, day slides into night, and the light which endows the poet's "sights" with "glories strung like beads" disappears; poised against this failing light, the scene takes on something of an elegiac cast. This quality has already been suggested by the past tense in which the entire catalogue proceeds.[8] We should note, however, that the poet has gone out of his way to generate this past tense: like the speaker at the end of Wordsworth's "Tintern Abbey," the poet of "Crossing Brooklyn Ferry" has contrived to look back on the scene in the midst of which we initially located him. We are entitled to wonder whether this carefully orchestrated loss of the very present mo-

ment whose glories the poem praises might not offer abundant recompense. In Wordsworth, the elegiac mode is itself the poet's compensation: awareness of mortality is humanizing, and "Tintern Abbey" accordingly propounds what might be called an elegiac humanism. But the elegiac aspect of the lines I have been considering is rather more muted than a reading of them out of context might suggest. In the course of the poem, Whitman invokes not only the capacity of recollection brought into play here, but also a magical power of repetition that, unlike Wordsworth's more delicate continuities, seems able to annul time and change and render elegy superfluous. The "present" scene the poem celebrates is not simply restored but also transformed through this ritual of repetition: reappearing as a function of the poet's word, it is purged of the distressing, disruptive energies the poem's third section records.

This dialectic is adverted to at the poem's opening. Whitman's agglutinative syntax makes grammatical relations difficult to parse; but if the "glories strung like beads on my smallest sights and hearings" are not simply appositive to what precedes the poet's mention of them, they are at least conditioned by it:

> The simple, compact, well-joined scheme—myself disintegrated, every one disintegrated, yet part of the scheme,
> The similitudes of the past and those of the future,
> The glories strung like beads on my smallest sights and hearings—on the walk in the street, and the passage over the river. (1856 211–12)

Here the immediate present is said to be governed by a structure of repetition that appears not only to insure its perdurance but also to master its heterogeneous energies.

The poem's succeeding line temporarily threatens this recuperative scheme, offering a more recalcitrant instance of mutability in an image of the poet's own impending death:

> The current rushing so swiftly, and swimming with me far away. (1856 212)

The first response to this crisis is Wordsworthian:

> The others that are to follow me, the ties between me and them,
> The certainty of others—the life, love, sight, hearing of others.
>
> Others will enter the gates of the ferry, and cross from shore to shore. (1856 212)

Here the poet's successors, who seem at first like usurpers, are quickly re-imagined as ephebes and inheritors instead; the poet folds them into a cycle of recurrent experience in which mortality is softened by the muted and metaphoric continuities characteristic of elegy. But such attenuations play a minor role in the poem. They are superseded by a scene of repetition that depends on a vision of language more akin to shamanistic word magic than to the avowedly metaphorical mode of Wordsworthian humanism:

> It avails not, neither time or place—distance avails not,
> I am with you, you men and women of a generation, or ever so many generations hence,
> I project myself, also I return—I am with you, and know how it is. (1856 212–13)

These declarations subdue time and change to the magical act of the poet's repeated manifestation, initiating "a play of presence and absence governed not by time but by poetic power" (Culler, "Apostrophe" 150). The protagonist caught in the poem's particular, contingent present disappears; the poet is reborn as an eternal presence generated by the word and embodying its recuperative power. Insuring the poet's perdurance, the apostrophes in "Crossing Brooklyn Ferry" also seem to quell the unruly energies that initially beset him: they subdue independent actions to the repetitive temporality generated by his word and subsume the objects of the harbor scene within the emanating presence his utterance seems to produce.

The long catalogue in section three performs similar functions, lending the present scene the contours the poem will praise. The tense in which the catalogue is couched contributes to this transformation. Whitman's litany is cast not just in the past tense, but in the imperfect rather than the preterite: as its opening declares, it renders only repeated events ("I too many and many a time crossed the river, the sun half an hour high" [1856 213]).[9] Unique acts attesting to independent initiative are replaced by a rhythm of recurrence already akin to the iterative mechanisms of language.

In other respects as well, this catalogue is less an elegy for an evanescent present whose vanishing the poet laments than a celebration of linguistic mastery. What we "see" is not so much a particular, valued scene, as the contours implied by a peculiar grammar—contours made visible, as it were, by means of the represented content Whitman's syntax traverses and thereby transforms. Whitman's true subject here is a power of repetition through which what he will mean by the present, and by presence, come into being.

This is not quite the triumph of culture over nature it might at first seem to be. Like Whitman's catalogues, all language recuperates the real, subjecting it to the power of the category; but it does not always dissolve the world into its own enunciatory rhythms with the manic insistence that typifies Whitman's litanies. In Whitman's characteristic tallies, the discrete categories designated by finite verbs and class names are themselves subjected to iterative syntactic mechanisms that blur the very boundaries such designations establish: all subjects become inflections of a single amorphous entity, all predicates aspects of a single ongoing process increasingly hard to distinguish from the energy of utterance itself.[10] Whitman's catalogue technique, that is, not only subjugates time and space; it also annuls the mode of experience structured by the finite verb and the polarized encounter for which the verb serves as fulcrum: the normative syntax that places a subject over against an object, articulating the particular shape of their relation in the predicate, is in several of Whitman's catalogues not so much permuted as subverted. The catalogues of *Leaves of Grass* thus pit their performative energies not simply against traits inherent in the natural world or against some neutral picture of such a natural stratum, but also against a pervasive structure of representation that itself already shapes and interprets what it depicts. Whitman's verbal transactions are thus an implicit critique of the shaping power of the sign and of the cultural field it constructs.[11] Foregrounding the vocative dimension of language in his catalogues, Whitman seems not only to dissolve the world into the word, but also to collapse the linguistic code and its authority into the apparently self-authorizing power of the enunciative position or speaker.[12] I will take up this latter reclamation project in chapter 4; but we should keep it in mind as we attend to the struggles with space, time, and multiplicity that in *Leaves of Grass* often displace this cultural agon.

3. Employing the syntactic deformations typical of Whitman's lists, the catalogue in section three of "Crossing Brooklyn Ferry" has the effect of producing sameness out of difference: overcoming opacity and distance, it functions to appropriate whatever it names.[13] As in many of Whit-

man's litanies, the theoretical possibility of repeating a given syntactic pattern *ad infinitum* seems here to be very nearly realized in practice. I quote at greater length from the passage cited earlier:

I too saw the reflection of the summer-sky in the water.
[. . . .]
Looked toward the lower bay to notice the arriving ships,
Saw their approach, saw aboard those that were near me,
Saw the white sails of schooners and sloops, saw the ships at anchor,
The sailors at work in the rigging or out astride the spars,
The round masts, the swinging motion of the hulls, the slender serpentine
  pennants,
The large and small steamers in motion, the pilots in their pilot-houses,
The white wake left by the passage, the quick tremulous whirl of the wheels,
The flags of all nations, the falling of them at sun-set,
The scallop-edged waves in the twilight, the ladled cups, the frolicsome crests
  and glistening,
The stretch afar growing dimmer and dimmer, the gray walls of the granite
  store-houses by the docks,
On the river the shadowy group, the big steam-tug closely flanked on each
  side by the barges—the hay-boat, the belated lighter,
On the neighboring shore the fires from the foundry chimneys burning high
  and glaringly into the night,
Casting their flicker of black, contrasted with wild red and yellow light, over
  the tops of houses, and down into the clefts of streets. (1856 213–15)[14]

The very sweep of Whitman's utterance here, compounded with a pervasive use of anaphora, induces a slightly dazed sort of attention that already makes particulars seem blurry.[15] But the attendant sense that objects are collapsing into each other derives as well from the particular patterns of syntactic suspension and repetition Whitman employs.

Diverse objects are blended in these lines by being made to occupy an identical grammatical position. This redisposition is begun in the third and fourth of the lines quoted above, through repetition of a single verb: the things presented are all made objects of discrete but congruent acts —they are all what the speaker "saw."[16] Beyond the fourth of the lines quoted, even the verb "saw" is omitted: the ensuing catalogue of object phrases, occupying ten long lines, thus all depends from a single verb; each object, located in a phrase whose grammatical function is entirely apposite to those which precede and follow, slides into an identical syntactic position. Ostensibly describing a receding visual field, this catalogue catches up the objects of the harbor scene into the fluid, centripetal space shaped by its grammar.[17]

Whitman's catalogue not only dissolves the spatial manifold in which discrete objects stand opposed; it also effaces the finite, transitive acts through which their relations are commonly structured. Whitman's catalogue ostensibly describes a world full of motion and change; but it annuls the force of the very doings it records, transforming acts performed by independent agents into varieties of a single, continuous process. As this phrasal catalogue depicts them, actions are denied syntactic force. They are characteristically rendered by participles or gerunds: "The stretch afar *growing* dimmer and dimmer"; "the fires from the foundry chimneys *burning* high and glaringly"; "The white wake *left* by the passage"; "the *ladled* cups"; "the *falling* of them at sun-set." Described by such verbals, the motions this passage records are no longer quite acts, and the entities to which they are ascribed no longer quite seem to be their agents.[18] Motions simply occur, tracing their trajectories through passive objects, flowing through the entire presented scene. This sense is re-enforced by the aural effect of Whitman's verbals: variously "swinging," "falling," "glistening," and "burning," things are drawn into a gradually accruing harmony through the loose rhyming of the words that describe the movements sweeping through them.

Effacing the independent status of actions, Whitman's gerunds and participles also elide their power to effect change: they suggest a strange variety of process that seems to continue performing itself in identical fashion on an always identical scene. Whitman's syntax shapes a zone of rhythmic, recurrent energies that tend toward an ideal limit of stasis.[19]

This catalogue also effaces the difference between the things it renders and the subject who names them. It does so by spinning out an extended sentence in the course of which both subject and predicate recede gradually from our attention. The rendered world thus no longer stands clearly opposed to an observer; the amorphous realm objects come to inhabit seems to be one into which the poem's agent, no longer easily locatable in relation to the landscape he describes, is himself being diffused.[20] Whitman's identification of the poet's physical presence with voice reinforces this confounding of the space Whitman's catalogues shape with the somatic terrain of the poet's own body. Mobilizing both the vocative pull of the word and the projective power of voice, this characteristic catalogue coordinates its centripetal and centrifugal energies, enacting a ritual of incorporation in which a contracting object world is subsumed within the poet's agglomerating interior.

The magical power thus ascribed to the word is perhaps conveyed most clearly by one of the syntactic features we already attended to, the catalogue's persistent deletion of the predicate. This grammatical anomaly negotiates a crossing from the world of the reality principle to the archaic space shaped by word magic. The power of action registered by the finite predicate is drained from the harbor scene and implicitly relocated in the ritual that names it; everything here is a function of the word, an aspect of the ongoing, undulant process indistinguishable from the poet's act of enunciation. Whitman's catalogue thus not only subdues the exterior scene to the poet's vocative powers; it seems also to generate the archaic space in which the objects he names now subsist.

It is a measure of the power *Leaves of Grass* ascribes to language that this internal space seems to be re-projected outward toward the end of "Crossing Brooklyn Ferry," shaping a no-longer alien external realm. (This reversal is also an instance of the sometimes confusing topological transformations that register and reify linguistic powers in Whitman's work.) "I reject none, accept all, reproduce all in my own forms," Whitman declares in "By Blue Ontario's Shore" (1856 180).[21] If the litany from section three of "Crossing Brooklyn Ferry" seems to mobilize the vocative pull implied in the opening of this declaration, the less typical but by no means uncommon catalogue in section nine suggests the productive, positional power announced at its close:

> Flow on, river! Flow with the flood-tide, and ebb with the ebb-tide!
> Frolic on, crested and scallop-edged waves!
> Gorgeous clouds of the sun-set, drench with your splendor me, or the men and women generations after me! (1856 219)

> Come on, ships from the lower bay! pass up or down, white-sailed schooners, sloops, lighters!
> Flaunt away, flags of all nations! be duly lowered at sun-set!
> Burn high your fires, foundry chimneys! cast black shadows at night-fall! cast red and yellow light over the tops of the houses! (1856 221)

Nearly everything the poet names in section three reappears unchanged in this closing cadenza. Commanding things to continue performing precisely those actions which the earlier catalogue had already presented as continuous, Whitman's imperatives make clear the power of language to generate as repetition what Whitman will mean by immediate presence. No longer withholding themselves as shifting objects assuming contingent configurations, the things the poet names reappear as functions of his word, unchanging presences shaped by and subject to its recuperative powers: "Keep your places, objects than which none else is more lasting!" (1856 221). In the archaic, magical universe of "Crossing Brooklyn Ferry," the ideal entities language names have thus become actual. And in the sometimes shadowy topological drama that organizes the poem's imaginative rhythms, the exterior space these objects occupy has been somaticized: "Suspend here and everywhere, eternal float of solution!" (1856 220). The things the poet names have once more assumed discrete form; but they seem now like entranced emanations of his voice, aspects of the labile body voice diffuses and re-incarnates.

Whitman's commitment to this space shaped by the magic word can be usefully contrasted to the persistent skepticism, in Wittgenstein's *Philosophical Investigations,* regarding the enticing regions language often seems to generate. There our tendency to confuse what Wittgenstein calls "surface grammar"—the logical space a particular syntax or expression implies—with a supposed "deep space"—an actual world conceived as sharing the properties thus suggested—is repeatedly chastened.[22] In Whitman's poems such depth is instead characteristically affirmed: the space the poet's stylized language shapes is called the world. Whitman's most explicit, dramatic declarations concerning what might be called the shamanistic resources of speech thus simply affirm the powers his poems widely display: "[I] have distanced what is behind me for good reasons," the poet declares summarily in "Song of Myself," "And call any thing close again when I desire it" (1855 55).

Not all Whitman's catalogues, of course, are single-minded attempts to project the imperial power of the word onto the world. In "Song of Myself," especially, heterogeneous elements are repeatedly introduced and allowed to deflect the poet's assimilative procedures. I shall take up in chapter 7 the way some of the catalogues in Whitman's first great poem oscillate between enacting and resisting the characteristic claims of Whitman's early editions. But it will be helpful to turn here instead to some catalogues in which efforts to suggest the performative powers of language take precedence, even more clearly than in "Crossing Brooklyn Ferry," over other concerns.

4. If "Crossing Brooklyn Ferry" is one of Whitman's more successful pieces, this is at least in part because the powers ascribed to the word are suggested there less obtrusively than in many of Whitman's other poems. The poet's vocative and performative powers are brought to bear on a single scene and seem to be describing or addressing encountered particulars even as they are busy transforming them. And as Richard Chase points out, the harbor scene is especially amenable to the sort of fluid vision Whitman's catalogues characteristically evoke (107–109). By contrast, some of Whitman's more strident catalogue poems have the peculiar virtue of making the linguistic assumptions at work in *Leaves of Grass* more explicit by flagrantly detaching them from the kind of representational supports "Crossing Brooklyn Ferry" provides. In such poems as the 1856 "Salut au Monde," the "scene" is unnervingly ency-clopedic: a staggering, seemingly random assortment of mountains, countries, continents, and peoples is pulled with gleeful insouciance from Whitman's grab-bag of names, to be processed by the agglomerating syntax brought to bear in "Crossing Brooklyn Ferry" on a single locale. The poet's palpable lack of first-hand acquaintance with the things he names has no discernible effect on his seeming ability to master and incorporate them; in "Salut au Monde" to name something is *ipso facto* to possess it, to "plant" it "permanently within." Whitman's catalogues thus gravitate naturally to apostrophe and the vocative:

> You, inevitable where you are!
> You daughter or son of England!
> You free man of Australia! you of Tasmania! you of Papua! you free woman
>   of the same!
> You of the mighty Slavic tribes and empires! you Russ in Russia!
> You dim-descended, black, divine-souled African, large, fine headed, nobly-
>   formed, superbly destined, on equal terms with me!
> You Norwegian! Swede! Dane! Icelander! you Prussian!
> You Spaniard of Spain! you Portuguese!
> [. . . .]
> You Sardinian! you Bavarian! you Swabian! Saxon! Wallachian! Bulgarian!
>   (1856 116–17)

The frenetic pitch reached toward the end of this passage clearly involves the poet in unintended self-parody: the initial patient, if rather clumsy attempts to establish credible moments of individual address are abandoned as Whitman frantically maximizes the centripetal pull of this language game. This bizarre moment nonetheless offers a distillation of Whitman's characteristic assumptions: in *Leaves of Grass* the name itself is inherently vocative, its power to produce the thing being magical rather than contextual and contingent. What might be called vocative etiquette thus turns out to be dispensable. Eliding the "you" as these lines reach their climax, Whitman's locution of course still implies it; this elision nonetheless suggests a shift toward that magical vision of language in which name and thing are conflated—the poet need no longer speak *to* the world because his word now *speaks* it. Here the vocative blends into the performative it always implies.

In *Leaves of Grass* even utterances cast in the indicative thus possess an implicit vocative pull. This effect is of course reinforced by the syntactic patterns I have been calling centripetal:

I see the high-lands of Abyssinia,
I see flocks of goats feeding, I see the fig-tree, tamarind, date,
I see fields of teff-wheat, I see the places of verdure and gold.

I see the Brazilian vaquero,
I see the Bolivian ascending Mount Sorata,
I see the Gaucho crossing the plains, I see the incomparable rider of horses
     with his lasso on his arm,
I see over the pampas the pursuit of wild cattle for their hides.
[....]
I see the regions of snow and ice,
I see the sharp-eyed Samoiede and the Finn. (1856 112–14)

Despite the animadversion to vision here, observed specificity is less the subject of these lines than the object of their enucleating energies. If to name, in *Leaves of Grass,* is to "see," it is also to summon and possess.

This pervasive vocative pull has an inherently essentializing effect: objects are lifted from the contingent, transitive relations in which they would otherwise be mired and summoned to the bar of the poet's timeless vision. Such essentializing power is intrinsic to the act of naming; but as the vocative dimension of Whitman's lists suggests, in *Leaves of Grass* it is characteristically conceived as a magical rather than merely intellectual resource. In the lines just quoted, this magical dimension is registered in a slight but repeated semantic disturbance common in Whitman's work: Whitman's "the" is equivocal in its representational import and thereby finally performative in its effect. A reading of these lines which takes Whitman's repeated "the" to be simply an ostensive gesture, the marker of what John Searle calls "singular definite reference" (72), feels increasingly awkward. The catalogue's panoramic outlook seems to enforce a corresponding generality in each of its local movements: we aren't firmly enough ensconced in any single locale for it to be credible we would understand which particular vaquero, or Bolivian, or Gaucho is being singled out simply by "the." Whitman's definite articles might thus be understood as cueing a series of class names. Yet the repeated reference to seeing demands ostensive interpretation: the poet gestures, it seems, at particulars. This representational conundrum implies its own performative solution. These lines, in effect, reify the paradox of their surface grammar, implying a magical space in which the poet's word has fused the class and the individual creature—in which the no-longer contingent individual possesses the ideal generality of the class, and in which the class possesses the solidity and specificity of the incarnate individual. This possibility, it should be stressed, no longer obeys the demands or constraints of either of the familiar language games to which these lines allude; according an implicit but nonetheless radical performative power to words, this passage enacts a series of "perceptions" that could exist nowhere but in language.[23]

According to Ernst Cassirer, just this surface grammar and the anomalous prospect it suggests characterize shamanistic speech. In *Language and Myth,* a monograph in which he argues that primitive religious categories are hypostatizations of ideal linguistic ones, Cassirer describes pantheistic deities as reifications of the class name:

There are several deities among the Coras who represent certain kinds of flowers, but are addressed as individual flowers. The same is true of all the Coras' demoniac creatures: the cicada, the cricket, the grasshopper, the armadillo are simply treated as so many individual wholes. If, therefore, ancient rhetoric names as one of the principal types of metaphor the substitution of a part for the whole, or vice versa, it is easy enough to see how this sort of metaphor arises directly out of the essential attitude of the mythic mind. But it is equally clear that for mythic thinking there is much more in metaphor than a bare "substitution," a mere rhetorical figure of speech; that what seems to our subsequent reflection as [*sic*] a sheer transcription is mythically conceived as a genuine and direct identification. (94)

Ideal abstractions are supposedly conjured up by shamanistic speech as actual, incarnate presences, bringing the diverse particulars of the world to the focal point designated and commanded by the name.

Like the enticing "deep space" Wittgenstein describes as a kind of *trompe l'oeil* effect produced by accidental similarities of surface grammar and the conflations of distinct language games they suggest, in *Leaves of Grass* the shamanistic powers of the poet's word are frequently implied by the sort of performative solution to a referential paradox we have just examined. Whitman's peculiar achievement thus slips away if we try to resolve the representational ambiguities of his syntax by appeal to most-likely-case scenarios. The otherwise exemplary analyses of Whitman's catalogue technique recently offered by James Perrin Warren, for example, go astray when Warren invokes such a literalized notion of poetic representation. Thus, for instance, in an analysis of section fifteen of "Song of Myself," Warren makes use of a sort of taxonomy of distinct representational cases in order to "solve" both the ambiguities of Whitman's use of the definite article—ambiguities which parallel those we have just attended to in "Salut au Monde" —and the poet's troubling mix of present-tense verb forms. Warren registers a possible reading of such a line as "The pure contralto sings in the organ loft," noting that "the definite article 'the' could indicate a generic noun phrase, while the simple present tense could indicate a stative verb phrase" ("Free Growth" 35).[24] But these possibilities are then dismissed because they contradict the representational procedures of some adjacent material, which employs the present progressive tense: "The one-year wife is recovering and happy having a week ago borne her first child." "Because the present progressive indicates the dynamic aspect of the verb," Warren notes

it would seem unlikely that the other verbs of the catalogue—all in the simple present tense—are stative. And since the generic noun cannot appear with a verb phrase in the present progressive tense, the personal agents must be taken as specific noun phrases.

If Whitman's use of the present progressive tense precludes the "timeless present" associated with the simple present tense, what sense of time does it allow? . . . A mixture of present progressive and simple present could occur in the instantaneous present . . . because both forms refer to an event as it is in the process of occurring. ("Free Growth" 36)

These deductions feel altogether too tidy. Here Warren regards Whitman's syntax as the transparent transcription of some observable reality which we should be able to delimit and recover. But Whitman often achieves his most dramatic effects precisely by breaking down this sort of contextual neatness. The long catalogue that opens section thirty-three of "Song of Myself" offers a more dramatic instance of just these characteristic conflations of ordinarily distinct representational possibilities. Whitman's opening proclamations locate what follows in a panoramic space: "My ties and ballasts leave me . . . . I travel . . . . I sail . . . . my elbows rest in the sea-gaps, / [. . . .] / I am afoot with my vision" (1855 57). In the passage's succeeding lines, individual agents and acts are pressured toward generic status not only because they appear in such a context, but also by means of Whitman's productive representational confusions. The poet is "afoot"

> Where the panther walks to and fro on a limb overhead . . . . where the buck
>   turns furiously at the hunter,
> Where the rattlesnake suns his flabby length on a rock . . . . where the otter is
>   feeding on fish,
> Where the alligator in his tough pimples sleeps by the bayou,
> Where the black bear is searching for roots or honey . . . . the beaver pats the
>   mud with his paddle-tail. (1855 57)

In this oneiric landscape each observed particular is also iconic; each individual creature is also an ideal, archetypal form. Each particular, grammatically "dynamic" act likewise repeats itself with the dreamlike inevitability implied by a stative reading of the verb, assimilating particular, finite actions to those iterative processes we are encouraged to identify with the poet's own performative energies.

This assimilation of discrete subjects and predicates to a single, rhythmic process ultimately indistinguishable from the poet's own enunciative act finds characteristic expression in the deverbal noun, another peculiar formation whose importance to Whitman's work Warren points out. Warren notes that these noun formations "from a verbal base" are more frequent in Whitman's poetry than the more common conversion of nouns to "denominal verbs" ("Real Grammar" 8). Moreover, Whitman's deverbal nouns include an unusually high proportion of "non-lexical" coinages ("Real Grammar" 9). Warren suggests astutely that these formations preserve a dynamic aspect because of their strangeness, so that "as a rule the forms balance precariously between the noun and the verb class" ("Real Grammar" 9). The urban scene rendered in section eight of "Song of Myself" suggests the agglomerative effect of such destabilized forms:

> *The blab* of the pave . . . . the tires of carts and *sluff* of bootsoles and *talk* of
> the promenaders,
> The heavy omnibus, the driver with his interrogating thumb, *the clank* of the
> shod horses on the granite floor,
> The carnival of sleighs, *the clinking* and shouted jokes and *pelts* of snowballs.
> *The hurrahs* for popular favorites . . . . the fury of roused mobs,
> *The flap* of the curtained litter. (1855 31–32; emphases added)

Detaching actions from particular agents, Whitman's deverbal nouns here recast finite, transitive acts as aspects of a diffuse, metamorphic process. Things, too, have been refashioned: discrete agents are replaced by loosely grouped, nominal accretions of this same omnipresent energy. The long catalogue from "Crossing Brooklyn Ferry" I examined earlier also makes use of such coinages, employing them in concert with participial modifiers that likewise suggest diffuse processes ("the white wake *left* by the passage"; "the *swinging* motion"). The harbor world is thus traversed by "the gradual *edging*," "the *falling*," and "the frolicsome crests and *glistening*." Like other key features of Whitman's catalogues, these deverbal nouns subdue the very contingencies they record, refashioning both substances and predicates into instances of a single agglomerating process.

5. In Whitman's early editions this archaic space is identified with the poet's own presence. Whitman's dialectic of the body is my subject in chapter 4; but I want at least to suggest here how his catalogue technique implies the sorts of somatic resources with which the poet is supposedly endowed. The collapse of discrete agents and acts into the undulant space shaped by speech implies correlative changes in the poet's body.

The image that concludes section thirty-one of "Song of Myself" alludes to the infantile scenario this melding of objects always recalls. A brief catalogue leads up to this scene, by means of just the sort of reification of linguistic functions we have been examining:

> In vain objects stand leagues off and assume manifold shapes,
> In vain the ocean settling in hollows and the great monsters lying low,
> In vain the buzzard houses herself with the sky,
> In vain the snake slides through the creepers and logs,

In vain the elk takes to the inner passes of the woods,
In vain the razorbilled auk sails far north to Labrador,
I follow quickly . . . . I ascend to the nest in the fissure of the cliff. (1855 55)

Whitman's final image here is vaginal and uterine. But the project thus suggested—of completing the child's researches by tracing existence back to its amniotic source—depends for its progress on the intertwining of infantile sexual registers with archaic dimensions of language. If the poet ascends to that fissure from which objects stream to "assume" the "manifold shapes" that populate the space of the Freudian secondary processes or reality principle, he works his way back to this threshold between division and agglomeration by means of one of Whitman's characteristic representational riddles. "The buzzard," "the snake," "the elk," and "the razor-billed auk" are all concrete universals, hypostatized class names imagined as magically incarnate particulars. Tracking manifold shapes that are already iconic, already embodiments of the idealizing word and its centripetal force, the poet thereby reascends to the boundary between the agglomerating realm of the primary processes and the spatial and temporal manifolds of the secondary ones, the borderline between a world of discrete identities and that undifferentiated plenum the catalogue's final image associates with an archaic somatic condition. The word magic on which the poet's ascent depends, we shall see in chapter 4, should be situated at precisely this threshold. Its crucial function is indeed to blur it, restoring an archaic mode of reception: through word magic the poet of *Leaves of Grass* seems to recover the agglomerating powers first experienced as a fusion with the maternal body. The separation the poet tracks back to its origin is both the division between self and other and the split between words and things.[25]

Leaves of Grass repeatedly suggests that these ruptures are one and the same. It does so in part by seeming to overcome them simultaneously, most dramatically in the catalogues that center on the poet's own body. Thus, for example, the beautiful litany that dominates the second section of "Song of Myself" not only seems to enucleate body boundaries, mingling inside and outside, self and other, in a manner closer to the primary processes than to the secondary ones; it does so in part by means of a word magic that fuses the thing with the word that names it, and with the poet's voice and breath. No catalogue of Whitman's offers a stronger sense of an undifferentiated, undulant, intensely somaticized space:

The smoke of my own breath,
Echoes, ripples, and buzzed whispers . . . . loveroot, silkthread, crotch and
  vine,
My respiration and inspiration . . . . the beating of my heart . . . . the passing
  of blood and air through my lungs,
The sniff of green leaves and dry leaves, and of the shore and darkcolored sea
  rocks, and of hay in the barn,
The sound of the belched words of my voice . . . . words loosed to the eddies
  of the wind,
A few light kisses . . . . a few embraces . . . . a reaching around of arms,
The play of shine and shade on the trees as the supple boughs wag,
The delight alone or in the rush of the streets, or along the fields and hillsides,
The feeling of health . . . . the full-noon trill . . . . the song of me rising from
  bed and meeting the sun. (1855 25–26)

The sense of amorphous unity that pervades this litany depends largely
on grammatical anomalies. Here Whitman completely suppresses predication, eliding the contingencies predicates record as well as the oppositions they structure.[26] The constative function of the catalogue is thus
suspended; this absence of statement serves in turn to foreground the
ritual, performative dimension of Whitman's tally. This performative
thrust is itself enigmatic: perhaps the catalogue blends together hitherto
discrete particulars, catching them up into the unity it seems to generate;
or perhaps it posits them, one by one, as aspects of its own unfolding.
These obverse activities, we shall see, can be thought of as complementary phases of a single ritual of repossession.

Here such performative resources consistently intertwine with somatic ones. Whitman's ritual naming alternates roughly between interior
and exterior phenomena; this unpredicated oscillation serves to establish
a sense of amorphous unity rather than any more firmly articulated
relation, dissolving the difference between self and other, body and
environment. Whitman's deverbal nouns are especially appropriate in
this context, since they suggest the existence of a pervasive kinesthetic
patterning that underlies all apparent particulars: the catalogue's somaticized space is shaped by "the beating," "the passing," "the snuff," "a
reaching," "the play"—provisional accretions of an always mobile
rhythmic activity. Defining a fantasmatic body no longer firmly separated from its objects, this archaic, labile realm exists for us in the
idiosyncratic syntactic and semantic procedures that name it.

This fusion of linguistic and somatic registers is suggested from the very beginning of the catalogue. The poet's body becomes a kind of rhythmically moving membrane; its crucial synecdoche is breath. This is the particular with which the catalogue begins, and to which it insistently recurs: "The smoke of my own breath"; "my respiration and inspiration"; "the sniff of green leaves and dry leaves." A rhythm of inhalation and exhalation is indeed the implicit model for the sort of pulsating space this passage suggests, in which objects seem ambiguously to attain either a detachment from or a fusion with the poet's body that are equally provisional; it is as if discrete particulars are caught up into the body, somaticized or desolidified, and then sent forth again as ductile emanations. For the pneumatic body this rhythmic relation to objects implies, eroticism is a version of auto-eroticism, object relations a kind of expansive, polymorphous narcissism: "A few light kisses . . . . a few embraces . . . . a reaching around of arms." Everything becomes an instance of what the poet's body "inspires" and "respires."

One of the items subjected to this rhythmic somaticizing is the poet's word, now provocatively physicalized: "The sound of the belched words of my voice . . . . words loosed to the eddies of the wind." "Belched" and "loosed" into the ductile space the catalogue renders, language takes up its place among the provisionally separate things the poet puts forth. Acquiring the status of physical phenomena, words might thus be capable of exercising a power over objects that is more than merely conceptual. Conversely, things themselves are transformed by this proximity to words: metonymic suggestion lends the poet's breath and body, and the objects he incorporates and re-projects, the ideal, abstract qualities of language. This idealization is crucial to the transformation the catalogue seems to perform. The ingestion and re-projection this passage implies can be attributed to body and breath only through an exorbitant troping of kinesthetic and respiratory powers. The rhythmic assimilation and expulsion presented here figure the vocative and positional powers of language, suggesting their magical force.

6. Like the body it evokes, however, word magic in *Leaves of Grass* hovers between vision and accomplishment; Whitman's projections of an archaic body and word are propelled by a desire to overcome the very splits of which the poet remains aware. This attempt to straddle the borders of two organizations, to resurrect lost satisfactions by employing

symbolic language until it reveals or restores the very powers from which it now separates us, can lead to a divided and anxious practice, a poetic idiom aware of its own expulsion from the very condition of which it dreams. Such equivocations, which undermine the poet's redemptive project yet are crucial to the greatness of Whitman's book, will be my subject further on. Whitman's troubled ambitions, however, sometimes find expression instead in a bellicose insistence, which is all the more irksome since, from our side of the breach between word and thing, or subject and object, they attempt to deny, the linguistic assumptions which underlie the poet's claims can seem simply outlandish.

It is perhaps for this reason that among Whitman's most insightful critics have been those most flabbergasted by his procedures. Whitman's frequently cavalier attitude toward representational concerns can be mind-boggling. His catalogues consistently omit sustained and sustaining context; for all the myriad things they encompass, these lists are concerned relatively little with depicting particular objects, evincing a strange shift of focus away from the very things Whitman's nouns are busy naming. This lack of concentrated attention, which ought to be a defect, turns out to be an essential resource instead, given Whitman's peculiar goals and assumptions. The tallies in *Leaves of Grass* typically work to break down the integrity and autonomy of hitherto independent objects, representing things as grist for the poet's linguistic mill; this end is best accomplished by naming objects as expeditiously as possible.

Such a procedure can give us the troubling sense that the poet is busy claiming identity with things he hasn't even bothered to glance at. F. O. Matthiessen's contrary assertions seem more generous than apt, describing only the very best of Whitman's catalogues rather than the bulk of them:

Whitman's excitement carries weight because he realized that a man cannot use words so unless he has experienced the facts that they express, unless he has grasped them with his senses. (518)

D. H. Lawrence's response seems more accurate, despite its racism, and for all its being a nasty joke at Whitman's expense:

As soon as Walt *knew* a thing, he assumed One Identity with it. If he knew that an Eskimo sat in a kyak, immediately there was Walt being little and yellow and greasy, sitting in a kyak.

Now will you tell me exactly what a kyak is?

Who is he that demands petty definition? Let him behold me *sitting in a kyak*. (166)

Marked by Lawrence's irascible wonder, these lines drive a wedge between knowing and naming, exposing the outrageousness of Whitman's working assumptions.

This emptiness of the knowledge provided by the name can make Whitman's practice seem like a prolonged exercise in tautology: claiming to do something substantial by naming objects, the poet is instead simply naming them. Knut Hamsen suggests this tautological quality of Whitman's work:

His tabulated poetry, those impossible reiterations of persons, states, household furniture, tools, articles of dress . . . reveal not a spark of poetic talent. When Whitman celebrates a thing he says right in the first line that he is celebrating that thing—in order to say in the next line that he celebrates a second thing, in the third line a third thing—without celebrating it in any way except by naming it. He does not know more of anything than its name, but he knows many names. (Quoted in Schyberg 104)[27]

Quentin Anderson offers a more explicit if more paradoxical formulation:

We may put it that nothing in the world offered any resistance to his consciousness of it. Neither multiplicity nor futurity nor the past nor physical remoteness nor any kind of apparent dissonance daunted him. His consciousness prescribed no limits; whatever he had the power to be conscious of he was conscious of. This also sounds aberrant, but it is the very quality of the Person's sense of the world. ("Whitman's New Man" 29)

Whatever Whitman had the power to name he might name, and he had the power to name anything whose name he knew.

Whitman's catalogues can thus resemble the enticing "deep tautologies" from which Wittgenstein's language philosopher retrieves the speculator in words (Pears 87). A demystified stance will register the poet's pronouncements as self-referential grammatical remarks masquerading as synthetic judgments—"I see the Brazilian vaquero" amounting to no more than the metacomment "I name the Brazilian vaquero." Yet this apparently tautological assertion will strike the believer in word magic as the exercise of a substantial power—"I name the Brazilian vaquero" meaning, in its turn, "I see and possess the vaquero by naming him." Despite their frequent lack of credibility (or, sometimes, interest) as series of empirical assertions, Whitman's catalogues do not simply collapse into the self-reflexive tracing of logical grammars so long as we entertain the hypothesis of word magic: we will then construe the formulaic predications in which the poet indulges as acts of ritual performance bearing directly on the world.[28] Whitman is willing to take up a great deal of space writing what amounts to tautology in the register of symbolic language, in order gradually to evoke that other, archaic dimension shaped by this magical mode of conceiving the word.

Suggesting a relation between the body and its objects that differs drastically from the sort we know, word magic conjures up a fantasmatic space in which the intervals traversed by desire have collapsed back into punctual satisfaction. The transfigured eroticism such space implies is a crucial focus of Whitman's early editions. Yet archaic satisfactions are not quite made present in *Leaves of Grass;* Whitman's evocations of blissful merging typically seem to waver, hovering between instantaneous, hallucinatory gratification and the sense of lack they should dispel.[29] In the liminal space through which the poet moves, touch never quite becomes incorporation; the other is not quite reducible to an aspect of the self; and desire never quite dissolves into continuous gratification. This spacing is also linguistic: the word remains sign rather than talismanic synecdoche; the poet's speech act, which should be the magical production of presence, threatens to lapse into mere designation instead.[30] The catalogues of Whitman's first two editions typically strive to suggest the resources of the full word. But the emptiness that haunts them is also Whitman's subject, as is the desire in which this lack entangles him. As Paul Zweig movingly recounts, Whitman haunted the Crystal Palace exhibition that came to Manhattan in 1853, soaking up not only the industrial wonders of the age but also the ambience of young men; he went home and wrote down their names in the same notebooks in which many of the catalogue poems took shape (212). Throughout the 1850s, Whitman periodically commemorated similar rambles in such laconic tallies:

Johny (round faced—in Dunbar's and engine house—full eyes) and liquid
Pete (smallish—looks a little like 5th av Billy Folk

Wm Vanderbergh, (young fellow, sick, sandy complexion Fulton av. near
   City Hall
Tom Riley (handsome Irish fighter
John Kiernan (loafer young saucy looking pretty goodlooking. (NUPM 1:251)[31]

Stretching on for several pages, this list grows increasingly poignant.[32] Should we read it as performance or designation, possession or indication, vehicle of fulfillment or of desire? What does it mean to name something, to bestow or utter a name? Whitman's catalogues articulate desire in the very foundering of performance, in the failure of the word magic of which they dream.

Such haunted doubling will occupy us further on. I want to turn next to Whitman's attempts to embed the word magic we have been considering in a representational context that will make it seem credible. The imaginative universe of Whitman's early editions can be understood as a reification of the vision of language I have been attending to, a building out of the space Whitman's notion of the word implies. Whitman's cosmological musings serve to hypostatize, and thereby naturalize, the verbal powers the poems display; *Leaves of Grass* is indeed, as Whitman remarked to Traubel, "a language experiment" (quoted in DBN 3:729n3439). Crucial to this cosmic projection will be the notion of "indication" we glanced at a moment ago. Ordinarily applied to systems of representation, such as language, this term comes in Whitman's poems to characterize the world itself: in *Leaves of Grass* the world becomes a kind of sign system, and the reality it points to is the word. We need to trace this governing chiasmus and take note of its consequences.

Notes

1. Schyberg has regularized the rather bizarre punctuation of this passage as it appears in Barrus (64).
2. On incorporation as a crucial trope for and goal of Whitman's procedures, see Anderson, *Imperial Self*, especially 157–61. I am indebted as well to Dorothy Gregory; see especially 33–49.
3. On the primary processes, see Freud, "Formulations Regarding the Two Principles in Mental Functioning," *Collected Papers* 4:13–21.
4. On the relation between affirmation and denial in *Leaves of Grass*, see Anderson, "Whitman's New Man" 37–41.

5. See Thomas 107–8 and Erkkila 38 for related discussions of the connection between "Crossing Brooklyn Ferry" and Whitman's earlier newspaper piece.

6. My slide here from the hazards of urban life to the more encompassing difficulties of object relations approximates Whitman's own. While such slippage sometimes blurs the political acumen of *Leaves of Grass* by suggesting that intractable social problems are amenable to regressive, fantasmatic solutions, it also accounts for much of the poetry's lure.

7. See for example Edwin Miller, *Walt Whitman's Poetry* 202.

8. James Miller notes the time shift; he draws attention as well to the "lurid" quality of the light which engulfs the scene. See *Critical Guide* 83.

9. On this point see Thomas 103.

10. I here follow Anderson: "It is, I believe, a central observation about Whitman that he undermined such structures as are said to be the basis of signification in Lévi-Strauss's *Savage Mind*. His use of species was not to discriminate, his use of human functions and relations had the end of agglomeration, his use of place did not effect distinctions" (*Imperial Self* 95).

11. The formal features of *any* representational code, that is, are already performative. See chapter 4, below, for an extended account of the relation between such normative syntax and the cultural register Lacan and Kristeva call the symbolic.

12. Hence Paul Fry's evocation of the poet's "calling": the vocative functions as a sign of the poet's access to linguistic powers more primordial than those mobilized by socially mediated signs (3, 12). See also Culler, "Apostrophe" 139–43.

13. Anderson fastens his attention firmly on this overriding effect of Whitman's catalogues: "It is mere grammatical pedantry to think of his catalogues as having the end of inclusion: at their brilliant best, they are successful efforts to melt things together, to make the sum of things ring with one note" (*Imperial Self* 95); "Whitman offered the sensation of lapsing into everything as the greatest of gifts; he was the prime poet of uncreation. Like a shaman making a puppet to represent the enemy to be destroyed, he dowers his world with only so much quiddity as he can dissolve, or cants each created thing on the slope of process down which it will slide to oblivion" (*Imperial Self* 94). In what follows, I spell out the syntactic aberrations that enact such effects. My account is indebted to two essays by James Perrin Warren: " 'The Free Growth of Metrical Laws': Syntactic Parallelism in 'Song of Myself,' " and "The 'Real Grammar': Deverbal Style in 'Song of Myself.' " I have benefited, as well, from comments Warren provided on a draft of my "Whitman's Tropes of Light and Flood." Basil De Selincourt's sensitive early response to the catalogues includes some brief but astute remarks on Whitman's syntax; see *Walt Whitman: A Critical Study* 124–55, especially 149–51. Other useful accounts of the poet's catalogue tech-

nique include Lewis, especially 51; Schyberg, especially 100–105; Coffman; Marki, especially 195–99; and Byers 111–12.

14. I have retained the period which ends the first of these lines in the 1856 text; but the editors of the *Variorum* construe this as a broken comma; see V 1:219.

15. See Marki 195 for a related discussion of Whitman's use of repetition.

16. As Warren suggests, such semantic repetition helps create the insistent "rhythm of syntactic parallelism" that characterizes Whitman's catalogues ("Free Growth" 32).

17. Warren stresses the importance of such "phrasal" catalogues in Whitman's work and astutely suggests that they typically seem to absorb the very things they render. See "Free Growth" 40.

18. Warren also stresses Whitman's elision of finite verbs, noting the temporal blurring produced by the resulting "stative" grammar; but he suggests that Whitman's use of deverbal nouns re-introduces a sense of activity into the catalogues; see "Real Grammar" 11–16. Such deverbal nouns, however, both transmute finite actions into continuous processes and weaken the sense of specific, individual agency; in contrast to simple transitive declarations, such constructions render a world no longer shaped by competing agents and their acts.

19. Marki (196) notes the way Whitman's catalogues seem to dissolve temporal distinctions.

20. So, as Warren suggests, "the poetic self expands, absorbing . . . . places and events" until "the activity of expanding becomes more important than the objects absorbed" ("Free Growth" 40).

21. The "I" here is literally America. But Whitman's identification of the nation's geographic expanse with the poet's own body is persistent: see for example the 1855 Preface, especially 7.

22. See Wittgenstein 47–51; also Pears 115–27.

23. This figmentary "perception" generated by language is memorialized in John Ashbery's "Scheherazade," a poem which might be understood in part as an ironically inflected homage to Whitman: "But most of all she loved the particles / That transform objects of the same category / Into particular ones, each distinct / Within and apart from its own class" (*Self-Portrait in a Convex Mirror* 9).

24. I quote here the CRE text Warren uses rather than the 1855 version; the differences are minimal: see CRE 41 and V 1:16. On the stative and the dynamic see Warren, "Real Grammar" 6–7.

25. I take up these assertions in chapter 4, below. See Kristeva, *Desire in Language* 174, 187, and 217–18; *Revolution in Poetic Language* 43–48 and 54–55; and *Powers of Horror* 52–53.

26. See Durand, "Whitman, le rythme, le sujet de l'écriture" 69–71 for a related discussion of the effects of Whitman's suppression of predication here.

27. Schyberg quotes from Knut Hamsen, *Fra det moderne Amerikas Aandsliv* (Copenhagen: n.p., 1889) 79.
28. See Wittgenstein 25 and 90.
29. Freud describes hallucinated gratification, which obviates frustration and delay, as the mode of satisfaction proper to the primary processes; see "Formulations Regarding the Two Principles in Mental Functioning," *Collected Papers* 4:14.
30. On the talisman or kosmos see Fletcher 82–92.
31. The list of names from which I have taken this brief selection occupies NUPM 1:247–62. Grier dates most of the notebook in which this list appears to 1857. NUPM 1:227–28 contains a similar list assigned by Grier to 1855 or 1856. NUPM 1:230–32, from the same notebook, contains a draft of portions of "Crossing Brooklyn Ferry."
32. Shively (51–54) sees these lists of names as celebratory, construing them as a tally of consummated assignations; see also 55–62. For the contrary view see Zweig 188–97.

3. Indications and Crossings: Light and Flood

Flood-tide of the river, flow on! I watch you, face to face,
Clouds of the west! sun half an hour high! I see you also face to face.
—"Crossing Brooklyn Ferry," 1856 211

Scattered throughout Whitman's early editions are what might be called the first rumblings of a cosmologizing imagination. It is not until the 1870s, when Whitman published "Passage to India," that these issue in the full-blown cosmic fantasizing that increasingly dominates the later poetry. Yet even in such early poems as "Crossing Brooklyn Ferry" we encounter images that imply the presence of at least a roughly traced cosmology. Full of such unfamiliar entities as "the float," a "due emission," and "a necessary film," this cosmic system will need some explaining. But it is probably more important to assess its significance for the early editions of *Leaves of Grass*.

Approaching Whitman's early poetry through the perspective enforced by the later work, one tradition of Whitman criticism accords such cosmic doctrine a central place. Noting the importance of the "imaginative fusion of the poet and the reader" in "Crossing Brooklyn Ferry," James Miller thus goes on to suggest that this merging figures an insight of a more essential order: "The reader's feeling, at the end of the poem, that he and the poet are interfused represents his emotional insight into the world of spiritual unity" (*Critical Guide* 80). "The chemical figure," Miller goes on to argue concerning Whitman's "float forever held in solution" (1856 216), "evokes a vivid picture of the abstract concept that underlies the entire poem" (85). But in "Crossing Brooklyn Ferry" the poet's energies are not easily subdued to such abstractions; the few lines in the poem that support this reading simply won't bear such weight. The order of priorities Miller suggests—poet's presence as trope for an underlying religious or cosmic vision—might better be reversed: rather than spelling out a coherent, systematic doctrine, Whitman's cosmological musings amount to a malleable repertoire of tropes and assertions, deployed so as to accord language and the poet's voice the powers Whitman's catalogues and evocations of the poet's presence suggest.

In Whitman's later work, cosmic speculation serves to focus our contemplation on a remote sphere from which we have supposedly come and to which we will return after death; his performative energies flagging, the poet posits a world beyond this one in which his still unrealized aspirations will be fulfilled. In the early editions of *Leaves of Grass,* Whitman's intermittent cosmologizing instead functions heuristically, building out a sense of our present world the poems' own characteristic transactions imply. In "Crossing Brooklyn Ferry," Whitman's most dramatic announcement concerning the "float" focuses directly on the here and now of the harbor scene: "Suspend here and everywhere, eternal float of solution!" (1856 220). The cosmic agents called on in the poem are likewise related intimately to the poet who invokes them, coming to figure his powers rather than making up for their waning. As Whitman's imperative in the line just quoted implies, the "eternal float" is made to "suspend here" by means of the poet's word: the "float" is a name for the space generated by Whitman's catalogues, and the cosmogonizing powers that shape the harbor scene are the poet's emanating presence and the voice on which it is modeled. In the early editions of *Leaves of Grass,* Whitman's cosmologizing functions as part of a sublime economy rather than a mystical vision: it helps structure a romantic transumption, a crisis of blockage and recovery in which initially external, competing forces are internalized as types of the poet's own power.[1]

This sublime economy is cued to depictions of light and flood; the poet's sometimes quirky cosmologizing is thus grounded in what almost feels like empirical fact. Both light and flood are ultimately regarded as deficient precursors of the poet's transfiguring word. But they are also set against one another, lending cosmic scope to the conflicts in which the poet is immersed. If Whitman's catalogues subdue recalcitrant objects to the inclusive power of the word, overcoming the multiple and the contingent, his light imagery serves to consign such separate, unstable forms to the status of simulacra. Illuminating only the surfaces of things, light also projects their outlines or images, creating a baffling mix of partially illumined objects and figmentary forms. It becomes Whitman's crucial metonymy for *natura naturata*—the world of seemingly discrete entities apprehended as an array of surfaces that conceal interiors and block our access to them. Like the images cast by light among which they appear, these surfaces are themselves regarded as misleading signs: they are said merely to "indicate" or poorly represent the force of *natura naturans* that has produced and now lurks within them. Associated with the insides such exteriors sequester, this animating force is typically figured in Whitman's work as a flood that creates all individual forms from out of its ceaseless flowing. Visionary moments in Whitman's work often begin with a welling up of this cosmic liquid: it results in the momentary dissolution of blocking surfaces and the ecstatic mingling of no-longer bounded forms.

The poet might well be assigned the prophetic task of recording such glimpses of an earthly paradise. But in the early editions of *Leaves of Grass* we repeatedly discover him lurking about to assist its progress: caressing and laving, his fluid body seems to be an essential catalyst in these visionary reactions. It is in his pneumatic guise, however, that the poet comes truly into his own: not only are breath and voice associated systematically with the natural power of flood, appearing as aspects of or substitutes for it; in Whitman's early editions *natura naturans* is ultimately a trope for the productive, performative force of language.

The world of surfaces amid which the poet moves is thus finally conceived as a series of signs pointing not simply to the sequestered flood of *natura naturans* but also to the living word. In a sublime transumption central to the imaginative economy of *Leaves of Grass,* world and word are thus reconceived as outside and inside, appearance and essence, respectively: the world has become the mere sign of itself; the word produces the world itself. This chiasmus of words and things hyperbolizes the ritual power of utterance displayed throughout the early editions of *Leaves of Grass;* it paradoxically naturalizes the power of the poet's word by making created nature a function of language. This naturalization is one crucial function of Whitman's sometimes baroque and improbable cosmic musings.

But Whitman's preoccupation with the supposed deficiencies of the natural world, and with the word's power to overcome them, can also be regarded as a displacement of more intimate and threatening difficulties. Positing a cosmological ground for the word, Whitman occults the social provenance of language, the symbolic status of its powers, and the socially mediated meaning and value of its objects and acts. Extricating the poet from pressures by which he has been conspicuously beset, this positioning of the word also implies that his speech might redeem a social realm from which its powers no longer derive.[2] Yet the cultural threats the poet would thereby evade are indirectly registered in the very image cluster that should serve to lay them to rest. The characterization of created nature as a realm of images serves only in part to assuage the poet's apprehensions, by implying both the merely illusory status of all that opposes his dominion and the word's priority to it. This proliferation of images simultaneously expresses anxiety, provoked by a debacle that is cultural rather than natural: Whitman imagines a world engulfed by simulacra, a symbolic order encroaching with something like inexorability on things themselves. His positioning of the poet's word as the cure for nature's odd fall into representation thus allays anxieties about the word by projecting them onto the world—disquietudes the vision of proliferating representations comes close to admitting. I will conclude my look at the imaginative structure centering on light and flood by noting how it registers some of these doubts; the cultural dilemma to which they point will be my subject in the following chapter. First I want to trace Whitman's image cluster in something like the terms it proposes.

1. Associating the world of visible forms with the action of light that reveals it, Whitman hyperbolizes its bewildering qualities. But he also levers appearances into the position of phantasmagoria: the bounding surfaces that delimit each object and mark its otherness are assimilated to the images and shadows produced by the play of light upon them. Suggesting that such otherness is delusive or at any rate accidental, Whitman's light imagery attributes it ambiguously to either a deficient mode of apprehension or a flawed sort of incarnation. Descending from outside and illuminating surfaces only, proliferating images rather than penetrating to the animating presence such surfaces conceal, light epitomizes an alienated mode of knowledge. Yet the opaque surfaces light is consigned to displaying or duplicating are themselves unnatural impediments: Whitman repeatedly figures them as accretions that perversely trap the life force lurking within them. The enigmatic creation myth in "Crossing Brooklyn Ferry" seems to associate such confinement with the action of light, apparently attributing the creation of bounded bodies to

an original instance of cosmic illumination: the created world of opaque forms seems to be figured as a collection of images projected from above by light. This peculiar equivocation—between false apprehension and degraded incarnation—turns out to be richly evocative. As we shall see in chapter 4, its resonance depends ultimately on Whitman's vision of socialization, which fastens not only on the separation of the body from its objects but also on the split between word and thing that inaugurates symbolic language and consciousness, debacles Whitman sees as related.

"Crossing Brooklyn Ferry" can provide us once more with a distilled version of Whitman's characteristic imaginative transactions. We need to remember, though, that the harbor scene is presented from the perspective of a sublime reversal supposedly already accomplished as the poet addresses us: his descriptions derive much of their frequently sanguine quality from this transfigured relation. Yet this transmuted scene is still disturbed by the muted presence of troubling forces. There are only a few references to the action of light in the poem, but these are disposed so as to color our reception of adjacent material. Light is the crucial source of the splendor that provokes the poet's ecstacy, despite a complementary reference to sound: "The glories *strung like beads* on my smallest sights and hearings [...]" (1856 212; emphasis added). But these brilliant auras—clustered on objects, perhaps, like dew—are conspicuously ephemeral. In the recurrent scene the poet evokes, the declining sun is "half an hour high" (1856 213), and in the poem's third section the light it projects grows "dimmer and dimmer" (1856 215). This light is also fitful in its operation: in section six the poet recalls that "The dark threw patches down upon me also, / The best I had done seemed to me blank and suspicious" (1856 216). The metaphorical status of this "dark" which descends on the poet augments the importance of images of light and shadow rather than diminishing it: the scene's shifting, evanescent light becomes Whitman's crucial metonymy for the mode of relation it conditions.

From the vantage of the poem's conclusion, that relation is an unnatural one. In "Crossing Brooklyn Ferry" light illumines a shifting, unstable scene filled with a multitude of creatures and objects apparently divorced from the subject who surveys them; the poet has been relegated to transcribing vicissitudes he does not control. This limitation may well strike us as inevitable. Yet the poem enacts a reversal in which it is supposedly overcome: "planting" the objects of the harbor scene "permanently within," the poet annuls their otherness and their changeability in a single gesture. "Crossing Brooklyn Ferry" thus suggests that the instability vision records is a function of its separation from the objects it apprehends and of the transitive relations it is therefore consigned to rendering: the mode of apprehension conditioned by light sees only the extrinsic, the merely contingent.

The long catalogue that dominates the poem's third section is framed by images that lend the entire scene something of the quality of Plato's cave. Its opening draws our attention to the play of light that illumines the harbor:

> I watched the December sea-gulls, I saw them high in the air floating with
> motionless wings oscillating their bodies,
> I saw how the glistening yellow lit up parts of their bodies, and left the rest in
> strong shadow. (1856 213)

Light slides over shifting surfaces, forming unstable patterns and providing glimpses of the object that are partial and virtually random.

The poet turns next to the river's surface, encountering not actual objects but figmentary forms produced by light:

> I too saw the reflection of the summer-sky in the water,
> Had my eyes dazzled by the shimmering track of beams. (1856 213–14)

The shapes which shimmer on the river are like outsides with no insides. Here Whitman's pervasive sense of the gap between surface and interior reaches a giddy limit: the interior is no longer simply inaccessible but has ceased to exist.

Heightening the deficiencies which already characterize the poet's apprehensions of the object world, this concentration on projected shapes also implicitly attributes his difficulties to the operation of representation light brings into play. In the scene shaped by light, our attention is diverted from the thing itself to a dazzling image that substitutes for it; introducing a mediating term between subject and object, light confounds their relation. As the poem elsewhere makes clear, the sun from which light emanates is also conceived as this alienating third: instigating a detour through the forms it projects, the sun is the source of mediations that deflect or displace the protagonist's observations rather than facilitating them.[3] Apparently, the poet is alienated from the objects he contemplates by representation, or by the distant source from which it emanates.

This detour seems not only to intervene in the poet's relation to objects, but also to structure his contemplation of himself. Light can represent objects where they are not, usurping their power of self-presentation by disseminating their images:

> Had my eyes dazzled by the shimmering track of beams,
> Looked at the fine centrifugal spokes of light round the shape of my head in the sun-lit water. (1856 214)

The poet gazes here on his own detached image; produced by the sun, this vision of his proper grandeur appears before him with a certain alienated majesty. If this haloed, seemingly light-emitting shape tropes the generative force of the poet, being an avatar of that Apollo figure whose romantic lineage goes back at least to Collins, this visionary power now stands over against him and must somehow be reclaimed.[4] If the poet's apprehension of objects detours through an alienating third, so too does his vision of himself: appearing as an image cast by the sun, identity itself has been hollowed out.

Coming at these lines from a different angle and associating them with two phrases from Whitman's enigmatic creation myth—one evoking the "float" and one asserting that each person "came, or comes, or shall come, from its due emission" (1856 218)[5]—Quentin Anderson reads this scene of what might be called natural alienation in terms of an occulted sexual scenario:

> He has been "struck from the float forever held in solution"; that is, he is defined as an identity by the power of the sun which images his head in the water, or is the creation of a particular seed of the paternal "float" or semen. ("Whitman's New Man" 20)[6]

The Oedipal structure Anderson adduces here helps account for the psychic resonance of the whole image cluster centering on light, coloring not only passages like this one but also the mythic drama in which the poet challenges the sun.[7] In this context the invasive or aggressive aspects of the poet's determination to fuse all creatures and objects into his fluid form are offset by the liberating effects of this gesture: negating the distance between subject and object, the poet thereby also annuls the interior distance and alienation to which all selves are subjected in the realm ruled by light and shaped by the detour through representation it inaugurates. The paternal metaphor to which Anderson appeals alerts us to the symbolic force of this myth of natural redemption.

The lines that conclude the long stanza of "Crossing Brooklyn Ferry" to which we have been attending, however, figure not our liberation from the reign of light but the phantasmagoria by which those under its rule are haunted. The scene turns demonic, as the poet observes:

> On the neighboring shore the fires from the foundry chimneys burning high and glaringly into the night,
> Casting their flicker of black, contrasted with wild red and yellow light, over the tops of houses, and down into the clefts of streets. (1856 215)

Images of nothing that exists, these violently shifting shapes epitomize the delusive quality of the world shaped by light. Representation has the dangerous capacity to usurp the proper place of things themselves, ensnaring us in a realm of insubstantial images.

If representation intervenes in our apprehension of the object world, and of ourselves, a similar doubling has apparently befallen the physical world, deforming incarnate objects themselves. Susceptible to being represented in images cast by light, the objects of the harbor scene are implicitly regarded as representations. In *Leaves of Grass* an explicitly semiotic vocabulary establishes this connection; it calls attention to itself since it tends to sit awkwardly in passages of physical description. Cued to the word "indicate," this terminology suggests that Whitman's cosmic musings are crucially concerned with the way signification shapes the world. Rather than being a nominalist gesture, though, this habit of attention instead serves to lever the poet's specially empowered words into the privileged position of things, by first showing that things themselves are already compromised by the semiotic operation we normally attribute to words.

Like Whitman's light imagery, his semiotic vocabulary also stresses the opacity of visible surfaces. A short stanza later deleted from the seventh section of "Crossing Brooklyn Ferry" characterizes the relation between such surfaces and the depths that lurk within them in terms of the operation of indication:

Every thing indicates—the smallest does, and the largest does,
A necessary film envelops all, and envelops the soul for a proper time. (1856
   218)[8]

Whitman's juxtaposition here suggests that it is by means of a "necessary film" that "every thing indicates." Enveloping "all," this "film"
seems to be a trope for opaque surfaces. Since it more particularly
"envelops the soul for a proper time," it can also be associated with the
body, epitomized by its surfaces; incarnation, blockage, and indication
are for Whitman intimately connected. A line from the poem's ninth
section suggests the self-division to which objects have thus been subjected: "Appearances, now or henceforth, indicate what you are!" (1856
221). Hidden behind their surfaces, things "indicate" themselves rather
than revealing what they are directly.

Such passages serve to relegate visible objects to the status of signs,
opposing outsides to insides as signifiers to signifieds. The operation of
indication that performs this signifying relay offers knowledge that is
sketchy and imperfect:

Whither I walk I cannot define, but I know it is good,
The whole universe indicates that it is good,
The past and present indicate that it is good. ("To Think of Time," 1856 341)

Indication provides a sign of something it cannot present directly, substituting for a thing which itself remains absent or inaccessible.[9] Whitman's
semiotic vocabulary thus displaces the organicist vision with which *Leaves
of Grass* is commonly associated: rather then being the expressive flow-
ering of the inside, the outside is a signifier veiling a signified it simultaneously indicates and sequesters. The visible world becomes an enigmatic text that rebuffs deciphering:

And I cannot put my toe anywhere to the ground,
But it must touch numberless and curious books
Each one scorning all that schools and science can do fully to translate them.
   (UPP 2:70)

The interpretive labor this book of nature both requires and frustrates
is one of the poet's generic tasks. Sometimes he works patiently, putting
up with the distance imperfectly bridged by indication while awaiting
the visionary breakthrough that will make recourse to this deficient
operation unneccesary:

> Spots or cracks at the windows do not disturb me,
> Tall and sufficient stand behind and make signs to me;
> I read the promise and patiently wait. ("Faces," 1855 127)

Sometimes he urges us to tolerate this gap with similar patience, offering a vision of eventual reconciliation that he can express for now only in the tantalizing mode of paradox:

> Will the whole come back then?
> Can each see the signs of the best by a look in the lookingglass? Is there nothing greater or more?
> Does all sit there with you and here with me? ("A Song for Occupations," 1855 92)

Yet more characteristically, the poet resolutely sets about overcoming such divisions, burrowing through indicative surfaces. "Song of the Open Road" thus invokes a figure whom the poet himself elsewhere incarnates:

> Only the kernel of every object nourishes;
> Where is he who tears off the husks for you and me?
> Where is he that undoes stratagems and envelopes for you and me? (1856 229)

Persistently and sometimes frantically kinetic, such images of physical penetration seem at first to be at odds with those aspects of Whitman's presentation that assimilate the physical world to the problematics of the image or sign. Yet in passages such as these, the created world is oddly figured as *encrusted*. It is characterized by dried-out surfaces, lifeless accretions that block all flow and animation—excrescences left, as it were, by an incomplete process of molting, shells that have not quite dropped away and now disguise and entrap what lurks within them. Like Whitman's explicitly semiotic vocabulary, his topographic mapping of objects replaces expressivity with an opposition between inside and outside that subverts such organic continuity.

The resistant, congealed physicality that characterizes objects in their fallen mode is sometimes explicitly associated with the production of deceptive signs: opacity amounts to misrepresentation, and can be figured as an ironized, dissimulating discourse. The 1855 poem "Faces" opens with a prolonged description of an urban crowd that modulates into remarkable grotesqueness:

> This now is too lamentable a face for a man;
> Some abject louse asking leave to be . . cringing for it,
> Some milknosed maggot blessing what lets it wrig to its hole. (1855 125)

Yet such deformity is shortly equated with deception and thus partly relieved of the sense of gruesome quiddity that made it so troubling:

> Features of my equals, would you trick me with your creased and cadaverous
>   march?
> Well then you cannot trick me.
>
> I see your rounded never-erased flow,
> I see neath the rims of your haggard and mean disguises. (1855 125–26)

The 1855 Preface likewise associates surfaces with stratagem and deceit, thus equating the overcoming of otherness with the bringing forth of unsullied originary force:

> The poets of the kosmos advance through all interpositions and coverings
>   and turmoils and stratagems to first principles. (1855 17)

The 1856 "By Blue Ontario's Shore" connects such deceptive surfaces with an irony that covers the logos:

> I swear I will not be outfaced by irrational things!
> I will penetrate what it is in them that is sarcastic upon me! (1856 200)

In such passages, incarnate creatures and objects seem to be parts of a blotted book of nature, a *natura naturata* that has become a devious, hostile wilderness of signs.[10] If the protagonist's concentration in section three of "Crossing Brooklyn Ferry" on images projected by light serves both to epitomize and to impugn our ordinary mode of apprehension, these passages suggest that such images and the awareness they condition merely reproduce the deficiencies of incarnate creatures and objects; representation has already befallen the thing itself. The light that produces delusive images and reflections replicates appearances that are themselves mere signs of an already sequestered presence.

This vision of incarnate forms as deficient representations or deceptive signs is admittedly at odds with an important strand of Whitman's pronouncements about the body. From his earliest notebooks on, Whitman frequently proclaims the inseparability, the interdependence, or even the identity of "body" and "soul." In an early notebook entry he declares that a healthy or "perfect" body not only houses the soul but makes it manifest:

The effusion or corporation of the soul is always under the beautiful laws of physiology—I guess the soul itself can never be anything but great and pure and immortal; but it makes itself visible only through matter—a perfect head, and bowels and bones to match is the easy gate through which it comes from its embowered garden, and pleasantly appears to the sight of the world. (UPP 2:65)

"Song of Myself" often imagines the body of the poet in just such terms. While the objects depicted in "Crossing Brooklyn Ferry" can only indicate what they are, being shrouded in surfaces that veil the very interiors they signify, in "Song of Myself" the poet's body is supposedly innocent of such division between inside and outside:

If I worship any particular thing it shall be some of the spread of my own
    body;
Translucent mould of me it shall be you. (1855 49)

This "translucent" body is free of the doubling that divides other bodies against themselves; it shares and embodies the divinity that characterizes the soul: "Divine am I inside and out, and I make holy whatever I touch or am touched from" ("Song of Myself" 1855 49).

This supposed identity of body and soul persists as an important element in Whitman's work at least until 1860, though as we shall see the body of which such identity might be predicated is by then no longer characteristically the poet's own. This identity is forcefully declared in the 1860 text of "I Sing the Body Electric." There the poet concludes a long—and unintentionally oppressive—listing of body parts with the fervent declaration:

O I say now these are not the parts and poems of the body only, but of the
    Soul,
O I say these are the Soul! (1860 302)[11]

This moment of particular vehemence, however, is also one of hovering doubt. The very insistence of Whitman's declarations suggests the troubling prospect they ward off: the parts of the body might *not* be the "parts" of the soul; the outside might fail to be the inside, becoming instead the alienated form in which it is entrapped. The fact that Whitman's "now," in the first of these lines, can be read as performative heightens this sense of the errancy to which the body is subject: the poet's declaration vigorously re-aligns body and soul, correcting the slippage to which their relation is always liable. The body is a contested site in Whitman's early editions, struggled over by natural powers in mythic narratives, and by the cultural forces such cosmic stories trope.[12]

By the time Whitman wrote the transitional 1860 edition, his attentions had begun to shift to the afterlife about which his later work ruminates; in the new poems composed for this volume, the distinction between bad and good body accordingly most often corresponds to a contrast between here and hereafter. As Harold Aspiz points out, Whitman draws on the notion of "the permanence of the immortal 'real body' [which] was an article of spiritualist faith" during the period (178), envisioning the extrication of an immortal body from its mortal coil. The fervor of these passages derives at least in part from the way this spiritualist doctrine helped Whitman imagine a body that might be neatly detached from the sort of self-division his descriptions in the first two editions of *Leaves of Grass* sometimes register:

> I absolve you from all except yourself, spiritual, bodily—that is eternal,
> (The corpse you will leave will be but excrementitious.) ("To One Shortly to Die," 1860 398)[13]

In the first two editions of *Leaves of Grass*, Whitman more often thinks of the expendable body as deformed covering than as internal waste matter, and thus as a kind of misleading sign. And his characteristic effort is to spy out the presence of a good body lurking beneath encrustations rather than to teach us about its emergence in another sphere.[14] A number of passages thus enact a kind of stammering desynonymization: it highlights Whitman's divided vision of the body by awkwardly trying to sort out and schematize it. The difficulty of envisioning the physiology Whitman propounds in the following passage from the 1856 poem "Assurances" is one indication of the overdetermination of the body in his work, its investment with multiple and often diametrically opposed meanings:

> I do not doubt that from under the feet, and beside the hands and face I am cognizant of, are now looking faces I am not cognizant of—calm and actual faces. (1856 265)

If Whitman imagines a good body which incarnates the soul, this temple of flesh characteristically manifests itself only by shucking off a bad or "excrementitious" body which deforms or degrades it.

How might this debacle happen? There are various answers to this question in Whitman's work. While Whitman's later editions reserve possession of a good body for other spheres, in the early *Leaves of Grass* entrapment in a bad body is a pervasive but not quite necessary consequence of earthly incarnation. Aspiz has demonstrated Whitman's often ambivalent interest in several of the medical pseudo-sciences of his era, with their obsessively manichean visions (109–79). These discourses advocated a variety of strenuous regimens to guard the bodily temple from self-abuse; they characteristically linked bodily purity with "natural" appetites, degeneration with the depraved tastes spawned by culture. While the detailing of purgative regimens is a much more common feature of Whitman's journalism and notebook jottings than of *Leaves of Grass,* the association of socialization with alienation from one's own body pervades his poetry as well as prose. But in the poems it assumes the status of a debacle for which mere health fads turn out to be a grossly inadequate remedy; the task of redeeming the body from cultural entanglements provokes rather more drastic measures in *Leaves of Grass.* This cultural scenario is not rendered overtly in the cosmic drama centering on light. But while the fall from good to bad body is attributed there to natural rather than social causes, it is associated with the aberrant category I have been calling natural representation, with the eruption of images and their virtual usurpation of the place of things themselves. In "Crossing Brooklyn Ferry" this fall into the realm of simulacra is given a sort of diagrammatic neatness, a definitional force it is tempting to read as a covert registration of the constitutive split between nature and culture. Representation, at any rate, can be said to constitute the scene ruled by light in which the protagonist is initially immersed; it is implicitly the origin not only of his apprehension but of all that he sees as well.

If Whitman's concentration on reflected shapes implies the pervasive role of representation, two short passages more firmly establish its constitutive function by pondering what might be called the boundary between representation and what precedes it. Two lines I took note of earlier depict this threshold as unapproachable:

I too saw the reflection of the summer-sky in the water,
Had my eyes dazzled by the shimmering track of beams. (1856 213–14)

These lines insist on the inaccessibility of the sun (in part by not mentioning it, instead naming the sky where it resides). Among the things
which cannot be directly apprehended is thus the very power that inaugurates representation; like the images it projects for our perusal, the
sun is available to us only in the figmentary form of an image displayed
on water. Unable to grasp presences directly and consigned to observing
their images, shadows, or indicative surfaces, we are also apparently
incapable of beholding the source of such mediation. What dazzles here
is, as it were, representation itself: barred from the threshold and the
difference it inaugurates, we are *inside* representation. In "Crossing
Brooklyn Ferry" only the poet in his mythic guise will be exempt from
this interdiction and its effects.

Defining our apprehension, representation seems also to constitute
the incarnate world we apprehend. Enforced by the semiotic vocabulary
Whitman applies to surfaces, this vision of creatures and objects as
themselves representations may be universalized by some lines near the
end of section five of "Crossing Brooklyn Ferry" which adduce an
enigmatic creation myth:

I too had been struck from the float forever held in solution,
I too had received identity by my body. (1856 216)

Whitman's trope here of the body as "struck" into existence surely
appeals in part to the notion of a solid substance being precipitated from
a fluid solution. That is at least the primary sense of a passage from
Whitman's notebooks which these lines in the published version modify:

I too was struck from the float eternally [?] held in solution.
I too was cohered and received identity through my body. (NUPM 1:230)[15]

Whitman's subsequent deletion of "I too was cohered" might be
explained as a useful compression; but it also has the effect of rendering
the sense of "struck" ambiguous. Keeping in mind the poem's dominant
tropes, Quentin Anderson thus argues that these lines also figure bodies
as the images or shadows cast when some primordial substance is "struck"
by a light source (*Imperial Self* 159). If this is plausible even as a
secondary reading, then in the poem's cosmic myth the act which gives
us birth, which places us in the opaque bodies that divide us from one

other, is also the birth of representation; to be "struck from the float" into particular incarnation is already to have fallen into the condition of the image, to be doubled and self-divided. Incarnate selves are thus subject to further acts of representation which are simply related falls, repetitions of this original replication. The fall from good to bad body is on this account not simply an accident that might befall us; in the realm ruled by light it has always already occurred.[16] A fable that makes subjection to representation and the self-division it occasions constitutive, we shall see in chapter 4, turns out to be very much in keeping with Whitman's vision of the body in culture, though not quite of the body as such—as the poet's struggle with the sun in "Crossing Brooklyn Ferry" already makes clear, his task is indeed to bring about another sort of incarnation. Yet the global status of the fall into representation makes the repossession of the body an apocalyptic project in *Leaves of Grass*. While standing as synecdoche for a supposedly natural force, flood carries this apocalyptic burden in Whitman's work.

2. In *Leaves of Grass* flood ultimately figures the powers of the poet's word; Whitman's cosmology is shaped by the very vision of language it ostensibly serves to guarantee.[17] This chiasmus of words and things motivates even those mythic formulations which give a naturalized name to the power that will redeem the surface world of created nature.

In Whitman's later work the dissolving of separateness which flood brings about is reserved for the afterlife on which poems like "Passage to India" expatiate. But in his early editions flood is a force that might transfigure our present world. In "Crossing Brooklyn Ferry," we have seen, the poet orders the float, in which all things supposedly subsist before assuming separate form, to "suspend here." In the 1860 "Starting from Paumanok," his speech does not simply command but instead gives voice to the immanent power with which flood is associated: "I permit to speak / Nature, without check, with original energy" (1860 8).[18] We will turn in a moment to this crucial relation between *natura naturans* and the poet's voice. We need to attend first to the topology these lines imply.

Like the voice that is lent to it here, flood is imagined as subsisting within individual creatures and objects; their bounded shapes offer only deficient indications of the single living presence that has produced them and that animates them still. This topological fable is not quite compatible with the creation myth that seems to relegate incarnate forms to the status of images or shadows. But Whitman is not, after all, a cosmological poet in the sense in which we might speak, for example, of Dante as being one. These two divergent topologies have enough in common for Whitman's purposes: imagining the visible appearances that set one self over against another either as projected images or as opaque, indicative surfaces, they both construe separate, bounded forms as deficient signs of a sequestered presence it is the poet's task to help liberate.

Images of flooding thus almost always have chiliastic implications in Whitman's work.[19] Lyrical visions of a redeemed natural world typically figure it as pervaded by a flood that dissolves individual surfaces; rightly incarnate or rightly apprehended, the objects created by the flood of *natura naturans* would share its qualities. Separate, solid substances are described, in these moments, as fluid and unbounded:

> Earth of the slumbering and liquid trees!
> Earth of departed sunset! Earth of the mountains misty-topt!
> Earth of the vitreous pour of the full moon just tinged with blue! ("Song of
>   Myself," 1855 45)

Or they blend with the surrounding atmosphere, a medium that seems to combine the qualities of flood and breath:

> Hefts of the moving world at innocent gambols, silently rising, freshly
>   exuding,
> Scooting obliquely high and low. ("Song of Myself," 1855 50)

Such ecstatic moments, though, offer no more than visionary glimpses of a condition that has vanished or has not yet come to pass. Like the cosmology of Emerson's *Nature*, Whitman's trope of emanating flood and the mythic narrative it implies give the entrapment of presence inside recalcitrant surfaces the form of a fall: the animating liquid that courses within discrete shapes ought properly to have suffused them completely, but has instead receded, leaving a world of congealed and bounded creatures in its wake.[20] Whitman's images of dried-out or calcified surfaces thus not only suggest that appearances are disguises or misrepresentations. They also associate the formation of such merely indicative crusts with the recession of flood or animating force: the lapse into signs is brought about by the withdrawal of animating, living presence. We might therefore want to read the natural cataclysm in which flood recedes as a mythopoeic account of the fading of the natural or the organic that attends the passage into the symbolic universe of culture.

The association of the poet's voice and presence with the flood of *natura naturans* thus serves to include him in a *peripeteia* in which the perils of culture are overcome. Yet the world his word produces is hardly natural. Whitman manages to have it both ways: associating flood, *natura naturans,* and voice, his image cluster both naturalizes the word and transfigures the natural by means of the powers of language.

The link between voice and flood is crucial to the equational structure of Whitman's work.[21] A loose association of sounds and voices with varieties of liquefaction pervades Whitman's work. In section twenty-one of "Song of Myself," the poet pauses to attend to sounds which already enact the "merge" that is the poem's project:

> I think I will do nothing for a long time but listen,
> To accrue what I hear into myself—to let sounds contribute toward me.

> I hear bravuras of birds, bustle of growing wheat, gossip of flames, clack of
>   sticks cooking my meals.

> I hear the sound I love, the sound of the human voice,
> I hear all sounds running together, combined, fused or following. (1860 59)[22]

This association is frequently given cosmogonic status: voice becomes interchangeable with flood as a trope for *natura naturans* in Whitman's work. Prior to articulate language, this mythic voice assumes the form of an eternal lull or hum, a cosmic music or murmur that weaves the entire visible world from out of its regular, breath-like "pulsations." The 1869 "Proud Music of the Storm" presents this vision explicitly, though the poem is marred by the bathos and unwieldy, involuted syntax of Whitman's later period. Here the "strong base" is both a foundation or origin and the low, throbbing tones on nature's "great organ," a sound associated in turn with flood:

> Now the great organ sounds,
> Tremulous—while underneath, (as the hid footholds of the earth,
> On which arising, rest, and leaping forth, depend,
> All shapes of beauty, grace and strength—all hues we know,
> Green blades of grass, and warbling birds—children that gambol and play—
>   the clouds of heaven above,)

The strong base stands, and its pulsations intermits not,
Bathing, supporting, merging all the rest—maternity of all the rest. (V 3:576)[23]

Sound and voice are also associated with the interior spaces where Whitman imagines the flood of animating presence as lurking. As I shall show in detail in chapter 5, Whitman's topological literalism thus provides the unlikely priority he assigns to language with an imaginatively compelling if ultimately questionable basis: since voices emanate from interior spaces, Whitman declares that the essential animating energies of individual creatures are expressed by the sounds that well up out of them.[24] Produced by and modeled on the voice, the poet's presence incarnates this animating force, making it manifest. This tie is suggested by Whitman's characteristic images for the poet and his powers. The poet's ability to redeem fallen creatures is repeatedly figured as an infusion of animating breath—"You there, impotent, loose in the knees, open your scarfed chops till I blow grit within you" ("Song of Myself," 1855 70)—and thus assimilated to the breath-like pulsations of the "strong base." This breath is itself a kind of liquid—"I dilate you with tremendous breath . . . . I buoy you up" (1855 71)—just as the pulsations of nature's "base" are also a flood, ceaselessly "bathing, supporting, merging all the rest." And in "Crossing Brooklyn Ferry," the power "which fuses me into you now, and pours my meaning into you" (1856 219) must be imagined both as a voice that flows through time and space to address us, and as a gigantesque, personal dispensation of the animating powers of flood.

3. This pouring of the poet's presence is apocalyptic: *natura naturans* perfects itself as language, and in the figure of the poet who incarnates the word. This apotheosis of living, animating presence makes representation dispensable, putting an end to the mediations it exacts.

In "Crossing Brooklyn Ferry" the poet's apotheosis is thus figured as the reclamation of both light and flood. The poem's opening foreshadows these triumphs, staging an imaginative confrontation between the poet and the apparently alien powers that govern the harbor scene:

Flood-tide of the river, flow on! I watch you, face to face,
Clouds of the west! sun half an hour high! I see you also face to face.
    (1856 211)

Others, it is true, will also "watch the run of the flood-tide" (1856 212); but they will not quite be said to engage in the squaring-off implied by "face to face."[25] And the scene's ordinary inhabitants, with their "downcast eyes"—the protagonist in his merely finite guise among them —will hardly approach the presumption and power of this redeemer who looks at the sun directly and as a rival.

The poet's confrontation with the powers of light is the more overt of these struggles. In the course of the poem he replaces the sun and assumes its role: Whitman's visionary pronouncements imply the poet's assumption of powers which resemble but also transfigure those of light. His ascent to the sun's position is suggested by a slightly awkward locution in which Whitman proclaims his presence. He is not simply looking "at" us:

> Consider [. . .] whether I may not in unknown ways be looking *upon* you!
> (1856 220; emphasis added)

This invisible figure now looks down upon us from a height; he replaces the sun, whose less innocent sequestering led to those moments in which "the dark threw patches down *upon* me also" (1856 216; emphasis added). This juxtaposition neatly suggests the reversal of position and power the poem negotiates.

The announcements in which the protagonist declares his presence also imply his assumption of powers of emanation which rival the sun's projection of light. And the capacities the poem goes on to ascribe to all in fact depend for their realization on this figure floating regally above us:

> Keep your places, objects than which none else is more lasting!

> We *descend upon* you and all things, we arrest you all. (1856 221; emphasis added)

These powers, it should be clear, not only resemble but also redeem those exercised by light. The poet supposedly "arrests" and stabilizes things themselves rather than trafficking in mere images and shadows.

Implied throughout "Crossing Brooklyn Ferry," both the reclamation of the sun's powers and the liberation from representation and its defects thereby achieved are more dramatically presented in sections twenty-four and twenty-five of "Song of Myself." Here the sun's power, initially figured as a threat, is explicitly internalized, being recognized as a type of the poet's own greater force. The sublime crossing from blockage to introjection occurs in the shift from one section to the next:

The earth by the sky staid with . . . . the daily close of their junction,
The heaved challenge from the east that moment over my head,
The mocking taunt, See then whether you shall be master!

[25]26
Dazzling and tremendous how quick the sunrise would kill me,
If I could not now and always send sunrise out of me.

We also ascend dazzling and tremendous as the sun,
We found our own my soul in the calm and cool of the daybreak.

My voice goes after what my eyes cannot reach,
With the twirl of my tongue I encompass worlds and volumes of worlds.
  (1855 50)

Whitman passes swiftly here from images of the sun's daunting power to explicit confrontation, but then to a calm, assured expansion of the image of the poet as sun-god which moves beyond conflict into a sublime landscape in which the sun's force has become a figure of the poet's own.[27] The image of the poet as light-bringer, finally, is subjected to a shift that approaches catachresis to reveal voice as the ultimate source of the sublime power light can trope.[28]

Two lines that appear further on in "Song of Myself" repeat this internalization. There the poet not only introjects the sun's power but also redeems its deficiencies:

Flaunt of the sunshine I need not your bask—lie over,
You light surfaces only . . . . I force the surfaces and the depths also.
  (1855 70)

Implicitly here, as explicitly in the earlier lines, voice is the source of the poet's power; and what voice can do, *these* lines make clear, is penetrate to normally inaccessible interiors. The poet overcomes the detours of representation—the illumination of mere surfaces and the replication of misleading images—inaugurated by the sun; his voice both fathoms and forces living presence, making it manifest or giving it expression.

If the poet can overcome the detours of representation, liberating the living presence hitherto locked up inside the things upon which he descends, that is because he himself supposedly epitomizes or incarnates the animating power of *natura naturans*. In the 1855 "Song of the Answerer," his advent is accordingly figured as a dramatic, catachretic mingling of light and flood:

> Him all wait for . . . . him all yield up to . . . . his word is decisive and final,
> Him they accept . . . . in him lave . . . . in him perceive themselves as amid light,
> Him they immerse, and he immerses them. (1855 129)

Here the poet who incarnates light also transfigures it, turning it into a living medium in which others may be immersed; it has become a kind of flood. The power of light to produce detached images disappears; instead, this flooding light conveys the poet's animating presence.[29] The opacity and distance epitomized by images, precipitated by the rule of the sun, and attributed to representation are apparently overcome.

We might therefore wish to understand the poet as a mythic figure who reverses our fall into culture and heals the breaches that attend it, returning us to natural immediacy. But if the poet's task can be described as the banishing of representation by what *Leaves of Grass* invites us to think of as living presence, we need to note that presence and the flood that figures it have themselves been transformed. The presence produced by apostrophe seems to incarnate the visionary possibility toward which Whitman's poems repeatedly point, a prospect prefigured by all those ecstatic glimpses of "slumbering and liquid trees" and "Hefts of the moving world at innocent gambols, silently rising, freshly exuding." Whitman's insistence on the poet's invisible but incongruously embodied presence suggests that this figure is not only a pouring of the flood, but simultaneously a body rendered fluid by the force he also is—a part of created nature wholly animated and dissolved by the cosmic liquid that wells up through it. Given the remarkable time-scheme these apostrophes inaugurate, this pouring of flood must also be seen as eternal; filling all persons and objects, it is a flood-tide that knows no ebb, an energy that can expend itself ceaselessly without diminution.

This magical figure is what *Leaves of Grass* wants to mean by living presence: all other presences turn out to be partial, adulterated avatars of the force this figure incarnates and conveys. In "Crossing Brooklyn

Ferry" it is thus the poet himself with whom nature is said to flood us: its fluid force, we recall, "fuses me into you now, and pours my meaning into you." In Whitman's work presence is the presence of voice and word. The poet redeems all those he addresses and all the things he names by catching them up into the apocalyptic time and space defined by his magical utterance.

4. It is of course a major paradox of Whitman's work that the deficiencies attributed to representation are supposedly overcome by language, that the poet's word restores what representation ruins. We shall be concerned from here on with this paradox and its implications.

The slippery relation between the poet's word and the supposedly natural disaster it reverses is suggested in the very pattern of images that articulates Whitman's enabling chiasmus of words and things. We noted that, just as the poet is a light beyond light, so too he is a flood beyond flood. If he outdoes natural light by being a source of animating presence rather than mere representation, he outdoes flood by being a living presence that never wanes. But if the poet redeems light by adding to it powers figured as flood, he likewise transfigures living presence by deploying powers very much like those of light. The poet's declarations, that is, create a seemingly eternal presence by means of a mechanism of iterability that is quite close to the capacity for replication that characterizes the image. The figure who supposedly liberates us from representation possesses an uncomfortable affinity to the figmentary shapes refracted through the harbor scene of "Crossing Brooklyn Ferry" by the action of light, which can multiply a single presence into innumerable simulacra. This connection is one Whitman's work resolutely denies. Yet the ambiguous role of representation in his imaginative universe is suggested not only by this disturbing resemblance, but also by the ambivalent status the image itself is accorded in such poems as "Crossing Brooklyn Ferry."

As we saw, the poem depicts the image in its negative aspect as a source of alienation and confusion: detaching appearance from object, it can prolong that appearance in the absence of the object that was its source, captivating us with an illusory form. Yet a line we already glanced at strangely invokes the image and invites it to play a benign and reliable role:

> Receive the summer-sky, you water! faithfully hold it till all downcast eyes
> have time to take it from you! (1856 220)

This command marks a rather striking reversal of an earlier description
of reflection we also took note of:

> I too saw the reflection of the summer-sky in the water,
> Had my eyes dazzled by the shimmering track of beams. (1856 213–14)

The very reflection which dazzled the protagonist is now said to facilitate
apprehension; representation becomes a cure for the fallen mode of
experience of which Whitman has made it the paradigmatic cause. Confronting a bewildering array of images and shifting accidents, Whitman
surprisingly appeals to the benign or faithful image.

What is the status of such a recuperative procedure in Whitman's
work? We can answer this question provisionally by noting the realm of
experience in which the image is commanded to play its newly beneficent
role. It does not play such a role in the fallen world depicted in "Crossing Brooklyn Ferry," the world "looked back on," for example, in
section six. Nor is it invoked within the visionary space inaugurated by
the poet's apostrophes, speech acts which are characterized as the advent
of direct and unmediated presence. The poet's presence is indeed so
immediate as to deny us that minimal detachment required for forming
a visual image or representation: the protagonist in his mythic guise
seems to undo the distance and difference that make representation both
possible and necessary.

Yet the alienation dramatically annulled by the poet's presence can
evidently be partially recuperated by the very procedure of imaging or
representing that is said to have caused them. The protagonist's invocation of the restaurative image characterizes the ambiguous realm of the
poem's ninth section, in which his command that the water "receive"
the summer sky occurs. There the poet himself appears neither as the
tormented figure depicted in sections five and six nor as the omnipresent
form who fills us by addressing us. He has exercised the powers of the
word which the poem's visionary scenes enact and has occupied the
labile form modeled on voice; but he has now come back to his particular present moment and is once more lodged in his finite, bounded body.
This return might best be understood as Whitman's attempt to suggest
the compatibility, though not the identity, of the prospects suggested by
the poet's reborn presence and the experience of those who inhabit more

restricted bodies; the poem's conclusion both intimates and delays the apocalypse toward which its earlier energies move. The benign image, that is, plays its role in the oddly provisional space and time of the poem's ninth section—a space and time on the point of effacement, on the verge of dissolving into the apocalyptic scene implied by the presence who is "with you now." Suffusing us with himself, the poet will inaugurate a mode of experience in which the image or reflection will be wholly dispensable.

Or at least they ought to be. But the reversal which allows the image to be the temporary cure for the very ills of which it has also been said to be the cause might lead us to wonder whether the range of this expedient might not extend further than Whitman declares. The redemption of what is called representation by further imaging or representation bespeaks, at the very least, the divided function of this term, suggesting in turn that its relation to the immediate presence it supposedly occults may not be one of simple opposition.

I anticipate here entanglements that will concern us further on: they trouble Whitman's efforts to detach the poet's presence from all that he should redeem, compelling the grandiose, comic, and anxious practice that shapes the mobile textures of *Leaves of Grass*. I want to turn now to the cultural scenario from which this presence claims to rescue us, attending to the anxieties it provokes and the self-divided identity it shapes. The traits of the presence produced by speech can be best understood as a response to these pressures.

Notes

1. See Bloom, "The Internalization of Quest-Romance." Weiskel, *The Romantic Sublime*, also takes up the problem of the relation between external agents and the poet's own powers, relating them to Oedipal structures; see especially 167–204. See also Hertz, "The Notion of Blockage in the Literature of the Sublime," *The End of the Line* 40–60.
2. According to Mikhail Bakhtin, lyric poetry elides the social saturation of language in order to subject resistant minority cultures to centrist tendencies (*Dialogic Imagination* 269–88). But in *Leaves of Grass* the vision of natural language serves primarily to undermine the claims of the dominant culture. For a discussion of Whitman's critical use of the concept of the natural, see Thomas 117–47 and Pease, *Visionary Compacts* 119–33. Julia Kristeva

associates the disruptive aspect of the poetic function with the archaic register she calls the semiotic; see chapter 4, below.

3. I draw here, of course, on Jacques Lacan's notion of the Other; see especially "The Meaning of the Phallus," *Feminine Sexuality* 74–85.

4. See Bloom's discussion of Collins's "Ode on the Poetical Character," *Visionary Company* 7–15, especially 11–14.

5. The second passage is not present in CRE; it disappeared from the poem in 1881. See V 1:222.

6. Anderson here modifies his own earlier and more sanguine reading of the corolla image: in *Imperial Self* he sees it as a figuration of the poet's imperial powers, "an image in the water from which radiates the whole of being" (94).

7. In *Imperial Self* Anderson reads light, float, and semen as part of a single image cluster; see 157–59.

8. These enigmatic lines were deleted in 1881 (see V 1:222); they have engendered a good bit of confusion and disagreement, and any reading of them is conjectural. See for example Anderson, *Imperial Self* 128, and James Miller, *Critical Guide* 88.

9. The crucial distinction here is between indication and expression, and it is a fairly common one. See for example Derrida's account of indication in Husserl, in *Speech and Phenomena:* "Whenever the immediate and full presence of the signified is concealed, the signifier will be of an indicative nature" (40). See chapter 5, below, for an extended discussion of expression and indication in Whitman's language theory.

10. On the importance of the notion of signs in Whitman's work, see Kenneth Burke, "Policy Made Personal: Whitman's Verse and Prose—Salient Traits" 90.

11. I here quote the 1860 rather than the original 1855 text. The section from which these lines are taken was added to the poem in 1856; the suggestion of performative utterance cued by Whitman's "now" first appears in 1860. See V 1:132.

12. Discussions of the image of the body in *Leaves of Grass* have tended to emphasize Whitman's radical commitment to sexuality, slighting the struggles in which this effort to validate a visionary sense of the body involves the poet. Matthiessen, for example, comments at length on the celebratory aspects of Whitmanian sexuality, while mentioning potentially disturbing aspects only in brief asides. Asselineau is especially vehement: "He feels himself indisputably united with his fellow-men by the desires of his flesh" (2:6). See also Kinnaird 26–27. A notable exception is Anderson, who stresses the discomforts that help determine Whitman's compensatory vision of the body: see especially *Imperial Self* 104. See also Aspiz, especially 3–33.

13. See also "A Song of Joys" 1860 266.

14. This difference in focus between the 1860 edition and the two that precede

it is strikingly illustrated by the revisions Whitman made in the 1860 text of "Assurances"; see V 1:248–49.

15. The bracketed interpolation here is the editor's.

16. My reading of Whitman's fragmentary incarnation myth is supported by other material in the published version of "Crossing Brooklyn Ferry" that offers a similar vision of the body as entrapping rather than expressing the soul. Much of this material is more harshly negative in the published version than in the notebook manuscript (NUPM 1:230–31); the vision of incarnation-as-representation made possible by the deletion of "cohered" as a gloss for "struck" thus seems to be part of a systematic darkening of the poem's account of the body. Despite the poet's declared intention to offer a panegyric to the life of the senses, the published version of "Crossing Brooklyn Ferry" presents a vision of incarnation that is in many respects grim.

17. The image of *natura naturans* as a liquid force, as well as the notion that the poet can release its flow, also figures prominently in Emerson's "The Poet," an early version of which Whitman heard Emerson deliver in New York in 1842 (Kaplan 101); see for example Emerson 3:12–13. My analysis of this image cluster is indebted to Charles Feidelson's remarks on the relation between flood and voice in Whitman's work: see especially 18–20.

18. These lines are part of a group that Whitman moved from "Starting from Paumanok" to the opening section of "Song of Myself" in 1881; see V 2:276. The assertion of the intimate tie between *natura naturans* and the poet's own speech here is very much in keeping with that poem, though atypical of the new work Whitman was composing by the 1880s.

19. Hartman uncovers a similar use of flood imagery in Wordsworth; see *Unmediated Vision* 29–35.

20. See Emerson 1:42.

21. The term "equational structure" is Kenneth Burke's; see *Philosophy of Literary Form* 77–102.

22. I quote here from the 1860 text, which makes more explicit the blending that accompanies the introjection of sound: "running together, combined, fused or following" is not present in 1855 or 1856; see V 1:36.

While this cluster of images linking flood, *natura naturans*, and sound functions programmatically in Whitman's work, it seems to be based on an intuitive enjoyment of the aural. This responsiveness is perhaps most evident in the late prose work *Specimen Days*, where it is also least programmatic or mythologized; passages describing Whitman's delight in sounds briefly enliven an otherwise often lethargic and diffuse memoir. See PW 1:118–54, passim.

23. I quote the 1871 *Leaves of Grass* text; the poem originally appeared in the *Atlantic Monthly*, February 1869. "Base" is Whitman's habitual spelling for a musical "bass": line 84 of the same poem, for example, praises "The clear, electric base and baritone of the world" (CRE 406; V 3:578). While this cosmic "base" and the merging it effects are still important to the later

work, by 1871 Whitman is no longer committed to imagining the poet's voice and breath as forms of this cosmic force, or to insisting that it can be activated here and now.

24. Such mythic vocal effusions do not of course quite correspond to any actual, articulate language. See chapter 5, below, for a detailed account of Whitman's efforts to bridge this gap.

25. On the biblical resonance of these lines see Strom.

26. There are no section numbers in the 1855 text from which I quote.

27. Anderson aptly characterizes this reversal: "the writer, a body defined by light from the sun, sends out a light which itself defines other bodies, including the sun at day break" (*Imperial Self* 146).

28. This passage concludes by apparently dismissing voice in favor of the poet's silent presence. But this elusive presence is itself a hypostatization of voice. See chapter 4, below.

29. A similar pattern is at work in the 1855 preface. Whitman adverts there to the poet as a kind of light beyond light—"High up out of reach he stands turning a concentrated light" (1855 9)—the unusual powers of which are again troped as flood: "As the attributes of the poets of the kosmos concentre in the real body and soul and in the pleasure of things they possess the superiority of genuineness over all fiction and romance. As they emit themselves facts are showered over with light" (1855 17).

4. The Embodied Voice

[Emerson] must have known as well as I knew that it would have been decenter to throw the book away than to mutilate it.

—Whitman, quoted in WWC 3:440

Who is the hero of *Leaves of Grass?* From where do his powers derive, and in which of the protagonist's multiple guises can they be exercised? Whitman's sliding lexicon makes such questions hard to answer. "I do not doubt that from under the feet, and beside the hands and face I am cognizant of, are now looking faces I am not cognizant of—calm and actual faces," the poet declares in a passage from the 1856 poem "Assurances" we looked at in chapter 3; "I do not doubt that interiors have their interiors, and exteriors have their exteriors—and that the eye-sight has another eye-sight, and the hearing another hearing, and the voice another voice" (1856 266). Whatever we make of these rather mind-boggling assertions, we ought at least to note that they invite us to discriminate among various meanings of Whitman's standing terms. If the Whitman of the early work can rightly be called a poet of the body, he becomes its celebrant only by detaching a certain body he wants to valorize from another body he does not at all mean to value.[1] This effort leads to some surprising cleavages: in the 1855 and 1856 editions, the figure produced by voice, who possesses only a tenuous relation to the solidity of flesh, is the crucial instance of the body Whitman is committed to praising; his powers stand in marked contrast to the frequently displayed predicaments of ordinary incarnate selves. This cleavage organizes "Crossing Brooklyn Ferry." Diane Middlebrook reminds us that the poem's protagonist speaks, so far as we can observe, to none of the fellow passengers among whom we see him, but only to us (110). This rhetorical focus is ostensibly motivated by his desire to convey to future auditors the glories of the harbor scene and the freely available pleasures of the libidinized body that receives all persons and objects "with free sense." Yet the visionary eroticism the protagonist invites us to share may paradoxically come into existence only by virtue of the announcements that proclaim it and the scene these addresses define.

The tone of Whitman's apostrophes typically implies that this communion proceeds from entirely generous motives.[2] These declarations sound self-confident and forceful, as the poet sweeps aside all possible demurs; or they tease us toward acquiescence with a gently taunting quality. But a brief aside that makes up most of the fourth section of "Crossing Brooklyn Ferry" lets us glimpse the indispensable role this scene plays in the constitution of the very powers it announces. Directly preceded and followed by the poet's buoyant apostrophes to us, this passage is tentative and wistful. It too consists principally of declarations made from the strange "present" produced by such announcements. But it is not addressed to us:

> I loved well those cities,
> I loved well the stately and rapid river,
> The men and women I saw were all near to me,
> Others the same—others who look back on me, because I looked forward to them,
> The time will come, though I stop here today and tonight. (1856 215)

This stanza registers displacements that turn out to be crucial to the poet's project. The first three lines possess an elegiac quality we may well find peculiar: they look "back" on the places "loved," and on those the protagonist "saw," regarding them now as absent; at the poem's opening, the protagonist is in the midst of the very people and things whose disappearance he here laments. Like the Wordsworth of "Tintern Abbey" in this respect, he takes pains to lever himself into this odd vantage, employing elaborate rhetorical staging.[3] It will thus be important to account for the vanishings recorded here by attending to the turbulent contacts between the man aboard the ferry and his cohorts, described in section six: the poet's lament here turns out to be less anguished than the scene it mourns. If the first three lines thus record the loss of a present moment that is perhaps well lost, the fourth declares the poem's key compensatory economy: it replaces the city, the river, and the passengers aboard the ferry with the poet's envisioned audience. Here, however, the expansiveness and generosity that typify the poet's apostrophes, suggesting that his relations with us have a wholly altruistic character, are not in evidence. Instead the poet acknowledges that he has made a careful investment: "Others the same—others who look back on me, *because* I looked forward to them." The specifically envisioned repayment of attention here briefly foregrounded lies at the heart of all Whitman's transactions with his intensely imagined future audience.

That the poet is striking an imaginative bargain with futurity is confirmed by his later resort to an overtly economic metaphor to characterize his relation to us: "What thought you have of me, I had as much of you—I laid in my stores in advance" (1856 218). The economy at work in such exchanges is clearer in this line, since the poet here engages us directly by means of apostrophe, performing his crucial transaction rather than merely describing it. Whitman's folksy locution ought not to distract us from what is being declared: the poet here expresses satisfaction concerning a disposition of emotional capital that at first seems prodigal but turns out to be parsimonious instead; what looks like expenditure is really investment and savings. The poet seems not simply to imagine our imagining of him, but to impinge on us directly—so at least the peculiar present tense and the intimate tone imply. Naming a scene his focus on generic future companions rather than particular present ones makes infinitely renewable, this bargain seems to insure the poet against mutability.

It also offers an extraordinary rate of return. The poet's payoff derives from the ambiguous "you" with whom his bargain has been struck, a "you" made to seem not only inclusive but also immediate and intimate. Aboard the ferry, too, the poet saw others who were "all near me"; yet they were of course all near each other as well. The intensity and range of their attachments, that is, must be thought of as similar to the protagonist's own: either intense but therefore limited in extent, or diffuse but correspondingly mild. But in this other scene, Whitman's tone implies, the poet is near you, and you are near him—yet "you" are, or is, everyone. If "you" pay as much attention to him as he does to "you," then his stores have indeed been laid in wisely: his rate of return is directly proportionate to the size of his audience.[4] This peculiar economy depends on Whitman's figure of voice and the vaporous presence it implies. The self to which these rewards accrue, that is, has itself been transfigured by this visionary self-capitalization. Both omnipresent and elusive, the figure created by such announcements escapes from the torments and limitations by which the man who rides the ferry is conspicuously beset.

Yet if we come back from this apostrophic scene to the passage we had been considering, we can note not only the possible benefit to the protagonist of such an imagined bargain, but also its tenuous status and the consequent vulnerability of the figure who envisions it. The poet there hovers suspended, in two different forms, between what "Crossing Brooklyn Ferry" invites us to call his past present and his future present, and perhaps either was or will be, but is not "now" quite near anyone. He is willing to give up the present moment aboard the ferry, with all its deficiencies, in order to strike that bargain with futurity by means of which he has become, or will become, the omnipresent, omnipotent, and confidently expansive figure who elsewhere addresses us. But we listen here to someone who sounds palpably displaced; the juggling of scenes and tenses and the tentative, wistful tone make us aware of how dependent this figure is, for all his powers, on the concluding of his bargain, the participation of his audience in this eternal, reciprocal moment of "looking (back and forward) on." Whitman's final line masterfully clinches this sense of the poet's own momentary hesitancy and lack of mastery. The passage, an aside in its entirety, closes with a further aside, marked off, in 1860 and thereafter, by Whitman's always carefully disposed parentheses:

(The time will come, though I stop here to-day and to-night.) (1860 382)

Here a wrenching shift of attention lands the protagonist back in the moment aboard the ferry, and in his finite, particular body. This "here" is a specific, limited here, and the moment in which he speaks these words, not yet eternal, is "to-day" or "to-night." The poet stops here, briefly, much as the soul in St. Augustine's allegory stops for temporary respite, in lodgings not its own, on its journey back home to God (Augustine 9–10). Yet unlike Augustine's pilgrim, who must endure this condition until death brings about his translation from here to hereafter, the poet of "Crossing Brooklyn Ferry" will acquire "here" and "now" the transfigured body in which he can hover everywhere forever. He will assume this form by means of the direct addresses to his audience this particular passage eschews: "The time" which "will come," here briefly regarded as in the future, is the poem's own oxymoronic eternal moment.

Atypically, this passage lets us glimpse both the gap between the poet's antithetical guises—a gap his apostrophes efface—and the intensity of his need to cross it. Before following the poet across this divide, we need to develop our sense of just what he is intent on putting behind him.

The Poet of the Body

1. Like the objects of the harbor scene in "Crossing Brooklyn Ferry" and the images cast on the river that come to epitomize them, the protagonist we glimpse in their midst is defined by representation. A phrase from the poem's sixth section makes explicit the cultural resonance of this ostensibly cosmic dilemma. There the poet who "looks back" on the socialized interaction which the section describes affirms that he too

> Played the part that still looks back on the actor or actress,
> The same old role, the role that is what we make it, as great as we like, or as
>   small as we like, or both great and small. (1856 217)

The epithet that begins the second of these lines has an odd proleptic force: as great or as small as we make it, we still play "The same old role," a sweeping designation that very nearly cancels out the variety the line goes on to adduce. While the section as a whole exhibits a similar tension between possibility and foreclosure, it is the latter that increasingly dominates this portrait of social life. Throughout Whitman's work, the particular role we happen to play turns out to be less important than the fact of our having assumed a socially structured identity.[5]

Whitman's designation of social life as a scene of acting or role playing is of course in one sense rather banal. Yet in *Leaves of Grass* this trope is invested with an unusual range of meaning through association with both the vision of representation that helps organize Whitman's work and the fantasmatic body topology with which it intertwines. In its context in "Crossing Brooklyn Ferry," Whitman's image indeed serves to characterize not only our identities as actors on the social scene but also our sequestering in the finite and bounded bodies we occupy once we have been "struck from the float." The separation of subject from object, as well as the division of the body between bounding surfaces and inaccessible interiors, may well strike us as inevitable. But Whitman associates these with an accession to socially structured identity that *Leaves of Grass* vigorously contests. In the imaginative universe of the poetry, the attempt to free us from subjection to socialization and the psychic self-division it entails turns out to be inseparable from the task of redeeming our bodies, not only from the encoding that has divided them into acceptable and shameful zones but also from the impermeable bounding surfaces that divide one body from another. The realm from which culture separates us thus assumes profoundly archaic contours in Whitman's work. And it is approached by means of an archaic logic of sliding associations, in which our escape from any of the mediations associated with representation implies our liberation from them all.

The same sort of slippage, however, characterizes our subjection: the psychic self-division attendant on socialization is persistently accompanied by a violation of the body that seems to follow as a nightmarish consequence. The socialized body indeed has its own peculiar topology in *Leaves of Grass*. The protagonist immersed in socially mediated interactions inhabits a body that seems itself to be traversed by representations; it sometimes seems to be nothing more than an unstable, fragmented space in which conflicting images collide. The socialized body is thus a more drastic version of the fallen body I described in chapter 3, a body split between pristine animating essence and indicative surface. In those passages in which the cultural source of our self-division becomes explicit, so too does the constitutive status of its effects: in social life a system of representations is internalized, defining a self rather than merely hindering its manifestation. In *Leaves of Grass* the division in self-presence thereby created is frequently registered by, or projected as, a shadowy figure to whose omniscient gaze body and self are subject. This unlocatable presence and the gaze that emanates from it seem like ghostly embodiments of the alien codes that structure us; they precipitate the sense of lack or incompletion this shaping inaugurates. Both the poet's fallen body and his relations with other people are haunted by this lack, and by the elusive Other who exacts it.[6]

Section six of "Crossing Brooklyn Ferry" presents us with a condensed depiction of these inter-related difficulties. Both the poet's encounters with others and his awareness of his own body are marked by anxiety;

both are haunted by the subjection of selves and their acts to cultural encoding. Some of these anxieties are less directly displayed than others; like the long catalogue from section three we examined in an earlier chapter, much of section six has been retrospectively revised or recolored. Since the figure generated as an image of voice ought to epitomize our own proper powers, Whitman is faced with the difficult task of suggesting both the differences and the continuities between the poet's magical and ordinary forms. The passages that depict the life of the finite figure we see aboard the ferry are therefore oddly divided: sometimes frankly condemning or tormented, their more frequent celebratory air conceals anxiety provoked by the refractory elements of experience depicted, yet also expresses the poet's delight in a scene already partly transformed by the powers of the poet in his other guise. This divided attitude shapes the section's concluding stanza. There overt celebration very nearly masks residual distress:

> But I was a Manhattanese, free, friendly, and proud!
> I was called by my nighest name by clear loud voices of young men as they saw me approaching or passing,
> Felt their arms on my neck as a stood, or the negligent leaning of their flesh against me as I sat,
> Saw many I loved in the street, or ferry-boat, or public assembly, yet never told them a word,
> Lived the same life with the rest, the same old laughing, gnawing, sleeping,
> Played the part that still looks back on the actor or actress,
> The same old role, the role that is what we make it, as great as we like, or as small as we like, or both great and small. (1856 217)

Erotic experience is the center of this stanza. Yet what begins as an expansive hymn to sensuality dwindles to a much more reticent close. In this "same life" lived "with the rest," it seems, the protagonist shares principally an imagined common isolation and lack of fulfillment—"the same old laughing, gnawing, sleeping."[7] The passage is marked by the poet's desire to overcome this reticence and the gulf between self and other it confirms. Yet what blocks the unconsummated encounters the poet laments is not simply circumstantial. The stanza's opening lines are characterized by just the sort of division I noted a moment ago: an overtly celebratory air hovers over both surreptitious transformation and suppressed edginess. The poet's transformations can serve as a key to his anxiety, since they work to efface its sources.

Like the long catalogue of the poem's third section, the grammar of this passage is disposed so as to elide transitive acts. Others may touch the poet, but they are not said to do so: instead, he notes, he "felt their arms on my neck." Yet while the actions of others are rendered as a predicate ascribed to the speaker, Whitman's technically transitive verb is hardly active in tenor. If nobody quite seems to do anything to anyone else here, that is because agents as well as acts have been enucleated. Declining to designate persons as it reaches the stanza's erotic center, Whitman's idiom instead registers depersonalized *disjecta membra* and then a diffuse, eroticized process, described by one of the poet's typical verbals: "*the negligent leaning* of their flesh." Such dissolving bodies mingle in nearly all Whitman's most exuberant erotic scenes. "Hair, bosom, hips, bend of legs," the poet intones in "I Sing the Body Electric," "negligent falling hands—all diffused . . . . mine too diffused" (1855 119). This visionary sense of the body and its agglomerative powers reaches its ecstatic limit in evocations of the labile presence projected by apostrophe. Whitman is certainly a great erotic poet. But the eroticism celebrated in his work is typically regressive, diffusing the threatening qualities of sustained, individuated encounter; few such encounters are dramatically realized in his poetry.[8] These characteristic lines from "Crossing Brooklyn Ferry" work to efface both transitive relations and the circumscribed and separate selves that must resort to them.

Yet the stanza records not only the poet's attempted transformations, but also the oppositional structure that balks them. Whitman associates this impediment with representation. Explicit in the final two lines, this focus is implied throughout. As we saw in chapter 3, in *Leaves of Grass* concentration on obtrusive surfaces that block or veil remote interiors articulates a topology Whitman systematically links to the rule of images; here Whitman's idiom very nearly detaches such surfaces from any sustaining identity or interiority. I suggested a moment ago that this attention to *disjecta membra* serves in part to elide the individuality *Leaves of Grass* finds threatening. But Whitman's imagery possesses a double valence and obeys the double logic of over-determination. This litany accords anatomical fragments an eerie autonomy, suggesting the mysterious and somewhat frightening aspect encounters assume in the scene governed by "the same old role." In this passage, that is, enucleation serves as symptom as well as cure: the poet's dissolution of others wards off relations that are frightening partly because the selves who enter into them are no longer quite whole, having been subjected already to a fragmentation which the poet's imagery simultaneously expresses and seeks to transfigure.

The section's more overtly negative middle stanza, at any rate, describes the poet himself, in his "past" incarnation, as suffering from just such self-division. Rendered as a violent psychomachia and thus linked to the problem of representation, its sources are clearly social:

> It is not you alone who know what it is to be evil,
> I am he who knew what it was to be evil,
> I too knitted the old knot of contrariety,
> Blabbed, blushed, resented, lied, stole, grudged,
> Had guile, anger, lust, hot wishes I dared not speak,
> Was wayward, vain, greedy, shallow, sly, a solitary committer, a coward, a
>   malignant person,
> The wolf, the snake, the hog, not wanting in me,
> The cheating look, the frivolous word, the adulterous wish, not wanting,
> Refusals, hates, postponements, meanness, laziness, none of these wanting.
>   (1856 216–17)

The figure we glimpse in these lines is anxious, incomplete, and internally fragmented; he is rendered as a crowd of cacophonous desires, disorganized drives subsumed in no discernible unity. The interior space depicted here is a metonymic collection of impulses—"anger, lust, hot wishes"—or of the grotesque incarnations, like figures from an antimasque, into which they seem to reify—"the wolf, the snake, the hog." Body and self are composed of a horde of competing, disturbing representations.

Not only the self-division, but also the sense of incompleteness to which these figurations of conflicted desire attest are condensed into the image of the "solitary committer" permitted to appear in the 1856 version of this passage—a figure whose onanism seems in context like anything but the blissful narcissism Whitman elsewhere projects.[9] This solitary committer—the twenty-eighth section of "Song of Myself" will shortly help us confirm it—traverses or traces his own body while affecting himself with the internalized images of others, his desires for whom this passage represents as tormenting and self-fragmenting. His body is the site on which he plays out unsatisfied drives; it is neither integral nor proper.

The impulses which here seem to inhabit the protagonist like a band of usurpers might thus perhaps be understood as internalized representations of so many external encounters, whether actual or fantasized, to which he is still drawn. Yet what divides the self depicted in these lines is not only such desires, but also the cultural proscriptions that regulate them;[10] these strictures seem to re-shape not only the protagonist's awareness but also his very body. Sprinkled among Whitman's litany of culturally received terms condemning recognizable, familiar sins—"lied, stole [. . .] had guile, anger"—are oddly phrased descriptions of what seem to be physical acts: "I too knitted the old knot of contrariety"; "Was [. . .] a solitary committer." Various sorts of evidence suggest that the first of these self-portraits alludes to sexual intercourse, the second, as I already suggested, to masturbation.[11] But it is probably less important to identify the particular acts referred to than to note the tortuous, periphrastic idiom that describes them: Whitman's awkward phrases themselves repeat the uncomfortable process through which the body is structured and cathected by means of the morally charged vocabulary mapped onto it.[12] Quentin Anderson has best described the resultant dialectic of the body in Whitman's work:

> we are of course aware that the body is shaped by cultural use and expectation. The labor I have attributed to Whitman is therefore a labor of undoing, unmaking, not simply a stepping out of doors all naked. (*Imperial Self* 104)

This marking of the body by culture exacts not only self-division but also an eerie loss of autonomy. The 1856 poem "By Blue Ontario's Shores" makes this fall from completeness the hinge between nature and culture, though the poet protests it: "I will see if the fishes and birds are to be enough for themselves, and I am not to be enough for myself!" (1856 201). The opening lines of the section of "Crossing Brooklyn Ferry" we have been considering likewise suggest that this sense of lack is constitutive of the self in culture, linking it to a surveillance presented as global. In these lines, which we examined in chapter 3, an enigmatic, alien power intervenes in the poet's private communings. It appears as a kind of shadow, a flicker or lapse of light that feels like a negative judgment, emanating from the source of representation:

> It is not upon you alone the dark patches fall,
> The dark threw patches down upon me also. (1856 216)

These dark patches of course have a principally psychic import, and are glossed accordingly as a kind of self-interrogation:

> The best I had done seemed to me blank and suspicious,
> My great thoughts, as I supposed them, were they not in reality meagre?
> [. . .] (1856 216)

This darkness falling from on high suggests a self-examination that does not feel wholly internal; it structures an identity that is not wholly self-contained. The poet is subject to a kind of disembodied gaze of which he is conspicuously aware: the gaze, we might say in Lacan's terms, of the Other, a fantasmatic embodiment of the internalized cultural code that structures him, and by means of which he names and defines himself, now re-projected outward.[13] This gaze sets up a kind of relay through which self-presence must pass. Subjected to it, the poet is no longer enough for himself, no longer complete.

2. Such incomplete, haunted figures turn up repeatedly in the early editions of *Leaves of Grass*; the poet himself is conspicuous among them. Both the tormenting self-division and the uneasiness concerning others that characterize the protagonist in section six of "Crossing Brooklyn Ferry" recur in these self-portraits. Both are conditioned by the gaze and the subjection to encoding it embodies.

One of Whitman's most turbulent renditions of the poet comprises the "headlands" passage that makes up the twenty-eighth section of "Song of Myself." Here the anxiety that often tinges Whitman's ebullient eroticism emerges as outright panic. Depictions of the poet's own body and of the bodies of others are densely and disturbingly intertwined: auto-eroticism and eroticism "proper" become virtually indistinguishable; neither seems integral or self-contained.[14] Both are marked by a lack that neither can make good, a loss that structures them according to anxieties neither can resolve.

The passage that suggests such unsettling notions follows one of the poet's characteristic claims to possess the sort of amorphous and absorptive presence with which we are already familiar:

> To be in any form, what is that?
> If nothing lay more developed the quahaug in its callous shell were enough

> Mine is no callous shell,
> I have instant conductors all over me whether I pass or stop,
> They seize every object and lead it harmlessly through me. (1855 53)

The archaic, polymorphous body proclaimed here seems to know neither self-division nor the division between self and other. But a sudden admission follows:

> I merely stir, press, feel with my fingers, and am happy,
> To touch my person to some one else's is about as much as I can stand.
> (1855 53)

Both anxiety concerning others and awkward awareness of one's own articulated body intervene here; they are registered in the peculiar attention to body boundaries revealed in the odd, fastidious locution, "To touch *my person to* some one else's." The poet's admission in these lines leads directly into section twenty-eight, whose opening leaves it ambiguous whether he does indeed subject himself to the touch of another here:

> Is this then a touch? . . . . quivering me to a new identity,
> Flames and ether making a rush for my veins,
> Treacherous tip of me reaching and crowding to help them,
> My flesh and blood playing out like lightning, to strike what is hardly
>   different from myself,
> On all sides prurient provokers stiffening my limbs,
> Straining the udder of my heart for its withheld drip,
> Behaving licentious toward me, taking no denial,
> Depriving me of my best as for a purpose,
> Unbuttoning my clothes and holding me by the bare waist,
> Deluding my confusion with the calm of the sunlight and pasture fields,
> Immodestly sliding the fellow-senses away,
> They bribed to swap off with touch, and go and graze at the edges of me,
> No consideration, no regard for my draining strength or my anger,
> Fetching the rest of the herd around to enjoy them a while,
> Then all uniting to stand on a headland and worry me.
>
> The sentries desert every other part of me,
> They have left me helpless to a red marauder,
> They all come to the headland to witness and assist against me.
>
> I am given up by traitors;
> I talk wildly . . . . I have lost my wits . . . . I and nobody else am the greatest
>   traitor,
> I went myself first to the headland . . . . my own hands carried me there.

You villain touch! what are you doing? . . . . my breath is tight in its throat;
Unclench your floodgates! you are too much for me. (1855 53–54)

The third line from the end here seems to make masturbation the precursor of eroticism "proper," implying their common structure as well. But eroticism and auto-eroticism are more confusingly confounded in the stanza's opening: it is hard to tell one from the other not quite because they are homologous, but because the boundary between them is weirdly permeable. The stanza's first line leaves it unclear which side of this boundary the poet begins on: the source of "a touch" is left disturbingly ambiguous by one of Whitman's typically mystifying deictics ("Is *this* then a touch?").[15] Rather than solving this referential confusion, we need to note how the resultant ambiguities shape both eroticism and auto-eroticism, rendering them anxious and self-divided. In this passage the self is already another, while the other is already a stand-in for the otherness of the self.

If we try to stabilize the passage by reading it as a description of auto-eroticism, the instability of auto-erotic experience itself quickly obtrudes. While the passage's opening accords conspicuous attention to the poet's own body sensations, these are soon personified and thus endowed with an eerie autonomy ("Flames and ether making a rush for my veins, / Treacherous tip of me reaching and crowding to help them"). These personified sensations (if that is what they are) then modulate into what feel like other persons—"prurient provokers" "behaving licentious toward me." These "provokers," in turn, exacerbate the body's own self-division and alienation. They impinge on the personified "fellow-senses" who, under the influence of these outsiders, turn into others themselves, a kind of fifth-column within the poet's own body: "They bribed to swap off with touch, and go graze at the edges of me"; "Then all uniting to stand on a headland to worry me." At the heart of auto-erotic experience we thus discover what seem to be a recollected other-eroticism[16] and other, recollected presences. Past encounters have helped turn the body into a site of anxious desire, an agitated, no longer integral terrain seemingly belonging to others rather than to oneself; here auto-eroticism is a kind of compulsive re-tracing of this alienated landscape.

Yet erotic encounters with others are no more self-contained than the auto-eroticism that repeats them—at least if we read this passage as a rendition of eroticism "proper." The presences registered in these lines are themselves rather shadowy; the person or persons to whom the passage's elusive touch might belong indeed seem hardly to matter here. Both excitement and the orgasm to which it points seem to promise not union with another but recovery of a psychic and bodily integrity now experienced as lacking: others are engaged here in "Straining the udder of my heart for its withheld drip," an oddly imaged act whose peculiar pronominal distancing ("its") implicitly figures these juices as also withheld from the poet himself. It is as if these mysterious others, who do everything "as for a purpose," held the key to a missing wholeness that might be recovered through them: the protagonist, so to speak, might come to himself through their aid. But such restoration proves elusive: his "confusion" is said to be "deluded" rather than resolved by "the calm of the sunlight and pasture fields" offered up to him as an image of his own impending tranquility. And as the section progresses, more dramatic confusions ensue. Immediately following the lines about "prurient provokers," which offer the passage's most forceful registration of others, the poet's attention focuses back inward, in lines I discussed above, to describe a somatic landscape traversed by sensations at once autonomous and unstable. Erotic encounters with others thus turn into hallucinatory replays of a tormented auto-eroticism: re-tracing a body terrain already traversed by self-division, already anxiously eroticized in relation to itself, these adventures compound such estrangement rather than curing it. Eroticism "proper" seems to be a doomed attempt to restore what auto-eroticism ought to have been.[17] Having helped provoke a loss of self-completion, others may seem to be guardians of a lost object and to promise its restoration, becoming objects of desire; but they cannot make good this lack. What has been lost has apparently not been lost in them.

The body that is the site of such apparently unfulfillable desire has been turned into a complexly articulated structure. The after-glow of section twenty-nine is accordingly disturbed by an image that presents both sexuality and the body it shapes as economies:

Parting tracked by arriving . . . . perpetual payment of the perpetual loan.
    (1855 54)

It is possible to read both halves of this line as announcing the kind of positive cash flow seemingly appropriate to the post-orgasmic scenario of this section: expenditure and agitation are apparently followed by repayment and renewed self-possession. The rest of the passage works to establish just such a mood of tranquil restoration:

Rich showering rain, and recompense richer afterward.

Sprouts take and accumulate . . . . stand by the curb prolific and vital,
Landscapes projected masculine full-sized and golden. (1855 54)

Whitman's final two lines here imagine ejaculation as leading directly to the creation of golden progeny: this parthenogenetic image denies the very alienation that characterizes the turbulent sexuality of the preceding section.[18]

Yet if we attend more closely to the line that precedes these buoyant assertions of self-recovery, we can discover a more recalcitrant economizing of body and self. While the first of Whitman's phrases figures recompense as following expenditure, self-recovery as following loss of self ("Parting tracked by arriving"), the second instead depicts these as simultaneous and indeed as constant: "perpetual payment of the perpetual loan." Whitman's placid affirmations are thus disturbed by the very structure this post-orgasmic moment at first seems to efface: the body does not merely make use of, but is itself structured by or as exchange; not an organic unity or a harmonious self-presence, it is an economy. Given the perpetual, confusing circulation of resources figured here, moreover, this economy confounds debtor and creditor rather than distinguishing between them. And whichever role the protagonist might play, his partner in this transaction remains unspecified. The body is thus structured as a debt that is ambiguously either unrecoverable or unpayable; in either case, this debt organizes eroticism around a lack, a continual loss of self-presence and self-completion.

Given the context in which Whitman's figure appears, it is tempting to call this debt biological. But the calm yet ecstatic agricultural images that close the section associate the natural with restored self-presence; the structure that disturbs such self-possession, lurking as it were in the midst of a purely biological bliss, would thus seem to be of a different order. We can discover traces of this other register in section twenty-eight. The portion of this passage in which Whitman's description is most charged with desire, in which the poet seems most nearly ready to be seduced into willing participation, is also marked by an ambivalent recitation of condemnatory terms:

> On all sides prurient provokers stiffening my limbs,
> Straining the udder of my heart for its withheld drip,
> Behaving licentious toward me, taking no denial.

There is a difficult-to-determine ratio of harshness and humor, self-castigation and self-satisfaction in these lines, condensed in the words "prurient" and "licentious"; it registers the mix of anxiety and excitement that characterizes the passage as a whole. What provokes this ambivalence here are the morally charged epithets with which the poet names his seducers, mobilizing cultural sanctions that govern and structure the body, its desires, and its acts. Nor are such strictures wholly external: not only does the poet mouth them himself; the ambiguously auto-erotic context suggests that it is at least in part the poet's own impulses that are thus categorized. The self-satisfaction lurking in the poet's repetition of these terms, as we shall see in a moment, is one response to the transgressive quality of his acts. But the very phrases that declare the protagonist's attraction also ward it off or warn him against it, in an effort to defend against desires that threaten the careful regulation of the body and thus feel as dangerous as they are intense. Whitman's homosexual orientation may have bearing here: an explicitly transgressive sexuality may sometimes seem most palpably to threaten socially sanctioned images of the body and to disorganize a self both drawn to and defended against such a cataclysm. But as Freud reminds us, the universal encoding and regulating of sexual activity attests to an inherent tension between eros and civilization; certain carefully coded sexual acts, he suggests, are provisionally and partially enlisted under the cultural order, keeping social and psychic disturbance within tolerable limits but by no means eliminating them.[19] The tension provoked in this scene might thus be understood as an extreme but not otherwise aberrant dramatization of the disruptions sexuality precipitates.[20]

These seem to provoke rather more anxiety than pleasure. Organized by the demands of a source outside itself, the body is experienced here as a site subject to perpetual surveillance: a kind of disembodied gaze broods over this scene of unspecified erotic activity, jealously protecting its threatened terrain. Such observation is implied in part by the oddly divided perspective that characterizes the section as a whole. This remarkable description is both heavily somaticized and disconcertingly panoramic: it suggests an unstable, shifting combination of tactile and visual awareness, the first magnifying the body and seeming to experience it from within, the second, as it were, miniaturizing it to view it from above. The passage's highly charged material is thus also weirdly objectified: the body is both a locus of intense, disruptive sensation and a prostrate form splayed out and displayed to a remote, disembodied gaze.

Like the regulatory vocabulary the poet himself mouths, this objectifying gaze has been internalized; it is after all the poet's own fantasy to which we attend here. His mounting excitement is thus experienced as a threat to the self's stability:

> The sentries desert every other part of me,
> They have left me helpless to a red marauder,
> They all come to the headland to witness and assist against me.

These "sentries" are not simply senses, though they appear in proximity to the "fellow senses" mentioned earlier; their function is to guard a threatened structure, defending it from impulses and acts that are made to seem invasive and alien. And despite their momentary dereliction, these sentries are planted permanently within: the very passage that describes their lapse of vigilance is itself intently on guard, bracing itself against impending catastrophe.

Played out beneath this gaze, the protagonist's sexuality is triply anxious; it is culpable, dangerous, and unavailing. In this passage the body's convulsive excitement comes close to provoking terror. It seems to threaten a system of cultural sanctions mapped onto the body, a structure defended as if it *were* the body; here orgasm feels not simply like transgression, but like abjection.[21] If this highly charged scene is nonetheless marked by intense excitement as well as intense discomfort, that may be because the structure eroticism threatens to disrupt is itself a source of anxiety. The body disturbed by desire and threatened with what feels like a loss of propriety is a body already alienated and improper, already estranged by being organized for the gaze; as we saw above, erotic activity dramatically heightens this sense of a lost bodily integrity or a lost object. The simultaneous presence of terror and attraction here is thus a measure of the lack that marks the body in culture; disruption and disorganization seem to promise the recovery of a vanished wholeness. Yet as we have seen, the erotic activity bent on restoring a missing completion instead continually rediscovers the lack it promises to overcome. The poet of *Leaves of Grass* is thus committed to searching out an eros prior to the gaze and the mediation it installs in the space of what should have been simple self-presence.

3. In Whitman's early editions writing is a crucial trope for this process of erotic encoding registered by the gaze. I will take up the implications of this figure at length in chapter 5; it helps link Whitman's vision of culture to his language theory, in which writing also plays a key role. Since we will be turning shortly to the cultural redeemer produced by and modeled on voice, however, I want to suggest here briefly some of the associations the opposing mode of writing possesses in Whitman's work.

The troubled protagonist of Whitman's 1855 poem "The Sleepers" is caught up in an often disturbing erotic economy; his involvement is associated with writing and reading, in a difficult passage that seems to connect these activities with mediation and self-division. Rather than offering a full explication of the poem, I want to focus on this erotic network and the image that condenses its psychic import.[22]

The poem's long opening movement displays a protagonist preoccupied by his troubling relation to others, and to the dense dream space they occupy:

> I wander all night in my vision,
> Stepping with light feet . . . . swiftly and noiselessly stepping and stopping,
> Bending with open eyes over the shut eyes of sleepers;
> Wandering and confused . . . . lost to myself . . . . ill-assorted . . . . contradictory,
> Pausing and gazing and bending and stopping. (1855 105)

Despite the initial contrast between his open eyes and the closed eyes of the sleepers, the poet turns out to be "lost to himself," "confused," and "ill-assorted" precisely because he is enmeshed in the oneiric web of which they are part; his conspicuous consciousness turns out to be consciousness of this dream world and his involvement in it. His open eyes soon droop, as if he has entered a hypnagogic trance:

> I stand with drooping eyes by the worstsuffering and restless,
> I pass my hands soothingly to and fro a few inches from them;
> The restless sink in their beds . . . . they fitfully sleep. (1855 106)

Whitman gestures here at lending his protagonist the healing powers that define the poet-shaman of *Leaves of Grass*.[23] In "The Sleepers," however, the transfiguring effects of the poet's touch are pretty much absent until the poem's salvific ending. For the most part, the poet seems neither capable of unifying the poem's disturbing material nor unitary himself; he is simply a site through which still unsubdued dream material passes.[24] Like a dreamer, the poet indeed seems not only to be the space in which desires are registered, but also to assume the various positions conjured up to embody their fulfillment. He appears for a moment in a conspicuously masculine role: "Onward we move, a gay gang of blackguards with mirthshouting music and wildflapping pennants of joy" (1855 107). But he occupies a feminine position as well:

> I am she who adorned herself and folded her hair expectantly,
> My truant lover has come and it is dark.
>
> Double yourself and receive me darkness,
> Receive me and my lover too .... he will not let me go without him.
>   (1855 107)

The richly imagined scenario that follows this invocation offers a concentrated instance of such instability rather than a resolution to it. Materializing and dissolving, the shapes that appear there are less persons than possible erotic positions:

> He whom I call answers me and takes the place of my lover,
> He rises with me silently from the bed.
>
> Darkness you are gentler than my lover .... his flesh was sweaty and
>   panting,
> I feel the hot moisture yet that he left me.
>
> My hands are spread forth . . I pass them in all directions,
> I would sound up the shadowy shore to which you are journeying.
>
> Be careful, darkness .... already, what was it touched me?
> I thought my lover had gone .... else darkness and he are one,
> I hear the heart-beat .... I follow . . I fade away. (1855 107)

Here persons appear as unstable incarnations of erotic functions, temporary embodiments of an obscure but seemingly inexorable sexual momentum; first the lover and then the poet himself fade into the ambience in which this confusing scene unfolds, returning to the matrix of desire that gave them briefly individuated existence.[25]

Though it appears in the midst of the increasingly distanced portraiture that works to subdue such haunting material, the enigmatic reference to reading functions as a reprise of the disturbing involvements I have been tracing:

> I turn but do not extricate myself;
> Confused . . . . a pastreading . . . . another, but with darkness yet. (1855 109)

Whitman's elliptical grammar makes the phrase about reading tricky to gloss. But "pastreading" might be most plausibly interpreted as a neologistic predicate-nominative: "[I am] a pastreading"—I am myself a reading of what is past.[26] This past would presumably consist of the fragmented and seemingly foreign dream material the poem records, which seems to predate its individual embodiments. The poet himself would be simply the composite of all the erotic inscriptions he reads, enigmatic desires that tie him to others as functions of the same erotic writing or code; he would be a text, or a fragment of one.

Another odd phrase, earlier in the poem, similarly associates the poet's participation in an erotic economy with signs: the mysterious "journeymen divine" are said to "lift their cunning covers and *signify me* with stretched arms" (1855 106; emphasis added). This peculiar locution seems not simply to make access to erotic invitation a matter of semiotic competence; if we read "me" as a direct object rather than as an indirect object appearing in an elided construction, the poet's initiation amounts to his becoming a sign himself.[27] A line that appears between these two passages describes the poet as just such a mark, a trace shaped by patterns that traverse him: "Perfume and youth course though me, and I am their wake" (1855 108).[28]

While the final sections of "The Sleepers" ward off such intimations, a subsequently deleted passage that leads into these closing cadenzas in the 1855 edition both offers a bitter protest against such erotic inscription and associates it with patriarchal authority. The passage follows a number of rather sentimentalized anecdotes that pit personal feeling against the sometimes obscure social pressures that disperse individuals and foreclose possibilities for intimacy:

> Now Lucifer was not dead . . . . or if he was I am his sorrowful terrible heir;
> I have been wronged . . . . I am oppressed . . . . I hate him that oppresses me,
> I will either destroy him, or he shall release me.

Damn him! how he does defile me,
How he informs against my brother and sister and takes pay for their blood,
How he laughs when I look down the bend after the steamboat that carries
    away my woman. (1855 111)[29]

This tormented scenario, of course, alludes to the sanctioned institutional violence of slavery. Yet this political drama, evoked with a sentimentality not atypical of Whitman's references to public events in *Leaves
of Grass*, functions also as a displaced version of the psychic coercions
with which the poem has been more intensely concerned. This displacement paradoxically allows such intimate pressures to be registered with
unusual force: despite the awkwardness involved in Whitman's attempt
to ventriloquize the voice of a slave, the passage is remarkable for its
agitated and vehement rebelliousness, attitudes rarely displayed overtly
in *Leaves of Grass*. But the paternal prohibition railed against here
provokes anxiety throughout Whitman's work; the coding of persons
and positions Whitman associates with this paternal function is perhaps
responsible for the sense of obscure foreboding that haunts the intense
but bewildering erotic scenarios that dominate the poem's opening sections.[30]

A long passage from the 1855 Preface preoccupied with sexual transgression makes this anxiety more overt; there too it is provoked by the
constitutive role played by inscription in erotic life. The emotional valence of the passage is admittedly difficult to determine: Whitman is
ostensibly celebrating a cosmic mechanism rather than lamenting a social one, educating his audience in the virtues of Emersonian compensation and the machinery of reincarnation that supposedly effects it. But
the loss of autonomy the passage details provokes increasing agitation:

Only the soul is of itself . . . . all else has reference to what ensues. All that a
person does or thinks is of consequence. Not a move can a man or woman make
that affects him or her in a day or a month or any part of the direct lifetime or
the hour of death but the same affects him or her onward afterward through the
indirect lifetime. The indirect is always as great and real as the direct. The spirit
receives from the body just as much as it gives to the body. Not one name of
word or deed . . not of venereal sores or discolorations . . not the privacy of the
onanist . . not of the putrid veins of gluttons or rumdrinkers . . not peculation or
cunning or betrayal or murder . . no serpentine poison of those that seduce
women . . not the foolish yielding of women . . not prostitution . . not of any

depravity of young men . . not of the attainment of gain by discreditable means
. . not any nastiness of appetite . . not any harshness of officers to men or judges
to prisoners or fathers to sons or sons to fathers or of husbands to wives or
bosses to their boys . . not of greedy looks or malignant wishes . . . nor any of
the wiles practiced by people upon themselves . . . ever is or ever can be stamped
on the programme but it is duly realized and returned, and that returned in
further performances . . . and they returned again. (1855 19–20)

As it progresses, this jeremiad seems nearly to escape the poet's
control. Enacting the repetition it describes, the passage becomes less an
explanation of the law that governs such recurrence than an instance of
its working. Actions initiated voluntarily ("Not a move can a man or
woman make") are said to recur with daemonic inevitability ("but it is
duly realized and returned, and that returned in further performances
. . . and they returned again"); detailing such repetition, Whitman falls
into a hypnotic enumeration of particulars that obscures the cosmic law
they supposedly instance. Approximating what we would now call repetition compulsion, this litany seems to be under the spell of a mechanism
it cannot properly name.

Whitman's runaway catalogue lists a series of demeaning and dangerous interactions weighted heavily toward sexual infraction. Yet it is not
precisely an incautious entering into sexual acts that is said to propel the
uncanny recurrences in which the will is lost and autonomy is eroded.
What initiates such inexorable repetition is not the act itself but the
word that attaches to it: "Not one *name of* word or deed [. . . .] ever is
or ever can be *stamped on* the programme but it is duly realized and
returned." Here body and self are envisioned as a kind of *tabula rasa* on
which a text is imprinted; they are structured by the condemnatory and
quasi-juridical vocabulary inscribed upon them. Paradoxically, such inscription leads not to avoidance but to inexorable recurrence: eroticism
consists in the compulsive repetition of culturally proscribed, daemoni-
cally charged scenes and acts. The guilt that evidently attends this process is perhaps less interesting than the uncanny loss of autonomy it
suggests. Subject to a cultural writing that constitutes sexuality, the self
is structured as the endless re-reading and re-inscription of an introjected
text.

4. In Whitman's work castration is another name for this subjection to
encoding and the fading of self-presence it exacts. Castration turns up in

the 1855 poem "Faces" as a seemingly inappropriate and highly charged image. The poem as a whole, we should recall, both offers instances of physical degradation that Whitman associates with the fall into representation and prophesies the restoration of a natural body not thus compromised. A list early on in the poem, which prophesies such redemption, presents a disturbing mix of grotesque physical description and what might be called psycho-social allegory. It suggests that the locus of deforming representations is cultural, and that their distorting powers extend to the body as well as the mind:

Sauntering the pavement or crossing the ceaseless ferry, here then are faces;
I see them and complain not and am content with all.

Do you suppose I could be content with all if I thought them their own finale?

This now is too lamentable a face for a man;
Some abject louse asking leave to be . . cringing for it,
Some milknosed maggot blessing what lets it wrig to its hole.

This face is a dog's snout sniffing for garbage;
Snakes nest in that mouth . . I hear the sibilant threat. (1855 124–25)

A subsequent image, which we examined in chapter 3, associates such lurid features with disguises, misrepresentations of an original animating energy the poet claims to discern lurking beneath these grisly surfaces:

Features of my equals, would you trick me with your creased and cadaverous
   march?
Well then you cannot trick me.

I see your rounded never-erased flow,
I see neath the rims of your haggard and mean disguises.

Splay and twist as you like . . . . poke with the tangling fores of fishes or rats,
You'll be unmuzzled . . . . you certainly will. (1855 125–26)

The poet's glimpse of a "rounded never-erased flow" beneath apparent monstrosity is a typically Whitmanian saving grace. Further on in the poem, though, this dialectic of surfaces and interiors acquires darker implications. As in "Crossing Brooklyn Ferry," representation comes to inhabit the inside:

Spots or cracks at the windows do not disturb me,
Tall and sufficient stand behind and make signs to me;
I read the promise and patiently wait. (1855 127)

Detailing Whitman's interest in the pseudo-sciences of his day, Harold Aspiz persuasively associates the "promise" the poet reads here with a millennium to be inaugurated by eugenics (139). Yet in *Leaves of Grass* the notion of the body as sign typically has bleaker connotations, suggesting blockage as well as promise. We should accordingly note that the "tall and sufficient" figures the poet claims to glimpse fail to make themselves entirely visible: partially obscured by "spots and cracks," they must make signs to the poet—merely "indicating," we may say in Whitman's own terminology, what they are. The poet, not yet in presence of such self-sufficient forms, must read and decipher the signs that represent them. Here nothing escapes the mediation of signs: that which is not itself a sign must make one. The social landscape, in its entirety, is a space defined by representation.[31]

Though it is dispelled at the end of "Faces" by one of Whitman's typical closing cadenzas, this is the focal vision toward which the poem converges. Its upbeat opening portraits, of "Faces of friendship, precision, caution, suavity, ideality" (1855 124), thus delay a recognition toward which the poem soon gathers:

The face of an amour . . . . the face of veneration,
The face as of a dream . . . . the face of an immobile rock,
The face withdrawn of its good and bad . . a castrated face,
A wild hawk . . his wings clipped by the clipper,
A stallion that yielded at last to the thongs and knife of the gelder.
[. . . .]
This now is too lamentable a face for a man. (1855 124)

Though he may seem to be merely one citizen among many, one empirical possibility among others and an improbable one at that, the figure with the "castrated face" toward whom this catalogue converges can be seen as a synecdoche for the entire poem and its burden.[32] Like those trapped behind cracked and spotted windows and reduced to making signs, this figure "withdrawn of its good and bad" has lost its natural expressiveness. The poet sees only a kind of blank surface, a mute sign; something is missing or at least deeply sequestered. That lack is troped as a violent severing, a castration. This image is startling; but it resonates with the complex of concerns I have been considering. Deprived of bodily integrity and propriety, deformed by a violence that is a mark of the law and of the structuring of eros by that law, the castrate is the very figure of our subjection. Castration, organizing Freud's discourse as a threat the anxiety attending on which generates the adult male's psychic topography, is read by Jacques Lacan as fact: as symbolic fact, the cultural and psychic mark of our insertion as subjects in the symbolic order, and of the loss of self-presence this origin of subjectivity entails.[33] "One part of himself," as the Lacanian journal *Scilicit* puts it,

is thrown up as the residue of his entry into the field of the Other—part-objects, or detachable parts of the body, whose structure is based on a feature of anatomical division due to its homology with signifying divisions. It is at the junction of these two registers that the subject, because he is subject to speech, pays the tribute of his pound of flesh to the Other. (Lacan, *Feminine Sexuality* 119–20)

Culture, Lacan argues elsewhere, not only gives us our (alienated) subjectivity by giving us the language we speak; it also speaks through us or writes us down:

it is not only man who speaks, but that in man and through man *it* speaks (ça parle), that his nature is woven by effects in which is to be found the structure of language, of which he becomes the material. . . . (*Ecrits* 284)

Culture writes with us by making us lexemes in a combinatory: in kinship systems, or in the Oedipal structures that remain to us of them.[34] Castration, of which circumcision would be the ritual enactment, is the psychic and symbolic mark of this constitutive expropriation, at once sexual and linguistic.

The castrate's appearance in "Faces"—in the same poem that later focuses on deformities characterized as disguises or deficient representations, and on the nearly occluded sign-makers said to lurk within such indicative surfaces—implies similar conjunctions, which *Leaves of Grass* will confirm. The castrate is one whose body is shaped by signs; our use of signs, and our subjection to them, is itself castration.[35]

What would a body be that escaped such symbolic debt? The figure produced by the poet's apostrophes is Whitman's crucial attempt to conjure up such a presence. It offers exemption from the anxieties I have been describing and embodies the crucial desires about which the early editions of *Leaves of Grass* cohere.

The Body of the Poet

1. In the vision of unfallen incarnation we examined in chapter 3, the body is a temple of self-presence, identical to the soul. In Whitman's

work this dream of a redeemed body depends for its realization on the figure of the poet generated by apostrophe. A grandiose pronouncement from the 1860 "Starting from Paumanok" displays this reliance of a supposedly universal possibility on the peculiar case made to stand as surety for it. There Whitman declares the inseparability of body and soul, giving this intertwining and the divinizing of the body it implies the form of a general truth:

> Behold! the body includes and is the meaning, the main concern—and includes and is the Soul. (1860 17)

Whitman's opening imperative lends this line its torque, which derives from the ambiguous deictic function of "Behold!" It is of course possible to construe command and accompanying gesture as an especially striking though by no means unique instance of Whitman's sententiousness: the poet might point at a supposed universal truth hanging, as it were, in front of our noses. But he might instead be gesturing at himself. His global assertion would then derive from and extend what seems true of his own remarkable body: the proclaimed identity of body and soul would codify a mode of incarnation the poet's barely material presence suggests. This mode is defined by the same "Behold!" that draws our attention to him: apostrophic as well as deictic, Whitman's command inaugurates an encounter in which we come face to face with a figure who is perforce invisible.

Such ambiguous pointing is a typical feature of Whitman's evocations of the poet's presence, and is crucial to their effect. It is not simply general case and particular instance that these deictics confound. Whitman's enigmatic ostensive gestures confuse and ultimately conflate a number of ordinarily distinct entities; the fusions thus suggested define the transfigured body on which Whitman's redemptive vision depends. In an apostrophe from "Song of Myself" which we glanced at in chapter 1, the poet directs us firmly toward a physical presence that turns out to be elusive:

> This is the press of a bashful hand . . . . this is the float and odor of hair,
> This is the touch of my lips to yours . . . . this is the murmur of yearning.
>   (1855 42)

The uncanny quality of these proclamations derives in part from the paradox of the poet forcibly drawing our attention to a body we cannot see or feel. But it depends as well on a conflation born of our resultant need to take up slack. Failing to locate a body, we fasten our attention on the words that announce it, in whose presence we more palpably are; Whitman's deictics seem to be pointing at themselves. Referring ambiguously to either body or language, such announcements effectively fuse them; they suggest that the poet's body has been reduced to the barely physical presence of his word; conversely, they imply that language has become incarnate, that in the poet's advent the word is made flesh. Supposedly touching us here, the transfigured presence defined by this fusion is remarkable for its lability and lightness. In such passages there seems to be no distance or difference among the words themselves, the sensuous "murmur" that proclaims them, and the elusive and barely material "press of a bashful hand" or "touch of my lips" into which words and voice seem always able to condense.

This conflation governs Whitman's redefinition of the body. Lending the poet extraordinary qualities and powers, it also serves to exempt him from the difficulties by which the man aboard the ferry and other localized versions of Whitman's protagonist are conspicuously beset: the body that incarnates speech wards off the debt I have been calling castration.[36] This saving association of body with word and voice is by no means peculiar to *Leaves of Grass,* though Whitman's version of it is certainly extreme. If, as Freud suggests, unconscious fantasies of castration are culturally pervasive, so is a compensatory fantasy, centering on an image of voice, that seems to preserve the body's integrity; the appeal of the poet's presence may derive largely from the way this figure embodies and dramatically intensifies a shared fantasmatic structure.[37] We need both to build out this vision of the transfigured body defined by word and voice, traced briefly in chapter 1, and to attend to its cultural resonance.

Another passage organized by dramatic but ambiguous pointing suggests some of the key implications of the identification of the poet's presence with his word. Similar to the line from "Starting from Paumanok" we looked at above, Whitman's address here is more explicitly epiphanic, directly announcing the poet's self-manifestation. It occurs in "Song of Myself":

Behold! I do not give lectures, or a little charity;
When I give, I give myself. (V 1:62)[38]

Proudly unveiling a presence we cannot see, Whitman's opening imperative, which once more performs a deictic function, of course contains an element of burlesque. The lack of possible uptake can make such supposed acts of revelation seem either comic or poignant, suggesting the poet's inability to produce the presence he proclaims. The humor and pathos of these moments is my topic in chapter 6; they are crucial to *Leaves of Grass*. But these qualities possess a never quite resolvable relation to the visionary intensity such announcements also generate, a dimension the very lack of uptake here can be read as sustaining rather than compromising. What might be conceived of as missing can also be thought of as superfluous baggage: this invisible figure is like a body reduced to its numinous core, a presence no longer "excrementitious," having shucked off the detritus the body is liable to become.

Here again, our sense of the poet's presence as a kind of zero-degree incarnation depends on the passage's ability to identify body with word, a conflation achieved once more by Whitman's opening deictic and its characteristically elusive referent. The subsequent dissociation of "myself," the presence we have been invited to behold, from mere "lectures" is partly humorous, since it seems at first to undo the identification between body and language on which the passage's power depends. Yet this distinction paradoxically ends up sustaining the crucial tie between body and word, or a certain kind of word. Lectures and other such referential verbal activities, we shall see in chapter 5, are in *Leaves of Grass* typically opposed not to silent presence but to performative utterance. Whitman's opening "Behold!" is itself performative, seeming to guarantee the fusion between body and word the passage implies: produced by language, the poet is consubstantial with it.

This apparent capacity for self-production through performative utterance is crucial to the poet in several respects. As we shall see further on, it seems to leave him free from the sexual and symbolic shaping to which he would otherwise be vulnerable. More broadly, it apparently allows him to initiate, sustain, and repeat his advent, independent of external circumstances or contingent events. He thus becomes a creature of a different stripe: reproducing himself at will, he is an ideal presence immune to the vicissitudes that affect all merely material objects. The word with which this presence is conflated is the model for such repetition: conveyed and embodied by it, the poet seems to sustain his identity unchanged through countless manifestations.

Whitman's canny use of performative locutions manages to imply this recurrence and suggest its power to generate an ideal presence exempt from change; the invariant scene to which his proclamation gives rise is no longer exactly contingent. "When I give, I give myself": in context, this has less of an air of coquetry than of definition, Whitman's "when" implying a global "whenever" and its inevitable corollary rather than an infrequent occurrence tantalizingly both proferred and postponed. This "whenever," moreover, is now: if "Behold!" is performative, it initiates the revelation the succeeding line goes on to specify. The poet thus manifests himself, through an always identical transaction, whenever the performative power that seems to inhere in these phrases is activated by a new encounter with them. Through the invariant words with which his presence has been conflated, he incarnates himself in always identical form.

Hovering between epiphany and con job, such performatives dramatically intensify the principle Jacques Derrida calls iterability—the capacity of (re-)generating the same.[39] The very notion of an ideal object, of a form of being immune to time and change, is according to Derrida a product of this power of repetition:

this ideality, which is but another name for the permanence of the same and the possibility of its repetition, *does not exist* in the world, and it does not come from another world; it depends entirely on the possibility of acts of repetition. It is constituted by this possibility. Its "being" is proportionate to the power of repetition; absolute ideality is the correlate of a possibility of indefinite repetition. (*Speech and Phenomena* 52)

This possibility is inseparable from language: iterability, Derrida reminds us, defines the word (and is defined by it); (only) the word or name repeats itself as the same through its successive embodiments.[40]

This production of ideal forms is also of course an act of mastery: positing repeatable entities, we generate a world we can control. Whitman's catalogues are a massive celebration of this power. But his apostrophes give it more striking embodiment. They suggest a bizarre temporality in which interval and succession have collapsed into the endless repetition of a single event and moment; the figure who manifests himself by means of such addresses has dissolved the very manifolds in which contingent events unfold. These carefully calculated declarations thus encourage us to construe the idealizing power of language in a magical mode. Whitman's apostrophes wed the inherent iterability of the word to the supposed power of the poet's performative utterance magically to repeat a single speech act forever, encoding this aberrant possibility into such poems as "Crossing Brooklyn Ferry." As a result, the purely ideal content language generates is apparently transformed into an unchanging and idealized presence literally produced for us as we attend to the utterance that names him.

Such reifying of the ideal contents generated by the word is according to Derrida a pervasive tendency, though *Leaves of Grass* certainly takes it to extremes. Language and repetition, Derrida suggests, give rise to the very notion of essence, of the thing itself set off from what can now be thought of as its accidents.[41] What is, what has being—rather than what merely appears, subject to the vicissitudes of circumstance—is the ideal, unchanging content I can call up before me and make present in the word. Immune to change, this ideal form never fails to present itself at my behest. Thus as Derrida suggests, "this determination of being as ideality is paradoxically one with the determination of being as presence" (*Speech and Phenomena* 53). *Leaves of Grass* subscribes to this double determination. Whitman's catalogues, we saw, seem to liberate objects from their entrapment in the shifting guises of appearance, allowing them to present themselves fully and immediately to the poet, to reveal "what [they] are." And his apostrophes convey to us what we are repeatedly invited to call a presence: they present the poet himself, freed from the contingencies in which he was hitherto mired. Presence in Whitman's work is finally the presence of this ideal being shaped by the word and supposedly given concrete physical embodiment through a magical disposition of it.

In *Leaves of Grass* voice is both the medium for this incarnation and the crucial synecdoche for the transfigured body thereby created. I suggested in chapter 1 that Whitman's appeal to voice helps authenticate the poet's claims of immediate presence, since it makes them tautological: voice already implies the proximity of the figure whose manifestation Whitman's declarations claim to perform. Reducing space to the modest intervals actual speech can traverse, Whitman's figure of voice also plays a key role in the temporal shell game that simultaneously collapses time and generates the immutable presence who masters it. Voice seems to make immediate a recurrence the word makes possible, activating here and now the invariant event the poet's phrases name. An oral announcement, Walter Ong reminds us, "exists only when it is going out of existence," only in a particular moment (*Interfaces* 136).[42] Paradoxically, it is partly by playing on this evanescence of oral address that Whitman's apostrophes manage to convert the general iterability of the word into what seems to be the magical recurrence of an event that cancels time. "Who knows but I am as good as looking at you now, for all you cannot see me?" (1856 218). Here what voice authenticates as present event defines a moment impossible to limit or pin down: right now is also forever.

Voice also defines the presence it seems to produce. As we noted in chapter 1, one of its crucial functions is to bridge the distance between body and word, material and ideal forms. In the 1856 poem "To You" the poet declares: "now I place my hand upon you, that you be my poem, / I whisper with my lips close to your ear" (1856 206). The poet's whisper here seems to generate what I earlier called a zero-degree incarnation, a body brought forth as accent and breath, as the scarcely material flesh which the ideal word, now voiced, has apparently put on. Supposedly transmuting all those who come into contact with it, lifting them up to the status of poem or word it already enjoys itself, this presence modeled on voice is the magically active synecdoche for a new mode of embodiment *Leaves of Grass* invites us to imagine as potentially universal.

In this respect, too, Whitman's work offers an explicitly magical version of a pervasive, typically unconscious fantasy. Voice, Derrida suggests in his critical reading of Husserl, whose work he regards as a distilled version of the phonocentrism pervasive in Western culture, implies and comes to define a sort of substantial ideality, a new sort of being or body. It seems both to idealize material objects and to incarnate ideal signifieds.[43] I need to adumbrate briefly this twofold operation, since the resonance Whitman's figure of voice possesses depends in large part on it.

According to Derrida, the crucial model for idealization within the Western tradition expounded most explicitly in metaphysics is the way voice seems to transform the material aspect of language itself, the sensible signifier. In the phenomenology of Husserl, which from Derrida's vantage epitomizes the tradition rather than overturning it, the voice that accomplishes this transformation is not quite the literal, physical voice; it is rather the fantasmatic voice of interior monologue, which seems to shelter the word within the speaker's own body:

It is not in the sonorous substance or in the physical voice, in the body of speech in the world, that [Husserl] will recognize an original affinity with the logos in general, but in the voice phenomenologically taken, speech in its transcendental flesh, in the breath. . . . (*Speech and Phenomena* 16)

Given the often improbable imaginative configurations that organize *Leaves of Grass,* this silent voice may have more in common with the poet's speech than is at first apparent. The association of the poet's voice with breath is pervasive. And in section five of "Song of Myself," speech reduced to the pneumatic perfection of a "lull or hum" is generated by the "valved voice" of the poet's own soul, an agent of internal colloquy rather than public address. Linked to the inner precincts of the poet's body and his inner monologue, his voice is also paradoxically associated with ours. So at least the peculiar topology suggested by a key passage in "Crossing Brooklyn Ferry" implies: "what is more subtle than this [. . .] / Which fuses me into you now, and pours my meaning into you" (1856 219). The poet's meaning or word supposedly comes to inhabit us, as if it constituted our own silent speech.

According to Derrida, such inner speech seems to transform the signifiers that it sequesters. Repeated within the sacrosanct precincts of the body, as breath, the signifier seems to shed its inert physicality. And it no longer appears in external time and space, among contingent, material supports. What Derrida calls the "flesh" of this vocal signifier generated by inner monologue thus possesses—and defines—a peculiar sort of "materiality":

The phenomenological voice would be this spiritual flesh that continues to speak and be present to itself—*to hear itself*—in the absence of the world. (*Speech and Phenomena* 16)

It is just such a mode of being—devoid of opacity and redeemed from circumstance, caught up into the body and thus no longer foreign—that the speech of *Leaves of Grass* is devoted to generating.

This new mode of being turns out to be what we mean by ideality: the vocal signifier constitutes the possibility of what we think of as ideal objects. There is something of a paradox here: the founding distinction of semiotics places the signified concept over against the signifier and its materiality.[44] Yet according to Derrida it is only through the apparent sequestering of the vocal signifier within the body that we get a kind of fantasmatic image of ideality—of the mode of being, so to speak, ideal objects might enjoy. As its materiality seems to dissolve, the signifier appears to become a perfect transparency, through which the signified itself appears; yet this very transparency comes to define the signified as well (*Grammatology* 20). In the voice the signifier

phenomenologically reduces itself, transforming the worldly opacity of its body into pure diaphaneity. This effacement of the sensible body and its exteriority is *for consciousness* the very form of the immediate presence of the signified. (*Speech and Phenomena* 77)

The idealizing operation performed by voice is thus paradoxically also an act of embodiment; the wearing away of material dross is also the incarnation of an ideal form, a putting on of flesh by the word. In this image of voice, the purely mental contents through which we organize the world and gain indirect mastery over it acquire a kind of actuality, transforming our sense of what the actual might be.

As the illogical slide from signifier to signified in the quotation from Derrida seems meant to suggest, this building out of the apparent phenomenology of voice is always a fantasmatic operation, a kind of magic thinking that inflects our awareness of objects and bodies. In *Leaves of Grass* this characteristically unconscious fantasy becomes the basis for proclaimed fact. If voice always implies the sequestering of the word within the body and thus the generation of a sort of idealized inner duplicate of the external world, Whitman's catalogues suggest that the latter has simply collapsed into the former; the taking of the signifier into the body as voice is construed as a magical power to incorporate the object itself.

The body in which things thus supposedly take up residence has also been redefined. Here too Whitman builds out a magical version of the topology voice suggests. According to Derrida voice is the source of and model for the punctual unity that characterizes our image of the proper body. It generates the sense of immediacy or transparency that produces consciousness as self-presence and creates a fantasmatic body in their image:

As pure auto-affection, the operation of hearing oneself speak seems to reduce even the inward surface of one's own body; in its phenomenal being it seems capable of dispensing with this exteriority within interiority, this interior space in which our experience or image of our own body is spread forth. (*Speech and Phenomena* 79)

The body image generated by the silent voice of interior monologue thus seems immune to the articulation and opacity that characterize both the literal, biological organism and the body shaped by culture.[45] In *Leaves of Grass,* we saw in chapter 3, such transparency is a conspicuous attribute of the poet's presence.

The role played by voice in generating this transfigured body can be suggested by juxtaposing two of Whitman's notebook fragments. The first offers a prescription for successful "composition," adjuring the poet to attain "A perfectly transparent, plate-glassy style" (CW 9:34). This looks like a neoclassical formula, and it seems to restrict the function of the word rather than celebrate its generative power: language, attaining its proper transparency, simply shows the thing itself. But a second quotation uses strikingly similar terms to discuss the quality the body might attain in poetry: "A poem in which is minutely described the whole particulars and ensemble of a *first-rate healthy Human Body*—it looked into and through, as if it were transparent and of pure glass— and now reported in a poem" (NUPM 1:304).[46] The body is also properly transparent, and shows itself only by attaining the very "plate-glassy" quality that lets the word show *it.* There is thus a more intimate relation between language and body, signifier and signified, than a simple linear passage from representer to represented would account for: the proper body is reconceived according to the transparency or ideality Whitman ascribes to the proper signifier.[47] As we have seen, this linguistic transparency is itself generated by voice.

In *Leaves of Grass* such transparency governs not just a fantasized image of the body's interior, but the body of the poet in its entirety, his "translucent mould" (1855 49). It thus characterizes his presence to others as well as his sense of self-presence:

> Divine am I inside and out, and I make holy whatever I touch or am touched
> from. (1855 49)

This magical transparency depends on a magically empowered voice. Projected by and as speech, the poet's presence assumes the qualities that seem to define the sacrosanct interior domain from which speech emanates; identified with voice, the poet's body might be said to present its interior directly, having sloughed off the bounding surfaces that confine the body within definite limits and block our access to such inner regions. This presence, so to speak, is all self-presence. It can accordingly penetrate to and confound itself with ours. Free of the opacity that characterizes both the appearance of others and our experience of our own unredeemed bodies, the poet supposedly melds with and transfigures us as well. Impinging on us as voice and the transparent interiority voice defines, he seems to flow effortlessly into and through flesh apparently no longer resistant or opaque; recalling us to our proper bodies, this image of voice and the recovered self-presence it defines speak to and restore our own.

This body defined by voice seems exempt from the often cataclysmic reshaping to which other bodies in *Leaves of Grass* are conspicuously liable. The threats the poet's presence keeps at bay are symbolic as well as biological; as is characteristic of Whitman's work, the features that define the poet's physical presence imply correlative changes in what might be called his psychic terrain. In Whitman's portraits of sexuality, we have seen, the anxieties provoked by these registers intertwine. The poet's presence is apparently exempt from the constraints imposed by both. The self-production of which he is supposedly capable should be understood as a kind of parthenogenetic power: it lends him an autonomy and completion which the very fact of our immersion in sexed reproduction erodes.

This latter process receives a divided estimate in Whitman's work: celebrated with a bravado that can sometimes seem quite forced (as in "Children of Adam"), it also provokes less overt anxieties. In "Crossing Brooklyn Ferry," sexual reproduction implicates the self in the ceaseless ebb and flow of generations figured by the river's tides, a trope that conveys the inexorable sweep of such energies and the individual's attendant subjection to massive rhythms of begetting and death. A more opaque image from the poem's tormented sixth section, which we glanced at earlier, seems also to focus on this process: "I too knitted the old knot of contrariety" (1856 217). To knit the old knot isn't primarily to engage in the masturbatory act various critics discern here, though masturbation plays out some of the anxieties the phrase condenses.[48] It is rather to take up one's place in the weaving of always unweaving generations, the sexual knot of the procreation of male and female selves. The line echoes a haunting, oneiric passage from "Song of Myself":

> Urge and urge and urge,
> Always the procreant urge of the world.
>
> Out of the dimness opposite equals advance . . . . Always substance and
>   increase,
> Always a knit of identity . . . . always distinction . . . . always a breed of life.
>   (1855 26–27)

These shadowy "opposite equals" looming "out of the dimness" suggest the archaic, impersonal energies that propel reproduction, out of which any sexed identity is "knit." The re-appearance of this same trope in "Crossing Brooklyn Ferry" in effect introjects this impersonal scene: less spontaneous agent than conduit, the poet becomes the site through which these massive energies trace their continuation; traversed and constituted by them, he is neither unitary nor self-contained.[49]

The ambitions announced in an odd entry from one of Whitman's early notebooks can be understood as an attempt to imagine a way out of this involvement. The aspiration is one Whitman found it difficult even to state:

Could we imagine such a thing—let us suggest that before a manchild or womanchild was born it should be suggested that a human being could be born [. . . .] (UPP 2:76)[50]

Syntactic hitches let us see that even Whitman is having trouble thinking this thought. But he is determined to think it: sexual difference ought to be a mere accident, a secondary or surface quality, and the primordial, undifferentiated identity it replaces should be recoverable. Neither "manchild" nor "womanchild," this visionary "human being" not yet marked by sexual difference is apparently unaffected by that process of generation out of which it presumably emerges: complete in itself, it seems self-sufficient and virtually self-created. The poet who achieves rebirth by announcing his presence in the poems incarnates such visionary ambitions. Though we are likely to imagine this figure as a man rather than a woman, it nonetheless fulfills much of what Whitman's notebook entry seems to want to mean. Generating himself through a magical exercise of his own spontaneity, the figure shaped by apostrophe does not owe his existence to forces outside himself; his identity is neither constituted nor compromised by powers that exceed his own self-presence.

In *Leaves of Grass* those forces are cultural as well as physical, as the passages we have been considering themselves imply. Conflating infant body and adult identity, the socially resonant terms "manchild" and "womanchild" fuse biological difference with the assumption of gendered roles. The knot knitter of "Crossing Brooklyn Ferry" is likewise associated with the symbolic as well as the biological construction of selves. This connection is partly a function of context: in section six, contiguity links the poet's anxiety at taking up his place in the process of reproduction with the shaping of sexual identity by cultural constraints. But the figure of knitting itself suggests such cultural inscription: in the context of *Leaves of Grass* it should be associated with the many forms of writing engraved on body or psyche, tracings that mark the self with the discourse of the Other. The poet who can reproduce himself in invariant form by speaking apparently no longer owes his identity to this mechanism; he no longer knits the knot of contrariety, and the gendered writing of the symbolic code should no longer re-write itself through him.

The presence generated by apostrophe indeed seems immune to such inscription in every sense. If the body generated by voice seems to be, so to speak, all interior, it has dissolved the very surfaces that would leave it vulnerable not only to surveillance but to more obviously violent forms of interference as well. I have in mind the circumcision or tattooing rituals that are the symbolic equivalents of castration. Such overt aggression is rather more crudely literalized than the modes of cultural inscription *Leaves of Grass* invites us to ponder. But to point out the poet's invulnerability to it is to remind ourselves that his body offers us an image of profound privacy: an inside without a surface, it incarnates a sacrosanct, inviolate self-presence.

The poet's relation to the word seems to be similarly private. If voice authorizes fantasmatic images of incorporation, providing a mode in which the outside world is taken into the body, it can also suggest inviolate self-communion.[51] In inner monologue, Derrida notes, the vocal signifier seems to be generated in an autonomous act. Meaning seems not to depend on or to be borrowed from socially generated structures:

The logos can be infinite and self-present, it can be *produced as auto-affection*, only through the *voice:* an order of the signifier by which the subject takes from itself into itself, does not borrow outside of itself the signifier that it emits and that affects it at the same time. Such is at least the experience—or consciousness—of the voice: of hearing (understanding)-oneself-speak [*s'entendre-parler*]. (*Grammatology* 98)[52]

Effacing the role of the Other in constituting my signs, voice elides the breach in self-presence which the detour through an alien word effects. We saw that in *Leaves of Grass* an internalized vocabulary is made responsible not only for the alienation of consciousness but also for the body's self-division and expropriation; in several key passages in Whitman's work an introjected word seems to divide inner body space by inhabiting it. Exempt from surface engraving, the presence identified with voice also seems immune to such internalized representations and the alien structure they encode. If voice can suggest a consciousness perfectly present to itself because wholly self-contained, in the magical universe of *Leaves of Grass* the body generated by voice shares this sublime closure.

The transactions initiated by this presence also seem exempt from interference; impinging on us, the poet draws us into a scene and moment seemingly sheltered within the sort of sacrosanct region his body defines. Descending upon us as an invisible presence, he seems not only to escape from the gaze but also to abrogate its function; hovering above us, the poet assumes the place of the Other, seeming to transfigure its role from a judicial to a gently seductive one:

> Closer yet I approach you
> [. . . .]
> Who was to know what should come home to me?
> Who knows but I am enjoying this?
> Who knows but I am as good as looking at you now, for all you cannot see
>   me? (1856 218)

Here the panoramic space of section six has been replaced by a hidden, protected scene; the remote, austere vantage that organizes Whitman's tormented portrait of social life dissolves into the intimate vision the poet's approach sustains. In "Song of Myself" the magical privacy of this scene exempt from surveillance is explicitly if paradoxically contrasted to more public modes of relation the poet supposedly by-passes:

> This hour I tell things in confidence,
> I might not tell everybody but I will tell you. (1855 43)

The charmed quality of this encounter is defined by the presence that precipitates it. It depends in part on the reduction of public, objectified time and space which the poet's apparent ability to project himself to us implies. But it derives as well from an implicit identification of the protected space his advent produces with interiority. The space into which the poet seems to fold us is like the sequestered, inviolable inner body space which voice defines.

2. As such passages begin to make clear, the transparency I have been associating with the sign is not the only crucial feature of the presence generated by voice. Important to this figure's appeal, the punctual self-production voice seems to enable does not wholly define him; it is not only the poet's capacity to reproduce himself as the same that makes him seem uncanny. Whitman's evocations of the poet's presence often stress what feels like an obverse quality: no sooner embodying himself than he dissolves, the poet is remarkable for his slipperiness and fluidity —"In me the caresser of life wherever moving . . . . backward as well as forward slueing," he declares in "Song of Myself" (1855 35). A passage from the 1855 "Song of the Answerer" we looked at in chapter 3 offers a more explicit panegyric to the topologically giddy space this dissolving body inaugurates:

> Him all wait for . . . . him all yield up to . . . . his word is decisive and final,
> Him they accept . . . . in him lave . . . . in him perceive themselves as amid light,
> Him they immerse, and he immerses them. (1855 129)

Beginning as an account of the poet's imperial power, these lines slip gradually into an evocation of a less masterful identity. The lack of stability that characterizes the topology of Whitman's final line may indeed strike us as disconcerting: the familiar transaction in which the poet subsumes others by means of his word modulates into a scenario more difficult to picture, in which subject and object immerse or dissolve one another. Here neither the poet's body nor the bodies with which it mingles seem like embodiments of the ideal word or instances of the stabilization of otherwise fluid processes the sign's iterability makes possible. This stabilizing power appears in *Leaves of Grass* as word magic; it is associated in Whitman's work with the sort of mastery declared at the passage's opening, in which a punctual identity internalizes its objects. As we have seen, voice is both the model of such punctuality and the agent of the apparently magical incorporation by means of which things are caught up into the body and lent the transparence voice lends it. The labile somatic space rendered at the end of the passage turns out also to depend on voice; but it evokes a more archaic relation between vocal production and body image. In word magic the representational function of language is simultaneously employed and denied: as the catachrestic mingling of light and flood here implies, the power to depict things is conflated with the power to generate them; this productive power is supposedly matched by an assimilative one. The vocal activity that precedes word magic, we shall see, is not yet involved in representation, and the body it defines is not yet distinguished from its objects. This anterior organization is also crucial to the appeal exerted by Whitman's figure of voice; it lends resonance to the word magic that transmutes and extends it.

Residues of this archaic register persist in adult language, according to Julia Kristeva; linguistic textures that foreground these persistent traces of an archaic oral mode, she also suggests, serve to evoke the now superseded sense of the body that once intertwined with them.[53] Focusing on what might be called the fantasmatic implications of stylized verbal practice, as well as on the properly infantile roots of such interrelated linguistic and somatic structures, her account can help us unpack the range of implication Whitman's figure of voice possesses. As we shall see in chapter 5, Whitman himself appeals explicitly to the notion of the archaic in his expository writings on language: the powers he claims for the word, which are absent from the languages around him, he ascribes to primitive languages and the speech of American "aborigines." The recovery of such vanished linguistic powers, moreover, is ambiguously said either to depend on or to make possible a restored relation to our bodies. Yet Whitman's remarks on primitive cultures say little about the bodies of their members—nor could the traits of the poet's own labile, pneumatized presence credibly be ascribed to the bodies of tribal peoples.[54] By contrast, the psychically archaic register Kristeva describes is characterized by body images that resemble in important respects the body generated by the poet's catalogues and apostrophes.[55] Moreover, the verbal behavior to which she attends possesses several of the same features Whitman attributes to the language of primitive cultures—traits contemporary linguists tend no longer to discover there. It will therefore prove helpful to map one sort of archaism onto another. In intellectual discourses during Whitman's time, as in popular modes in our own, the categories of the primitive and the infantile intertwine with and displace each other: together they provide a storehouse of images for a mode of identity prior to the sorts of anxious self-division *Leaves of Grass* details.[56] If the labile presence of the poet produced by voice sometimes bears less resemblance to actual archaic organizations than to what Kristeva describes as our shared evocation and retrospective recasting of them in fantasy, this distortion may imply not only an urgent need to imagine and recover a mode of identity clearly preferable to that shaped by culture, but also the merely figmentary status of such a supposed alternative.

In section two of "Song of Myself," Whitman evokes just the sort of fluid somatic space we can profitably associate with an archaic psychic register. I discussed this passage already in chapter 2, and need only recall a portion of it here:

> The smoke of my own breath,
> Echoes, ripples, and buzzed whispers .... loveroot, silkthread, crotch and vine,
> My respiration and inspiration .... the beating of my heart .... the passing of blood and air through my lungs,
> The sniff of green leaves and dry leaves, and of the shore and darkcolored sea-rocks, and of hay in the barn,
> The sound of the belched words of my voice .... words loosed to the eddies of the wind,
> A few light kisses .... a few embraces .... a reaching around of arms. (1855 25–26)

Whitman's reference in the penultimate line to voice and words, both suggestively physicalized, alerts us to naming as the agent of incorporation and re-projection here, making the passage in part an instance of the word magic that was my subject in chapter 2. Yet this somaticized catalogue is characterized by the sort of layering that typifies Whitman's renditions of the poet's presence. The punctual retrieval and reproduction of clear and distinct entities made possible by a linguistic representation conceived as magical co-exists with a blurrier sense of the body the passage also manages to evoke. Like the self-contradictory topology of "Song of the Answerer," which confounds container and contained, this passage also suggests a labile space in which body and *umwelt* dissolve into one another. The incorporative mastery made possible by word magic slides over into a messier, less punctual relation between vocal and somatic energies, and between the body and its objects.

The term "object" indeed hardly seems applicable here, since subject and object fade into a single circulating movement of somaticized fragments. Kristeva's name for this archaic space is the *chora*, a realm organized in part by

the relations (eventually representable as topological spaces) that connect the zones of the fragmented body to each other and also to "external" "objects" and "subjects," which are not yet constituted as such. (*Revolution in Poetic Language* 28)

As in Whitman's catalogue, these "relations" prior to distinct subject and object take the form of the somatic rhythms that link these zones. Kristeva terms this organization the semiotic:

Rhythm, a sequence of linked instants, is immanent to the *chora* prior to any signified spaciousness: henceforth, *chora* and rhythm, space and time coexist. (*Desire in Language* 286)

Registering only as patterns of energic movement what will later come to be distinct exterior objects and interior body sensations, the space shaped by this activity is

an essentially mobile and extremely provisional articulation constituted by movements and their ephemeral stases. We differentiate this uncertain and indeterminate *articulation* from a *disposition* that already depends on representation. . . . (*Revolution in Poetic Language* 25)[57]

It may be something of a paradox to suggest that Whitman's language, which is entoiled in representation, evokes a somatic state prior to the stabilization representation effects, a state structured instead as what Kristeva calls "a pulsating *chora* . . . a rhythmic but nonexpressive totality" (*Revolution in Poetic Language* 40). But Kristeva argues that this archaic organization is recalled by the traces of infantile vocal behavior still present within adult language deployed for symbolic purposes. Properly semiotic oral performance, not yet involved in the production of sounds as signs, is organized by principles independent of those imposed by the demand for signification. Traces of such patterning persist in adult speech; to the extent that they are foregrounded, they disturb symbolic representation or deflect attention from it, engaging our energies elsewhere.

We need therefore attribute to Whitman neither a merely instrumental stance toward form nor the sort of single-minded willfulness such an approach implies; we need not suggest that he cogitated a special language to depict an archaic body whose traits he had already meticulously enumerated. Kristeva's notion of the semiotic instead implies that the verbal practice of the poems is constitutive and not merely reflective of Whitman's vision of the body. Vocal behavior, at least, plays such an active role in the original formation of the *chora:* if the semiotic is organized by rhythm, that rhythm is as much oral as muscular: "the *chora* precedes and underlies figuration ... and is analogous only to vocal or kinetic rhythm" (*Revolution in Poetic Language* 26). Marked heavily by vocal structures which resemble those that organize the *chora,* the language of *Leaves of Grass* does not simply offer us a symbolic representation of an archaic body, but is itself inflected by archaic processes; it does not merely display but instead generates through its very structure the sense of the body the poems imply. In order to isolate such archaic elements in Whitman's work, I need to adduce briefly some of the characteristics of a properly semiotic vocal activity.

One of the first vocal behaviors, Kristeva notes, is the child's laughter. Intimately intertwined with body sensations and kinesthetic activities, the laugh helps shape the rhythmically structured space it also remarks:

the semiotic disposition makes its start as riant spaciousness. During the period of indistinction between "*same*" and "*other,*" infant and mother, as well as between "subject" and "object," while no space has yet been delineated (this will happen with and after the mirror stage—birth of the sign), the semiotic *chora* that arrests and absorbs the motility of the anaclitic facilitations relieves and produces laughter. (*Desire in Language* 283–84)

This laughter modulates into proto-linguistic activity, which thus possesses a kinesthetic basis. Rhythmical, patterned vocalic activity at first develops independent of the function of sound as sign. Kristeva notes the importance of

the first vocalizations and echolalias concomitant to the constitution of the semiotic *chora:* glottal stops and stress (a play on intensity as well as on frequencies of vowel sounds). (*Desire in Language* 287)

While Whitman's language of course signifies, traces of such archaic vocal play are nonetheless quite evident in his poetry. They are of course discoverable in all language, providing the basis for the pleasure in oral patterning activated by verse. But Whitman's catalogues tend to foreground such pre-symbolic structures: their long litanies of object phrases eclipse predication, drawing attention to rhythmic sequences of words relatively unburdened by syntactic obligation. Such vocalic patterning is even more notable, though, in some of Whitman's notebook fragments, where the symbolic function of language seems to have virtually disappeared. The best example is perhaps the brief one isolated and commented on by Matthiessen: "Cantaloupe. Muskmelon. Cantabile. Cacique City" (CW 10:36). The last two items in this list, Matthiessen suggests, are associated with each other and with what precedes solely through phonic variation (530).[58] Another notebook list mingles such vocal play with stronger symbolic connections:

Loveblows. Loveblossoms. Loveapples. Loveleaves. Loveclimbers. Loveverdure. Love Vines. Lovebranches. Loveroot. Climber-blossom. Verdure, branch, fruit and vine. Loveroot. Juice Climber. Silk crotch. Crotch bulb and vine. Juicy, climbering mine. Bulb, silkthread crotch and [. . . .] (CW 10:10)

The lack of concern here with getting something said carries over into the published passage toward which this list of echolalia modulates, the catalogue from section two of "Song of Myself" we attended to a moment ago:

Echoes, ripples, and buzzed whispers . . . . loveroot, silkthread, crotch and vine. (1855 25)

If the agglomerating, porous space this passage evokes resembles the *chora,* this archaic zone is shaped in Whitman's poem, as it is in a properly semiotic organization, by vocalic play that tends to echolalia.

The pre-symbolic activity such passages recall, Kristeva notes, helps energize and organize the emerging symbolic function that gradually restructures infantile vocal behavior:

beginning with the "first point of psychic organization," light-giving marker or mother's face, which produced laughter along with the first vocalizations, the future speaker is led to separate such points into *objects* (transitional at first, then simply objects) and add to them *no longer laughter but phonation—* archetype of the morpheme, condensation of the sentence. As if *the laughter that*

*makes up space had become, with the help of maturation and repression, a
"place name." (Desire in Language 287; emphases in original)*

Emerging from infantile laughter and echolalia, such rudimentary
versions of the signifying function are still clearly embedded in the
rhythmic somatic activities those first vocalizations helped structure. The
holophrastic utterances that characterize this phase dramatically combine symbolic and semiotic resources:

While it is true that pseudomorphemes and even pseudophrases emerge during
this period, they remain holophrastic: they are vocalizations, they designate
the place or object of enunciation (the "topic"), whereas the motor or vocal gesture (intonation) serves as predicate (the "comment"). (Desire in Language 287)

Whitman's phrasal catalogues oddly resemble this topic-comment
format, though they do not literally conform to it. Characteristically
leaving behind the predicate that technically governs the ensuing list,
they effectively resolve themselves into a series of objects or "place
names" accompanied by rhythmically expressive but non-predicating
"comments." They thus evoke the archaic moment in which discrete
objects are first being constituted or separated out from the sort of labile
semiotic space Whitman's rhythmic utterances also recall. From our
own vantage, however, it is the provisional status of this separation that
is most striking, a feature suggested in part by the catalogues' cumulative rhythm: effacing the kinesthetic specificity of the "comment,"
these litanies present "topics" that are less discrete entities than emergent aspects of a pervasive, still largely undifferentiated rhythmic continuum.

Suggested by Whitman's catalogue technique, this archaic somatic space
shaped by vocal activity is more directly rendered in numerous passages
in *Leaves of Grass*. It is evoked, for example, not only in the explicitly
somaticized litany from section two of "Song of Myself," but also in the
crucial fifth section of the same poem. There the poet recalls the advent
of his soul as a sexual partner, a description that has shocked some
critics while delighting others, provoking debates about whether the
physical presence described in the passage really tropes a spiritual one,
or the reverse. We should remember, though, that the poet's soul is
invoked as a voice:

> Loafe with me on the grass . . . . loose the stop from your throat,
> Not words, not music or rhyme I want . . . . not custom or lecture, not even
>   the best,
> Only the lull I like, the hum of your valved voice. (1855 28)

Voice, I suggested earlier, defines in Whitman's work a presence simultaneously ideal and incarnate; it thus implies a paradoxical reconciliation of the very scandal the passage provokes.

More important for our present purposes, the figure of voice that presides over this section also effectively renders moot debates about whether the erotic scenario into which the passage modulates is auto-erotic or depicts the poet as ravished by a partner. The voice invoked here, we can note, is not yet involved in the production of "words" or articulate language: themselves instances of echolalia, the "lull" and "hum" in which the poet's "valved voice" engages serve as synecdoches for an archaic oral activity governed by pleasure in vocal effusion rather than by the representational exigencies of the symbolic function; the rhythmic, labile body associated with such vocalization influences the sexuality of the rest of the section, in which adult erotic activity emerges from, overlays, and then dissolves back into the diffuse somatic sensations that characterize the agglomerating body space of archaic experience. The space of the *chora* itself, we should recall, is one in which the very distinctions between self and other, auto-eroticism and eroticism "proper," are not yet operative.

Though they are evident here, the anxieties they tend to provoke are annulled by the image of voice that governs this encounter. This scene is thus the virtually perfect obverse of the terrifying sexual scenario displayed in the poem's twenty-eighth section. Rather than rediscovering a lack that makes each the unavailing supplement of the other, auto-eroticism and eroticism "proper" are here fantasized as complementary facets of a sexuality paradoxically still conditioned and protected by the archaic organization from which it emerges. The auto-eroticism registered as the somaticized lull and hum of the valved voice, and thus still organized by the diffuse rhythmic processes of the *chora,* seems free from the sense of self-division so evident in section twenty-eight, as if it were not yet structured by symbolization or the Other. While the erotic encounter with a partner that seems to follow departs more clearly from such archaic indistinction, it still benefits from the agglomerating sensuality associated with primitive vocalization. From the section's beginning, the agent who will become the poet's partner has been distinguished provisionally by direct address: "I believe in you my soul." Yet this other initially seemed part of a fluid, somaticized space that encompassed the poet's body, a space shaped by its own lull and hum. Splitting off from the labile region it thus not only belonged to but also helped generate, the figure called soul initiates an encounter reminiscent of the pleasures of this apparently superseded organization from which it emerges. The movement from auto-eroticism to eroticism "proper" thus manages to be simultaneously more definite and less disturbing than in section twenty-eight:

> I mind how we lay in June, such a transparent summer morning;
> You settled your head athwart my hips and gently turned over upon me,
> And parted the shirt from my bosom-bone, and plunged your tongue to my
> barestript heart,
> And reached till you felt my beard, and reached till you held my feet. (1855
> 28–29)

Like the auto-eroticism that precedes it, this encounter is luxuriantly expansive, unmarked by either the sense of self-division or the defensive posture toward others that characterize the later section.

Whitman's succeeding stanza recalls the source of such assurance. There the clarity of subject-object positions briefly apparent in the lines above is abruptly subverted, as the grammatical subject is ambiguously either displaced by hyperbaton or simply omitted. It is unclear who is where or who does what to whom:

> Swiftly arose and spread around me the peace and joy and knowledge that
> pass all the art and argument of the earth. (1855 29)

Here a phrase that overtly obeys the boundary between self and other covertly elides it: blurring the clarity made possible by the unambiguous disposition of the symbolic function, Whitman's line confuses subject and object as well as transitive and reflexive verbs, generating the sort of labile space the rest of the stanza's more orderly symbolic language goes on to characterize. In context, the confounding of subject and object the stanza's opening line achieves thus suggests a feeling of fluid unity rather than the scary confusion of section twenty-eight. We can rightly regard such tranquility as marking another of Whitman's efforts to evoke post-orgasmic bliss. But we should note as well that the shift, between stan-

zas, from clarity to a confusion of agency reminiscent of archaic processes suggests that two perspectives are overlaid in the entire scene.
Activated here toward the section's end by fuzzy grammar and evoked
at the beginning through an image of archaic voice, the agglomerative
processes of the *chora* condition the dream-like renditions of adult sexuality sheltered between them. Distinct partner though it be, the difficult-
to-locate and expansively stretching body that settles on top of the poet
itself possesses a protean quality akin to the archaic fluidity activated by
voice. The elusive activity initiated by this figure, we should also note,
assumes its most definite form as a displaced act of fellatio. Here such
oral eroticism recalls or reactivates the "lull" and "hum" of the "valved
voice": orality links vocal and sexual activity, also fusing an archaic
somatic register and an adult sexuality fantasized in its light.[59] Whitman's evocation of the semiotic organization structured by voice allays
the anxieties provoked by the otherwise similar configurations depicted
in section twenty-eight.

Most apparent in such overtly erotic scenes, which are regularly linked
to explicit images of voice, this enchanted sense of a labile body is also
evoked by the linguistic textures in *Leaves of Grass* that foreground the
modes of vocal patterning Kristeva details. Yet Kristeva herself characterizes this sort of blissful vision of archaic processes as compensatory
fantasy; the infantile organization she calls the *chora* is by no means
equivalent to the idealized self-completion we tend to project back onto
it. Lability is not simply a source of pleasure:

the archaic relation to the mother, narcissistic though it may be, is from my
point of view of no solace to the protagonists. . . . For the subject will always be
marked by the uncertainty of his borders and of his affective valency as well. . . .
(*Powers of Horror* 63)

While *Leaves of Grass* is on rare occasions caught up in the terror such
an unstable organization can provoke, Whitman characteristically offers
just such a rapturous image of the body experienced as the site of
agglomerating energies.

　　Not simply fortuitous errors, such reconstructions perform the crucial
task of providing us with an image of identity exempt from the sort of
alienation *Leaves of Grass* records: "The edenic image of primary narcissism is perhaps a defensive negation elaborated by the neurotic subject

when he sets himself under the aegis of the father" (*Powers of Horror* 63). "Neurotic" is more synonym than antonym for "normal" here; Kristeva's crucial contrast is with the psychotic, who has refused the cultural compact, subjection to the father's law, and the alienated subjectivity accorded those under its rule, instead actually inhabiting the unstable realm others recast in fantasy.

Yet *Leaves of Grass* does not simply elaborate the sort of compensatory image Kristeva describes. In Whitman's imaginative universe the poet neither consistently retreats to a region sheltered from the patriarchal function nor accepts the usual terms of the bargain that seals our subjection to it. If Whitman evokes an archaic body not yet regulated by symbolic language or the law, he also claims to project a punctual body by means of word magic: both this figure and the magic language that produces it seem to usurp the law's power rather than merely evade its purview. This figure indeed seems not only to preserve crucial attributes of the semioticized body extolled in Whitman's most blissful evocations, but also to fuse them with the stabilizing mastery of a symbolic function that word magic recasts and reclaims for the self. *Leaves of Grass* thus imagines a mode of identity capable of transfiguring the social relation rather than avoiding it, a figure who might exercise power in the cultural sphere without suffering the alienation which participation there exacts. This is Whitman's explicitly magical embodiment of the figure of voice analyzed by Derrida, a transparent, self-present identity that punctually retrieves, internalizes, and re-disposes its objects. We are now in a better position to understand this figure as a liminal one. In what follows, I want to situate it more precisely in relation to both the organization it preserves and the one it wards off, by looking in detail at another crucial contrast between semiotic and symbolic registers.

Like the archaic complex that word magic extends, the debacle it avoids encompasses both body and language. The threats to which these are subject are adumbrated in Whitman's work by a crucial organizing image we looked at earlier, that of castration. Castration, we saw, explicitly figures the disaster to which the socialized body succumbs. A brief passage from "Song of Myself" thus associates subjugation with emasculation, phallic self-possession with social revolt:

[I] make short account of neuters and geldings, and favor men and women fully equipped,

> And beat the gong of revolt, and stop with fugitives and them that plot and
> conspire. (1855 47)

In "Faces," we saw, contiguity links castration more specifically with subjection to signs. This initially improbable association is complemented by Whitman's vision of a different sort of signifying activity that might avoid or indeed protect against emasculation, a vision reflected in a series of pronouncements employing castration imagery to characterize what might be called threats to the body of Whitman's book. "To a cipher," Whitman opined to Traubel in Camden, "that's all: what does a man come to with his virility gone?" (WWC 3:321). Whitman had Leaves of Grass in mind here: the loss of virility he praises himself for having avoided is "either" metaphorical "or" associated, through a kind of contagious magic, with the act of writing and the image of the body proffered by the book. Whitman's pronouncements about Leaves of Grass tend toward a vehemence that suggests such magic thinking. Recalling Emerson's proposed excision from the forthcoming 1860 edition of Leaves of Grass of the most provocative passages of "Children of Adam," which represent what Whitman there calls the phallic "work of fatherhood" (1860 290) with unusual if rather mechanical explicitness, he declared to Traubel: "He must have known as well as I knew that it would have been decenter to throw the book away than to mutilate it" (WWC 3:440). Given such insistence on the phallic integrity of Leaves of Grass, one of Whitman's remarks concerning the economy between the author's body and his book also possesses a resonance beyond its immediate medical context; discussing the cost to his health of the Civil War hospital visits that resulted in Drum-Taps and Specimen Days, Whitman averred: "My body? Yes—it had to be given—it had to be sacrificed" (WWC 3:582). This sacrifice of the poet's body to the book is balanced by its resurrection in the book:

> In the best poems re-appears the body, man's or woman's, well-shaped,
> natural, gay,
> Every part able, active, receptive, without shame or need of shame. ("A Song
> of the Rolling Earth," 1856 322–23)

This resurrected body, without shame and natural in every part, is what we might call an uncastrated body. Why should the birth of such a presence require the sacrifice of the body Whitman already possessed? Why should it take place in a book? Why, in the crucial case of the poet's apostrophes, should this uncastrated body need to appear not just in words, but as a word? Why, conversely, should the book be the crucial place in which phallic integrity is menaced? What—we need to ask in order to pursue the economy I have been tracing between body and vocal production—might a castrated word be, or an uncastrated one?

These last questions concern the relation of the sign to what it names. Like the pronounced oral patterning characteristic of semiotic vocalization, archaic versions of this tie help structure the *chora,* implying a primitive experience of the body and its objects. In order to suggest how word magic recasts and extends such primordial material, I need to offer an account of both the semiotic relation between sound image and object which word magic modifies and the later, firmly symbolic one it resists. This latter relation of word to thing entails a disjunction between subject and object formalized by syntax itself; this constellation is what Whitman will come to mean by castration.

In properly semiotic vocalization, Kristeva suggests, there *are* no objects distinct from the sounds themselves. Vocal activity in the *chora* is not yet structured by the representational function of language; the utterance does not yet stand for a thing that differs from it: "The *chora* is a modality of signifiance in which the linguistic sign is not yet articulated as the absence of an object and as the distinction between real and symbolic" (*Revolution in Poetic Language* 26).[60] The thing for which the sign might stand, indeed, does not yet exist as such: paradoxically, the distinct object the sound will come to represent will be separated out from the flux of the *chora* only by virtue of the nascent operation of representation itself; the object is firmly isolated and detached from the subject who apprehends it only as the sound becomes the sign of a thing.[61]

The shift to this representational mode, and to the split between signifier and signified, sound image and intentional object, that makes it possible is by no means abrupt; the gradual constitution of objects goes hand in hand with a gradual renunciation of our original relation to vocal production. In order for the sound to be able to stand for a thing, it must in effect cease being a thing itself. We must, at least, curtail our intense involvement in the production of sound itself in order to invest our attention in its representational capacities: energy must be withdrawn from sound production as physical act, so that the word can become the sign of something else—something external or something absent. This development is also a renunciation; what must be renounced is the pleasure of auto-eroticism. Sounds on their way to becoming stable signifiers, Kristeva notes, at first represent only in part the external objects they are gradually coming to denote; they also act as "representations of an 'interior object,' an internal perception, an eroticization of the body proper during the act of formulating the word as a symbolic element" (*Desire in Language* 217). It is this auto-erotic component of vocalization that must be abandoned or repressed, in order to facilitate the expeditious use of sounds as (neutral) signifiers representing the detached objects that populate the codified symbolic universe in which our desires will henceforth be played out.[62]

This re-orientation, however, is never absolute. Obvious disturbances in symbolic language are often precipitated by a dramatic lifting of just this repression. The speech of schizophrenics, Freud argues in some seminal remarks on the psychic consequences of language acquisition, is marked by a re-investment of energy in the signifier itself: treating this oral entity as a thing in its own right, the schizophrenic breaks the symbolic link that binds it to its signified, thereby severing his own ties to the shared symbolic universe signification subtends (*Collected Papers* 4:133). The passages in Whitman's poems and notebooks dominated by echolalia and other sorts of oral play and patterning are instances of a controlled regression to just such a primitive investment.

The attraction of such regressive possibilities suggests the costs of the re-orientation they resist—costs not simply cancelled by the huge benefits conferred by the symbolic function or the frightening aspects of the organization it supersedes. Redefining our relation to our bodies as well as to our speech, these costs amount to what I have been calling castration. The movement from semiotic vocalization to symbolic language, from the word as somatic object to the word as neutral sign of a thing from which it is detached, precipitates a shift from auto-erotic *jouissance* to a contingent and partial pleasure in external objects. The objects precipitated out of the *chora* sunder its unity. Moreover, these objects isolated by the word and detached from the self are also lost *in* the word. Established by representation, they are accessible only in relations mediated by a cultural order that originates elsewhere and is never itself accessible. They are, that is to say, symbolic objects: appearing as instances of culturally defined entities, they have being, meaning, and value only within a symbolic circuit of exchange. One enters this circuit only by relinquishing unmediated access to the unique, the physical, and the real: whatever remains unnamed within this system is effectively dissolved or faded by it. It is in this sense that symbolic language is a language in which the object has been lost, or a language that sequesters the object. The auto-eroticized body shaped by the semiotic succumbs to this fading: like the vocalization that helps structure it and provokes its pleasure, it is occulted by the symbolic mediation that gives stability in exchange.

As we have seen, these are just the losses by which the protagonist of Whitman's early editions is haunted. Enforced by the separation of signifier from signified which symbolic language and culture demand, these losses are also exacted by the very syntax of our speech. This syntactic component of castration is worth noting, since it will help us characterize both the resistance involved in Whitman's overtly aberrant catalogue constructions and the more ambiguous stance implied by the syntactically normal utterances in *Leaves of Grass* that nonetheless seem to subvert through word magic the very separations syntax ordinarily enforces.

Syntax, Kristeva argues, repeats and makes explicit the divisions already precipitated by the opposition of signifier and signified. If the signifier divorced from the signified it represents already posits a detached object, the syntactic operations of predicating and judging make explicit both this positional act or "thesis" inherent in naming and the separation this "thetic" mode entails: the object is firmly isolated from the subject who names it through the limiting attribution of the predicate. The opposition between noun phrase and verb phrase, according to Kristeva, is thus the mark within syntax of the subject-object split established by the thetic act of positing, though the two divisions are admittedly not perfectly homologous: "syntax is the ex-position of the thetic. The subject and predicate represent the division inherent in the thetic; they make it plain and actual" (*Revolution in Poetic Language* 54).[63]

Syntax also isolates a subject; moreover, it alienates the very subject it precipitates. It is through the act of positing formalized by accession to syntax, Kristeva argues, that a discrete subject is stabilized by being set over against the object: "for every signified transcendental object, there is a transcendental ego, both of which are givens by virtue of thetic operation—predication and judgment" (*Desire in Language* 130). The subject, that is, is paradoxically a function of the judgment that emanates from it: "the ego constitutes itself only through the operating consciousness at the time of predication: the subject is merely the subject of prediction, of judgment, of the sentence" (*Desire in Language* 130). Symbolic language, Lacan thus notes, generates the subject only at the price of "splitting" it: "the first split . . . makes the subject as such distinguish himself from the sign in relation to which, at first, he has been able to constitute himself as subject" (*Four Fundamental Concepts* 141). He discovers himself not as an autochtonous self-presence (though he may fantasize himself as one) but as a term located within an already constellated field organized by available predicates: what Kristeva calls the "open combinatorial system" (*Revolution in Poetic Language* 43) relating subjects and objects through the thesis is superimposed on and stabilized by the structure of culturally sanctioned relations.[64] The stabilized subject who manipulates syntax is thus also an object shaped by the syntax of culture: "his nature," to recall Lacan's phrase, "is woven by effects in which is to be found the structure of language, of which he becomes the material" (*Ecrits* 284). Whether or not he need fear literal castration, he is already fantasmatically castrated: separated from the objects precipitated out of the *chora* and lost in the word, he also encounters himself as an identity generated elsewhere. "Through the effects of speech," Lacan notes, "the subject always realizes himself more in the Other" (*Four Fundamental Concepts* 188). This alienation is registered as "the lack that constitutes castration anxiety" (*Four Fundamental Concepts* 73).[65]

Such global formulations sound rather different from Whitman's protestations. Yet this castrated subject is very nearly the exact equivalent of the mode of identity *Leaves of Grass* seeks to annul: the sunderings generated by the signifier-signified split and formalized by our accession to syntax are very close to those implied by Whitman's condensing figure of "the same old role." This trope, I argued earlier, comes to suggest not only the poet's subjection to social shaping but also his consignment to an uncomfortable body that brings him into awkward and anxious relation to others. This conjunction at first seems odd, since it conflates contingent social sanctions and what at least appear to be the immutable topological facts that structure our interactions in the oppositional form of the subject-object polarity. Yet this unlikely identification of cultural and topological constraints may reflect Whitman's sense that our images of the body are themselves shaped by syntax, and are thus part of a global cultural grammar. According to Kristeva, at any rate, the subject-object polarity is precipitated only through an accession to positional language formalized by a syntax that also alienates the subject, dividing it against itself. The poet's relation to others may reflect or repeat the anxiety of this origin, in which both an alienated subject and its objects are generated within an already organized symbolic field. Just this complex of events, we saw, appears repeatedly in Whitman's depictions of the not-yet-liberated protagonist of *Leaves of Grass*.

Whitman's catalogue constructions, which disrupt the syntactic norms that formalize such supposed disasters, might perhaps be construed as a resistance not only to castration but also to the symbolic order that exacts it. The syntactically disruptive practice of modern experimental writing, at least, should according to Kristeva be understood in such insurrectionary terms. Whitman's verbal textures sometimes resemble this artistic practice even more closely than they do the properly infantile vocalizations of the *chora* which these texts also recall.[66] Violating the syntactic closure that subtends the symbolic, such experimental texts aggressively re-activate the semiotic, resurrecting traces of an unstable but still uncastrated body.

They do so in part by failing properly to posit and detach objects, a failure weirdly compatible with just the sort of incessant naming of things characteristic of Whitman's catalogues. Whitman's procedure does invoke the positional force of the word. Like the texts Kristeva describes, however, his litanies tend to stall, repeating a single syntactic unit by finding, say, a substitute noun phrase rather than promptly fulfilling syntactic demands with a verb phrase:

> The blab of the pave . . . . the tires of carts and sluff of bootsoles and talk of
> the promenaders,
> The heavy omnibus, the driver with his interrogating thumb, the clank of the
> shod horses on the granite floor. (1855 31–32)

Here, as Kristeva suggests, "the syntactic division (modified-modifier, NP-VP . . .) is disrupted" (*Revolution in Poetic Language* 55). Such disruption might be understood as an implicit refusal to acknowledge the very grounds of social commerce or to participate in it, since it rejects "one function of language though not the only one: to express meaning in a communicable sentence between speakers. This function harbors coherence . . . or, in other words, social identity" (*Desire in Language* 131). Such disrupted enunciations certainly refuse the received relational categories articulated by available, acceptable predicates. According to Kristeva they also abort the positing or separating out of the very things they name: suspending the complementary structure of noun phrase plus verb phrase, they thereby subvert the subject-object division it formalizes. Hovering at the threshold of the positional, these litanies suggest just the sort of ambiguous space I discussed in chapter 2: provisionally projected objects still seem to be part of the subject who names them.

This failure to detach objects firmly is also implied by the breakdown of representational closure syntactic incompletion suggests. The orderly construction of the verisimilar scene posited by a subject-predicate pair is interrupted; the symbolic function seems to be disturbed by energies of a different order:

This ellipsis or syntactic *non-completion* can be interpreted as the thetic break's inability to remain simply intra-syntactic—a division within a signifying homogeneity. A heterogeneous division, an irruption of the semiotic *chora*, marks each "category" of the syntactic sequence and prevents the "other" from being posited as an identifiable syntactic term. . . . (*Revolution in Poetic Language* 56)

Frustrating signification and organized instead by iterated syntactic fragments, such texts seem to dissolve the world of discrete objects posited by syntax back into the rhythmic, somaticized space their recurrent pattern suggests. Provisionally posited objects are no sooner named than they are eroded by the "instinctual rhythm" that organizes the text. Like emphasis on sound as an autonomous value, syntactic non-completion is thus also, according to Kristeva, an "attempt to dissolve the first social censorship—the bar between signifier and signified" (*Revolution in Poetic Language* 63). Not firmly isolated by complete acts of positing, "things" seem to be simply provisional, unstable accretions of the somatic energies voice helps shape. As such, they are subject to the sort of rhythmic structuring that organizes the space of the *chora*, the rough alternation of centripetal and centrifugal energies that a less archaic register will isolate and formalize as the vocative and positional powers of symbolic language:

The entire gamut of partial drives is triggered within the chora underlying the text, endlessly "swallowing"/rejecting, appropriating/expelling, inside/outside. The real object is never posited as lost, lacking. . . . instinctual rhythm simultaneously posits and passes through the object. . . . drives pass through the body as well as the surrounding natural and social configuration. (*Revolution in Poetic Language* 99)

> Echoes, ripples, and buzzed whispers . . . . loveroot, silkthread, crotch and
> vine.

Like the pattern of syntactic recurrence that structures such a text, its referential procedure can thus also be thought of as anaphoric. Since the aborted speech acts that make it up fail to posit discrete scenes successfully, the text instead evokes the single, somatic locus shaped by vocal rhythm itself:

when instinctual rhythm passes through ephemeral but specific theses, meaning is constituted but is then immediately exceeded by what seems outside meaning. . . . The processes' matrix of enunciation is in fact *anaphoric* since it designates an elsewhere: the *chora* that generates what signifies. (*Revolution in Poetic Language* 100)

In *Leaves of Grass,* as we saw in chapter 2, this hovering sense of anaphora serves to dissolve an often staggering amount of material back into a space, shaped by enunciation, indistinguishable from the poet's agglomerating body:

> Where the panther walks to and fro on a limb overhead . . . . where the buck
> turns furiously at the hunter,
> Where the rattlesnake suns his flabby length on a rock . . . . where the otter is
> feeding on fish. (1855 57)

Cueing their iterating syntactic fragments to the single word "where," these lines and those that follow them make location their explicit topic; but their incomplete acts of positing have the effect of dissolving spatial as well as syntactic position. Like the more recent texts Kristeva analyzes, the sections of *Leaves of Grass* organized by such stylized disruption not only resist the divisions I have been calling castration but also subvert the symbolic order that requires them.

Or at least they seem to. But we should note that, unlike the modernist texts Kristeva discusses, Whitman's catalogues tend to fulfill their syntactic commitments. Whereas the former initiate syntactic structures but fail to complete them, Whitman's typical litanies hypnotically suspend and thereby transfigure the very requirements they technically satisfy. Thus, for example, the long catalogue of apparent syntactic fragments excerpted just above turns out finally to modify a main clause that passes grammatical muster: "Where the panther walks to and fro on a limb overhead [. . . .] I tread day and night such roads" (1855 57, 60). Despite what grammar tells us, however, in this litany the very act of predication or positing lodged in the main clause is effectively engulfed by the distended anaphoric structure that organizes the catalogue as a whole, negating the firm separation of subject from object predication implies. By contrast to the staunchly incomplete utterances Kristeva analyzes, on the other hand, Whitman's grammatical closure does posit a name for all that precedes: gathering the catalogue's anaphoric energies under the sign of a coherent self, it brings these rhythmic processes to the punctual focus of a dominant "I."[67] Co-opting or commandeering normative grammar instead of rebelling against it, Whitman's litanies seem to meld the profoundly archaic structure of the *chora* with a different, liminal vision of the poet's body and word, implying a relation to the cultural order that is transformative rather than insurrectionary.

This transformative relation is suggested even more strongly by Whitman's proclamations of the poet's presence. Rather than disrupting syntax, these performative utterances revel in the positional power it codifies. Yet they re-imagine the very operations in which they engage: the poet's performatives subscribe to the grammatical requirements that insert us in a circuit of symbolic identities, yet claim to annul the very bar between signifiers and signifieds that in fact generates both the objects of cultural exchange and the subjects who engage in circulating them. These pronouncements, that is to say, are instances of word magic, and they owe their attraction in part to the relation between speaker and symbolic order they imply. Itself a hyperbolic version of the positional power that organizes this realm, word magic suggests that we can exercise such force without paying the price of castration, acceding to the benefits of the symbolic without foregoing archaic satisfactions. We might do so by speaking a still uncastrated word. Word magic thus claims to carry forward into symbolic language traits peculiar to a transitional stage between semiotic and symbolic modes; in the fantasy it sustains, the threshold between these organizations is effectively effaced. We can see how this is so by pinpointing more precisely the stage in the shifting, fantasmatic relations between language and object that word magic reverts to and seems to extend.

The invariant connections between signifiers and signifieds required by symbolic language, we saw above, codify links of sound images to intentional objects that develop only gradually. At first, we noted, these associations are weakened by intense investment in sound itself: the link between a sound and the external object it will come to denote must compete with an interfering association between the sound and the auto-erotic pleasure its production evokes. The development of symbolic language thus demands a progressive eroding of our investment in the physical aspects of vocal production and the somatic satisfactions these afford. Yet for a time, it turns out, intense investment in sounds facilitates rather than retards their progressive binding to objects, by lending the connection between these a fantasmatic meaning. The tie between word and thing, that is, is accorded a strength it will soon no longer possess: given the continuing sense of the word as physical presence, what will become the purely symbolic, conventional tie between signifier and signified is registered as a literal, physical bond of word and thing. Connected to an external object but still strongly associated with a somatic process or presence, the word is experienced as a fantasmatic fusion of these disparate entities.[68]

This fantasmatic structure centers on the mouth; the particular form it takes depends on a primordial association between ingestion and vocalization. The metonymic connection between these two activities provides the basis for a vision of naming as literal, physical incorporation that only gradually gives way to the construction of a ruling metaphor that posits language as *like* ingestion since it, too, affords a kind of possession of the object. As Nicolas Abraham and Maria Torok suggest, in an argument congruent in many respects with Kristeva's:

Learning to fill the void of the mouth with words constitutes an early paradigm of introjection. Clearly this cannot occur without the constant presence of a mother who herself possesses language. Her constancy ... is the necessary guarantee of the meaning of words. When that guarantee is assured, and only then, words can replace the mother's presence and give rise to new introjections. First the empty mouth, then the absence of objects become words, and finally experiences with words themselves are converted into other words. Thus the original oral void will have found a remedy for all its wants through their conversion in linguistic intercourse with the speaking community. . . . Thus food absorption, in the literal sense, becomes introjection in the figurative sense. To achieve this transition, presence of the object must be superseded by auto-apprehension of its absence. Language . . . makes up for that absence by *representing* presence. . . . ("Introjection—Incorporation" 6)

The fantasized conflation of word and thing is thus also temporary, and rejection of it is crucial; both the reality principle and the circuit of cultural exchange we come to call reality require the effective renunciation of this identification. The entities supposedly literally incorporated in the word must be recognized as symbolic objects neither subject themselves to this sort of physical possession nor directly fused with the physical realm they help us negotiate. And our attachment to this physical stratum (first experienced by the infant as subject to literal ingestion) must be largely replaced by an investment in the shared symbolic entities culture circulates and the shared symbolic introjections that link us to this system of exchange. Based on the renunciation or repression of the primordial identification of ingestion and vocalization, incorporation and naming, the symbolic order must thus be, in Abraham and Torok's phrase, "a 'community of empty mouths' " ("Introjection—Incorporation" 6). The empty mouth indeed becomes a crucial synecdoche for the subject's body, a body for which the object is now lost. No longer experienced as present in the word, the object is detached from the subject; no longer susceptible to magical incorporation, it will return only via a circuit of exchange and only as symbolic: either as a word, or through words that give it a culturally mediated meaning and value.[69]

It is just these castrations that word magic resists. Obeying the syntactic structures that formalize our symbolic relation to objects, word magic appeals surreptitiously to the very incorporative metaphor the symbolic compact demands that we renounce, collapsing introjection back into incorporation. That renunciation is always fragile, since as Maria Torok suggests

il existe un niveau très archaïque où les deux mécanismes, devenus si opposés par la suite, pouvaient encore se confondre. [a very archaic level exists where the two mechanisms, afterwards so opposed, could still be intermingled.] (Torok, "Maladie du deuil" 722)

Le fantasme d'incorporation apparaît donc comme le premier mensonge, l'effet du premier langage rudimentaire. [The fantasy of incorporation thus looms as the first lie, the effect of the first rudimentary language.] (Torok, "Maladie du deuil" 722)

We are accordingly always susceptible to

The fantasy of incorporation [which] aspires to accomplish [appropriation] by magic, as it were, by carrying out in a literal sense something that has meaning only in a figurative sense. . . . In the magic of incorporation, then, one finds . . . demetaphorization (taking literally what is meant figuratively). . . . ("Introjection—Incorporation" 4–5)

Less overtly disruptive and less profoundly archaic than the schizophrenic speech analyzed by Freud, since it retains the binding of word to thing such behavior elides, this incorporative fantasy nonetheless involves withdrawal from the social sphere, being indeed a kind of raid on its objects.[70] Paraphrasing Abraham and Torok in his introduction to their work, Derrida thus speaks of "the *catastrophic* reversal that will occur with the fantasy of incorporation. That fantasy transforms the oral metaphor presiding over introjection into a *reality*" (*Fors* xxxviii).

Related but not simply identical to this incorporative fantasy, the constellation of putative linguistic powers Freud condenses in the term "word magic" can be thought of as less disruptive and less archaic in turn. In Whitman's imaginative universe, at least, the magical fusion of word and thing is deployed in order to re-project objects as well as to incorporate them: the things drained from the social sphere are given back, at least provisionally, in transfigured form.[71] In *Leaves of Grass*, moreover, the incorporative fantasy at the root of word magic co-exists with less cataclysmic versions of verbal sorcery, passing over into the more general "omnipotence of thought" Freud adduces as a synonym for his term.[72] Regressive designs are thus implicit within but do not always overtly dominate the myriad scenes shaped by magical utterance in Whitman's work; archaic material often inflects what looks like a social scenario without violently disturbing it. The poet of *Leaves of Grass* deploys word magic not to destroy the social bond but to redeem it, cancelling its costs by effacing the boundary between symbolic and semiotic registers.

Kristeva's vision of the aggressive, adversarial stance implicit in works that erode the division between signifier and signified thus needs at least some refurbishing to be applicable to Whitman:

since poetry works on the bar between signifier and signified and tends to erase it, it would be an anarchic outcry against the thetic and socializing position of syntactic language. It depletes all communities, either destroying them or identifying with the moment of their subversion. (*Desire in Language* 174)

It is not only the anarchist who "works on the bar between signifier and signified." So does the shaman. The semiotic weakens both representation and sociability, by making vocalization, so to speak, its own object. The shaman instead operates a ritually controlled evocation of the tie between word and thing that symbolic language must repudiate. Claiming to efface the separation of signifier from signified that in fact makes symbolic language and the symbolic compact possible, he seems thereby to revitalize culture, recovering the natural grounding of social forms by displaying the magical power of ritual utterance over nature. Whitman's protagonist is less comfortably ensconced in culture: he wields word magic in order to suggest that the castrations exacted by symbolic language have no power over him. Yet he seems thereby to restore to us not only the bodies but also the social relations that should have been ours.[73]

Leaves of Grass thus aims both to reclaim culture for us and to recover more archaic modes of our being for culture. Effacing the threshold between the symbolic realm and what precedes it, the poet creates a continuity in which not only word magic but also the earlier organizations Kristeva describes seem compatible with social requirements. It is in terms of this blurring of boundaries that we can best understand what initially seems a peculiar polarity in Whitman's depictions of the poet's body, an oddity noted by more than one critic. Quentin Anderson has astutely remarked the reciprocity of what he calls active and passive poles in these portraits (*Imperial Self* 139–60); more recently, M. Jimmie Killingsworth has pointed to the paradoxical characterization of the poet in terms of both phallic bravado and a receptivity he calls feminine (60–87). We might better term it archaic, and recall that the labile somatic space of the semiotic is gradually succeeded by a body image organized by both the punctual incorporation and the punctual self-production word magic seems to enable. Embodiment of the word and of the patriarchal power of positing, this fantasmatic body is phallic. In *Leaves of Grass*, indeed, it is the phallus itself; yet it characteristically dissolves back into the *chora* out of which it rises.[74] Instances of word magic typically shade over into just the sort of semioticized verbal practice that attenuates positional power; the poems thus seem to mingle the body images these contiguous registers imply. Yet the ambiguous presence thereby created presides over a transfigured cultural space Whitman invites us to call America.

3. This body defines what the body should be. This is so despite both the relative infrequency of the performative announcements that seem to generate the poet's presence by means of his word and the tendency of Whitman's catalogues to leave implicit the somatic basis of the collapsing space they evoke. The figure directly identified with voice epitomizes a vision of incarnation much more widely at work in Whitman's poems. Given the importance with which I am endowing this presence, it is probably prudent to offer some indication of the prevalence of his avatars in the early editions of *Leaves of Grass*.

Appearances of the poet himself in what might be called his overtly generic guise recall the presence produced by apostrophe and the transfiguring powers of voice most strongly. "I know I have the best of time and space—and that I was never measured, and never will be measured," the poet vaunts in "Song of Myself" (1855 79). Alluding to a power of diffusion that in *Leaves of Grass* is dramatically enacted as a power of speech, such proclamations are frequently supplemented by overt declarations of the poet's pneumatic prowess: "I inhale great draughts of space," Whitman proclaims in "Song of the Open Road" (CRE 151; V 1:229).[75] Serving here to collapse intervals but elsewhere instancing the poet's power to flow through them, these appeals to breath evoke through metonymic suggestion the vocal and linguistic capacities that in fact underwrite them: incorporation and effusion, we noted in chapter 2, are magical, somaticized versions of the vocative and positional modes of language.

Voice is also the implicit model for the peculiar topology that organizes the poet's mythic transactions with objects. An unlikely boast in "Song of Myself" thus owes both its evocative power and its admittedly tenuous coherence to an unstated appeal to voice; like a passage from

"Song of the Answerer" we looked at earlier, it paradoxically images the poet as "both immersed and immersing" (Anderson, *Imperial Self* 132):

> I fly the flight of the fluid and swallowing soul,
> My course runs below the soundings of plummets. (1855 61)

Suggesting both the penetrative power that would allow him to flow into us and the fluidity of an inner body space in which we might be melded, voice is also the model for the sort of lability that might allow the poet to assume these apparently contradictory guises.

Like these mythic versions of the poet, the bodies of others we glimpse in Whitman's panoramic portraits of American life often possess some of the traits of the presence produced by apostrophe, though in more attenuated form. At their most ecstatic, these evocations are marked not by attention to strenuous physicality, but by what F. O. Matthiessen aptly calls the poet's "enjoyment of relaxed buoyant existence" (568); the scenes of labor or recreation that fascinate the poet are full of the sort of undulant, rhythmic movement epitomized by the labile presence of the poet himself. Matthiessen's analysis of this portraiture is still unsurpassed. Noting "the regressive, infantile fluidity, imaginatively polyperverse, which breaks down all mature barriers" (535), he suggests that these qualities typify the bodies of others as well as Whitman's own: "his epithets of movement reveal the very kind of limber indolence that was so characteristic of his own body" (569).[76] A parallel suggestion takes a more revealing form: "a similar index to the range of his plastic skill in creating movement," Matthiessen notes,

is provided in the concluding passage of 'Song of Myself':

> I effuse my flesh in eddies, and drift it in lacy jags.

Such effusion conditions the slow-paced action that his loose rhythm can encompass best. (569)

Here "effusion," an unlikely process to assign to solid bodies, is made the imaginative key to Whitman's portraiture, a reading that emerges from just the sort of evocation of the poet's own presence to which we have been attending. Matthiessen thus implies the order of influence I am claiming for Whitman's vision of the body: the figure of the poet modeled on voice—a body emerging from speech, or dissolving back

into it, as here at the close of "Song of Myself"—defines the characteristics toward which all bodies ought to tend.

A few of the figures that populate *Leaves of Grass* come closer to
embodying such fluid energies than even Whitman's selective cataloguing of observable labor and play will permit; they serve as bridges
between the mythic body of the poet and the finite bodies rendered in
the book's panoramic portraits of American life. Two of the most memorable of these figures appear in Whitman's protean comedy of incarnation, "Song of Myself." The "friendly and flowing savage" of section
thirty-nine combines a labile body with a magical performative power
that has been displaced from word to bodily gesture, making it seem
especially archaic; he is clearly an avatar of the poet's magical presence
(1855 69–70). The "twenty-ninth bather" of section eleven has also
been identified with the poet—but in his reticent rather than his transfiguring aspect. Edwin Miller thus sees her as Whitman's most poignant
self-portrait (*Walt Whitman's Poetry* 94); Ivan Marki stresses that she,
like the lonely man who created her, fulfills her desires only in imagination (155). Such attenuations are appropriate to note. But we
should note as well that her elusive body resembles the poet's effusing
one:

> Dancing and laughing along the beach came the twenty-ninth bather,
> The rest did not see her, but she saw them and loved them.
>
> The beards of the young men glistened with wet, it ran from their long hair,
> Little streams passed all over their bodies.
>
> An unseen hand also passed over their bodies,
> It descended tremblingly from their temples and ribs. (1855 34)

The barely physical contact that characterizes this imagined encounter is
not only an index of Whitman's furtiveness, though it is surely that in
part. Whitman's twenty-ninth bather inhabits a body reduced to what it
should properly be; it is just such a transparent form that Whitman's
proclamations of the poet's presence claim to incarnate.

Such alter-egos help suggest that the poet's magical presence is the limit
to which all bodies ought to tend. A few of Whitman's depictions of the
poet himself, however, seem to belie the crucial role I am assigning to

language and voice in defining the body; so do some of his pronouncements about presence. Whitman sometimes seems to be suggesting that words are superfluous, since silent presence already conveys as much or more than they are able to:

your very flesh shall be a great poem and have the richest fluency not only in its words but in the silent lines of its lips and face and between the lashes of your eyes and in every motion and joint of your body [. . . .] (Preface, 1855 11)

But such pronouncements are trickier than they appear. What may seem to be a dismissal of language in favor of presence turns out on closer examination to be an assertion that presence is already language. This odd notion depends on Whitman's appeal to the hermetic doctrine of a language of nature, a topic to which we shall turn in chapter 5. The point I want to make here is simply that praise of silent presence is not necessarily incompatible with a vision of the body that centers on the word, however odd this conjunction may seem.

My assertion that the language on which the redeemed body is modeled is pre-eminently oral—that it is an image of voice and not just a vision of the word that defines the poet's presence, even when that presence is said to be silent—may seem odder still. Section twenty-five of "Song of Myself," which concludes with an evocation of just such a silent presence, indeed makes some apparently disparaging remarks not just about language but more specifically about voice. At one point the poet apostrophizes "speech," which has supposedly just addressed him, in order to admonish it:

Come now I will not be tantalized . . . . you conceive too much of articulation.

Do you not know how the buds beneath are folded?
Waiting in gloom protected by frost,
The dirt receding before my prophetical screams. (1855 51)

I shall be arguing in chapter 5 that such apparent dismissals of speech are also more equivocal than they seem, focussing not on language and voice as such but only on certain of their productions. We can at least note here the presence of a verbal irony whose object is not immediately apparent: the slight over-formality of both "prophetical screams" and "you conceive too much of articulation" sits oddly not only with the more lyrical second and third lines but also with the passage that precedes them. There the poet reports the words that "speech" supposedly spoke to him: "It provokes me forever, / It says sarcastically, Walt, you understand enough . . . . why don't you let it out then?" (1855 51). This demotic American voice ascribed to "speech" hardly resembles either the "prophetical screams" that supposedly exemplify the poet's attempts at visionary language or the rather fastidious idiom in which he now deprecates them. What gets paraphrased and evaluated in the lines quoted above may thus be not speech itself but only a degraded version of it. An earlier demur is likewise equivocal: "Speech is the twin of my vision. . . . it is unequal to measure itself" (1855 50). This may mean that speech, which can't measure its own value, doesn't know its proper limits. But it may suggest instead that the language game of measuring is of a different and lesser order than the linguistic activities in which the word exercises its full and proper force. The contrast between the performative powers of voice and the merely representational or indicative uses of words, I shall argue in chapter 5, is crucial to Whitman's tracts on language. The provisos here are accordingly preceded by some lines extolling the penetrative powers of voice and the mastery voice affords:

> My voice goes after what my eyes cannot reach,
> With the twirl of my tongue I encompass worlds and volumes of worlds.
>   (1855 50)

What thus turns out to be a highly equivocal critique of speech is followed at the section's conclusion by praise of a silent presence whose contrast to voice may likewise be only apparent:

> Encompass worlds but never try to encompass me,
> I crowd your noisiest talk by looking toward you.

> Writing and talk do not prove me,
> I carry the plenum of proof and every thing else in my face,
> With the hush of my lips I confound the topmost skeptic. (1855 51)

Simply noting the opposition declared here between language and the poet's silent presence fails to account for the uncanny quality of this passage, which depends instead on their conflation.[77] Contrasted to the writing literally in front of us and the talk to which we have supposedly been attending, this invisible face performing an admonitory hush of lips we cannot see is more than slightly unnerving. This invisibility is subtly insisted on by the poet's avowal that he is "looking toward you," since

this look is one we would be hard pressed to return. Like the elusive
body pointed at by Whitman's deictics, this hovering but unlocatable
figure who cannot be "proved" by mere "talk" is evoked by and modeled on voice. The silent body praised in *Leaves of Grass* is a body
defined by speech.

This *de facto* conflation of voice with silent presence in the very
passages that draw our attention to the supposed difference between
them is responsible for some of our more spectacularly sublime encounters with the poet. Like a series of passages we looked at earlier, such
scenes are characteristically cued by deictics with no discernible object,
or imperatives ordering us to engage in acts with the poet that have no
possible uptake. "As Adam Early in the Morning" provokes a shiver by
commanding us to look on and touch a body we cannot see or get
hold of:

> Early in the morning,
> Walking forth from the bower, refreshed with sleep,
> Behold me where I pass—hear my voice—approach,
> Touch me—touch the palm of your hand to my body as I pass,
> Be not afraid of my body. (1860 314)

Here body and voice are metonymically associated but also explicitly
distinguished. Yet the body we are directed to behold and touch is
present only in the accents of these words; in this uncanny moment we
put our hands, as it were, to a voice, registering the magical presence
voice implies.

A dramatic passage near the end of "So Long!," the concluding poem
of *Leaves of Grass* since 1860, likewise achieves its effect by declaring
the distinction between word and body while depending on their virtual
equivalence. Whitman contrasts the poet's "songs" to the silent presence
who appears as the book's closing revelation:

> My songs cease—I abandon them,
> From behind the screen where I hid, I advance personally, solely to you. (V
>   2:451)[78]

This magical figure is produced by subtracting voice from person, an
operation the net result of which, in these particular circumstances,
might well be calculated as zero. Named instead as the book's crucial
"one," the poet himself, it is the numinous limit Whitman will call

presence, a translucency taking the form of the very thing supposedly deducted from it: the poet emerges here as pure energy and (speech) act, devoid of mass or dross. In *Leaves of Grass* the final, silent presence on whom our attention rests is present as voice and word.

This presence defines what the body ought to be. Yet however undulant their movements, this figure's avatars are necessarily compromises between the powers voice suggests and the limitations both our finite bodies and the shaping to which they have been subjected entail. The presence conjured up by apostrophe is nowhere else in *Leaves of Grass* thus perfectly incarnate: "Song of Myself" is the comedy of this difference; "Crossing Brooklyn Ferry" offers a starker, more schematic version of it. Appearing in his own right as a figure of power, this magical presence is for us an image of desire. Yet while he marks our distance from what we ought to be, he also seems to be poised on the brink of effacing this gap: leaving us in some sense in the divided world that was always ours, the poet's presence nonetheless implies that our relation to the powers that dispose us, and thus to ourselves and our bodies, has already begun to be altered; were the performative magic marshaled by his words ever wholly realized, the world would collapse into the visionary, archaic space his own body implies.

The gap between what the body ought to be and what it is thus reappears in *Leaves of Grass* as a gap afflicting the word. Poised between representation and performance, or between a merely conventional performative force and a performative power that is properly magical, the poet's speech hovers before an apocalyptic prospect that seems always about to be fulfilled. It is indeed this fissure in the word that lends *Leaves of Grass* the divided qualities that define it, suspending the poems between figure and fulfillment, desire and power, comic or haunted and authentically visionary modes.

Whitman's forays into language theory end up revealing the sources of such difficulties. Bent on liberating a speech capable of exercising the powers to which the poems aspire, by paring away the supposedly accidental attributes of language that undermine such force, these writings instead suggest the inevitable intertwining of what Whitman thinks of as objectionable and desirable traits; despite themselves, they provide an invaluable taxonomy of all that frustrates what should be the poet's magic word. We thus need to turn to Whitman's writings on language:

both to see how deeply speculations about the word permeated the poet's imagination and to isolate the particular linguistic features that in his view compromise the supposed resources of speech. Returning to *Leaves of Grass* in chapter 6, we will find just these features at play in Whitman's speech acts, lending them the complex, ambivalent resonance that makes the equivocal fate of Whitman's program the very basis of his greatness as a poet.

Notes

1. On this dialectic of the body in Whitman's work see Anderson, *Imperial Self*, especially 102–16.
2. Whitman criticism has tended to offer a similar account of the poet's motivation, regarding these apostrophes as touching evidence of Whitman's generosity; the scene in which the poet communicates his ecstatic vision to us is assumed to play no central role in shaping the mode of apprehension it announces. See for example Edwin Miller, *Walt Whitman's Poetry* 209, and James Miller, *Critical Guide* 80. A more tantalizing account of Whitman's apostrophes is offered by Richard Collins, who suggests that they allow the poet to re-create himself, transcending time and space, by impinging on his audience. Yet Collins goes on to assert that Whitman means to "by-pass" language, which he supposedly sees as arbitrary and inadequate. While according the poet's apostrophes a more central role, recent criticism still tends to idealize the motives that impel them. See for example Pease, "Blake, Crane, Whitman, and Modernism" 76–78; Larson 7–30; and Kronick 92–117.
3. I take up the contrasts between the two poems in chapter 6, below.
4. On the transcendental self as a mode of identity that internalizes the market economy from which it supposedly escapes, see Anderson, "Property and Vision in Nineteenth-Century America." See Calabrese for an extended consideration of Whitman's career in terms of the problematic Anderson develops.
5. Killingsworth notes "the tone of submission that lies beneath the rather enigmatic last lines of the 'dark patches' passage" (53–54).
6. On the relation of the Other to the symbolic code see Lacan, "The direction of the treatment and the principles of its power" (*Ecrits* 226–80), especially 233, and "The subversion of the subject and the dialectic of desire in the Freudian unconscious" (*Ecrits* 292–325), especially 305; see also Mac-Cannell 55. On the Other and the gaze see Lacan, "Anamorphosis," *Four Fundamental Concepts* 79–90, especially 84. On lack, see Lacan, "The

Subject and the Other: Alienation," *Four Fundamental Concepts* 203–15.

7. See NUPM 1:231 for the notebook draft these published lines revise. See also chapter 3, note 19, above.

8. On this point see Anderson, *Imperial Self* 102–104; Edwin Miller, *Walt Whitman's Poetry,* 20–23; and Black 125–37.

9. This figure, intensely charged for Whitman, appears only in the 1856 text; see V 1:221. Many critics have commented on the auto-erotic bases of Whitman's art.

10. Edwin Miller notes that the poet's confession in this stanza reads like a catalogue of the seven deadly sins (*Walt Whitman's Poetry* 206).

11. See 119–20 for a consideration of "the old knot of contrariety."

12. Killingsworth (52–53) makes a related point about the 1856 *Leaves of Grass* as a whole, an observation that arises out of his discussion of this passage.

13. On the Other and the code see especially Lacan, *Ecrits* 233. "Conscience" is too restrictive a name for the mechanism at work here; see for example Freud's distinction of the agency of the super-ego from the function of conscience, *New Introductory Lectures* 53. But Freud's super-ego may also be too circumscribed a concept for what is figured in these lines, though Whitman's fantasy of vulnerability to apprehension has affinities with Freud's description of that agency's function. While Lacan's Other has something in common with Freud's super-ego, its etiology is different and its purview is larger; this aggrandizement might be regarded as the complement of Lacan's suspicion of ego psychology. See for example Lacan's "correction" of standard translations of Freud's classic formulation of the task of the ego, ("Where id was, there ego shall be" [*New Introductory Lectures* 71]): " 'There where it was' . . . I would like it to be understood, 'it is my duty that I should come to being' " (*Ecrits* 129); see also *Four Fundamental Concepts* 44.

14. Killingsworth (36–37) notes this intertwining, though he does not read the passage as disturbing.

15. Killingsworth (36) makes a similar point.

16. I use this awkward neologism in the absence of a suitable term: "hetero-eroticism" and "homo-eroticism" both restrict the range of possible reference inappropriately.

17. I mean to suggest here that the question of the relative priority of auto-eroticism versus eroticism "proper" becomes moot, since both have been restructured by the symbolic function; neither is any longer "complete." But the related problem of the order of development of ego libido and object-cathexes is itself one to which Freud gave a series of shifting answers. See James Strachey's commentary in "Appendix B: The Great Reservoir of Libido," *The Ego and the Id* 53–56.

The uncomfortable confusion between auto-eroticism and eroticism "proper" that marks section twenty-eight is even more pronounced in the notebook passage Whitman later revised for "Song of Myself"; see UPP 2:72.

18. I follow Anderson here: see *Imperial Self* 117. I also have in mind a passage from Beverly Dahlen's prose poem *A Reading 1–7:* "having a thought the same as having a baby. it comes from inside, unreal. the fountain. that's what we remember. we were supposed to be golden. each one a savior. that would redeem it. no one told us so" (20).

19. See *Civilization and Its Discontents,* especially 56–62. The uncircumscribed eroticism called *jouissance* would have no place in such a structure. As the Lacanian journal *Scilicit* suggests: "That the Other should ... act as guarantee is the founding condition for any possibility of exchange, and what must be given up to this is the *jouissance* of the subject. The castration complex thus designates the passing of *jouissance* into the function of a value, and its profound adulteration in that process" (Lacan, *Feminine Sexuality* 120).

20. "Eroticism," Georges Bataille suggests, "always entails a breaking down of the established patterns. . . . of the regulated social order basic to our discontinuous mode of existence as separate individuals" (quoted in Bernstein 53; the ellipses are Bernstein's).

21. I have Kristeva's usage in mind here: the abject is what threatens the boundary between the symbolic universe of "clean and proper" subjects and objects and all that must remain outside it for it to remain itself; see *Powers of Horror* 1–18.

22. Among recent critics, Larson (59–72) and Killingsworth (15–27) each offer extended accounts of the poem that sometimes intersect with the reading I offer, though proceeding from different vantages. See also Richard Chase 54–57.

23. On this point see Aspiz 172–73.

24. On this point see Larson 60–62.

25. I am indebted here to the account of fantasy offered by Laplanche and Pontalis: see "Fantasy and the Origins of Sexuality."

26. See Larson 65.

27. See Killingsworth 18 for a discussion of some related ambiguities at work in the phrase "signify me."

28. Larson (63) makes a similar point about this line.

29. These lines are not present in CRE; they disappeared from the poem in 1881. See V 1:116.

30. On the political aspects of this passage, which are emphasized more forcefully in an earlier notebook version, see Erkkila, *Whitman* 122–24. My analysis here is also indebted to Larson (67–68) and Killingsworth (23–34); see also Marki 238–39. Edwin Miller (*Walt Whitman's Poetry* 81–82) stresses the Oedipal resonance of the passage, which Erkkila also mentions.

31. For Whitman as for the contemporary medical and eugenicist discourses Aspiz summarizes (183–209), it is primarily careless or perverse social

practices that degrade the body; in "Faces," contiguity clearly associates both the need for signs and the body's status as a sign itself with social oppression and the deformation of the body it causes.

32. Anderson astutely suggests this figure's exemplary position: "One can be out of one's 'place' in one's own body, just as one may have a 'castrated face,' an epithet I take from the poem 'Faces.' The way in which you, so to speak, occupy your body, is involved" (*Imperial Self* 142).

There are of course more sanguine portraits of American citizens sprinkled throughout Whitman's work. My point is that the vision of the body they partially suggest is fulfilled by the poet's own magical presence; this figure, I shall be arguing below, offers us an image of a body exempt from symbolic shaping; its difference from the degraded bodies on which "Faces" focuses, like the difference between good and bad bodies throughout Whitman's work, is thus not merely contingent. "Castration" is a crucial trope for this structural cleavage.

33. Freud summarizes this constitutive function of castration in "The Passing of the Oedipus-Complex" (*Collected Papers* 2:269–76).

34. On Oedipus as the remnant within Western bourgeois society of more complex kinship systems that articulate culture and inscribe the self within it, see Lacan, *Ecrits* 66–68 and 142.

35. I mean to suggest, of course, not that Whitman and Lacan are somehow equivalent, but that Whitman is the scandalized critic of a structure very like the one Lacan explicates.

36. On the relation between performative utterance and the denial of castration, see Durand, "The Anxiety of Performance" 173–74.

37. On the prevalence of fantasies of castration that characteristically remain unconscious see Freud, *Analysis of a Phobia in a Five-Year-Old Boy, Collected Papers* 3:152n2. See also Laplanche and Pontalis, *Language of Psycho-analysis* 58–61.

38. I cite the 1871 text here. Until 1871, the second of these lines declared less dramatically, "give out of myself." This is one of a small number of instances in which Whitman, after 1860, made minor revisions in earlier poems that bring out more sharply features of the poet's presence crucial to the world of the first three editions, features with which Whitman was no longer concerned in the new poems he was writing. He may have been motivated by a sense of what the poem, as written, already implied.

39. I take up the scandalous aspect of Whitman's performatives in chapter 6, below.

40. On the ideal rather than material status of that which can be repeated and recognized as the same, see Saussure's discussion of phonic identity, 107–110. Derrida insists repeatedly on the circular relation I adumbrate here between language and iterability: his critiques of language-origins theories often turn on just this problematic. See especially "The Linguistic Circle of

Geneva," *Margins of Philosophy* 137–53, and the reading of Rousseau, *Grammatology* 95–316.

41. I take up Derrida's analysis of the relation between name and essence, and its pertinence to Whitman's language theory, in chapter 5, below.

42. Ong's work on voice and writing can function as a useful explication of Whitman's vision of voice and presence, since Ong shares and makes explicit several of the assumptions also at work in *Leaves of Grass*. In addition to *Interfaces of the Word* see also *Presence of the Word*, especially 111–75, and *Rhetoric, Romance, and Technology*.

43. As Derrida's studies of Artaud, among other writings, suggest, fantasies centering on voice are not confined, in his view, to philosophy, but pervade Western images of the body. See "La parole soufflée," *Writing and Difference* 169–95, and "The Theatre of Cruelty and the Closure of Representation," *Writing and Difference* 232–50. Derrida's work should also make us suspicious of the impulse to see logocentrism as a Western disease to which non-Western peoples are supposedly immune. I have in mind especially Derrida's critique, in his reading of Lévi-Strauss, of the anthropologist's compensatory fantasies concerning the racial other; Derrida describes these as an occupational hazard endemic to anthropology (see *Grammatology* 101–40). While for Lévi-Strauss, as Derrida notes, it is the fall into writing of which the non-European Nambikwara are supposedly innocent, for contemporary academics reared on post-structuralism the characteristic temptation is instead to exempt non-Western peoples from the very logocentrism which efforts to exile writing have helped preserve; Cultural Studies sometimes displays this post-Derridian version of the impulse to romanticize the cultural or racial other. The reifying of linguistic powers, and of the sense of self-presence voice suggests, may be temptations to which all speaking beings are vulnerable.

44. In *Grammatology*, among other places, Derrida offers a critique of the way this dichotomy has been mobilized; see especially 12–13.

45. Derrida's analyses of the problematic of the body in the work of Artaud are pertinent here; see note 43, above.

46. Harold Aspiz (67–68) shows that one basis for this notion of a "transparent" body is the anatomy chart, a source of inspiration for the laying bare of body parts that occurs in the long catalogue which in 1856 and thereafter concludes the text of "I Sing the Body Electric," the poem Whitman is evidently pondering here. But transparency nearly always has visionary implications in Whitman's work, as the published litany in which this notebook fragment apparently issues bears out; the poem offers a transfiguration rather than a mere redaction of anatomical material: "O I think these are not the parts and poems of the body only, but of the soul, / O I think these are the soul!" (1856 179). In 1860 and thereafter, this act of transfiguration is brought out more strongly, by means of performative utterance:

"O I say now these are not the parts and poems of the body only, but of the Soul, / O I say these are the Soul!" (1860 302). See V 1:132.

47. I develop this point more fully in chapter 5, below.

48. See for example Edwin Miller, *Walt Whitman's Poetry* 206.

49. I here follow Anderson's suggestion that Whitman is intent on rejecting the sense of the self as founded upon "a fatally dialectic base" ("Whitman's New Man" 19).

50. This peculiar fragment is immediately preceded in Whitman's notebook by some pronouncements about individual freedom as the basis of American society. Such a juxtaposition suggests something of the complex intertwining of ideological and fantasmatic modes in Whitman's work; political material sometimes opens out into the sort of extravagant speculation this quotation exemplifies, and sometimes serves as a cover for it. While this intertwining does not belie Whitman's intense political commitments or the political preoccupations and implications of *Leaves of Grass*, it may well color our reception of particular, ostensibly political pronouncements. I take up these issues in chapters 6–8, below.

51. For a discussion of fantasies of privacy in the work of John Ashbery that intertwines with my argument here, see my "Private Language: Ashbery and Wittgenstein."

52. This passage goes on to note a corollary I take up in chapter 5, below: "That experience lives and proclaims itself as the exclusion of writing, that is to say of the invoking of an 'exterior,' 'sensible,' 'spatial' signifier interrupting self-presence" (*Grammatology* 98).

53. Kristeva thus argues for the pertinence of infantile linguistic organizations to the study of adult speech; see *Desire in Language* 278.

54. Though the "friendly and flowing savage" of "Song of Myself" is an attempt to make just such a connection; see 149.

55. Edwin Miller and Stephen Black both stress the regressive aspects of Whitman's work. But I am particularly indebted to Quentin Anderson here, as well as to Dorothy Gregory; see chapter 1, note 8, above.

56. See for example Emerson's remarks on the child and on "aboriginal" man in "Self-Reliance" 2:29 and 48–49.

57. Kristeva explicitly situates her notions of the *chora* and the semiotic in relation to Freud's primary processes; see *Revolution in Poetic Language* 25. On primary and secondary processes see Freud, "Formulations Regarding the Two Principles in Mental Functioning," *Collected Papers* 4 13–21.

58. Matthiessen's remarks on Whitman's verbal textures are always astute, as is his sense of the relation of verbal and muscular rhythm in *Leaves of Grass*; see especially 517–36 and 564–77.

59. Zweig (253) notes the eroticizing of voice in the passage.

60. "Significance" is Kristeva's coinage. In his introduction to *Revolution in Poetic Language*, Leon S. Roudiez explains: "what we call *significance*, then,

is precisely this unlimited and unbounded generating process, this unceasing operation of the drives toward, in, and through language" (17).

61. See Saussure 111–13; this sense of the constitutive role of symbolic language pervades Kristeva's account.

62. "This instinctual drive will later be replaced, due to repression, by the sign representing (erasing) it within the communicative system" (*Desire in Language* 217). The Kristeva essay I draw on here, "Giotto's Joy" (*Desire in Language* 210–36), employs the Freudian classification of "word-presentations" and "thing-presentations" rather than Saussure's signifier/signified antinomy; the slippage between these terminologies is not crucial here. See Freud, "The Unconscious," *Collected Papers* 4:98–136, especially 127–36.

63. On the Lacanian mirror stage as a preliminary version of and necessary precondition for such symbolic and syntactic stabilization, see Kristeva, *Revolution in Poetic Language* 46–47.

64. See Lacan's discussions of "points de capiton," including *Ecrits* 303.

65. If the body part whose expropriation comes to figure this lack is genital, that is due, according to Lacan, to the homology of signifying and sexual structures; it is on the basis of sexual difference, as elements in kinship systems, that culture appropriates and counts with us: "the genital drive is subjected to the circulation of the Oedipus complex, to the elementary and other structures of kinship" (Lacan, *Four Fundamental Concepts* 189).

66. In *Revolution in Poetic Language,* an English translation of Kristeva's doctoral thesis, Kristeva devotes sustained attention to the work of Mallarmé and Lautréamont.

67. The foregoing applies to catalogues that end with a main clause. Many of Whitman's litanies instead begin with the main clause, subsequently spinning out a series of grammatically parallel phrases; these phrases also effectively transmute the symbolic closure they ostensibly obey. For an extended discussion of such a catalogue, see chapter 2, above.

68. This organization thus conflates not only the signifier/signified or sound-image/intentional-object pair, but also intentional object and physical thing. On the crucial role of this last antinomy in symbolic language, see Saussure 65–66 and 114–22, and Lacan, *Ecrits* 149–52.

69. See Lacan's classic formulation concerning need, demand, and desire, *Feminine Sexuality* 80–81.

70. According to Abraham and Torok, the archaic fantasy of incorporation is revived by catastrophic, psychically unacceptable events that make introjection unbearable; incorporation thus involves a rejection or "encrypting" of aspects of our relations to others and our shared world. See "Introjection—Incorporation" 4–5.

71. Quentin Anderson stresses the importance of incorporative fantasies in Whitman's poetry: "incorporation and even engorgement qualified the body which was the poet's scene" (*Imperial Self* 104). See also Edwin Miller: "Though rarely observed, the regressive nature of Whitman's imagery is

clear. His protagonists are ingesting experience—'*absorbing*' is one of his favorite words—in a manner suggestive of the child at the mother's breast" (*Walt Whitman's Poetry* 62). See also Black's brief but suggestive comments on "magic words," 72–73 and 166.

72. See Freud, *Totem and Taboo* 75–99, and "The Uncanny," *Collected Papers* 4:393–94.

73. For an extended discussion of Whitman's poetry in relation to shamanism see Hutchinson, especially xi–xxviii and 26–57.

74. See Sedgwick 205 for a discussion of the phallic attributes of the poet's body.

75. I quote the CRE text here; until 1871, "air" rather than "space" concludes the line.

76. Matthiessen credits this last observation to Jean Catel.

77. Larson's reading of this passage (93–98) is congruent in several respects with the one I offer here. For a different view of the passage, which is nonetheless compatible with the trajectory of my argument, see Durand, "The Anxiety of Performance" 168.

78. I quote from the 1867 rather than the 1860 version, from which the concluding "solely to you" is absent. This final apostrophe activates the presence the line asserts; it does so by implicitly appealing to voice and address as evidence of presence. The very final lines of the poem conclude Whitman's book on a similar note, though the relation declared there between presence and death is a troubling one (I take it up in chapter 6, below): "Remember my words—I love you—I depart from materials, / I am as one disembodied, triumphant, dead" (1860 456).

5. Writing and Representation

He completes no poems, apart and separate from himself. . . . His lines are pulsations, thrills, waves of force, indefinite dynamics, formless, constantly emanating from the living centre, and they carry the quality of the author's personal presence with them in a way that is unprecedented in literature.

—Burroughs, "The Flight of the Eagle" 235–36[1]

After all there's something better than to write: that's not to write: writing is a disease.

—Whitman, quoted in WWC 3:358

Camden

1. One of the many ironies recorded by Horace Traubel, mostly unconsciously, in his mammoth record of Whitman's last years in Camden is the vision it proffers us of the poet of the voice awash in the exotic sea of his own archives. Justin Kaplan masterfully renders the weird landscape over which Whitman hovered:

From boxes and bundles in the storeroom, from the big iron-banded double-hasped trunk that had been with him in Washington and now stood against the bedroom wall, he released drifts and billows of paper. He had kept every imaginable variety of written and printed matter: manuscripts, old letterheads and billheads thriftily saved and written over, faded scraps of writing paper and even wallpaper pinned, pasted, or tied together in ragged bundles that had a before-the-flood look, notebooks and diaries, many of them homemade, scrapbooks, letters received and drafts of letters sent, printer's proofs and samples, photographs, memoranda, circulars, receipts and accounts rendered, official documents, clippings from magazines and newspapers. With an occasional shoe or wad of stamps or stick of kindling mixed in haphazardly, this tide churned in a widening semicircle in front of Whitman's chair, seeped into the corners of the room and under the furniture and was tracked out into the hallway.

Year after year, Whitman stirred his archive with the crook of his cane. Relics of personal history floated to the surface. (16)

Despite the haphazard attitude such clutter seems to imply, Whitman took an intensely proprietary interest in this bizarre heap of memorabilia. His growing intimacy with Traubel was indeed expressed largely through his increasing willingness to confide to his would-be Boswell the task of curating the documents through which he rummaged, many of which bore directly on the poet's own life. As years passed, Whitman gradually worried into shape the self-portrait he charged Traubel with preserving, exercising the same sort of care which, for all their looseness and informality, he lavished on his poems as *Leaves of Grass* labored toward its authorized "deathbed" version. As Kaplan notes, the life to be offered for posterity's inspection was continually re-traced and adjusted:

Sometimes Whitman was hardly conscious of reshaping his past to make it conform to the ample, serene and masterful identity he achieved long after. Sometimes he reshaped his past deliberately, just as he reshaped *Leaves of Grass* over the course of nine editions in order to give his life as well as his work a different emphasis. Ever since his stroke he had been editing his archives. . . . Some manuscripts he carefully altered, destroying single pages, effacing or disguising identifications, transposing genders, changing "him" to "her" or a man's initials to a number code. By the time he died scarcely a period in his life had not been "revised" in one way or another. Some periods had practically ceased to exist so far as intimate documentation was concerned. (19)

More was involved in such reconstructions than a cautious concern for leaving an uncompromising record of one's doings behind one. As Quentin Anderson has compellingly argued, Whitman was still at work inventing "the Person"—that ideal being given birth in the poems, mimed awkwardly in the actual life, but approximated more closely, it was to be hoped, in the hagiography through which that life would be remembered ("Whitman's New Man" 49).[2] Whitman had made the creation of such a Person the principal aim of his poetry:

to express by sharp-cut self assertion, *One's-Self* & also, or may be still more, to map out, to throw together for American use, a gigantic embryo or skeleton of Personality, fit for the West, for native models [. . . .] (CORR 1:247)[3]

A notebook entry I quoted in chapter 4 suggests the remarkable aspect this Person produced by a poem might attain:

A poem in which is minutely described the whole particulars and ensemble of a *first-rate healthy Human Body*—it looked into and through, as if it were transparent and of pure glass—and now reported in a poem—(NUPM 1:304)

The devoted admirers who gathered around the poet in Camden sometimes claimed to discover this numinous quality in Whitman's own person. Their testimonials are perhaps more a tribute to the poetry's power than a reflection of the actual physical attributes of the author of *Leaves of Grass*. Whitman's friend John Burroughs, for example, inflects what purports to be physical description with a range of associations clearly provoked by an encounter with the poetry:

Then there was a look about him hard to describe, and which I have seen in no other face,—a gray, brooding, elemental look, like the granite rock, something primitive and Adamic that might have belonged to the first man; or was it a suggestion of the gray, eternal sea that he so loved, near which he was born, and that had surely set its seal upon him? (*Whitman: A Study* 62)[4]

We need not be inordinately suspicious to find this hard to credit as a description of the man Burroughs visited in Camden. Burroughs' portrait here, of Whitman as a kind of primitive, cosmic force, recalls the omnipotent presence on whom the poems center, "the source from which the power and action emanate" (Burroughs, "The Flight of the Eagle" 237–38).[5]

The even more exorbitant rhetoric of Whitman's friend and apologist William O'Connor thus turns out to be even more apt. Writing to Burroughs in 1866, O'Connor opined: "And your thought is also mine —he is an incarnation" (quoted in Barrus 35).[6] Bizarre as the description of an actual person, this makes more sense as a misplaced but incisive characterization of the poet-hero of *Leaves of Grass*: generated by performative utterance, this figure seems to be the living embodiment of the word.[7]

This magical presence, we have seen, supposedly overflows the boundaries of the work that produces him. The Camden inner circle was thus by no means alone in positing the existence of an actual person who would correspond to the figure evoked by the poems. As Kaplan relates, Whitman received countless letters from men and women who extrapolated wildly from their imaginative encounters with the poet of *Leaves of Grass*:

In 1860 a total stranger, Susan Garnet Smith of Hartford, informed him that after reading *Leaves of Grass* she felt "a mysterious delicious thrill!" and decided it was her destiny to bear him "a noble beautiful perfect manchild."

My womb is clean and pure. It is ready for thy child, my love. Angels guard the vestibule until thou comest to deposit our and the world's precious treasure. . . . Our boy, my love! Do you not already love him? He must be begotten on a mountain top, in the open air.

He wrote "? insane asylum" on the envelope of her letter, but admitted that if Susan was "insane" so were "Song of Myself" and "Children of Adam." Like a number of other women (and men) who responded to his poems and had their lives changed as a result, she was in part the victim of an innocent literal understanding. (329)[8]

It was a literalism the poems had been designed to elicit. No less sophisticated a reader than the English woman of letters Anne Gilchrist, who in 1870 published an important and astute review of Whitman's work praising its depiction of female sexuality, apparently also responded to Whitman's poetry, from the first, in something like the extravagant terms she later employed to characterize its effect: Whitman's poems, she wrote, were "his actual presence," provoking "each reader to feel that he himself or herself has an actual relationship to him" (quoted in Kaplan 333). This was no mere figure of speech: in 1876 she had set out for America, intent on marrying a man she had never met.[9] Whatever their degree of literary sophistication and whatever the extent of their personal acquaintance with the poet, all these devotees seem to have taken their cue from the poetry's central assertion, identifying Whitman himself with the living presence *Leaves of Grass* claims to produce.

While readers of *Leaves of Grass* thus extrapolated from the poems and often made claims on the actual man that would have been awkward to honor, Whitman busied himself in Camden with the obverse task of funneling himself back into the world of the poetry. He seems to have been nonplussed as often as pleased by the avid uptake the poems generated, nervously dodging such especially intrepid literalists as Gilchrist while tinkering with the shape of the ideal figure to whom his readers had responded.[10] Such reticence may have resulted in part from the poet's increasing age. It seems also to have been a function of the vicissitudes of Whitman's private life: rather than trying to play the person the poems conjure up, on the whole Whitman settled in his Camden years for basking indirectly in the admiration and amorous fervor this figure provoked, while struggling in private with the less apocalyptic but still turbulent erotic ambitions that occupied him personally. Meanwhile he retraced the outlines of the personage as whom he would be remembered, a somewhat toned-down, increasingly desexualized avatar of the poet-hero of *Leaves of Grass*. Surrounded by acolytes as he hovered over his archive, Whitman existed simultaneously as an image-taking shape in an authorized text laboriously gleaned from mountains of heterogeneous documents.[11] The garrulous but cagey old man who emerges in the course of Traubel's study was conjuring up in front of their noses the figure by which those who gathered about him in Camden often seem mesmerized; the poet of presence was dissolving himself into his own idealized representation.[12]

This testamentary gesture might initially seem peculiar to Whitman's last years in Camden.[13] But some of the poet's remarks to Traubel let us see it as part of a more general economy Whitman himself seems to have regarded as central to his make-up. These comments sit strangely beside the most dramatic pronouncements of *Leaves of Grass.* "I and mine do not convince by arguments, similes, rhymes," Whitman had declared there to his audience; "We convince by our presence" ("Song of the Open Road," 1856 233). Yet as we have seen, the man who once described himself as "*furtive* like an old hen" (Carpenter 43) also implied a far from direct relation between this presence and the person with whom it might be supposed to be simply identical: "My body? Yes —it had to be given—it had to be sacrificed [. . .]" (WWC 3:582). "I consider it a Whitman trait," the poet of presence also remarked unnervingly to Traubel, "the ability to tide over, to lay back on reserves, to wait, to take time" (WWC 4:331).

2. The secret Whitman thus hinted at to Traubel turns out to be the secret of writing; in Whitman's imagination the economy between living presence and representation around which these last remarks circle, an operation characterized by substitution and delay, is persistently associated with the functioning of texts. In his Camden years Whitman was still sufficiently drawn to the central claim of his early editions—that the poems generate a literal, living presence—both to wish sometimes that this suspect mode had played no role in his life's work and to downplay its actual contribution. His intermittent complaints about writing indeed conceal as much as they divulge about its function in *Leaves of Grass:* expressing generalized anxiety about this mode while skirting the issue of how it might have facilitated the poet's manifestation, Whitman alternately groused to Traubel about the supposed impotence of texts— complaining about the disadvantages of having decided to write a book rather than lecture to people directly—and railed against the illicit, seductive powers writing and the mere representations it disseminates manage to wield.

Sitting in Whitman's Camden house amid the clutter Kaplan describes, which at the poet's behest he devoted years to sorting and preserving, Traubel might be imagined to have found such remarks perplexing; they suggest something of the haunted quality of the Camden project, at the center of which the poet of voice and presence excoriated writing and representation while sitting perched over a mammoth editorial enterprise. *With Walt Whitman in Camden,* though, betrays no trace of such perplexity. Part of the strangeness of the Camden transactions derives from the way members of Whitman's inner circle seem to have been able to slide dreamily between the different roles they were called upon to play. The early editions of *Leaves of Grass* had been solitary productions; admitted now to Whitman's workshop, Traubel and his friends were both assistants and audience, both producers and consumers of the myth of the poet's presence. Traubel, especially, seems to have been sufficiently mesmerized by the figure he helped re-touch to have remained blithely unaware of how that being's creator, who labored at his side, employed means that ought to have vitiated their ends. The issue of writing is the crucial case in point. While Whitman and Traubel dirtied their hands with it in Camden, the poet-hero of *Leaves of Grass* on whom their ideal person was based remained wholly innocent of such compromising involvements.[14] That at least was the story the poetry told, and Traubel would hardly have been the first reader of *Leaves of Grass* to be transfixed by it. In such poems as "Crossing Brooklyn Ferry," the uncomfortable Camden economy, in which writing is both overtly employed and energetically excoriated, is replaced by outrageous, insouciant denial:

> We understand, then, do we not?
> What I promised without mentioning it, have you not accepted?
> What the study could not teach—what the preaching could not accomplish is accomplished, is it not?
> What the push of reading could not start is started by me personally, is it not? (1856 219)

The uncanny figure who emerges in *Leaves of Grass* creates himself precisely by virtue of this disclaimer. What would otherwise be an ordinary representation thereby becomes instead a magical presence. What would otherwise be an economy, in which the author substitutes an idealized image of himself for his actual person, becomes instead an act of sublime self-manifestation: the figure who can present himself where others can merely represent themselves is *ipso facto* the mythical redeemer of time and space who stands at the center of *Leaves of Grass.*

Still railing to Traubel against writing, but by now up to his neck in it, the older man editing his oeuvre in Camden occasionally relaxed his intransigence. He even let lapse his rigorous exclusion of writing from the central transactions of *Leaves of Grass*—as if to make peace there too, at last, with this mode and the attenuations it implied, or as if he felt the fiction of the poet's presence was no longer worth the risk of absurdity the poetry's disavowals of writing ran. Revising his poems again for a forthcoming 1881 edition, Whitman deleted the last of the lines just quoted from "Crossing Brooklyn Ferry";[15] like other small but significant changes he made in the poem, this excision has the effect of allowing the figure of the poet to slip from the status of magical presence to that of inspiring representation, a diminution not unlike the strategic retrenchment over which Traubel unwittingly presided.

A Living and Full-Blooded Man

1. More ambitious and resolute, the poet of Whitman's early editions is correspondingly more vulnerable to the role played by writing in his work. This is so despite the panache with which writing and reading were originally banished from such poems as "Crossing Brooklyn Ferry": everything the poet should be and all he should be able to do are haunted by writing. The poet's tone indeed finally suggests this vulnerability, which is registered in the very bravado with which he attempts to deflect it.

The divided estimate Whitman offered Traubel in Camden, which focuses on writing's illicit powers as well as its supposed impotence, suggests that what Whitman sometimes thinks of as the text's simple inability to produce a living presence is perhaps the most straightforward, but ultimately not the most threatening problem with Whitman's *de facto* dependence on writing in *Leaves of Grass.* This inability is nonetheless damaging enough to Whitman's claims to merit excluding writing from the imaginative universe of the early editions.

The world of the early *Leaves of Grass* is shaped by the poet's magical advent, which abrogates space and time and subjects the world to his extensible identity. Any involvement with writing undoes these transformations. The distinction between the presence implied by voice and the sort of ordinary representation produced by writing thus matters in part because it implies a stark correlative contrast: the contrast between a magical transfiguration and the lack of one.[16] The denials of writing and reading that recur throughout Whitman's early editions can be understood in part as expressions of such a schematic opposition. The simple exteriority of writing to voice, and of the representations writing proffers to the presence voice announces, organize one strand of Whitman's remarks about writing and reading.

Whitman thus dismisses writing because it fails to effect the sort of spatial transformation the presence produced by voice implies. Rejecting print as his medium, he makes it responsible for perpetuating the very intervals the poet should overcome:

> This is unfinished business with me . . . . how is it with you?
> I was chilled with the cold types and cylinder and wet paper between us.
>
> I pass so poorly with paper and types . . . . I must pass with the contact of
> bodies and souls. ("A Song for Occupations," 1855 87)[17]

Writing also conspicuously fails to overcome the temporal separation of writer and reader.[18] Abandoning the fiction of voice that animates the poems, one day with Traubel, Whitman thus lamented his decision to write *Leaves of Grass* rather than set up as an itinerant lecturer, since

> I needed to reach the people: I could have done so at once, following out this method, instead of subjecting myself to the terrible delays—the murderous delays [. . . .] (WWC 3:467)

Assigned atypically in this late remark to his poems, such disabling dependence on writing had been rigorously excluded from the imaginative universe of Whitman's early editions. Whitman's comment to Traubel indeed still displays the residual effects of the very myth it appears to renounce: his hyperbolic phrasing suggests the sort of epiphany the poetry's image of voice sustains, envisioning not the ordinary appearance of an ordinary person but an apocalyptic advent disastrously prevented by writing. As the texture of this passage still implies, what writing threatens for Whitman is not simply the ability to get one's message to people now rather than later, but the eternal moment on which his imaginative vision depends.

It is Whitman's image of voice, that is, which suggests that the poet's power is magically self-renewing. And it is through breath and voice that the poet can apparently convey this self-sustaining force to us; an implicit association with voice governs nearly all Whitman's claims concerning his poetry's redemptive effects. A passage in "The Flight of the Eagle," an essay on his work Whitman helped John Burroughs compose for the latter's *Birds and Poets,* thus appeals indirectly to an image of voice in order to make credible some surprising assertions concerning the poetry's power to contain and communicate personal energies that have apparently become perpetual:

He completes no poems, apart and separate from himself. . . . His lines are pulsations, thrills, waves of force, indefinite dynamics, formless, constantly emanating from the living centre, and they carry the quality of the author's personal presence with them in a way that is unprecedented in literature. (235–36)

This vision depends on detaching the poet's word from the inert text in which it might seem to be lodged:

Consider, you who peruse me, whether I may not in unknown ways be looking upon you! ("Crossing Brooklyn Ferry," 1856 220)

The poet's presence, evoked here by an apostrophe whose implicit dismissal of the book we are reading suggests by contrast the proximity of a voice to which we attend, attains its uncanny quality through just this rejection of writing.[19]

We can thus repeatedly find Whitman extricating the preternaturally active power he associates with voice from the writing of which *Leaves of Grass* is at least apparently composed:

the qualities which characterize *Leaves of Grass* are not the qualities of a fine book or poem or any work of art but the qualities of a living and full-blooded man [. . . .] You do not read, it is someone that you see in action [. . .] or racing along and shouting aloud in pure exultation. (CW 9:22)

The inertia Whitman sloughs off here is the inertia of representation. Disengaging himself from writing, the poet becomes the eternally active presence who apparently dominates not only *Leaves of Grass* but also the space beyond it. Voice transfigures a world for which the poems provide not a mere image but a magical synecdoche.

2. As the intricate intertwining of assertion and disclaimer in such passages ought already to make clear, however, the supposedly straightfor-

ward opposition between the book and the poet's voice and body only begins to describe the status and function of writing in *Leaves of Grass;* it tells us what Whitman would like the relation between writing and the poet's presence to be. The Camden transactions, which make massive use of the very tool Whitman continues to excoriate, suggest a more intimate and unsettling connection. The presence produced in the poems inherits his powers not quite by repudiating writing but instead by employing surreptitiously the very techne whose role the poet denies: the figure of the poet is a kind of hallucination produced by keeping invisible the role writing plays in its production.

This dependence of the poet's presence on writing, and on the representation for which it stands, is not merely contingent, not simply an avoidable liability incurred through the vocational accident of having chosen to write a book. What Whitman means by presence is a function of representation: the poet becomes magical, exceeding the capacities of ordinary persons and defining what presence should be, by enlisting the resources of representation. I suggested in chapter 4 some of the crucial associations writing and representation possess for Whitman, noting the supposed degradations entanglement with them implies. Making use of these mechanisms to enable his advent, the protagonist of *Leaves of Grass* becomes yet another instance of the sort of symbolic entity from whose coercive power he can supposedly free us, suffering himself from the alienation he apparently cures.

This uncomfortable intertwining haunts not only the poet's presence, but also the notion of voice and the vision of word magic enlisted to produce it. If a certain kind of language—I have been calling it castrated—precipitates our alienation, the poet's uncastrated word supposedly exempts him from such fading. Yet this uncastrated language may turn out to be impossible to isolate from the fallen word: just as Whitman's book helps constitute what we are led to call the poet's presence, so the castrated language associated with writing surreptitiously lends its resources to the seemingly antithetical speech for which that presence stands as surety. It is in this sense that the entangling of voice with writing in *Leaves of Grass* points to an impasse that is more than merely contingent: the magic word that generates the poet's presence achieves its apparent transfiguring power by suppressing its dependence on the very linguistic mechanisms from whose alienating dominance the poet should liberate us.

One crucial task of Whitman's forays into language theory is to deny the necessity of this entanglement, and thus to sustain the possibilities the poet's word and presence seem to embody. Like his poems, Whitman's expository remarks on language are organized by a contrast between writing and voice: the apparently straightforward opposition between these modes is enlisted to help keep his other crucial distinctions in place. Whitman's attempts to isolate a language defined by the resources of voice aim to liberate a magical performative speech from the degradation that has apparently befallen ordinary language, a language supposedly denatured and emasculated by being submitted to writing; this extrication should serve in turn to distinguish the poet's redemptive presence from the dangerous representations by which other, socialized selves have been captivated, and which, indeed, they have become.

Exercising a magical power of incorporation and positing, this unfallen idiom would be a symbolic language that has retained the fantasmatic resources of the semiotic *chora*. The sign and its meaning would still be functions of the rhythmic, vocalic features with which the individual speaker can endow them; they would still be molded by the kinesthetic matrix of the speaker's body, a matrix that in the moment of enunciation supposedly also replicates the organic structure of the creature or thing the word names, a structure lurking in the word itself. The word would thus be doubly expressive, and in the act of pronouncing it subject and object would be effectively fused.

The other language is instead indicative: having allowed its vocal, expressive resources to be enervated by writing, it is tied to neither speaker nor object, merely representing entities to which it possesses no intrinsic connection. Occulting living presences rather than revealing them, this indicative language delivers us over to an alienating symbolic space filled with the autonomous representations it spawns.

Yet the distinctions Whitman would like to suggest between these two languages turn out to be difficult to maintain. Sometimes his contrasts depend on characterizations that seem improbable. Sometimes a putative opposition collapses, as features supposedly reserved for or consigned to one language turn up rather unmistakably within the other. And to the extent that this effort to detach one form of language from another seems unconvincing or proves untenable, the very liabilities that characterize the fallen language shaped by writing also necessarily inhabit the supposedly organic, oral word Whitman wants to oppose to this mode. Evident in Whitman's language theory, this unintended crossing of categories is reflected in his poems as well. Its consequences for a reading of *Leaves of Grass* have little to do with any mere dismissal of Whitman's theories or arguments. Haunting the poet's most dramatic performative gestures, this entanglement leads to the sorts of equivocation that mark the visionary but extremely mobile idiom of Whitman's poems; his language theory details the crises that motivate these hesitations, lending them an urgency that might at first seem surprising.

Whitman's attempt to distinguish fallen language from the poet's redemptive speech includes arguments about both the appropriate function and the proper nature of words. The first centers on an opposition between the performative powers of language and its supposedly degraded use for merely constative or representational purposes. The second is cast as a distinction between expressive and indicative words, between organic names wedded to the presences they conjure up and arbitrary signs limited to representing things they do not comprehend and cannot present. Whitman thus associates both the forsaking of language's appropriate task and the loss of its proper status with a fall into representation. He thereby makes castrated language part of an embracing cultural mechanism that entangles us in images and symbolic artifacts; the poet's unfallen utterance, by contrast, should fasten words again to things, restoring to us the organic and integral presences culture has sequestered and allowing us to resume this proper status ourselves. In his language theory Whitman associates all these antinomies with the crucial opposition between voice and writing; yet all prove as difficult to sustain as the supposedly obvious contrast between these two modes. In what follows, I shall take up in turn Whitman's distinctions between performative and constative utterance, between organic and arbitrary signs, and between the poet's word and presence and the images and artifacts with which culture ensnares us. We need to pay special attention to the way the axial but unstable opposition between voice and writing intertwines with these supposed polarities.

A proviso is in order. The full range of Whitman's remarks on language is admittedly less cohesive than the structure of claims and enabling distinctions I will adduce. The looseness of Whitman's formulations has several causes. The notes Traubel assembled as *An American*

Primer, which have been re-edited as the definitive *Primer of Words,* are hardly a finished piece of writing; yet they are as close as Whitman comes to a manifesto on language conversant with his practice in the poems.[20] The poems themselves discourse on linguistic matters in the midst of other concerns; we can hardly expect a perfectly consistent terminology to emerge from such glancing attentions. *Leaves of Grass,* moreover, regularly moves between visionary and practical contexts— between what The Poet ought to be able to do and what the actual poet does. Thus, for example, while writing is repeatedly said to play no part in the crucial transactions performed by *Leaves of Grass,* Whitman also sometimes casually refers to his poems as writing. The value of such other important terms as "sign" and "indication" can also wobble, as Whitman moves between visionary and practical, or technical and casual, modes. Faced with such inconsistencies, I have tried to make principal use of those works and passages that are engaged in relatively sustained and intent examination of linguistic issues, though I have occasionally given in to the temptation of marshaling the quotable stray assertion.

Performatives and Constatives

1. Despite the staggering amount of material he generated over the course of his career, Whitman could sometimes be despairing or dismissive about language: "such emotional revolts," he remarked to Traubel:

against you all, against myself: against words—God damn them, words: even the words I myself utter: wondering if anything was ever done worth while except in the final silences. (WWC 4:13–14)

Yet even such "final silences," I argued in chapter 4, are in *Leaves of Grass* conditioned by a magical presence dependent for its redemptive attributes on association with language and voice. If Whitman's occasional diatribes against language thus end up suggesting despite themselves his commitment to a world shaped by the word, such sweeping invectives are in turn far less common than is often supposed: what might look like wholesale dismissals of language are characteristically more limited, discriminating attacks on certain kinds of linguistic behavior; they have the aim of guarding the powers of language against the etiolations to which the supposedly degraded use of words leaves them liable.

The language theory of the 1856 "A Song of the Rolling Earth," the Whitman poem that gives most sustained attention to linguistic issues, is admittedly tricky to gloss.[21] At one point the poem opposes ordinary language to "substantial words":

> the substantial words are in the ground and sea,
> They are in the air—they are in you. (1856 322)

I shall take up this hermetic notion of substantial words further on. Here I want to concentrate instead on the poem's list of the linguistic activities such words pre-empt. Possessed of these strange substantial words, the "rolling earth" apparently need not busy itself with most of the language games that occupy ordinary speakers:

> The earth does not argue,
> Is not pathetic, has no arrangements,
> Does not scream, haste, persuade, threaten, promise,
> Makes no discriminations [. . . .] (1856 324)

The poet himself is sufficiently impressed by the earth's substantial words to want to abandon some of his own linguistic activity, which complements the language behavior the rolling earth eschews:

> I swear I will never henceforth have to do with the faith that tells the best!
> I will have to do with that faith only that leaves the best untold. (1856 331)

Such discursive forays are in any case unavailing, the poet not being able to "tell the best" even when he tries. His attempts to do so result in an emasculation of his crucial pneumatic powers:

> When I undertake to tell the best, I find I cannot,
> My tongue is ineffectual on its pivots,
> My breath will not be obedient to its organs,
> I become a dumb man. (1856 330)

These passages dismiss a good deal of ordinary language behavior. But it does not necessarily follow that the poem rejects the efficacy of all human speech. Poets or "sayers" are indeed declared able to employ substantial words:

> The great masters, the sayers, know the earth's words, and use them more
> than the audible words. (1856 323)

We will see further on how "sayers" can render substantial words themselves audible, making them available for human consumption. Even so modified, however, such words apparently cannot be employed to "tell the best"—at least the poet of "A Song of the Rolling Earth" cannot so employ them. Rather than deciding that Whitman's poet-hero is not yet a master sayer, we might better suggest that "telling" isn't an appropriate way to use the earth's words. What "A Song of the Rolling Earth" rejects is not language, not even human language, but certain kinds of words and certain linguistic activities with which Whitman associates them. Like the poet who cannot "tell," the rolling earth, past master of substantial words, refuses to engage not in language but in a number of language games: in arguing, arranging, screaming, hastening, persuading, threatening, promising, and discriminating. Between them, poet and rolling earth reject what J. L. Austin would call locution, perlocution, and the sort of illocution whose force is social rather than magical (for Austin, the only kind).

Telling, and perhaps arranging, are instances of locution, which Austin also calls constative utterance: they offer reports or representations of conditions subsisting independent of the words themselves and are judged according to the criteria of truth and falsity, of the representation's conformity or lack of conformity to the state it represents (Austin 1–3, 94–95). Arguing, screaming, hastening, and persuading fit Austin's category of perlocution—employing language in order to get people to do something (Austin 101–2). Threatening, promising, and perhaps arranging are illocutions, or what Austin more typically calls performatives: they do something *in* saying something (Austin 99–100).[22] Yet like the more obvious case of performing a clearly bounded ritual such as a marriage ceremony or the christening of a ship, threatening and promising are performatives operative only within the symbolic sphere of social reality. I duly apprise you of my intention to do x upon your doing y or not doing z; the act I thereby perform has symbolic, sometimes judicial standing rather than direct physical power or magical force, though both its uptake and its perlocutionary side effects may leak over into the physical sphere (I might accost you in carrying out my threat; you might hit me over the head to preempt its uptake). All of these language games are rejected by both poet and rolling earth in favor of those mysterious substantial words which apparently are employed in another fashion.

Before going further, we should recall our distinction between the practical and visionary contexts of *Leaves of Grass*. Over the course of Whitman's book, the poet engages in an awful lot of telling, persuading, and promising, throwing in some arguing, screaming, and threatening as well. But none of these moments present the poet in his mythic aspect or display him exercising his paradigmatic function: the poet's defining task is the uttering of words possessing magical performative force. It is in light of this shamanistic power that the merely symbolic, socially efficacious language games dismissed in "A Song of the Rolling Earth" seem to be inadequate or degraded uses of words.

In *Leaves of Grass* Whitman's attacks on the constative are particularly biting. Given the poet's apparent power to act on the world directly by speaking, language that limits itself to a merely discursive or representational function, making reports about conditions it has not itself caused and does not change, has flagrantly relinquished its true calling. Whitman depicts such language not only as powerless but also as disastrously self-enclosed: unable to impinge on the world directly, it becomes circular; beginning by referring to a universe that stands outside its compass, it ends up referring to itself. Whitman's jibes at such supposedly impotent and ultimately self-reflexive discourse are typically withering. Early in "Song of Myself" he dismisses mere "talkers":

> I have heard what the talkers were talking . . . . the talk of the beginning and
>   the end,
> But I do not talk of the beginning or the end. (1855 26)

Like Emerson, Whitman here lances the idea that meaning and value are lodged in the past or future, on which the present would thus depend. Yet the compulsion to refer present events to another time, in light of which they might be interpreted, is here tied to the notion, wrongheaded for Whitman, that language can do no more than offer reports, generating true or false propositions about or "talk *of*" something beyond its dominion. Speaking about a world to which it merely refers, such language never takes hold of that world but instead simply exfoliates, endlessly deferring encounter with the very things of which it speaks. Such propositional language thus entoils us in a labyrinth: "I have heard what the talkers were talking, the talk [. . . .]" As Whitman's disparaging epithet "talkers" already implies, "talk *of*" something is finally just talk about talk.[23]

Whitman typically associates such impotent, self-enclosed discourse with texts. Writing, which reports spoken language, indeed comes to epitomize language which itself merely makes reports. Thus in section two of "Song of Myself," immediately following the long catalogue in which the poet assimilates and transfigures all he names, Whitman both contrasts such visionary transactions to the degraded activity of ferreting out represented content from poems and links this goose-chase to writing and reading. Whitman teases those who go scurrying after "meaning"—who regard the poem as a report about something beyond the words themselves and the personal power and presence words rightly used are able to convey:

> Have you practiced so long to learn to read?
> Have you felt so proud to get at the meaning of poems?
>
> Stop this day and night with me and you shall possess the origin of all poems.
>   (1855 26)

Reading sends us chasing after an absent speech act it merely represents, just as constatives offer us a truth to which their language merely refers. This association pervades Whitman's work:

> For it is not for what I have put into it that I have written this book,
> Nor is it by reading it you will acquire it. ("Whoever You Are Holding Me
>   Now in Hand," 1860 346)[24]
>
> There is something that comes home to one now and perpetually,
> It is not what is printed or preached or discussed . . . . it eludes discussion
>   and print,
> It is not to be put in a book . . . . it is not in this book,
> It is for you whoever you are . . . . ("A Song for Occupations," 1855 90)

Writing thus becomes Whitman's crucial instance of a disaster to which talk is also liable—the fall from performative utterance, in which the word is the present exercise of the speaker's own force, to mere representation, in which language is directed toward something outside itself and beyond the speaker's control. In the magical universe of *Leaves of Grass,* this identification acts as a kind of ritual containment: what is epitomized by writing is therefore (or thereby) essentially foreign to speech, though speech enervated by writing may be liable to it; preying upon speech, writing supposedly renders it susceptible to disasters from which it might otherwise have been immune.[25] Section two of "Song of Myself" thus ends by associating books with a spectral power that seems to initiate rather than merely accompany the loss of personal force which characterizes the fall into the labyrinth of reference:

> You shall no longer take things at second or third hand . . . . nor look through the eyes of the dead . . . . nor feed on the spectres in books. (1855 26)

Here contiguity feels like magical contagion: Whitman's line implies that culture seduces us into substituting somebody else's reports for our own perceptions and active powers by employing the necromantic art of writing. I shall have more to say further on about the vampiric figures that haunt this passage and the living death inflicted by the books out of which they rise up. Protecting us from them, the poet might seemingly also save us from lapsing into the emasculating use of language for merely constative or reportorial purposes, a fall that has supposedly come to haunt speech to the extent that writing infects it.

2. Magical performative power should thus define the language that has not foolishly bartered its natural resources for cultural seductions. Such power should be available to those whose voices have not been emasculated by the sorts of degraded involvements writing represents. The poet of *Leaves of Grass,* who supposedly does not write, defines this saving remnant; his performative power seems to make constative utterance superfluous. Here it is important to distinguish once more between the practical and visionary guises of Whitman's work. The poet's language is of course engaged in representing (it is finally entangled more inextricably in representation than Whitman would like to believe). But this representational function is effectively upstaged, since *Leaves of Grass* dramatically obtrudes the poet's performative powers on our attention. Those powers are as extreme as the disasters from which the poet is supposedly immune. Obeying the formulaic logic of magic thinking, the opposition Whitman sets up between constative utterance and magical performative power makes one a kind of ritual opposite of the other. If representation is disastrously self-enclosed, the poet's performative word

enjoys a special power over things that is based on a specially intimate connection to them.

The identification of proper word use with performative force pervades Whitman's work. A dramatic passage from *The Primer of Words* is particularly explicit, and especially boisterous. It needs to be read with the distinction between technical and casual usages in mind; its designation of the performative poet as a "writer" is highly atypical, running counter, as we shall see further on, to a diatribe against writing that traverses the *Primer* and helps organize its crucial distinctions:

A perfect writer ~~will~~ would make words ~~do any thing that any thing can do~~ sing, dance, kiss, copulate do the male and female act, bear children, weep, bleed, rage, stab, steal, ~~sw~~ fire cannon, steer ships, ~~play overtures of music perform operas,~~ sack cities, ~~shoot trot on h~~ charge with cavalry ~~or artillery~~ or infantry, or do any thing that ~~any thing~~ man or woman or the natural powers can do. (DBN 3:742)[26]

Whitman's assertion here of the virtual equivalence of words rightly used with "natural powers" is not just gratuitous hyperbole: it works to lever performative language from the status of symbolic cultural transaction to that of physical act, according words a shamanistic power over things themselves.

This contention that words properly employed have magical power over things is sometimes supplemented by the stranger suggestion that such words *are* things:

As a sprig from the pine tree or a glimpse anywhere into the daylight belittles all artificial flower work and all the painted scenery of theatres, so are *live words* in a book compared to cunningly composed words. (CW 9:159–60; emphasis added)

Not simply a way of dramatizing a distinction between spontaneous and premeditated language, Whitman's opening contrast here between natural and cultural production serves to confer a more radical power on "live words": the passage establishes an opposition between things themselves and representations, and then implies that this division might fall not between objects and the words attached to them but within the domain of language itself.[27] Those who employ language for representational purposes wrongly assume a separation between words and a world of real objects supposedly beyond their reach; words used rightly erase this catastrophic split.

This contention that words share thinghood with things indeed turns out to be a rather mild version of their proper consanguinity. Whitman's characteristic aim is not to set words on an equal footing with objects but to suggest their fusion. He is interested, that is, not simply in suggesting the substantiality of the word, but in asserting its consubstantiality with the thing and its resultant talismanic power. In Whitman's work the magical force of language supposedly derives from this fusion:

A perfect user of words uses things—[...] they exude [...] in power and beauty from him—miracles from his hands—miracles from his mouth [...] things, lilies, clouds, sunshine, woman, poured consciously—things, whirled like chain-shot-rocks, defiance, compulsion, houses, iron, locomotives [...] the oak, the pine, the keen eye, the hairy breast, the Texas ranger, the Boston truckman, the [...] woman that arouses a man, the man that arouses a woman. (*The Primer of Words*, DBN 3:740)

The confusion here between words and things—the whole catalogue might be a list of either, or of one *as* the other—is hardly casual; it both underwrites and illustrates the performative power the passage asserts. As we have seen, in *Leaves of Grass* this archaic fusion of word and thing lends the poet's performative utterances their uncanny quality.

In Whitman's work, moreover, the word is not simply a part of the thing: it is the germ from which the whole will grow, a synecdochic essence endowed with magical productive force. A notebook fragment makes this generative function of language even more explicit than does the quotation above from the *Primer:*

From each word, as from a womb, spring babes that shall grow to giants and beget superber breeds upon the earth. (UPP 2:84)[28]

Despite the sometimes vehement tones of the *Primer*—the quotation about making words fire cannon and charge with cavalry or infantry is a good example of such bluster—the poet's performative word is thus not to be thought of as aggressive or adversarial. Able to generate the thing, the word which is its essence can also supposedly restore it to health or help bring to fruition its organic potential. The tremendous force of the poet's utterance thus supposedly differs from the coercive power wielded by the symbolic language of culture: the poet's naming recalls creatures and objects to their innate course of development rather than imposing extrinsic structures upon them; it can liberate us from the violence of culture, which characteristically divides us against ourselves by implanting alien proclivities within us.

This saving word must be oral rather than written. Writing, engraved on a surface itself, epitomizes for Whitman not only the constative, but also the mere externals which representation is characteristically confined to depicting. In *Calamus* the poet's own momentarily forbidding "exterior" is thus ambiguously either his silent visage or his text:

> Recorders ages hence!
> Come, I will take you down underneath this impassive exterior—I will tell
>   you what to say of me. (V 2:380)[29]

As Whitman's gesture at direct address in these lines implies, this liberating descent is accomplished by voice. Here supposedly taking us down to an otherwise inaccessible interior, voice more typically projects this sacrosanct region outward, bypassing opaque surfaces by expressing animating energies as sound.

This vision of voice depends on an appeal to topology. Proceeding from an interior that lends it its resonance, voice as it were makes the structure of that inner region audible.[30] But in Whitman's work voice is given the trickier task of expressing the animating energies not only of the speaker from which it emanates but also of everything he names. It is not immediately obvious how the voice of one creature possesses the sort of intimate connection to the interior of another that would make this expressive function possible. Whitman tries to bridge this gap through a theory of organic naming: the true name of each creature must somehow condense the organic energies its own voice manifests; lurking in the name, these resources should be recoverable by a speaker properly endowed. The dichotomy we have been examining, between the linguistic activities of constative and performative utterance, thus demands a parallel distinction between opposing *kinds* of words: between arbitrary and organic names, indicative and expressive signs. Repudiating the merely representational uses of language, Whitman seeks also to dismiss the indicative or arbitrary element in semantics, in individual words themselves. Writing epitomizes this sphere of language as mere designation; as we shall see, the poet's own specially endowed voice is the privileged medium of language in its proper, expressive mode.

Expression and Indication: Organic and Arbitrary Signs

Whitman's attempt to disengage organic, expressive names from the mass of merely arbitrary, indicative words in which they are supposedly mired is perhaps the most crucial struggle prosecuted in his writings on language. This effort, however, seems to run counter to other important aspects of Whitman's speculations on words. In taking up Whitman's distinction between organic and arbitrary signs, which serves to dismiss a vast range of language behavior while empowering the poet's magical speech, I want therefore to juxtapose this centripetal impulse to the centrifugal, demotic vision of language Whitman also develops. The conflict between these two notions of words, I shall try to show, is more apparent than real; in Whitman's language theory the unruly demotic energies reshaping the American idiom paradoxically serve to empower the poet's special speech by liberating it from the synchronic structures to which it would otherwise be subject; what might be called Whitman's practical concerns thus end up serving his visionary ambitions.

It will also prove instructive to place Whitman's claims for expressive, organic signs in the context of some of the other linguistic theories promulgated in his period, both reputable and shady. Several of Whitman's key claims about language are aberrant with respect to the historical philology of his own time and not simply when set against the structural linguistics of ours. These aberrations sit side by side in Whitman's work with views that would probably have passed muster among the period's foremost philologists; both Whitman's modifications of such respectable theory and his dramatic departures from it are indices not so much of his lack of understanding as of his own urgent agenda.[31]

Involving a vision of the poet's relation to culture as well as to the word, that agenda brought Whitman's musings on language into conflict not only with the working premises of historical philology but also with the enabling assumptions of an earlier American debate. Both Whitman's language theory and the social vision with which it comports can be seen as extreme versions of more widespread transcendentalist claims that likewise challenged federalist premises. In his important recent study of the ongoing argument during the first seventy-five years of the republic over the future of the American language, David Simpson notes that transcendentalist theorists broke with a governing postulate of the federal period and its immediate aftermath when they posited some sort of organic or natural tie between the word and the thing it names. The nominalist presuppositions they thereby called into question, Simpson points out, had firmly situated language as a social institution, a product of contingent human agreements rather than a natural fact. Debates about particular linguistic practices and programs for language reform had hitherto focused on their social and political rather than their supposed ontological implications; what mattered about linguistic practices was how they mediated the relations between social groups, not how they might restore an unmediated connection between the individual and some source prior to social conflicts or accords (Simpson 230–37). It is just such a source for individual perception and power that Whitman is intent on liberating from the social shaping of selves the federal debate took for granted. His language theory offers a hyperbolic version of the characteristic transcendentalist claims Simpson describes (244–45): a defense of linguistic innovation compatible with populism turns out to empower the rare "great soul" who can liberate the organic resources of words; recovering such roots, the extraordinary individual is freed from the trammels of culture, its symbolic structures and its ideological divisions; he may perhaps free us in turn. Whitman's departures from federalist assumptions are thus motivated in part by the millennial anti-institutionalism and visionary individualism that played important roles in the political and social rhetoric of the period.[32] As we shall see, however, the magical powers Whitman reserves for exceptional individuals are ultimately enlisted for ends not easily identified with even this utopian strand of American political life: the incorporative space the poet's powers supposedly sustain is less a utopian version of Jeffersonian agrarianism or its artisan republican variant than an archaic universe miraculously restored.

It is this magical vision of the word, as well as the role he accords the gifted individual in recovering such power, that places Whitman's musings on language beyond the bounds not only of the federalist debate Simpson describes but also of the philological research in which he took such avid interest. While the historical philologists I shall attend to were not always so firm in distinguishing nominalist and realist perspectives as were the descendants of Locke who shape Simpson's earlier American scenario, Whitman ends up espousing an extreme linguistic realism that would surely have shocked them as well. It would probably also have fuddled some transcendentalists. Simpson notes that the varieties of realist argument put forward by transcendentalist theories of language were typically carefully hedged (235–40). Recent work on Emerson indeed goes further, suggesting that what looks like a statement of realist assumptions can instead be taken as a sophisticated performance of something much closer to a nominalist theory of metaphor as (cognitive and cultural) power; on this reading Emerson's essays move gradually toward direct assertion of a view his earlier rhetorical practice already implies.[33] Yet it is undoubtedly the strand of linguistic realism which at least overtly dominates the early work that had the greatest impact on Whitman. The relation between Emerson's speculations and Whitman's vision of language is thus tricky to compute; I take it up in chapter 7, in connection with a use of metaphor in "Song of Myself," atypical in *Leaves of Grass,* that responds to nominalist as well as realist strands in Emerson's work. Here, I want to focus on the realist claims that dominate Whitman's language theory and the mastery they accord the poet.

I argue in what follows that Whitman concocted his vision of a language that would liberate and empower the poet by deftly mixing the postulates of academic philology with more speculative, often dubious contemporary theories. Since this mix is complex and my account of it rather detailed, a prolepsis of my argument may be helpful.

As James Warren has shown, Whitman was interested not only in the sort of diachronic change to which historical philology attended, but also in less common attempts to construe such change as progress, a program that typified not pioneers like Wilhelm von Humboldt but popularizers like Christian Bunsen and Maximilian Schele de Vere, both of whom Whitman had read.[34] More particularly, Whitman characteristically commented enthusiastically not on the sort of inexorable phonetic change charted by Bopp,[35] but on the unruly semantic innovations that preoccupied students of the American language. He tended to see such changes as freeing speech from settled constraints and thus as liberating language from the rules imposed by "grammarians" and other conservative guardians of culture. In a more visionary mode, he could equate this liberation from arbitrary restriction with the redemption of the word from its fallen status as merely arbitrary sign, envisioning the recovery of its supposed organic resources. Whitman thus managed to combine the kind of optimistic vision of linguistic progress he encountered in

Bunsen and Schele de Vere with a reclamation project more in keeping with the notion of linguistic degeneration espoused by August Schleicher. Part of the attractiveness of Schleicher's account derived from its resemblance to a vision of the word it did not explicitly espouse: Schleicher's work stirs up our recollection of the story of a lost adamic language, a language that might be recovered from out of the confusions of Babel. In Whitman's speculations, it is just such a language that the liberating progress of American English might enable us to retrieve.

The Primer of Words thus mingles attention to academically respectable historical philology with interest in the heterodox, hermetic tradition John Irwin describes in *American Hieroglyphics:* Whitman is in search of something like the silent, hieroglyphic "language of nature" in which things themselves are already words. Yet as Irwin notes, he combines this hermetic vision of a silent natural language with a commitment to voice (99–110). Here Whitman follows the lead of an extensive contemporary interest in what Charles Kraitsir called "glossology"— the doctrine of a motivated connection between the thing and the sound that represents it. This doctrine was not restricted in Whitman's time to the hermetic spheres to which post-Saussurian linguistics has consigned it: a firm commitment to the wholly arbitrary nature of the connection between signifier and signified is not to be found even in the work of such a precursor of structural linguistics as Humboldt.[36] Reputable linguists, though, tended to be circumspect about both the proportion of semantic activity such a supposedly motivated connection might account for and the nature of this tie: they characteristically regarded the sound of the word as having a motivated connection not to the essence of the object but only to the speaker's emotional response to it; the connection between the word and the thing itself, while not entirely arbitrary, was thus mediated rather than direct.[37] Whitman's doctrine of organic, expressive sound in effect combines the hermetic notion of a language of nature with such glossological presumptions: the word is organically connected to the thing and not just to our concept of it; but this connection obtains between the thing and the vocal sign rather than inhering in some silent natural language.

In Whitman's vision of language it is thus voice that can realize the organic, expressive potential concealed in words. This expressiveness has been lost through inattention—through our treating words as no more than convenient designations to aid in our commodification and exchange of things. Writing, as we might expect, not only exemplifies but is made a crucial cause of this fall from expression to indication. That fall might be reversed by one who remains uncontaminated by print and devotes his attentions instead to recovering the resonance in words that writing destroys.

If Whitman steps beyond the bounds of serious philological discussion by according the single speaker a determinative role in shaping the progress and fate of language, his particular version of linguistic individualism turns out to be extraordinary by nearly any standards. The speaker who would recover the organic resources of words needs remarkable vocal prowess as well as single-mindedness. Such oral resources, in turn, might be possessed only by one who has steered clear not only of writing but also of all those psychic and bodily self-divisions for which writing comes to stand: it is finally only the poet or one who possesses an uncastrated, pneumatic body like his who is capable of breathing into words and thereby retrieving them from the death to which writing leaves them liable.

This is in part a fortunate limitation: it is important to Whitman to distinguish clearly between the poet's use of words and the characteristically coercive demands of other speakers, and to insist that this difference is one between authentic power and mere trickery. Yet a language theory that guarantees the resources of the word by means of the poet's person is on shaky ground: the poet's body, I argued in earlier chapters, is created by hypostatizing the apparent powers of language; in Whitman's work the supposed powers of the word thus create the very creature who is then said to guarantee their efficacy. It is more useful to think of this pattern of argument as tracing a closed circle than as being merely contradictory. Whitman's work centers on a language and body that define each other, a structure that folds back on itself and remains inaccessible to those outside who might try to re-enter it; I have been calling this circle the archaic.

1. Much of both *The Primer of Words* and the longer, even more loosely organized notebook now called *Words*[38] details Whitman's enthusiastic, often sophisticated response to the historical philology that dominated the linguistics of his day. A portion of *Rambles among Words*, by Whitman's acquaintance William Swinton, which the poet may well have helped compose,[39] opens with a quotation from Wilhelm von

Humboldt that suggests what fascinated Whitman about this phase of linguistics:

An idiom is an organism subject, like every organism, to the laws of development. One must not consider a language as a product dead and formed but once: it is an animate being and ever creative. . . . (265)[40]

Stressing continuous renewal rather than settled structure, the organicist metaphor Humboldt employs here provoked intense debate among nineteenth-century linguists, who argued about the legitimacy of its possible implications. The faction of philologists historian and critic Hans Aarsleff considers the period's most regressive marshaled the organicist metaphor to argue for the complete autonomy of linguistic development, its freedom from merely "historical" change or "political" history" (Aarsleff 31–37). While we might expect Whitman, too, to be nervous about the influence of contingent political and social developments on what were after all the poet's tools, he characteristically celebrates the effects of technological and political change on language. As Whitman describes them, these unruly pressures are registered principally in the growth of new vocabulary. Whitman's notebooks are filled with catalogues that attest to his lively, sustained interest in such linguistic innovation and variety. He frequently wrote down lists of the technical terms belonging to particular trades: one of his notebook entries offers more than a hundred sailing terms, complete with definitions (DBN 3:818–22). Others note slang expressions, presumably recently heard: "shin-dig," "spree," "bender," "bummer" (DBN 3:693).

This interest in contingent, historically generated semantic change can be found in the writings of philologists less committed to a literalized interpretation of the notion of linguistic organicism than the faction Aarsleff rebukes; it is a recurrent if minor strand in Humboldt's work.[41] But it played a special role in debates about the American language: Whitman would surely have noted assertions in the work of University of Virginia linguist Maximilian Schele de Vere about the fructifying effect on vocabulary of the new ranges of experience America offered (Schele de Vere 195). As Simpson argues, this espousal of American linguistic innovation came to play an important part not only in the sometimes boisterous claims for American cultural independence but also in arguments about the appropriate internal social and political profile of the republic; the American debate stressed the supposed connection between unbridled linguistic change and populist upheaval (Simpson 32, 46). Nationalist and populist strands dove-tailed in the rhetoric that contrasted American democracy with European "feudalism," an often polemical dichotomy that helped motivate Whitman's enthusiastic espousal of linguistic change. Whitman's examples of linguistic innovation accordingly focus on the American idiom, whose grandly "lawless" growth supposedly not only furthered the nation's efforts to shuck off "ultramarine" political and social encrustations but liberated the energies of the common people from domestic regulation as well.[42]

Whitman sometimes praises semantic innovation as a response to the generalized ferment of American life:

These States are rapidly supplying themselves with new words, called for by new occasions, new facts, new politics, new combinations.—[. . .] Far plentier ~~words~~ additions ~~are needed~~ will be needed, and, of course, will be supplied. (*The Primer of Words*, DBN 3:734)

This celebration of the new can amount to simple boosterism. Whitman is capable of inventorying the country's rapidly growing word stock as if it were a kind of economic indicator:

<u>Factories, mills, and all the processes of hundreds of different manufactures,</u> grow thousands of words. (*The Primer of Words*, DBN 3:747)

In such moments he resembles the very apostles of industry he excoriates in *Democratic Vistas*.

More typically, however, Whitman sees semantic change as reflecting and furthering political reform rather than indiscriminate economic expansion. His espousal of the contemporary American craze of finding native names for native realities is motivated more by the populism he considered the central feature of the American political tradition than by blind enthusiasm for the new or mere xenophobic rejection of things European.[43] The desire to consolidate and extend America's relative freedom from hierarchical constraint marks Whitman's sometimes cranky program for the reform of American place names:

Many of the Counties in the State—and ~~in all the Eastern~~ in other States—must be re-named

---

What is the name of Kings' County [. . .] or of Queens County to us?—or St. Lawrence County?

Get rid as soon as convenient of all the bad names—not only of counties, rivers, towns,—but of persons, men and women—(*Words,* DBN 3:701)

Objecting to names that commemorate a king, a queen, and a saint, Whitman here positions linguistic change as both expression and instrument of the demotic energies that might challenge such centralized institutional authority.

We can understand this aspect of Whitman's writings on language as a celebration of the centrifugal energies such semantic changes manifest and further. There was perhaps a logic to such verbal innovation:

What do you think words are? Do you think words are ~~arbitrary~~ positive and original things in themselves?—No: Words are not original and arbitrary in themselves.—Words are a result—they are the progeny of what has been or is in vogue. (*The Primer of Words,* DBN 3:736)

But it was not a logic susceptible to any single, simple formula, nor did it obey the demands of any single principle or center of power. One of the chapters of Swinton's *Rambles* which Whitman is supposed to have helped compose is quite explicit in its enjoyment of such uncontrollable diversification:

And here a spinal fact is the composite character of our language: to what new realizations is it lifted in America! The immense diversity of race, temperament, character—the copious streams of humanity constantly flowing hither—must reappear in free, rich growths of speech. (288)

Such energies interest the writer of this part of *Rambles* at least in part because they are opposed to the sort of social and political conservatism that also found expression in narrow linguistic scholarship:

The theory of English scholars and literateurs, for hundreds of years, has been the theory of repression. They have discouraged and cramped the spontaneous expansions of the Language. . . . (289)

This demotic, anti-authoritarian interpretation of linguistic change is also explicit in Whitman's "Slang in America":

Language, be it remember'd, is not an abstract construction of the learn'd, or of dictionary-makers, but is something arising out of the work, needs, ties, joys, affections, tastes, of long generations of humanity, and has its bases broad and low, close to the ground. Its final decisions are made by the masses [. . . .] (PW 2:573)

This understanding of linguistic innovation as inherently political was by no means unusual. Impassioned advocacy of democratic ferment may not have been typical of academic philology; but even Humboldt occasionally praised dialect as a source of "strength and vigor in a language and a nation" and saw support for it as leading to "rapport between the upper classes and the masses" (*Humanist without Portfolio* 243–44).

Another way of construing linguistic change important in the American context, however, was explicitly ruled out by Humboldt. He considered the notion that change constituted progress, together with the frequent corollary that progress meant movement toward teleological fulfillment of the potentials of the word, as vulgarizations of the interest in diachronic processes that characterized historical philology (*Linguistic Variability* 1–6). As Warren points out, this teleological vision helps organize the work of two linguists important to Whitman, Christian C. J. Bunsen and Maximilian Schele de Vere (*Walt Whitman's Language and Style* 21–28). A Hegelian stance explicitly governs Bunsen's massive *Outlines of Universal History, Applied to Language and Religion*.[44] Schele de Vere also tended to interpret linguistic change as progress, and to see both linguistic innovation and the expansionist political energies with which it supposedly went hand in hand as phases in a universal development.[45]

Embracing this teleological vision,[46] Whitman managed to fuse it, more dramatically than Schele de Vere had done, with his interest in the unruly demotic energies linguistic change was also said to reflect and further. There is something of a contradiction here, or at least a tension: Whitman construes linguistic innovation as the liberation of centrifugal energies that have escaped the control of any single, central authority, and, simultaneously, as concerted progress toward a single goal. Whitman resolves this apparent dilemma, in part, through appeal to the commonplace transcendentalist distinction between imposed and organic structure: what looks like order is only the arbitrary imposition of capricious authority; what seems to be anarchy obeys a deeper logic that will one day be evident. A passage from the *Primer* that contrasts the sort of historical changes traced by philology to the linguistic fixity defended by rear-guard grammarians thus associates such seemingly chaotic innovation with the covert working of an intrinsic, organic law:

The Real Grammar will be that which declares itself a nucleus [. . .] of the spirit of the laws, with ~~perfect~~ liberty to all to carry out the the [*sic*] spirit of the laws, even by violating them, if necessary.—The English Language is grandly lawless like the [. . .] race who use it.—Or Perhaps—or rather breaks out of the little ? laws to enter truly the higher ones It is so instinct with that which underlies laws [. . .] and the purports of laws, ~~that I think~~ it ~~goes toward the destinati~~ refuses all petty interrup~~tu~~ptions in its way ~~toward~~ purports.—(DBN 3:735)

Freedom from meddling authorities, however, turns out to be a goal of this mysterious progress rather than just an instrument that furthers it. If on the one hand demotic energies help advance the course of teleological development, on the other hand what such development brings about is apocalyptic liberation from a constraint Whitman figures as simultaneously linguistic and political. What might be called the practical politics involved in Whitman's championing of linguistic populism thus facilitates not only a teleological vision of language but also a millennialist political prospect supposedly enabled by linguistic reform. The project of shucking off particular hierarchies and traditions passes over into a determination to put an end to all culturally imposed restrictions; Whitman often suggests that this goal can be achieved through a liberation movement focused on words. Whitman's language theory is thus pulled beyond the bounds of academic philology in part by the terms of an American political rhetoric to which the poet enthusiastically contributed: espousing what looks like radical individualism, Whitman accords it the teleological privilege and millennial resonance which the Revolutionary re-crafting of the jeremiad lent the notion of freedom.[47] A passage from the *Primer* that begins by arguing for the replacement of "ultramarine" names and the old hierarchies they help keep in place accordingly modulates into a visionary idiom that implicitly identifies such linguistic renovation with the advent of the chiliad:

The great proper names used in America must commemorate ~~what dates from~~ things belonging to America, and dating thence [. . . .] Because What is America for? [. . .] To commemorate the old myths ~~and goddesses~~ and the gods? [. . .] To repeat the Mediterraneanean [*sic*] here? Or the uses and growths of Europe here?—No;—(Nä-o͞-o͞) but to destroy all ~~them~~ those ~~growth~~ from the purposes of ~~mankind~~ the earth, and to erect a new ~~world~~ earth in their place. (DBN 3:755)

What I have been calling the centrifugal aspect of Whitman's language theory thus combines practical populism with a utopian vision of the end of fallen culture; part of Whitman's enthusiasm for the turbulent undermining of authority manifest in American English as well as in American political and social life is attributable to his equation of such subversion with the end of all systematic codification and restraint, and with the millennial prospect with which this liberation from arbitrary control was associated in American political discourse. A linguistic stance that in a practical context involves championing one class over against another, or appealing to one seat of linguistic authority rather than another, thus translates in Whitman's utopian vision into the notion of a language liberated from all competing social pressures and all need for political adjudication. The sort of specific semantic changes that on Whitman's own account both reflect and prosecute ideological struggle are enlisted to support a vision of language in which the word and its speaker have been freed from all such collective shaping; the demotic energies that liberate language from institutional control supposedly return it to the individual as an unmortgaged possession subject solely to his or her independent will.

Both this linguistic state of nature and the political possibilities to which it seems to attest are very much out of keeping with the federal debate over language Simpson describes, in which both conservative and demotic interests regarded words as necessarily socially saturated, so that escape from the pull of competing interests at work in them was scarcely imaginable. Moreover, their resemblance to the utopian strand of contemporary political rhetoric that Sean Wilentz and Betsy Erkkila describe as a radical recasting of the Jeffersonian tradition by New York artisans turns out to be partial and problematic.[48] If a utopian intensification of the Jeffersonian "relocation of sovereignty in the individual rather than the state" (Erkkila 26) structures a millennialist political vision Whitman shared with his more radical contemporaries, both the role he assigned to language in attaining this prospect and the part he accorded the poet in realizing the resources of the word and bringing them to bear on his fellow citizens are less easily assimilated to the demotic politics of the period. As we shall see further on, the word freed from conservative codification and restraint supposedly recovers and deploys a variety of magical powers, shaping a regressive space we can comfortably subsume within neither Jeffersonian nor radical working-class discourse. Whitman's notion of who can and cannot wield those powers is also hard to reconcile with demotic concerns or equate with American political utopianism. It would be an over-simplification to claim that Whitman's interest in diffuse, historically conditioned linguistic change is simply a Trojan horse inside of which the imperial poet will be found lurking, since his fascination with such disorderly processes seems quite genuine. But the centrifugal forces enthusiastically traced in Whitman's notebooks on language turn out to enable a dramatic concentration of power: in Whitman's writings on language it is not the masses but the gifted individual speaker or "great soul" who makes optimal use of the freedom from regulation and constraint demotic energies make possible; despite Whitman's occasional demurs, this figure is less exemplary than exceptional, and the universe his powers shape may be the fulfillment not so much of American consensus and community as of the desire to abrogate the need for them.[49]

If Whitman's claims concerning the poet's special powers have a problematic relation to his own demotic rhetoric, they are patently out of keeping with the reputable linguistic discourse of his day: in Whitman's language theory individual initiative rather than the massive, impersonal processes traced by philology is the crucial source of linguistic revitalization. His vision of what such renewal might achieve is also aberrant by contemporary standards as well as modern ones.

The power Whitman accords the gifted individual speaker in realizing the resources of the word is a dramatic instance of the way the imaginative demands of *Leaves of Grass* helped shape the agenda for the language theory, disturbing Whitman's often faithful redaction of the reigning assumptions of academic linguistics. When wearing his practical hat, Whitman was perfectly attentive to strictures against viewing the individual as a crucial source of linguistic change:

No art, no power, no grammar, no combination or process can originate a language; it grows purely of itself, and incarnates everything. It is said of Dante, Shakespeare, Luther, and one or two others, that they created their languages anew; this is foolish talk. ("America's Mightiest Inheritance" 56)[50]

Yet in his visionary guise, Whitman could temporarily ignore the very perspective to which he was elsewhere committed. Following Schele de Vere in arguing that the paring away of inflectional markers that characterized romance languages was to be understood as progress rather than decay,[51] Whitman was in part simply taking a demotic stance, since he associated the syntactic permutations which the loss of such inflections encouraged with "freedom":

Thus individualism is [...] a law of modern languages, and freedom also.—
The words are not built in, but stand loose, and ready to go this way or that.
(*Words*, DBN 3:723)

Here "individualism" seems to signify no more than individual choice
with regard to usage, a freedom that implies no special powers for
special speakers. It turns out, however, that some will make better use
of such freedom than others:

Drawing language into line by rigid grammatical rules, is the theory of the
martinet applied to the ~~most ethereal~~ processes of the spirit, and to the luxuriant
growth of all that makes art.—It is for small school-masters, not for great souls.
(*Words*, DBN 3:666)

Whitman's characterization here of the vast machinery of diachronic
change as "the processes of the spirit," which may sound polemical or
simply purple to our ears, was common parlance—similar phrasing
turns up regularly in Humboldt. But his accompanying suggestion that
"great souls" are specially exempt from regulation is rather more brash,
as is the implication that this freedom derives from their special responsibility for a presumably teleological progress.

The extreme power Whitman accords the gifted individual in furthering linguistic development is matched by a truly visionary notion of the
sort of language he is to make available. Having had his own powers
stimulated by the demotic energies that begin to set words free from
conservative rules and restraints, the "great soul" is to clinch this liberation by discovering resources in the word no more available to populist
innovation than to grammatical pedantry. The word is to be anchored
firmly to an organic, natural basis in things; the cultural and historical
vicissitudes that Whitman enthusiastically traces thus paradoxically facilitate the vision of a language beholden to neither history nor culture.

Something of this visionary prospect is occasionally discernible even
in Whitman's descriptions of the semantic changes being fueled by technological growth and thus usually associated in his work with demotic,
centrifugal impulses rather than with the poet's supposed special powers.
In what may or may not be displays of merely playful exuberance,
Whitman attributes a kind of organic expressiveness to the words coined
to keep pace with industrial innovation. He endows these words with
solidity and imagines them as sharing the qualities of the things they
name. Enthusing over the semantic effects of the growing iron industry,
he suggests:

They are ponderous, strong, definite, not indebted to the antique—they are ~~iron~~ iron words, wrought and cast.—I ~~consider~~ see them all good, ~~and~~ faithful, ~~trem sturdy,~~ massive, permanent words.—I love well these iron words of 1856. (*The Primer of Words*, DBN 3:747)

Another quotation from the *Primer,* though, gives witty expression to what will elsewhere be crucial doctrine: it is the poet or specially adept individual who realizes this organic resonance lurking in new words. Here Whitman displays the sort of daft enthusiasm that characterizes the poet of *Leaves of Grass* at his most winning—simultaneously earnest and aware of his own outlandishness, both visionary and comic. His claims nevertheless sit strangely in the quasi-discursive context of the *Primer:*

Kosmos-words, Words of the ~~Enlargement~~ Free Expansion of Thought, History, Chronology, Literature [. . .] are ~~becoming~~ showing themselves, with ~~grand large and~~ foreheads muscular necks and breasts [. . . .] These gladden me!—I put my arms around them—touch my lips to them. (DBN 3:739)

As the lovemaking here implies, it will turn out to be the poet's body and not just his "great soul" that can free the organic resources lurking in language and thus restore words to the consubstantiality with things this passage so outrageously figures; Whitman's visionary notion of the word is at once a vision of the body. It will seem more explicable, if perhaps no less unsettling, that the powers of language should depend on the poet's body for their realization once we have seen in detail what the organic resources of the word are supposed to be.

2. One indication that the powers Whitman wants to claim for the word are visionary is the apocalyptic time scheme his account of their realization implies. This apocalyptic structure suggests dramatically how Whitman's language theory exceeds the practical linguistics I have so far been detailing; it serves to differentiate the poet's crucial recuperative powers from the unruly demotic energies that can help set them in motion. It also provides an instructive instance of Whitman's willingness to jettison the strictures of historical philology in order to sustain the poet's supposedly magical speech and its atavistic resonance.

A provisional way to distinguish the poet's magical powers from populist energies might be to suggest that while the people fuel linguistic expansion and development, the poet instead supposedly recovers a prior state of the word, undoing the mediations of culture and restoring language to its natural condition. This is something of an over-simplification, however: in Whitman's narrative, as we have seen, both the apparently heterogeneous linguistic changes fostered by the populace and the poet's more discriminating transactions serve teleological ends. It is thus more precise to describe the time-scheme implied by Whitman's musings as circular, and to note that both people and poet help propel language along this route: exhibiting a structure common to apocalyptic discourse, Whitman's language theory envisions a development that is ultimately a return to origins, to an essence prior to contingent historical change. But while the masses and the linguistic turbulence they generate help move language toward this apocalyptic juncture, in Whitman's vision it is only the poet or others like him who can take the crucial steps that complete the circle, turning progress into the restoration of an edenic condition we ought not to have lost.

The progressive commitment evident in Whitman's discussions of semantic change thus dove-tails in his writings on language with an interest in more recursive processes, to which the poet has a privileged relation. Historical philology is enlisted to support both these preoccupations. But the vision of restoration toward which Whitman's language theory gravitates depends on less reputable strands of philological speculation than does his consideration of linguistic progress; intent on justifying the poet's powers and the escape from fallen history they should make possible, Whitman abandons his often scrupulous respect for the provisos set forth by scientific linguistics. His vision of the organic language the poet is to recover is an extreme version of an adamicism Aarsleff regards as a kind of distorted image of philology; rigorous historical philologists had to attack adamicist premises precisely because an imaginatively unfettered interpretation of philological research might appear to lend support to such assumptions.

Humboldt's analysis of the changing status of the linguistic sign can serve as a case in point. His remarks might seem to encourage adamicist speculations: according to Humboldt, the arbitrary status of the sign is a historical development, gradually replacing a motivated connection between word and thing; such motivation characterizes languages in their earliest phases of development rather than in their maturity (*Linguistic Variability* 111, 241–43). I shall take up Humboldt's own highly circumspect account of the nature of this connection, which would have disappointed adamicist enthusiasts, further on, when I can contrast it directly to Whitman's own more extravagant musings. Only highly selective attention to Humboldt's writings, however, would allow one to assume that the recovery of this vanished connection between word and thing was part of philology's agenda. According to Humboldt the decay of such a tie is by no means an unequivocal disaster: "luxuriant voluptuousness" of sound impedes rather than furthers the conceptual mastery that is the principal function of the word (*Linguistic Variability* 67, 144). It is hardly Humboldt's aim to set about trying to restore such motivated connections in order to retrieve language from some presumed degeneration. Academic philology indeed characteristically ruled out speculation about the presumed traits of a lost original language supposedly radically different from historically observable ones, insisting that the principle of uniformitarianism that guided practical research also govern theoretical reflection (Aarsleff 297–317). Thus Humboldt suggested that the original cause of language is itself an unfathomable mystery—an assertion with consequences for enthusiasts seeking a supposed lost language since it was just such a transparent motivation of linguistic structures that they hoped to discover at a temporal origin (*Linguistic Variability* 4). Even Schele de Vere, who as we have seen was himself something of an enthusiast when it came to ascribing a teleological goal to linguistic change, warned of the futility of seeking to track language to its beginnings (19).

Such strictures were necessary, according to Aarsleff, precisely because historical philology had rekindled speculation concerning the resources of lost languages; like the doctrine of the magical powers of the sign, the vision of a vanished speech in which no longer available powers had been freely exercised hovers at the edges of respectable debate during the period, ironically fueled by academic research. One had only, so to speak, to run the machinery of historical linguistics backwards in order to be something of an adamist. Or more precisely: coupling diachronic study with a *Weltanschauung,* one learned to trace languages to their roots, not simply to map linguistic change but instead to validate notions of systematic progress or decay. Accounts of supposed linguistic degeneration tended to be the more boldly speculative: committed to finding their way back to the point before linguistic decline had commenced, unfettered theorists posited a period of linguistic activity different in kind from the observable changes philology traced; Schleicher's suspect distinction between "linguistics" and "philology" turns on just such a difference.[52] The vision of linguistic degeneration this sort of taxonomy could be made to support also possessed a resonance that belied its apparently pessimistic import, since it offered the tantalizing prospect of recovering and restoring a lost adamic language. Even Schleicher, whom Aarsleff characterizes as a dangerous combination of diligent practical researcher and rhapsodic theorist, stops short of attributing an adamic mastery of word over thing to pre-historic language —he posits the existence of several early languages rather than the single, singularly empowered one of the biblical account (Schleicher 2). Yet philological success in tracing the words of contemporary languages to their common roots fueled a revival of just such adamicist speculations, variously hedged and modified, among those less tethered to the constraints of an academic discipline than Schleicher. Historical philologists thus did repeated battle against the misappropriation of their work by romantic enthusiasts (Aarsleff 24–26, 316–17).

Whitman managed to position himself on both sides of this controversy. We can find him scrupulously resisting the lure of a lost original language and insisting that speculation concerning it is inherently vacuous:

Language cannot be Traced to First Origins.—Of the first origins of language it is vain to treat, any more than of the origin of men and women, or of matter, or of spirit. ("America's Mightiest Inheritance" 56)

Yet something very like this attempt turns out to be central to his vision of the word. The characteristic task of Whitman's "great soul" is precisely the recovery of a lost organic tie between word and thing; he is to rescue language from the degraded state in which the connection between them seems to be merely a matter of social convention. The enthusiastic espousal of linguistic progress in *The Primer of Words* thus meshes oddly with a vision of the supposed degeneration such development is to overcome: Whitman combines the teleological speculations he discovered in Bunsen and Schele de Vere with an adamicist project fueled by a view of linguistic decline Schleicher's account helped make credible.[53] Simpson notes that the vision of progress *as* restoration was a fairly typical feature of American polemics: Noah Webster, for example, argued that the apparent innovations of American "yeomen" were in fact a return to older practices abandoned in England under pressure from foppish urban grammarians. What Webster had it in mind to recover, however, was well within the scope of human memory: American English was bringing about a return to the linguistic good taste of the reign of Queen Anne (Simpson 65–66). Whitman, by contrast, envisions recovery of a language less like Anne's than Adam's.

Like other enthusiasts who appropriated and modified the approaches and results of academic philology, Whitman thus marshaled historical distinctions to defend a vision of language that was ultimately ahistorical. In the account of adamicist arguments that follows in the next sections, we will often find Whitman and other proselytizers making selective appeal to philological evidence, enlisting it to paint an edenic portrait of what language once was, hence what it intrinsically is or ought to be. In Whitman's speculations, which are typical in this regard, diachronic evidence is characteristically solicited to enable the poet to sort through and evaluate aspects of synchronic structure. If academic philologists held that present languages were modifications of older ones, elements of which could be found lurking within current formations, Whitman suggests that neglected traces of lost linguistic powers subsist in American English, supposedly making possible the recovery of an older, unfallen speech. In practice Whitman wields this diachronic razor quite freely: his reclamation project often amounts to dividing present language into desirable and undesirable aspects, a quarantine operation justified as the separation of originary, authentic features from those artificially imposed.[54] More broadly, an implicit appeal to adamicist premises governs nearly all Whitman's speculations on the poet's special relation to the word: in what follows, the apocalyptic vision of a lost but recoverable origin in which language is still at one with nature lies behind and justifies even those discriminations not overtly concerned with linguistic change.

3. Both adamicist assumptions and the way highly selective appeal to diachronic data was enlisted to support them are most dramatically evident in arguments mounted by Whitman and several of his contemporaries concerning the supposedly deteriorating relation between sound and sense, the name and the thing it names. But I want to turn first to another topic in which Whitman was also passionately involved. Less overtly concerned with diachronic change than with synchronic struc-

ture, it will help to make clear both the threats Whitman's adamicism wards off and the condition it should protect or restore. Fallen language and culture, we saw in chapter 4, are made responsible in Whitman's work for a pervasive alienation that ought to be avoidable: generating symbolic entities that become the objects we desire and dividing us against ourselves by implanting such entities within us as well, they occult the unique, the intrinsic, and the natural, overlaying them with a taxonomy of artificial forms. Whitman's effort to disentangle organic from arbitrary signs accordingly intersects with a polemic against the classifying power of fallen language, an aggressive, culturally coercive force Whitman contrasts to the supposed resources of the proper name. Proper names suggest to Whitman the possibility of a language that innocently expresses the essence of each individual creature or thing. They seem to imply that linguistic classification is an avoidable and therefore nefarious violence: while the classifying powers of language generate the coercive representations culture imposes, the proper name exemplifies linguistic resources that supposedly might have saved us from these disasters.[55] We shall see shortly how Whitman's vision of proper names is specifically edenic: describing a language that is not ours, it also defines a world that could not be our own. Whitman's remarks, however, obscure this impossibility: the proper name is insistently made to define what the word (and the world) should be.

Whitman's writings on language make the slide from the proper name into classification a crucial instance of the supposedly merely contingent fall from expression to indication. While according to Whitman the expressive sign has an intrinsic connection to what it signifies and makes the object's organic energies manifest, the indicative sign possesses a merely arbitrary relation to its object and is thus devoid of such resources.[56] In Whitman's account the act of categorization exemplifies this lapse. Intent on naming an object in order to make it available for practical manipulation rather than to express its uniqueness, fallen culture designates the thing by means of a term already in circulation, a word the object must share with other entities that acquired this designation though equally capricious procedures; ignoring the object's intrinsic characteristics, such indicative terms dispose it arbitrarily, dropping it into gerrymandered groups.

In Whitman's account the proper name avoids such violence—or at least it ought to. Attentive to the individual entity, the proper name should express something inherent in it rather than foisting an alien structure upon it:

Names of cities, islands, rivers, new settlements, &c. These should / must assimilate in sentiment and in sound, to something organic in the place, or identical with it. (*Words,* DBN 3:705)

It turns out, however, that the propriety of the proper name, which should epitomize the authentic resources of language, is peculiarly vulnerable to the encroachments of classification, from which it must be vigilantly protected: the proper name has an unnerving tendency to become a kind of surreptitious class name. In Whitman's writings on language it is indeed paradoxically the lapsed proper name rather than the class name that comes to exemplify the interrelated evils of designation and classification.

Sometimes Whitman treats the loss of organic expressiveness that can befall the proper name as a kind of accident, the result of mere carelessness, or of ignorance as to what is at stake in the problem of naming. We are often content to hit on an indicative name rather than struggling to divine an organic one:

What is the curious rapport of names? [. . .] I have been informed that [. . .] there are [. . .] people who say ~~that~~ it is not important about names, ~~or words~~ —one word is as good as another [. . .] if the designation [. . .] be understood. —I say that nothing is more important than names. (*The Primer of Words,* DBN 3:753–54)

Here the fall from expression to indication that can plague even the proper name is attributed to innocent misunderstanding. Elsewhere, however, this slippage seems to further malign purposes. Indicative names can be purposely employed to denature the unique object, subjecting it to the alienating violence of social structure by consigning it to a strategically motivated rather than merely accidental grouping. Such imperial interference is simultaneously linguistic and political. The key category of the American place name is thus Whitman's crucial instance of such tampering:

California is sown thick with the names of all the little and big saints
   —(Chase them away and substitute aboriginal names

   What is the ~~strange charm~~ fitness [. . . .] What the ~~fitness~~ strange charm of aboriginal names?—Monongahela [. . .] it rolls with venison richness upon the palate. (*The Primer of Words*, DBN 3:752)

This extravagant praise of aboriginal names is attributable in part to the sort of political boosterism I noted above: Whitman aims to free America from all linguistic evidence of foreign influence.[57] But ultramarine names are supposedly foreign in a more profound sense, just as native names are native in a more radical way. Aboriginal names are supposedly indigenous not only to the region but also, as it were, to the particular things they name. I shall take up further on Whitman's argument for this supposed organic bond between proper name and unique object which aboriginal names exemplify; it depends on a tie between vocalization and organic structure this quotation already implies. In contrast to such supposedly intrinsic names, the "foreignness" of the European words affixed to the American landscape consists most profoundly in their merely arbitrary relation to the things they name, an arbitrariness their transplantation from old circumstances and uses insures. These names are not truly proper: here the fall from the aboriginal name to the merely arbitrary foreign one is also implicitly a fall from the proper to the class name, which assimilates unique native places and objects to alien categories and thus annexes them for imperial use.

This violence has been inflicted on American persons as well as American places. Whitman of course inveighs against such imperial aggression. But his program for rectifying it shares the crankiness that often characterizes his plans for reform:

What [. . .] is there in the best aboriginal names? What [. . .] is there in strong words of qualities, bodily, mental,—a name given to the [. . .] cleanest and most beautiful body, or to the offspring of the same?—What is there that will conform to the genius of These States, and to all the facts [. . .] ?—What escape [. . .] with perfect freedom, without affectation, is there from the shoals of Johns, Peters, Davids, Marys,

Or on what other names happy principle, popular and fluent, shall could other words be prefixed or suffixed to these, to make them show who they are, and what land they were born in, what government [. . .] which of The States, and what genius, mark, blood [. . .] times [. . .] have coined them with their own strong-cut coinage? (*The Primer of Words*, DBN 3:744–45)[58]

This invective is directed in part at the sort of ultramarine influence Whitman also condemns in his consideration of American place names.

Yet in this instance too, the transplanted European name comes to symbolize the class name; the political annexation inveighed against here is also the expropriation of the unique and proper by means of the category, from the trammels of which Whitman concocts an elaborate program to free American citizens.

This concern for the proper governs the passage despite the absence of any overt claim to be able to restore to Americans the edenic perfection of the truly proper name. In the "practical" context of imagining reforms that might begin to undo the damage already caused by ultramarine names, Whitman indeed envisions an elaborate inflectional system that apparently might rebuff the imperial interests advanced by foreign names only at the cost of exacerbating another linguistic catastrophe: he proposes to reclaim Americans from the European names arbitrarily imposed upon them by supplementing this foreign taxonomy with a more minutely detailed indigenous one. The very laboriousness of this effort suggests that the aim of such reforms is not solely political: European influence, after all, might be more easily repudiated by simply replacing the stock of foreign names with an equal number of "aboriginal" ones. Whitman's bizarre vision of names modified by multiple supplementary markers should thus also be read as a paradoxical effort to overcome the dangers of classification by means of more classification. This paradox registers both the intensity of Whitman's discomfort with the power of the category and the elusive status of an edenic limit he can approach only by means that at least temporarily exacerbate the very ills they should cure. Whitman struggles to reverse the fall from linguistic propriety into the violence of classification by concocting a taxonomy so minutely detailed as to merge, at some asymptotic limit, into the visionary prospect of the truly proper: the category finely enough tailored to fit only a single object would as it were dissolve into a truly proper name.

The fantasy of the properly proper name is thus indeed an edenic one, applicable only to Eden: as David Simpson reminds us (218–19), the commutable relation between word and object which defines the proper name as inalienable private property is conceivable only for a circumscribed, finite field of objects—a sacred or ritual space much like the one to which Whitman's catalogues try to reduce profane multiplicity. Short of that field and that limit, the effort to restore the proper must make use of improper means. Whitman here not only implicitly equates the violence of cultural imperialism with the linguistic violence of categorization; the violence of the category, in turn, seems to be one from which naming and language can be only laboriously and provisionally separated.

Yet this pervasive entangling of the proper name in the evils of categorization turns out to possess ambiguous significance. On the one hand, it can suggest the elusiveness of the proper within language, and thus the shaky status of a linguistic doctrine centering on it: the very notion of the proper is in danger of evaporating as the fall into the class name turns out to have compromised (nearly) all supposed instances. Yet on the other hand, this slippage of the proper name into the surreptitious class name can paradoxically be enlisted to suggest that the supposed authentic propriety of a few aboriginal words properly defines language: the mass of names that lack the traits these aboriginal words seem to possess can be disqualified as not really being proper names at all. The fact that categorization turns up even within the proper name, that is, can be construed as enabling rather than compromising an attempt to define the resources of language on the basis of the proper: occurring within the domain of the proper name itself, the lapse into categorization that characterizes the mass of language can be regarded as contingent rather than inevitable; it seems attributable to cultural imperialism rather than structural necessity.

The fiasco of improper proper names is accordingly balanced in Whitman's work by a vision of class names which obey the proprieties that (should) define the proper name itself. A bizarre notion of commutability derived from a strictly untenable view of the proper name organizes Whitman's consideration of all nomination and all word use; his vision of semantics is implicitly governed by this determination of the truly proper name as the proper mode of language. This attempt to extend the rules that ought to govern the proper name to the entirety of language makes clear that what motivates the distinction between the proper name and the category is hardly the effort to formulate an objective and sustainable linguistic taxonomy. It is instead the need to imagine an entire language defined by an elusive limit: the limit of one representer per represented, a vision of absolute uniqueness and propriety somehow to be sustained in and by the word. This global aspiration responds to and seeks to reverse the violence of a linguistic and cultural imperialism that seems equally pervasive.

Whitman's attempt to make all language conform to the commutable relation between word and object that should define the proper name is implied by a series of strange pronouncements that overtly take up the problem of precise classification rather than the perfect propriety which the authentic proper name should insure. The strangeness of these pronouncements is perhaps a function of this displacement. Their vehemence seems motivated at least in part by a concern that does not surface overtly: passionately arguing that words themselves must be protected from the violence of being lumped indiscriminately together, Whitman thereby struggles to subdue indirectly an aggression he elsewhere blames words for inflicting on things. We may thus find him insisting punctiliously on the absolute uniqueness and propriety of the individual word, fending off the partial synonyms that make semantics the description of a complex network of overlapping terms. Words themselves should be accorded the respect proper to persons and things, which is, precisely, respect for the unique or proper:

> One beauty of words is exactitude:—To me, each word out of the   that now compose the English language, has its own meaning, and does not stand for any thing but itself—and there are no two words that are the same and any more than there are two persons the same. (*The Primer of Words*, DBN 3:736)

In the notebooks assembled as *Words,* we can find Whitman at work warding off a complementary contamination. If in the *Primer* no two words are to possess overlapping meanings, in *Words* multiple meanings of a single term must also be ruled out (here Whitman misuses "synonyms"):

> Of course the word "Indian" does not belong apply to the American aborigines. —It originated—An Indian is a man or woman of the [. . .] southern and eastern half of Asia. It confuses and vexes language to have these such synonyms with contra-meanings. (DBN 3:709)

The fact that Whitman is here pursuing a visionary agenda is indicated by the contrast between these remarks and a quotation the practical student of contemporary linguistics clipped out and pasted into an earlier page of *Words*. Nothing surrounding the extract suggests disapproval:

If it be a sign of richness in a language that a single word is used to express many quite different things, the good old English may be regarded as the Rothschild of languages. For instance, how many significations lie in that single monosyllable *box*? (DBN 3:684)

Repudiating such slippage, Whitman in his visionary guise commits himself instead to the utopian project of making words themselves exhibit—and thus perhaps sustain—perfect distinctness and autonomy.

The visionary status of this program is strikingly suggested by the awkwardness of Whitman's attempts to imagine how it might be put into practice. The project of the proper lies behind Whitman's remarks concerning frequency of word use as well as those about punctilious categorization. But the implicit attempt to make actual discourse exhibit the commutable relation between word and individual object which authentic proper names supposedly sustain leads to provisos that are palpably outlandish. Each word, according to Whitman, must occupy its own proper place, and no key word may be repeated:

> (One single name belongs to one single place only—as a word a a keyword of a X book may be best used only once in a book.
> In most instances A characteristic word once used in a poem, speech, or what not, is then exhausted [. . .] he who thinks he is going to produce effects by piling freely using strong words, is but a ignorant of words. (*The Primer of Words*, DBN 3:750)

What governs Whitman's bizarre opening strictures here is the implicit (and impossible) vision of language as reducible to the paradigm of the proper name: it is only the (truly) proper name that might have a single, irreplaceable referent. But the propriety of the proper name which is Whitman's implicit model for all word use here is itself extravagantly construed: like the unique being it names, the word supposedly belongs in only a single place (though this is strictly inconceivable); it should be as incapable of duplicate appearances as the singular living being to which it would thus be indissolubly wedded.

We can see clearly here what the paradigm of the proper name is meant to protect, and what it staves off: in this vision, language simply reflects the contents and contours of existence; the discrete orders brought into being by discourse disappear. The violence from which Whitman here protects the word is thus a violence for which all words except the truly proper name are elsewhere made responsible: the violence of indiscriminate repetition or application, an aggression against the unique and proper creature and occasion.

Whitman's account implies that words protected from such violence will also be innocent of it, a consequence that obeys the rules of magical rather than logical thinking. Words used as if they were proper names should acquire the protective virtues of the proper name; no longer repeated indiscriminately, they would no longer designate indiscriminately either. But Whitman's vision in the *Primer* of the way proper use transforms status goes further. The commutability of name and thing that ought to govern all word use not only wards off the violence words otherwise do to things; it also empowers the word by fusing it with its object. Whitman's admonition against having a single word appear in more than a single place is thus followed by some surprising assertions concerning the pay-off for such punctilious word use:

A ~~great~~ true composition in words, ~~is~~ returns the human body, male or female— that is the most perfect composition, and shall be best-beloved by men and women, and shall last the longest, which slights no part of the body, and repeats no part of the body. (*The Primer of Words*, DBN 3:750–51)

Whitman's closing proviso here makes it clear that more is involved in these remarks than a plea for physical frankness. If no part of the body is to be ignored in "perfect composition," no part is to be repeated either. It is this one-to-one relation of word to thing, and not simply lack of squeamishness, that "returns the human body," a result which thus seems to consist of more than renewing our respect for and comfort with the flesh. In the magic that lurks here, words reserved for a single occasion, and naming a single object, should cease being mere designations, sharing the qualities and attaining the quiddity of what they name. In Whitman's language theory words treated as if they were things become consubstantial with them; the word used properly conjures up the presence of the object with which it is fused.

This power is of course extreme. But it is not to be confused with the sort of power the fallen word wields; indeed it serves to exorcise that fallen power, protecting and presenting the unique, irreplaceable object rather than occulting it within a culturally generated category. Yet the awkwardness of Whitman's attempt to imagine a language in which each word would be restricted to a single appearance and wedded to a single object suggests that the elusive paradigm of the truly proper name tells us less about language than about the anxieties our subjection to it provokes. The proper name sustains a dream of escape or exemption: from repetition and multiple application as the proper mode of language; from the power of the transposable category over the unique creature and occasion; from the coercive force an imposed nomenclature exerts over everything it names.

Whitman's efforts to make language display the intrinsic or the proper thus respond to the anxieties detailed in *Leaves of Grass* at the price of ignoring the linguistic relativism characteristic of the most sophisticated contemporary language theory.[59] Humboldt, for example, argues that the proper name characterizes nomination only at some unrecoverable origin: each sound or single-syllable word, he suggests, originally corresponded to a discrete impression, its meaning being as unique as the individual object that provoked it (*Linguistic Variability* 242–43). But he insists that a phenomenon more truly characteristic of language soon takes over: the sound provoked by a particular impression is attached to others through the principle of analogy central to language, enlisting what was once a proper name to do the work of the category. As in Whitman's account, this loss of propriety is also a loss of expressivity, a slide into designation as well as classification:

This phenomenon, whereby a language, following a general analogy, applies sounds appropriate to specific cases to other cases to which they are strange can also be found in other parts of its operation. (*Linguistic Variability* 243)

Unlike Whitman, however, Humboldt presents this shift as inevitable and irreversible; nor does he bemoan its occurrence.

We might indeed read such passages as offering a heuristic fable rather than a literal historical account: Humboldt may be making assertions about structural necessity in the guise of a temporal narrative; to call something an original but unrecoverable trait may be not to lament its passing but instead to remark its structural inadequacy, its incapacity to perform the work of symbolic language. According to both Aarsleff (150) and Paul de Man (*Blindness and Insight* 112–41), accounts of the origins of language were read as just such parables of structure during the period in which they were written. But Aarsleff further argues that philology's diachronic focus made it increasingly difficult for mid-nineteenth-century readers to understand such narratives in the heuristic terms their authors had intended (150–63), with the result that academic linguists younger than a liminal figure like Humboldt dismissed remarks about origins as naive speculations ungrounded in empirical research, while enthusiasts embraced them as literally valid accounts pointing the way back to vanished traits that ought to be recoverable. The latter response helps motivate Whitman's consideration of the proper name, whose function as true naming has supposedly been progressively oc-culted by an aggressive categorizing system that ought to have been avoidable and should be eradicable. As we shall see further on, Whitman explicitly appeals to the putative traits of vanished (or nearly-vanished) languages in order to sustain this vision of the proper name as the proper mode of language.

We are in a position to understand this selective appeal to diachronic data as a way out of the structural impasse I have been analyzing: despite itself, Whitman's synchronic account reveals the same incapacity of the proper name to define the field of language that Humboldt's diachronic parable may have been designed to suggest. Jacques Derrida, whose interpretation of the genre of the origins essay is more skeptical than Aarsleff's or de Man's, assimilating the mode itself to what they regard as its subsequent misreading, understands Rousseau's *Essay on the Origin of Languages* to be making a similar appeal to diachronic narrative to evade what the text itself reveals to be structural necessity. Mingling paraphrase and critique, Derrida displays the vision of propriety articu-lated by Rousseau, which is a milder version of the one I have tried to uncover in Whitman's work, as a kind of *Fata Morgana* of the word. He reminds us as well of what this mirage is designed to protect:

the first substantives were not common but proper nouns or names. The abso-lutely literal [*propre*] is at the origin: one sign to one thing, one representer per passion. (*Grammatology* 278–79)

Which supposes that there might be ... something like a unique sign for a unique thing, a supposition contradictory to the very concept and operation of the sign. To determine the first sign in this way, to found or deduce the entire system of signs with reference to a sign which does not belong to that system, is to reduce signification to presence. (*Grammatology* 284)

What the proper name ought to sustain is presence: the pristine integrity of the thing itself, not yet annexed to something else or divided against itself to serve alien purposes. If Derrida suggests here that efforts to justify the primacy of proper names on a systematic or taxonomic basis will always prove awkward, an alternative argument for the perdurance of the unique thing within language thus remains available: any evidence of an organic, intrinsic tie between word and object will suggest that the thing itself can be made present in and by the word. If the effort to ward off expropriation by suggesting that all word use might conform to the model of the proper name remains unconvincing, Whitman thus attempts to ground the vision of the proper as the essence of language in a more radical sort of propriety: the proper name is not only the private property of the object; it is also proper or native to it, emanating from and not just attaching to the creature or thing it names. As Simpson suggests, this vision of the word as proceeding from the thing is a drastic denial of the social provenance and ideological power of language (234–35). Skirting taxonomic difficulties, it cancels the coercive aspect of nomination by making the name a function not of cultural projects but of the natural object itself.

It is of course hard to find more than sporadic and questionable evidence of such organic links between word and thing in actual languages. Here, however, diachronic data—or selective and skewed instances of it—is readily available to the enthusiast. Seeking to sink the word in the thing, Whitman finds some support in discussions of the motivated status of the sign among reputable linguists. But he also draws on the host of less scrupulous speculations these analyses helped spawn. Since this aspect of Whitman's language theory is crucial to the poet's largest claims, it is worth situating his vision of the motivated status of the sign in this historical nexus.

4. Whitman's vision of a language that emanates from things has much in common with the notion of a "language of nature" that enjoyed currency in American transcendentalist circles and their environs. Interest in such a natural language was owing largely to the efforts of American Swedenborgians; the concept is evoked powerfully in the work of Sampson Reed. According to the hermetic tradition Reed expounds, as Philip Gura explains, "at the Creation God had impressed into the fabric of nature a set of correlatives, or symbols, which man, after discovering the creative power of his mind, could read with a new and ever-increasing clarity (84–85)."[60] "There is a language," Reed thus suggested,

not of words, but of things . . . . everything which is, whether animal or vegetable, is full of the expression of that use for which it is designed, as of its own existence. If we did but understand its language, what could our words add to its meaning? (*Growth of the Mind* 46)

This language of nature was a language of truly proper names: "Everything which surrounds us is full of the utterance of one word, completely expressive of its nature. This word is its name . . ." (*Growth of the Mind* 47).

Despite the glancing reference to utterance here, this heterodox tradition devalues the spoken word in favor of the language of gesture, as John Irwin shows in *American Hieroglyphics*. According to Reed the "language of nature" was the language of Eden, and it precluded the need for human speech: "Adam and Eve knew no language but their Garden" ("Oration on Genius" 11).[61] Adam's primary language skill, that is, was knowing how to read the analogical, spiritual significance God had written on or implanted in his creatures; Adam's communication supposedly consisted simply of the ostensive gestures by which he shared his delight in these intrinsic meanings with the equally adept reader Eve.[62] Within this tradition, as Irwin suggests, the birth of human speech constitutes a lapse from the edenic union of Adam with the objects of his garden and of language with the intrinsic spiritual meanings to which gesture had modestly drawn attention: the fall is "a discontinuity whose linguistic equivalent is the substitution of the arbitrary language of spoken words for the prior and necessary language of natural signs" (Irwin 34).

Whitman's notion of organic names clearly owes much to this tradition. We cannot be sure that he read Reed, or that he knew Elizabeth Peabody's translation of the French Swedenborgian Guillaume Oegger's *The True Messiah*, a crucial source for Emerson's "Nature."[63] But Swedenborgianism was much discussed in the circles Whitman frequented; Floyd Stovall takes the poet's acquaintance with its basic tenets for granted (228–29).[64] As Irwin persuasively suggests (29), a prelapsarian "language of things" seems to be what Whitman has in mind in his enigmatic references to "substantial words" in "A Song of the Rolling Earth":

Human bodies are words, myriads of words (1856 322)

Air, soil, water, fire, these are words,
I myself am a word with them [. . . .] (1856 323)

Devoted to recovering such substantial words, the poem at least appears
to share Reed's suspicion of human speech:

> I swear I begin to see little or nothing in audible words!
> I swear I think all merges toward the presentation of the unspoken meanings
>   of the earth! (1856 329)

Yet as Irwin also suggests, Whitman's work combines the notion of a
language of nature with a commitment to voice:

Whitman's attempt to regain the original language of natural signs, his effort to
replace "audible words" with "the presentation of the unspoken meanings of
the earth," involves the paradoxical use of phonetic signs to restore the unspoken
(nonphonetic) language of pictographic ideograms. . . . it is in light of the Romantic concept of song as the transcending of the mediation of spoken language
through spoken language that Whitman's effort to transform the physical into
the metaphysical must be understood. (38)

This notion that voice might recover the language of nature is indeed
central to Whitman's work; but as we shall see it is less paradoxical than
Irwin suggests. First, Whitman's commitment to the hermetic doctrine
of signatures or natural writing, a doctrine the hieroglyphic craze helped
revive, is more ambivalent than Irwin implies. Second, his passionate
espousal of the organic properties of sound and of oral language grows
out of a systematic argument for the expressive powers of the phoneme,
an argument promulgated by both academic and hermetic linguists during the period. Third, the yoking of this notion of expressive orality with
the doctrine of a language of nature is less aberrant than Irwin suggests:
we can discover a similar conjunction in such a central source as Boehme
and find it in Emerson as well.

Detailed by Irwin, Whitman's enthusiasm for Champollion's decoding
of the hieroglyphs is undeniable, as is his interest in the doctrine of
natural signatures with which a hermetic interpretation of hieroglyphic
script comported (20–24). Yet hermetic writing is still writing; as I
argued in chapter 3, Whitman's response to the vision of nature as
emblem book is accordingly ambivalent. His depiction of a hieroglyphic
book of nature is often marked by the sort of impatience that characterizes his reaction to indicative signs: though its emblems are supposedly
motivated rather than arbitrary, even nature's hieroglyphs signify a pres-

ence they do not make manifest. As Whitman depicts it, the natural emblem typically lacks the quality of revelation it possesses in Reed's account, approaching instead, in its opacity, the blankness of the "husk" or indicative surface. We can recall a passage from an early notebook in this regard; it mingles awe with a quotient of frustration:

> And I cannot put my toe anywhere to the ground,
> But it must touch numberless and curious books
> Each one scorning all that schools and science can do fully to translate them.
> (UPP 2:70)

In the comic world of "Song of Myself," the poet sometimes reacts to the signs that resist deciphering with staunch good humor and a resolve to do his level best. He can sound like an odd mix of prophet and grammar schooler:

> And I know I am solid and sound,
> To me the converging objects of the universe perpetually flow,
> All are written to me, and I must get what the writing means. (1855 43)

Yet the absence of direct revelation leaves even the resilient hero of "Song of Myself" confronting a hieroglyphic text whose opacity can be haunting. In section six the poet reads a dark fatality it seems to be his fate to accept rather than overcome:

> A child said, What is the grass? fetching it to me with full hands;
> How could I answer the child? .... I do not know what it is any more
>   than he
> [....]
> Or I guess it is a uniform hieroglyphic,
> And it means, Sprouting alike in broad zones and narrow zones,
> Growing among black folks as among white,
> Kanuck, Tuckahoe, Congressman, Cuff, I give them the same, I receive them
>   the same. (1855 29)

The darkness and wonder discernible here are provoked not only by the death the poet believes he reads in this "uniform hieroglyph," but also by the still elusive meaning of such mortality, the difficult legibility of this natural text.

Sometimes, as in this section of "Song of Myself," the poet attributes the difficulty he encounters in deciphering such natural hieroglyphs to his own incapacities. More characteristically, though, his troubles appear to derive from an intrinsic defect in the text he tries to read. Outside the comic context of "Song of Myself," as I suggested in chapter 3, this deficiency tends to provoke not good-humored patience but a grim resolve to break through the blockage it causes. The poet's generic task is not to read nature's emblems but to burrow through them and reclaim the presences they signify. So in "Song of the Open Road" the "incomprehensible" surfaces of the book of nature are implicitly to be peeled away rather than perused:

> The earth is rude, silent, incomprehensible at first—nature is rude and incomprehensible at first,
> Be not discouraged—keep on—there are divine things, well enveloped
> I swear to you there are divine things more beautiful than words can tell!
> ("Song of the Open Road," 1856 231)

Nature's surfaces are indeed sometimes depicted not as hermetic signs that encrypt sense but instead as non-sense. Such images are a kind of catachresis of the trope of nature as emblem book:

> The great poet submits only to himself. Is nature rude, free, irregular? If nature be so, do you too be so. Do you suppose nature has nothing under those beautiful, terrible, irrational forms? (CW 9:162)

Within the hieroglyphic tradition Whitman modifies, the emblematic surface or signature attests to the object's divine provenance, while our inability to decipher it is the mark of our own fallen nature. For Whitman, by contrast, the emblematic surfaces of objects are unnecessary sources of blockage, and their illegibility is more often attributed to the fallen, divided status of the object than to our incapacities. Writing, even "hieroglyphic" writing, is thus to be cast aside in favor of the actual presence it attests to but does not directly reveal. Rather than being rendered unnecessary by the book of nature, human language—or at least the poet's language—must instead restore the deficiencies of nature's text or by-pass the necessity for reading it. As the recurrent topological trope that intertwines with Whitman's depictions of the book of nature already implies, it is voice that will perform this crucial task. Emanating from inside the creature or object, voice and sound are supposedly direct, unmediated expressions of its animating energies or intrinsic structure; unfallen human language—which is oral language—supposedly repeats such expressive effusions.

It is the poet's task to restore this expressive stratum to words now apparently devoid of an organic tie to the things they name, words whose misuse as mere tokens or designations has obscured this crucial feature. Despite Whitman's ambivalent interest in the notion of hermetic script and the doctrine of signatures, in his work such abuse of the oral resources of the word is epitomized—or perhaps even engendered—by writing.

Whitman's notion that proper human speech reproduces the sounds and hence the essential energies of the creatures and objects it names was characteristically repudiated by the period's professional linguists. But it found a kind of partial support in the widespread, respectable belief in the motivated status of the oral sign. If the heterodox tradition Irwin recapitulates ascribed a natural, organic connection with objects or essences only to such hermetic written signs as the hieroglyph, associating oral language with the fall into arbitrary designation, a contrary but equally visionary tradition thus also persisted in Whitman's time. It enjoyed the advantage of being able to find in the work of professional linguists attenuated versions of a doctrine whose radical implications a properly unfettered understanding might restore.

I suggested earlier that even Humboldt does not subscribe to the notion that the phoneme is purely arbitrary. He is, however, rather circumspect concerning both the nature of the connection between signifier and signified and the proportion of semantic data this tie might account for; as I noted, he also posits a gradual decline of such a motivated tie between the name and the thing it denominates, a shift he remarks without lament. Pure onomatopoeia, traditionally the trump card of theorists wishing to demonstrate the motivated nature of the linguistic sign, is for Humboldt a kind of fictive limit, never wholly realizable in articulate human language; it is in any case, he remarks a bit scornfully, rather crude (*Linguistic Variability* 52).[65] Yet Humboldt accords some role to what he calls "indirect imitation": similar objects supposedly tend to receive names sharing common sounds, and there is, in a number of cases, at least some imitative basis for these shared features (*Linguistic Variability* 52–53). More commonly, however, the designation of a range of related objects by similar-sounding words lacks even such imperfect imitative rationale: the sign is characteristically motivated with respect to the system of signs but not with regard to the thing it denotes (*Linguistic Variability* 53). Moreover, according to Humboldt, even words with some imitative basis modify this feature by incorporating the speaker's emotional response to the thing he names; it is for this reason, among others, that pure vocal imitation does not occur in language (*Linguistic Variability* 35).[66] Yet Humboldt suggests that even the mediated connection between word and object was once sufficiently natural for language to be naturally understood (*Humanist without Portfolio* 249). Such connections between sounds and the impressions that provoked them supposedly still lurk in the roots of our polysyllabic words, though we no longer hear or understand them (*Linguistic Variability* 242–43). While Humboldt notes this loss he is not intent on recouping it; the principal business of language is a cognitive mastery such sensuous immediacy can impede rather than foster.

Similar claims and provisos can be found in both Schele de Vere and Bunsen. Like Humboldt, Schele de Vere posits a motivated connection between sound and meaning, though unlike his predecessor he seems rather enthused by the prospect of retrieving and deciphering such ties: the philologist, he declares

must . . . inquire into the reasons why such forms, and no others, have been chosen to express such ideas. Proceeding from the fundamental truth, that in the working of the divine mind of man, nothing is casual or arbitrary, he must try to trace the correspondence between the outer form and the inner meaning— between word and idea, and thus engage in the doctrine of sounds. (199)

Schele de Vere does not allow this archaeological enthusiasm to obliterate the other crucial limitation Humboldt had placed on the doctrine of the motivated sign. Research into the connection between sound and sense will never restore a direct, unmediated tie between word and thing or recover a language that gives direct expression to the animating energies of the things it names. Interjections and onomatopoeia cannot possibly be, as enthusiasts would have it, the keys to such an original natural language, since they are not language at all: "unarticulated sounds are not words" (21).

Bunsen puts this more forcefully, enlisting an ethnocentric observation alien to the spirit of Humboldt's linguistic relativism to clinch an otherwise broadly Humboldtian point: "no imitation of nature exists in language any more than does expression of sensation. The interjections are no parts of speech, any more than the 'clicks' of the Hottentots (passionate interjections) are articulate sounds" (2:132). Nor can articulate language originate in pure onomatopoeia (2:130). Bunsen thus firmly denies the existence of any direct, expressive tie between name and object. While there is an analogical relation between the phoneme and the way some quality of the object impresses the speaker, the connection between the name and the thing itself is merely indicative:

It is not that the sound is imitated, or the purely animal sensation is *expressed,* but the object is *indicated* by the imitation of a quality by which the mind perceives it. . . . (2:132; emphases added)

Yet in Bunsen as in Schele de Vere, these restrictions set limits to an enthusiastic interest in the motivated status of the phoneme. "Every sound," Bunsen maintains, "must originally have been significative of something," obeying an "inward necessity, not an arbitrary or conventional arrangement" (2:81). The relation between sound and sense, Bunsen believed, inhered in a connection between the emotional response a creature or object provoked in its human witness and the physiological experience of producing different phonemes by activating various portions of the mouth (2:90, 132).

This vision of a motivated connection, however mediated, between meaning and sound possessed an allure speculators on language found hard to resist. Such a borderline figure as Charles Kraitsir, whose work was published and championed by Elizabeth Peabody and influenced a climactic passage of Thoreau's *Walden,* thus combined respect for the mediated status of the tie between word and thing with enthusiastic espousal of a cranky educational program designed to make this connection accessible once more (to young schoolchildren!) and thus retrieve language from the supposedly degenerate condition in which the relation between sound and sense appears merely arbitrary.[67] Positing the same sort of connection between an initiating impression and the physiology of a vocal response as Bunsen describes, Kraitsir is bold enough to hazard a kind of dictionary of phonemes or "germs" and to analyze words not merely into their component signifying syllables but also into these supposed primordial parcels of organic, physiological sense. Of labials, for example, Kraitsir opines:

They betoken the following phenomena and things: the secondary or tertiary, the level or horizontal, the broad, wide, parallel, moving, visible, effected, mealy, superficial, palpable, meeting, mounting, both multum and minus, measure, middle, falling, flowing, fluttering, flattening, flame, blood, etc., in short, things that are liplike. (168)

Kraitsir is adamant about the natural, and therefore invariant, status of such connections: "all *germs* have an inherent, natural, absolute, organic meaning . . ." (209).

This intrinsic meaning, though, has been progressively obscured. New words—for reasons Kraitsir does not quite satisfactorily explain—often violate this natural signifying system:

These elements [germs], though imbued with absolute, organic significance, have been differently used or abused by wordwrights. . . . (171)

More important, careless pronunciation has allowed the tie between sound and sense that inheres in words (or in words not coined by abusive namers) to slip away, since the aural properties of the very germs in which this connection inheres have been perverted by misguided speech habits. Kraitsir does not take this degradation calmly:

Of what importance is the mis-pronunciation which is about 150 years old?— Of what importance are dysharmony, cacophony, falsehood, the cutting off from other nations, and all other evil things connected with, and resulting from, the vulgar practice? (39)

According to Kraitsir the causes of this slippage are intellectual, moral, and aesthetic deficiency or perversity (124). But linguistic degeneration itself gravely exacerbates the defects from which it results:

How should a senseless dislocation of sounds, letters, and ideas remain without baneful consequences to the life of humanity? (79)

The injuries inflicted to the sense of hearing (which amount to a deafness for the elegancies of harmony and melody);—nay—a perversion of the very moral sentiments,—are among the fruits of the customary methods of teaching the *Ai, Bee, See.* (44)

Kraitsir's ire here is directed at the neglect of phonics in the teaching of reading. Unlike such enthusiasts of spelling reform as Noah Webster, however, Kraitsir held out against tampering with English orthography to give each letter a single sound and thus make the written word represent its oral counterpart in straightforward fashion. For the current oral form of the word is itself the target of Kraitsir's reformist energies, and present spelling, which preserves older, more organic pronunciation, is the key to restoring this original propriety. What was needed was therefore a complex instructional system in which children would first be taught the "proper" sounds of the phonemes together with the graphic representations which still possess an invariant, commutable relation to these original, authentic phonemic values; pupils would thereby simultaneously be taught to read phonetically and to pronounce English words "correctly." Only then would they be reminded of the current pronunciation of the word they had just been taught to read and properly pronounce; both the gap between correct and incorrect pronunciations and the distortion of orthographic (and etymological) good sense required to twist the written word into its current oral embodiment would presumably engender intense abhorrence and inspire the young student with ardor for reform—of pronunciation rather than spelling (59–60). Kraitsir's whole account is itself marked by the sort of zeal a vision of the motivated status of the sign tends to provoke—an enthusiasm fostered by the surmises of figures like Humboldt despite the provisos with which academic linguists took care to surround them.

While Kraitsir thus espoused reform designed to restore indirect motivation to the sign, he respected the line drawn by academic philologists between articulate human language and pure imitative effusion. Benjamin Taylor, a less influential but still symptomatic American enthusiast, reversed this pattern of restraint and indulgence. Having little to say about linguistic rehabilitation, Taylor's odd *Attractions of Language, or a Popular View of Natural Language, in all its Varied Displays, in the Animate and Inanimate World; and as Corresponding with Instinct, Intelligence and Reason* blurs the boundary between the expressive, natural cry and articulate, conventional human speech. Taylor is not so bold as to erase it entirely:

These voice or vowel sounds, are the fluid *material* of all artificial language, which would naturally flow on, in a current of continuous sound, did not the skill of man, form, limit and distinguish it. On the other hand, the mouth-sounds or consonants compose all that is strictly *artificial* in spoken language; here the superiority of our race is clearly seen. (183)

Despite the enthusiasm for artifice expressed here, a predominant thrust of Taylor's book is the attempt to deny that the introduction of convention marked by consonantal interruptions of vocalic flow constitutes an exile of articulate human language from the domain of natural, expressive sound. The difference between these two realms is said to be one of degree rather than kind:

between natural and artificial language, there is no intermediate chasm, or
bridgeless gulf to be o'erleaped; but the transition is easy, and the connection
indissoluble. (182; quoted in Simpson 239)

Interjections are accordingly rehabilitated; regarded as part of the lan-
guage-system proper, they suggest the possibility of sustaining natural
expressivity within codified speech. Since the interjection is

the expression of emotion, rather than of thought, if we continue to give it a
name and a place in artificial language, it must be as the *link* that binds the two
great divisions together. (183)[68]

Onomatopoeia is also resuscitated:

The waterfall, is suggested to him, and a sound involuntarily escapes his lips; it
may be *dash* or *roar*, but whatever it is, it is an *imitation*, and by the assistance
of gesture, is understood by his companion. (175)

The passage from such expressive imitation to articulate naming is presented with no hint of rupture: "That sound became a word, and that
word a name . . ." (179).

Lurking behind the enthusiasms of Kraitsir and Taylor, as a kind of
ideal limit at which they might converge, is the notion of adamic language or the language of nature. If language at its origin was directly
imitative, as Taylor suggests, and if the sounds made by nature's creatures are as expressive of their natures as human phonemes, according
to Kraitsir, are of human responses, then there must have been a primordial language in which the essential energies of all nature's creatures
were directly repeated by human speech. This primordial language ought
to be recoverable. The language of nature, that is to say, might have
been oral, and attention to euphony might restore it.

This notion of a spoken language of nature is at odds with the particular
hermetic lineage Irwin traces. Oegger's *The True Messiah*, for example,
is quite explicit in connecting oral language with the fall. The language
of nature, Oegger insists, is "quite distinct of that which consists in
sounds which are articulated by means of the elasticity of the air, and
which have merely a conventional meaning" (84). But such a crucial
seventeenth-century source for the tradition of a language of nature as

Jacob Boehme engages in painstaking analyses of biblical passages along lines very much like Kraitsir's. Less circumspect than Kraitsir, in fact, Boehme glosses the word of God rather than the word of man and thus claims to fathom the essence of created things and divine acts rather than the essential principles of the human reaction to them. According to Boehme the sensations that occur in the mouth when we pronounce God's word aloud are a kind of vocal emblem of the hermetic meaning of the divine acts those words represent. Glossing "In the beginning created GOD heaven and earth," for example, Boehme remarks of "created" (Schuff):

For the teeth *retain* the word, letting the spirit go forth *leisurely* between the teeth. This signifieth that the astringent quality holdeth the earth and stones *firmly* and fast together; and yet, for all that, *letteth* the spirits of the earth spring up, grow and bear blossoms out of the astringent spirit; which signifieth the *regeneration or restitution of the spirits of the earth*. (*Aurora* 466)

God's other book is likewise a talking one. Like the biblical word, all animal nature reveals its essential properties in its sounds:

Therefore the greatest understanding lies in the signature, wherein man . . . may not only learn to know himself, but therein also he may learn to know the essence of all essences; for by the external form of all creatures, by their instigation, inclination and desire, also by their sound, voice, and speech which they utter, the hidden spirit is known; for nature has given to everything its language according to its essence and form, for out of the essence the language or sound arises, and the fiat of that essence forms the quality of the essence in the voice or virtue which it sends forth, to the animals in the sound, and to the essentials [vegetables] in smell, virtue, and form. (*Signature of All Things* 12)

In the animal kingdom it is sound that reveals essence. This expressive quality can persist in the sounds of human language:

if the spirit opens to him the *signature,* then he understands the speech of another; and further, he understands how the spirit has manifested and revealed itself (out of the essence through the principle) in the sound with the voice.

. . . for with the sound or speech the form notes and imprints itself into the similitude of another; a like tone or sound catches and moves another, and in the sound the spirit imprints its own similitude, which it has conceived in the essence, and brought to form in the principle.

. . . and with this signature he enters into another man's form, and awakens also in the other such a form in the signature; so that both forms mutually assimilate [*sic*] together in one form, and then there is one comprehension, one will, one spirit, and also one understanding. (*Signature of All Things* 9–10)

Articulate human speech thus shares the expressiveness of God's two speaking books. Moreover, as the positing here of a human power of auditory "comprehension" or "understanding" that results in the merging of speaker and hearer already implies, unlike animal sound human language—at least in its prelapsarian state—can capture and repeat the essences of others as well as expressing the speaker's own. Thus in Boehme's account Adam's language is characteristically conceived as oral rather than gestural; in this tradition the sounds of the names he bestows, like the phonemes of the divine word, convey the essences of what they name:

For as Adam spoke for the first time, he gave names to all the creatures according to their qualities and inherent effects. And it is truly the language of all nature, but not every many knows it, for it is a secret, a mystery.... (quoted in Aarsleff 60).[69]

This tradition lies behind crucial passages in Emerson's "The Poet," an early version of which Whitman heard Emerson deliver in New York in 1842 (Kaplan 101):

Like the metamorphosis of things into higher organic forms, is their change into melodies. Over everything stands its daemon, or soul, and, as the form of the thing is reflected by the eye, so the soul of the thing is reflected by a melody. The sea, the mountain-ridge, Niagara, and every flower-bed, pre-exist, or super-exist, in pre-cantations, which sail like odors in the air, and when any man goes by with an ear sufficiently fine, he overhears them, and endeavors to write down the notes, without diluting or depraving them. (*Collected Works* 3:15)

As is typical of Emerson's fables, the end of this passage has an equivocal import: its story of slippage is one we might well choose to read as a parable of structural necessity rather than as a straightforward account of a contingency which careful attention might evade. In Whitman's theory, by contrast, such dilution is indeed a depravity, and it ought to be avoidable. Emerson's casual association here of such slippage with writing becomes a crucial tenet for Whitman, as does the need to steer clear of this (supposedly contingent) practice and the linguistic debility it triggers. Conversely, Whitman insists on the power of the extraordinary voice to restore the natural sounds locked up in the mute words of books or lost because of the sort of disregard for euphony

Kraitsir excoriates. More systematically committed to the notion of expressive sound than to the doctrine of a silent language of nature from which speech would mark a fall, Whitman asserts that sound reveals the essential natures of the things from which it emanates. Like Benjamin Taylor or the Emerson of "The Poet" (but less circumspectly), he argues for a continuity between such expressive effusions and articulate human speech. Like Kraitsir, he champions a program of educational reform that supposedly will restore our aural tact and our vocal capacities, permitting us to re-activate the expressive strata now dormant in words. Yet while this reform is to be generally disseminated throughout America's schools, its ultimate object will be realized only by the poet himself: the expressive potential of the adamic word will be recovered by the pneumatic powers of a body that has kept aloof from the related linguistic and cultural disasters for which writing is made to stand.

5. Whitman's most sustained poetic treatment of linguistic issues, the enigmatic "A Song of the Rolling Earth," promulgates this vision of an oral language of nature. This is so despite both the poem's suspicion of the "audible words" of ordinary human speech and its occasional equation of "substantial words" with physical things themselves, a conflation which evokes the hermetic doctrine of signatures espoused by Oegger or Reed. Various lines in the poem display these latter tendencies:

> Human bodies are words, myriads of words
> [. . . .]
> Air, soil, water, fire, these are words
> [. . . .]
> Syllables are not the earth's words,
> Beauty, reality, manhood, time, life—the realities of such as these are the earth's words. (1856 322–23)[70]

Both the association of substantial words with the divine writing of the book of nature evident here and the attendant dismissal of oral language, however, sit side by side in the poem with more extensive evocations of an elusive natural speech. What in Reed is an aberrant image of voice at odds with the dominant doctrine of God's eloquent silence—"Everything which surrounds us is full of the *utterance* of one word, completely expressive of its nature" (*Growth of the Mind* 47; emphasis added)— becomes the central organizing trope in Whitman's vision of a language of nature.

This connection between voice and natural language is presaged early in the poem by a pair of lines that overtly deal with the provenance of "substantial words" rather than their mode:

> the substantial words are in the ground and sea,
> They are in the air—they are in you. (1856 322)

The topological motif adduced here, which modifies the simple identification of physical objects and substantial words elsewhere in the poem, associates such words with depths rather than surfaces. A later passage goes on to suggest the connection, pervasive in Whitman's work, between such interior spaces and the sounds that emanate from them:

> The earth does not exhibit itself nor refuse to exhibit itself—possesses still *underneath*,
> *Underneath* the ostensible sounds, the august chorus of heroes, the wail of slaves,
> Persuasions of lovers, curses, gasps of the dying, laughter of young people, accents of bargainers,
> *Underneath* these possessing the words that never fail. (1856 325; emphases added)

The first of these lines sustains Whitman's topological motif, its opening paradox issuing into a contrast between surfaces and something "underneath" them that by the passage's end turns out to be "words." This sequestering accords with hermetic doctrine, as does the implication that such words will "exhibit" themselves only to a special sort of discernment. But this discernment turns out to be aural rather than visual: the initial topological distinction gives way in the passage's succeeding lines to a contrast concerning sound rather than sight, an opposition between "ostensible sounds" and the words "underneath" them. Whitman's phrasing here seems to point not to the sort of difference between sound and silence Irwin's tracing of hermetic tradition might lead us to expect, but to a distinction between sounds that are "ostensible" and those that are not. "Underneath" thus bears an acoustic sense compatible with its topological one: the sounds being made within visible forms are also too faint to be heard by those not specially trained to listen for them; yet to the practiced ear they can be heard "underneath the ostensible sounds." As in the tradition articulated by Reed, each of these substantial words is a kind of living synecdoche of the thing itself, the distillation of its unique essence. But in Whitman's redaction the substantial word captures this essence by condensing the living creature's diffuse vocalic activity, crystallizing the supposedly primordial, indissoluble link between oral effusion and organic energy into a discrete and bounded vocal signature. While even Boehme had prudently restricted the domain of such vocal signatures to the animal kingdom, associating the signatures of vegetables and minerals with their silent substantial forms instead, Whitman enthusiastically extends the notion of vocal substantial words to all of nature. As we saw in chapter 3, his cosmology figures the productive force of *natura naturans* as a voice; "A Song of the Rolling Earth" seems likewise to endow all *natura naturata*, whether animate or inanimate, with its signature sound.[71]

Whitman's most detailed evocations of the vocal effusions such substantial words supposedly recoup are those which depict the sounds made by the poet himself. The most memorable of these passages is one we looked at in chapter 4, the poet's apostrophe to his soul in section five of "Song of Myself":

> Loafe with me on the grass. . . . loose the stop from your throat,
> Not words, not music or rhyme I want. . . . not custom or lecture, not even
>   the best
> Only the lull I like, the hum of your valved voice. (1855 28)

Steering clear not only of discursive activity and designation but even of the division of vocal performance into discrete words, this voice emits a continuous stream of sound unmarked by the articulations that establish recognizable units of sense only by sacrificing organic expressiveness. Expending itself in the present without reserve, this effusion seems indistinguishable from the animating energies that shape the body from which it emerges: it is the body as breath and the breath become vocal, the *pneuma* as the origin of language in pure, unmediated expression.

Yet what makes this lull or hum the purveyor of presence, the perfect expression of the organic energies of the creature from which it proceeds, also marks the poet's *neume* as not yet being language.[72] Lacking articulation, this continuous flow of sound will not be repeatable except in some ideal total repetition: having no boundaries or units, it cannot be called back except in its entirety. Like the notion of the properly proper name, the vision of a speech originating in a pure expressive stream of sound is thus in danger of foundering on the problem of iterability central to language; the word must be transposable and repeatable in order to be a word. This requirement seems to undermine the possibility of an unmediated, expressive relation between the signifier and the individual creature or occasion; it threatens to exclude from language all that is unique and organic, occulting expression with indication and subduing the proper to the category. It is not clear how vocal effusions might be crystallized into iterable "substantial words" without losing their unmediated relation to process and presence.

As we saw already by watching Benjamin Taylor struggle to deny its import, this gap between vocal effusions and the bounded, repeatable units created by consonantal articulation marked, for the linguistics of Whitman's day as for that of our own, the split between nature and culture, between natural animal sound and conventional human language. Seeking like Taylor and others with adamist leanings to elide this rift and its significance, Whitman employs the effective (if suspect) tactic of displacement: he makes the shift from one register to the other occur within nature itself and thus diffuses its import. Into the gap between expressive vocal streams and those actual names which designate a creature but fail to express its animating energy, he inserts the substantial words of the earth—now inaudible vocal signatures that compress expressive effusions into single, repeatable words. Appearing in nature, such articulate sound would still be natural; according to our common and sometimes barely conscious mythologies, it would thus still be directly expressive, not yet instituting the mediations we associate with culture.

This doctrine of natural articulation also implies that the expressive language of nature might still be ours. If the language of nature already consists of bounded, iterable words, then the difference between natural sound and human speech is no longer structural; it thus ought to be merely contingent. An elliptical passage in the opening section of "A Song of the Rolling Earth" accordingly attributes to "the masters" the power to translate the earth's substantial words. Here Whitman declines to specify the procedures such masters employ, instead offering a gnomic formulation that approaches catachresis:

> The workmanship of souls is by the inaudible words of the earth,
> The great masters, the sayers, know the earth's words, and use them more
>   than the audible words. (1856 323)

But a passage further on that attributes such powers of translation to the poet himself begins to unpack this paradox of a human language that employs (initially) "inaudible words":

> This is a poem for the sayers of the earth—these are hints of meanings,
> These are they that echo the tones of souls, and the phrases of souls;
> If they did not echo the phrases of souls, what were they then? (1856 330)

Here the "echo" which is the poet's speech seems to be a crucial increment rather than a mere copy or attenuation: apparently amplifying what we can think of a bit crudely as the decibel level of the hitherto "inaudible" "tones of souls," it not only adds expressive names to the vocabulary of an otherwise indicative human language but at the same time liberates creatures and objects from the entrapment to which the faintness of their own vocal efforts would otherwise consign them. Whitman's vision of language makes much of the topology that figures expressive sounds as lurking "underneath" impassive exteriors, lacking the volume to emerge, and of the salvific role thus accorded the human speech able to recover and amplify these vocal productions.

Positing such a promethean role for the "masters," Whitman elsewhere seeks to enlarge the realm of such expressive naming, extending it to the sphere of actual languages. Or almost actual: Whitman accomplishes this expansion by making selective use of the diachronic data of comparative philology to support what detailed synchronic analysis would suggest are untenable assertions. Striving to suggest that perfectly expressive words of the sort "the masters" supposedly employ can be discovered among the mass of merely indicative words that make up current languages, he enlists philological arguments concerning the decreasing motivation of the sign to justify apocalyptic claims about the speech of the "red aborigines," whose rich, supposedly onomatopoetic words still designated many of the place names in Whitman's America.[73] In Whitman's account, not much else of these aboriginal languages remains: their syntactic rules and discursive practices drop conveniently from view, leaving only those tantalizing, apparently primitive proper names. Whitman advocates recovering and using as many of these as possible, hoping thereby to make available to American English the powers of a nearly vanished speech which consisted entirely, it might well have seemed, of organic, expressive signs. In "Starting from Paumanok," Whitman indeed effectively claims that the onomatopoetic words of Indian languages do not merely imitate or approximate, but perfectly repeat natural sounds, directly presenting the essential animating energies such sounds supposedly purvey. Like the "substantial words" of the earth, which they apparently duplicate, these names would thus crystallize each unique individual presence into a single expressive word:

> The red aborigines!
> Leaving natural breaths, sounds of rain and winds, calls as of birds and animals in the woods, syllabled to us for names,
> Okonee, Koosa, Ottowa, Monongahela, Sauk, Natchez, Chattahoochee, Kaqueta, Oronoco.
> Wabash, Miami, Saginaw, Chippewa, Oshkosh, Walla-Walla,
> Leaving such to The States, they melt, they depart, charging the water and the land with names. (1860 20)

Here the troubling gap between pure expressive effusions and articulate, iterable words is supposedly bridged within human language rather than in the sacrosanct realm of nature; but it is once more crossed in remote territory exempt from close scrutiny. Without absolutely effacing it, Whitman is thus free to preserve the distinction between natural sound and codified human language even more tenuously than Taylor had. It is registered only in a single word in the second of these lines, which marks a slight breach between the perfect repetition of expressive sounds and mere imitative approximation: "calls *as* of birds and animals." This very line opens with a less circumspect formulation: "Leaving natural breaths, sounds *of* rain and winds." In keeping with this euphoric opening rather than with the momentary qualification that follows it, the phrase that ends Whitman's line registers the crucial transposition such perfect repetition has supposedly accomplished: now "syllabled to us for names," natural sounds have become miraculously iterable; Indian languages can apparently graft consonantal articulation to vocal effusion without expressive loss, making the energies and essences of all things available for human speech and human use.[74]

This vision of an articulate speech able to translate expressive sounds without slippage seems to accomplish what Whitman's taxonomic struggle with proper and class names could only awkwardly suggest: the organic words of such a tongue would ground language in the proper, directly presenting the unique creature and its intrinsic qualities. They would thus make categorization and the discourse that mobilizes it unnecessary, liberating us from their coercions. This bracing corollary of Whitman's vision of organic naming is adduced in a passage from the *Primer* whose implications for semantic theory are rather staggering:

Names are a test of the esthetic and of spirituality [. . . .] A delicate [. . .] subtle something there is in the right name—an undemonstrable nourishment that ~~soothes a~~ exhilirates [*sic*] ~~and nurishes~~ [*sic*] the soul [. . . .] Masses of men, unaware what they smoothly [?] [. . .] like, lazily inquire what difference there is between one name [. . .] and another.—But the few fine ears of the world decide for them also and recognize them [. . . .]

~~As~~ All that immense volumes, and more than volumes, can tell, are conveyed in the right name. (DBN 3:756)[75]

Despite Whitman's reference to "fine ears," the difference he insists on between "right names" and the shoddy alternatives accepted by "masses of men" involves more than simple mellifluousness. "Right names" supposedly convey, in a single expressive word, all that "immense volumes" can "tell." Here Whitman's axial opposition between truly proper names and the coercive categories foisted on things by class names and manipulated in predication and judgment assumes its most radical form. Discourse and the aggressions it mobilizes are supposedly rendered unnecessary by the organic name, which expresses the essence of the object, out of which all its proper attributes will flower: "<u>All lies folded in names,</u>" Whitman suggests elsewhere in the *Primer* (DBN 3:755). "Right names" supposedly contain in their very phonemes the entire manifold of predicates that (properly) pertain to the creature or object.[76] Whatever discourse adds to this plenitude it adds nefariously; injecting foreign attributes into a harmonious and self-sustaining structure, it disrupts what would otherwise be a proper organic unfolding.

As I argued above, however, Whitman is interested not in promulgating precise linguistic distinctions—whether synchronic or diachronic—but in sustaining the capacities all language ought to possess: he is less concerned to isolate the supposed powers of some limited segment of language than to extend their domain, suggesting that the resources manifest in one place are latent elsewhere. He accordingly discovers the expressive powers exemplified by American Indian place names lurking within words less conspicuously onomatopoetic. The poet, after all, should be able to deploy expressive language without having to confine his speech to a few exotic place names.

When it comes to the mass of American English, however, the distinction between indicative and expressive language characteristically no longer corresponds to a difference between one kind of word and another. It typically depends instead on the way any given word is employed. A single word can fall from expression to indication if it is used improperly; conversely, its expressive resources can be restored by a speaker properly attentive and appropriately endowed. This modification seems dictated in part by the demands of credibility. Whitman needs to maintain the force of a distinction that becomes increasingly tenuous the more it is extended: perusal of a dictionary, for example, would hardly yield obvious principles for detaching the vocabulary of an expressive English language from an indicative one. Perhaps more important, though, is the fact that this altered criterion not only extends the domain of organic language but simultaneously restricts it. Or more precisely: the focus on proper use extends the range of organic vocabulary while limiting the roster of those able to activate it. Whitman thus preserves the axial distinction between the poet's liberating speech and the mass of social language whose oppressive effects his word is to undo.

6. In Whitman's language theory this distinction between the abusive and redemptive use of words is mapped onto a contrast between writing and voice. If the rightness of "right names" derives from their origin in natural sounds, Whitman's paradigm for the loss of expressive resources is the passage from sound to silence; writing becomes the crucial instance of a repetition that denatures what it repeats. This association obeys a logic with which we are by now familiar: what is patently true of writing ought not to apply to its apparent opposite, speech. Like other features of Whitman's language theory, this focus on the harmful effects of written repetition serves to displace the difficulties associated with the sign's iterability from the realm of structural necessity to that of supposedly contingent practice. The gap between continuous vocalic effusions

and the articulated sounds that are repeatable only because they inter-
rupt this flow and subject it to codification, generating the word by
sacrificing expressive immediacy, is elided by drawing attention instead
to a parallel but supposedly avoidable rift: silencing voice, writing severs
the word from its apparent fusion with living presence. If written repetition is thus responsible for depriving language of its organic resources,
voice should be able to repeat words without such slippage; according
to Whitman voice can indeed reverse the emasculation of the word
writing exacts.

If the poet of "A Song of the Rolling Earth" claims to be able to
deploy the earth's "substantial words" or "echo the tones of souls," he
thus makes perfectly clear that writing cannot effect this expressive
repetition:

> The truths of the earth continually wait, they are not so concealed either,
> They are calm, subtle, untransmissible by print. ("A Song of the Rolling
>   Earth," 1856 324)

Silent itself, writing epitomizes the carelessness for expressive sound that
also supposedly characterizes the use of words for discursive purposes;
in "A Song of the Rolling Earth" the impossibility of transmitting the
earth's words in writing thus parallels the poet's inability to "tell the
best."

In the *Primer*, Whitman associates writing not only with the fall into
discourse and designation but also with the nefarious work of classification. Whitman indeed figures writing as something like classification
squared: if classification occludes things by imposing categories generated by the language system upon them, writing occults objects altogether, since those mesmerized by this practice supposedly devote their
energies to codifying words themselves. Obsessive concern for orthography thus comes to figure the self-enclosed quality of a language detached
from its source in expressive natural sounds and employed to sustain a
social, symbolic order that is itself a product of such emasculated discourse and the classifications it generates. Whitman associates this mania
for the law of the letter, which kills the spirit of living speech, with
morbidity and impotence:

> The spelling of words is subordinate.—To Great Excessive nicety Morbidness
> about for nice spelling, me and tenacity for or against some one letter or so,
> means dandyism and impotence in literature. (DBN 3:740)

Whitman's closing trope here suggests the loss of performative force that supposedly accompanies such self-enclosed attentions. In the *Primer* the activity of writing comes to epitomize not only the squandering of proper power but also the impossibility of restoring it by means of reforms that fail to attend to the expressive sounds in which the word's authentic resources inhere:

But it is no small thing, ~~nor easy~~; ~~not a~~ no quick growth; ~~It is~~ not a ~~mere~~ matter of rubbing out one word and ~~of~~ writing another.—~~The~~ Real names ~~do not~~ never come so easily. (DBN 3:755)

The substitution of one written word for another will always be unavailing, since the new term, like the old, has been fashioned with the same lack of regard for oral values that disqualified its predecessor. Suggesting nervous correction rather than adamic inspiration, Whitman's image (and graphic practice!) here seems to make writing responsible for turning language into a palimpsest. Writing would thus itself be the disaster it anxiously tries to cure, the catastrophe it initiates being precisely that of substitution: the replacement of one particular written word for another cannot reverse but instead merely repeats an initial, disabling exchange of silence for sound, indicative writing for expressive voicing. All writing substitutes for a voice supposedly fused with living presence, a voice whose expressive powers it cannot convey.

Writing is thus the impotent circulation of castrated words. Not only misguided attempts at linguistic reform but also the characteristic diction of books supposedly reflects this crucial debility. Even Whitman's "practical" remarks concerning the differences between oral and written language thus contribute to mapping the split between organic expression and sterile artifice onto the distinction between speech and writing:

Books themselves have their peculiar words—~~all words,~~ namely those that are never used ~~except in books~~ in living speech, in the real world, but only used in the worlds of books.—Nobody ever actually talks as books and plays talk. (DBN 3:735)

The relatively moderate tone of this pronouncement, oddly enough, is perhaps a function of the very absoluteness of the contrast Whitman here claims to bemoan; the exaggerated distinction between spoken and written diction serves to circumscribe writing and its damaging effects. What most troubles Whitman is not the separation of one sort of language from another but their interpenetration. Writing is dangerous not because it establishes a distinct sphere of impotent language but because it tends to prey upon and emasculate speech: while writing can never restore authenticity to words, it can drain their proper powers from them.

The loss of connection to the living and the organic precipitated by writing is thus more threatening when it befalls the otherwise healthy word subjected to the pen and committed to paper, enervating its expressive resources and reducing it to designation. Scornful though he may be of those who propose orthographic reforms, Whitman accordingly inveighs to Traubel against "the damnable practice" of bad penmanship and the "infamous yawning gulf" it creates (WWC 4:303). This condemnation of a particular kind of writing seems peculiar, given Whitman's characteristic blanket rejection of the mode itself: here he tries in effect to insure writing itself against the disaster for which he has made it the paradigmatic cause, or at least to arrest the falling away from presence and power it occasions. If there is a note of horror in Whitman's phrasing that feels hyperbolic, it may thus register a worry which the reformist concerns announced here displace. What presents itself as an exaggerated fear about the possible slippage of designation to which illegible scrawls can lead, that is, might be understood as the indirect expression of anxiety about a more fundamental and less eradicable threat: what characteristically worries Whitman about writing is not the practical fear over the blotting of a particular designation, but the fall into designation itself, a debacle all writing precipitates. Whitman's vehemence may thus register a sense that the attempt to minimize the linguistic damage writing does by monitoring writing itself is inherently futile. It seems also to reflect uneasiness over his own involvement with this mode—an involvement that should have been avoidable, though the harm writing inflicts is not.

If the Camden transactions sometimes reveal Whitman's uneasy immersion in writing and in the liabilities for which it stands, the language theory of the 1850s adamantly associates the poet with the powers of voice. These powers include the ability to repair the loss of expressiveness which the word subjected to writing suffers. Speaking not only Indian place names but also the degraded, apparently merely indicative words in common circulation, the poet and others like him re-activate the expressive potentials of language, conjuring up the vocal streams which words originally crystallized and resurrecting the living energies such effusions convey.

Not just any voice, though, can retrieve words from the slide into designation writing precipitates. This task can be accomplished only by a speaker endowed with superb vocal equipment, an endowment of course epitomized by the gargantuan pneumatic prowess of the poet of *Leaves of Grass*. Possessors of "superb vocalism" (DBN 3:752) are said to animate words much as Whitman's poet-hero animates the living creatures into whom he infuses his transfiguring breath; they breathe into names, reactivating the expressive powers of the original vocal performance of which each name is a residue:

The ~~heart~~ subtle charm of beautiful pronunciation is not in dictionaries, grammars, marks of accent, ~~or any~~ formulas of a language or ~~any thing in the~~ any laws or rules.—The ~~heart~~ charm of ~~all~~ the beautiful pronunciation of all words, of all tongues, is ~~a~~ in perfect, flexible vocal organs, ~~flexible~~ and in a developed harmonious soul [. . . .] All words, spoken ~~by~~ from these, have ~~superb~~ deeper sweeter sounds, new meanings, impossible on any less terms.—Such meanings, such sounds, continually wait in ~~all words,~~ every word that exists—in these words,—perhaps slumbering, ~~not worked~~ through years, ~~perhaps~~ closed from all ~~easy,~~ tympans of temples, ~~and~~ lips, brains, until ~~the that of~~ that comes which has ~~that~~ the quality ~~of that none wa~~ waiting patiently ~~in~~ in ~~that~~ the words.—~~and seem~~ [?] ~~never to die.~~—(*The Primer of Words*, DBN 3:745)[77]

The semantic doctrine toward which Whitman works his way here, in which the intonational resources of the superb vocalist supposedly make possible the creation of "new meanings," and in which meaning itself is equated with "sound," is rather stunning; but it derives from the theory of organic names in which it is embedded. As the passage makes clear, the well-endowed voice does not so much invent unprecedented meanings as re-activate senses "slumbering" in the words themselves, expressive strata lurking in the sounds once uttered by particular creatures and captured in the onomatopoetic words coined by inspired aboriginal namers. These expressive resources fall dormant once the word passes over into designation, a disaster this passage once more associates with writing—even a writing which tries to offer cues for speech ("not in dictionaries, grammars, *marks of accent*") or the writing of the poet's own text ("Such meanings, such sounds, continually wait in [. . .] every word that exists—in these words,—perhaps slumbering [. . .] through

years"). Language thus supposedly depends for its health on the resources of individual utterance, which can free words from that impov-
erished condition in which mere designation has replaced expressive
mastery.

Whitman sometimes associates such liberating "vocalism" with the
sort of demotic, centrifugal energies he regards as one important source
of linguistic renovation. In his chauvinistic mode, he can go so far as to
prophesy the general diffusion of such vocal powers throughout the
American populace:

The Americans are going to be the most fluent and melodious voiced people in
the world—and the most perfect users of words. (*The Primer of Words,* DBN
3:732)

He can also urge adoption of educational reforms supposedly able to
bring about this dissemination, though his recommendations share the
awkwardness that typifies his attempts to implement a visionary prospect through a practical program:

What vocalism most needs in these States, not only in the few choicer words and
phrases, but in our whole talk, is ease, sonorous strength, breadth, and openness.
Boys and girls should practice daily in free, loud reading—in the open air, if
possible [. . . .] let your organ swell loudly without screaming—don't specify
each syllable or word, but let them flow—feel the sentiment of what you read
or say, and follow where it leads. ("America's Mightiest Inheritance" 60)[78]

It is not simply the ungainliness of such reformist schemes, however,
that limits Whitman's enthusiasm for spreading "superb vocalism"
throughout the land. The probably unintentional hint of phallic power
in the preceding passage ("let your organ swell") registers an attribute
of voice that is elsewhere explicit doctrine: words invigorated by voice
are procreative. It is not only schoolchildren whose access to this spermatic power might provoke misgivings. Whitman is ultimately more
concerned to circumscribe than to diffuse the resources with which voice
is invested in his work.

The phallic power of voice, and the anxiety occasioned by the prospect of others wielding it, are both conveyed by an agitated passage from
"Song of Myself." There the always unstable "soldering" of active-
passive poles onto masculine and feminine positions is particularly fluid,[79]
a lability provoked not only by Whitman's own conspicuously malleable
erotic identifications but also by the circumstance that in this scene the

phallic position is invested in voice and can thus assume especially protean embodiment:

> A tenor large and fresh as the creation fills me,
> The orbic flex of his mouth is pouring and filling me full.
>
> I hear the trained soprano .... she convulses me like the climax of my love-
>   grip;
> The orchestra whirls me wider than Uranus flies,
> It wrenches unnamable ardors from my breast,
> It throbs me to gulps of the furthest down horror,
> It sails me .... I dab with bare feet .... they are licked by the indolent
>   waves,
> I am exposed .... cut by bitter and poisoned hail,
> Steeped amid honeyed morphine .... my windpipe squeezed in the fakes of
>   death. (1855 52)

Here occupying the passive rather than the active, phallic position the poems customarily reserve for him, the poet is penetrated by voice, which "wrenches unnamable ardors" from him, disposing him "wider than Uranus flies." In this final erotic pun, an embedded pronominal adjective tentatively stabilizes the scary slide from active to passive, briefly suggesting a scene in which someone else assumes the passive role and the poet himself, perhaps, momentarily takes up the position of phallic power. It is not insignificant that this oblique re-assertion of mastery depends on an apostrophe coded into the passage by Whitman's word play, a speech act the poet performs. For if the "ardors" the otherwise passive protagonist experiences remain "unnamable," this blockage is occasioned by his loss of use of the very organ speech acts require, an organ which in this passage others employ to invade him: "my windpipe squeezed in the fakes of death." The dangerous (if attractive) passivity figured here is the passivity of being "voiced"; it is an uncharacteristic position the poet of *Leaves of Grass* does not choose to experience too often.[80]

Whitman's language theory is designed to make the recurrence of such an event unlikely. The powers of voice with which Whitman sometimes aspires to endow the general populace are more typically restricted to the exceptional few:

What beauty there is in words! What a lurking curious charm in the sound of some words!— Two or three Then voices! Five or six times in a lifetime, (perhaps not so often,) voices you have heard such from men and women speak in such

~~towering~~ such ~~perfect~~ voices, as they spoke the most common word! (*The Primer of Words*, DBN 3:732–33)

It is indeed characteristically the poet rather than others who can be found exercising his pneumatic powers by performing the sorts of echo-lalic effusions he has recommended to America's schoolchildren:

I amuse myself by exercising my voice in recitations, and in ringing the changes on all the vocal and alphabetical sounds. (*Specimen Days*, PW 1:158)[81]

Like his fantasized ephebes, the poet works here at blurring the codified articulations that purchase indicative precision at the cost of expressive impoverishment. In the context of the late prose piece *Specimen Days*, such vocalizing is regarded as a pleasant pastime or, at most, a regimen for health. But in Whitman's earlier work, while apprentices blur pho-nemes and syllables to improve their own equipment, the poet and his occasional peers bring their already perfected prowess to bear on words in order to transfigure language itself. Exempt from the rules that emas-culate voice and inhibit attempts to recapture its expressive powers, they are linguistic over-men:

Language must cohure [*sic*]—it cannot be left loosely to float [. . .] to fly away. —Yet all the ~~laws~~ rules of the accents and inflections of words drop before a perfect voice—~~it~~ that may follow the rules, or be ignorant of them—it is indifferent which. (*The Primer of Words*, DBN 3:738–39)

It is on such heroic figures that Whitman's language theory ultimately depends. We need to investigate the source of their remarkable powers.

7. As we might by now expect, the capacity to transfigure language does not come with practice alone; performing vocal trills in the open air turns out to be a necessary but hardly sufficient part of the vocalist's regimen. Whitman's additional requisites for linguistic mastery, which are arduous indeed, obey a double necessity with which we are also familiar: validating the supposed ability of individual speakers to redeem the word by positing an unshakable foundation for their powers, these taxing requirements simultaneously restrict to a chosen few the ability to exercise the authentic performative force of language.

In the *Primer* Whitman thus supplements the program of vocal gym-nastics sketched above with some vehement stipulations regarding the safeguarding of the vocalist's body. We are thereby reminded that voice and the organic language it supposedly recovers ward off disasters that are not only linguistic; efforts to insure linguistic, vocal, and bodily purity and propriety intertwine regularly in Whitman's work. But the *Primer* gives this pervasive connection the more particular form of a cause-and-effect relation, making vocal prowess depend on the possession of a proper body. Voice can restore organic expressiveness to words only if voice itself remains a natural, unpolluted organ, a status it can retain only if it is lodged in an organism equally natural and pure. The redeemer who would reclaim the expressiveness and propriety of words must thus steer clear not only of writing, but also of all those involvements for which writing comes to stand in Whitman's work, entanglements that deform the body and thereby emasculate the voice as surely as writing itself denatures the word:

All sorts of physical, moral and mental deformities are inevitably returned in the voice. (DBN 3:738)

Drinking brandy, or gin, beer, is generally fatal to the perfection of the voice;— A Meanness of mind, and all is the same;—Gluttony, in eating, of course the same; a thinned habit of body, or a rank habit of body—masturbation, inordinate going with women, total and spoil sternly rot the voice. Yet none no man can have a great vocalism, whose amiab who has no experience of love woman who with woman and no who has no experience with man [*sic*].—The voice is rich with the exp arousing with final fibre and xxxxx charm of the voice, follows the chaste experience drench of love. (DBN 3:737)

We are clearly in the realm of magic thinking here. Both the agitated phrasing and the range of behavior specified in Whitman's apotropaic litany might well remind us of the passage from the 1855 Preface concerning the "name[s] of word[s] or deed[s]" that "stamped on the programme" are "duly realized and returned, and that returned in further performances . . . and they returned again" (1855 19–20). If we except the final, idealized stipulation of the necessity of experiencing the "chaste [. . .] drench of love"—an oxymoronic description which mingles reticence and braggadocio in a manner reminiscent of "Children of Adam," and which, like the latter, seems like a piece of counter-phobic bravado[82]—this list, like the passage from the Preface, does not simply adjure abstinence from over-indulgence but anxiously wards off all manner of entanglements and the daemonic power they apparently unleash, protecting what it seems to imagine as the perfect autonomy and self-sufficiency of a clean and proper body.[83] It is only from such a body that a redemptive voice might emerge.

It is worth noting in passing that these proclamations inadvertently register the precarious status of the redeemer they envision, enlisting mechanisms in his defense that threaten the very autonomy for which he ought to stand. As in the Preface, what menaces self-presence and self-completion in this passage turns out to be not just interaction with others but also the introjection of a regulatory structure that makes the body a function of something outside itself. Both the daemonic repetitions of the Preface and the stamping with which they are associated are apposite here, as is the cultural origin of this mechanism of inscription that divides the self: here too it is implicitly not just impulse but the cultural coding and control of desire, and the obsessions to which they lead, that violate the vocal purity and bodily integrity Whitman anxiously tries to protect. This is so despite his invocation of a moralized vocabulary to condemn what threatens the vocalist's autonomy. Recognized explicitly elsewhere in Whitman's work as a threat, cultural proscriptions are here paradoxically deployed to ward off interactions they have themselves helped to make threatening: as in the Preface, the moral armature overtly enlisted to control behavior is ultimately part of what provokes anxiety in this agitated passage rather than the key to assuaging it; Whitman's condemnatory terms themselves undermine the propriety they are called on to guard. This paradox is a kind of mirror-image of a problem I shall take up further on: if the vocalist is compromised here by the very sanctions Whitman enlists, elsewhere he turns out to be constituted by mechanisms he claims to rebuff. In either case, the propriety for which this figure should stand is violated by gestures that ostensibly sustain it; he comes into being as a function of alien powers against which he ought to defend.

Like many of Whitman's pronouncements about the body, these declarations are thus as ambivalent as they are evocative. For the purposes of my present argument, however, their import is as follows. On the one hand, such attempts to guarantee the powers of the word by grounding them in a body exempt from self-division conform to the logic of Whitman's language theory: it makes sense that only the possessor of a self-sufficient body might retrieve for language the organic power of the proper name, freeing the word from entanglements by which he himself supposedly remains uncompromised. Yet this appeal is nonetheless awk-

ward, since something very like circularity hovers over Whitman's meditation on body and voice here. It appears that voice has the power to
recall words to their proper meanings, activating an idiom which can
extricate us from the trammels in which culture and fallen language
otherwise entoil us, only if it proceeds from a body somehow already
exempt from such entanglement. We can at least note that the sort of
person on whom the linguistic argument of the *Primer* converges and
finally depends begins to look very much like a fantasy figure concocted
to embody, already, immunity to just the kind of self-division and loss
of propriety from which the language theory and its vision of organic
names appeared at first to offer a more reasoned basis for exemption.

Elsewhere in the *Primer,* Whitman offers an additional glimpse of the
vocalist that seems initially to solve such difficulties, suggesting how this
figure might have managed to maintain the august aloofness from dangerous interaction the passage we have been considering makes a requisite for his redemption of words. Yet despite itself, the passage displays
this aloofness as an endangered trait, defended by troubling means. This
entry from the *Primer* has the virtue of making more explicit the vision
of identity with which Whitman's language theory intertwines. Yet it is
ultimately compromised by an even keener version of the troubling
circularity it seems at first to resolve. Here Whitman's forbidding caveats
concerning the bodily temple in which voice is enshrined are supplemented by some rather daunting positive requirements:

Latent, in a great ~~writer,~~ user of words, must actually be all passions, crimes,
trades, animals, stars, God, sex, the past, night, space, metals, and the like—
because these are the words, and ~~if~~ he who is not these, plays with a foreign
tongue, ~~talking xxx~~ turning helplessly to dictionaries and authorities. (DBN
3:742)[84]

Specifying the source of the vocalist's powers, these declarations also
suggest how he might steer clear of the self-dividing desires he can
indulge only at the cost of his resources: this figure need not embroil
himself in transitive relations and the codes that structure them, since he
contains all his objects in himself. This vision of completeness and self-
sufficiency displays dramatically the magical mode of identity Whitman's apparently demotic and open-ended musings on language are
ultimately enlisted to sustain; more than just a pure and healthy physical
specimen, this "great user of words" shows a strong family resemblance
to the poet of such pieces as "Crossing Brooklyn Ferry." Apparently

composed in 1855 or 1856, when Whitman's poet-hero was just being concocted, the *Primer* not only makes explicit the linguistic resources this redeemer can marshal but also shows the necessity of his birth.[85] Outside the enchanted spheres of the natural expressive effusion, the "substantial words" of the earth, and the onomatopoetic proper names of aboriginal languages, this passage suggests, it is only a magically agglomerating body like the poet's that can fully awaken the expressive properties dormant in what are otherwise merely indicative words.

Though startling, this grounding of authentic language in a magically incorporative body conforms to a logic Whitman's theory of naming and his doctrine of expressive sound imply. Organic names, after all, supposedly condense the vocal effusions of the things they name, effusions expressive of the unique organic matrices from which they emerge. The voice able to re-activate this perfectly expressive stratum should accordingly emanate from a body capable of duplicating the kinesthetic resources which the name supposedly crystallizes. That body should be able to transform itself into, or else should already contain, all the creatures and things to whose expressive names it aspires to give voice.

This arduous requirement is in part a fortunate limitation: evoking the protean poet of *Leaves of Grass,* it makes the redemption of language depend upon him and enforces a very strict boundary indeed between the organic idiom to which he gives voice and the mass of ordinary language that facilitates social exchange. Yet as much in keeping with the spirit of Whitman's enterprise as this final dependence of the word on the body of the poet may be, it is nonetheless a shaky foundation for the language theory the *Primer* tries to expound. It is awkward enough that Whitman keeps his essential theoretical distinctions in place by appealing in the supposedly discursive context of the *Primer* to a fantasmatic figure modeled on the poet of the imaginative universe of *Leaves of Grass.*[86] It is more uncomfortable still that the person on whom the powers of language ultimately depend is brought into being, in the poems, precisely by voice. The voice that supposedly generates the presence of this linguistic savior, the *Primer* lets us know, might possess the magical powers requisite for such an act only if it emanates from the very sort of body that, in the poems, it apparently creates.

The fact that the poet-hero of *Leaves of Grass* owes his existence to the supposed functioning of the very linguistic powers of which the *Primer* makes him the implicit guarantor is neatly suggested by the form his presence in the poems takes. The poet, I suggested earlier, is a kind of zero-degree incarnation, a figure not only produced but also defined by his vocal attributes: "one in whom you will see the singularity which consists in no singularity" ("Leaves of Grass: A Volume of Poems Just Published" 25), the poet in his mythic guise is a kind of generic being, a voice hypostatized as a living presence. But the powers of voice are then guaranteed by this hypostatization.

The passage from the *Primer* I have been considering also offers evidence of this reification, displaying once more the slippery sense of causality it involves. If the "great user of words" must already possess, "latent in" himself, all that he is to name, it is hard to imagine what form such internalization might take other than the possession of the words themselves and the symbolic introjection those words make possible; it is difficult to conceive a credible meaning for Whitman's assertion that is not simply tautological. It is not only the general difficulty of imagining such internalization as anything other than figurative that encourages us to read Whitman's formulation as tautology. Here the powers of the word are guaranteed by being grounded in what we might choose to regard as a magically agglomerating body: such a body would be capable of the sort of literal incorporation that would give Whitman's claims here substantive meaning. But in Whitman's work this body can be sustained only if the magical powers of language already obtain: throughout *Leaves of Grass,* the poet's assimilative powers are registered precisely as the powers of the word.

If the order of causality Whitman details between a magical, incorporative body and a magic word is thus finally circular, this pattern is hardly a sign of mere meaninglessness. Instead it traces a powerful closure, a structure that circles back on itself, rebuffing our attempts to re-open and re-enter it. In this archaic realm, language and body define each other: voice produces echolalic effusions inseparable from the somatic rhythms of the body from which they emanate, articulating a space not yet separated into subject and object. Proper to the semiotic *chora,* this fantasmatic intermingling of body and voice, and of self and other, is partially sustained by the liminal practice of word magic evoked in the *Primer* and the poems; the magic word should ward off the emasculating divisions enforced by the indicative sign and the symbolic order it structures.

The circularity endemic to Whitman's account is thus powerfully evocative. Yet a language theory that finds its justification in the incorporative, semioticized body of the poet begs the very questions it purports to solve. The gap between expressive effusion and articulate, codified language, as well as the difference between an organic speech endowed with magical performative force and a fallen idiom that merely refers to what it names, are supposedly bridged by an archaic body we might continue to possess only if these rifts have already been healed; a fantasmatic body defined by the *chora* is made to guarantee the magical powers of the symbolic word.

The fragile distinctions sustained by this presence organize both *The Primer of Words* and *Leaves of Grass*. The poet's body and the notion of vocalism it is enlisted to guarantee prevent the liabilities attributed to fallen, symbolic language from defining the sign as such. They ward off the possibility that all language trades in designations; that the paradigmatic noun is the arbitrary class name and not the expressive proper one; that classification and coercion pervade the field defined by language. All naming would then, in the sense Kenneth Burke has established, be rhetoric and persuasion.[87] All performance, in Austin's terms, would possess merely social, symbolic force.

What separates good from bad language would thus be almost nothing. This is so not only because of the circularity I have been tracing. As we shall see, the traits of the magical presence associated with the adamic word are themselves troubling. This difficulty is by no means insignificant: the poet's presence is not only the crucial source from which the adamic word emanates, but also the key instance of what it can produce. In *Leaves of Grass* the deficient entities circulated by fallen language are explicitly measured by contrast to this figure. What stands opposed to constative utterance or discourse, representation or designation, is not simply another form of naming or another linguistic mode, but the poet himself. In "A Song for Occupations" it is thus the poet's presence that supposedly abrogates the detours of representation:

> I bring what you much need, yet always have
> [. . . .]
> And send no agent or medium . . . . and offer no representative of value—
>   but offer the value itself. (1855 89)

In "Song of Myself" as well, this presence is itself the visionary meaning all discourse gropes to report:

> Man or woman! I might tell how I like you, but cannot;
> And might tell what it is in me, and what it is in you, but cannot;
> And might tell that pining I have—that pulse of my nights and days.

> Behold! I do not give lectures, or a little charity;
> When I give, I give myself. (V 1:62)[88]

This claim is repeated in "Song of the Open Road":

> I and mine do not convince by arguments, similes, rhymes,
> We convince by our presence. (1856 233)

We can thus measure the space between fallen and unfallen language by seeing how well the poet's presence keeps them apart. Producing but also produced by unfallen language, not only the guarantor but also the prime example of its power, this presence ought not of course to be compromised—or constituted—by the characteristics that define the fallen word. Epitomized by writing, those negative features also structure the related phenomena of the mechanism and the image, and the related operations of repetition and representation. Contrasting these to the poet's presence and to the working of the unfallen word that produces him, Whitman means thereby to validate the linguistic possibilities with which this figure is fused. Yet in detailing these contrasts, Whitman's exposition is not simply bothered, as heretofore, by the unlikeliness of some of his attributions. Instead his polarities tend to collapse into one another, to the extent that it will prove nearly impossible to distinguish the poet from all he should serve to lay to rest.

Presence and Representation

In Whitman's work the axial distinction between the poet's presence and the entities spawned by fallen language is registered in part in terms of the problem of power. Himself the incarnation of the organic word, the poet can supposedly convey to us the living energies it crystallizes. Neither emerging from nor expressing such animating force, the productions of fallen discourse are mere simulacra; lacking living, organic reality themselves, they ought to possess no power over that reality, or over us.

This neat opposition, however, structures only part of Whitman's treatment of symbolic productions. Whitman also repeatedly rails against the power fallen language manages to exercise, struggling to bring us to our senses by arguing that this force is illegitimate; our worship of the symbolic entities generated by the fallen word is idolatrous. Yet the exaggerated power Whitman sometimes accords such idols suggests that he himself is hardly immune to their seductions. His brusque dismissals of arbitrary language and its productions modulate into more agitated attempts at expulsion; entities and operations sometimes characterized as impotent turn out to possess a nearly fatal attraction and to exercise an almost fatal power, from which not only others but also the poet himself must be saved. This hyperbolic treatment of the powers of fallen language can be understood in part as a tacit recognition that its supposedly illicit or illusory constructs define us. But it registers as well the disturbingly intimate relation these productions turn out to possess to the poet's own presence. The phobic quality of Whitman's rhetoric can perhaps best be explained as a function of this contagion and the uneasiness it inspires: not only do symbolic entities possess an almost inescapable power; this resisted power may constitute the poet himself.

Intent on warding off such conclusions, Whitman makes writing the crucial instance of the duplicity that lends the arbitrary word a force it should not possess; our enchanted worship of texts epitomizes the idolatry which the simulacra generated by fallen language inspire. Fallen language and its untoward effects, in turn, become synecdoches for the representations of all kinds that dominate culture and the force they exercise over us; Whitman ascribes dangerous seductive powers to all manner of symbolic entities and artifacts. While his singling out of writing should serve to exempt the poet, who supposedly does not indulge in it, from Whitman's indictment against the fallen word, this broader focus suggests the scope of the domination from which he can therefore free us. Yet the poet's presence may turn out to be hard to distinguish not only from the entities generated by writing but also from the myriad representations that surround and define us; this would-be liberator would thus himself be a product and a part of the very system of symbolic domination he supposedly resists. In what follows, I will first take up Whitman's opposition between the poet's presence and the writing that epitomizes fallen language, turning next to the broader problem of the troubling relation between the real things supposedly produced by his magic word and the variety of representations that emasculate us.

1. Whitman's efforts to dismiss writing often turn on an opposition between the organic resources of voice and the supposedly merely mechanical efficacy of a merely mechanical medium. Unconnected to living presence rather than emerging from it as the voice does, writing substitutes structures of its own making for the organic entities it cannot fathom. This substitution is sometimes said to make writing and its productions impotent. The techne of writing can achieve only technical reforms, wielding a degraded perlocutionary power incapable of true performative effect:

> States!
> Were you looking to be held together by the lawyers?
> By an agreement on a paper? Or by arms?
>
> Away!
> I arrive, bringing these, beyond all the forces of courts and arms,
> These! to hold you together as firmly as the earth itself is held together.
>
> The old breath of life, ever new,
> Here! I pass it by contact to you, America. (["States!"], 1860 349)[89]

As Whitman's closing deictic and the apostrophic scene it activates imply, his political argument here turns on an opposition between voice and writing. Voice, which emanates from an interior, possesses a performative force that helps further organic unities; writing, an inert mark on a surface, effects conjunctions that are merely superficial.

Yet such mechanical structures manage to counterfeit the powers of living organisms. Devoid of animating impulse, they nonetheless exercise a bizarre sort of initiative: obeying the will or functioning as the proxy of no living agent, they nonetheless continue relentlessly to act. In Whitman's work all manner of cultural artifacts can acquire this daemonic power. But writing is the crucial instance of it. Possessing no life of its own, the text nonetheless regenerates itself, impinging on the present moment and the living creatures whose energies ought to shape it. Repeating itself inexorably, the text and the mechanical energies it conveys do not merely displace the properly self-sufficient presences on which they impinge. Finally, we shall see, they hollow them out from within. Like other cultural mechanisms, writing replicates by lodging within us till it takes possession of us.

At the very least, writing enervates the presences it affects, robbing them of their active force:

> Have we not darken'd and dazed ourselves with books long enough? ("Passage to India," CRE 421; V 3:574)

This stupefying effect turns out to be a comparatively minor evil. Impinging on the present from out of the past, writing possesses a power that is eerie because it is the power of something no longer alive; the images Whitman chooses for suggesting the dangerous action of such ghostly repetition are exorbitant enough to be startling. Our fascination with texts is figured as a perverse, unhealthy commerce with the dead. Bewitched, the living expend their energies "pressing the noses of dead books upon themselves and upon their country [. . .]" ("Letter to Ralph Waldo Emerson," 1856 353). This cadaverous anthropomorphism tells only half the story of our relation to books. If texts weigh on us like corpses, this oppressive effect is matched by the benefit they do the dead whose words they preserve. Writing sustains the dead whose words live through it by a process of repetition that might be called vampiric: drained of their very animation by this debilitating intercourse, the living become automatons who serve as mouthpieces of the deceased. If Whitman declares in "Song of Myself" that, in reading books, we feed on the merely spectral—"nor look through the eyes of the dead . . . . nor feed on the spectres in books" (1855 26)—these spectral presences, which resurrect themselves only by virtue of our mesmerized cooperation, feed on us as well.

This enervating exchange is sometimes figured as violent encroachment. Writing can stifle speech, throttling the breath and the living presence it sustains. An oddly ferocious image from the 1856 "Letter to Ralph Waldo Emerson" suggests this force: "Here also formulas, glosses, blanks, minutiae, are choking the throats of the spokesmen to death" (1856 351). But the power of writing sometimes assumes a form that is more disturbing precisely because it is less violent and overt. Rather than choking or stifling voice, writing can instead insinuate itself into speech, draining its resonance. Repeating words written down by others, we speak writing, losing the proper powers of voice:

(And who are you—blabbing by rote, years, pages, languages, reminiscences,
Unwitting to-day that you do not know how to speak a single word?).
("Myself and Mine," 1860 225)

In Whitman's imagination the word written down and then repeated by
others who have read it is no longer proper—it is pronounced through
a kind of ghostly ventriloquism, in which the dead speak through the
mouths of the living. Such words are not so much uttered as echoed, and
have themselves been hollowed out by death.[90]

This commerce with the dead not only saps the voice. It also enervates
the body:

Investigating here, we see, not that it is a little thing we have, in having the
bequeath'd libraries, countless shelves of volumes, records, &c.; yet how serious
the danger, depending entirely on them, of the bloodless vein, the nerveless arm,
the false application, at second or third hand. (PW 2:425)

Engaged here in *Democratic Vistas* in formulating a social critique that
is often trenchant, Whitman gives writing its due, ambivalently acknowledging its benefits.[91] Yet even in the pragmatic context of the *Vistas,*
writing retains something of the magical force poems and *Primer* accord
it: such uncanny power is registered here in Whitman's description of
the "bloodless" and "nerveless" body enervated by reading.

This metaphor of reading and writing as debilitating disease is frequent in Whitman's work; it suggests the peculiar intimacy of the danger
writing represents:

After all there's something better than to write: that's not to write: writing is a
disease. (WWC 3:358)

Denouncing the dangers of this illness to Traubel, Whitman includes
himself among the infected:

In most of us I think writing gets to be a disease. We scribble, scribble, scribble
—eternally scribble: God looks on—it turns his stomach: and while we scribble
we neglect life. (WWC 1:350)

As Whitman's insistently iterative phrasing here suggests, the disease of
writing is characterized by repetitive, obsessive behavior. When it comes
to writing, though, repetition compulsion is not only a symptom; repetition, we have seen, is itself the source of the anxiety writing provokes.[92]
The disease of writing thus produces behavior that fuels this infection

rather than simply manifesting it; once exposed to writing, we are progressively debilitated by our own compulsive acts.

In another pronouncement recorded by Traubel, Whitman offers an even more sinister version of the threat to bodily integrity posed by the disease of writing, and by the repetitive behavior of which this illness consists. Writing insinuates itself into our interiors, preying upon the pneumatic body:

> The trouble mostly is that writers become writers and cease to be men: writers reflect writers, writers again reflect writers, until the man is worn thin—worn through. (WWC 1:195)

Whitman's trope of reflection here equates the repetitions effected by writing with the diffusion of images. In the context of Whitman's work, to suggest that the text is an image is to insist that the powers exercised by its replicating form are scandalous: like the image, the text is a mere simulacrum; nothing itself, it should possess no power except that of reminding us of its original and returning our attention to it. This "original" is of course the speech act writing records—or at least it should be. But here Whitman traces a perverse lineage: the origin of writing and the images it disseminates may itself be an image or text. In Whitman's estimation texts that have thus bartered away an authentic genesis in living speech should be utterly powerless. So in a somewhat querulous literary estimate, derivative poems—mere reflections—are said not to perdure as "living" poems might:

> Rhymes and rhymers pass away—poems distilled from other poems pass away,
> The swarms of reflectors and the polite pass, and leave ashes. ("By Blue Ontario's Shore," 1856 194)

Yet in the passage from Traubel, Whitman suggests that the supposedly merely illusory power of the copy or reflection somehow manages to bring about a disastrous effect. The end result of such scribbling, of the further repetition of mere writing, is not simply that the productions of such a writer "pass away." Instead, this replication of written images is said to exercise a dreadful power, though it recoils upon the writer rather than acting on others. The author is himself hollowed out by such bewitched activity: "the man is worn thin—worn through." Attending to images, he becomes a mere image or shadow himself. Associated with the image, with a nothing or non-presence that insinuates itself within us like a disease, writing and repetition not only captivate but also come to destroy us. Once activated, they devour voice and presence inexorably, eating them away from within.

The anxiety registered in such passages may derive not only from the seemingly cataclysmic nature of this invasion, but also from its virtual inescapability. In Whitman's work the threat posed by writing turns out to be both intimate and pervasive. The overwrought quality that frequently characterizes Whitman's depictions of the effects writing has on voice and presence might thus be understood as resulting in part from denial: what may be structural necessity assumes the form of a disaster whose lurid features both reflect the poet's attempt to make it seem foreign and authorize his insistence that it remain so. "Usurpation," Derrida suggests, both registering and displacing the force of a melodrama to which Whitman would thus be very much committed, "necessarily refers us to a profound possibility of essence.... How was the trap and the usurpation possible?" (*Grammatology* 40). How could writing and the repetition for which it stands come to inhabit the voice and dispossess it of its proper powers? Or how could they not.

The repetition that hollows out speech would thus constitute language, defining the fate not only of the misguided writer entoiled in literary history and discipleship, but of any self shaped by the word. Rather than depending on the speaking subject's pneumatic powers to animate and fill it, language would instead generate him by dividing him against himself: it would turn voice into an echo and consciousness into a kind of palimpsest. Hyperbolic or hysterical though it may seem, Whitman's association of writing and repetition with a debt exacted by the dead thus perhaps figures an essential truth, a prospect less escapable than even his uncanny images suggest. The dead may be said to speak through the mouths of the living insofar as they possess a prior relation to the language in which the living articulate themselves and their desires; giving voice to this language, the living are themselves hollowed out by death, structured by a non-presence that defines what presence can be, depriving it of its autonomy and propriety.

2. Whitman's images of writing infiltrating voice, however, serve to relegate an intertwining they too record as pervasive to the status of a

disaster. If writing is Whitman's figure for the contingency of enervating repetition, and of the fading of self-presence such repetition exacts, the poet's word and presence are the crucial instances of a language and identity that supposedly escape these debacles. Yet even the poet's pristine vocalism turns out to be liable to the infections for which writing serves as a carrier. And his presence can be hard to distinguish from the captivating but counterfeit figures writing and repetition produce. Whitman must, at least, protect the poet's word from exposure to writing and its echoic effects with particular vigilance; and he must painstakingly detach the poet's form from the images generated by ordinary repetition, with which it might all too easily be confused. Here too the danger of usurpation—or of simple confusion—implies "a profound possibility of essence." The lurid features writing and repetition assume in Whitman's work may thus serve not only to suggest that the disasters they inflict are avoidable, but also to deny their intimate relation to the poet's own voice and presence.

The poet himself repeatedly insists on his independence from such compromising involvements. He proclaims himself the champion of the present moment, of a here and now wholly adequate and self-contained:

> Happiness not in another place, but this place . . not for another hour, but
>   this hour. ("A Song for Occupations," 1855 96)

And he fends off the repetition that hollows out speech and turns the living into phantoms:

> I am the poet of reality
> I say the earth is not an echo
> Nor man an apparition. (UPP 2:69)

These pronouncements should both accomplish and exemplify the repudiations they announce. Animated by the poet's voice, they ought to possess the performative force proper to language, bringing about our liberation rather than merely describing it. But in order to do so, they must themselves already fulfill the condition they declare. The echo robs the word of its proper force; turning present speech into a repetition of and reference to prior utterance, it saps performative power and consigns language to the degraded task of representation. The magical force of the poet's word—as well as his own bodily integrity—thus depends on his immunity to the echoic effects he deplores: the poet "puts today out of himself with plasticity and love" ("Song of the Answerer," 1855 130) only by preserving inviolate his own living speech.

Whitman insists on this lack of infection repeatedly; his very vigilance, however, suggests the poet's susceptibility to the dangerous influences from which he claims to free us. Whitman's bragging declarations of originality should be understood at least in part as an effort to keep at bay this contagion that threatens the poet's voice: in denying that the poet is subject to influence, Whitman is not so much seeking to insert himself into the canon as to detach himself from the filiations canons both reflect and sustain. Thus he notes approvingly of the writer of *Leaves of Grass,* in his own anonymous "review" of the 1855 edition: "He makes no allusions to books or writers; their spirits do not seem to have touched him [. . .]" ("Leaves of Grass: A Volume of Poems Just Published" 24). The anxiety lurking in this magisterial pronouncement becomes more overt in a more private context; in a notebook entry Whitman warns himself: "Make no quotations and no reference to any other writers" (CW 9:4). Whitman's absolutism here makes this repudiation resemble a magical rite of expulsion; it suggests the intimacy of the threat such declarations ward off.

If Whitman is worried about the way repetition and the echo seem able to compromise the poet's word and presence, the suggestion that these operations might contribute to or constitute them is even more disturbing. Yet like his efforts to protect the poet's own speech from outside interference, his attempts to distinguish the poet's power over others from the illicit powers of repetition end up suggesting the intimate relation between these supposedly inimical forces. The poet may declare himself to be the champion of the present moment; but his continuing power over us depends precisely on his ability to repeat his presence. The dichotomy between the poet and what he opposes would thus not quite amount to a difference between a living presence firmly ensconced in its own present moment and an echo or repetition: it would depend instead on a subtler distinction between two kinds of repetition. Whitman's diatribes against writing are motivated in part by the precariousness of this opposition; the urgency with which writing and its powers are exorcised is a function of the clearly vital place of repetition in Whitman's own poetry. The poet subdues others to his omnipresent form much as writing is said to impinge on future readers and take possession of them; but the poet, supposedly, does not write.

In Whitman's work the difference between good and bad repetition thus turns on a difference between voice and writing. While writing embalms an utterance, unnaturally preserving it after the living presence that animated it has died, voice emanates from an actual living presence, conveying its energies to us. And while writing insinuates the past into the present and turns the living into mouthpieces of the dead, the poet's announcements—both uttered and heard by us "now"—supposedly subdue both past and future to an eternal moment their own recurrence defines. Like a counter-magic fighting off the influence of the dead, these pronouncements seem to secure us in a living present restored to its proper integrity by means of a speech whose power of good repetition fends off the repetition effected by writing.

Unlike the bad repetition which hollows out self-presence, the repetition of the poet's living word thus restores self-presence to us. While the writing that repeats itself through us drains our voices of their resonance and our bodies of their strength, the poet supposedly pours his magically repeating word inside us in order to renew our bodily integrity and reactivate our own vocal powers. Welling up within us as he fuses himself into us, the poet's words are the ideal form of our own:

> It is you talking just as much as myself . . . . I act as the tongue of you,
> It was tied in your mouth . . . . in mine it begins to be loosened. ("Song of
>   Myself," 1855 82)

The magical repetition of which the poet's living speech seems capable thus not only preserves presence by fighting off the bad repetition effected by writing; this good repetition defines what living presence is. The poet's apparent power to reproduce himself as the same, I argued in chapter 4, makes him seem like the magical incarnation of an ideal form, a self-sustaining being immune to interference; unaffected by extrinsic forces or contingent events, he is what he is, presenting himself fully and directly. Repetition of the wrong sort devours the living; but living presence becomes what it is by virtue of (another sort of) repetition.

This distinction is as crucial to the poet's project as it is precarious: it prevents the poet's announcements from being another instance of the very mechanisms from which he should save us. Whitman accordingly associates this dichotomy between good and bad repetition with a contrast which both seems to shore it up and underlines its importance—one between presence and representation. While writing is the copy of an utterance rather than the utterance itself, speech is a present act and attests to a living presence. I argued earlier that Whitman's manipulation of this dichotomy between writing and voice is designed to sustain a possibility which the contrast between them does not ordinarily imply: while the bad repetition operated by writing cheats us by producing a mere image or simulacrum of the living word, counterfeiting the speaking presence in which that word should originate, the good repetition effected by the poet's voice magically reproduces the actual presence of the poet himself.

The poet's word thus apparently fends off a treachery Whitman often equates with culture. Flooding us with a presence who defines what presence is, or situating us firmly among the actual objects his performatives supposedly produce, the poet's announcements keep at bay the simulacra in which culture would otherwise enmesh us, steering us clear of a welter of symbolic entities that are supposed to serve but instead overshadow organic presences and usurp their powers, ultimately devouring both our objects and ourselves. Yet this crucial opposition threatens to collapse under the weight of the shaky distinction it ought to shore up. The dichotomy between the poet's presence and the simulacra spawned by culture turns out to be as tenuous as the contrast between good and bad repetition. A similar difficulty compromises Whitman's broader effort to distinguish the full range of the poet's performative announcements, and the variety of real presences they supposedly produce, from the degraded operation of representation and the idols it imposes on us. The poet's power is always disturbingly close to the power of bad repetition enjoyed by the reflection or image, and this proximity must repeatedly be denied.

3. Like his consideration of writing and repetition, Whitman's estimate of the representations that dominate symbolic space is divided. Like texts, representations are sometimes said to be impotent, though we may be duped into according them a force they do not inherently possess. But Whitman himself often endows representations with exorbitant powers —powers virtually indistinguishable, indeed, from those supposedly exercised by the poet's own presence or marshaled by his performative word.

Like his treatment of writing, Whitman's analysis of representations includes an account of the seemingly inexplicable fascination they manage to compel. Substituting itself for the thing it represents, the representation irresistibly draws our attention to itself rather than directing us to the creature or object for which it stands. We come to value the representation as if it were the thing itself.[93] This pathological fascination is as pervasive as it is unnatural. The poet must repeatedly retrieve us from it:

> Have you reckoned the landscape took substance and form that it might be painted in a picture?
> Or men and women that they might be written of, and songs sung?
> Or the attraction of gravity and the great laws and harmonious combinations and the fluids of the air as subjects for the savans?
> Or the brown land and the blue sea for maps and charts?
> Or the stars to be put in constellations and named fancy names?
> Or that the growth of seeds is for agricultural tables or agriculture itself? ("A Song for Occupations," 1855 91)

This allure is especially scandalous when it seduces us into preferring representations to ourselves: we wander in a space filled with apparently autotelic images, idols that seem neither to refer to nor leave room for the human creatures who have been taught to efface themselves before them. The poet tries to put an end to this perversion by reminding us of the proper relation between images and those who create them:

> All doctrines, all politics and civilization exurge from you,
> All sculpture and monuments and anything inscribed anywhere are tallied in you,
> The gist of histories and statistics as far back as the records reach is in you this hour—and myths and tales the same;
> If you were not breathing and walking here where would they all be?
> The most renowned poems would be ashes . . . . orations and plays would be vacuums. ("A Song for Occupations," 1855 92)

Our attention must repeatedly be disengaged from the representative substitute and recalled to its living source:

> This printed and bound book . . . . but the printer and the printing-office boy?
> [. . . .]
> The well-taken photographs . . . . but your wife or friend close and solid in your arms? ("Song of Myself," 1855 74)

Like writing, the representation of whatever sort tends not only to divert our attention, but to wear away our lives as well. Dominated by it, culture amounts to fetishism: it trains us to adore the sign and devalue the thing it signifies; we serve the representations that ought to serve us.[94]

The intimacy of this threat is registered in the poet's own susceptibility to it. Whitman privately warns himself against such emasculating idolatry, just as he elsewhere forbids himself all reference to other writers:

Poet! beware lest your poems are made in the spirit that comes from the study of pictures of things—and not from the spirit that comes from the contact with real things themselves. (CW 9:10)

While Whitman's attacks on representation often seem motivated by pragmatic concerns, warning us of a danger in order to enlist our support in eradicating it, his sense of personal susceptibility to the very threat from which he hopes to protect others begins to imply the sort of inextricable entanglement we saw at work in his jeremiad against writing. The poet's tone can indeed imply that the power symbolic forms exercise over us is inexorable. "Respondez!," a poem first published in 1856 and prudently excluded from Whitman's "deathbed" edition, is a vitriolic diatribe against a culture infatuated with representations. Yet a note of terrified fascination gradually emerges from beneath the tone of violent invective:

Let nothing but love-songs, pictures, statues, elegant works, be permitted to
    exist upon the earth!
[....]
Let shadows be furnished with genitals! Let substances be deprived of their
    genitals!
[....]
Let books take the place of trees, animals, rivers, clouds!
[....]
Let the portraits of heroes supersede heroes!
[....]
Let the reflections of the things of the world be studied in mirrors! Let the
    things themselves still continue unstudied!
Let a man seek pleasure everywhere except in himself! Let a woman seek
    happiness everywhere except in herself! (Say! what real happiness have
    you had one single time through your whole life?) (1856 319–21)[95]

What begins as a jeremiad demanding repentance and reform modulates here into something more closely resembling a transfixed recitation of inevitabilities.

Whitman's denigration of representations, his repeated insistence that they possess no legitimate power in themselves, is thus the less revealing facet of his polemic. Expending much energy to convince others that they have been duped by a sleight-of-hand by which he remains unmystified, Whitman elsewhere reveals that he too is prey to such trickery. Few of those he seeks to warn, indeed, would ascribe such extreme powers to representations as he sometimes does himself.

Whitman often attributes indirect, perlocutionary power to representations: words affect our notions of what they name. In *Democratic Vistas,* for example, he argues for renovating "the idea of the women of America, (extricated from this daze, this fossil and unhealthy air which hangs about the word *lady*) [. . .]" (PW 2:389). But he sometimes accords representations a more startling power—a power of which the ominously equipped shadows in "Respondez!" already give some hint. Representations can supposedly affect living beings directly, exercising a force that is magical rather than merely conventional. Whitman suggests, for example, that models of the human form can adversely affect the physiology of actual babies about to be born, the representation not simply affecting our ideas but insinuating itself into the very act of procreation.[96] Attractive statues will help produce attractive babies, while caricatures will lead to human deformities:

Exaggerations will be revenged in human physiology. Clean and vigorous children are jetted and conceived only in those communities where the models of natural forms are public every day . . . (Preface, 1855 17–18)

And I say that clean-shaped children can be jetted and conceived only where natural
forms prevail in public, and the human face and form are never caricatured.
("Says," 1860 419)

We can read these passages as a kind of nightmare, in which a distinction that keeps the poet's crucial values in place collapses. When Whitman inveighs against representations because they seduce us into ignoring things themselves, he blames them for blurring our sense of categories whose essential stability is nonetheless not in question. Here, however, representations very nearly beget presences. We can understand this genealogical confounding either as a spectacular instance of nefariousness and perversion or as the disintegration of the very opposition between representation and presence that energizes such notions of invasion and betrayal. These passages conjure up a landscape in which *there are* no presences that are not also representations, in which the very distinction between real and symbolic objects no longer obtains. Or rather: here what we take to be organic presences or things themselves are the progeny of representation. Passages that might be interpreted as invectives against an avoidable threat can thus also be read as an oblique admission of the constitutive role played by representation in shaping our objects: the things we call presences have themselves been produced by representation.

In Whitman's work the poet himself rises up as a presence supposedly immune to this contamination; the real things he claims to generate by means of his word are important ancillary cases. But Whitman's nightmare of a world filled by the offspring of magically active statues can also be read as a bad dream about the poet's own powers. Like his treatment of writing and repetition, that is, this anxious vision obliquely registers not only the pervasive role played by representation in shaping cultural space, but also an intimate, uncomfortable affinity between the presences produced by the poet's own magic word and the symbolic entities that replace real things. In these passages mere caricatures, possessing no inherent, organic relation to what they represent, are accorded a striking power: they can alter the interiors or essences of the creatures whose outer forms they misrepresent. This power of the caricature or false sign is indeed nearly identical to the force elsewhere reserved for true expressive signs or for the speech of the poet who realizes their organic resources: the power of magical performance, the ability to generate the things one names simply by naming them.

Revising Whitman's preferred view of the influence exercised by symbolic forms—whose apparent force ought to be illusory—this *de facto* intertwining of the powers of representations with the powers of the poet's own word also unsettles the vision of organic language Whitman struggles to convey. The tremendous power organic language supposedly wields is said to be wholly natural. Yet if the powers representations exercise are in passages like these not merely acknowledged but exaggerated, this exaggeration perhaps measures not only Whitman's nervousness about cultural coercion but also an uncomfortable sense of his own grandiose ambitions. Briefly according to representations a frightening version of the sweeping powers the poet claims to wield for wholly generous purposes, such passages register the terrors of a world in which the energies of others have become as formidable as the poet's own, their ambitions as imperial. Not easily distinguishable from the powers exercised by representations, the powers of the poet's speech would thus be deprived of that special benignity and innocence Whitman typically claims for them. Not thereby reduced to impotence, his word would enter and compete for the symbolic space in which representations, constituting namable presences, shape us by recruiting us to their particular, interested versions of who we are.[97]

Despite Whitman's protestations, his work offers ample evidence of this unsettling resemblance between the poet's word and presence and all they should serve to lay to rest. We might, for example, note a striking similarity between the perversely fascinating representations against which Whitman warns us and the poet's own imaginative labors. It is Whitman, after all, who devises the daring chiasmus between words and things that levers language into the position of a thing itself while relegating objects to the status of simulacra. Few representations work harder than a poem like "Crossing Brooklyn Ferry" to efface the existence of a world beyond their borders or to claim that the landscapes they fashion merit our exclusive attention; like those dangerous representations which spawn subsequent productions that refer back to them rather than to "things themselves," "Crossing Brooklyn Ferry," which generates the present as the Möbius strip or eternal moment the poem's apostrophes name "now," is an ideally self-perpetuating structure. The figure of the poet such speech acts produce—Whitman's key instance of a living presence supposedly uncontaminated by representation—is indeed the crucial case of this disconcerting resemblance between the products of magic language and the simulacra from which they should save us.

4. The clearest evidence of this confounding is the circumstance that the poet's presence, while seemingly produced by voice, in fact owes its existence to writing. Said to block the poet's manifestation, writing enables it; said to compromise his powers of self-creation, writing constitutes them. Writing generates the poet—but only as the obverse of what he is declared to be. The poet's presence defines what presence should be by simultaneously perfecting and occulting the operation of representation that brings it into being.

Whitman's repeated denials that writing and reading play a role in the poet's manifestation serve to ward off this confounding of presence and representation. We should recall both the insistence with which this denial is made in Whitman's work and the sort of collapse it keeps at bay. Writing does not attest to the poet's actual, living presence: it repeats words spoken in another place and time and offers us only the representations of speech and the personal presence speech implies. It must be ruled out of the poet's imaginative universe, among other reasons, because it fails to effect such a magical emanation, leaving the poet caught in the compromised body he longs to transfigure.

Yet the techne that threatens the poet's redeemed presence also makes it what it is—or what it seems to be. That presence does not, as Whitman would have it, appear in a text by accident or incidentally; it achieves its seemingly magical power precisely by helping itself to the resources of a writing whose role the poems must deny. This point is perhaps an obvious one; but it bears a bit of spelling out, since Whitman is committed to making it hard to see.

The poet's voice and presence, I suggested earlier, seem to annul space by traversing it. Actual voices, of course, have limited powers of diffusion. But the voice that augments itself with writing seems able to convey everywhere the presence to which voice attests. The written voice speaks from a distance our act of reading renders close; it conflates the elsewhere from which it announces itself and the "here" in which we receive it. The intimate, strangely spaceless space of such poems as "Crossing Brooklyn Ferry" arises largely from this textual circumstance. The apparent ability of Whitman's mythic voice to diffuse itself through time and thus collapse it depends more obviously on recourse to a text; only the voice that has helped itself to the resources of writing and representation speaks and repeats its words eternally.[98]

The vaporous body that can fuse itself into us is also created through Whitman's canny manipulation of a text. Actual voices, of course, project themselves from bodies that remain finite and bounded. In Whitman's text, however, there *is* no body, but only the haunting illusion of an unlocatable voice. Paradoxically, the voice we seem to hear as we read, unencumbered with an actual body, can therefore define an implicit body wholly modeled on its own characteristics. Defined not only by fluidity but also by an eerie transparency, this disembodied body makes the poet "one in whom you will see the singularity which consists in no singularity" ("Leaves of Grass: A Volume of Poems Just Published" 25). Such an essentialized form comes into being only through the text, which transmutes effacement into idealized presence—or into an ideal image or sign. Immune to the vicissitudes that continually reshape all material existents, since he resurrects himself whenever a reader encounters his words, the poet can repeat his advent eternally in identical form. This power of repetition, which makes him what he is, is virtually indistinguishable from the power Whitman excoriates texts for exploiting. Yet it endows the poet with the perfect autonomy and propriety that make him the incarnation of what *Leaves of Grass* means by presence.

The figure Whitman claims to generate might thus be defined as a being possessing precisely those positive traits and powers that characterize the image, even though, by virtue of some powerful magic, it is a living being instead. Voice, which attests to actual presence, figures this magic in *Leaves of Grass*. Writing, which epitomizes the representational function of the word, should play no role in the poet's manifestation. Admitted overtly into the universe of *Leaves of Grass,* it should destroy the redemptive figure its surreptitious use seems to create. At least as ordinarily practiced and understood, writing would perfect the poet's presence, and define what presence is, through recourse to an image or simulacrum. In *Leaves of Grass* presence would fade into its sign.

Yet just as Whitman envisions a magical operation which employs the powers peculiar to representation to constitute not an image but a living presence, so too he proposes a writing that is not simply writing. Ascribing an oxymoronic status to his poems and to the volume in which they appear, Whitman would have us regard *Leaves of Grass* as a book that is somehow not a book, but the actual bodily presence of its author:

> Camerado! This is no book,
> Who touches this, touches a man. (V 2:452)[99]

These announcements hover between outright, outrageous denial of the very existence of the book we are reading and an implicit claim to transmute what reading is, very nearly making explicit the precarious transaction on which the poet's presence depends. As the delicate rhythm of repudiation and revelation here suggests, the visionary prospect *Leaves of Grass* claims to actualize ultimately hinges on a paradoxical mode of communication as crucial to Whitman's project as it is difficult to conceive: the poet's exemplary mode of existence depends on the possibility of a peculiar kind of inscription that effaces itself on demand, metamorphosing into a living presence conveyed to us as surely as representations are disseminated by ordinary writing.

Oblique references to this special sort of writing are sprinkled throughout Whitman's work, inflecting even remarks not directly concerned with the poet's presence. I earlier cited a contrast between "live words in a book" and "cunningly composed words" (CW 9:159–60).[100] There Whitman seems to be making a simple distinction between words —whether spoken or written—that arise spontaneously and those that have counterfeited their occasion and thereby forfeited their naturalness and immediacy. Yet a liberating if not quite logical inference hovers in Whitman's locution. There should be a relation between the occasion and spirit in which writing is composed and its mode of perdurance. Implicit in Whitman's phrasing is the notion that a text dashed off rather than cunningly composed, the innocent and as it were incidental transcription of spontaneous speech, might sustain the fusion with living presence voice supposedly enjoys, also reaping the ancillary benefits that derive from writing yet being compromised by none of the defects that characterize that mode as it is ordinarily practiced.[101]

Whitman's repeated pronouncements concerning the way *Leaves of Grass* was composed should be understood in this light. A mythical linguistic possibility lies behind such seemingly workmanlike statements as the following:

I avoid at all times the temptation to patch up and refine, preferring to let each version or whatever go out substantially as it was first suggested. (WWC 1:64–65)

It lurks as well in his repeated declaration that *Leaves of Grass* was composed in a natural, spontaneous atmosphere, an assertion that might seem simply to propound a kind of aesthetic athleticism:

I have read these leaves to myself in the open air, I have tried them by trees, stars, rivers,
I have dismissed whatever insulted my own soul or defiled my body ("By Blue Ontario's Shore," 1856 196)[102]

These avowals are matched by commands that the book be read only in such a setting: "read these leaves in the open air every season of every year of your life [. . .] dismiss whatever insults your own soul, and your very flesh shall be a great poem [. . .]" (Preface, 1855 11). It is as if the spontaneity and similarity of the different occasions of writing and reading could somehow unite them, abrogating the delays, distances, and mediations that characterize texts. Effacing itself because of its nearly incidental character, such writing would become a voice, and thus a presence.

But writing is writing. And despite Whitman's espousal of an almost transparent, almost incidental variety of text which would apparently perform the neutral task of simply conveying the protagonist's presence without diminishing his powers, the role played by writing in constituting this figure is hardly the innocent one such an envisioned mode implies: lending its resources to voice, writing creates Whitman's poet. And like anyone else, Whitman cannot write without being liable to the negative traits of this mode—traits he himself spells out, in a repeated exorcism that serves finally to specify in some detail the linguistic features that compromise the magical powers his image of voice seems to sustain, returning the poet to the very space he claims to transcend. Whitman's need to make use of writing to mobilize the supposed resources of voice alerts us to an entangling which further slippery distinctions between one sort of text and another are a bit too obviously gerrymandered to stave off: the poet's presence, which should free us from the sway of representations, owes its apparently liberating qualities to the very mode it should redeem.

5. I have been arguing that this debacle is more than merely contingent; it obeys a necessity at work in all Whitman's musings on what presence should be. To point to the role of writing in *Leaves of Grass* is thus not simply to note that the poet's presence isn't quite a presence but is rather, sadly as it were, the representation of such a presence; though the poems gain much of their power by denying it, that point is finally obvious to all but the most fervent acolyte.[103] It is instead to suggest that the perfected presence who apparently escapes the alienation imposed by representation is generated as a fictive limit of representation itself. Whitman's figure of what we would be were we not subjected to the mediating structures of culture is a kind of hallucination produced by the very mechanisms from which it seems to save us.

If this is so, then this figure embodies not the supposedly proper relation between representation and presence he is invoked to sustain, but its opposite. The vision of presence for which the poet stands is in certain ways peculiar, just as the transactions that seem to produce him manipulate representation to generate presence in a manner far from common. Yet in his tricky relation to representation as in other crucial respects, this figure turns out to be oddly exemplary. Representation, we think, ought to be ancillary to presence: neither blocking its manifestation nor constituting our images of it and thereby compromising what it seems to be, representation should lead us obediently back to the real presence for which it stands. Walter Ong's formulation of this pervasive view is as benign as the process he describes:

In its internal dynamics, imitation is amiably self-destructive: if the imitation is totally successful, the product is indistinguishable from nature. (*Interfaces* 283–84)

In Whitman's work the relation between representation and presence, insofar as it is admitted to obtain at all, seems to resemble that offered in Ong's happy account; but it is made more gratifying still by being given a magical cast. In the universe of *Leaves of Grass,* representation is not merely "indistinguishable" from presence but can apparently produce it; writing, if it plays any role in the poems, does not simply counterfeit but supposedly metamorphoses into the voice that attests to the advent of the poet's person. Given a more important role to play when it is given any role at all, representation in *Leaves of Grass* thereby becomes all the more "amiable": making no claims on its own behalf, it supposedly yields up its place completely to presence without encroaching on its proper priority.

The story the poems want to tell is thus a more atavistic and resonant version of the account Ong offers. Jacques Derrida's formulation of the relation between representation and presence is more trenchant; less in keeping with Whitman's aspirations, it is more attuned to the economy that both enables and troubles them. Summarizing a common view we might attribute either to Whitman or Ong, Derrida manages simultaneously to unsettle it, suggesting that representation produces the very presence its apparent effacement seems to restore:

perfect representation should represent perfectly. It restores presence and effaces itself as absolute representation. This movement is necessary. The telos of the image is its own imperceptibility. When the perfect image ceases to be other than the thing, it respects the thing and restores originary presence. (*Grammatology* 297–98)

The ironic torque here is lodged primarily in Derrida's last sentence, and especially in his formulation of that fictive limit at which "the perfect image ceases to be other than the thing." Displaying the magic thinking that sustains Whitman's vision of presence and lies behind more attenuated versions of it as well, this paraphrase subverts the logic it offers to repeat: it implies that "the thing itself" is itself an image. What we mean by presence, that is, is a function of representation. This is assuredly so in *Leaves of Grass:* the iterability that generates the proper, self-sustaining form which qualifies in Whitman's work as presence is inseparable from representation.

This ideal form, Derrida suggests, can never find its match in the physical object or be embodied by it; representation produces an image of presence that will always remain, so to speak, behind things. If the sign gives birth to the hallucinatory possibility we call presence, it thus also generates the notion that the opaque, shifting surfaces before us poorly represent such presence, indicating it only by separating us from it. The idea of presence is thus inseparable from the supposed cataclysm of its loss:

> representation does not suddenly encroach upon presence; it inhabits it as the very condition of its experience. . . . The interior doubling of presence, its halving, makes it appear as such. . . . (*Grammatology* 312)

Whitman's chiasmus of words and things, which plays a crucial role in structuring the imaginative universe of *Leaves of Grass,* offers what we might want to call an amiable transumption of the predicament Derrida here views as inescapable. It ascribes the divisions that on Derrida's account inhere in representation to a supposedly remediable defect in things. In Whitman's work, we have seen, material objects are themselves called "representations," in part to suggest their deficiency, their difference from the proper entities language names. This nomenclature also serves to efface, through semantic displacement, the operation of representation that generates the ideal forms hypostatized as presences.

Voice is Whitman's figure for this crossing: incarnating language and wedding it to living presence in the poet's apostrophes, Whitman's image of voice seems to realize the chiliastic prospects the word implies. Writing undoes this chiasmus: naming the sign as sign, it reveals the poet as a representation. What according to Whitman is a contingent if all too common fate, to which we are led by fallen culture, thus assumes the form of a necessity, enacted most dramatically in the very speech acts that supposedly evade it. "The signifier," Jacques Lacan suggests,

makes manifest the subject of its signification. But it functions as a signifier only to reduce the subject in question to being no more than a signifier, to petrify the subject in the same movement in which it calls the subject to function, to speak, as subject. (*Four Fundamental Concepts* 207)

the subject manifests himself in this movement of disappearance that I have described as lethal. . . . I have called this movement the *fading* of the subject. (*Four Fundamental Concepts* 207–208)

Producing Whitman's image of voice as a function of representation, writing makes proclamations of the poet's presence instances of this fading. Apocalyptic though their tone may often be, these speech acts are an unwilling if not unwitting instance of the paradox Lacan acerbically describes; they reduce even the supposedly transfiguring identity they generate to the status of a castrated subject, or a sign.

Yet even this sign of identity, this image of voice, is resonant. It is what remains to us of the proper bodies we once possessed, or that we imagine were ours. Not yet enacting the apocalypse it imagines, representing this body but not yet presenting it, *Leaves of Grass* offers us, ambiguously, an image of recovery, or an image as loss.

Though they do not make it overt or incorporate it within the poet's project, Whitman's poems nonetheless hint at this attenuation associated with writing; they can afford to do so since, while such intimations imply the still unrealized status of the poet's redemptive aspirations, they do not radically compromise his integrity. His possible exercise of the aggressive powers for which writing comes to stand is a darker feature of *Leaves of Grass,* about which the poems are less forthcoming. Said to effect our exodus from the field of fallen culture and the mediations of the symbolic code, the poet and his word can be understood as triumphant instances of their working; the poet's presence, after all, is itself symbolic, its being as well as its meaning dependent on a social circuit of exchange. Far from impotent, such symbolic forms—Whitman tells us himself—are active and indeed coercive, usurping the place of the natural, the intrinsic, and the proper. Whitman often comes close to calling this usurpation culture; the poet is part of it.

Only rarely does this sense of complicity surface in Whitman's work. Admission that the presence generated in the poems is himself a product of the symbolic order and an instance of its powers and seductions is most sustained in the *Calamus* sequence that first appeared in the 1860 *Leaves of Grass*. Strenuous denial of this relation is more typical of Whitman's first two editions. Struggling to realize his magical powers and make good his performative claims, the poet-hero of the 1855 and 1856 *Leaves of Grass* is seemingly threatened with impotence rather than uncomfortable responsibility: if the transfigurations he announces do not quite come off, he appears to be a wistful figure possessed of noble aspirations, rather than a trafficker in rhetoric and persuasion like anyone else. Not only the visionary power, but also the pathos and humor of Whitman's early editions are thus generated by the poet's claims to renounce the fallen language games by means of which ordinary speakers cajole and coerce us. While the aggressive implications of the poet's entanglement in writing and representation are resolutely suppressed in the early editions of *Leaves of Grass,* the melancholy and comic ones periodically relieve the apocalyptic intensities of the performative project Whitman will not permit them to redirect.

To suggest that the unfallen word Whitman envisions repeatedly collapses into the fallen language from whose effects the poet should liberate us is thus hardly to assume a dismissive stance toward the poetry. Disquieting suggestions concerning the poet's word hover throughout Whitman's work, not only in the diatribes that try to discount them, but more valuably in the mobile, divided tone of local pronouncements. Extreme claims concerning the power of the word organize the imaginative universe of *Leaves of Grass;* yet at its best, Whitman's poetry accommodates the hesitations, equivocations, and brusque but vulnerable assertions we might expect a simultaneous commitment to and suspicion of such visionary claims to generate; at times the most programmatic of poets, Whitman is elsewhere the reluctant ironist, comedian, or elegist of his own project. Rather than coming to rest with the truism that Whitman's work never quite performs what it claims to, we need to trace this play of avowal and doubt through his poetry. Despite what *Leaves of Grass* declares, the poet's voice and

presence exist for us as an exuberant but troubled attempt at performance, and as a surreptitious but sustained meditation on their own
possibility.

Notes

1. Quoted in Anderson, "Whitman's New Man" 18. As Anderson points out,
   Whitman collaborated on this chapter concerning his work. See "Whitman's
   New Man" 11.
2. Steven Calabrese offers an important account of Whitman's extended efforts
   to turn the Person into a marketable commodity.
3. Letter to William D. O'Connor, January 6, 1865.
4. See also Burroughs, *Notes on Walt Whitman as Poet and Person* 56.
5. Quoted in Anderson, "Whitman's New Man" 44.
6. This remark pre-dates Whitman's Camden years. O'Connor was part of the
   poet's earlier Washington circle; see Kaplan 287–89.
7. Richard Maurice Bucke, the Canadian alienist who was another close friend
   and staunch supporter, thus suggested in a similar vein: "With Walt Whitman, his outward life, his inward spiritual existence and his poetry, were all
   one; in every respect each tallied with the other" (*Walt Whitman* 51).
8. Kaplan's account derives from WWC 4:312–14. See also WWC 4:212,
   4:234, and 1:49–50.
9. Gilchrist's review appeared in the Boston *Radical,* under the title "English
   Woman's Estimate of Walt Whitman." Written in 1869, it appears in *In Re
   Walt Whitman* (41–55) as "A Woman's Estimate of Walt Whitman." Having fended off Gilchrist's initial advances, Whitman became friendly with
   Gilchrist and her children and came to admire her greatly; see Kaplan 330–
   33 and 364–67, and Erkkila 312–16. Whitman's response to Gilchrist was
   of course colored by his sexual orientation; but it is of a piece with his
   general nervousness about the reactions *Leaves of Grass* provoked. Discussing another such letter, received some years before, with Traubel, Whitman
   remarked: "It's one of the confessions [. . .] I get confessions every now
   and then: from women, from men: they seem to inure to the kind of work I
   do: I don't as a rule know what to do with them: they mainly amaze me [.
   . . .] I haven't read it myself for years: take it along, anyhow: I want you to
   have it: it belongs with the other riff-raff you have" (WWC 4:212).
10. As Erkkila notes, "Whitman cautioned her [Gilchrist] not to confuse 'an
    unauthorized and imaginary ideal Figure' with the 'plain personage' of Walt
    Whitman" (Erkkila 313). More than a little disengenuous, Whitman here
    blames a confusion that threatened to become personally embarrassing on
    Gilchrist's imagination rather than his own; he thus manages both to avoid
    repudiating the Person and to stave off the awkward consequences this
    figure produced. Erkkila quotes from CORR 2:170.

11. On the split between Whitman's sometimes tormented private life and his carefully controlled transactions with the Camden circle see Anderson, "Whitman's New Man" 47.

12. In his discussion of Rousseau, Derrida explores this economy, of which Rousseau was explicitly aware. "Let us note that the economy is perhaps indicated in the following," Derrida suggests: "the operation that substitutes writing for speech also replaces presence by value: to the *I am* or to the *I am present* thus sacrificed, a *what* I am or a *what I am worth* is preferred. . . . I renounce my present life, my present and concrete existence in order to make myself known in the ideality of truth and value" *(Grammatology* 142). As we might expect, Whitman claims to conflate presence and value: "[I] send no agent or medium . . . . and offer no representative of value—but offer the value itself" ("A Song for Occupations," 1855 89).

13. In Camden Whitman devoted money as well as time to insuring his perdurance. He scandalized a group of English benefactors by taking the money they had collected to relieve his supposed destitution and lavishing it on an enormous mausoleum (Kaplan 25, 49–52).

14. Anderson implies a similar tension. Discussing the collection of clippings reprinted as part of the apparatus of *Walt Whitman's Autograph Revision of the Analysis of Leaves of Grass (For Dr. R. M. Bucke's Walt Whitman),* he remarks: "When we turn to the Appendix we are of course confronted by a montage of clippings of the sort that filled his scrapbooks in his cluttered Camden nest. The reader is invited to witness the process of assemblage for himself, for here, whatever our views of the Person, he may be said to have risen up, and been revealed" ("Whitman's New Man" 49).

15. The last of these lines disappears from the poem in 1881; see V 1:223.

16. Anderson, among others, thus notes Whitman's "assertion of an agency more inclusive and unmediated than print" *(Imperial Self* 120). See also Edwin Miller, *Walt Whitman's Poetry* xv.

17. This intimation that the poet has just by-passed his text, or is about to do so, was deleted from the poem in 1881; see V 1:83–84.

18. As Walter Ong notes in a remark in keeping with the spirit of Whitman's work, in writing "the person who produces an utterance has been more and more effectively distanced from the person who takes in the utterance" *(Interfaces* 288). Ong thus suggests, as Whitman might, that "death presides at both ends of the writing operation. The basic reason is that the person being addressed as present is in fact absent, and because, obversely, the author is not present to his reader although his words will be" *(Interfaces* 239).

19. Breitwieser (133–34) draws attention to the uncanny effect of Whitman's manipulation of voice and writing.

20. *An American Primer* was published in 1904; see DBN 3:728–29n3439.

21. In the 1856 edition the poem appears under the awkward but revelatory title "Poem of The Sayers of The Words of The Earth."

22. Difficult-to-classify cases such as "arranging" serve Austin's purposes though they appear to frustrate them: rather than struggling to developing a neat taxonomy, Austin is intent on demonstrating the overlapping of his categories and hence the role played by illocutionary or positional force in *any* utterance: "To perform a locutionary act is in general, we may say, also and *eo ipso* to perform an *illocutionary* act" (98).

23. Whitman's much-vexed notion of "indirection" has bearing here. As both Feidelson and Anderson have noted, "indirection" can be understood as a procedure which subverts language-as-statement; it abrogates the notion that a world exists beyond or removed from language itself. See Feidelson 18–21 and Anderson, "Whitman's New Man" 15–21.

24. Here in *Calamus* what has been left out of the book is of course in one sense the explicit declaration of the poet's homosexuality. But like other things that matter to Whitman, the poet's sexuality ought to be a present force rather than a condition to be reported on: what we need to acquire is not knowledge of the poet's sexual preferences but an immediate experience of his body.

25. This is of course the symptomatic structure Derrida has adumbrated. See especially his analysis of Rousseau, *Grammatology* 97–268.

26. In quoting from the *Primer* I have reproduced many of the tentative formulations Whitman later crossed out (as indicated in DBN), though in a number of cases I have replaced these with bracketed ellipses.

    As we shall see, Whitman's designation here of the master of performative power as a "writer" is highly uncharacteristic; I take it to be what I earlier called a "casual" characterization. The passage which immediately follows this one in the *Primer* crosses out "writer," preferring the phrase "great [. . .] user of words"; see 241.

27. At odds with the myth of voice that animates *Leaves of Grass,* this notion of "live words" that appear in a book is nonetheless in keeping with the need to salvage the text that is sometimes admitted to convey the poet's presence to us. See 262–64.

28. On Whitman's fascination with the supposed power of the word to evoke the thing, see Asselineau 2:232 and Matthiessen 556.

29. I quote here from the 1867 rather than the 1860 text.

30. Ong's description of the relation between sound and interiority can serve to adumbrate the apparent phenomenological basis for Whitman's extravagant proclamations: "a field of sight suggests always a beyond or a beneath which is not seen. By contrast, sound gives perceptions of interiors as interiors without their being opened up into surfaces: I can tap an object and learn thereby whether it is solid or hollow" (*Interfaces* 122).

31. While I have come to rather different conclusions, I have benefited greatly in my consideration of Whitman's language theory from the work of James

Perrin Warren; see especially *Walt Whitman's Language and Style,* particularly 1–90. Warren's important book, *Walt Whitman's Language Experiment,* appeared as the present study was going to press.

32. On the intensification of millennial anti-institutionalism and radical individualism during the antebellum period see Ziff 28–29, Fredrickson 7–20, and Bercovitch, *American Jeremiad* 132–75. On their Revolutionary antecedents, which Simpson's account of the federal period scants, see Bercovitch, *American Jeremiad* 93–131 and Erkkila 12–27.

33. I have in mind especially Julie Ellison's *Emerson's Romantic Style,* though her terminology differs from the one I make use of here. See also Pease, *Visionary Compacts* 220–34.

34. On Whitman's interest in Bunsen and Schele de Vere, see Warren, *Walt Whitman's Language and Style* 5, 25–26; and Stovall 162–65, 213.

35. See Aarsleff 13, 16, 294, and 386.

36. See Saussure 67–70 for his classic formulation concerning the arbitrary bond between signifier and signified.

37. Such a mediated tie between word and thing is also posited in the great speculative essays on language origins by Herder and Rousseau: see Herder, *Essay on the Origin of Language,* especially 99–119; and Rousseau, *Essay on the Origin of Languages,* especially 11–16.

38. For a description of this notebook see DBN 3:664n3436.

39. See NUPM 5:1624–26, and Warren, "Whitman as Ghostwriter" and *Walt Whitman's Language and Style* 3–10, for a history of the scholarly controversy concerning the authorship of chapters 11 and 12 of *Rambles;* both Grier (NUPM) and Warren attribute at least some role in their composition to Whitman. While I occasionally quote from these chapters in what follows, none of my main contentions concerning Whitman's language theory depends principally on material garnered from this source.

40. Though the passage is attributed in *Rambles* to Humboldt, according to Warren it appears not to be a precise quotation; but it resembles closely a passage from *Linguistic Variability* 27; Warren cites another translation of the same passage, *Humanist without Portfolio* 280. See Warren, *Walt Whitman's Language and Style* 11.

41. See for example *Linguistic Variability* 72, 145–46, 154–55, and 188.

42. Whitman applies the term "lawless" more particularly to slang; but slang functions for him as a kind of synecdoche for the linguistic innovation for which he praises American speech; see "Slang in America," PW 2:572–77.

43. On the extravagant period enthusiasm for native place names see Simpson 118–21 and 206–209.

44. See for example 1:36.

45. See Schele de Vere 14, 91–93, 106–107, and 238–39. I am indebted here to Warren; see especially *Walt Whitman's Language and Style* 21–28. Schele de Vere's argument is rather complex, since the assertion that linguistic progress is furthered by political conquest must be reconciled with the

apparently opposing contention that it is the languages of conquered peoples rather than conquering ones which eventually come to dominate the linguistic mixtures that result from political occupation; see 116–25.

46. See Warren, *Walt Whitman's Language and Style* 30, for an account of Whitman's interest in linguistic teleology.

47. On the cultural importance of teleological claims for the American Revolution and American liberty see Bercovitch, *American Jeremiad* 133–34. As Bercovitch points out (*American Jeremiad* 135), an insistence on the distinction between mere license and the sort of liberty that served teleological ends was also a staple of American political rhetoric in the period following the Revolution. Whitman's interest in demotic ferment thus locates him in the more liberal camp within the American consensus Bercovitch describes. The centripetal energies of the poet, however, mark not so much a countervailing conservatism, still within that consensus, as a desire to escape politics altogether. See chapters 6–8, below.

48. On artisan republicanism and its Jeffersonian background see Erkkila 12–27 and Wilentz, especially 61–106.

49. I mean to suggest the strain involved in trying to contain Whitman's fantasies of the poet within the sort of figural recuperation of individualism Bercovitch describes as a staple of American rhetoric (a recuperation in which the political thinker of *Democratic Vistas* enthusiastically participates, and toward which the poet of *Leaves of Grass* also gestures): "In virtually every one of the countless biographies of American heroes, for example, the author insists that 'true individualism' is not something unique —not a Byronic or Nietzschean assertion of superiority—but an exemplum of American enterprise: a model of progress and control that typifies the society as a whole" (Bercovitch, *American Jeremiad* 156). On the American tendency to recast revolutionary or romantic "individuality" as American "individualism," and thus to harness potentially radical energies for the task of developing communal consensus, see also Bercovitch, "Emerson, Individualism, and the Ambiguities of Dissent" and "The Problem of Ideology in American Literary History." I take up the complex relation of Whitman's poet figure to this dialectic in chapter 8, below.

50. In "Slang in America," similarly, Whitman approvingly quotes Arthur Symons concerning "languages, in the construction of which whole peoples unconsciously co-operated, the forms of which were determin'd not by individual genius, but by the instincts of successive generations [. . .]" (PW 2:574).

51. On Schele de Vere's and Whitman's interpretations of inflectional leveling see Warren, "Real Grammar" 4–6.

52. See Aarsleff 13–14 and 293–99, and Warren, *Walt Whitman's Language and Style* 14–16.

53. I am indebted here to related assertions by Warren; see *Walt Whitman's Language and Style* 21–28.

54. I am indebted to Warren for the notion of Whitman's strategic mixing of synchronic and diachronic linguistics, though my sense of both the particular combination Whitman concocts and the purposes it serves differs markedly from his; see *Walt Whitman's Language and Style* 21.

55. Irwin (32) notes Whitman's valorization of proper names.

56. On Whitman's use of the term "indication" and its status as a deficient mode of signification that fails to produce the presence or express the intrinsic qualities of the things it signifies, see chapter 2, above.

57. See for example DBN 3:756.

58. It is something of a paradox that Whitman chooses the trope of coining here to figure the influences that supposedly give each person his or her own unique identity. Perhaps this paradox registers, in displaced form, the difficulties of attempting to recover the proper in language.

59. On relativism as a crucial principle for Humboldt see Aarsleff 345–47.

60. For accounts of Reed's influence on Emerson, see Strauch v–xiii and Gura 79–86.

61. On Reed's view of the superfluousness of human speech in a prelapsarian state, see also Gura 83.

62. Reed explains: "They had nothing to communicate by words; for they had not the power of concealment. The sun of the spiritual world shone bright on their hearts, and their senses were open with delight to natural objects. . . . What had they to *say?*" ("Oration on Genius" 11).

63. On Oegger's influence on Emerson see Gura 86–87.

64. On Whitman's relation to Swedenborgianism see also Irwin 30.

65. For the classic structuralist position on onomatopoeia see Saussure 69.

66. On this point see Aarsleff 346–47.

67. See Gura 126–29 for a seminal discussion of Kraitsir, and 129–36 for an account of Thoreau's appropriation of Kraitsir's doctrines in the railroad-cut passage in *Walden*.

68. See Saussure 69–70 for a structuralist account of interjections.

69. See *Aurora* 541–42. Aarsleff (78n51) cites an apposite passage from Boehme: "Now, that Adam stood in the image of God and not that of the beasts is shown by the fact that he knew the property of all the creatures and gave names to all the creatures according to their essence, form, and property; he understood the language of nature as revealed *and articulated* word in all essence, for the name of each creature has its origin here" (emphasis added). See Boehme, *Mysterium Magnum* 1:134. Aarsleff 59–61 cites parallel passages from other seventeenth-century tracts.

70. The last two lines quoted here appear only in the 1856 text; see V 1:266.

71. Whitman's notion that even inanimate objects produce expressive sounds seems to derive from a sense of the relation between sound and structure akin to that adduced by Ong; see note 30, above.

72. On the *neume*, which Whitman's lull and hum resembles, see Derrida:

With this exemplary model of a pure breath *(pneuma)* and of an intact life, of a song and an inarticulate language, of speech without spacing, we have, even if it is placeless [*atopique*] or utopian, a paradigm suitable to our measure. We can name and define it. It is the *neume:* pure vocalization, form of an inarticulate song without speech, whose name means breath. . . . (*Grammatology* 249; bracketed interpolations are the editor's)

As I suggested in chapter 4, above, this mythologized image of voice is perhaps the model for the very self-presence it seems to present:

To speak before knowing how to speak, not to be able either to be silent or to speak, this limit of origin is indeed that of a pure presence, present enough to be living, to be felt in pleasure [*jouissance*] but pure enough to have remained unblemished by the work of differance, inarticulate enough for self-delight [*jouissance de soi*] not to be corrupted by interval, discontinuity, alterity. (*Grammatology* 249; bracketed interpolations are the editor's)

73. On the nineteenth-century vogue for American Indian languages, and on the traits lent by enthusiastic Anglos to such seemingly paradisal speech, see Simpson 202–29. See Abrams 95 concerning romantic commonplaces about American Indian languages.

74. Note too that these aborigines "depart, *charging* the water and the land with names." Both magnetic and juridical in its implications ("I charge you"), this word suggests a performative force simultaneously natural and cultural.

75. The question marks enclosed in brackets are the editor's; bracketed ellipses are mine.

76. Derrida's description of the fictive limit at which language would not yet be discourse but would express in single words all that discourse labors to reconstruct has bearing here. He is both paraphrasing and undermining the views of Rousseau:

Between prelanguage and the linguistic catastrophe instituting the division of discourse, Rousseau attempts to recapture a sort of happy pause, the instantaneity of a full language, the image stabilizing what was no more than a point of pure passage: a language without discourse, a speech without sentence, without syntax, without parts, without grammar, a language of pure effusion, beyond the cry, but short of the hinge [*brisure*] that articulates and at the same time disarticulates the immediate unity of meaning, within which the being of the subject distinguishes itself neither from its acts nor from its attributes. It is the moment when there are words ("the words first used by mankind")—which do not yet function as they do "in languages already formed" and in which men "first gave every single word the sense of a whole proposition". . . . But language cannot be truly born except by the disruption and fracture of that happy plenitude, in the very instant that this instantaneity is wrested from its fictive immediacy and put back into movement. It serves as an absolute reference point for him who wishes to measure and describe difference within discourse. One cannot do it without referring to the limit, always already crossed, of an undivided language, where the proper-infinitive-present is so welded to itself that it cannot even appear in the opposition of the proper noun and the verb in the infinitive present. (*Grammatology* 279–80; the bracketed interpolation is the editor's)

The supposed link between sound and sense Whitman adduces in the passage from the *Primer* was a commonplace in the rhapsodic treatments of Native American languages that flourished in mid–nineteenth-century America (Simpson 210–11). But Whitman is less typical in linking other commonly noted features of "aboriginal" languages with this onomatopoetic quality. The "fitness" of native place names was often attributed to their adjectival, epithetic origin (Simpson 209). And their ability to convey what would otherwise require separate predication was explained by their "syncretism": place names were often formed by joining a noun and verb phrase into a single, lengthy compound word (Simpson 220). In Whitman's account the properties with which etymology and syntactic agglutination have thus endowed the name are attributed instead to its aural features alone:

All aboriginal names [. . .] sound good [. . . . I] was asking for something savage and luxuriant, and behold here are the aboriginal names. I see how they are being preserved. The[y] all are honest words—they give the true length, breadth, depth— They all fit,—Mississippi!—how the word rolls winds with chutes—[. . .] it [. . .] rolls a stream three thousand miles long;—Ohio, [. . .] Connecticut, Ottawa, [. . .] Monongahela [. . .] all fit. (*The Primer of Words* DBN 3:743; bracketed interpolation is the editor's; bracketed ellipses are mine)

Humboldt notes the syntactic agglutination of American Indian languages but regards it as a defect (*Linguistic Variability* 112).

77. All but the first sentence of this notebook entry has been struck through with two vertical lines; the entire passage nonetheless appears in Traubel's *American Primer;* see DBN 3:745n3345.

78. Linked here to an awkward effort at reform, this attack on articulation was a commonplace of speculative romantic and pre-romantic linguistics. Compare Rousseau's assertion that progress in articulation accompanies a loss of expressive accent (16); like Whitman, Rousseau associates writing with this shift (21–22). Herder, in a similar vein, points out that accent or intonation is unwritable (93) and characterizes writing as the mere corpse of living speech (94–96).

79. On the relation between the active-passive and masculine-feminine polarities see Freud, "The Development of the Libido and the Sexual Organizations," *Introductory Lectures* 327; and "Femininity," *New Introductory Lectures* 101–3.

80. Another conspicuous instance of such passivity, section twenty-eight of "Song of Myself," is part of the extended sequence the scenario quoted here initiates.

81. Here Whitman's oxymoronic "alphabetical sounds" implicitly dissolve writing back into voice.

82. Whitman's vision of a "chaste [. . .] drench of love" derives in part from

eugenicist polemics (see Aspiz 183–209), an origin incompatible with neither phobic nor counter-phobic qualities.

83. I take this phrase from Kristeva, or more precisely from Leon S. Roudiez, her English translator; see *Powers of Horror* viii.

84. Here Whitman's revisions serve to stress the associations of indication with writing, and expression with voice, that pervade the *Primer*.

85. On the dating of the *Primer* see DBN 3:728–29n3439, and Warren, "Dating Whitman's Language Studies."

86. Conversely, both the attempt to justify in the discursive context of the *Primer* the sorts of linguistic powers the poems display and the appearance there of a figure very much like the poet of *Leaves of Grass* suggest that Whitman would like to regard the poetry's sometimes outlandish transactions as something more than mere fiction.

87. See for example *Philosophy of Literary Form* 3–8.

88. I quote the 1871 text here. Prior editions all offer slight modifications of the less striking 1855 version of the final line: "What I give I give out of myself."

89. Note that Whitman's "Here!" is performative, activating the passing on of the "breath of life" to which words and voice seem to attest.

90. On recitation as the loss of proper speech see Derrida, "La parole soufflée," *Writing and Difference* 169–95, especially the discussion of the figure of the prompter (souffleur), 176–81.

91. For other, more positive estimates of the practical benefits of writing and the technology that reproduces it, see "Letter to Ralph Waldo Emerson," 1856 349; "Starting from Paumanok," 1860 21; and "Song of the Exposition," V 3:618.

92. On repetition as a mechanism independent of the recuperative procedures of the symptom see Freud, *Beyond the Pleasure Principle,* especially 6–17. Jettisoning the supposed biological basis of this compulsion to repeat and of the death drive with which Freud associates it, Lacan understands these in terms of the "fading" of the subject exacted by accession to the symbolic; see *Four Fundamental Concepts* 53–64 and 197–208. See also Hertz, "Freud and the Sandman," *The End of the Line* 97–121.

93. This fetishistic valuation of the representation may be ineradicable: "It is perhaps unavoidable that, when a subject confronts the factitiousness of object relation, when he stands at the place of the want that founds it, the fetish becomes a life preserver. . . . But is not exactly language our ultimate and inseparable fetish? And language, precisely, is based on fetishist denial ('I know that, but just the same,' 'the sign is not the thing, but just the same,' etc.) and defines us in our essence as speaking beings. Because of its founding status, the fetishism of 'language' is perhaps the only one that is unanalyzable" (Kristeva, *Powers of Horror* 37).

94. I here use the terms sign and thing, rather than signifier and signified, in an effort to paraphrase Whitman's argument, in which the continuing avail-

ability of something prior to, and unaffected by, the process of signification is of paramount importance.

95. Because of the parallelism that governs this passage, the last of these lines implies that the transition from narcissism to object relations is somehow equivalent to a fall into representation. On the connection between these shifts, see chapter 4, above.

96. Whitman seems to draw here on contemporary eugenicist beliefs about the effects of the psychic and moral states of the participants on the offspring of intercourse; see Aspiz 193–206. Espoused by psuedo-science or not, this belief that thoughts directly determine physical reality is an instance of magic thinking, inflected here by anxiety.

97. On the recruiting of subjects to ideological positions see Althusser, "Ideology and Ideological State Apparatuses."

98. See Ong, *Interfaces* 136.

99. I quote here from the 1867 text; the 1860 version lacks the "Camerado!" which makes this utterance an apostrophe.

100. See 180, above.

101. On "good" writing see Derrida, *Grammatology* 17.

102. See also WWC 3:148–49.

103. Though Whitman's work encourages just such extravagant responses. See above, 163–65.

6. Inscriptions

Mr Burke rouzed the indignation of all ranks of men, when by a refinement in cruelty superiour to that which in the East yokes the living to the dead he strove to persuade us that we and our posterity to the end of time were riveted to a constitution by the indissoluble compact of a dead parchment, and were bound to cherish a corse at the bosom, when reason might call aloud that it should be entombed.

> —Wordsworth, "A Letter to the Bishop of Landaff" 1:48

> Nor, perchance—
> If I should be where I no more can hear
> Thy voice, nor catch from thy wild eyes these gleams
> Of past existence—wilt thou then forget
> That on the banks of this delightful stream
> We stood together. . . .

> —Wordsworth, "Tintern Abbey," *Poems* 1:361

America does not repel the past or what it has produced under its forms or amid other politics or the idea of castes or the old religions . . . accepts the lesson with calmness . . . is not so impatient as has been supposed that the slough still sticks to opinions and manners and literature while the life which served its requirements has passed into the new life of the new forms . . . perceives that the corpse is slowly borne from the eating and sleeping rooms of the house . . . perceives that it waits a little while in the door . . . that it was fittest for its days . . . that its action has descended to the stalwart and wellshaped heir who approaches . . . and that he shall be fittest for his days.

> —Whitman, Preface, 1855 5

> Closer yet I approach you,
> What thought you have of me, I had as much of you—I laid in my stores in advance,
> I considered long and seriously of you before you were born.
> Who was to know what should come home to me?
> Who knows but I am enjoying this?
> Who knows but I am as good as looking at you now, for all you cannot see me?

> —Whitman, "Crossing Brooklyn Ferry," 1856 218

> Why should not we also enjoy an original relation to the universe?

> —Emerson, *Nature, Collected Works* 1:7

"To read apostrophe as sign of a fiction which knows its own fictive nature," Jonathan Culler suggests, "is to stress its optative character, its impossible imperatives: commands which in their explicit impossibility figure events in and of fiction" ("Apostrophe" 146). Understood in this way, Culler notes, apostrophe and other modes of poetic address that seem to exceed the powers of ordinary speech are neither mystified nor demystified, involving instead an investment in mystification that simultaneously registers its contrary ("Apostrophe" 153). That being so, our task as readers of apostrophe and similar lyric speech acts is to attend to this play of investments and adduce what might be called its imaginative rhythm: granted that such gestures are not merely mystified, we need to ask what sort of stake they have in the enchantments they set in motion, and how they react to whatever works to disenchant them.

We might begin to position Whitman in this regard by placing the lines above from "Crossing Brooklyn Ferry" over against the poem with which Culler ends his account of apostrophe, Keats's "This living hand":

> This living hand, now warm and capable
> Of earnest grasping, would, if it were cold
> And in the icy silence of the tomb,
> So haunt thy days and chill thy dreaming nights
> That thou would wish thine own heart dry of blood
> So in my veins red life might stream again,
> And thou be conscience-calm'd. See, here it is—
> I hold it towards you. (Keats 503; quoted in Culler, "Apostrophe" 153)

According to Culler the poem's crucial achievement is its ability to vanquish the skepticism which the final claim to presence is likely to provoke. "The narrator," Culler notes,

> contrasts his life with his death, proleptically predicting that when he is dead the reader will seek to overcome his death, will blind himself to his death by an imaginative act. We fulfill this icy prediction, not by seeking actually to sacrifice our lives that Keats might live, but by losing our empirical lives: forgetting the temporality which supports them and trying to embrace a purely fictional time in which we can believe that the hand is really present and perpetually held toward us through the poem. ("Apostrophe" 154)

Keats's poem may turn on a harsher dialectic than Culler suggests. It can be argued that the poem in some sense demands our lives precisely by making it impossible to ignore that it has itself already sacrificed Keats's. Associating living presence with voice but more especially with deixis, the poem conversely weds failed deixis to death, contrasting "This living hand, now warm and capable / Of earnest grasping" with the dead hand, incapable of such a gesture, which may come to "haunt" us. Though an image of voice implies the poet's presence at the lyric's close, it is the failure of the deictic gesture on which the final proclamation turns that works Keats's chilling effect: it is the absence of the hand, rather than the fiction of its presence, that haunts us, a result brought about less by an achieved mystification than through its collapse. This demystification of course initiates a fiction of its own: we should indeed speak of the fiction of the absence of the hand, or of its ghostly dissolving, rather than simply of its failure to appear, since it is, as it were, the vanishing of a hand never literally there in the first place that activates the rather terrifying proleptic power of Keats's poem. This disappearance precipitates "This living hand," at its close, into the condition of epitaph; as the hand evaporates, the fiction of voice to which the lyric appeals seems to lapse into mute inscription. This lapse is very like what the poet has predicted will be passed on to us. If his prophesy in a sense comes true, that is because it names a condition to which the poem's own economy of address subjects us: calling on us to animate the speaker's voice and presence by lending ourselves to the prosopopoeia which generates the poem, Keats's text recruits us to a community of supposed personhood whose dissolution not only prefigures but seems to precipitate our own.[1] Here voice and inscription are disposed so as to yield an illusion not only of presence but also of its fading.

Though there is a quotient of irony in invoking the title of Geoffrey Hartman's seminal essay in such a context, "False Themes and Gentle Minds" thus describes a romantic rhetorical and imaginative rhythm pertinent to Keats's poem (*Beyond Formalism* 283–97). Here disenchantment is essential to the poem's achievement of a sparer—if in this case more ominous—enchantment. Rather than warding off demystification, "This living hand" not only invites but indeed depends on it.

Whitman's typical apostrophes are more solicitous of the enchantments they initiate. My epigraph from "Crossing Brooklyn Ferry" is characteristic in this regard. Outrageously making invisibility an attribute of the poet's living presence rather than letting it be registered as the condition that undoes his claims, this passage avoids the reversals that structure "This living hand," restraining any tendency to demystification and enlisting it with minimal disruption into a fiction by no means purged of its naive implications.[2] It is not until the 1860 edition of *Leaves of Grass* that Whitman regularly associates the insubstantiality of the poet's presence with death. Until then, if inscription is occasionally allowed into the imaginative universe of the poems, its negative implications are vigorously denied; in the 1855 and 1856 *Leaves of Grass,* Whitman seems bent on detaching the poet's words from the condition of epitaph rather than letting them lapse into such ominous monumentality.

The dialectical relation to archaic sources Hartman makes central to romantic mythopoeia, that is, seems not to be crucial to the achieved fiction of *Leaves of Grass;* the poems of Whitman's early editions seem less intent on purifying such energies than on retrieving them intact. This project does not quite place Whitman outside the problematic Hartman understands as energizing romanticism: the impulse toward purification, Hartman suggests, coexists in an unresolvable tension with the daemonization it struggles to tame (*Beyond Formalism* 289). As we shall see, however, Whitman's stance does locate him over against the paradigmatic position Hartman assigns the Wordsworthian project of demystification.[3]

One sign of Whitman's commitment to the sort of archaic resonance Wordsworth struggles to purge is the way *Leaves of Grass* fends off the very notion of fiction Culler invokes. Culler points out that the fictive status of lyric apostrophe is characteristically hard to keep clearly in view, since "apostrophe is different in that it makes its point by troping not on the meaning of a word but on the circuit or situation of communication itself" ("Apostrophe" 135). But Whitman's campaign on behalf of the supposedly literal status of the poet's addresses is especially zealous. The image of voice conjured up by his repeated denial that writing plays any role in his poems serves to suggest that the linguistic powers displayed in the poems are more than merely fictive, implying the poet's ability to recover the archaic energies lurking in words. The poet seems to liberate magical performative power from debased involvement with the constative; expression from indication; the shamanistic powers of the proper name from the coercions of the category; and the living presences produced by the magic word from the representations culture would teach us to value in their place.

As we saw, Whitman's discursive tracts on language are likewise intent on demonstrating the poet's special access to these linguistic resources. Suggesting that Whitman would like to regard as literal the powers which the poet's apostrophes epitomize, these prose writings possess a vehemence which implies as well that the gesture of disenchantment is not one the poetry will invite or accommodate comfortably. Yet the awkward entanglements we uncovered in Whitman's language theory suggest that *Leaves of Grass* is likely to end up subjecting the poet's magical claims to the very purgation they resist. The poems themselves record similar entanglements repeatedly. Indeed, while Whitman's prose tracts adamantly repudiate writing and the lapses for which it stands, his poems often seem to register awareness not only of the role writing plays in producing the poet's image of voice, but also of the melancholy implications this intertwining possesses. Rarely made explicit, an unsettling self-consciousness about their own status seems to lurk within many of the poet's most buoyant pronouncements: what Whitman's language theory suggests despite itself, through a troubling circularity, the poems of *Leaves of Grass* reveal in the self-divided quality of individual speech acts. The bravado of the poet's declarations can pass over very delicately into a more quizzical and vexed awareness. It is as if the voice to which the universe ought to resound suddenly heard itself with an eerie detachment, sensing that it was not quite bringing off the magical transaction its performative utterance declared. This sudden sense of distance often seems to be provoked by an ambiguous awareness of the role played by writing in purveying the poet's word; typically undeclared, this awareness seems to hover in the poet's tone. This is tone, of course, in something of a catachrestic sense: it is as if the resonance of the poet's pronouncements were hollowed out by the muteness and monumentality of inscription; or as if Whitman's image of voice had always to free its exuberant accents from the shadow of a writing threatening to darken its claims.

This flickering recognition amounts to demystification of a sort. But in Whitman's early editions a purifying of the poet's fictions is resisted rather than welcomed: almost never allowed to redirect his project or prompt a redefinition of what his presence means, it characteristically provokes anxiety or melancholy; the accents that attest to it are typically wistful, and the comedy it can occasion is characteristically a rueful one. These responses form a kind of surreptitious counterpoint to the expansive self-confidence with which the poet's presence is typically proclaimed; they suggest the importance to *Leaves of Grass* of a canny but precarious mystification. Brooding over the poems' own mode furtively but obsessively, *Leaves of Grass* confirms the central place Whitman's myth of language holds in his imaginative vision: not only the poet-hero but also the author of *Leaves of Grass* seems to have invested his identity to a remarkable degree in a dream of the word, and of the kinds of self-presentation and command of others it ought to make possible. Sensing themselves as writing, Whitman's visionary pronouncements momentarily waver, leaving the poet in a space he does not command and cannot redeem.

Inventories

This displacement of the poet's speech-acts by writing can often be quite subtle. But I want to begin with a rather massive version of the sort of wavering I have in mind; less carefully managed than the delicate modulations of tone that enrich Whitman's apostrophes, it suggests by its sheer preponderance the way the performative vision that animates *Leaves of Grass* remains vulnerable to the ills it ought to cure.

Sending a copy of Whitman's book to Carlyle in 1856, Emerson attached a mischievous and now famous disclaimer: "after you have looked into it, if you think, as you may, that it is only an auctioneer's inventory of a warehouse, you can light your pipe with it" (Slater 509). "I expect him to make the songs of the nation," he is supposed to have remarked more acerbically some years later, "but he seems to be contented to make the inventories" (quoted in Schyberg 104). Emerson surely had Whitman's notorious catalogues in mind here, as Ezra Pound perhaps did too when he claimed that, having always recalled that there were about twenty pages of good poetry in all of *Leaves of Grass,* he found on going back to locate them that he couldn't rediscover which ones they were.[4] Like Emerson's increasingly dour equivocations, Pound's predicament suggests something of the unpredictable mix of exhilaration and exasperation we can often feel reading Whitman; even the most enthused encounter with the poet's massive lists is likely to be overtaken by a sense of tedium at unexpected and not necessarily consistent junctures. Some of Whitman's catalogues, of course, are more successful than others. Yet to an unnerving degree almost all these litanies are subject to odd slippages of focus; these seem due less to momentary lapses of attention or sympathy on the part of the individual reader than to a difficulty endemic to the catalogues themselves. It is as if what holds our attention is likely suddenly to evaporate, or to metamorphose into something altogether less compelling. There are surely various ways to account for this slippage. But we might understand it in part as a function of the slide from magical performance to constative utterance, or from expressive naming to mere indication, to which these lists seem conspicuously liable. The resonance and power which the names the poet intones often seem to possess can simply disappear, turning what we had been registering as a vocative drama or a ceremony of positing into an arid list; rather than assimilating or animating the things they name, Whitman's catalogues then seem merely to enumerate them. Understood as inventory rather than magical act, the massive litanies of *Leaves of Grass* can be rather bleak.

Serving to hedge the poet's bets, the mobile, frequently comic tone that pervades "Song of Myself" helps insure the catalogues there against such effects. But the sort of lapses I have been describing are by no means peculiar to Whitman's weaker poems or confined to his later work. In lines Whitman added to the 1855 poem "A Song for Occupations" for the 1867 edition, the poet introduces the daunting catalogue that had always composed most of the poem's fifth section with an assertion that makes explicit the performative, or at least perlocutionary, task about to commence:

> Strange and hard that paradox true I give;
> Objects gross and the unseen Soul are one. (V: 1:93)

The first printing of the poem already concludes Whitman's long list of the paraphernalia of American trades by summing up what the catalogue should have accomplished or at any rate made convincing:

> In them the heft of the heaviest . . . . in them far more than you estimated, and far less also,
> In them, not yourself . . . . you and your soul enclose all things, regardless of estimation. (1855 96)

One need not cower in the seemingly limited sphere of one's individual identity, that is, since that identity in fact subsumes all things.[5] This incorporative trope is one with which readers of *Leaves of Grass* are of course familiar. Yet the catalogue framed by these declarations seems gradually to dissipate the vocative energies that might accomplish such ends; the poet's word seems to lose itself among the myriad acts and appurtenances its ritual force was to subsume:

> House-building, measuring, sawing the boards,
> Blacksmithing, glass-blowing, nail-making, coopering, tin-roofing, shingle-dressing,
> Ship-joining, dock-building, fish-curing, flagging of sidewalks by flaggers,
> The pump, the pile-driver, the great derrick, the coal-kiln and brick-kiln,
> [. . . .]
> The blast-furnace and the puddling-furnace, the loup-lump at the bottom of the melt at last, the rolling-mill, the stumpy bars of pig-iron, the strong clean-shaped T-rail for railroads,
> Oil-works, silk-works, white-lead-works, the sugar-house, steam-saws, the great mills and factories,
> Stone-cutting, shapely trimmings for façades or window or door-lintels, the mallet, the tooth-chisel, the jib to protect the thumb,
> The calking-iron, the kettle of boiling vault-cement, and the fire under the kettle,
> The cotton-bale, the stevedore's hook, the saw and buck of the sawyer, the mould of the moulder, the working-knife of the butcher, the ice-saw, and all the work with ice,
> The work and tools of the rigger, grappler, sail-maker, block-maker,
> Goods of gutta-percha, papier-maché, colors, brushes, brush-making glazier's implements,
> The veneer and glue-pot, the confectioner's ornaments, the decanter and glasses, the shears and flat-iron,
> The awl and knee-strap, the pint measure and quart measure, the counter and stool, the writing-pen of quill or metal, the making of all sorts of edged tools,
> The brewery, brewing, the malt, the vats, every thing that is done by brewers, wine-makers, vinegar-makers,
> Leather-dressing, coach-making, boiler-making, rope-twisting, distilling, sign-painting, lime-burning, cotton-picking, electro-plating, electrotyping, stereotyping,
> Stave-machines, planing-machines, reaping-machines, ploughing-machines, thrashing-machines, steam wagons. (V 1: 93–95; CRE 216–17)[6]

This staggering enumeration continues for another eight long lines. Its cumulative effect is less bracing than stupefying: Whitman's list seems finally simply to detail the incapacitating proliferation of industrial instruments it ought to redeem. Our sense here of a sort of massive inertia is surely attributable in part to the recalcitrance of the "gross" objects Whitman's list includes, a property to which the poet explicitly draws our attention and makes the occasion of his paradox. But it probably results as well from the very mania for inventorying that ought not only to register this riddle but also to intimate its visionary resolution: it is hard to read all the way through this catalogue without coming to regard it as merely a Herculean exercise in stock-clerking. The inertia that overtakes this litany, that is, derives partly from a troubling sense of the distance between all these words and the things they name: what ought to be a ceremony of re-possession seems to collapse into a merely indicative enumeration. Thus understood, Whitman's words simply re-trace a dispersive, metonymically organized space, rather than re-gathering it into the poet's imperium by means of the ritual power of utterance.

A failing to which the poet's catalogues are always liable, this slippage may be precipitated here by the absence of the sort of extended phrases, set firmly in parallel relation by strongly marked anaphora, which Whitman usually employs. The litanies in *Leaves of Grass* depend for their success on the suggestion of ceremonial status such insistently iterative procedures establish. They rely as well on the sense of voice these ritualized locutions imply: in *Leaves of Grass* it is voice that re-activates the magical powers of the word, re-animating the expressive energies lurking in the names of things.

What undermines this concluding list from "A Song for Occupations" is thus also writing. If the apparent slippage from expression to indication here is precipitated by an increasing sense of distance between word and thing, this awareness is provoked in turn by a gradual dissipation of Whitman's image of voice and the resultant foregrounding of the writing literally in front of us. As Walter Ong points out, "Writing and print distance the utterer of discourse from the hearer, and both from the word, which appears in writing and print as an object or thing" (*Interfaces* 283). Regarded with the sort of detachment print invites, the poet's inventory seems to be an exercise in the mere designation or indication writing stands for in Whitman's work.

Like this slide from performance to indication, another, closely related lapse can afflict Whitman's catalogues. Viewed as performance, these litanies seem to relocate productive power in the poet's own present act, canceling the precedence which the concatenated world of things would otherwise possess. Regarded as designation, Whitman's lists instead enumerate what pre-exists them, detailing a priority they are powerless to reverse.

Not simply an agon between name and thing, this struggle for priority is also a battle over words themselves. As performance, Whitman's litanies take power over the word as well as the world, making language the magical instrument of the poet's will; as indication, his catalogues repeat words whose significance is not his to determine and whose power over things is not primarily his to dispose.[7] Thus emptied out, the poet's enumerations confirm rather than contest the already-spoken condition of the word and the already-bespoken status of the things it names.[8] Naming the body, the catalogue from "I Sing the Body Electric" makes dramatically clear that this battle for linguistic priority is also a struggle against alienation.[9] It is a struggle the poet seems to lose:

> Head, neck, hair, ears, drop and tympan of the ears,
> Eyes, eye-fringes, iris of the eye, eye-brows, and the waking or sleeping of the lids,
> Mouth, tongue, lips, teeth, roof of the mouth, jaws, and the jaw-hinges,
> Nose, nostrils of the nose, and the partition,
> Cheeks, temples, forehead, chin, throat, back of the neck, neck-slue,
> Strong shoulders, manly beard, scapula, hind-shoulders, and the ample side-round of the chest,
> Upper-arm, arm-pit, elbow-socket, lower-arm, arm-sinews, arm-bones,
> Wrist and wrist-joints, hand, palm, knuckles, thumb, forefinger, finger-balls, finger-joints, finger-nails,
> Broad breast-front, curling hair of the breast, breast-bone, breast-side,
> Ribs, belly, back-bone, joints of the back-bone,
> Hips, hip-sockets, hip-strength, inward and outward round, man-balls, man-root,
> Strong set of thighs, well carrying the trunk above,
> Leg-fibres, knee, knee-pan, upper-leg, under-leg,
> Ankles, instep, foot-ball, toes, toe-joints, the heel,
> All attitudes, all the shapeliness, all the belongings of my or your body, or of any one's body, male or female,
> The lung-sponges, the stomach-sac, the bowels sweet and clean,
> The brain in its folds inside the skull-frame. (1856 177–78)[10]

What ought to be a ritual of repossession, a healing and re-animating of the body by means of pneumatic energies endowed with restorative force, comes to seem instead like an obsessive enumeration, a sort of mad, encyclopaedic cataloguing of the *disjecta membra* which the alienated body subjected to cultural encoding has become. As the poet's words seem to fall from voice to writing, the precedence which the catalogue seeks to reverse stays where it was, with the surrounding world Whitman's language belatedly names, in the received terms that shape our sense of it.

For the most part, the possible lapses to which we have been attending threaten these litanies without re-inflecting them: Whitman's catalogues rarely register their equivocal status in discernible modulations of voice. Yet in the occasional lists that foreground Whitman's transumptive claims by explicitly declaring them, the poet's triumphant accents sometimes seem tinged by another tone:

> See! steamers steaming through my poems!
> See, in my poems immigrants continually coming and landing,
> [....]
> See, pastures and forests in my poems—See, animals, wild and tame—See, beyond the Kanzas, countless herds of buffalo, feeding on short curly grass,
> See, in my poems, old and new cities, solid, vast, inland, with paved streets, with iron and stone edifices, and ceaseless vehicles, and commerce. ("Starting from Paumanok," 1860 21)

Visionary in their implications, these exuberant declarations of the poet's power are nonetheless marked by a quotient of pathos or slightly melancholy wit; it is occasioned by the very belatedness this catalogue claims to overcome.

Prolepsis

What might be called a drama of prolepsis is thus central to the equivocal speech acts that organize Whitman's work. If Whitman's catalogues both register and contest the priority of world and code to the poet's own utterance, his apostrophes can be understood as more dramatic attempts to escape the foreclosure this belatedness entails: they project the poet into another scene at which he is, so to speak, the first to arrive. This priority is often the explicit subject of the poet's declarations to us:

> What thought you have of me, I had as much of you—I laid in my stores in advance,

I considered long and seriously of you before you were born. ("Crossing Brooklyn Ferry," 1856 218)

Seeming to liberate the poet, these addresses simultaneously threaten to subjugate us; here the poet seems to wield over others the very power from which he himself supposedly escapes. Kerry Larson thus draws our attention to "the insistently *proleptic* drive behind these solicitations" (18).[11] He also astutely notes that the poet's repeated insistence that he comes not to dominate but to emancipate us paradoxically insures this subjugation, since exercising the power the poet proclaims, of "awakening the dormant will of the second person—the slumbering 'glory of you' ... amounts to paralyzing it" (47). "Bad faith or a case of self-interest masquerading under the guise of a disinterested generality," Larson goes on to argue, "is ... not the real issue here ..." (53). As we shall see, this gesture of exculpation may well be too sweeping; but it does alert us to the complexity of both Whitman's ambitions and his consequent predicament. As we have seen in other connections, the poet of *Leaves of Grass* can often be found deploying the very mechanisms his work seems devoted to defusing.

Larson construes this awkward impasse as an instance of the American political dilemma with which Whitman's work sometimes struggles —the paradoxical task of trying to posit an originary national compact that is indissoluble without being constraining.[12] Useful since it points out the explicitly political implications of address in Whitman's work, such a reading nonetheless runs the risk of enlisting the poet's performatives in a constitutional drama at the cost of unduly restricting the range of implication of this figure of presence and the proleptic powers he exercises and struggles to re-define. The poet and the encounter he initiates condense concerns that are broadly ideological but hardly circumscribed by what we ordinarily mean by politics. What the poet himself seems to become as he addresses us is not comfortably comprehended under the rubric of political individualism; and the perils he claims to ward off are too broadly defined to be equated with the political targets of even a radically individualist political iconography. Whitman's polemical distinction between voice and writing, we saw in chapter 5, implies that the poet's apostrophes by-pass not just institutionalized modes of political mediation but a cultural mechanism pervasive enough to take writing as its image: it is, indeed, the power of images and representations that the poet's voice and presence ought to render nugatory. Whitman depicts these mechanisms not simply as dangerous, but as necromantic instruments deployed by the vampiric dead: enticing us into a worship of symbolic forms that pre-empt the proper priority and organic growth of living presences, writing and representation inflict a kind of living death on those they infect.[13]

The poet's presence can supposedly awaken us from this lethal enchantment. Whitman's figure of voice, we saw, bespeaks the poet's ability to exercise power of a different kind, power which can liberate us from simulacra by restoring what they destroy: he comes among images as the essence of living presence, freeing us from our bewitched idolatry.[14] The proleptic power of Whitman's apostrophes is thus wholly benign, since what the poet pre-empts is not other presences but the symbolic structures that would violate their proper autonomy.

Yet the uncomfortable disclaimers of coercive intent to which Larson draws attention suggest an entanglement our own examination of Whitman's language theory has also revealed: the poet's presence may be an instance of precisely the sort of preemptive authority Whitman warns us against, and he may liberate us from our old idolatries only by imposing new idols upon us. Making surreptitious rather than overt use of the symbolic mechanisms he claims to banish, in order to perform what we are thereby seduced into calling our liberation, the poet of *Leaves of Grass* may not simply, as Larson suggests, commit some of the aggression he would like to obviate; he may subject us to a fiercer enchantment rather than introducing a finer, more purified one.

If the living voice Whitman claims to project would incarnate the liberating power to which he aspires, while writing epitomizes the symbolic structures from which he supposedly frees us, the image of voice able to occult its dependence on the very writing Whitman repudiates is the vehicle of this enchantment. Yet Whitman's attempt to sequester writing is not wholly successful. His figure of voice thus sometimes intimates the equivocal relations among what ought to be the poet's enabling dichotomies. In the poet's apostrophes, the crucial distinctions between the performative and constative, expression and indication, proper living presence and symbolic construct or simulacrum can seem to hover, suspended, short of the dramatic resolution to which Whitman's image of voice should attest. Seeming sometimes to suspend the poet's powers as well, this irresolution may instead reveal the troubling status of an authority by no means vitiated or renounced.

Characteristically no more explicit in Whitman's apostrophes than in his catalogues, such equivocations are nonetheless registered intimately in these addresses to us: they seem to re-inflect the poet's utterance, or to lend it a strangely hovering accent. Entering the universe of *Leaves of Grass* surreptitiously, the ambiguities that trouble the poet's magic word seem to haunt his declarations and the project they supposedly further, rather than provoking a dialectical reversal or initiating a sparer, demystified fiction.

We can clarify this stance toward disenchantment, and see what is at stake in the particular vision of priority Whitman struggles to sustain, by juxtaposing such speech acts to the very different strategies of Wordsworth in a poem like "Tintern Abbey." As in Whitman's work, demystification is associated in Wordsworth's poem with the passing of voice into text. Though "Tintern Abbey" leaves this connection implicit, we can indeed contrast Whitman's characteristic investment in a figure of voice to Wordsworth's commitment to what might be called a figure of writing. Redeeming more primitive enchantments, writing in "Tintern Abbey" figures a mode of perdurance and a mechanism of influence that are explicitly symbolic—and thus, for Wordsworth though not for Whitman, a proleptic power no longer constraining or pre-emptive. Whitman's figure of voice thus wards off attenuations Wordsworth celebrates; a purging or purifying of imagination that *Leaves of Grass* registers only indirectly, and with anxiety or melancholy, is Wordsworth's explicit theme. As we shall see further on, however, discomfort concerning the proleptic power exercised by their own words is nonetheless a burden these poets share.

Wordsworth: "Tintern Abbey"

Discussing "The Ruined Cottage" in *Wordsworth's Poetry*, Geoffrey Hartman suggests that "the theme of the completed poem is the humanized imagination ..." (140). This description is equally applicable to "Tintern Abbey," which thus occupies a late stage in the embracing dialectic Hartman's classic study traces through Wordsworth's work. "Wordsworth's great claim," Hartman argues there concerning the prior phase of this dialectic, "is that the imagination can be naturalized, and that the 'heroic age' of its naturalization [eventually] saves it from being lost to human life" (210). Nature, in Hartman's well-known account, liberates the poet's imagination from the sudden, violent intensities Harold Bloom calls "sublime solipsism";[15] but it comes gradually to be seen as the type rather than the literal source and guarantee for continuities that are accordingly recognized as communal and symbolic.

This taming of sublime power, Hartman notes, is always precarious. Wordsworth achieves it only by skirting persistent intimations he finds troubling: "Nature, time, memory, and poetry itself, can only fitfully bind an imagination which is radically in excess of nature as of every socializing principle" (211). Hymned in Wordsworth's recollection of the Simplon Pass (Prelude 1850 6.592–616),[16] this sublime power more characteristically provokes misgivings; according to Hartman it is indeed often disavowed, appearing in Wordsworth's early work, especially, not as the poet's own possession, but displaced and disguised as an encroaching and terrifying natural force. I want to come back, toward the end of this chapter, to Hartman's account of this earlier stage in Wordsworth's dialectic, since traces of such frightening sublimity persist even within the purified myth of symbolic continuity worked out in "Tintern Abbey." Troubling Wordsworth's sustaining, humanized vision of cultural transmission, these intimations of less gentle power may mark not so much the difficulty of socializing the imagination as the unsettling persistence of violently pre-emptive social mechanisms from which imaginative power can never be wholly detached. Leaves of Grass, itself archaic in its aspirations, is more overt in warding off hostile atavistic powers with which the poet's own magical capacities might be confused; but "Tintern Abbey" has not simply left behind such haunted ground.[17] Given the degree to which Wordsworth's and Whitman's visions of poetry are opposed, they indeed conceive in surprisingly similar terms the social mechanisms from which it needs to be disentangled. Whitman's anxieties thus emerge as not simply aberrant; but it is possible that what provokes them can be redressed neither by political action nor by a poetic program that exceeds it.

We need to turn now, however, to the myth of human continuity that dominates "Tintern Abbey" and the writing that figures it, in order to distinguish this version of romantic dialectic from the more archaic ambitions that animate Leaves of Grass and the figure of voice evoked to sustain them. "For Wordsworth," Paul de Man notes in an early essay

that takes issue with the crucial role Hartman accords nature in Wordsworth's work, yet seems far more compatible with Hartman's account
than do the severer intimations of de Man's later writing,

> the relationships towards time have a priority over relationships towards nature;
> one finds, in his work, a persistent deepening of self-insight represented as a
> movement that begins in a contact with nature, then grows beyond nature to
> become a contact with time. The contact, the relationship with time, is, however,
> always a negative one for us, for the relationship between the self and time is
> necessarily mediated by death; it is the experience of mortality that awakens
> within us a consciousness of time that is more than merely natural. ("Time and
> History in Wordsworth" 16–17)[18]

It is just this shift that "Tintern Abbey" records and responds to.
While *Leaves of Grass* celebrates an eternal present centering on the
poet's presence and apparently regenerated by word magic and the
power of voice, in "Tintern Abbey" the present moment is instead the
site of a precarious and partial renewal, provoking a dialectic of relin-
quishment and recovery that effectively gives up presence for what can
be sustained beyond its loss.[19] Temporality and the attenuations our
awareness of it provokes condition the poem's subdued affirmations
from its opening. Wordsworth's title already suggests the "vacillating
calculus of gain and loss, of hope and doubt. . . ." which Hartman
regards as the poem's subject (*Wordsworth's Poetry* 27): "Lines Composed a Few Miles above Tintern Abbey, on Revisiting the Banks of the
Wye during a Tour. July 13, 1798" (*Poems* 1:357). This elaborate,
conspicuously circumstantial heading doubly inscribes the vatic present
of lyric utterance within a temporal structure that conditions the poem's
claims. It makes the poem's present a commemoration or quest for
recovery of a prior incident outside the bounds of lyric speech. It further
qualifies this lyric performance by emphatically projecting it, too, into a
past, not only dating its occurrence but conflating enthusiasm and transcription, present inspiration and an act of written composition which
conserves such afflatus for future use.

Implied by Wordsworth's title, this preoccupation with time, and with
a structure of attenuated repetitions that can mitigate but not overcome
its force, lends the poem a reflective, ruminative intensity which manages
to seem both celebratory and somber. It is the sense of wonder that
predominates in Wordsworth's opening lines, which dwell on the precar-

iousness of even such contingent and partial recovery as the poet discovers and seeks to preserve:

> Five years have passed; five summers, with the length
> Of five long winters! and again I hear
> These waters, rolling from their mountain-springs
> With a soft inland murmur.—Once again
> Do I behold these steep and lofty cliffs,
> That on a wild secluded scene impress
> Thoughts of more deep seclusion; and connect
> The landscape with the quiet of the sky. (*Poems* 1:357–58)

Like the cliffs which join this re-encountered scene with the tranquil expanse above it, suggesting the possibility of a deeper, more inward sequestering than the poet's present perception alone provides, the poem itself will be a medium of connection, positing the continuities that sustain us. But it is also a meditation on their fragility, a quality suggested in part by the rhythm of hesitation and recovery that characterizes Wordsworth's delicately enjambed blank verse; the penultimate line here indeed poises on a verb positioned so as to problematize the very project it names.[20]

Imaged in the natural scene and renewed by encounter with it, the tenuous continuity "Tintern Abbey" struggles to affirm does not inhere there; it is neither guaranteed nor fulfilled by a natural presence that rejuvenates itself or a present moment in which the poet might be thought to recover it. Partly a hymn to ongoing life or natural presence, "Tintern Abbey" is more crucially a celebration of mind as "a mansion for all lovely forms" (*Poems* 1:361), of the power to generate the images or representations that perdure beyond the extinguishing of immediate presence. We are told that the peculiarly human sustenance the poet has obtained from the scene he now revisits was paradoxically released not by immersion in the landscape but by separation from it:

> These beauteous forms,
> Through a long absence, have not been to me
> As is a landscape to a blind man's eye:
> But oft, in lonely rooms, and 'mid the din
> Of towns and cities, I have owed to them
> In hours of weariness, sensations sweet,
> Felt in the blood, and felt along the heart;

And passing even into my purer mind,
With tranquil restoration. . . . (*Poems* 1:358)

Figured as a reaction to urban life and hence as contingent, the alienation that precipitates what Wordsworth here describes as a purification of sensation turns out to be necessary to the continuities the poem celebrates, as does the removal the poet seems likewise to lament. Further on in the poem, anticipated absence encroaches even on the poet's present experience: the significance of the present scene inheres in its future power to sustain the poet who will have lost it. The landscape indeed rises up before the poet less as an impinging presence than as a clarified or resolved image, and it is precisely as an image he will be able to recall that the scene is valued:

And now, with gleams of half-extinguished thought,
With many recognitions dim and faint,
And somewhat of a sad perplexity,
The picture of the mind revives again:
While here I stand, not only with the sense
Of present pleasure, but with pleasing thoughts
That in this moment there is life and food
For future years. . . . (*Poems* 1:359)

Here both the present moment and the actual presences one might be supposed to recover there are virtually effaced as discrete categories. The present becomes the site in which one hopes for memory, and presences take on meaning as the images from which they are here made virtually indistinguishable. Representation seems not simply to survive the extinguishing of present perception, but to extinguish perception itself.[21]

"Tintern Abbey" nonetheless skirts the sublime transumption that would celebrate this image-making faculty as self-sustaining and self-delighting. More nearly hymned in the ninth section of the Immortality Ode, the "obstinate questionings / Of sense and outward things, / Fallings from us, vanishings" (*Poems* 1:528) are in "Tintern Abbey" displaced onto a shadowy Miltonic figure, hovering in a passage I quoted above. This Miltonic ghost is conjured up in order to exemplify an imaginative stance antipodal to the poet's own: "These beauteous forms, / Through a long absence, have not been to me / As is a landscape to a blind man's eye." Further on, Wordsworthian imagination is likewise positioned over against the transumptive visionary intensity avowed, for example, by the Keats of "Ode to Psyche," who can "see, and sing, by

my own eyes inspired" (365).[22] Wordsworth does gesture at the sort of
profound interiorizing of outward forms and external powers we associate with such sublimity:

> And I have felt
> A presence that disturbs me with the joy
> Of elevated thoughts; a sense sublime
> Of something far more deeply interfused,
> Whose dwelling is the light of setting suns,
> And the round ocean and the living air,
> And the blue sky, and in the mind of man. (*Poems* 1:360)

These lines hover uneasily between hymning nature and celebrating an
imaginative power that might introject it in totality and thus make us
independent of further transactions with the external world. Disrupting
the easy harmonies suggested here by parallel structure, Wordsworth's
preposition "in," in the final line, accomplishes a sudden intensification
and suggests a peculiarly human sort of immanence: mind, rather than
being simply another site in which vitalizing power can lodge, can
apparently internalize both the totality of things seen and the force that
animates them. Yet such intimations of radical power are followed
almost immediately by a characteristic demur:

> Therefore am I still
> A lover of the meadows and the woods,
> And mountains; and of all that we behold
> From this green earth; of all the mighty world
> Of eye, and ear,—both what they half create,
> And what perceive; well pleased to recognize
> In nature and the language of the sense
> The anchor of my purest thoughts, the nurse,
> The guide, the guardian of my heart, and soul
> Of all my moral being. (*Poems* 1:360)

As the idiom of the last two lines here suggests, in context these qualifications are less important as an epistemological credo than as an ethical
one: registering the claims a contingent and changing world makes upon
imaginative power, this avowal of reciprocity modulates directly into the
poem's hymn to the humanized imagination.

This Wordsworthian vision of imagination not only renounces the more
intense pleasures of the sublime. It also succeeds intoxications for which

sublimity itself provides a substitute: the demystified visionary poetry that can see, and sing, by its own eyes inspired has already given up word magic for a realm of representation imaginatively compelling enough to eclipse the world it can no longer directly master. Denominated in "Tintern Abbey" as the heady delights of youth, the pleasures relinquished by both the sublime and the humanized imagination resemble in important ways the ecstasies the poet of *Leaves of Grass* claims to restore:[23]

> For nature then
> (The courser pleasures of my boyish days,
> And their glad animal movements all gone by)
> To me was all in all.—I cannot paint
> What then I was. The sounding cataract
> Haunted me like a passion: the tall rock
> The mountain, and the deep and gloomy wood,
> Their colours and their forms, were then to me
> An appetite; a feeling and a love,
> That had no need of a remoter charm,
> By thought supplied, nor any interest
> Unborrowed from the eye.—That time is past,
> And all its aching joys are now no more,
> And all its dizzy raptures. Not for this
> Faint I, nor mourn nor murmur; other gifts
> Have followed; for such loss, I would believe,
> Abundant recompense. . . . (*Poems* 1:360)

Here ear as well as eye plays its part, the "sounding cataract" effectively supplementing Wordsworth's explicit focus on immediate visual pleasure. Yet this is not yet "the mighty world / Of eye, and ear,—both what they half create, / And what perceive," since the very tension between perception and imaginative creation is not yet operative. Thought, apparently, has not yet detached itself from the immediate scene, or at least is not aware of having done so. If the poet "cannot paint / What then I was," this supposed incapacity is thus not merely a hyperbolic assertion of his present distance from his former self. Instead it registers, in displaced form, a paradigmatic shift: the poet cannot represent a self not yet consciously immersed in or defined by representation.[24] Appearing to the youth as "all in all," nature is still experienced as a festival of immediate living presence in which all things, himself included, share. The passage recalls, though its vision is not quite identical to, the archaic Whitmanian world of interpenetrating subjects and objects.

I have been arguing that voice is the key agent of this fusion in *Leaves of Grass*. It is crucial to the abandoned stage Wordsworth depicts here too, though in "Tintern Abbey" its importance is left implicit, being suggested in part by the defining role textual transmission plays in the contrasting mode of identity the poet comes to assume. Registered in this passage in the haunting sound of the cataract, itself an equivocal image, the association of the one life within us and abroad with voice and sound is more overt in another important evocation of this superseded mingling of self and world. I have in mind what is by now a *locus classicus* in Wordsworth criticism, the requiem for the boy of Winander, composed, like "Tintern Abbey," in 1798:[25]

> There was a Boy; ye knew him well, ye cliffs
> And islands of Winander!—many a time,
> At evening, when the earliest stars began
> To move along the edges of the hills,
> Rising or setting, would he stand alone,
> Beneath the trees, or by the glimmering lake;
> And there, with fingers interwoven, both hands
> Pressed closely palm to palm and to his mouth
> Uplifted, he, as through an instrument,
> Blew mimic hootings to the silent owls,
> That they might answer him.—And they would shout
> Across the watery vale, and shout again,
> Responsive to his call,—with quivering peals,
> And long halloos, and screams, and echoes loud
> Redoubled and redoubled; concourse wild
> Of jocund din! . . . (*Poems* 1:362)

If Wordsworth's recollection of the earlier self who had first come to Tintern Abbey offers a more muted, almost somber version of this boisterous echoic play, that may be because the cataract-haunted youth he recalls there is already faintly troubled by intimations that are thrust upon the boy of Winander more starkly:

> And, when there came a pause
> Of silence such as baffled his best skill:
> Then, sometimes, in that silence, while he hung
> Listening, a gentle shock of mild surprise
> Has carried far into his heart the voice
> Of mountain-torrents; or the visible scene
> Would enter unawares into his mind
> With all its solemn imagery, its rocks,

Its woods, and that uncertain heaven received
Into the bosom of the steady lake. (*Poems* 1:362)

These lines trace an intricate dialectic: its operative notions are silence, voice, imagery, and reflection. Distancing the boy from the natural world in which he was immersed, the eerie silence of this scene metamorphoses even more strangely into voice. Distant and devoid of any intimation of call and response, this voice might be described, only a bit too schematically, as the voice of *natura naturans* rather than of *natura naturata*. Suddenly manifest in and as itself, rather than appearing through a multitude of discrete creatures and objects, Nature simultaneously declares its integrity and detaches itself from the boy who intuits it; the birth of the peculiarly human power to intuit or posit a structured totality, as well as the individual phenomena that compose it, is also the origin of human self-consciousness and difference. This birth might also be called a fall: it is marked by a paradigmatic shift in the boy's attentions, from unselfconscious immersion in immediate presence to involvement with images and representations. From what "Tintern Abbey" names the aching joys of the eye, the boy passes to the sobering stillness of "solemn imagery," a phrase suggestive of reflective distance. Call and echoic response are likewise replaced by a more somber and inward transaction, in which "the visible scene / Would enter unawares into his mind," a process perhaps epitomized by the final instance Wordsworth offers us of it: the boy's mind internalizes "that uncertain heaven received / Into the bosom of the steady lake." Here an expanse suggestive of totality, and of idealization, is explicitly made available to the boy as an image. The accompanying sense of tranquil restoration, though, is shadowed by a hint of delusion: the "uncertain" heaven seems stabilized, but thus also transmuted, as it appears as a reflection in what Wordsworth calls the "steady" lake. Wordsworth's verb "received" likewise manages to seem both comforting and faintly troubling. Suggesting a deep sequestering broadly appropriate to the lake itself but not to the particular operation of optical reflection described here, it both implies and problematizes a profound interiorizing Wordsworth's work consistently associates with imagination. This stanza of "There Was a Boy" thus poises on a birth into the human universe of images and representations which involves, ambiguously, both the appearance of the world as a totality and the fading, or at least the transmutation, of everything in it.

Characteristically ambivalent, Wordsworth typically struggles to re-gard this falling away from natural presence as fortunate. "There Was a Boy," however, poises at a liminal moment: Wordsworth leaves the boy uncomfortably suspended both above the natural scene and, as it were, above the natural self still literally immersed in it ("he hung / Listen-ing").[26] The poem barely intimates that the totality the boy glimpses attests to an active power that is his own: a power akin not to *natura naturata* but to *natura naturans,* the imaginative power which can bind up disparate forms into a whole of its own making.

Stopping far short of the sort of claims for imaginative autonomy that characterize Wordsworth's meditation on the crossing of Simplon Pass (indeed killing off the boy before he might make them), "There Was a Boy" also leaves unrealized the binding of imaginative power to human continuities and communal concerns. The poem is characteristic, how-ever, in its preoccupation with this latter project. Typically regarding the moment detailed in "There Was a Boy" not only as an access of creative energy but also as a falling away from the supposedly unmediated pleasures of a former stage, Wordsworth struggles to conceive of the imaginative power of totalization as fulfilling itself not in an abrupt, self-starting individual act but in the building out of a human universe whose continuities might replace the natural ones from which we have been reft. Seeking a transmissibility which might make up for the self-renew-ing life of nature, Wordsworthian imagination must renounce the sub-lime autonomy that characterizes its most intense manifestations and bind itself to the project of symbolic transmission that for Wordsworth defines human culture and human selves.

It is partly the lack of such symbolic connection that is registered in the regret that haunts the close of "There Was a Boy." Blockage afflicts not only the boy who "hung / Listening" but also the poet who should be his imaginative heir:

> This boy was taken from his mates, and died
> In childhood, ere he was full twelve years old.
> Pre-eminent in beauty is the vale
> Where he was born and bred: the churchyard hangs
> Upon a slope above the village-school;
> And, through that churchyard when my way has led
> On summer-evenings, I believe, that there
> A long half-hour together I have stood
> Mute—looking at the grave in which he lies! (*Poems* 1:363)[27]

Despite the closing focus on his own muteness, what the poet lacks here is not so much voice as writing. Conspicuous by its absence, particularly in the context of a poetic corpus littered enough with such inscriptions for a number of critics to regard them as Wordsworth's crucial metonymy for poetry itself, is any mention of an epitaph.[28] The boy, as the poem presents him to us, never recovers from the silence that overtakes the world of mimic hootings in which he was formerly immersed. While the poet mourns the loss of this unreflective immediacy, what he requires in order to carry on is not the joy of the boy's innocent effusions but the record of an altered language that might have succeeded them and acknowledged their demise.[29] Like the boy's abruptly truncated career, the poet's speechlessness is thus paradigmatic: perhaps suggesting a reflective interval, it may instead imply a more profound disorientation; the poet who confronts the boy's fall from voice to blank silence lapses into a transfixed state that threatens to put an end to poetry itself.[30]

While an image of voice is Whitman's crucial figure for an individual power immune to natural contingency and scornful of the compensatory mechanisms of culture, Wordsworth thus characteristically renounces voice for writing, a shift that accommodates fate rather than defying it. If his poetry is epitaphic, Wordsworth's epitaphic mode not only marks the place of death but conspicuously internalizes it, a difficult gesture that harbors abundant recompense; in Wordsworth's poetry mortality tells us who we are since it occasions the transmission that makes our identity sustainable.

"There Was a Boy" displays not this recognition but the need for it. If the poem is itself epitaphic, it comes too late to mediate the gap between voice and silence effectively; or, to put it differently, the boy of Winander dies too early, before he can see the virtue of writing an epitaph or before he knows what such an inscription might say. While Wordsworth's *Essays on Epitaphs* suggest that memorials composed by and frankly attributed to the bereaved are more suitable than those in which the dead themselves supposedly address us (2:60–61), "There Was a Boy" is by no means alone in Wordsworth's poetic corpus in the sense of insufficiency that haunts this belated gesture: the poems that in effect supply inscriptions for unlettered monuments characteristically seem to struggle to redeem the dead from an otherwise unremitting and frightening muteness that threatens to consume those who confront this blankness as well. Despite what the *Essays on Epitaphs* declare, in Wordsworth's imaginative universe one might ideally write one's own epitaph. One would at least pass on to one's inheritors the material with which to compose one; paradoxically, this would consist less of the particulars of one's life than of the assurance that one had already entered into what might be called an epitaphic attitude. What one might pass on, that is, turns out to be the sense of transmissibility itself, a symbolic legacy that for Wordsworth comes to seem virtually synonymous with culture.

This is precisely what the poet of "Tintern Abbey" does. A poem that seems to begin as a celebration of natural renewal and modulates into a hymn to imaginative power thus ends as a ritual of human continuity. Despite the lack of any overt reference to epitaph, the poem culminates with an extravagantly funereal gesture: emptying living presence and voice into testamentary inscription, the poet assumes his own death in order to ensure the transmission that will annul it. Engraving his own epitaph, so to speak, here and now in his sister's heart, he gives himself up to the symbolic circuit in which he will survive.

"Tintern Abbey" evokes this symbolic continuity quite explicitly as an alternative to the self-delighting and self-renewing natural totality the poet may possibly have posited more than perceived, a whole from which his positional power has in any case separated him:

> well pleased to recognize
> In nature and the language of the sense
> The anchor of my purest thoughts, the nurse,
> The guide, the guardian of my heart, and soul
> Of all my moral being.
>   Nor perchance,
> If I were not thus taught, should I the more
> Suffer my genial spirits to decay:
> For thou art with me here upon the banks
> Of this fair river; thou my dearest Friend,
> My dear, dear Friend; and in thy voice I catch
> The language of my former heart, and read
> My former pleasures in the shooting lights
> Of thy wild eyes. . . . (*Poems* 1:360–61)

This displacement and the partial repetition it achieves of the poet's experience modulates into the more ambitious project of bequeathing that concludes "Tintern Abbey." It demands a more drastic curtailment:

                    and, in after years,
When these wild ecstasies shall be matured
Into a sober pleasure; when thy mind
Shall be a mansion for all lovely forms,
Thy memory be as a dwelling-place
For all sweet sounds and harmonies; oh! then,
If solitude, or fear, or pain, or grief,
Should be thy portion, with what healing thoughts
Of tender joy wilt thou remember me,
And these my exhortations! Nor, perchance—
If I should be where I no more can hear
Thy voice, nor catch from thy wild eyes these gleams
Of past existence—wilt thou then forget
That on the banks of this delightful stream
We stood together; and that I, so long
A worshipper of Nature, hither came
Unwearied in that service: rather say
With warmer love—oh! with far deeper zeal
Of holier love. Nor wilt thou then forget,
That after many wanderings, many years
Of absence, these steep woods and lofty cliffs
And this green pastoral landscape, were to me
More dear, both for themselves and for thy sake! (*Poems* 1:361–62)

These lines are quite moving. Yet what the poet proffers Dorothy
here might be regarded as either a gift or an affliction; it is probably
fairest to see it as both. The cost to Dorothy is an instance of the burden
that transmission imposes on inheritors: we will take it up when we
turn, toward the end of this chapter, to the aggression lurking in both
Wordsworth's and Whitman's bequests. If this passage nonetheless invites Dorothy to think of the repetitions it envisions as a legacy offered
rather than as an entailment enjoined upon her, that view is at least
partially justified by the fact that Wordsworth here passes on not just
his particular memories and demands but a vision of transmissibility
itself.

     This transmission exacts its price from the poet as well as from his
sister. It is epitomized by the very inscription which allows him to
survive. If Dorothy is to become the poet's faithful reader, renewing his
experience by remembering and repeating his words in his absence, he
must turn himself into her writer, a task the poem associates with the
willing introjection of death. Chastening the resonance of voice by subduing it to the condition of epitaph, the poet effectively reduces himself

here and now to what he must become in order to survive: he transmutes
his life and his presence into the transmissible words through which he
will endure, defining himself through the scene of his death and the
bequest that his demise will activate.[31] This gesture, both severe and
sustaining, is the crucial legacy the poet passes on to his sister; he
predicts that it will at some later date sustain her too, by defining her as
it has come to define him.

This transaction condenses and dramatizes a logic that for Wordsworth, as for Whitman, very nearly defines the space of culture—a
bargain Wordsworth accepts and internalizes, but of which Whitman
wants to want no part. If the poet of "Tintern Abbey" will survive in an
epitaph, through signs, then he will survive as a sign, sustained in a
symbolic circuit. And if he can perform this substitution, that must be
because it has in a sense already occurred; the poet must already have
taken up his place as part of a communal network of images and
representations. "Tintern Abbey" embraces this initiation and the relinquishing of self-sufficiency that attends it: they are registered in the
poet's intently envisioned sacrifice of his own living presence, a dissolution which strangely fulfills the poem's burden of good hope.

If this description seems too unremitting or too bleak, that is partly
because I have made it so impersonal. Wordsworth insists that his
affectional bond to his sister is crucial to the humanizing compact "Tintern Abbey" initiates. The mechanism that permits the poet's survival
may be pervasive enough to define culture. But in Wordsworth's poem
this global mechanism takes the form of the intensely personal transmission with which "Tintern Abbey" concludes; it is crucial to Wordsworth
to insist that he will survive only if Dorothy's love for him makes her a
willing participant in a shared enterprise.

As we shall see further on, this personal ethos typifies Wordsworth's
vision of poetic and cultural transmission. The contrast between his
work and the characteristic ambitions of *Leaves of Grass* in this regard
will prove instructive. In Whitman's poems, reliance on particular intimacies and the fidelity they can generate is meticulously excluded. The
responses of the poet's auditors need not be solicited because they are
apparently compelled, by a performative idiom and the living presence
supposedly poured into us by the ritual it activates: according to Whitman's governing myth we can never escape either the poet's insights or

the imperial and amorous figure who is their burden. Appealing to his sister, Wordsworth pins his hopes on a personal bond rather than on the sort of structural necessity Whitman's poems seem to enforce.

It is possible, of course, to overstate the humanized and humanizing aspects of Wordsworthian transmission; Wordsworth himself may indeed be committed to such overstatement. One might well not want to be Dorothy, or to have one's future responses enjoined in this way. Yet the distinction between Whitman's performatives and the optatives and exhortations with which "Tintern Abbey" concludes is important even if it does not quite bespeak a contrast between constraint and freely exercised choice. As Hartman suggests, optatives can be considered as attenuations of ritual address, modulations from an archaic magical universe into a demystified space in which daemonic powers have been at least partly relinquished in favor of explicitly symbolic ones (*Beyond Formalism* 287–88).

Writing is Wordsworth's condensing figure for this supposedly humanizing transformation of power. In "Tintern Abbey" inscription foregrounds the symbolic status of cultural continuities, drawing attention as well to what this purification should perfect—the reciprocity of writer and reader, of the dead and the living, a mutuality that for Wordsworth not only makes possible the connections that sustain us but also gives them their value. Whitman, writing in a moment when he is not yet with us, imagines a magical speech in which he will be ever-present to us. Wordsworth, addressing Dorothy on the occasion of their shared visit to the Wye, conjures up his own effacement and death, compelling the recitation or re-reading of his words which is not only their characteristic mode but also their imaginative burden.

Speech Acts

In the archaic universe voice shapes in *Leaves of Grass,* the poet's presence thus sloughs off the cultural bargain Wordsworth celebrates; apparently invulnerable to contingency and loss, the poet has no need of the symbolic structure that partially recuperates them. But Whitman's figure of voice is made possible by writing. The attenuations Wordsworth accepts accordingly haunt *Leaves of Grass* despite the poet's insistent ebullience. Writing means for Whitman very much what it means for Wordsworth: it displays the poet's reliance not only on representation but more particularly on a mechanism of cultural transmission Whitman repeatedly excoriates. Claiming to free us from the mediating cultural structures that preserve us only at the price of turning us into images ourselves, *Leaves of Grass* thus hovers between performing this liberation from representation and merely representing it. Whitman's announcements of the poet's presence are poised between a transumptive word magic and a belated constative mode whose assertions are belied by recalcitrant fact, between the revelation of a living presence uncompromised by signs and the melancholy or comic display of just such signs. Purveying Whitman's figure of voice, writing indeed threatens to reduce the poet's presence to a sign itself: turning present address into epitaph, it displays or exacts the fading of the self-sufficient identity to which voice should attest.

Rarely acknowledged overtly, this economy might be thought of as afflicting a poet who remains unaware of its working. But Whitman's mobile idiom often seems to register the poet's own sense of the ambiguous status of his project. This is especially true with respect to the lapse of power writing in part represents: as we shall see further on, Whitman is less uncomfortable with suggestions that the poet's noble powers have not quite been successfully exercised than with intimations that he has managed to wield a less innocent force, one ultimately difficult to distinguish from the authority from which it should free us. While acknowledgment of this darker power of the poet's word is difficult to discern in *Leaves of Grass,* quotients of pathos or rueful wit often lurk in the poet's visionary proclamations. They suggest that some of the doubts Whitman's claims tend to provoke among his readers can also preoccupy the poet, though in Whitman's first two editions they are almost never allowed to redefine what his advent means. In exploring such equivocations, it will be useful to return to some of the apostrophes we considered in earlier chapters, in order to judge the difference writing makes in the poet's declarations. We can often hear this difference in his tone.

1. In Whitman's apostrophes voice and writing situate the poet himself in quite different ways. In section forty of "Song of Myself," we saw in chapter 4, voice attests to and defines the transfiguring presence Whitman's declaration announces:

Behold! I do not give lectures, or a little charity;
When I give, I give myself. (V: 1:62)[32]

We might hear this address as mixing visionary intensity and braggadocian delight: revealing the splendidly invisible presence who defines what presence is, the poet seems to revel not only in his conjuring powers but also in the stupefaction likely to attend our difficult apprehension of this marvel. Whitman's deictic "Behold!," I argued, suggests an act of transubstantiation for which stupefaction might well be an appropriate initial response. The lack of a visible body here forces us to look for the poet in his word; seeming to fulfill Whitman's visionary ambitions, the figure of voice to which our search leads suggests that we will indeed find him there—a living presence, both embodied and ideal, now rising up before us. But another possible source of stupefaction lurks in these lines. Rather than taking this transaction as an instance of successful magic, we might instead regard it as a case of what J. L. Austin charmingly calls "infelicity" (14): our difficulty beholding the poet may bespeak not the profundity of his powers but the simple failure of his speech act. Any attention to these lines as writing will tend to provoke this sense of failed magic, disturbing the constellation Whitman's figure of voice suggests. Broadly affiliated with indication in Whitman's work, writing displays the indicative status of the poet's words with particular sharpness here: it reduces the elusive presence voice suggests quite simply to absence.

Absence itself, however, can be understood as attesting not quite to "infelicity," but instead to the working of a darker power than the poet intends to mobilize, of which he might be victim rather than agent. These lines may instance the operation of the necromantic cultural power Whitman associates with texts. The absence of a palpable body here might intimate a relation between poet and word that is a kind of demonic parody of the confluence Whitman's figure of voice implies. Rather than bespeaking the fusion of word and living presence, the announcement "Behold! [. . .] / [. . .] I give myself" can suggest that the identity named here has effectively been reduced to nothing but the words in whose presence we are. The indicative signs to which we give our allegiance, Whitman often complains, do not simply fail to produce living presences but come to define and thereby emasculate the selves whose places they usurp; falling under their sway, we no longer appear to others, or to ourselves, as living presences, but simply as signs. Whitman's announcements of the poet's presence would thus exemplify the very cultural mechanism from which they supposedly free us.

Similar ambiguities trouble many of the poet's announcements:

I and mine do not convince by arguments, similes, rhymes,
We convince by our presence. ("Song of the Open Road," 1856 233)

These lines, too, can seem to fracture into various voicings: we might think we hear in them a visionary intensity or the pride of triumphant revelation; a melancholy intimation of "infelicity" or a rueful comedy provoked by this same failure; or a rather more chilling sense that presence, for us, is simply the presence of signs.

How sharp an irony we discover in such passages will depend in part on whether we think of them as uttered or inscribed. Moreover, the question of whether we think of Whitman's speaker as sharing our ironic awareness may also turn on the role we attribute to writing: the voice we imagine we hear may itself be troubled by inscription and what it implies. In the cases so far before us, it is probably judicious to ascribe such disquieting awareness to reader more than to poet; while hints of comedy and melancholy do seem to lurk in these announcements, in context their boastful and visionary aspects are clearly predominant.[33] A number of Whitman's announcements of the poet's presence, though, seem genuinely equivocal in both tone and import: there the problems I have been worrying seem quite palpably to worry the poet as well. We are most apt to sense a hovering accent in the performatives that are most richly erotic; given Whitman's particular erotic bent, we need to attend especially to passages that conjure up not only an idealized, invisible presence but also the labile body that is the archaic precursor of such idealization. The more intent the poet seems to be on inhabiting and enjoying the polymorphous body his announcements imply, the more those announcements seem haunted by a sense of that body's ineffability.

A brief passage from "Song of Myself," which we attended to earlier from a different perspective, is perhaps most delicately poised between pleasure and pathos:

This is the press of a bashful hand . . . . this is the float and odor of hair,
This is the touch of my lips to yours . . . . this is the murmur of yearning.
   (1855 42)

The wistfulness of the poet's tone here in part reflects the characteristic furtiveness of Whitman's desire; but it also registers the equivocal status of the poet's claims to performative power, the longing of this language to be more than language. The amorous encounter the poet initiates here depends on Whitman's insistent conflation of body and word, a conjunction on which his deictics insist and to which an image of voice should attest. Yet we can hear in this voice an unhappy intimation of something that undoes its claims—a furtive sense of the distance between all these words and the body they name, but cannot quite manage to be.

It is admittedly awkward to specify the mechanism through which writing affects the tone of voice to which we respond here. We are used to attaching poems to "speakers," and to insisting on the distinction between the poet writing his poem and the speaker engaged in the speech act the poet represents. If Whitman characteristically conflates these two, for instance by calling his speaker "Walt Whitman," he may do so at least in part in order to occult the fictive status of the speech acts on which the poems focus and the role played by writing in facilitating the image of such acts. But in passages like this one, it is as if the poet's awareness of the text he was engaged in writing infiltrated the image of voice his poem projects: the distance between word and thing, and the merely indicative status of the linguistic sign, seem to trouble a speaker who, supposedly innocent of writing, should be immune to these supposedly avoidable deficiencies of the word as well. Writing and what it implies seem to darken what might otherwise be a purely visionary utterance.

Like the mechanism that might make Whitman's speaker aware of inscription, the precise effects of this awareness on tone are not easy to pin down. We might conceivably discern in these lines faint intimations of the icy recognition that structures Keats's "This living hand," though they provoke no dialectical reversal: the economy in which the sign takes the place of the presence it announces, rather than producing it, can indeed seem all the more inexorable because of the poet's insistent proclamation of a magic that should keep this reduction at bay. Yet a sense of stoic acceptance in the face of an inevitable fate is less apparent here than a wistfulness which suggests that the speaker believes that the failure of word magic which haunts these lines might well have been avoided. The poet's tone seems to hover equivocally among quiet triumph, seductiveness, and a poignancy provoked by the possible infelicity of these speech acts. Shadowed by a writing that calls into question the very presence they proclaim, these lines seem troubled by a melancholy sense of missed encounter, a feeling that the poet's transfiguring body may be dissolving even as Whitman tries to inhabit it and enjoy the labile eroticism it should make possible.

In such erotically charged passages, the poet seems to waver between a lability that promises the delights of a not yet Oedipalized sexuality and an utter evaporation that pre-empts the very assignation with which these addresses entice us. We can thus understand the elusiveness of this figure of presence as an ambiguous sign: it both renders the somatic instability of an archaic body and marks the poet's inability to recover it. Seeking to reclaim the powers of word magic but perhaps displaying instead the purely symbolic status and power of the sign, Whitman's apostrophes also suggest the unattainability of the polymorphous body they struggle to resurrect, a body prior even to the word magic that both supersedes and recalls it. Intent on restoring the body as a presence unmarked and unmediated by signs, Whitman's declarations might always enact the occulting of this pre-symbolic body instead; it might always be only a collection of signs with which we are left. The hint of melancholy we can hear in these announcements registers not only the possible failure of the poet's word magic but also the dissolution of the archaic body this magic should evoke, a fading exacted by the very words that name it. The pathos of this doubled sense of naming haunts Whitman's image of voice throughout *Leaves of Grass*.

2. Poised between the magical production of a reborn body and its vanishing, such announcements in Whitman's first two editions typically register this latter effect only in equivocal accents that lurk behind the poet's leading tone. In the 1860 *Leaves of Grass*, however, Whitman's attitude toward the poet's presence has itself become ambivalent, and his relation to his earlier fictions is frequently wary. Both the *Calamus* sequence and the Sea-Drift poem "As I Ebb'd with the Ocean of Life," we will see in chapter 7, sharply repudiate Whitman's figure of presence, though in quite different ways. A number of the other poems composed for the 1860 *Leaves*, though, attenuate Whitman's authorizing myth without rejecting it. Focusing overtly on the mechanisms that simultaneously create and dissipate the poet's presence, they stop short of renouncing this figure and his powers.

In these poems Whitman's apostrophes frequently advert directly to the existence of the writing that threatens to block the poet's advent or simply dissolve him. Insisting that *Leaves of Grass* is not a book, or else that the text we are reading is about to metamorphose into a voice and a presence (or is doing so now) such announcements nonetheless tend to brood over the economy Whitman's appeal to voice had earlier served to occult, probing an act of transformation whose power had depended on the ease with which apostrophe seemed to accomplish it. In 1860, moreover, this problematic transfiguration is repeatedly associated with the poet's death. There are surely several reasons for this intensified concentration on mortality. Whitman's new focus on genital rather than infantile, polymorphous sexuality implicates the poet in the generational economy he had earlier seemed to evade. At the same time, this edition also offers strong intimations of the spiritual interests which increasingly preoccupied the poet; several 1860 poems tentatively adduce the oceanic afterlife on which such later pieces as "Passage to India" dilate. Yet in the 1860 edition death also images a fate Whitman's figure of voice seems increasingly to precipitate rather than elude: it names the fading, made palpable by writing, which reliance on the sign exacts. In the production of Whitman's ideal figure of presence, manifestation and dissolution come increasingly to seem inseparable.[34]

The melancholy that haunts previous announcements of the poet's presence is accordingly more evident in several parallel declarations in 1860; it appears not just as an undertone, but as a persistent response the poet must register overtly, tempering his characteristic ebullience. A brief evocation of the poet's presence in "Starting from Paumanok" compresses this movement, focusing more on affirmation than dejection; but it adverts to the death that must be suffered in order to attain the effusing body the poet celebrates:

> O Death! O for all that, I am yet of you, unseen, this hour, with irrepressible love,
> Walking New England, a friend, a traveller,
> Splashing my bare feet in the edge of the summer ripples, on Paumanok's sand. (1860 18)[35]

We are likely to imagine this unseen body dabbling its feet in Long Island's waters as itself rather fluid; it seems to have purged itself of the stolidity of flesh. Associated with presence but also, explicitly, with death, this figure must suffer dissolution and pass through absence in order to become what it ought to be. Declared overtly here, this detour organizes all Whitman's proclamations of the poet's presence, taking the form of the writing that purveys those announcements; the poet must pass through images or signs, if not simply into them, to become what Whitman calls presence. In these lines death displays the reliance of what we mean by presence and identity on a mechanism which precipitates a fading of all that is not the word. If Whitman's announcements of the poet's advent, with their focus on lability, also evoke a being prior to this birth and this death, they do so only by means of the very signs that accomplish or exact it.

The haunting leave-taking on which *Leaves of Grass* comes to rest, in 1860 and thereafter, inhabits such paradoxes more fully. In the closing sections of "So Long!" Whitman dwells on the overlapping of what produces the poet's presence and what dissolves it; his declarations of the poet's triumphant manifestation are difficult to tell from poignant admission or lament.

The best-known lines in the poem are probably those that ambiguously either disavow or claim to transubstantiate the poet's book. We have already attended to these proclamations:

> This is no book,
> Who touches this, touches a man. (1860 455)

In later editions, an awkward ritual salutation makes more explicit Whitman's apostrophic mode here, a dimension which serves to disentangle a numinous presence from Whitman's book by appealing to the living voice apostrophe implies:

> Camerado! This is no book,
> Who touches this, touches a man. (V 2:452)[36]

The succeeding stanza goes on to adduce the sort of labile body voice can also define:

> O how your fingers drowse me!
> Your breath falls around me like dew—your pulse lulls the tympans of my ears,
> I feel immerged [sic] from head to foot,
> Delicious—enough. (1860 455)

This passage manages to seem both overstimulated and poignant. Evoking the polymorphous pleasures of the *chora* and lending them the unfocused, global intensity that would now be called *jouissance,* Whitman's heavily somaticized description simultaneously functions to make the visible a little hard to see; it thus oddly suggests the elusiveness of the archaic encounter that might produce the sense of surfeit the poet declares.

In "So Long!" this elusiveness haunts evocations of both the archaic body lost through signs and the punctual presence whose dramatic manifestation supposedly frees us from their dominion. The melancholy lurking in the passage just considered is also evident in the lines that conclude the stanza that precedes them. There the power to conjure up the living presence implied by apostrophe, to draw it up out of the book, belongs not to the poet himself but to death:

> [Camerado!] This is no book,
> Who touches this, touches a man,
> (Is it night? Are we here alone?)
> It is I you hold, and who holds you,
> I spring from the pages into your arms—decease calls me forth. (1860 455)

If the impediment represented by writing gives way to an actual presence here, this figure's advent paradoxically takes the form of a dissolution. It is this paradox, as much as the sense of furtiveness that often attaches to eroticism in *Leaves of Grass,* that accounts for the wistfulness so strongly registered in the third and forth of these lines: asking whether we are here alone is in part a displaced way of asking if we are here at all, a doubt still reflected in the insistence that, in the next line, tries to keep it at bay. The poet, it would seem, becomes the embodied presence who defines what presence and body should be only by trading one absence for another, passing through writing only by passing into death.

Or very nearly so. But "So Long!" struggles to place the poet at the threshold between these two absences, and thus, as it were, to protect him from both. The poet hovers on the brink of a death he both anticipates and holds back from:

> So I pass—a little time vocal, visible, contrary,
> Afterward, a melodious echo, passionately bent for—death making me undying,
> The best of me then when no longer visible—for toward that I have been incessantly preparing. (1860 455)

We have here what looks like cosmic doctrine, and the labile, caressable presence conjured up out of the book for our delectation in other stanzas might seem to be simply identical to the immortal soul adverted to in the second and third of these lines. But this is supposedly not quite the case:

> What is there more, that I lag and pause, and crouch extended with unshut
>   mouth?
> Is there a single final farewell?
>
> My songs cease—I abandon them,
> From behind the screen where I hid, I advance personally, solely to you. (V
>   2:451)[37]

It is this figure stalling at the edge of death, rather than the inhabitant of an afterlife the poem also imagines, who epitomizes presence in *Leaves of Grass*. I suggested in chapter 4 that this silent presence is defined by the very voice supposedly subtracted from it. This image of voice, in turn, acquires its elusiveness and its apparent ideality from its proximity to the conditions with which it is not to be simply confused: to the writing out of which it emerges and the death into which it will shortly dissolve.

In the poem's very last lines, the poet is once more defined by his closeness to a fate that has not yet quite claimed him. Death is, as it were, the limit to which the body emerging from writing, and produced as an image of voice, ineluctably tends—a limit at which it cannot quite arrive without ceasing to be what it is. This slight but crucial distance is described as the space of a resemblance that is not yet a perfect identity, of an "as":

> Dear friend, whoever you are, here, take this kiss,
> I give it especially to you—Do not forget me,
> I feel like one who has done his work—I progress on,
> The unknown sphere, more real than I dreamed, more direct, darts awaken-
>   ing rays about me—*So long!*
> Remember my words—I love you—I depart from materials,
> I am as one disembodied, triumphant, dead. (1860 456)

Having supposedly passed through writing to appear to us as a transfigured presence, the poet here hovers just short of a definitive dissolving that would leave his body available to being represented but not to being presented directly. Having just emerged from signs and on the verge of passing once more under their sway, he becomes, by virtue of this double proximity and this double danger, what presence should be.

In these closing sections of "So Long!" both imagery and tone draw out such equivocations, calling our attention to the paradoxes at which apostrophe in *Leaves of Grass* typically hints more obliquely. The ideal presence which should redeem us from signs takes its power from its reliance on them; the labile, archaic body that precedes such ideality now exists for us only in a linguistic practice that simultaneously evokes and occults it. The poet voices these intimations indirectly throughout *Leaves of Grass*, often in the very pronouncements that should keep them at bay; they are audible, though often only faintly, in the pathos and humor that register a felt lapse from magical performative power.

3. Like the poet's own presence, the redemptive encounter to which he calls us turns out to be highly equivocal. In the first two editions of *Leaves of Grass*, this assignation supposedly renders unnecessary the sort of symbolic transmission Wordsworth invokes. The charmed scene into which Whitman's apostrophes fold us depends for its contours on an image of voice.

Even in "So Long!" the poet who has very nearly dissolved into his own image holds back from the economy to which Wordsworth sternly subjects himself: the haunting encounter between poet and audience shapes a tenuous idyll that delays the death Wordsworth invites; it seems to render superfluous the symbolic transmission, epitomized by writing, that in "Tintern Abbey" introjects mortality and thus allows a figurative survival beyond it. Prior to 1860, Whitman's apostrophes typically insist more adamantly on the poet's ability to create a magical meeting that protects both poet and audience from such attenuation: supposedly preserving the poet from the dissolution over which "So Long!" lingers, these direct addresses seem to create a repeating event and a protected space that rescue us too, not only from natural change and contingency but also from the rule of representation that partially subdues them. In poems such as "Crossing Brooklyn Ferry," we saw in chapter 3, our reliance on signs is displayed as exacting a price the poet is unwilling to pay. His advent seems to liberate both himself and his auditors from the public space ruled by light and defined by images, a space in which we can avail ourselves of the stabilizing powers of representation only by being subjected to them ourselves. One of the crucial functions of the scene inaugurated by the poet's apostrophes, we noted in chapter 4, is to shelter us from this realm, and from the fading of self-presence it exacts, by sequestering us in an agglomerating zone indistinguishable from the poet's own polymorphous body. Granting a kiss or a touch where Wordsworth offers a last will and testament, Whitman supposedly initiates us not into a cultural circuit that will preserve us through others, provided we reduce ourselves to the signs that symbolic operations can transmit, but into a magical space that obviates the need for such mediations and exempts us from the cultural stipulations that regulate our access to them.

The tenuous difference between such interchanges and the symbolic economy they claim to by-pass is nonetheless registered in the role writing plays in the poet's apostrophes. The text of *Leaves of Grass* threatens to dissolve the charmed encounter Whitman's image of voice defines, fracturing it into separate occasions of writing and reading. Or, if Whitman's written text can be said itself to constitute a single transaction in which both writer and reader participate, it is a symbolic one rather than a magical communion.

Whitman's late poem "Souvenirs of Democracy," which focuses overtly not only on an act of inscription but more particularly on the poet's last will and testament, thus does not so much abandon a possibility as lay bare the paradoxical conditions that have subtended it from the first. The poem is interesting not only for what Whitman now admits, but also for the way such admissions intertwine with what he continues to proclaim. Organized around a questionable opposition with which we are already familiar—one between two sorts of writing—"Souvenirs of Democracy" adamantly contrasts the opposing consequences of these different modes, distinguishing between a merely symbolic transmission and the liberating encounter the poet's text supposedly initiates:

> The business man, the acquirer vast,
> After assiduous years, surveying results, preparing for departure,
> Devises houses and lands to his children—bequeaths stocks, goods—funds
>   for a school or hospital,
> Leaves money to certain companions to buy tokens, souvenirs of gems and
>   gold;
> Parceling out with care—And then, to prevent all cavil,
> His name to his testament formally signs.
>
> But I, my life surveying,
> With nothing to show, to devise, from its idle years,

Nor houses, nor lands—nor tokens of gems or gold for my friends,
Only these Souvenirs of Democracy—In them—in all my songs—behind me
leaving,
To You, whoever you are, (bathing, leavening this leaf especially with my
breath—pressing on it a moment with my own hands;
—Here! feel how the pulse beats in my wrists!—how my heart's-blood is
swelling, contracting!)
I will You, in all, Myself, with promise to never desert you,
To which I sign my name,

Walt Whitman [signature]
(CRE 615)[38]

Admitting the necessary entangling of Whitman's crucial transactions with the symbolic mechanisms from which they should save us, the poem cannily focuses on the material aspect of the poet's procedures, hoping thereby to suggest that an actual presence might be transmitted by them. Blown on or bathed by the poet's breath and pressed between his hands, the "leaf" that holds his writing can supposedly regenerate a trace of his presence. It is with this trace that we are invited to commune.

The encounter thereby initiated supposedly offers us an alternative to the transmission detailed in the poem's opening stanza. Mediated by public, juridical structures and epitomized by the unregenerate writing that purveys them, this symbolic transaction is made to seem both sadly impersonal and slightly rapacious. The inheritance the businessman bequeaths is never quite redeemable from the symbolic mechanisms that make his legacy transferable: the poem displays that fading of real presences into symbolic entities with which Whitman is persistently concerned. Accumulated in part in the symbolic forms of "stocks" and "funds" and transmitted via the symbolic efficacy of a last will and testament, this legacy in at least one instance gets cashed in simply for more conspicuously symbolic objects: "tokens, souvenirs of gems and gold." In other cases, less tautological operations occur: funds, for example, are turned into "a school or a hospital." Yet the impersonality that haunts these transactions seems to be one from which the partners themselves will never successfully emerge. Brought into relation by symbolic objects and the legal instrument that insures their proper disposal, the businessman and his heirs seem sundered by the very transmission that binds them. In contrast to the poet, a living creature defined by pulse and breath, the businessman is himself reduced to a purely juridical function:

> And then, to prevent all cavil,
> His name to his testament formally signs.

There is something faintly ghastly in this exercise of control as Whitman's diagrammatic description presents it. Those affected by the testament's stipulations do not so much interact with a person as submit to a name or sign. This power of a symbolic agent and event to govern persons haunts Whitman throughout *Leaves of Grass*.

"Souvenirs of Democracy" nonetheless hovers over the possible resemblance between the transaction the poet initiates and the mechanisms from which it should save us. Whitman ends by proclaiming the poet's advent and conjuring up the intimate scene his presence should inaugurate; but this final performative is qualified by a final paradox. Adhering to the procedures of the will and testament whose import he claims to redefine, Whitman closes not by revealing a presence but by appending his signature. We are left not quite with a living person but instead with his legal proxy—the mark not only of his absence, but also of the symbolic structures that make such fading more than merely contingent. The occasion to which we are called by the poem thus vacillates between the saving intimacy Whitman's image of voice seems to shape and the sort of codified symbolic transaction inscription might activate.[39]

Despite the ostentatious repudiation of writing in Whitman's earlier work, what we might call the signature also troubles the chiliastic proclamations of the poet's presence that occur there. Our confrontation with Whitman's text intimates not simply the poet's failure to appear, but also the symbolic, mediated, and broadly institutional status of the supposedly purely personal transactions to which he calls us.

4. Like the poet and the scene he initiates, the audience summoned by apostrophe to commune with him also possesses a highly ambiguous status. Turning once more on Whitman's image of voice and its relation to writing, this ambiguity is often starkest in passages that point directly to Whitman's text and try to face down its consequences. In "Souvenirs of Democracy," the businessman's last will and testament seems to reduce to virtual ciphers not only the businessman himself but also those who assume his legacy. While the poet's advent is meant to protect us from the fading that attends this sort of symbolic transmission, we saw that the signature that initiates his bequeathing of presence activates the very sort of procedure that presence claims to by-pass: called to the

intimate, charmed communion that will preserve our sacrosanct individuality, we are summoned to this encounter by an impersonal and essentially juridical instrument. Yet if the poet's performative were to succeed, its effect would be not symbolic but magical: producing the poet's living presence out of his breath-leavened text, "Souvenirs of Democracy" would draw us into the intimate scene the poet's signature, meanwhile, simultaneously promises and belies.

The different effects on us of these different transactions, between which "Souvenirs of Democracy" is poised, are registered in the instability of the very pronoun that names us:

> To You, whoever you are, (bathing, leavening this leaf especially with my breath—pressing on it a moment with my own hands;
> —Here! feel how the pulse beats in my wrists!—how my heart's-blood is swelling, contracting!)
> I will You, in all, Myself, with promise to never desert you. (CRE 615)

Here Whitman's shifter names the individual addressed by an image of voice and summoned to the magical, intimate transaction that might preserve his or her uniqueness. But it names at the same time the anonymous, generic addressee defined by participation in the codified transmission activated by the signature.[40]

Epitomized in "Souvenirs of Democracy" by the legal instrument of the will and testament, such codification and the fading of individuality it exacts are more broadly associated in *Leaves of Grass* with writing. If address in Whitman's poems often seems designed to court the sort of anonymity writing implies, that may well be in order to display the poet's power to rescue us from it. Yet in Whitman's book the "you" salvaged by apostrophe is always in danger of fading back into the field of inscription from which the poet's magical voice has called it. This is so even in the encounters shaped by apostrophe in Whitman's first two editions, despite the typical absence there of the sort of overt reference to writing that organizes "Souvenirs of Democracy."

While Whitman's earlier apostrophes typically finesse their resemblance to the mechanisms of symbolic transmission from which they should exempt us, their seductive appeal nevertheless turns on their equivocal difference from the more public procedures they recall, a distinction likewise left unstated, perhaps since our divining of it will be one sign of our election. Suggesting, in their strangely universal applicability, the scope and defining power of codified public instruments, the

poet's announcements enlist an image of voice to transform the procedures to which they allude, thereby transforming as well the "you" to
whom they speak.

The gesture in which the poet who has apparently been addressing a
multitude suddenly singles out an intimate partner is a characteristic
feature of Whitman's apostrophes:

> O my comrade!
> O you and me at last—and us two only. ("Starting from Paumanok,"
>   1860 22)

I noted in chapter 2 some of the benefits that accrue to the poet by virtue
of the paradoxical "you" suddenly focused on here. Suggesting direct
address but diffusing themselves through writing, these pronouncements
conjure up a "you" simultaneously intimate and universal: as unique as
the single addressee the intimate tone implies, yet as numerous as the
audience reached by Whitman's text.

The poet's tone in such passages suggests that the surplus of erotic
enjoyment Whitman's trope of voice thereby seems to secure is by no
means incidental to such moments. The gentle seductiveness that characterizes these addresses is very much a function of the peculiar scenario
Whitman's apostrophes create: the poet's tone reflects the amorous assurance which accrues to the lover who has mastered this metamorphosis of writing into speech, the poise of the man with a limitless supply of
available partners.

Such assurance often lends the poet's overtures an air of relaxed
confidence, and a slightly teasing, flirtatious quality virtually unique to
Whitman:

> This hour I tell things in confidence,
> I might not tell everybody but I will tell you. ("Song of Myself," 1855 43)

This declaration indeed makes its trick of mode the occasion for its
flirtatious innuendo: Whitman's election of "you," a selection made
from a field of "everybody," is a seductive gesture that turns on the
magical transformation of the text which everyone may read into the
tender and intimate voice that apparently addresses a single, chosen
partner.

This seductive announcement of our personal election is repeated in
several of Whitman's apostrophes, turning always on this trick played
with their mode:

Whoever you are, now I place my hand upon you, that you be my poem,
I whisper with my lips close to your ear,
I have loved many women and men, but I love none better than you. ("To
    You," 1856 206–207)

Clearly enjoying this seduction, Whitman here also asserts that the partner he calls to himself is thereby transformed. Like the erotic benefits that accrue to the poet, the way these apostrophes seem to transfigure those he addresses is also a crucial source of their appeal. Whitman's curious claim here that this transformation involves turning the "you" into the poem itself can be understood in part as an effort to identify audience as well as poet with the word. But it serves more particularly to recreate us as selves shaped by the charmed occasion into which the poet's speech seems to draw us: the poet's apostrophes seem to call us from the public realm organized by codified institutional practices, sequestering us in an intimate space devoid of such mediation. As we noted, the transmutation we thereby undergo is registered in the emergence of a singular, seemingly unique "you" from a plural, essentially anonymous one. Called from the matrix of Whitman's public text by the poet's voice, we are summoned to assume our sacrosanct individuality.

Such mesmerizing effects already rely on a remarkably sophisticated manipulation of tone, and of the curious possibilities of Whitman's fictive mode. Yet the play of writing and speech that generates Whitman's scenario of seduction and liberation has its sadder underside. It suggests itself as we sense the poet's voice falling back into the writing from which these accents emerge. Draining Whitman's "you" of its tenuous individuality, this slide into writing renders poignant the intimate tone of the implied speaking voice. The anonymity of a generic addressee nearly always haunts these locutions, for all their more confident and winsome qualities. It threatens to leave the poet face to face with his book, seeking a lover effectively reduced to the indeterminate features of an anonymous audience of readers; and it seems to abandon those readers to the condition from which the poet's voice should have called them.

Like other, related moments of fading in *Leaves of Grass,* this lapse is not quite contingent. Address, of course, is not always so dramatically menaced by writing or so liable to abrupt transformation by what writing implies; but that is because it does not always depend so directly on writing to produce its effects. The power of the apostrophes I have been considering derives not simply from direct address but also from the way such speech acts both allude to and seem to transfigure more public occasions and forms. It is precisely the apparent ability of these announcements to transform a global transaction into an intimate, private one that lends them their seductiveness and their redemptive force: they thereby seem to transfigure a field of symbolic interactions rather than simply to occur someplace within it. Facilitated by writing, the global scope the poet's apostrophes commandeer is an instance of the power of representation to organize a general field through mediating, and codified, transactions. If the poet borrows this power in order to deny its hold over us, his apostrophes are thus liable to turn into an especially dramatic exhibition of the very mechanisms they hope to exorcise. I argued in chapter 5 that the poet's pristine presence is a function of the representational economy it seems to transcend. The individuality of those the poet addresses, supposedly rescued and revealed as sacrosanct by his apostrophes, likewise depends on a symbolic realm that severely qualifies it. In Whitman's apostrophes this dependence is registered in the way an identity whose uniqueness is defined by its emergence from a field structured by writing seems to fade back into the matrix from which it came. Like the dissolution of the body the poet wants to speak into being and inhabit, this fading of the lovers he addresses and hopes both to enjoy and to save is a source of the melancholy that lurks in Whitman's announcements to us.

"None Shall Escape Me"

This lapse of individuals into the blank, anonymous features of a kind of generic identity shaped by global symbolic mechanisms is one of the terrors to which the imaginative universe of *Leaves of Grass* is especially liable. A contrast to Wordsworth's work will once more prove instructive. While this fear is not, as we shall see a bit further on, one from which Wordsworth is wholly free, it is very much mitigated by his commitment to a determinedly personal mode of symbolic transmission: in Wordsworth's work symbolic forms supposedly sustain individual identity rather than subverting it. Whitman neither accords symbolic transactions this sustaining power nor embraces the sort of personal interdependence Wordsworth sees them as fostering. The peculiar combination of desires and fears that shapes the relation between poet and audience in *Leaves of Grass* thus stands out with special sharpness when juxtaposed to the vision of transmission that animates Wordsworth's poetry.

Wordsworth typically conceives our recruiting to cultural compacts as an initiation into sympathy and mutuality, rather than a subjection to a system of binding precedents. While symbolic mechanisms in *Leaves of Grass* seem to reduce the particular transactions in which individuals engage to instances of a generic and essentially anonymous operation that subverts identity, Wordsworth conversely tends to imagine the symbolic field as nothing but a collection of the sort of individual ties celebrated in "Tintern Abbey." The community depicted in "The Brothers," for example, is to be understood not as a concatenation of institutions, rules, and laws, but as a network of individual relations and individual narratives of personal connection and fidelity. In the village graveyard to which the alienated prodigal Leonard returns, there are thus no tombstones, since as the Priest explains, "We have no need of names and epitaphs; / We talk about the dead by our fire-sides" (*Poems* 1:406). As Leonard rightly concludes:

> Your Dalesmen, then, do in each other's thoughts
> Possess a kind of second life: no doubt
> You, Sir, could help me to the history
> Of half these graves? (*Poems* 1:407)

Though the absence of palpable inscription is crucial to the ethos Wordsworth evokes here, the passage by no means turns on the sort of agitated rejection of writing characteristic of *Leaves of Grass*. While here in "The Brothers" social cohesion and continuity are sustained by talk, the image of voice Wordsworth's passage celebrates is hardly Whitmanian: voice is devoted to repeating its part of a communal narrative. An easy commerce between voice and writing thus typifies Wordsworth's work. If the poet of "Tintern Abbey" saves Dorothy mnemonic effort by writing his legacy down, in "The Brothers" the living, so to speak, return the favor, keeping the dead alive in memory through their own faithful voicing of what amounts to an unwritten text. This permeable border between voice and writing bespeaks the amicable relation not only between the living and the dead, but also between individual and communal energies. Neither expressing autonomous individuality nor enacting its fading by means of an inscription conceived as anonymous and global, the commemorative recitations described in "The Brothers" embody a communal space that is simply the sum of individual relations or of the narratives that preserve them, enriching the living by connecting them to the dead.[41]

In Wordsworth's work the overlapping symbolic ties that make up cultural space are thus not simply intimate: apparently innocent of coercive sanctions, they also depend on individual uptake, on a freely-bestowed fidelity that seems to make communal coherence a contingent and indeed precarious achievement sustained principally by individual feelings of inter-dependence and mutual regard. "Tintern Abbey," I noted earlier, draws attention to this supposed freedom through the optative or hortatory, rather than performative, mode of the poet's closing address to Dorothy, and more broadly in the solicitude with which he envisions her future life. Wordsworth's portrait of social compacts thus lends them the same sort of respect for contingency and individual circumstance that characterizes his vision of imagination: the poet for whom eye and ear half create but also half perceive is concerned to temper power as much as to celebrate it, whether it be the sublime power of poetic imagination or the social power at work in testament and transmission.

Paradoxically, *Leaves of Grass* is no more comfortable with this sort of freedom than it is with the sweeping symbolic powers such contingency might mitigate. This double suspicion can help us isolate the opposing pressures Whitman's apostrophes are designed to resist and the resultant tensions that trouble the relation between poet and audience which these speech acts organize. While Whitman characteristically excoriates symbolic transactions for the inexorability of their functioning and the consequent reduction of identity to a kind of cipher, the mode of individuality he struggles to sustain is in certain respects peculiar: it ought, for example, to be self-sufficient rather than dependent on others, immune to the individual initiative exercised by other selves rather than vulnerable to it. Like most of the crucial features of the imaginative universe of *Leaves of Grass*, the relation between self and other governed by Whitman's image of voice thus possesses profoundly archaic appeal. Centering the powers of the word on the poet's own self-starting speech act, word magic detaches them from the governing cultural structures that give us limited symbolic power in exchange for the loss of autonomy

Whitman sometimes tropes as castration. Yet the magic word simultaneously frees the poet from dependence on the sort of individual uptake Wordsworth celebrates, a contingency that would seem to be in his interest since it apparently indicates the less than total subjection of individuals to the proleptic power of cultural mechanisms. In one sense this paradox is perfectly resolvable: for Whitman, I suggested in chapter 2, the contingent, transitive acts that take place in the symbolic realm ruled by light are instances not of individual freedom and initiative but of our subjection to a cultural grammar that dictates the forms our supposedly freely chosen relations can assume. Yet the poet who aspires to protect us from the symbolic structures that violate our proper autonomy nevertheless finds himself in the awkward position of initiating transactions whose effects can be difficult to tell from the dangers he warns us against. Obviating the poet's dependence on others, word magic in *Leaves of Grass* enforces on Whitman's audience a necessity no less total than that he attributes to symbolic functions, though we are to think of it as beneficent rather than constraining.

My contention that the poet is nervous about the freedom his audience might be able to exercise is apparently belied by Whitman's repeated attempts to impress on us a sense of this very liberty. Certainly the best known, and probably the most touching examples of this insistence appear near the end of "Song of Myself":

> I lead no man to a dinner-table or library or exchange,
> But each man and each woman of you I lead upon a knoll,
> My left hand hooks you round the waist,
> My right hand points to landscapes of continents, and a plain public road.

> Not I, not any one else can travel that road for you,
> You must travel it for yourself. (1855 80)

> I am the teacher of athletes,
> He that by me spreads a wider breast than my own proves the width of my
>   own,
> He most honors my style who learns under it to destroy the teacher.

> The boy I love, the same becomes a man not through derived power but in
>   his own right. (1855 81)

The 1860 "Poets to Come" likewise insists that what the poet of *Leaves of Grass* imposes on us is our own freedom:

> Leaving it to you to prove and define it,
> Expecting the main things from you. (1860 187)

I will come back to these lines further on; the "it" which ends the first of them has a rather surprising antecedent that strangely circumscribes the liberty the poet bestows, making our assumption of it difficult to tell from constraint. Kerry Larson has in any case persuasively demonstrated this disturbing aspect of the poet's attempts to expostulate with us concerning our freedom; he argues that Whitman is at least as nervous about such independence as he is solicitous of it (7–29, 39–55). As Larson notes (49), declarations of our liberty are thus often given paradoxical formulation:

> I teach straying from me, yet who can stray from me?
> I follow you whoever you are from the present hour;
> My words itch at your ears till you understand them. (1855 81)

The pre-emptive aspect at work in such equivocal assertions sometimes predominates quite clearly:

> None shall escape me, and none shall wish to escape me. ("A Song for Occupations," 1855 89)

More particularly, while the poet repeatedly insists that we have the liberty to improvise future transactions of our own, he is characteristically less enthusiastic about according us an equivalent degree of freedom in our dealings with him. The apparently magical transactions initiated by apostrophe seem to exempt the poet from the sort of contingent and anxious interactions depicted in the troubling sixth section of "Crossing Brooklyn Ferry."

As we might expect, it is voice that suggests the irresistibility which should characterize the poet's performative transactions with us. Whitman's figure of voice indeed implies that we play no active or essential role in the poet's advent: the powers of diffusion proper to voice do not depend on somebody else's hearing its words; in *Leaves of Grass* the poet's announcements supposedly diffuse not just a living sound but also a living presence. Able to project himself by means of his word, the poet would have no need of us in order to effect his perdurance. If he nonetheless takes trouble to convey his visionary understanding to us, he does so, it would seem, so that we can share his marvellous secret.

The poet's amorous ambitions likewise seem to be satisfied by this figure of voice whether or not we wish to cooperate in the trysts his announcements initiate. Voices place their auditors in a singularly passive position, seeming to penetrate to their interiors without waiting for active participation or assent. The body modeled on voice should share these undissuadable powers.

Yet the text which produces this figure of voice undercuts the poet's claims to self-sufficiency, returning him to relations that are contingent rather than magical and suggesting his dependence on the very audience his vocal prowess seems to make incidental to his survival and pleasure. Said to be diffused by voice, Whitman's utterance depends for its reach on unacknowledged acts of reading: the poet's ideal form is resurrected only as we read his text; we sustain the imperial figure voice seems to create, the presence that seems to produce itself through an act of parthenogenesis. Slipping from the magical status of living presence Whitman claims for him, the poet dependent on reading survives, despite himself, as the sort of image or sign Wordsworth celebrates, and by virtue of the kind of symbolic transmission that in "Tintern Abbey" is explicitly said to rely for its success on freely granted individual uptake.

Whitman sometimes overtly acknowledges this uncertain relation and its crucial role. In such moments, the writing and reading usually banished from the poet's universe are openly admitted into its confines: they serve, in part, as a sign of the poet's dependence on other people. As we shall see in the following chapter, such admissions are most frequent in Whitman's 1860 *Calamus* sequence. In the 1855 and 1856 *Leaves of Grass*, by contrast, we can sense this dependence for the most part only in the undertones that disturb the poet's declarations—and only, as it were, as we remove ourselves from the sphere defined by his voice and its emanation. We can feel the poet's need for us in "Crossing Brooklyn Ferry," despite what he declares, though it lurks far behind the leading tone:

> It avails not, neither time or place—distance avails not,
> I am with you, you men and women of a generation, or ever so many generations hence,
> I project myself, also I return—I am with you, and know how it is. (1856 212–13)

The magical figure who dominates "Crossing Brooklyn Ferry" seems to dissolve if we think about reading these lines. We can then perhaps hear a subdued but finally urgent entreaty here: a plea for our assent, our cooperation in this scene by virtue of which the poet may perhaps become the trope of what he declares himself already literally to be— the omnipotent figure capable of such a transfiguring act.

We can sense this need for our participation, as well, in a passage we considered already from "Song of Myself":

> This hour I tell things in confidence,
> I might not tell everybody but I will tell you. (1855 43)

The poet's voice speaks in a magical space its accents render near, and to those compelled into the circle of its intimacy. But it speaks in a text which disperses that space again, to others its words may sometimes manage to master, but over whom its powers remain contingent rather than assured.

In the first two editions of *Leaves of Grass,* this dependence of the poet on his audience provokes melancholy rather than Wordsworth's subdued celebration. To fall from a magical universe into a symbolic one is partly to give up self-sufficiency and power, and this is an attenuation the Whitman of the early editions does not willingly accept. Insofar as the symbolic realm can be characterized by the freely elected intimacy Wordsworth makes central to it, we can understand Whitman as rejecting a cultural compact to which Wordsworth gladly subscribes.

Wordsworth: Epitaphs

This contrast tells us a good deal about the imaginative stance of *Leaves of Grass.* Yet simply to oppose Whitman's insistent atavism to what can be made to look like Wordsworthian demystification is to miss an important anxiety these poets share. Wordsworth's vision of freely chosen personal fidelity wards off intimations about cultural transmission that possess a surprising resemblance to Whitman's more overt denunciations. Idealizing symbolic compacts, Wordsworth tries to elide both their proleptic power and their global scope, defusing the very dangers Whitman openly records and resists. This shared anxiety registers a peril more unsettling than mere external threat. As we shall see, Wordsworth's vision of beneficent transmission is troubled by the always equivocal relation between a pre-emptive version of symbolic continuity he struggles to banish and the humanized mode he espouses. Wordsworthian transmission may perpetuate some of the dominations it hopes to leave behind; its nobler pleasures may always be tinged with a less laudable enjoyment of the coercive powers it ostensibly repudiates. Similar ambiguities lurk in the compact initiated by the poet of *Leaves of Grass*. In Whitman's work the writing that both facilitates and undermines the liberating magic of the poet's apostrophes may function, not simply to diminish his powers, but to mark these as powers of another kind. Despite the melancholy which awareness of the poet's dependence on inscription characteristically provokes in *Leaves of Grass*, writing intimates not only the poet's failure to free us but also his exercise of the sort of coercive symbolic force he claims to liberate us from. While Wordsworth and Whitman offer very different pictures of the sort of influence poetry exercises and the sort of effect it can achieve, their notions of what it ought *not* to do thus turn out to be strangely similar. And for both poets, this vision of what poetry should not do—which is also what culture should not do and what the poet can supposedly help it to stop doing—turns out to be hard to isolate from what poetry does.

A careful look at Wordsworth's covert anxieties concerning cultural transmission can thus serve to acquit *Leaves of Grass* of the charge of indulging a merely idiosyncratic phobia; registered even in Wordsworth's very different body of work, which celebrates our reliance on symbolic compacts, the price Whitman more conspicuously laments may be one he accurately describes. Wordsworth's difficulties detaching the legacy poetry bequeaths from the cost exacted by what is supposed to be cultural transmission of the wrong sort will also prove instructive for an appraisal of *Leaves of Grass*. The poet's apostrophes may be a dramatic instance of an aggressivity generally at work in cultural transmission, and not simply a peculiarly unattractive manifestation of Whitman's supposedly aberrant omnivorous egotism.

In Wordsworth's work the sustaining legacy offered by epitaph does not simply overcome silence. This is admittedly the most overt threat against which Wordsworthian transmission is marshaled: the loss of voice that befalls alter egos such as the boy of Winander, marking what might be called existential intimations, characteristically finds restitution in the communal text that replaces lost natural continuities with symbolic ones. Coming upon a haunted and silent spot, such epitaphic pieces as the early "Lines (Left upon a Seat in a Yew-tree)" (*Poems* 1:254–56) strive to rescue the dead from muteness, and to humanize the unspeaking landscapes they inhabited, by recovering a lesson they did not have the insight or foresight to transmit. Yet the Wordsworthian text also takes the place of another, more dangerous transmission.

The power of the wrong sort of inscription, specifically the wrong sort of epitaph, to subvert rather than sustain us is the burden of a *locus classicus* of Wordsworth studies, from the third of the *Essays upon Epitaphs:*[42]

Words are too awful an instrument for good and evil to be trifled with: they hold above all other external powers a dominion over thoughts. If words be not (recurring to a metaphor used before) an incarnation of the thought but only a clothing for it, then surely will they prove an ill gift; such a one as those poisoned vestments, read of in the stories of superstitious times, which had power to consume and to alienate from his right mind the victim who put them on. Language, if it do not uphold, and feed, and leave in quiet, like the power of gravitation or the air we breathe, is a counter-spirit, unremittingly and noise-lessly at work to derange, to subvert, to lay waste, to vitiate, and to dissolve. (2:84–85)

It is not quite clear who will be poisoned or dissolved here—the dead who should be preserved inviolate in memory or the living who should be upheld by a reverent relation to them, a relation the epitaph should support. But Wordsworth takes pains to make the source of such devas-tation perfectly explicit: words that clothe or disguise the writer's thought rather than incarnating it are responsible. According to Wordsworth such degraded epitaphs threaten to corner the market, overwhelming authentic expression:

Energy, stillness, grandeur, tenderness, those feelings which are the pure emana-tions of nature, those thoughts which have the infinitude of truth, and those expressions which are not what the garb is to the body but what the body is to the soul, themselves a constituent part and power or function in the thought—all these are abandoned for their opposites,—as if our Countrymen, through successive generations, had lost the sense of solemnity and pensiveness (not to speak of deeper emotions) and resorted to the Tombs of their Forefathers and Contemporaries only to be tickled and surprised. (2:84)

As the by-now voluminous commentary on these passages has shown, this crucial but questionable opposition between two sorts of language condenses tensions central to all three of the *Essays*.[43] I will come back briefly, a bit further on, to the problematic notion of the proper relation between language and thought, and between communal discursive practice and individual identity, posited by Wordsworth's contrasting figures of body and garment. But I want to turn first to what the very notion of improper expression serves to occult.

In the *Essays* Wordsworth blames the dangerous slippage between feeling and expression on perverse literary taste:

Would we not recoil from such gratifications, in such a place, if the general literature of the Country had not co-operated with other causes insidiously to weaken our sensibilities and deprave our judgements? (2:84)

He suggests that "vicious diction" (2:86), especially in the form of neoclassical antitheses designed to display compositional cleverness rather than to reveal true feeling, has become an incapacitating distraction. Yet the counterfeiting of authentic feelings for the dead emerges in the *Essays* as a threat both pervasive and urgent enough to make literary habit a curious source for it:

These suggestions may be further useful to establish a criterion of sincerity, by which a Writer may be judged; and this is of high import . . . no faults have such a killing power as those which prove that he is not in earnest, that he is acting a part, has leisure for affectation, and feels that without it he could do nothing. This is one of the most odious of faults; because it shocks the moral sense: and is worse in a sepulchral inscription, precisely in the same degree as that mode of composition calls for sincerity more urgently than any other. (2:70)

The urgency of this call for sincerity would seem to bespeak a peculiar difficulty occasioned by the epitaph. If epitaphic writing is peculiarly liable to the counterfeiting of appropriate sentiments, that may be because such feelings struggle against others deemed less proper. As the curious epithet "killing" in the passage above already implies, what Wordsworth presents as bizarre lapses of decorum can be understood instead as eruptions of a persistent, if persistently disavowed, aggression directed against the dead.[44] At the very beginning of the first of the Essays, Wordsworth suggests that epitaphs, or at least the monuments on which they are inscribed, originate as a defense against just such aggressivity:

Almost all Nations have wished that certain external signs should point out the places where their dead are interred. Among savage tribes unacquainted with letters this has mostly been done either by rude stones placed near the graves, or by mounds of earth raised over them. This custom proceeded obviously from a twofold desire; first, to guard the remains of the deceased from irreverent approach or from savage violation: and, secondly, to preserve their memory. (2:49)

Throughout the *Essays,* the opposed impulses enumerated here—to preserve the dead in memory or to do violence to them—tend implicitly to intermingle. Though Wordsworth does not put it this way, epitaphs are thus constantly tempted to perform the very sacrilege they were invented to forestall. While he deploys the phrase with other, particular compositional faults in mind, Wordsworth's "general recommendation that they who have offended or may be disposed to offend in this manner would take into serious thought the heinousness of their transgression" (2:92) can thus serve as a formulation of the intensely ambivalent feelings provoked by the epitaphic enterprise. In this respect, at least, the fault of improper epitaphs is not that they are mere garments rather than true incarnations of the writer's feelings: the problem is with the feelings themselves.

The *Essays* give some indication, however, that such aggressive sentiments are not entirely inappropriate. The turbulent emotions and divided agenda of the epitaph writer may respond to disquieting intimations concerning the dead, as this curious passage suggests:

Amid the quiet of a Church-yard thus decorated as it seemed by the hand of Memory, and shining, if I may so say, in the light of love, I have been affected by sensations akin to those which have risen in my mind while I have been standing by the side of a smooth Sea, on a Summer's day. It is such a happiness to have, in an unkind World, one Enclosure where the voice of detraction is not heard; where the traces of evil inclinations are unknown; where contentment prevails, and there is no jarring tone in the peaceful Concert of amity and gratitude. I have been rouzed from this reverie by a consciousness, suddenly flashing upon me, of the anxieties, the perturbations, and, in many instances, the vices and rancorous dispositions, by which the hearts of those who lie under so smooth a surface and so fair an outside must have been agitated. The image of an unruffled Sea has still remained; but my fancy has penetrated into the depths of that Sea—with accompanying thoughts of Shipwreck, of the destruction of the Mariner's hopes, the bones of drowned Men heaped together, monsters of the deep, and all the hideous and confused sights which Clarence saw in his Dream! (2:63–64)[45]

Here the disturbing passions Wordsworth glimpses are ostensibly relegated safely to the past, since he imagines them as troubling the dead during their lives. Yet they turn the Sea itself, Wordsworth's figure for the graveyard where the dead now reside, into something like Lear's terrible ocean.

Elsewhere in the *Essays*, this agitation carried into the grave seems to well up from it to consume the living. I have in mind the passage, already quoted, on language as "counter-spirit," and in particular the image of the poisoned coat that serves to figure the killing effects of the wrong sort of words. As Paul de Man reminds us, this is the coat of Nessus ("Autobiography as De-Facement," *Rhetoric of Romanticism* 80).[46] This garment was a grim legacy offered by the dying to the living: given by the centaur Nessus to Deianeira, it was meant to poison her husband Heracles, who had just inflicted on Nessus a mortal wound (Graves 2:193). While the passage in the *Essays* overtly concerns the harm done by living writers of epitaphs, either to the dead or to those who read of them, a more archaic dread of the magical violence the dead may do the living thus lurks here. As Wordsworth notes elsewhere in the essays, with a disapproval we are now in a better position to understand, epitaphs can also take the form of inscriptions supposedly offered not by the living but by the dead themselves, from beyond the grave (2:60–61); such a transmission, Wordsworth's figure here implies, may inflict a mortal wound. It is to this threat of violence, in part, that the aggression of the living responds.

In de Man's seminal reading of the *Essays*, the violence Wordsworth attributes to improper epitaphs is thus made to characterize the mode itself. De Man locates this violence more particularly in "the latent threat that inhabits prosopopeia," epitaph's organizing trope:

namely that by making the death [*sic*] speak, the symmetrical structure of the trope implies, by the same token, that the living are struck dumb, frozen in their own death. The surmise of the 'Pause, Traveller!' thus acquires a sinister connotation that is not only the prefiguration of one's own mortality but our actual entry into the frozen world of the dead. ("Autobiography as De-Facement," *Rhetoric of Romanticism* 78)[47]

Despite Wordsworth's efforts to attribute it to depraved literary practice and thus relegate it to the status of perversion, a similar sense of threat haunts the vision of benign transmission articulated in the *Essays*, suggesting that epitaph may always in part inscribe an act of violence perpetrated not only by the living against the dead but also by the dead against the living. We can understand this latter violence as the product of a will to perdure, and of the consequent claims an older generation makes on a younger one, in trying to live through it and more particularly in entailing the very possessions and privileges it ostensibly bequeaths. But this personal passion both fuels and is fueled by the global cultural energy Lacan calls the passion of the signifier. If lending a voice and a face to the dead seems to exact a reciprocal fading of our own speech and visage, which should be simply palpable and present, that may be because the perdurance of the dead as part of a shadowy community of address that makes claims on us intimates not only the symbolic status of identity but also its entailment by the social configurations that precede every individual. As the image of the coat of Nessus itself implies, the danger in perverse epitaph, or simply in epitaph, is thus finally not that of a divorce between feeling and expression, inside and outside, or individual experience and communal practice, but rather of an intimate relation between them that is the reverse of what we think it ought to be: it is as if, reversing the logic of Wordsworth's figure, the body were always in danger of becoming the result or "incarnation" of the garment (as if clothes made the man). Both enabling and disenabling, this power of the coat of Nessus, of the dead and of the structure their writing transmits, not simply to uphold but in another sense to constitute and thereby fade the living, is persistently skirted in Wordsworth's work. Yet if silence and existential anguish are the external threats against which epitaph is marshaled, this double violence, at once personal and more broadly cultural, always remains as a threat internal to epitaph itself, troubling a notion of transmission which can never be wholly detached from it.

As in Whitman's work, the lurid contours this danger assumes in the *Essays upon Epitaphs* may be partly a function of denial. In several of Wordsworth's poems, the threatening aspect of the epitaph or monument is more overt and the dangers it represents are more nearly inescapable; in such cases the poet responds more stoically.

The first of Wordsworth's commemorative "Matthew" poems is prefaced by the following headnote:

In the School of ————— is a tablet, on which are inscribed, in gilt letters, the Names of the several persons who have been Schoolmasters there since the foundation of the School, with the time at which they entered upon and quitted

their office. Opposite to one of those Names the Author wrote the following
lines. (*Poems* 1:380)

The epitaph the poet composes is thus an answer to, or an attempt to
rescue Matthew from, not simply the silence of mortality but the inscription of an insufficient or improper memorial.[48] The poem's conclusion
makes this clear, with a kind of tough-minded wonder:

> —Thou soul of God's best earthly mould!
> Thou happy Soul! and can it be
> That these two words of glittering gold
> Are all that must remain of thee? (*Poems* 1:381)

Here the reduction of individual identity to the impersonality of the
letter is presented with a kind of schematic simplicity that suggests the
inexorable, a fate epitomized or exacted by epitaph. Or epitaph of the
wrong sort: the whole sequence of Matthew poems can be understood
in part as an attempt to restore the body this coat of Nessus wastes. Yet
as the fiction of the headnote itself implies, in a sense the poet's project
is offered as a kind of marginal gloss on this passion of the letter rather
than an alternative to it. Wordsworth's closing "must" likewise suggests
a fatality the poem can mitigate but not evade, a fatality that seems to
lean into the future and appears to have designs on the poet himself.

The long narrative poem "Michael" also proposes itself as a beneficent, sustaining transmission:

> Therefore, though it be a history
> Homely and rude, I will relate the same
> For the delight of a few natural hearts;
> And, with yet fonder feeling, for the sake
> Of youthful Poets, who among these hills
> Will be my second self when I am gone. (*Poems* 1:456)

It would perhaps be untoward to describe the poem itself as a coat of
Nessus draped on Wordsworth's readers, though its burden turns out to
be rather severe. But we can at least note that this benign transmission
doubles and attempts to reverse the disastrous transmission the poem
narrates, a legacy likewise designed to be benign. I have in mind the
poem's central incident, the laying of a cornerstone by the shepherd
Michael and his departing son, an act the father regards as initiating a
covenant:

I knew that thou couldst never have a wish
To leave me, Luke: thou hast been bound to me
Only by links of love: when thou art gone,
What will be left of us!—But, I forget
My purposes. Lay now the corner-stone,
As I requested; and hereafter, Luke,
When thou art gone away, should evil men
Be thy companions, think of me, my Son,
And of this moment; hither turn thy thoughts,
And God will strengthen thee: amid all fear
And all temptation, Luke, I pray that thou
May'st bear in mind the life thy Fathers lived,
Who, being innocent, did for that cause
Bestir them in good deeds. Now, fare thee well—
When thou return'st, thou in this place wilt see
A work which is not here: a covenant
'Twill be between us; but, whatever fate
Befall thee, I shall love thee to the last,
And bear thy memory with me to the grave. (*Poems* 1:466)

Michael's closing provisions here, which soften the injunctions of the covenant symbolized by the sheep-fold whose cornerstone the son is to lay, are just the sort of humanizing gestures that characterize Wordsworth's own acts of transmission. Yet the demand of the covenant effectively over-rides the extenuations the father attaches to it, inflicting the very psychic violence he tries to mitigate; the covenant determines what the son must be in order to take up his place in a lineage by no means wholly softened or humanized.[49] Failing this injunction represented by the foundation stone, the son loses his place and his name, despite the father's good intentions:

Meantime Luke began
To slacken in his duty; and, at length,
He in the dissolute city gave himself
To evil courses: ignominy and shame
Fell on him, so that he was driven at last
To seek a hiding-place beyond the seas. (*Poems* 1:467)

It is at least in part the covenant that drives him there, a fact that lends the father's ensuing stoicism the proportions of tragedy rather than mere pathos:

He went, and still looked up to sun and cloud,
And listened to the wind; and, as before,

Performed all kinds of labour for his sheep,
And for the land, his small inheritance.
And to that hollow dell from time to time
Did he repair, to build the Fold of which
His flock had need. 'Tis not forgotten yet
The pity which was then in every heart
For the old Man—and 'tis believed by all
That many and many a day he thither went,
And never lifted up a single stone. (*Poems* 1:468)

This scene images the fate that haunts Wordsworth's epitaphic mode. To note the troubling overlap between the benign transmission to which Wordsworth aspires and the sort of ferocious, pre-emptive energies detailed in a poem like "Michael" is no more to accuse the poet of simple duplicity than to suggest that the shepherd's efforts to soften the compact with his son are merely hypocritical. But just as Michael assumes something of the archaic visage of a patriarch, despite himself, so too the poet cannot help but participate in, and benefit from, the very cultural coercions he struggles to personalize and humanize.

Traces of such coercive energies trouble even the gentle injunctions of "Tintern Abbey." The difficulty is not to overstate the case, or to discount the quotient of imaginative generosity that makes Wordsworth's exhortations moving. There is nevertheless something troubling about the detail with which the poet envisions both Dorothy's future state and her appropriate response to it. It is disturbing, too, that both envisioned circumstance and stipulated response so closely approximate Wordsworth's own as to very nearly reduce Dorothy to the condition of the poet's specular reflection. If there is just a hint of unctuousness in the tone of Wordsworth's closing cadenza, it may arise from an effort to deny this unpalatable aspect of the poet's desires, and of the transmission which furthers them. Despite genuine efforts to soften its effects, the poet's inscription exercises a positional authority that tends to be pre-emptive, a symbolic force associated more than once in Wordsworth's work with patriarchal power. Recalling the legal machinery of inheritance and entailment, the gesture of transmission with which "Tintern Abbey" closes may necessarily activate the proleptic authority of the name of the father.

Wordsworth: The Sublime

In Wordsworth's poetry the project of humanizing cultural transmission is not simply identical to the task of curtailing the individual power Wordsworth calls imagination; but we saw earlier that the two enterprises are related. The patriarchal authority lurking even in the closing section of "Tintern Abbey," conversely, resembles in its pre-emptive positional force the abrupt imaginative power that manifests itself as poetic sublimity. This similarity might lead us to modify Hartman's classic account of Wordsworthian imagination, which has so far stood us in good stead, in one salient respect; in doing so, we will in part be following the lead of some brief but suggestive remarks in Hartman's own later essays on Wordsworth, as well as the more extended argument of Thomas Weiskel's *The Romantic Sublime*. In *Wordsworth's Poetry*, we saw, Hartman argues that imagination must be bound and humanized because, as it manifests itself in moments of sublime influx, it reveals itself as a power prior to social compacts and destructive of them: it is in this sense that Bloom's notion of "sublime solipsism" is apposite to Hartman's analysis. We might instead suggest that imagination in its sublime aspect is dangerous, not because it abrogates social compacts, but because it recalls social powers of the wrong kind. The dialectic of the sublime, Weiskel argues at length in his immensely useful study, can be understood as a condensed version of the Oedipal drama. Wordsworth's ambivalence with regard to imagination may measure in part his uneasiness concerning the sort of unchecked patriarchal force also evident in what his work encourages us to think of as the wrong sort of epitaph and the wrong sort of transmission.[50]

A brief account of the career of Wordsworthian imagination in such Oedipal terms will prove useful here, in part because of the way this history differs in its details from Whitman's attempts to revise the Oedipal configuration. But the broad effort to posit poetry as an alternative to the Oedipal compact is a project these poets share. Moreover, the resemblance between poetic transmission and the Oedipal structure from which it should free us is likewise a burden by which both poets are troubled. This confluence suggests that poetic language may derive much of its power over us from the very mechanisms to which it often aspires to offer an alternative.

Hartman's germinal account in *Wordsworth's Poetry*, though, of

Wordsworthian imagination as an essentially autonomous power that must first be naturalized, and then humanized, neglects intimations that imagination is linked to cultural authority from the first. If imagination appears over against the poet, in both Wordsworth's early work and the descriptions of his childhood in *The Prelude*, assuming the guise of a hostile natural force that erupts in the midst of the landscape, this displaced violence supposedly registers the poet's discomfort with imaginative autonomy:

Nature's familiar aspect is eroded; quasi-apocalyptic creatures and visions emerge. This, we know, is a sign that imagination is beginning to reveal itself as a power separate from or even opposed to nature; yet it seems to Wordsworth as if nature, not imagination, were rising up against him. It is nature that is demonic. ... (*Wordsworth's Poetry*, 84–85)

A similar displacement, Hartman suggests, lends the crucial "spots of time" their brooding quality:

In episodes where the violation [of nature] is patent we can say that the spirit of place rises up in revenge against the violator. But where it is secret, as in the two spots of time (for no clear desecration has occurred), we must assume that the boy's very *awareness* of his individuality—a prophetic or anticipatory awareness nourished by self-isolating circumstances—reacts on him as already a violation. A sudden self-consciousness, transferred to outward things, is raised against him under the mask of nature. (*Wordsworth's Poetry*, 214–15)

Projection and denial, however, do not alone account for this rising up of sublime power over against the poet; nor is it quite imagination's autonomy that the spots of time reveal in displaced form. As Weiskel stresses, the Oedipal configuration of these moments is palpable (175–85). The power that confronts the poet can be understood as the power of the father, a cultural authority to be inherited and internalized only if one has first acknowledged its otherness and put oneself under its sway. The second of the spots of time, of course, centers overtly on the death of Wordsworth's father; it also concerns, Weiskel shows in his fine analysis, the boy's unstated intimations of this event (183). Desired as well as feared, the impending death of the father provokes, in self-imposed retribution, what the earlier "spot of time" calls a "visionary dreariness" (*Prelude* 1850 12.256), a sense that the natural scene is haunted by an obscure but menacing force:[51]

'twas a day
Tempestuous, dark, and wild, and on the grass

> I sate half-sheltered by a naked wall;
> Upon my right hand couched a single sheep,
> Upon my left a blasted hawthorn stood. (1850 12.297–301)

This configuration becomes a kind of knot to which the boy obsessively returns after his father's death:

> And, afterwards, the wind and sleety rain,
> And all the business of the elements,
> The single sheep, and the one blasted tree,
> And the bleak music of that old stone wall,
> The noise of wood and water, and the mist
> That on the line of each of those two roads
> Advanced in such indisputable shapes;
> All these were kindred spectacles and sounds
> To which I oft repaired, and thence would drink,
> As at a fountain. . . . (1850 12.317–26)

This sort of obsessive reversion to a haunted scene associated with a brooding power we might well term patriarchal also characterizes Wordsworth's preceding description of a "spot of time." There the relation between such obsessive return and a burdened Oedipal resolution is rather spectacularly overt. The terrain on which the poet encountered, not the gibbet where a murderer had been hanged, which had mouldered away, but the bare inscription of his name, carved in "monumental letters" (1850 12.241), and the adjacent spot, haunted by "visionary dreariness," on which he had seen the girl "vexed and tossed / By the strong wind" (1850 12.260–61) become with a bizarre appropriateness the preferred site of the poet's own later courtship rites:

> When, in the blessèd hours
> Of early love, the loved one at my side,
> I roamed, in daily presence of this scene,
> Upon the naked pool and dreary crags,
> And on the melancholy beacon, fell
> A spirit of pleasure and youth's golden gleam;
> And think ye not with radiance more sublime
> For these remembrances, and for the power
> They had left behind? . . . (1850 12.261–69)

This scene the poet re-treads, as Weiskel astutely notes, is a spot where, in the form of the bare letters of the executed murderer's name, "The order of law is inserted into the order of nature by means of writing"

(178). According to Weiskel it is this inscription and the law it bespeaks, even more than the particular facts of the murder or execution themselves, that had occasioned the boy's fear: "The element of panic enters the text with the appearance of the characters, as if they constituted the deep meaning of the grave, and not vice versa" (178). The young man who woos on this spot becomes a husband and father in his own right only by internalizing the law whose inscription he has witnessed here.

There are moments in Wordsworth's poetry, Weiskel suggests, when the poet seems ready to put on this ferocious power of the law himself, if rather uneasily. Commenting on the passage in Book XIII of *The Prelude* in which the poet visits the archaic ruins on the Plain of Sarum and conjures up a druidic ceremony, Weiskel remarks:

The Salisbury vision exhibits with stunning clarity Wordsworth's ambivalent relation to the archaic power of the Word. He is in part the victim of the vision; there is naiveté in his incantation; he doesn't know what will follow. But he also participates in the power, assuming the ancient role as if it were his inevitable due. That the vision presents such a contrast to his self-conception as poet serves to expose the partiality of that conception, though not its sincerity. (192)[52]

Something of this ferocious positional force associated with the name of the father persists in the crucial eruptions of poetic sublimity in *The Prelude*. A detailed account of such passages would of course have to take into consideration the important differences, noted by Hartman and Weiskel, between the poet's vision on Mount Snowden and his meditation on the crossing of the Simplon Pass, itself a prelude to the more ominous sublimities of Gondo Gorge.[53] But in both the Snowden and Simplon episodes, a self-starting power seems to the poet to erupt abruptly; and in both, this sublime imaginative power recalls the sort of positional force that also characterizes the patriarchal function, whether in its deific or human guise. I quote from the passage on the crossing of Simplon, since it presents a crux that merits consideration:

Imagination—here the Power so called
Through sad incompetence of human speech,
That awful Power rose from the mind's abyss
Like an unfathered vapour that enwraps,
At once, some lonely traveller. I was lost;
Halted without an effort to break through;
But to my conscious soul I now can say—
'I recognize thy glory': in such strength

Of usurpation, when the light of sense
Goes out, but with a flash that has revealed
The invisible world. . . . (1850 6.592–602)

Weiskel, who tends to associate Wordsworth's rather protean term "imagination" with what Hartman calls the "humanized imagination," rather than with mind in its more august and terrifying sublime aspect —which is what Hartman takes Wordsworth to mean by imagination proper—sees imagination as resisting both sublimity and Oedipalization here. I would suggest instead that Oedipal intensities are not always banished quite so firmly from Wordsworth's conception of the poet's task, and that this atypical passage is an instance not of a resistance to Oedipalization but of an internalization of the Oedipal compact, an internalization not usually so apparent in Wordsworth's work. The crux here is the term "unfather'd": assigned by the passage to imagination, this epithet is associated by Weiskel with the ego as well: "it is at once the ego's need and its attempt to be *unfathered,* to originate itself and thereby refuse acknowledgement to a superior power. The Imagination is not an evasion of the oedipus complex but a rejection of it" (203). Yet here the vapor of imagination rises up not as an emanation of the ego or the self, but as a blocking agent, an apparently external force that abruptly thwarts it. If imagination itself appears as "unfathered," glimpsed rising from the mind's abyss, that does not quite mean, therefore, that the self who glimpses this force is unfathered too. It is only by subjecting himself to this power prior to every individual that the poet puts it on; it is only by accepting this unfathered force that he acquires the power of positing or fathering, whether cultural or poetic. According to Wordsworth's account it is only later that this power is re-cognized as an attribute of "soul."

This bargain, Oedipal in its structure, is implicitly accepted in the meditation on Simplon, a passage Hartman rightly sees as exceptional. But Weiskel is surely correct to suggest that, for the most part, Wordsworth seeks to distance the poet's powers from the sort of patriarchal authority inherited here. What Hartman in *Wordsworth's Poetry* terms a naturalizing and humanizing of imagination, Wordsworth thus also displays as its feminizing: in his work idealized versions of a pre-Oedipal space and a maternal influence which can supposedly pass over into culture from it, unscathed, are marshaled against the terrors of the patriarchal sublime.

In *Wordsworth's Poetry* Hartman persuasively links the naturalizing of imagination in Wordsworth's work with the gradual disappearance of those incidents in which a threatening power suddenly erupts in the midst of a natural landscape. Brooded over in Wordsworth's early poetry as well as in the passages in *The Prelude* that recall the poet's early development, these frightening manifestations give way to descriptions of landscape that stress continuity rather than abrupt disjunction, omnipresent flux rather than sudden eruptions of power:

The obsession with specific place lifts from him or blends into a more generous conception of nature. . . . What happens here and now has happened before, and is elsewhere, everywhere. . . . This multiplying locus assumes a tremendous sweep and molds for itself a subtler form as the blank verse of the fragments becomes an exercise in fluidity. The strongest contrasts become blendings; new corridors are opened and hidden subsistencies revealed. (166)

In contrast to the sudden concentrations of force I have been associating with positional and patriarchal power, the fluidity of these gentler landscapes suggests a more archaic space not yet organized by such punctuality. What Hartman terms a contrast between apocalypse and nature can also be understood as an opposition between Oedipal and pre-Oedipal dispositions: like several of Whitman's catalogues, such passages of natural description evoke an idealized version of the register Kristeva calls the semiotic, an organization shaped by a relation to the mother's body not yet mediated by symbolic structures or regulated by paternal prohibition.[54] Among the passages in Wordsworth's work explicitly stressing the role of the mother in shaping this sort of space, the best known is probably the one from Book II of *The Prelude:*

> Blest the infant Babe,
> (For with my best conjecture I would trace)
> Our Being's earthly progress,) blest the Babe,
> Nursed in his Mother's arms, who sinks to sleep
> Rocked on his Mother's breast; who with his soul
> Drinks in the feelings of his Mother's eye!
> For him, in one dear Presence, there exists
> A virtue which irradiates and exalts
> Objects through widest intercourse of sense.
> No outcast he, bewildered and depressed:
> Along his infant veins are interfused
> The gravitation and the filial bond
> Of Nature that connect him with the world. (1850 2:233–44)

For most, access to this space is subsequently blocked:

> Such, verily, is the first
> Poetic spirit of our human life,
> By uniform control of after years,
> In most, abated or suppressed; in some,
> Through every change of growth and of decay,
> Pre-eminent till death. (1850 2:260–65)

In Wordsworth's account it is those still blessed by a special tie to the feminine who are best able to sustain this sense of deep interfusing supposedly once guaranteed by the maternal. Book XIV of *The Prelude* thus evokes the feminine as a principle that can continue to soften patriarchal sublimities within the social, symbolic space the name of the father rules. Wordsworth's paean to Dorothy insists that her saving grace rescued him from a ferocity that had already begun to claim him:

> Child of my parents! Sister of my soul!
> Thanks in sincerest verse have been elsewhere
> Poured out for all the early tenderness
> Which I from thee imbibed: and 'tis most true
> That later seasons owed to thee no less;
> For, spite of thy sweet influence and the touch
> Of kindred hands that opened out the springs
> Of genial thought in childhood, and in spite
> Of all that unassisted I had marked
> In life or nature of those charms minute
> That win their way into the heart by stealth,
> Still to the very going-out of youth,
> I too exclusively esteemed *that* love,
> And sought *that* beauty, which, as Milton sings,
> Hath terror in it. Thou didst soften down
> This over-sternness; but for thee, dear Friend!
> My soul, too reckless of mild grace, had stood
> In her original self too confident,
> Retained too long a countenance severe. (1850 14:232–50)

Here the gentle continuities that in Wordsworth's work characterize a natural space evocative of the pre-Oedipal and an infantile condition associated with the maternal are made to pass over without loss into the social relation between the poet and his sister. Wordsworth's relation to Dorothy, at any rate, is said to cure the poet of his obsession with those sublimities I have been calling patriarchal and linking to Oedipal transmission. In "Tintern Abbey," this gentler relation makes possible an act of bequeathing Wordsworth seems to understand as a feminized alternative to the Oedipal compact grimly depicted elsewhere in his work.

A good deal more might be said about the idealized images of both the maternal and, more broadly, the feminine Wordsworth invokes to authorize this vision of gentle continuity. But we can confine ourselves to noting that Wordsworth wants to locate a feminine principle free of sublime violence within symbolic culture and not just prior to it. Scarcely more comfortable with Oedipal transmission than is Whitman, Wordsworth thus manages to celebrate symbolic compacts, imagining a form of them supposedly innocent of patriarchal authority and its proleptic power. Yet as we have seen, the beneficent transmission he hopes to enact remains haunted by traces of just such coercive energies.

Power and Law

If Wordsworth defuses the threat of patriarchal power by imagining a symbolic, essentially textual transmission shaped by the feminine and thus supposedly exempt from Oedipal demands, Whitman by contrast invokes an archaic image of voice whose positional power is magical rather than symbolic; he thus aims to commandeer the power of the father rather than, like Wordsworth, to attenuate it. Like Wordsworth, Whitman retreats from the symbolic space governed by patriarchal authority to a fluid semiotic terrain that evokes an archaic relation to the mother. But Whitman seems more drawn than Wordsworth to the power lodged in positional and patriarchal authority, though he is certainly no less leery of its cost. He is, conversely, less intent on isolating a version of symbolic compacts he can affirm, less committed than Wordsworth to fostering benign symbolic mechanisms with recognizable connections to a network of existing institutions they might reform rather than subvert. This is so despite Whitman's attempts to associate the poet's presence with a visionary democratic prospect, since, as much recent criticism has shown, the community supposedly initiated by the poet's advent is meant to by-pass just such institutional mediation.[55] We might re-cast this formulation more broadly, describing Whitman's project as a paradoxical attempt to ground our sociality in a mode of relation not governed by common subjection to symbolic law or the castration it exacts. Whereas Wordsworth's search is for a transmission that is symbolic but not patriarchal, Whitman's demand is for a version of positional power that is inherent rather than culturally invested or inherited. Word magic is the privileged form of this fantasy; a connection to his audience that accords the poet tremendous power yet acquits him of the alienating effect and coercive intent Whitman identifies with symbolic mechanisms is the mode of relation such magic should permit.

This redemptive fantasy is of course attended by its own peculiar temptations. I have been arguing not only that both Wordsworth and Whitman aspire to a mode of relation that is not Oedipal, but also that the alternative transmission each proposes is finally impossible to isolate from the aggressions it should redeem. Given Whitman's particular fascination with the very positional power he dreads, this contagion is likely to be especially acute. While it is something of an overstatement, since such power is not without its attractions for Wordsworth too, we might almost say that coercive symbolic authority is a residue Wordsworth cannot quite manage to purge from his work, whereas in *Leaves of Grass* this supposedly repudiated force turns out in practice to be very difficult indeed to distinguish from the sort of power the poet seems only too pleased to wield. Despite both the winsome quality that characterizes the poet's declarations of his liberating manifestation and the melancholy that attends intimations of the collapse of this presence into just another sign, Whitman's apostrophes do not simply succeed, or fail, in freeing us from pre-emptive cultural mechanisms; they are themselves an instance of them, exacting the very fading from which Whitman wants to believe his declarations protect us.

The poet's apostrophes exercise this pre-emptive symbolic power most palpably as Whitman's image of voice seems to fade into writing; the text which suggests a melancholy lapse of the magical power Whitman associates with voice also reveals his exercise of power of another, less beneficent sort. We may of course already be uncomfortable with the magical scene into which voice seems to fold us: the archaic space voice initiates in Whitman's work is not without its terrors, among them the very eclipsing of boundaries which Whitman tends to see as an unmixed blessing since it dissolves the polar relations structured by the sign and governed by the law of the father. Our possible discomfort with the scenario shaped by the poet's voice, that is, is matched by Whitman's anxieties concerning the scene of symbolic transmission epitomized by writing: inscription subjects us to powers *Leaves of Grass* characteristically depicts in lurid terms. The poet who, despite his best intentions, ends up exercising a power mobilized by writing and unnervingly difficult to distinguish in its effects from the symbolic transmission against which he repeatedly rails is thus caught in a position that is compromising in more than one respect. He does not simply wield a power he hopes to attenuate since it provokes pragmatic misgivings; rather, he becomes an instance of the very thing he has violently excoriated and rejected. Calling into question the repudiation Whitman proclaims, the violence of his invectives against writing and representation implies that this resemblance may afford the poet a satisfaction no less intense than his distaste: suggestive less of simple disapproval than of powerful ambivalence, Whitman's diatribes against symbolic transmission seem to register a mix of anxiety and fascinated attraction. If Whitman's text precipitates the very fading of identity from which *Leaves of Grass* claims to preserve us, the poet is thus not simply caught up despite himself in a pervasive symbolic structure no speech act can quite leave behind, or entangled in aggressions endemic to political union which he attenuates as much as anyone can. Rather, the extreme anxiety provoked by mechanisms of symbolic transmission in *Leaves of Grass* is matched by the poet's intense if covert interest in wielding those mechanisms himself. While this may be a paradox, it is hardly an incomprehensible one: like those under the sway of a compulsion to repeat described by Freud near the opening of *Beyond the Pleasure Principle* (11), the poet gains a measure of control over the injury done him and the anxiety it provokes by repeating and reversing the scene of its transmission; shifting from passive to active role, he inflicts injury and anxiety in his turn, gaining a retrospective mastery over them at the price of passing them on.[56] We thus need to attend not only to the way inscription in *Leaves of Grass* can act to subject us, but also to the poet's investment in this aggressive aspect of his supposedly liberating transactions with us.[57]

One way to get at the uncomfortable intertwining of the poet's presence with the cultural operations from which it should free us is to recall both the untoward effects attributed to the dead in Whitman's work and the poet's disconcerting resemblance to these ominous figures. As we saw in chapter 5, Whitman associates writing and representation with those no longer alive, depicting these mechanisms as instruments that permit the dead to maintain a ghoulish existence at the expense of the living. We saw that Whitman expends a good deal of effort trying to detach the effects of the poet's presence from this sort of necromancy: we saw as well that the tenuous distinctions between bad and good repetition, and between representation and a living presence somehow fortified with the powers of the sign, end up suggesting the very affinity they ought to dispel. In "So Long!," we noted, the poet indeed acquires the qualities that elsewhere define him as the epitome of living presence precisely by hovering at the brink of a death that is not quite allowed to claim him.

Some portraits of the poet make this troubling resemblance even clearer. *Leaves of Grass* offers us occasional glimpses of a figure who has crossed the threshold at which "So Long!" stalls. These visions of a presence who ponders us from the kingdom of the dead suggest not simply that the poet's effect can be difficult to distinguish from the supposedly necromantic powers to which culture subjects us, but also that these are powers Whitman is not entirely averse to wielding. Despite the bracing aspect of these uncanny encounters, the poet assumes in them, if not quite the ghoulish aspect attributed to specters elsewhere in Whitman's work, at least the visage of the dead father:

> I but advance a moment, only to wheel and hurry back in the darkness.

> I am a man who, sauntering along, without fully stopping, turns a casual
>   look upon you, and then averts his face,
> Leaving it to you to prove and define it,
> Expecting the main things from you. ("Poets to Come," 1860 187)

Though it is the poet who averts his face here, the "casual look" that precedes this gesture invests it with sublimity rather than implying humility or submission. And the third and fourth of these lines, which we glanced at earlier, offer an especially troubling instance of the poet's claim that he confers on us our own liberty: the "it" we are to exercise our freedom defining turns out to be the poet's fleetingly revealed face; our initiative consists in filling in the contours of his visage. Like God or his patriarchal avatar, the poet turns on us a countenance we are not quite permitted to gaze on but are enjoined nonetheless to recall; we acquire our own identity by assuming what we can of his.

Another poem in the 1860 edition makes clear the effect such a transaction might have on us. Left implicit in the lines just quoted from "Poets to Come," the mesmerized gaze with which we are expected to look back toward this obscure but dominating figure is described overtly in a passage from "Starting from Paumanok" that also evokes the poet's ghostly visage. There the poet's audience is reduced to a condition disturbingly similar to that Whitman elsewhere ascribes to those under the sway of writing and the proleptic transmission it effects:

> See projected, through time,
> For me, an audience interminable,
>
> With firm and regular step they wend—they never stop,
> Successions of men, Americanos, a hundred millions,
> One generation playing its part and passing on,
> And another generation playing its part and passing on in its turn,
> With faces turned sideways or backward toward me to listen,
> With eyes retrospective toward me. (1860 6–7)

There is something quite disconcerting about this parade: "playing its part and passing on," each fleeting generation marches forward into oblivion, its eyes not even fixed on the stage it briefly inhabits but instead cast back toward the dead poet, who seems almost to direct this haunted procession. We are very close here to the sort of eerie pre-emptive effect Whitman rails against in his diatribes characterizing writing as an instrument of the dead. The passage also recalls the uncanny chiasmus of the living and dead de Man discerns in epitaph: here too, the prosopopoeia central to cultural transmission seems not only to confer a face on the dead, but to exact in exchange the animation of the living, feeding it to the poet who mesmerizes their gaze; in this passage it is the living rather than the dead who seem spectral.

These haunting passages have something of the feel of fleeting and equivocal admissions, as if Whitman was briefly drawn to suggest the ominous aspects of the transmission attributed to the poet's magical voice but purveyed by writing. Yet it may be ultimately more disconcerting that passages given a predominantly upbeat air can also imply this troubling resemblance between the poet's transactions and the pre-emptive cultural mechanisms they supposedly replace. It turns out, indeed, that the apostrophes which most fully detail the supposedly beneficent effects of the poet's presence often suggest most strongly the disturbing resemblance between our encounters with him and the symbolic transmissions they are designed to obviate.

As we saw in chapter 5, according to Whitman writing violates our proper autonomy, installing inside us an alien text written by the dead. This text supposedly pre-empts our own words and enervates the living voice that might speak them; transmitting the demands of the dead, it saps our vitality as well, wearing away our own living presence. Supposedly impinging on us as a living presence himself, the poet claims to restore our autonomy and integrity to us. Yet in the 1856 "Poem of You, Whoever You Are," Whitman's attempts to detail this restoration of selfhood uncannily repeat the alienating self-division they should heal:

> I only am he who places over you no master, owner, better, god, beyond
> what waits intrinsically in yourself. (1856 207)

The complex coercion here involves not simply a power relation between poet and reader but, more intimately, the implantation of a mode of identity not quite describable as a recovered autonomy or wholeness.[58] Despite the appearance of the reassuring term "intrinsically" here, the line describes not an organic identity but a divided one. Imagining this internal division as one between master and slave, owner and owned, social better and inferior, or god and human worshiper, this line also attributes to the poet's intervention the installation, or at least the activation, of this agonistic structure of selfhood: the poet does not quite deny that he places over us a master, an owner, a better, or a god, but only that each of these agents of control "waits" already within us, presumably biding its time to assume its due authority.

I am suggesting, of course, that the poet's attempts to restore our proper self-sufficiency turn out to resemble the operations by which culture creates a mode of self-policing identity no longer characterized by such autonomy: the line reads like a parable of the implantation of the super-ego. The irony at work here thus exceeds the properly political dilemma that cultural transmission necessarily turns on the power relations it sometimes wants to eschew; the very selves we think of as engaging in or escaping this coercive relation are products of it.

Some lines a bit further on in the poem offer another image for this generation of supposedly sacrosanct subjects. Recalling a trope deployed differently elsewhere in Whitman's work, they too manage to suggest the disturbing resemblance between the poet's transactions with us and the psychic violence they should heal:

> But I paint myriads of heads, but paint no head without its nimbus of gold-colored light,
> From my hand, from the brain of every man and woman it streams, effulgently flowing forever. (1856 207)

In the context of Whitman's work, these lines imply that the supposedly autonomous individuality the poet calls forth is simply another version of the culturally conferred identity from which we are apparently being preserved. Here the poet takes the place of the sun of "Crossing Brooklyn Ferry," painting the corolla of light it projects there, which installs us in the realm of images and representations. The poet's gesture dramatically repeats this subjugation. As Whitman's strangely doubled genitive construction implies ("From my hand, from the brain of every man and woman it streams"), we acquire the halo that will be made to symbolize our sacrosanct individuality only as we take up our places in a representation emanating from the poet—or from the Other, the resemblance between this scene and the one in "Crossing Brooklyn Ferry" suggests, an Other whose work the poet has here effectively been empowered to perform.

The poet's supposed ability to police the identity he thus confers also resembles a capacity "Crossing Brooklyn Ferry" associates with the sun and the light and darkness it projects. In "Crossing Brooklyn Ferry," we saw in chapter 3, the poet himself is provoked to painful self-interrogation by means of a shadow that impinges upon him suddenly. Declaring the poet's ascent to the sun's throne, Whitman is at pains there to insist that he will put an end to this sort of august interrogation, replacing it with saving emanations of his own transfiguring presence. But in a pair of lines from "Poem of You, Whoever You Are," the poet seems less intent on dismantling our self-division than on monitoring it:

> I pursue you where none else has pursued you
> [....]
> I track through your windings and turnings—I come upon you where you thought eye should never come upon you. (1856 208)

While the poem as a whole is emphatically committed to recalling us to the psychic integrity culture has obscured, the poet's ability to penetrate to our interiors nevertheless does not so much overcome as uncannily repeat and reinforce our subjugation to an otherness planted permanently within us.

If the poet's attempts to repair our integrity can thus end up repeating the process of our self-division, his claims to restore to us a world that has been occulted by misleading representations can likewise have the disconcerting effect of provoking the very fading of the real they supposedly cure. As we saw in chapter 5, according to Whitman the representations culture teaches us to revere tend to supplant things themselves, robbing us of our living world and recruiting us to a realm of simulacra Whitman characterizes as apparitions fobbed off on us by the dead. Yet the poet's warnings against this disaster seem to provoke or at least repeat it: claiming to dissolve the miasma in which culture shrouds us, he seems to be dissolving the world itself. The opening of "Poem of You, Whoever You Are" thus seems less liberating than preemptive:

> Whoever you are, I fear you are walking the walks of dreams,
> I fear those realities are to melt from under your feet and hands;
> Even now, your features, joys, speech, house, trade, manners, troubles, follies,
>   costume, crimes, dissipate away from you,
> Your true soul and body appear before me,
> They stand forth out of affairs—out of commerce, shops, law, science, work,
>   farms, clothes, the house, medicine, print, buying, selling, eating, drinking,
>   suffering, begetting, dying. (1856 206)

Whitman's tone here betrays something of the ferocity at work in such foreclosure: the hint of harshness in these lines suggests not just denunciation or invective, but the wielding of a more jealous power that itself exacts the dissolution against which the poet warns us. The poet, in effect, pre-empts our world, not so much preserving us from a rude awakening otherwise certain to befall us as precipitating it here and now: these lines seem to pull our realities out from under us, turning them into apparitions and thereby claiming them for the ghostly region the poet himself seems to inhabit. Whitman's catalogue technique, we can note in passing, is deployed here in circumstances that make its preemptive aspect apparent: if Whitman's litanies typically seem to collapse a dispersed object world into the poet, these lines make clear that things are thereby repossessed from their erstwhile owners.

A similar tension between salvific and aggressive impulses makes the 1855 "To Think of Time" an extended exercise in disturbing intimation. Pondering death, the poet is concerned to reassure us that we shall come through it unscathed; yet he is just as intent on disabusing us of our fondness for all that cannot pass through the eye of the needle with us:

> To think that the rivers will come to flow, and the snow fall, and fruits ripen
> . . and act upon others as upon us now . . . . yet not act upon us;
> To think of all these wonders of city and country . . and others taking great
> interest in them . . and we taking small interest in them.
>
> To think how eager we are in building our houses,
> To think others shall be just as eager . . and we quite indifferent.
> I see one building the house that serves him a few years . . . . or seventy or
> eighty years at most;
> I see one building the house that serves him longer than that.
>
> Slowmoving and black lines creep over the whole earth . . . . they never cease
> . . . . they are the burial lines,
> He that was President was buried, and he that is now President shall surely
> be buried. (1855 99)

These lines hover between stoic wisdom and a darker pleasure; partly a warning or an attempt to console us for the coming loss the poet depicts, they nonetheless seem to exact the very fading of the world they foresee.

The hint of satisfaction lurking here can be explained at least in part by the position at which the poet is once more implicitly poised: present to us as a disembodied voice discoursing on last things to those still under the sway of what precedes them, he seems to occupy a liminal vantage, being on terms no less familiar with the realm beyond the grave than he is with our own. His warning thus serves to wilt a world we might otherwise usurp when we succeed him, by willing it to us in mortgaged condition: things, as it were, come to share the death into which the poem's speaker seems about to pass.

They have in any event been reduced to the status of signs, a condition the poem's proleptic discourse likewise seems to precipitate as well as describe:

> Pleasantly and well-suited I walk,
> Whither I walk I cannot define, but I know it is good,
> The whole universe indicates that it is good,
> The past and present indicate that it is good. (1855 104)

As Whitman's semiotic vocabulary here suggests, the fading the poem both registers and provokes is linked to the hegemony of symbolic systems. The eschatological concerns that dominate the poet's statements accordingly screen a less disinterested, more agonistic cultural drama played out by his speech acts and the relation to us they establish. If our possession of our world is conspicuously contingent, that is in part because our universe is no longer simply physical; both our world and our selves take the form of a series of symbolic values which those who precede us not only determine but can also bequeath or withhold. In "To Think of Time" the poet puts on something of the power reserved for the dead who precede us in this lineage of entailments. Exercising the positional power to categorize and confer, his pre-emptive announcements not only mobilize but also covertly revel in the quotient of aggression at work in cultural transmission. Poised between the positions of the dead and the living, the poet escapes the foreclosure that pre-empts the latter by becoming one of the former and passing this injury on; bequeathing the conspicuously conditional inheritance he has himself been offered, he thereby retains a hold on it himself.

Throughout *Leaves of Grass,* we have seen, Whitman's governing trope for this pre-emptive symbolic transmission is writing. The appearance of the poet's supposedly magical voice in the text of Whitman's book thus always implies the sort of power relation made more overt in the passages we have been considering. If Whitman's image of voice evokes a mode of presence and a variety of bequest not compromised by the lack these passages display and the aggressivity it provokes, writing intimates more than the poet's inability to transcend or transmute these defects. The poet's transmission does not simply fail to free us by failing to occur: succeeding all too well, it subjects us to the coercions Whitman would like to be able to repudiate.

As we noted, Whitman's written apostrophes implicitly recall the very codified instruments their intimate tone and gestures at private address ostensibly by-pass. The power they manage to exercise may derive from just this resemblance to formally instituted transactions and the cultural authority they possess. Like Wordsworth's acts of poetic bequeathing in this respect, Whitman's apostrophes can in part be regarded as attenuated versions of more strictly codified and more clearly empowered instruments of social transmission: they both evoke the power of such mechanisms as the will and testament and lack their institutionally sanctioned authority. Yet both Wordsworth's and Whitman's acts of transmission also exhibit the proleptic power of such instruments in its most general form: what Wordsworth and Whitman claim to confer, or at least to uphold, is not a particular inheritance or right but subjectivity itself.[59] Yet they convey identity only in the alienated form they aim to cure. More intensely ambivalent about cultural authority than Wordsworth, Whitman is caught in an especially compressed and powerful version of this paradox.

Like the visionary and poignant aspects of the poet's apostrophes, this darker implication of Whitman's addresses is also revealed in their tone, though this register is never dominant. We can sometimes discern a certain residual coldness in these announcements, a sense of distance perhaps reflecting not just the anonymity intrinsic to written address, but also a hint of the poet's dark pleasure in imposing it on us. Like the instruments of transmission he excoriates, the poet recruits us to impersonal structures which predate our appearance and confer on us identities that are sustainable only because they are imposed. There is thus a quotient of sentimentality in the determination—Whitman's as well as ours—to hear the poet's apostrophes as either visionary or poignant. The melancholy that attends the collapse of the poet's apocalyptic claims also masks the symbolic power they wield, obscuring the quotient of satisfaction Whitman derives from this surreptitious exercise of control.

The end of the 1856 "Song of the Open Road" seems to poise among these various possibilities:

> Mon enfant! I give you my hand!
> I give you my love, more precious than money,
> I give you myself, before preaching or law;
> Will you give me yourself? Will you come travel with me?
> Shall we stick by each other as long as we live? (1856 239)

Like the contrasts in these lines between presence and law, eros and symbolic accumulation, the antinomy of seductive and poignant tones here is one with which we are familiar. As is customary in *Leaves of Grass,* such polarities are structured by an opposition between voice and writing. Yet Whitman's text implies not simply the dissolution of the visionary scene the poet announces, but also the working of another, less generous operation. Enticing us with what is supposed to be an elusive but literal presence, the poet initiates a symbolic transaction and recruits us to the kind of compact from which he claims to exempt us: we are persuaded here to give our allegiance to an image or sign, committing ourselves to just the sort of mediating cultural construct we are supposedly being invited to avoid. Moreover, our own anonymity matches the blankness of the figure who summons us. If Whitman's sentimentalized gesture at direct address ("Mon enfant!") seems to single us out and sustain our uniqueness, his text instead inaugurates one of those symbolic rituals in which our identity is stipulated in functional rather than individual terms: the gesture at personal intimacy, indeed, seduces us into foregoing what it seems to promise, initiating us into an anonymous transaction in which our identity will be sustained, in mediated form, only as its supposed uniqueness is relinquished and we become instances of the generic addressee Whitman's written deictic names. Despite Whitman's gesture at embrace, there is a certain emotional distance lurking in these lines; it registers an anonymity the passage is not simply unable to overcome but itself exacts.

The poet's active if ambivalent participation in this recruiting of subjects is more evident in announcements in which the performative dimension is more overt. An apostrophe from "Poem of You, Whoever You Are" which I quoted earlier thus possesses a rather chilling effect, though Whitman's gesture of election encourages us to overlook it:

> Whoever you are, now I place my hand upon you, that you be my poem,
> I whisper with my lips close to your ear,
> I have loved many women and men, but I love none better than you. (1856
>   206–207)

Whitman's text does not simply register the impotence of his figure of voice or wistfully return us to the public space from which that voice sought to summon us; here inscription, an instance of the generalizing operation from which the passage claims to exempt us, actively recruits us to the sort of symbolically mediated, culturally conferred identity such operations establish. If the poet's living hand, made magically present, would bestow on us a mode of identity exempt from such mediation, the dead hand conveyed by the text, the hand as image or representation, itself exacts the fading Whitman's gesture at intimacy seems to fend off. The melancholy which seems to attend the fading of the poet's own presence into his text serves in part to mask this pre-emptive aspect of the transmission he initiates. Word magic—which should counter symbolic transactions but which, in its inevitable failure, always ends up in practice collapsing back into them—thus registers not only the poet's wish to escape the strictures of the symbolic, but also his desire to wield its powers himself, in more drastic if supposedly more beneficent form.

Such symbolic power, though, lurks in Whitman's apostrophes only as an unacknowledged substratum. If the poet's hand is finally not so very different from the hand Keats thrusts toward us in order to haunt us, and if the poet's presence, like Keats's, is one we would like to imagine as living in order that it might cease being an avatar of the dead father, those are intimations *Leaves of Grass* resists rather than invites, avoiding the reversals Keats's poem exhibits to such disquieting effect.

Neither this entanglement nor Whitman's attempts to hide it should be understood as signs of mere hypocrisy. They suggest, instead, an ambition that is divided and a stance toward transmission that is deeply ambivalent. Whitman's apostrophes register not only his commitment to discovering a source of intrinsic authority anterior to culture, but also both the contrary desire to wield cultural power and the wish to ennoble it by purging its more disastrous effects; they reveal the poet's impulse to spare us the injury he has suffered, but also his urge to discharge his anxiety by passing it on. Wound to a tighter pitch than Wordsworth's "Tintern Abbey," or even "Michael," Whitman's apostrophes participate to a never quite determinable degree in the coercions they also want to resist, at once repelled and fascinated by a structure of transmission they occult yet exemplify.

We need to attend to this quotient of aggression, lest we over-idealize the effects of the poet's speech acts or the impulses that motivate them; we flatten out Whitman's addresses to us if we focus solely on his generosity, or on the melancholy that attends the failure of his noblest aims. But we also need to remember that the poet would like to transmute the very injury he inflicts. Like Whitman's figure of presence, the image of a transmission exempt from the coercions law imposes is not only unstable but also destabilizing; it holds out to us the elusive promise of an unalienating inheritance and an unalienated identity. Unrealized by *Leaves of Grass* and strictly unrealizable, the prospects suggested by the poet's apostrophes are properly utopian or apocalyptic, figures of desire and of unassuaged discontent. Yet the passages that evoke our liberation necessarily activate what balks desire and separates us from fulfillment.

Notes

1. De Man offers the classic account of this economy mobilized by epitaph and the prosopopoeia that organizes it: see "Autobiography as De-Facement," *Rhetoric of Romanticism* 67–81. See also Cynthia Chase, *Decomposing Figures* 83–89 and Debra Fried, "Repetition, Refrain, and Epitaph."
2. See Breitwieser 134–45 for a contrary reading. Breitwieser regards a program of demystification as central to Whitman's addresses to his audience.
3. See Hartman, "Wordsworth, Inscriptions, and Romantic Nature Poetry," *Beyond Formalism* 206–30, especially 225–26; and "Romantic Poetry and the Genius Loci," *Beyond Formalism* 311–336, especially 329: "Thus Wordsworth refuses to renew archaic modes. An unghostly poetry is born, a true vernacular, 'words that speak of nothing more than what we are.'"
4. Appropriately enough, I am unable to relocate this anecdote.
5. For a reading of this catalogue antithetical to the one I offer, see Thomas 12–22.
6. I cite the CRE text, which is more unremitting in its mania for enumeration than is the original 1855 version.
7. De Man regards this tension between performative and constative poles as intrinsic to all language: the positional power of the word, which suggests radical freedom since it seems to inhere in individual utterances and speech acts, depends on the prior existence of codes that make positing possible only by making position a function of differential structures that are already in place. For a concise summary of de Man's argument, see Chase, *Decomposing Figures* 94–98.
8. On the already uttered and the already bespoken see Bakhtin 293–94 and 331.
9. On this point see Larson 155–56.
10. This catalogue is not present in the 1855 text; see V 1:130–32.
11. Commenting on the end of "Song of Myself," Bloom notes a similar dynamic: "The hawk accuses Whitman of belatedness, of 'loitering,' but the poet is one with the hawk, 'untranslatable' in that his desire is perpetual, always transcending act. There, in the twilight, Whitman arrests the lateness of the day, dissolving the presentness of the present, and effusing his own presence until it is air and earth. As the atmosphere we are to breathe, the ground we are to walk, the poet introjects our future, and is somewhere up ahead, waiting for us to catch up" (*Poetry and Repression* 263–64).

12. See especially xiv–xxii, 14–20, and 56–59.

13. This vision of the dead preying upon the living is of course not unique to Whitman; related preoccupations indeed turn up repeatedly in the writings of the poet's post-revolutionary cohort; see Forgie 53. My point is not that Whitman did not share the political concerns of his era—of course he did —but that he redefines the dangers of cultural inheritance by which his generation was especially troubled in such sweeping terms that they exceed the scope of political adjudication, provoking an apocalyptic intervention likewise hard to regard as a trope for political action; see chapter 8, below. Even Emerson, who associates the burden of cultural inheritance that preoccupied his generation with the mechanism of writing, and who accords it inclusive rather than narrowly political scope, treats the problem of influence troped by the role of books as a dialectic intrinsic to culture rather than a nefarious interference to be overcome by magical means. On this aspect of Emerson's work see Larson's valuable account (30–39).

14. My interpretation of Whitman's apostrophes differs sharply here from Larson's. His response to the poet's claims to presence is on the whole dismissive: "he makes of himself a figure of voice impatient to overleap the constraints of representation altogether. . . . Yet . . . such calls to presence are bound to seem especially melodramatic and unearned" (85). I have been arguing, on the contrary, that the import of Whitman's apostrophes depends crucially on the contours Whitman's figure of presence appears to assume. In particular, the culturally provocative stance these announcements imply is bound up intimately with the archaic body image they suggest. Larson thus casts Whitman's ambitions and anxieties in comparatively restricted terms: "While not necessarily false, the picture of the American Adam sauntering down the road is deceptive so far as it encourages us to believe that what Whitman most needed from poetry was the assurance of a self–fathering authority free from the afflictions of personal and cultural belatedness" (56). This is, I take it, exactly what Whitman did need from poetry —though not, without qualifications, from political theory.

15. See for example "Emerson and Influence," *A Map of Misreading* 160–76, especially 166–72.

16. In quoting from *The Prelude* I cite book and line rather than page numbers; as a rule I quote the 1850 rather than the 1805 text.

17. On the intractable persistence of the daemonic and its centrality to Romance and Romanticism, see Hartman, "False Themes and Gentle Minds," *Beyond Formalism* 283–97, especially 289.

18. "Time and History in Wordsworth" was published in a special issue of *Diacritics* in 1987; the essay is a transcription of a lecture de Man delivered at the Christian Gauss Seminar in Criticism at Princeton in 1967; see "Time and History in Wordsworth" 4n1. I take up some of de Man's later remarks on Wordsworth on 334.

19. On this point see Ferguson 70.

20. On the resources of Wordsworthian blank verse see Hartman, *Unmediated Vision* 3 and 25.

21. I here follow Weiskel; see 141–42.

22. On Wordsworth's ambivalent relation to Miltonic blindness see Hartman, *Wordsworth's Poetry* 99.

23. Weiskel notes, however, that regressive tendencies are not wholly foreign to the Wordsworthian sublime, or what Keats called the "egotistical sublime," which Weiskel also denominates the "positive" as against the "negative" or "true" sublime; see especially 137, 150–64, 185, and 194–204. In general, I place less stress on the regressive aspects of Wordsworthian imagination than Weiskel does; I see it as more implicated in the sublimity and Oedipalization Wordsworth wants to resist; see 342–43.

24. Inasmuch as this youth is in his early twenties—Wordsworth's first visit to Tintern Abbey having occurred in 1793—we cannot understand his immersion in presence and lack of interest in "a remoter charm, / By thought supplied" as exactly literal; the autobiographical trajectory the poet traces is a kind of imaginative or temperamental recapitulation of an earlier psychic development.

25. On the dating of "Tintern Abbey" and "There Was a Boy" see *Poems* 1:953–55. The classic account of "There Was a Boy" is de Man's: see "Time and History in Wordsworth," especially 5–9, and "Wordsworth and Hölderlin," *Rhetoric of Romanticism* 47–65, especially 50–54. I am indebted as well to Ferguson 69, 167–70, and 242–49, and Hartman, *Wordsworth's Poetry* 19–22.

26. I here, of course, follow de Man: see "Time and History in Wordsworth" 7–8 and "Wordsworth and Hölderlin" 52–53.

27. Noting the "hangs" which describes the Churchyard, de Man suggests that the scene itself now reflects or repeats the boy's precariousness ("Time and History in Wordsworth" 8); moreover, the very presence of a compositional echo can be understood as an ironic allusion to the sort of reciprocity of call and response the boy had earlier enjoyed, which has lapsed into a muteness that claims the poet as well as the boy. On echo as trope in Wordsworth's work and more particularly in "There Was a Boy," see Ferguson 161–71.

28. On epitaph as a Wordsworthian figure for poetry see Ferguson, especially 155–72, and Hartman, *Wordsworth's Poetry* 12–13 and 20. De Man remarks, with typically mordant humor: "Hartman is quite right in saying that the poem ["There Was a Boy"] 'becomes an . . . extended epitaph' . . . though one might want to add that it is the epitaph written by the poet for himself, from a perspective that stems, so to speak, from beyond the grave. This temporal perspective is characteristic for all Wordsworth's poetry— even if it obliges us to imagine a tombstone large enough to hold the entire *Prelude*" ("Time and History in Wordsworth" 9).

29. In an earlier version of the poem, Wordsworth mourns his own passage from one state to another, rather than projecting it onto a boy who has

since literally died (see *Poems* 1:954–55, and de Man, "Time and History in Wordsworth" 8–9). This revision probably responds, as Hartman suggests, to the need for narrative closure (*Wordsworth's Poetry* 20); but it also serves to foreground the topos of transmission.

30. Hartman's remarks on the Wordsworthian topos of "the halted traveler" are pertinent here: see *Wordsworth's Poetry* 3–18.

31. On the characteristic fading of voice into inscription in Wordsworth's poetry, see Hartman, *The Fate of Reading* 161–63 and 289–92. Discussing Rousseau, Derrida outlines an economy similar to that set in motion at the conclusion of "Tintern Abbey": see chapter 5, note 12, above.

32. I quote the 1871 text, in which Whitman's deictic drama is sharpest; see V 1:62 for the various versions of this passage.

33. See, for example, the material surrounding the first passage just discussed (1855 70).

34. On Lacan's formulation of the relation between death and the sign see chapter 5, note 92, above. On the relation between death and the poet's presence in *Leaves of Grass,* I am indebted to comments by Donald Pease on a draft of "Whitman's Presence: Apostrophe, Voice, and Text in *Leaves of Grass,*" though my formulations depart from his suggestions in certain respects.

35. I read the "you" here as the audience of *Leaves of Grass;* the opening exclamation ("O Death!") might best be regarded as an ejaculation concerning but not addressed to death, though a modulation from one addressee to another is also possible.

36. I quote the 1867 text.

37. I quote the 1867 text, which introduces "solely to you."

38. I quote the original 1872 text, printed in CRE among the poems excluded from *Leaves of Grass.* The poem appears in the "deathbed" edition, in truncated form, as "My Legacy"; see the editorial note on CRE 615; for "My Legacy," see CRE 497–98.

39. On the undermining of animating intention and performative efficacy which the signature suggests, see Derrida, "Signature Event Context" 193–96.

40. Breitwieser (131, 136) points to the anonymity of the written "you," though he construes its import differently than I do.

41. Wordsworth's enabling fiction is thus that we choose writing, rather than it choosing us.

42. On the *Essays upon Epitaphs* see de Man, "Autobiography as De-Facement," especially 74–81.

43. On Wordsworth's opposing tropes of language as incarnation and language as garment, and the problematic status of the antithesis they figure, see de Man, "Autobiography as De-Facement" 79–91 and Ferguson 30–34. On the related passage in *The Prelude* (1850 5.426–59) concerning a drowned man and his garments, see Cynthia Chase, *Decomposing Figures* 14–29 and Warminsky 25–30.

44. This hostility can appear in the sort of compositional freaks Wordsworth frowns on, such as puns which make light of the deceased person's name:

> Palmers all our Fathers were
> I a Palmer lived here. (2:68)

It can lurk in the odd alacrity with which poetic closure seems ready to mime the ferocity of fate, producing an untoward comic effect:

> Aged 10 Weeks
> The Babe was sucking at the breast
> When God did call him to his rest. (2:93)

On this sort of effect see Fried.

45. Owen and Smyser, Wordsworth's editors, make this association to *Lear,* in addition to noting the explicit reference to *Richard III;* see *Prose Works of William Wordsworth* 2:106.

46. See also Cynthia Chase, *Decomposing Figures* 63 and 87.

47. See also Fried 617.

48. On this point see Ferguson 86.

49. As Lacan notes, speaking as it happens of the beneficent rather than the harmful effects of our insertion in the Oedipal configuration, the culture will tend to make good whatever is lacking in the particular familial case; see *Ecrits* 199, 217.

50. In his 1979 essay "Words, Wish, Worth: Wordsworth," Hartman takes up Oedipal aspects of Wordsworthian imagination; see especially 177–81, 193–95, and 200–205. So far as I know, though, the argument I am making here about Wordsworth's attraction to the feminine as a supposed alternative to Oedipal terrors is not one Hartman has advanced.

51. Hartman's brief but suggestive reconsideration of this passage in "Words, Wish, Worth: Wordsworth" notes the presence of such Oedipal material; see 211–12.

52. On the terrors of this passage see also Hartman, "Words, Wish, Worth: Wordsworth" 200–202.

53. See Hartman, *Wordsworth's Poetry* 42–48 and 60–67; and Weiskel 48–53, 153, and 194–204. Even the Snowden vision, though, is not lacking in the terrors, provoked by abruptly revealed power, characteristic of the "negative" sublime, which following Weiskel I have been associating with Oedipalization. Weiskel himself indirectly suggests this aspect of the Snowden passage: "It is inconceivable that Wordsworth should have given us the Mount Snowden vision without the *subsequent* editorializing in which he turns experience into emblem and takes possession" (53; emphasis added).

54. In his 1977 essay "A Touching Compulsion," Hartman stresses the association Wordsworth makes between natural landscape and the maternal term, though he does not focus there, as in *Wordsworth's Poetry,* on the sense of blending which I am associating with the register Kristeva calls the semiotic,

or on the possible contrast to Oedipalization and the sublime; see *The Unremarkable Wordsworth* 25–30. A general consideration of the tension between the Oedipal father and the pre-Oedipal mother, brought to bear very briefly on Wordsworth, can be found in his *Saving the Text;* see especially 75–107 and 151–54. On the "egotistical" sublime as a partial reversion to the pre-Oedipal and an attempted foreclosure of the paternal term, see Weiskel 150 and 162–64. On the negative or "proper" sublime as an evasion of the maternal and the pre-Oedipal, see Hertz, "The Notion of Blockage in the Literature of the Sublime," *The End of the Line* 40–60, especially 51–53. On the role of the maternal in Wordsworth, with specific reference to the passage I take up immediately below, see Ferguson 130–38; for a more severe estimate see Warminsky 22–25.

55. See for example Fredrickson 20–21; Grossman 203 and 208n28; Pease, "Blake, Crane, Whitman, and Modernism" 66; and Larson, especially xx, 28, and 246n7; Larson argues, though, that Whitman's ambivalent political views led him to re-instate a version of the very mediating mechanisms he had supposedly eliminated.

56. On repetition as a retrospective attempt to master anxiety, see the extended discussion in *Beyond the Pleasure Principle* 6–17. Though Freud argues for the theoretical independence from the pleasure principle of both the compulsion to repeat and the death drive which it supposedly manifests, his opening discussion focuses instead on the difficulty of detaching one from the other in practice; Whitman's apostrophes, certainly, institute a repetition in the service of pleasure. The converse, however, may also be true: Lacan's linking of repetition compulsion, and the fading or death that inhabits it, to the rule of the sign suggests that pleasure, for the human subject, may always be a pleasure in repetition, haunted by death. Enabled by inscription, the pleasure the poet derives from the perfectly iterable scene in which he appears to us is at any rate inseparable from an anxiety which provokes aggression, a pleasure written out under the sign of death.

57. On the aggressive aspects of the poet's apostrophes see Anderson, "Whitman's New Man" 39–47; Grossman 195; and, of course, D. H. Lawrence's classic account, especially 167. I am indebted as well to Larson (30–55). While Larson's lack of attention to the form the poet seems to assume in his addresses to us leads to a narrower interpretation of what it is Whitman intends to by-pass than the one I offer, I am in substantial agreement with his broadly deconstructive suggestion that the poet ends up perpetuating some of the coercions he claims to alleviate. My sense of this entanglement, though, is rather darker than Larson's. In keeping with his treatment of apostrophe as a device supposedly furthering Whitman's considered meditation on a political problem, Larson tends to regard the aggression mobilized by Whitman's addresses as an unavoidable hazard of constitution-making and cultural transmission, a coercion inseparable from the need for consensus. But as the lurid and frequently violent rhetoric provoked by the

problems of writing and representation in Whitman's work suggests, we need also to attend to both the extreme anxiety coercive transmission provokes in *Leaves of Grass* and the attendant fascination it compels. If we are willing to see the element of coercion in Whitman's relation to us, that is, we should also be willing (as Lawrence was) to see it as extreme; constitutional democracy surely asks less of us than the poet does. Whitman's apostrophes may thus have less to tell us about political praxis or the perils of constitution-making than about the terrors and aggressions socialization can inspire—responses which can of course be mobilized for ideological purposes. See chapter 8, below.

58. On this passage see Larson 51–52.
59. Larson (49) makes a similar point about Whitman.

7. Legacies

The poet is a god, or, the young poet is a god. The old poet is a tramp.
—Stevens, "Adagia," *Opus Posthumus* 173

Over the course of Whitman's career, the paradoxes to which we have been attending proved difficult to sustain. Tenuous itself yet never quite free of the liabilities it supposedly leaves behind, Whitman's image of voice pretty much vanishes from the poems written after 1860. The national cataclysm that for a time became the focus of Whitman's work, demanding attention to the sort of intractable material rendered in *Drum-Taps,* is certainly one reason for this disappearance. Yet the cosmic opinionizing that in turn succeeds Whitman's war poetry assuages not only his lingering doubts concerning the legacy of the nation's conflict, but also more intimate anxieties never quite laid to rest by the elusive vision of identity promulgated in the earlier work.[1] Parts of the 1860 *Leaves of Grass* also suggest that the mode of presence so exuberantly imagined in the prior incarnations of Whitman's book had itself come to seem untenable or inadequate; this re-valuation seems due only in part to the darkening of the American political horizon. The *Calamus* sequence struggles to accept a mode of identity shaped by the cultural demands and constraints from which the poet's earlier speech acts had seemed to exempt him, and to celebrate a transmission closer to the symbolic one proffered in "Tintern Abbey" than to the magical transactions initiated by the poet-hero of the 1855 and 1856 *Leaves of Grass.* The *Sea-Drift* poem "As I Ebb'd with the Ocean of Life" registers the enormous cost of this accommodation.

These pieces mark an end to the poetic project I have been tracing. Articulated most programmatically in several of the poems composed for the 1856 edition, that project first emerges in Whitman's comic masterpiece "Song of Myself," shadowed by the doubts and demurs that

366

re-appear more sharply in 1860. Before turning to *Calamus* and "As I Ebb'd," I thus want to look at Whitman's exuberant but equivocal beginning. The scope of "Song of Myself" offers the reservations that trouble Whitman's image of voice ample room to appear; but its comic mode tolerates such doubts with relative equanimity. Whitman's career thus begins with a poem that exhibits something like the play of mystification and demystification I have been relegating to the borders of his mythopoeic project. This peculiarity helps account for the poem's deserved reputation as Whitman's major achievement. The virtual disappearance of such flexibility in subsequent work marks Whitman's increasing commitment to enforcing his imaginative vision rather than probing the paradoxes it occasions.

"Song of Myself"

I think I could turn and live awhile with the animals .... they are so placid and self-
      contained,
I stand and look at them sometimes half the day long.

They do not sweat and whine about their condition,
They do not lie awake in the dark and weep for their sins,
They do not make me sick discussing their duty to God,
Not one is dissatisfied .... not one is demented with the mania of owning things,
Not one kneels to another nor to his kind that lived thousands of years ago
                                                    —"Song of Myself," 1855 55–56

Failing to fetch me at first keep encouraged,
Missing me one place search another,
I stop some where waiting for you
                                                    —"Song of Myself," 1855 86

"Song of Myself" is Whitman's comedy of incarnation; it revels in the paradoxes occasioned by the poet's effort to imagine the world either as the product of the magic word or as grist for its mill. In this first, buoyant ritual of vocal performance, the power of voice encounters multiple centers of resistance: both the assimilative and the idealizing tendencies I have been tracing through Whitman's work repeatedly founder on the quirky specificity of individual lives and objects. As both Richard Chase (59–66) and John Kinnaird (27–33) have argued concerning the peculiar virtues of "Song of Myself," Whitman is at this point in his career content to celebrate this tussle rather than determined to resolve it. Antipodal senses of "identity," both Chase and Kinnaird suggest, are thus played off against one another to principally comic effect: the poem takes pleasure both in individual quiddity and in the "merge" that intimates our commonness. From the vantage of my argument, this cosmic comedy takes the form of an unresolved struggle between the agglomerating powers of the performative word and the multiplicity it tries to transmute. Voice and the labile energies it evokes are pitted in the poem against solid bodies of whatever sort, whether they be the finite forms in which the poet himself assumes momentary embodiment or the bodies of others, which voice should propel toward the merge. But voice itself is the site of a similar struggle. The ritualized aspects of Whitman's catalogues, which evoke a sense of the word's performative power and seem to activate centripetal, assimilative energies, compete with a tendency to conspicuous, sometimes comically obtrusive metaphor, which diffuses such ritual force and delays the mastery it implies. "Song of Myself" also employs a mobile, frequently slangy idiom: it draws attention to the social provenance of words, subverting the sense of sacred utterance by recalling the profane and multiple uses of speech.

This sort of comic doubling, in which virtually every assertion and every desire is countered by its opposite, reflects in part the ebullience of beginnings. Yet the comedy of "Song of Myself" is matched by a delicate pathos likewise unsurpassed in Whitman's work, and we might also understand the poem's tendency to poise between alternatives both as a function of the difficulties that precipitate the poem's wistfulness and as a way of evading them. If "Song of Myself" seems confident enough in the poet's newly discovered power to await its full effect with equanimity, reveling meanwhile in all that temporarily resists his mastery, this tendency to irresolution is also a way of diffusing the dangerous aspects of that power. The poem's inclination to evade closure, that is, serves partly to mask the sorts of intimations we explored in the previous chapter.[2] Whitman's inventive capacities, we shall see, are lavished especially on devising multiple, and mutually subverting, versions of priority and prolepsis; the poem's wonderfully extravagant myth-making is in part a way of avoiding the darker aspects of a cultural transmission "Song of Myself" both resists and exemplifies.

1. If "Song of Myself" is Whitman's comedy of incarnation, it is none-theless shadowed by an anxious sense of what the body can become. The poem's vision of the body oscillates between the antipodal scenes of sections five and twenty-eight, both of which we have already exam-ined.[3] In section five, the recollected idyll on the grass defines flesh as a sort of erotic double of voice, of the luxuriant "lull and hum" of a speech prior to meaning and articulation; the body thus evoked seems itself to be innocent of segmentation and encoding. The stratified body depicted in section twenty-eight, by contrast, experiences desire as a sort of *sparagmos,* a violent fragmenting along lines of cleavage already marked out upon or within it.[4] Eroticism, we saw, seems in section twenty-eight both to threaten the cultural coding of the body and, in the panic this disruption provokes, to register the power of such inscrip-tion.

This dichotomy is typical of Whitman's first two editions. What is less characteristic is how far Whitman is willing to move, in a celebratory mode, along the continuum stretching between these polar possibilities. This flexibility depends on an outlook that is essen-tially comic: embodiment itself, as Kinnaird suggests, is in "Song of Myself" fundamentally ironic. Any incarnate form, however perfect, is already a tangible, finite version, and thus a limitation, of the pro-tean image of voice in which the poem revels. "Song of Myself" is dis-posed to celebrate the doubling that results, offering an ironical sense of the body as both a particular thing and a chamber for the voice which exceeds and dissolves such particularity. More convincingly than Whitman's subsequent poems, "Song of Myself" thus takes pleasure in the incarnate selves that resist the merge as well as in the voice that propels it, lavishing detailed attention not only on the poet's own body but also on the resilient, defiantly individual bodies of others. There are limits, however, to this revel: delighting not only in the sort of fluid bodies that stay closest to voice, but also in what we might call phallic bodies, which as it were stand up for themselves, the poem is nevertheless intent on warding off the encoding that de-prives the body of such independence, turning it into a site defined by lack.

"Song of Myself" begins with a voice assuming embodiment:

I celebrate myself,
And what I assume you shall assume,
For every atom belonging to me as good belongs to you.

I loafe and invite my soul,
I lean and loafe at my ease . . . . observing a spear of summer grass. (1855 25)

Here poet and audience, self and other, but also voice and body are brought into equivocal relation by Whitman's play on "assume." If these lines draw our attention to the problem of prolepsis or transmission—a topic to which we shall return—they also define "Song of Myself" as a comic exploration of identity, distributing the poet's self between the protean voice engaged in celebration here and the bodies this otherwise elusive agent puts on. The provocatively insouciant loafer supposedly mesmerized by the grass is the second of these incarnations; like the single spear he contemplates, he seems in his self-sufficiency suggestively phallic. The poet's prior incarnation is easy to miss, since it is nearly as fluid as the voice that generates it. Whitman's address to a possibly plural "you," in lines two and three, implies a process of vocal diffusion. In the magical universe inaugurated here it is not just the poet's words, but also the atoms he puts on, that radiate to all of us; they define his body as an emanating energy rather than a fixed and bounded form. It is not only the poet's discourse or its truth but also this labile body that we "shall assume": in the course of the poem we supposedly assimilate this presence, not only taking the poet's speech and breath into our interiors but thereby mingling his effusing body with our own.

This is the version of the body "Song of Myself" celebrates most easily. As I argued in chapter 4, the poem offers us numerous glimpses of what we might call a semioticized body, an elusive, indeterminate presence that evokes the archaic somatic space Kristeva terms the *chora*. The poet's ability to metamorphose from shape to shape in the course of "Song of Myself" itself suggests such lability. Several of the particular guises he dons are also conspicuously fluid. We have had occasion to notice some of these elusive incarnations already: the invisible presence who is "around, tenacious, acquisitive, tireless . . . . and can never be shaken away" (1855 31); the figure who can "fly the flight of the fluid and swallowing soul" and whose "course runs below the soundings of plummets" (1855 61); the rhythmically defined body, alternately absorptive and effusing, evoked by the catalogue of section two. There is also the body not wholly body of section four, which seems as impalpable as the transcendental decor on which it weirdly leans:

> Apart from the pulling and hauling stands what I am,
> Stands amused, complacent, compassionating, idle, unitary,
> Looks down, is erect, bends an arm on an impalpable certain rest,
> Looks with its sidecurved head curious what will come next,
> Both in and out of the game, and watching and wondering at it. (1855 28)

Section thirty-three likewise offers us a diffuse form whose vestigial discrete parts seem incongruous enough to occasion some quiet comedy:

> My ties and ballasts leave me . . . . I travel . . . . I sail . . . . my elbows rest in
> the sea-gaps,
> I skirt the sierras . . . . my palms cover continents,
> I am afoot with my vision. (1855 57)

In "Song of Myself" the bodies of those the poet encounters or imagines also frequently assume these dissolving contours. The twenty-ninth bather of section eleven and the "friendly and flowing savage" of section thirty-nine are perhaps the most extravagant of these portraits.[5] Whitman's catalogues likewise typically enucleate the bodies they render, catching them up into rhythmic patterns that seem to dissolve solid boundaries. As we saw in chaper 2, deverbal nouns, which put barely hypostatized processes in the grammatical place of things, contribute to this effect, as in the catalogue in section eight we looked at there:

> The blab of the pave . . . . the tires of carts and sluff of bootsoles and talk of
> the promenaders,
> The heavy omnibus, the driver with his interrogating thumb, the clank of the
> shod horses on the granite floor. (1855 31–32)

The second of these lines, however, offers some resistance to Whitman's characteristic dissolving of incarnate particulars into ambient rhythmic energies. Odd enough to snag our attention and momentarily impede the catalogue's forward flow, the phrase "interrogating thumb" focuses briefly on a body movement that seems quirky rather than common; it serves to isolate the omnibus driver, marking his identity as specific rather than shared. The catalogues in "Song of Myself," to which I will return, are full of such gestures. As we shall see a bit further on, the sense of quiddity Whitman's incongruous tropes suggest also characterizes several of the poem's more extended portraits; this celebration of the kinesthetic peculiarity and apparent self-containment of other bodies and selves is also relatively rare in *Leaves of Grass* outside "Song of Myself."

Such traits are more commonly attributed to the poet. They may for the most part be restricted to him since Whitman links these qualities to phallic prowess, as a passage I cited in chapter 4 makes clear:

> [I] make short account of neuters and geldings, and favor men and women
> fully equipped,
> And beat the gong of revolt, and stop with fugitives and them that plot and
> conspire. (1855 47)

The phallic completeness displayed here is associated in turn, in Whitman's early editions, with a power of self-production attributed to the word in its magic aspect: the power of positing, conceived in a magical rather than symbolic mode, should generate a self-sufficient subject rather than precipitate its fading. Phallic bravado and delighted self-containment thus properly belong to the poet: insofar as Whitman's work is governed by a mythopoeic imagination, it is the poet in his finite guise who incarnates the powers of voice and word.

Yet in "Song of Myself" Whitman is willing not only to lend these qualities on occasion to others, but also to probe the poet's own possession of them. The poet's proclamations of phallic self-delight can seem oddly insistent, suggesting that his vaunted self-completeness is, paradoxically, an adversarial stance:

> Showing the best and dividing it from the worst, age vexes age,
> Knowing the perfect fitness and equanimity of all things, while they discuss I
> am silent, and go bathe and admire myself.
>
> Welcome is every organ and attribute of me, and of any man hearty and
> clean,
> Not an inch nor a particle of an inch is vile, and none shall be less familiar
> than the rest. (1855 27)

As exclusive as it is exhaustive, this self-absorption should secure the body against the divisions imposed by the discourse the poet walks away from here; in "Song of Myself" the poet's phallic body is an answer to the self-divided, castrated body culture shapes.[6] As Thoreau was perhaps the first to note, the poet thus "occasionally suggests something a little more than human." "It is as if," he wrote Harrison Blake in the same 1856 letter, "the beasts spoke" (quoted in Untermeyer 965). This is of course a scenario to which "Song of Myself" turns in its search for the sort of self-sufficiency culture pre-empts:

> I think I could turn and live awhile with the animals . . . . they are so placid
>   and self-contained. (1855 55)

Such a vantage is not easy to occupy. Vital to the argument of "Song of Myself," the poet's assertions of phallic mastery thus tend nevertheless to the humor of the tall tale, lending Whitman's epic of incarnation a frequent air of comic bravado:

> You sea! I resign myself to you also . . . . I guess what you mean,
> I behold from the beach your crooked inviting fingers,
> I believe you refuse to go back without feeling of me;
> We must have a turn together . . . . I undress . . . . hurry me out of sight of
>   the land,
> Cushion me soft . . . . rock me in billowy drowse,
> Dowse me with amorous wet . . . . I can repay you. (1855 45)

In such passages, hyperbole draws attention to the exorbitant aspect of the poet's claims, ostentatiously making good the sense of lack that haunts the divided body.

In "Song of Myself" the comedy occasioned by the poet's proclamations of phallic self-sufficiency is not always of the rather boisterous sort evident in this last example. If the poet's phallic body provokes revelry, exhibiting a completeness that cultural inscription threatens, it can also occasion wistfulness, since it marks a limit of the very positional power it instances: any particular guise the poet assumes puts a stop to the metamorphic possibilities his hitherto disembodied voice suggests.[7] "The motif of 'Song of Myself,' " Richard Chase thus notes astutely, "is the self taking on a bewildering variety of identities and with a truly virtuoso agility extricating itself from each one" (66). The protagonist's delight in inhabiting a specific body mingles pleasure in the particular guise assumed with a satisfaction about which he is less forthcoming; as if he still abided elsewhere, apart from the limiting form in which we glimpse him, the poet seems to remain strangely unapproachable and inviolate.

The quotient of low-keyed comedy in section nine is thus occasioned by something like bemusement. Despite the joyous delirium described there, the poet seems to take pleasure not only in the form he assumes but also in the slight distance he preserves from it. Here voice itself seems oddly reticent, as if it spoke for another self still held in reserve:

> The big doors of the country-barn stand open and ready,
> The dried grass of the harvest-time loads the slow-drawn wagon,
> The clear light plays on the brown gray and green intertinged,
> The armfuls are packed to the sagging mow:
> I am there . . . . I help . . . . I came stretched atop of the load,
> I felt its soft jolts . . . . one leg reclined on the other,
> I jump from the crossbeams, and seize the clover and timothy,
> And roll head over heels, and tangle my hair full of wisps. (1855 32)

Manifest here as a sort of residual shyness toward the scene he describes, the poet's typically less than complete immersion in the particular forms he assumes receives explicit comment more than once in "Song of Myself." In section sixteen, an avowal of self-satisfied quiddity is preceded by a demur that makes it seem less dogmatic than quietly comic:

> I resist anything better than my own diversity,
> And breathe the air and leave plenty after me,
> And am not stuck up, and am in my place. (1855 41)

In section forty-two, the poet seems less proud of the particular place he assumes than surprised by it:

> . . . . A call in the midst of the crowd,
> My own voice, orotund sweeping and final. (1855 73)

Here voice, which should be the poet's inviolate core, seems momentarily to lose itself in the body in which it is temporarily ensconced: it seems ventriloquized, appearing as the voice of another, since it emanates unexpectedly from a particular, finite form. The humor occasioned by this imbroglio is peculiarly Whitmanian.

A bit further on in the poem, this sort of compromising specificity is mischievously dissolved. The particular self who proposes to stand up firmly and testify seems to metamorphose into an unstable multitude of identities before he can do so:

> It is time to explain myself. . . . let us stand up. (1855 76)

That at least is one possible reading of this line. Its humor would thus depend on playing off a slightly unctuous scenario, suggested by a reading of the "us" as a presumably tractable group of followers or believers, against a more richly comic one: the rising up of the poet's multiple selves seems giddily insurrectionary, subverting not only the decorum of the group meeting we are invited to imagine but also the very notions of testimony and identity this decorum reflects.

In a similar vein, section twenty reverts to the atomic literalism of the poem's opening in order to make explicit the comedy lurking in the paradox of incarnation first suggested there:

> Who goes there! hankering, gross, mystical, nude?
> How is it I extract strength from the beef I eat?
>
> What is a man anyhow? What am I? and what are you?
> All I mark as my own you shall offset it with your own,
> Else it were time lost listening to me. (1855 43)

Here the delicately weighed adjectives of the first line issue into the reductive literalism of the second, once more to humorous effect. In these lines voice accosts the embodied identity it has assumed, pondering what turns out to be an unstable composite in several respects: of seemingly self-sufficient quiddity and unsatisfied desire; of omnivorous egotism and universal intimations; of the flesh of other creatures, ingested, and the resultant body that is the self. Voice probes the contradictions in which incarnation has entangled it, bumping up against incongruous limitations of its own protean potential.

Alternating between comic bravado and comic reticence, these portraits of the poet in his phallic but finite guises thus bespeak both delight and uncertainty. Suggesting a self-sufficiency dependent ultimately on a vision of word magic, which would make the body the embodiment of voice and render it independent of everything outside the self, these passages simultaneously register not only the sense of limitation which these apparently self-generated yet finite forms imply, but also the attendant fragility of this dream of the self-sufficient body. Gazing with an odd detachment on forms he imagines himself to be, the poet hints at their vulnerability, their relation to an outside or an other that remains unassimilated and unmastered. It is as if the fantasy of the body as phallic, as self-contained and self-engendered, could not be played out without calling itself into question. That "Song of Myself" is nevertheless ready to celebrate this body is one measure of the poem's comic poise.

This fragile vision of self-completion is also explored through the poet's enchanted contemplation of other selves. The poem's comic tolerance for frequently incompatible perspectives and multiple centers of authority is evident in Whitman's willingness to discover what I have been calling phallic qualities in those the poet confronts. Celebratory like the poet's self-portraits, these glimpses of phallic exuberance nevertheless seem peculiarly intent. We should of course understand the poet's mesmerized attention to his phallic demigods as a sign of desire. But desire itself is in part a function of the precarious status of identity to which we have been attending. The poet's rapt contemplation of what appears to be the radiant self-sufficiency of others possesses an intimate and by no means simple relation to the problem of his own putative completeness. The phallic mastery the poet observes might perhaps serve to confirm, or else challenge, his own. But it may instead bring it into being. Thus while section twenty tendentiously declares that one self-contained identity can "offset" another, in "Song of Myself" this joyous struggle among rival potentates intertwines with a less overtly adversarial yet ultimately more unnerving relation between self and other. The passage from section twenty indirectly implies as much. The poet who must "extract strength from the beef I eat" becomes himself by incorporating someone or something else. Even this incorporative procedure, moreover, is put in question by the comedy we noted in these lines, which turns on the incommensurability between human identity and such absorptive physiological processes. No longer co-extensive with reality, the poet lodged in a particular body must transact relations with an outside, relations for which ingestion tends to become an awkward model. Fantasies of incorporation repeatedly generate comic incongruity in "Song of Myself," as the poet confronts the disparity between his image of voice and his finite body. In section thirty-one this body gets overburdened when it tries to realize literally the incorporative capacities which the vocative word suggests:

> I find I incorporate gneiss and coal and long-threaded moss and fruits and grains and esculent roots,
> And am stucco'd with quadrupeds and birds all over,
> And have distanced what is behind me for good reasons,
> And call any thing close again when I desire it. (1855 55)

Here the things the poet calls close, which ought to have been taken into
the body, end up stuck to its surface instead. Generated through a
literalized understanding of the powers of the word, the dream of incorporation founders on just those bounding surfaces which the poet's
image of voice seems to dissolve, boundaries that make palpable our
finite status and limited capacities.

Despite the poet's supposed ability to metamorphose from voice into
particular incarnate form, "Song of Myself" thus also implies another,
less parthenogenetic origin for his phallic body. Rather than reflecting
the punctual self-production word magic should make possible, the sense
of phallic self-completion would instead originate in a complex experience of other bodies. And even this paradoxically derivative self-sufficiency would depend, not on the magical incorporation of other selves
word magic can also suggest, but on the symbolic mechanisms of identification and introjection and their imaginary roots.[8] Partly a taunt and a
challenge, other seemingly self-sufficient identities more crucially serve
as models for the poet's own presumptive self-containment. Yet in doing
so, they unnervingly suggest that the poet owes his apparent self-sufficiency not only to others, but ultimately, as we shall see, to the social
circuit that sustains symbolic operations and determines their particular
configuration.

In the comic world of "Song of Myself," the pleasure the poet takes in
the exuberant physicality of others is mingled most clearly with a sense
of playful struggle. The eroticized passages that describe the labor or
play of those to whom the poet is attracted tend to focus on patterns of
movement idiosyncratic enough to offer resistance to the sort of absorptive impulses that dominate several of the poem's long catalogues. Like
his description of the driver with the "interrogating thumb," the poet's
contemplation of the butcher boy and blacksmiths in section twelve
seems to take pleasure not in a sense of imaginative or sensual merging
so much as in an implicit, eroticized tussle in which the other parries
such assimilation:

> The butcher-boy puts off his killing-clothes, or sharpens his knife at the stall
> in the market,
> I loiter enjoying his repartee and his shuffle and breakdown.

Blacksmiths with grimed and hairy chests environ the anvil,
Each has his main-sledge . . . . they are all out . . . . there is a great heat in the
   fire.

From the cinder-strewed threshold I follow their movements,
The lithe sheer of their waists plays even with their massive arms,
Overhand the hammers roll—overhand so slow—overhand so sure,
They do not hasten, each man hits in his place. (1855 34–35)

The enucleating energies typical of Whitman's work are not absent here: suggested most strongly by the wonderful coinage, a deverbal noun, describing the movement of the blacksmiths' torsos—"The lithe *sheer* of their waists"—the merge is also hinted at by the communal activity in which these workers engage. Yet the cadence on which the passage ends—its monosyllables establishing a slow, insistent distribution of spondaic stresses—suggests the persistence of syncopated, diverse energies rather than their dissolution: "each man hits in his place." Peculiar usages—"Blacksmiths with *grimed* and hairy chests *environ* the anvil" —likewise draw attention to a gritty physicality and a multiplicity of action and energy not reduced to any single flow. Similar elements are at work in Whitman's preceding description of the butcher-boy: his "shuffle" and "breakdown" evince kinesthetic energies that would be difficult to subdue, an effect nicely augmented by the present opacity of Whitman's terms (these dances no longer being popular ones).

All these bodies take palpable pleasure in their own individuality; it is one source of the eroticism that suffuses these descriptions. Part of the erotic tension here, however, is more properly poetic: it derives from a conflict between the absorptive energies at work in the poem's language and the muscular activities that resist reduction to them. Being of a linguistic order, these assimilative energies are not an overt feature of the represented scene. Yet in "Song of Myself" the poet's voice typically hints at their incipient embodiment: the struggle here, in part, is between the phallic bodies of others and the diffuse, semioticized body of the poet.

While the assimilative tendencies of the poet's idiom are less evident in the portrait of the African-American dray-driver that follows in section thirteen, the sense that this figure represents a taunt or challenge to the poet is stronger; it is established by devices analogous to those we have just examined. Motivated in part by racial stereotypes, the resultant sense of erotic agon is nonetheless fundamental to the poem's sense of the phallic body:

> The negro holds firmly the reins of his four horses . . . . the block swags
>   underneath on its tied-over chain,
> The negro that drives the huge dray of the stoneyard . . . . steady and tall he
>   stands poised on one leg on the stringpiece,
> His blue shirt exposes his ample neck and breast and loosens over his hip-
>   band,
> His glance is calm and commanding . . . . he tosses the slouch of his hat away
>   from his forehead,
> The sun falls on his crispy hair and moustache . . . . falls on the black of his
>   polish'd and perfect limbs.
>
> I behold the picturesque giant and love him . . . . and I do not stop there,
> I go with the team also. (1855 35)

Perhaps because Whitman's iterative syntax and the absorptive energies it suggests are pretty much absent here, the shadowy, labile body of the poet we often sense hovering over the represented scene, present as an image of voice even when not more directly depicted, seems to have disappeared. Instead, the passage gives us a brief, enigmatic glimpse of the poet in what appears to be another guise: "I behold the picturesque giant and love him [. . . .]" Section twelve offers us an equally brief but more explicit self-portrait: "From the cinder-strewed threshold I follow their movements." In both these descriptions, the poet is identified not with the assimilative energies of voice and the diffuse presence they imply, but as a profiled figure, a finite body placed over against the bodies to which he is drawn. In addition to the agon to which we have so far been attending—between phallic independence and the more archaic energies of the merge—these passages thus also focus on the relation between other selves and the poet in his discrete, embodied guise.

Recalling that the poet in his finite form is himself often depicted as phallic, we might want to treat such moments as instances of the impe-rial "offsetting" proclaimed in section twenty: carrying out the wealth of the Indies in order to bring home the wealth of the Indies, the poet would on this reading be capable of enjoying the phallic self-sufficiency of others because it tallies with his own. Whitman's vision of magic language is marshaled to sustain this independent origin of the phallic body. Yet in this poem of multiple myths and frequently incompatible intimations, a different genealogy for the poet's vaunted self-sufficiency can be extracted. In the line from section twelve quoted above, we glimpse the poet as a kind of profile oddly divorced from Whitman's image of voice, a conspicuously inconspicuous, marginal figure not himself characterized by the phallic attributes that mesmerize him. The brief evocation of the poet in section thirteen, while less striking, accords him a similarly peripheral and passive role. The slight sense of wistfulness that inhabits these passages might be said to emanate from this profiled figure. On this reading, encounters with phallic bodies offer not a reflection of the poet's self-sufficiency, but a model for it: rather than being encounters between offsetting equals, these passages are suffused by a desire that emanates from lack.

Other passages in "Song of Myself" make this specular etiology of identity more explicit. While the poet is sometimes said to create himself *ex nihilo,* he elsewhere tries on a variety of provisional guises: partly a celebration of democratic community, these identifications should also be understood as tentative exercises in self-construction. What the poet puts on is not just a possible social role but also a possible body, a form whose stereotypical qualities serve the cause not only of democratic idealization but also of phallic self-containment: the stylized bodies the poet assumes suggest an idealized body-integrity that is in some sense the poem's desideratum rather than its starting point.[9] It is thus not only republican enthusiasm that motivates Whitman's frequently sentimental portraiture:[10]

> Alone far in the wilds and mountains I hunt,
> Wandering amazed at my own lightness and glee,
> In the late afternoon choosing a safe spot to pass the night,
> Kindling a fire and broiling the freshkilled game,
> Soundly falling asleep on the gathered leaves, my dog and gun by my side.
>   (1855 32–33)

Far less compelling than Whitman's kinesthetically attentive portraits of butcher-boy, blacksmiths, and dray-driver, this clichéd attempt to imagine oneself as another, like other similar efforts in "Song of Myself," is nonetheless central to the poem's dialectic of the body. The poet here puts on a neatly cohesive identity that will indirectly underwrite the integrity of his own.

It should be evident that the imaginative transactions that organize a passage like this one are of a less archaic order than those which shape much of Whitman's work. We have here to do, not with a fantasy of incorporation, sustained by an appeal to the *chora* or the magical conflation of naming and ingestion that seems to restore this register, but with identification and introjection.

Some of the poem's more explicitly erotic reveries also abandon the fluid merging typical of Whitman's work. Instead they depict an economy of desire in which others, through their attentions rather than by virtue of the poet's magical absorptive powers, might bestow on him a completeness they seem to possess. In section fourteen, the poet's brief but intensely imagined passivity suggests not only a stylized femininity, but also an imaginary exchange in which he would acquire phallic attributes by seducing those who already possess them. The poet's passive posture is especially striking since it appears, in the first and third of the lines below, in the midst of an otherwise conspicuously phallic self-portrait—a self-portrait it effectively enables:[11]

> What is commonest and cheapest and nearest and easiest is Me,
> Me going in for my chances, spending for vast returns,
> Adorning myself to bestow myself on the first that will take me,
> Not asking the sky to come down to my goodwill,
> Scattering it freely forever. (1855 36)

Like the phallic portraits that precede it in the poem, this passage is poised between celebrating a putative self-sufficiency ("Scattering it freely forever") and displaying the economy that generates the illusion of it. Here the integrity of the poet's body, provisional rather than assured and reflected rather than originary, seems to depend not on an archaic completeness sustained by word magic, but on his insertion into an economy of desire whose inter-related positions he will come to occupy in proper turn. As the stylized gender roles adduced here imply, the poet's body image is a function not only of the body images of others, but also of the symbolic system by which those others have themselves been shaped, and through whose rituals they pursue the course of their desire. The specular origin of the phallic body thus ultimately leaves the poet vulnerable to mechanisms that "Song of Myself," like the rest of Whitman's work, is intent on resisting. As we shall see by examining some of the poem's grimmer portraits, this etiology makes apparent self-sufficiency a product of the very mediating social structures which a properly phallic body and proper identity should be able to dissolve.

Whitman's willingness to entertain a heterodox account of the poet's origins is perhaps the crucial instance of the comic equanimity that characterizes "Song of Myself." But the poem's good humor has its limits. So far as Whitman's portraits of the body are concerned, these are reached as the poet attends to those the culture has maimed or humiliated. Partly an index of Whitman's radical egalitarianism, these disturbing descriptions can also be understood as painful forays into the risks of self-fashioning. In the conspicuously fantasmatic universe of "Song of Myself," they serve in part to test out the consequences of the poet's intimation that his sense of his own body derives from a sequence of identifications, rather than springing full blown from his spermatic word.

Whitman's portraits of damaged bodies suggest that this process of internalization leaves the poet open to some frightening involvements. It is true that Whitman's claims to possess one identity with all those who suffer—"I am the man . . . . I suffered . . . . I was there" (1855 62)—do not always feel credible. They may indeed belie the comprehensiveness of social imagination to which they are meant to attest: focusing on images of broken bodies which the poet can supposedly assume as his own, these passages are typically far less attentive to the dense, and less accessible, social histories that shape the wounded selves with whom the poet claims to identify, histories that presumably differentiate the perceptions of these sufferers from the poet's intuitions of them. Yet a more general sense of the power of social mechanisms pervades these portraits nevertheless. By no means self-sufficient or self-contained, several of the bodies the poet observes are shattered testaments to the shaping power of political, ideological, and economic formations:

> The disdain and calmness of martyrs,
> The mother condemned for a witch and burnt with dry wood, and her
>   children gazing on;
> The hounded slave that flags in the race and leans by the fence, blowing and
>   covered with sweat,
> The twinges that sting like needles his legs and neck,
> The murderous buckshot and the bullets,
> All these I feel or am. (1855 62)

The demotic bonhomie that aspires to overcome such social violence simply by welcoming its victims back into the fold with open arms can feel rather forced;[12] so can attempts to evoke a genuinely individual sufferer with whom the poet supposedly communes as the perfect democrat.[13] The poem's portraits of social violence are indeed characteristically most successful when most generalized. Whitman is capable of a sort of allegorical portraiture not unworthy of Dante:

> Here and there with dimes on the eyes walking,
> To feed the greed of the belly the brains liberally spooning. (1855 73)

> They who piddle and patter here in collars and tailed coats . . . . I am aware
>   who they are . . . . and that they are not worms or fleas,
> I acknowledge the duplicates of myself under all the scrape-lipped and pipe-
>   legged concealments. (1855 74)

Attending to passages of similar violence though of a less allegorical sweep, Kerry Larson astutely points to the darker aspects of a contrast whose comic mode we noted earlier. These mangled bodies serve in part as foils for the poet's image of voice:

> the speaker roams through a gallery of presences helplessly trapped in the constraining form of their own bodies. . . . Holding up the body to view as infinitely woundable is here to uphold the invulnerable sway of an onlooker who is nothing but disembodied voice. . . . (140)

Yet as Larson implies (140), "Song of Myself" is by no means lacking in intimations of the poet's vulnerability to just such wounding. While the disembodied consciousness observing citizens "who piddle and patter" claims an affinity not with such degraded actuality but instead with an essence that supposedly remains inviolate beneath it, one of the poem's key moments of crisis is precipitated by intimations diametrically opposed to this sort of assurance:

> Askers embody themselves in me, and I am embodied in them,
> I project my hat and sit shamefaced and beg.

> I rise extatic [sic] through all, and sweep with the true gravitation,
> The whirling and whirling is elemental within me.

> [38]
> Somehow I have been stunned. Stand back!
> Give me a little time beyond my cuffed head and slumbers and dreams and
>   gaping,
> I discover myself on the verge of the usual mistake. (1855 68)

The middle stanza here, deleted after 1860, alleviates otherwise anguished recognitions. It unconvincingly suggests a visionary transcendence not only of the socially imposed sufferings the poet observes, his sympathy for which has become nearly unbearable, but also of identifications that by now possess rather terrifying implications.[14] These include, but are not limited to, the prospect that the poet's own body might be subjected to a literal wounding similar to that he observes. They encompass as well a sense of the dangers of identification: in a violent social space, the body image the poet assumes will necessarily be shaped by intimations of injury. The mutilated or degraded selves by whom he is haunted also suggest that the specular construction of the body, once begun, is difficult to circumscribe, making identity dependent on the very scenario the poet hopes to avoid: taking in the images of other bodies to constitute his own, the poet thereby opens himself as well to the violent social forces and coercive symbolic system that have shaped them. In such disastrous instances as those I have been detailing, this shaping involves a grotesque violation of autonomy and integrity. Like the sufferers he observes, the poet shaped by this social scene will in some sense also be radically maimed and incomplete.

Registering and responding to the damage done by both slavery and nascent capitalism,[15] and implying the need for a redeemed body politic that will not be guilty of such sins, passages like this thus also offer a painful version of the narrative of self-construction already implied in the poem's portraits of more triumphant selves. Attending to his phallic heroes, the poet takes from them a completeness whose borrowed or derivative status suggests his own lack; here such lack, violently marked on the bodies of others, is itself introjected. Far from being self-engendered, our apparent integrity is derived, a function not only of others but also of the entire social configuration of which they are part. Even the phallic body depends on the forces it seems to keep at bay.

Characteristically, the poems of Whitman's first two editions pull back from such disturbing intimations. They steer clear of the vicissitudes of introjection, instead marshaling the magic word as incorporative power in order to dissolve into the plenum of the self other bodies and the dangers they auger. Displaying a comic equanimity virtually unique in Whitman's work, "Song of Myself" celebrates an erotic agon of discrete bodies and selves, despite the disasters to which the identifications on which it turns can lead.

2. This equanimity concerning the body derives in part from Whitman's image of voice. Despite the vicissitudes of its attempts to find adequate embodiment, voice remains a privileged figure for identity in "Song of Myself." The poet's voice may have trouble dissolving others, or get temporarily enmeshed in a body itself. But neither the comic nor the more anxiety-provoking incongruities these adventures among incarnate particulars occasion quite dethrones Whitman's governing trope, since voice, in the poem, can recover itself by withdrawing from the very embodiments with which it flirts.[16]

The poem's openness to contradiction, however, is not limited to Whitman's explorations of the body. In "Song of Myself" voice also confronts dispersive tendencies closer to home. The ritual power of utterance is unsettled by a tendency to metaphor, which foregrounds the human rather than natural provenance of the word and suggests that its force is pragmatic rather than magical. Attention to slang, and to incongruous ranges of vocabulary wittily juxtaposed, further suggests that this pragmatic power is necessarily entangled with questions of cultural authority and can be wielded effectively only by those who attend to its configurations. The poet's utterance is thus immersed in the very social conflicts from which Whitman's stylized litanies seem at first to exempt it. Like the divided sense of the body "Song of Myself" explores, this probing of the poem's image of voice evinces a negative capability Whitman soon proved unable to sustain.

In the poem's catalogues, dispersive linguistic energies intertwine with a power of resistance ascribed to things themselves. Whitman's litanies are marked by the sort of attention to idiosyncratic detail we noted as well in some of his more extended portraits. Such detailing tends to focus on kinesthetic particulars, lending individual creatures and objects a solidity unusual in Whitman's work; the world the poet encounters can seem genuinely multiple and unassimilable. The long catalogue that dominates the poem's thirty-third section offers a number of these acts of attention: we encounter "the rye as it ripples and shades in the breeze"; the "low scragged limbs" to which the poet holds (1855 58); "the geese" that "nip their food with short jerks" (1855 59). Such observed particulars seem especially resistant to the dominant flow of Whitman's catalogues when they are conveyed by coinages or pithy misspellings, which lend the word something of the quiddity discovered in the thing: "At the cider-mill, tasting the sweet of the brown sqush"

(1855 59). Whitman obtains a similar effect by employing terms that have the air of being neologisms though they are not: "The prostitute *draggles* her shawl, her bonnet bobs on her tipsy and pimpled neck" (1855 39; emphasis added).

Like such idiosyncratic vocabulary, metaphorical terms can serve to draw our attention not only to the resistance creatures and objects offer to the poet's absorptive impulses, but also to the way language itself registers this resistance in the very act of trying to overcome it. This disturbance need not be spectacular to be effective: "Song of Myself" is sprinkled with terms that prove to be metaphorical only if we devote special attention to them; they quietly engage the pervasive otherness of things. A figurative dimension is just barely noticeable, for example, in Whitman's description of the rattlesnake in section thirty-three: "Where the rattlesnake suns his flabby *length* on a rock" (1855 57; emphasis added). Here the poet's struggle to name what he sees appears in the tension between a physical, concrete verb and adjective and the more abstract noun to which they attach, a noun which thus functions as a trope, a slightly awkward usage provoked by the foreignness of the creature the poet looks at. Slight displacements toward the figurative also mark the following: "the sharp-peaked farmhouse with its *scalloped* scum" (1855 57; emphasis added); "the mockingbird sounds his delicious *gurgles*" (1855 59; emphasis added).

The movement toward figure is not always so unobtrusive. "Song of Myself" is studded with the sort of conspicuously metaphorical terms a Wordsworthian or Coleridgean taxonomy would catalogue as examples of fancy rather than imagination, instances of figuration notable for their improbability and seeming inappropriateness:[17] "the alligator in his *tough pimples* sleeps by the bayou" (1855 57; emphasis added); "the ground-shark's fin cuts *like a black chip* out of the water" (1855 58; emphasis added). Such tropes provide a jolt of surprise that defamiliarizes the object, abruptly impeding the assimilative momentum of the poet's litanies by condensing the sense of strangeness that lurks in Whitman's less riveting figures. In such moments, creatures and objects seem to resist not only the poet but also the act of naming which has been provoked to such contortions in attempting to get a grip on them. One way to suggest how much at odds such fanciful tropes are with Whitman's characteristic practice is to note that the figures just cited would be perfectly at home in the work of Marianne Moore. Moore's bristly lists can be read as subversions of the sublime poetic of which Whitman's early editions offer a hyperbolic, because avowedly magical, instance. In "Song of Myself," though, Whitman plays Moore to his own shaman, impeding the very rituals of appropriation in which he engages.

The crucial source for the divided sense of the word that results is probably Emerson. Whitman seems on the whole to have read Emerson's essays with a tenacious literalism that was extreme if not unexampled. The vision of language we traced in chapter 5, which reaches a kind of apotheosis in contemplating the resources of the proper name, gets much of its impetus from the realist, correspondential strand of Emerson's work most evident in *Nature*. But as Julie Ellison argues, following Bloom, from at least the time of "The Poet" Emerson's work is marked by an extravagantly prodigal sense of metaphor, which comports with a nominalist rather than realist theory of language (195–208). As Ellison suggests, Emerson's delight in producing multiple figures, cascading series of images in which each trope displaces the one before it, can be understood as an expression of his growing sense of naming itself as displacement, as fertile misapprehension (166–74). Extravagant use of trope can suggest that the capacity of the word to grasp the thing is itself figurative—that our power, which lies in figuration, is nominal and pragmatic rather than being grounded in the order of things. Conspicuous metaphor can also serve to dramatize the peculiarly human temporality set in motion by language: if the name is a figure, it propels us toward a future by positing a vision which our own commitment to our tropes can help make true: "all language," Emerson suggests in "The Poet," "is vehicular and transitive, and is good, as ferries and horses are, for conveyance, not as farms and houses are, for homestead" (3:20).[18] This prospective, pragmatic power is quite different from the instantaneous mastery of the thing supposedly exercised by the so-called organic name.

A crucial source of pleasure in the passages from "Song of Myself" we have been examining, such capricious figuration and the nominalist vantage it implies soon virtually disappear from Whitman's work. The object loses the otherness that fanciful metaphor conspicuously violates and thus ultimately sustains; the name is rooted firmly, as if "untouched / By trope or deviation" (Stevens, *Collected Poems* 471), in the ritual power of the proper which an increasingly unrelieved verbal stylization implies.

The magical status of the poet's word in the poems that follow "Song of Myself" is suggested not only by stylized syntax and avoidance of conspicuous metaphor, but also by idiomatic pruning. "Poetic style," notes Mikhail Bakhtin in remarks applicable to the ritually oriented utterance of much of *Leaves of Grass*

is by convention suspended from any mutual interaction with alien discourse, any allusion to alien discourse.

. . . . It follows that any sense of the boundedness, the historicity, the social determination and specificity of one's own language is alien to poetic style, and therefore a critical qualified relationship to one's own language (as merely one of many languages in a heteroglot world) is foreign to poetic style. . . . (285)[19]

This commitment to the monologic, Bakhtin argues, places poetry in the service of political centralization and hegemony (287). Lyric utterance nonetheless sustains a fantasy that the poet's speech is exempt from such historical entanglement, its avoidance of competing discourses giving the illusion that

the word plunges into the inexhaustible wealth and contradictory multiplicity of the object itself, with its "virginal," still "unuttered" nature. . . . (278)

The vision of the poet as adamic namer is thus a recurrent figure for lyric authority:

Only the mythical Adam, who approached a virginal and as yet verbally unqualified world with the first word, could really have escaped from start to finish this dialogic inter-orientation with the alien word that occurs in the object. Concrete historical human discourse does not have this privilege. . . . (279)

Adamicism, we saw in chapter 5, is a crucial element in Whitman's prose tracts on language, which are also intent on explaining away the power of the "alien word" and "historical human discourse" to stand between the poet and such originary naming.

We saw as well, however, that Whitman's adamicism and the reclamation project it authorizes overlap with another, potentially competing vision of language. The untidy semantic and discursive jostling Bakhtin associates with the notion of heteroglossia, I argued, is ultimately made to subserve magical ends, paradoxically centering linguistic authority in the poet himself; but Whitman's interest in decentralized linguistic innovation, we noted, is not wholly attributable to such possibilities for dialectical reversal. "Slang in America" is particularly enthusiastic in its treatment of demotic speech, championing slang because it reveals populist linguistic energies that resist centralized authority and illustrates dramatically the socially saturated and politically interested status of any discourse.[20] The essay finds its match, among Whitman's poems, in the idiomatic mobility of "Song of Myself": revelling in the competing social visions registered by heteroglossia, Whitman plays the centralizing tendency of ritual address off against the dispersive fact of idiomatic conflict. Masterfully collaging myriad verbal textures or, when it wants to, juxtaposing incongruous ones to comic effect, "Song of Myself" performs that "dance of the intellect among words" Ezra Pound was later to call logopoeia (Pound, *Literary Essays* 25)—a practice Pound claimed, surely under the grip of an anxiety of influence, to have encountered only in Propertius and Laforge (Pound, *Literary Essays* 33).[21] The mode is quintessentially American, and the discursive melange of "Song of Myself" already anticipates the more ambitiously orchestrated cacophony of *Huckleberry Finn*.

"Song of Myself" offers ample evidence of Whitman's penchant for slang. His demotic terms are judiciously placed, being deployed for maximum leverage. The sudden shift in idiom such intrusions accomplish serves typically to re-direct whatever argument is in progress, the juxtaposed vocabularies mobilizing competing perspectives. Thus, for example, the solemnity toward which the poet's guesses about the grass in section six gradually modulate is deftly re-inflected by the sudden appearance of slang terms that lend an earthy quality and a suggestion of resilience to some otherwise somber lines devoted to detailing the return of earth to earth:

> Or I guess the grass is itself a child . . . . the produced babe of the vegetation.

> Or I guess it is a uniform hieroglyphic,
> And it means, Sprouting alike in broad zones and narrow zones,

> Growing among *black folks* as among white,
> *Kanuck, Tuckahoe, Congressman, Cuff,* I give them the same, I receive them
> the same. (1855 29; emphases added)

In "Song of Myself" this resistance suggested by slang is marshalled less often against natural threats than against such social dangers as pretension and undue refinement: "Washes and razors for foofoos . . . . for me freckles and a bristling beard" (1855 46). The attitudes thus lanced are themselves given idiomatic embodiment in the poem. Indeed the poet himself, or at least a certain range of his utterance, can become the object of this leveling tendency, as the context in which the term "foofoos" gets detonated makes clear:

> I am the poet of commonsense and of the demonstrable and of immortality;
> And am not the poet of goodness only . . . . I do not decline to be the poet of
> wickedness also.
>
> Washes and razors for foofoos . . . . for me freckles and a bristling beard.
>
> What blurt is it about virtue and about vice?
> Evil propels me, and reform of evil propels me . . . . I stand indifferent.
> (1855 46)

The beliefs expressed here are all of a piece, the jibe at "foofoos" fitting in smoothly with the other demotic sentiments expressed in these lines. Idiom, though, tells a different story. The speaker who can say "*I do not decline to be* the poet of wickedness also" is marked by his finicky locution as pretty much one of the foofoos he claims to scorn. It may thus be partly the discourse of the poet himself that provokes the exasperated, earthy question, "*What blurt* is it about virtue and about vice?" Likewise, the figure who can "stand indifferent" expresses a disinterested distance that is the very opposite of the impassioned leveling of the middle line, which directs its barb at all those who sound, we can suppose, like this stilted voice that claims to be on the side of moral and social inclusiveness.[22]

This example is instructive in a number of respects. It alerts us to the possibility that the ideological struggles into which slang and demotic idiom enter can be played out primarily through incongruities of diction, whose subtleties need not always receive overt thematic comment. And it shows that some of the poet's own utterances can become the object of demotic scorn. The fact that the poet can be at odds with demotic tendencies is a complication we might not have expected. It suggests an ambivalent social identification that itself becomes one of the poem's implicit subjects: idiomatic conflict draws attention to the poet's own tendency to standoffishness; entangled with questions of class, that tendency stands in the way of the merge, or at least of its social realization. Yet this clash of idioms also reveals the demotic as an ambiguous category in its own right: "Song of Myself" is willing to hazard the possibility that populist energies might prefer to impede the poet's assimilative urge rather than further it, a circumstance that has the odd effect of marking a troubling tension between the poetic program of *Leaves of Grass* and the class interests and ideological perspectives for which Whitman often claimed to speak. As we might expect, "Song of Myself" often associates slang with an earthiness and frank sexuality connected in turn to the theme of the merge: the demotic, in part, subverts the exclusiveness more "refined" idioms and attitudes seek to maintain. Yet since it serves as well to lance abstraction and generalization, the demotic also gets aligned with a contrary impulse toward resistant idiosyncrasy. The very presence of slang, indeed, serves to call into question the apparently transcendent authority of the stylized ritual utterance that propels the merge.

Conspicuous appearances of slang terms thus turn out to be the obvious high-points of a much more extensive verbal drama played out in the poet's own speech, a drama simultaneously idiomatic and ideological. Devoid of slang, one of the poem's earliest verbal tussles nonetheless anticipates the pyrotechnics of the later "foofoos" passage, subverting the poet's momentary pretensions and recalling him from a preachy and professorial role to his rightful place as demotic champion:

> Houses and rooms are full of perfumes. . . . the shelves are crowded with
> perfumes,
> I breathe the fragrance myself, and know it and like it,
> The distillation would intoxicate me also, but I shall not let it.
>
> The atmosphere is not a perfume . . . . it has no taste of the distillation . . . .
> it is odorless,
> It is for my mouth forever . . . . (1855 25)

The second verse paragraph here brings to a climax a drama also at work in the first. Like the Emerson of *Nature* as Richard Poirier mischievously describes him (68), the character who invites us out into the open air in this passage can himself sound like an inveterate denizen of the parlour: he calls air "atmosphere" and manages to contrast it to perfume in a phrase itself exquisitely distilled: "it has no taste of the distillation . . . . it is odorless." There is high comedy waiting around Whitman's line ending, as we bump into a very different voice and quite another sense of the world: "It is for my mouth forever." This voice seconds the assertions of its predecessor, but does so in such a way as to qualify those earlier remarks, letting us hear them as instances of the very attitude to which they claim to object. The first verse paragraph has quietly prepared this climax, playing off "breathe the fragrance myself" against the more earthy and emphatic "and know it and like it."

Here demotic intrusions save the poet from an inadvertent stiltedness which resists the merge. In section three, though, a popular idiom and the gritty physicality it suggests instead stick in the craw of the poem's assimilative tendencies:

To elaborate is no avail . . . . Learned and unlearned feel that it is so.

Sure as the most certain sure . . . . plumb in the uprights, well entretied,
    braced in the beams,
Stout as a horse, affectionate, haughty, electrical,
I and this mystery here we stand.

Clear and sweet is my soul . . . . and clear and sweet is all that is not my soul.
    (1855 27)

Insisting on physical specificities and our investment in them, the carpenter's lingo in the second of these lines also injects a class element into the passage, suggesting an ironic attitude toward the universe of abstractions. One such abstraction has just claimed that class differences are ultimately of no account: "Learned and unlearned feel that it is so." The working class idiom that follows qualifies the slight glibness of this inclusive assertion. We can note a similar strain, between an inclusive formulation and a pithy vocabulary that proves irreducible to it, in the passage's succeeding phrases. "I and this mystery here we stand" sums up, and thus thins out, the irascible pleasures articulated in the line above it: "Stout as a horse, affectionate, haughty, electrical." This line is itself a collection of irreconcilables, resistant to generalization. Its heterogeneity derives in part from the incommensurability of its categories, no two terms here being quite co-planar. But its prickliness is also idiomatic: "Stout as a horse" seems not quite to come out of the same mouth that says "haughty." At once idiomatic, conceptual, and political, and implying differences of outlook, ethos, and class, such multiplicity tends to impede the merge rather than further it.

The poem abounds in such lexical dramas, which are characterized by the sort of comic subversiveness to which we have just been attending. Thus in section twenty-one, the assertion "we have had ducking and deprecating *about enough*" (1855 45; emphasis added) comes to rest on a phrase that seems idiomatically at odds with what precedes; it might make us wonder whether the very term "deprecating" isn't itself an instance of the superior attitude the poet struggles to expel. Other contrasts are quieter, suggesting not an explosive conflict but the inevitable co-presence of divergent perspectives in a linguistic universe that is superimposed on a social one:

> Maternal as well as paternal, a child as well as a man,
> Stuffed with the stuff that is coarse, and stuffed with the stuff that is fine.
> (1855 40)

Supposedly illustrating the assertion of the poet's own diversity offered in the first of these lines, the demotic idiom of the second also serves to qualify it, deflecting the passage toward a comic register: it suggests the positioned status and thus the merely partial validity of any single formulation, even when that formulation itself asserts the value of multiplicity.

Whether such socially saturated locutions further or impede the poet's incorporative project in particular instances, their cumulative effect is thus to call into question the efficacy of ritual language and the centripetal aims for which Whitman deploys it in "Song of Myself." The relative absence of verbal play in the poems that follow, and more especially in those written after the appearance of the 1855 edition, is thus only in part a reflection of Whitman's declining inventiveness; it also marks a shift from a playful or ironic attitude toward the poet's program to a more insistent one. In their multiplicity, the divergent languages of "Song of Myself" suggest a variety that is irreducible, its very taxonomy remaining elusive. Alerting us to the social provenance of any idiom, such verbal multiplicity tends to undermine the air of ritual authority at which the poet's own speech often aims, reminding us that a hieratic language apparently prior to social disputes is in fact an instrument for prosecuting them. This priority to social formations, we have seen, is crucial to the poet's program: in the myth that propels "Song of Myself" as throughout the early editions of *Leaves of Grass*, the poet and his word ought not to be products of the social order, but should offer us an alternative to its coercions. Yet in "Song of Myself" the ritual language that might inaugurate this liberation itself repeatedly metamorphoses into varieties of socially located speech, undermining the very dichotomy between the natural and the cultural, the intrinsic and the imposed, which the poet claims to retrieve. Veering from one received idiom to another, the poet's speech risks relinquishing the magical priority of the ritual word and comes close to revealing instead its own social saturation and belatedness.

3. The idiomatic drama of "Song of Myself" thus intertwines with the poem's concern with prolepsis, a preoccupation we also saw troubling Whitman's vision of incarnation. Like the poet's body, his ritual speech often seems to be shaped and limited by the social order whose authority it should be able to pre-empt.

"Song of Myself" does not of course go so far as to cede firm priority to the social mechanisms from which the poet should free us; instead, it offers multiple versions of precedence and proleptic power. This tolerance for irresolution typically provokes the comedy that characterizes the poem: we can view it as both insurrectionary and tough-minded, since Whitman's humor contests dominant structures without claiming clear-cut victory over them. But the poem's conspicuous irresolution can also occasion wistfulness, and this response is cannier than might at first be apparent. The poet's inability to establish firm priority over the structures that shape us defers the chiliastic prospects he sometimes claims to usher in; but it thereby occults the uncomfortable implications of the poet's own power. The poet's wistfulness thus tends to be sentimental, since he benefits from the blockage over which he sometimes pines.[23] The vision of "Song of Myself" remains ultimately comic, irresolution and good hope enabling and sustaining each other.

The drama of such poems as "Crossing Brooklyn Ferry" is both more clear-cut and more uncomfortable. There the poet pre-empts the power of culture to pre-empt our self-sufficiency, interposing himself between us and the mechanisms that would otherwise control us. As we have seen, Whitman thereby runs the risk of revealing the poet as an instance of the very coercive authority from which he supposedly preserves us. "Song of Myself" in effect relinquishes such absolute priority in order to evade its consequences, a temporary expedient that helped Whitman produce his comic masterpiece. Here the poet no sooner claims priority than he cedes it. Generating the episodic, digressive structure that has baffled the rage to order of more than one critic,[24] "Song of Myself" concocts a series of multiple myths that keep power and priority circulating, displacing each claim to authority before its disturbing implications can be tallied. Yet Whitman is careful to vest power in the poet often enough to suggest that he has a special relation to it.

As in most of the major poems of the 1855 and 1856 editions, it is especially the proleptic force of cultural authority that the poet must combat. His attacks on the customs and laws that make claims on him typically share the boisterousness of his boasts of phallic autonomy, with which they intertwine:

> Whimpering and truckling fold with powders for invalids . . . . conformity
> goes to the fourth-removed,
> I cock my hat as I please indoors or out.

> Shall I pray? Shall I venerate and be ceremonious?
> I have pried through the strata and analyzed to a hair,
> And counselled with doctors and calculated close and found no sweeter fat
> than sticks to my own bones. (1855 43)

Religions and the gods they would place over us are supposedly likewise pre-empted by the originary force of the poet's phallic body:

> Magnifying and applying come I,
> Outbidding at the start the old cautious hucksters,
> The most they offer for mankind and eternity less than a spirt of my own
> seminal wet. (1855 71)

Such prodigious force, of course, presents dangers of its own. As we have seen, assertions of the poet's potency, which display his freedom from anterior powers, are thus incongruously paired with demurs concerning his possible designs on us:

> These are the thoughts of all men in all ages and lands, they are not original
> with me,

> If they are not yours as much as mine they are nothing or next to nothing,
> If they do not enclose everything they are next to nothing. (1855 41)

Yet the resounding authority of this renunciatory gesture, we followed Larson in noting, is itself rather troubling; it catches the poet up in a paradox akin to that propounded by the Cretan liar.[25]

If the poet's direct attempts to abjure the proleptic power he else-where declares thus turn out to be an ambiguous means of assuaging our anxieties, the repeated displacements to which the poem's multiple fables subject his claims are a subtler and more effective device. This tendency to prodigal myth-making is at work from the very beginning of "Song of Myself." Despite their remarkable air of brash cockiness, the poem's opening lines announce the poet's power in such a way as to qualify his claims to absolute priority; the myth we already noted here, of the poet as self-delighting origin, co-exists with another, implicit creation story. The poet's own identity is already doubled in Whitman's first line, which splits him into the antipodal roles of active subject and enigmatic object: "I celebrate myself." The claim of blissful self-containment is thus qual-ified in the very phrase that announces it, which suggests that the self is an elusive entity that precedes the poet's speech act, a priority which qualifies the transparency the line implies. This sense of divided identity also troubles the ensuing vision of the poet on moral holiday: "I loafe and invite my soul." Here the blithe meaning of an idiomatic phrase, which sustains the poet's claims to self-sufficiency, is played off against a more somber vision evoked by the literal sense of these words and the scene of invocation they conjure up. This expectant receptivity or wise passiveness also qualifies the claim of phallic equanimity that follows ("I lean and loafe at my ease . . . . observing a spear of summer grass").

Like his relation to himself, the poet's connection to us is articulated in a fragmentary narrative that remains sufficiently ambiguous to call into question the commanding precedence he seems to claim. It is not quite certain what fable we are being told:

> And what I assume you shall assume,
> For every atom belonging to me as good belongs to you. (1855 25)

We noted earlier that Whitman's play on "assume" confounds intellec-tual and atomic priority: it is not only the poet's ideas but also his atoms that we will put on, a conflation that works to make language and self indistinguishable from the order of nature. Thereby freed from the clutches

of culture, his emanating body and word might loosen its grip on us as
well. Yet which aspect of nature the poet himself should be identified
with remains a little uncertain. Whitman's image of voice serves to
connect the poet with the productive energy of *natura naturans,* apparently endowing him with the ability to generate the very body he assumes. But the term "assume" can also imply that the poet takes on an
obligation: the body he puts on would on this reading be imposed on
the poet rather than generated by him. He would be reduced to the
status of a created object—shaped, like the rest of us, by the power of a
natura naturans whose design passes through him. The implications of
this diminished status are not entirely mournful. Wrenching power from
culture, the poem's opening relocates it ambiguously either in the poet
or in a nature irreducible to him; the poet's claims to proleptic power
are tempered by an alternative myth, in which poet and audience alike
are subjected to an anterior force. Throughout "Song of Myself," the
oscillation between these accounts is managed in such a way as to
disperse the uncomfortable implications of the poet's precedence almost
as soon as they begin to gather.

Establishing the poem's oscillating rhythm of countervailing claims,
the next four sections of "Song of Myself" markedly display this sort of
equivocation. Section two tends to gather power to the poet himself,
implying its subsequent radiation to us: it leaves culture behind for a
nature which is then filtered through the absorptive and effusing body
defined by Whitman's long catalogue. The section accordingly ends with
one of those disclaimers of proleptic intent with which we are familiar;
the poet assures us that his absolute priority enables rather than pre-
empts our own ("You shall not look through my eyes either, nor take
things from me, / You shall listen to all sides and filter them from
yourself" [1855 26]).

He is not through backpedalling. The priority suggested so forcefully
in section two is succeeded by a spate of qualifications; the poet is
depicted in a variety of incongruous conditions and dispersed among
multiple myths of the self. Section three begins with a hymn to the
present ("There was never any more inception than there is now" [1855
26]) and ends with a praise of self-presence grounded in the poet's
phallic completeness ("Knowing the perfect fitness and equanimity of
things, while they discuss I am silent, and go bathe and admire myself"
[1855 27]). Yet in the interval between these sanguine assertions, Whit-

man broods over an ominous image of pre-emptive power. It subjects poet and audience alike to a sublime anterior force:

> Urge and urge and urge,
> Always the procreant urge of the world.
>
> Out of the dimness opposite equals advance .... Always substance and increase,
> Always a knit of identity .... always distinction .... always a breed of life.
>   (1855 26–27)

In keeping with the way the section begins and ends, these lines seem bent on subduing the menacing implications of the power they describe. We should note, however, that the threat they struggle to tame itself functions to alleviate a more troubling danger: the pre-emptive force of this shadowy sexual mechanism dissipates the oppressive aspects of the poet's own power, presenting a daemonic alternative to it.

If sections two and three equivocate by ambiguously assigning priority both to the poet and to alien agents, sections four and five conspicuously divide the poet himself. Section four threatens to turn him into the precipitate of the very cultural forces he had earlier seemed to ward off:

> Trippers and askers surround me,
> People I meet.... the effect upon me of my early life .... of the ward and city I live in .... of the nation,
> The latest news .... discoveries, inventions, societies .... authors old and new. (1855 28)

A demur intervenes:

> They come to me days and nights and go from me again,
> But they are not the Me myself. (1855 28)

This figure who redresses the poet's alienation, however, is immediately made to seem more than a little alien himself. We have looked at the section's succeeding lines already:

> Apart from the pulling and hauling stands what I am,
> Stands amused, complacent, compassionating, idle, unitary,
> Looks down, is erect, bends an arm on an impalpable certain rest,
> Looks with its sidecurved head curious what will come next,
> Both in and out of the game, and watching and wondering at it. (1855 28)

Repository of an elusive self-containment, this profiled character seems almost to prefigure the uncannily aloof icon of identity that hovers above the poet in "As I Ebb'd with the Ocean of Life." The "soul" of section five, who succeeds the "Me myself" depicted here, is certainly less forbidding; yet he too is now remote, and must be invoked. Partly a melancholy intimation of the divided status of the subject, such distant images of self-contained identity also serve to suspend the uncomfortable consequences of the poet's imperial energies, by delaying his definitive advent.

Despite such demurs, the poem's first five sections tend to center power and authority in the poet, qualifying but not radically undermining what seems to be a priority over nature as well as culture. Section six concludes what might be called the poem's overture (in section seven the poet launches out into the sort of panoramic social space that is most fully rendered in the catalogues, beginning his assimilative labor). There Whitman offers multiple myths of the poet's place that are at odds with the preceding images of his priority, assuaging our possible anxieties by conspicuously subjecting him to the same pre-emptive forces that limit us. Of all the movements of "Song of Myself," this section is poised most elaborately among competing accounts of precedence; it can serve as a synecdoche for the delicate irresolution achieved by the poem as a whole.

In relation to the poem's first five sections, the most obvious displacement of power in section six is from poet to nature: elaborating the central text "all flesh is grass," the section makes nature rather than poet the site of circulation and dissemination. Yet this vision of nature's priority is itself qualified. The ten sections that conclude "Song of Myself," which prepare for the final irresolution of the poet's leave-taking through a temporary intensifying of contrary claims, balance sweeping assertions of his precedence not only with equally sweeping denials of its pre-emptive power, but also with more unremittingly naturalized accounts of the forces governing development and decay:

Rise after rise bow the phantoms behind me,
Afar down I see the huge first Nothing, the vapor from the nostrils of death,
I know I was even there. . . . I waited unseen and always,

And slept while God carried me through the lethargic mist,
And took my time. . . . and took no hurt from the foetid carbon. (1855 77)

This ominous passage suggests that resigning priority to nature, while it serves to assuage the untoward implications of the poet's power, is ultimately no more tolerable than ceding it to culture. The vision of nature offered in these sections of the poem indeed hovers between the sublime dialectic just barely maintained here and a tendency to abjection, whose starkest emergence Kerry Larson (141–42) locates:

O suns . . . . O grass of graves . . . . O perpetual transfers and promotions .
    . . . if you do not say anything how can I say anything?

Of the turbid pool that lies in the autumn forest,
Of the moon that descends the steeps of the soughing twilight,
Toss, sparkles of day and dusk . . . . toss on the black stems that decay in the
    muck,
Toss to the moaning gibberish of the dry limbs. (1855 84)

The poem's opening sections are marked by less violent oscillations. Section six not only plays off nature against the poet more equivocally; it comes full circle by also slipping back and forth unobtrusively between tales of natural priority and cultural authority, thus assuaging the anxieties evident in the passage above, which have been provoked by the very vision of unrelieved naturalism to which the earlier section might also appear to subscribe.

The opening lines of section six establish the natural plenitude and attendant awe that encourage the negative capability which characterizes the section as a whole:

A child said, What is the grass? fetching it to me with full hands;
How could I answer the child? . . . . I do not know what it is any more than
    he. (1855 29)

A series of provisional, wonderfully prodigal attempts to answer the child's question follow. The phrase "or I guess," which cues the first few of them, suggests a tolerance for uncertainty that is quite moving; if it is motivated not only by faith and generosity, but also by a desire to evade the unpleasant implications of any single answer, that does not make it less so. Like the poem as a whole, these guesses begin with an extreme contraction that wittily centers all meaning and value on the poet himself:

> I guess it must be the flag of my disposition, out of hopeful green stuff woven.
> (1855 29)

The myth that succeeds this one likewise makes nature an index of something not merely natural. But it displaces the poet's primacy:

> Or I guess it is the handkerchief of the Lord,
> A scented gift and remembrancer designedly dropped,
> Bearing the owner's name someway in the corners, that we may see and remark, and say Whose? (1855 29)

Natural processes are here made to figure an order that transcends them. Ascribed to an elusive god ("Whose?"), the signature that marks nature with this law also implicitly subjects it to the cultural authority or patriarchal place from which such inscription emanates. Yet here too wit serves to qualify the poet's formulation even as he offers it. An index of negative capability, this evasiveness may also register discomfort. Whitman's next metalepsis may thus serve in part to disperse the anxieties typically provoked by cultural entailment in *Leaves of Grass*. It brings the section full circle, linking human kinship not with patriarchal authority and the sign but instead with natural cycles of birth and decay:

> Or I guess the grass is itself a child . . . . the produced babe of the vegetation.
> (1855 29)

While we tend to think of it as Whitmanian, this naturalism may itself provoke Whitman's discomfort. The next stanza employs the trope of the "uniform hieroglyphic" to subsume natural processes once more to an act of inscription that secures their meaning. Yet the demotic flavor lent these lines by the slang terms to which we attended earlier—"Kanuck, Tuckahoe, Congressman, Cuff"—prepares for the populist leveling of cultural distinctions that ensues: "I give them the same, I receive them the same" (1855 29). Here the linking of democracy and death, about which Lawrence complained (169–70), seems to possess implications of which Whitman is by no means unaware: perfect equality gets achieved only in the return of earth to earth, which is at once a dissolving of the order of culture back into the less punctilious order of nature.

As we might by now expect, the section's next line evades the starker implications of such natural processes. Ostentatiously drawing attention to the humanizing fantasies that already lurk in the preceding stanza's lending of voice to the grass, it also foregrounds the oscillating rhythm of the section's figuration, thereby intensifying it: "And *now* it seems to me the beautiful uncut hair of graves" (1855 30; emphasis added).[26]

The ensuing verse paragraph draws our attention to rhetoricity in another way:

> Tenderly will I use you curling grass,
> It may be you transpire from the breasts of young men,
> It may be if I had known them I would have loved them;
> It may be you are from old people and from women, and from offspring taken soon out of their mothers' laps,
> And here you are the mothers' laps. (1855 30)

Whitman dwells here once more on an image of natural process as prolepsis. Yet the apostrophe that organizes these lines has the effect of drawing nature into the universe of human speech, thus reversing the very priority to which the poet seems to defer. These lines indeed feel their way toward a possible common ground between the orders of nature and culture, trying to imagine a space organized by neither the symbolic law of the father nor the inhuman rhythms of a purely biological generation and decay. They do so in part by shifting attention from the earlier figures of patriarchal authority to a fleeting glimpse of the maternal, or more precisely an idealizing fantasy of it: coming briefly to rest on an image of mother and infant, these lines center human order on a scene apparently prior to the patriarchal inscription which will codify it. Yet as the oddly scrupulous pairing in the final two lines seems meant in part to imply—"from offspring taken soon out of their mothers' laps, / And here you are the mothers' laps"—this order which has not yet asserted sharp control over nature is not simply reducible to it either, instead offsetting and balancing natural processes, or intervolving with them. Or so the poet would have it, imagining grass and maternal laps as alternative, yet apparently reconcilable locations for human selves. But the rather touching awkwardness involved in trying to take literally the figure that sustains this prospect suggests something of the strain that attends the poet's attempt to treat human and natural universes as cooperative and commensurate: the poet's closing phrase registers the strangeness of the vision to which his hopes have led.

We can hear a related awkwardness in the apostrophe and prosopopoeia that organize the verse paragraph as a whole. Culler has alerted us to the sense of strain likely to emerge when poets address uncomprehending foliage. Yet a delicate melancholy, and a wistful humor, also play through these lines. Perhaps they register not so much the vatic struggle to get grass to understand as the more human reticence that helps motivate this displaced speech act: talking to nature is also a way of speaking circuitously rather than directly to human auditors. There is great tact and skill in the way Whitman handles the oblique interaction of these scenes of address. Like the displacements that organize the section as a whole, the awkwardness of the poet's apostrophe to the grass is made to reflect his diffidence with regard to questions of cultural order and authority. It suggests both his effort to draw out a benign principle of priority and succession and the impasse in which this project lands him: his rhetorical difficulties register the fragility of his vision of a non-coercive principle of succession and continuity. Indeed the poet can offer us, in lieu of anything more tangible, only this utterance, touchingly poised between human and natural auditors, as a problematic hint of how a non–pre-emptive order might feel. Yet it owes its appeal in part to the very impasse that prevents the realization of the prospect at which it points: it is only by suspending us between the disparate orders of nature and culture that the poet defers the unpleasant implications of each.[27]

In what follows, Whitman seems to ponder the quotient of awkwardness to which we have been attending. Speaking not to nature but to himself, the poet muses on the strangeness of his own figure, or of a literal reading of it:

> This grass is very dark to be from the white heads of old mothers,
> Darker than the colorless beards of old men,
> Dark to come from under the faint red roofs of mouths. (1855 30)

Continuing to probe the limits of his figure by attempting to take it literally, he next imagines the blades of grass as organs of speech. We might link these "uttering tongues" to the mothers with whom grass has recently been identified. Here too what is groped for is at least in part an organizing order that is not patriarchal, one based on expressive, effusive voicing rather than pre-emptive inscription:

> O I perceive after all so many uttering tongues!
> And I perceive they do not come from the roofs of mouths for nothing.
>   (1855 30)

Yet the effort to lift up nature into culture as living speech, and thus to ground human order in simple presence rather than proleptic hieroglyph or sign, once more proves elusive:

> I wish I could translate the hints about the dead young men and women,
> And the hints about old men and mothers, and the offspring taken soon out
> of their laps. (1855 30)

Paradoxically, this inability seems momentarily to offer an answer to the problem of priority and power. The poet turns to us, as if culture itself might be organized as an exchange of nothing more than tentative guesses, none countervailing another:

> What do you think has become of the young and old men?
> And what do you think has become of the women and children? (1855 30)

But as the quotient of sly teasing lurking in these questions implies, the preceding investigation of order and authority has made such a solution difficult to accept. The poet thus steps once more to the forefront. Addressing us rather than the grass, he both posits and calls his positing into question, simultaneously reasserting authority and attenuating its effect:

> They are alive and well somewhere;
> The smallest sprout shows there is really no death,
> *And if ever there was* it led forward life, and does not wait at the end to
> arrest it,
> And ceased the moment life appeared.
>
> All goes onward and outward . . . . and nothing collapses,
> And to die is different from what anyone supposed, and luckier. (1855 30;
> emphasis added)

In its unlikeliness, which makes it seem oddly conjectural despite the firmness at which Whitman gestures, the adjective on which the section ends can serve as an image for the delicate balance of assertion and forebearance on which "Song of Myself" would like the whole problem of power and precedence to come to rest.

The issue of priority thus kept unresolved in the opening sections of the poem continues to trouble its unfolding, provoking not only the ambivalent treatment of the body and the figurative and idiomatic variety we noted earlier, but also the sort of multiple fabulation to which we have just been attending. We can confine ourselves here to observing that "Song of Myself" ends with a final declaration of priority that manages to resolve the poem on a note of conspicuous irresolution. The imperial figure who stands front and center at the poem's opening dissolves at its close:

> The last scud of day holds back for me,
> It flings my likeness after the rest as true as any on the shadowed wilds,
> It coaxes me to the vapor and the dusk.
>
> I depart as air . . . . I shake my white locks at the runaway sun,
> I effuse my flesh in eddies and drift it in lacy jags.
>
> I bequeath myself to the dirt to grow from the grass I love,
> If you want me again look for me under your bootsoles.
>
> You will hardly know who I am or what I mean,
> But I shall be good health to you nevertheless,
> And filter and fibre your blood.
>
> Failing to fetch me at first keep encouraged,
> Missing me one place search another,
> I stop some where waiting for you (1855 85–86)

Not only does the poet fade away here into the mystery of process he initially seemed to concenter and resolve. His disseminating form also divides into air and grass, impalpable voice and compost of flesh. "Song of Myself" thus leaves us to ponder the still enigmatic contraries its opening appeared to fuse in the poet's revealed presence: of word and body, *natura naturans* and *natura naturata,* informing logos and formed, individuated matter. This fracturing of the poet's person also leaves us poised between two competing fables of prolepsis, already implicit in the poem's opening lines. Departing as air and dissolved into nature, the poet still retains the originary power implied by the pervasive association among atmosphere, breath, and voice; we can expect him to reappear as present, performative utterance. Yet he also persists as grass, the product of an atomic circulation whose source and meaning section six has rendered conspicuously opaque.

Figuring the poet both as creative and created nature and hovering between antipodal fables of priority and power, this final section of "Song of Myself" also finds other ways to leave equivocal the effect the poet's precedence might have on us. The diffuse presence we are directed to seek out seems to lead us out into an open, uncharted space and to promise that we will discover there the key to all being, including our own. Yet as Harold Bloom has noted, the poet's ability to locate himself in a mysterious spot that is not only the object of our quest, but is also somehow always up ahead of us, evinces an uncanny priority (*Poetry and Repression* 263–64).

Characterizing "Song of Myself" and recurring occasionally throughout the 1855 *Leaves of Grass,* this sort of delicate suspension, at once comic, poignant, and deeply uneasy, gives way in the 1856 edition to less balanced and often more vehement resolutions. There the poet typically comes unambiguously before us, assuming the imperial guise that makes him master not only of his auditors but of nature and culture as well. Declaring that he comes as voice, the poet insists on his beneficent effect; the role played by inscription in constituting the identity which supposedly saves us from signs is resolutely suppressed.

This myth plays only a minor role in most of the poems Whitman wrote for his 1860 edition. There the poet is less concerned with his ability to come before us than with the priority of inscription to his own voice and person. Quite palpably the product of the symbolic mechanisms his earlier incarnations appeared to keep at bay, he now characteristically devotes himself to probing the source of this inscription and trying to reconcile himself to its effects.

Calamus

> Mankind has always dreamed of seizing and fixing that fleeting moment when it was permissible to believe that the law of exchange could be evaded, that one could gain without losing, enjoy without sharing. At either end of the earth and at both extremes of time, the Sumerian myth of the golden age and the Andaman myth of the future life correspond, the former placing the end of primitive happiness at a time when the confusion of languages made words into common property, the latter describing the bliss of the hereafter as a heaven where women will no longer be exchanged, i.e., removing to an equally unattainable past or future the joys, eternally denied to social man, of a world in which one might *keep to oneself.*
> —Lévi-Strauss, *The Elementary Structures of Kinship* 496–97

If we read Whitman as a political poet and the first two editions of *Leaves of Grass* as political discourse, the 1860 *Calamus* sequence might seem to mark a dramatic retreat from the public sphere, suggesting a sharp contraction of the poet's sympathies. The *Calamus* poems sometimes put forward this reading themselves:

> But now take notice, land of the prairies, land of the south savannas, Ohio's land,
> [. . . .]
> For I can be your singer of songs no longer—One who loves me is jealous of me, and withdraws me from all but love,
> With the rest I dispense—I sever from what I thought would suffice me, for it does not—it is now empty and tasteless to me,
> I heed knowledge, and the grandeur of The States, and the example of heroes, no more,
> I am indifferent to my own songs—I will go with him I love,
> It is to be enough for us that we are together—We never separate again.
> ("Long I Thought That Knowledge Alone Would Suffice Me," 1860 354–55)[28]

Going farther than Whitman himself does here, Betsy Erkkila views this proclaimed turn from politics to privacy as itself a symptom of political malaise:

> This poem is usually cited as evidence that Whitman's crisis of the late 1850s was brought on by a homosexual love relationship. But the poem may also suggest the reverse: that his crisis of faith in the "grandeur of the States" precipitated his turn toward the privacy of love. . . . (*Whitman the Political Poet* 152)

> Like the divided nation in which South was breaking from North and private interest was prevailing over public interest, Whitman's separate person had seceded from the democratic en masse. (*Whitman the Political Poet* 154)

Kerry Larson concurs:

> Better, it appears, to resign his commission now, circa 1858, than to see it rendered meaningless in the immediate future. Petulant and bitter, he elects to "go with him I love, / It is enough for us that we are together." At least it can be said of them, in a tone closer to reproach than consolation, that "we never separate again." (169)

While there is undoubtedly a degree of truth in this suggestion of a relation between political disillusion and the poet's withdrawal to the privacy of "paths untrodden" (1860 341), the correlation Erkkila and Larson offer in these passages is suspiciously tidy. Assigning politics the role of cause and affectional life that of effect, they here reduce Whitman's love poetry to the status of mere compensation or displacement.[29] Committed to this reading, Larson manages to hear emotional contraction in the poet's very tone: the whole sequence, in his view, is marred by the petulance and bitterness he discerns in the lines from "Long I Thought" quoted above.

These lines are not among the sequence's strongest, and their tone, not fully controlled, is accordingly difficult to gauge. But they might better be faulted for being sentimental or ostentatiously demonstrative than for the qualities Larson locates in them. Likewise, the *Calamus* sequence as a whole runs the risk of occasionally aggrandizing and over-simplifying the new emotional gamut to which the poet self-consciously attends; but these are faults provoked by a new-found emotional expansiveness, and not by the sort of bitter withdrawal Larson hears. Paradoxically, the scenic contraction of *Calamus*, its relinquishing of the panoramic scope that typifies the 1855 and 1856 *Leaves of Grass* in favor of a series of sheltered encounters "by margins of pond-waters" (1860 341), facilitates a strengthening of the poet's bonds to others.

Something of this emotional expansion is evident even in the pointed renunciations of "Long I Thought." In this poem Whitman both aggrandizes and over-simplifies the commitments of the poet of the first two editions of *Leaves of Grass;* his reasons for doing so seem complex. Both alluding to and briefly enacting his earlier role as bard of the nation in another passage, Whitman may in part be trying to sum up neatly and thereby ennoble a period of his career he is presumably putting behind him. He would thus also be magnifying the sacrifice he makes for love: in the tradition of Propertius, for example, he would validate the strength of his feeling by pointedly giving up an epic career for a lesser lyric one. Yet the lines that announce this noble renunciation also subtly undermine the grandeur they ostentatiously relinquish, implying a critique of the poet's prior career. Whitman's apostrophes in "Long I Thought" are peculiarly, indeed comically, awkward:

> But now take notice, land of the prairies, land of the south savannas, Ohio's land,
> Take notice, you Kanuck woods—and you Lake Huron—and all that with you roll toward Niagara—and you Niagara also,

And you, Californian mountains—That you each and all find somebody else
     to be your singer of songs,
For I can be your singer of songs no longer [. . . .] (1860 354)

This boisterousness both complicates and qualifies the political commitment it foregoes. The project of political poetry as Whitman sometimes
aspired to practice it is made to seem both overblown and, in the felt
strain involved in apostrophe here, curiously abstract and remote. The
poet's political claims thus appear as the questionable counterpart of a
bardic role with which we are, by 1860, quite familiar: here made to
seem comic, the poet's sweeping address to the continent characteristically generates the omnipresent figure capable of subsuming it. The
troubling impersonality of this process, which in a sense forecloses the
very relation it appears to inaugurate, is suggested not only by these
lines but also by the contrasting idiom that succeeds them:

   I am indifferent to my own songs—I will go with him I love,
   It is to be enough for us that we are together—We never separate again.
      (1860 355)

Perhaps a bit too self-conscious and a bit too proud of their own delicacy
and tact, these closing lines nonetheless suggest an intimacy that appears
as something of a relief after Whitman's bellicose apostrophes. Here
what might be called a tonal contraction registers an intensification of
sympathy and involvement. Avoiding direct address, Whitman ends the
poem by speaking of his beloved rather than to him; in contrast to his
preceding declamations, which they help evaluate, these understated
assertions suggest a more complex and sustained relation, a tie that is
both rich and vulnerable.

   How we evaluate the intimacies of Calamus thus depends in part on
what we make of the bardic stance of Whitman's first two editions: we
are likely to dismiss Calamus as merely private if we praise Whitman's
earlier poetry for being public and political. Complementary simplifica-
tions accompany these complementary views. To interpret the subsuming presence of the 1855 and 1856 editions as a trope for political union,
as Whitman sometimes did himself, is to ignore the more regressive
satisfactions this figure affords. Lewis Hyde's work on gift economies
should thus be applied to Leaves of Grass with more caution than either
Hyde or Larson observe. Whitman might sometimes wish to say of

himself what Hyde says of the divine intermediaries of myth, but we need not say it for him:

I have come to think of the circle, the container in which the gift moves, as its "body" or "ego." (16)

Aborigines commonly refer to their own clan as "my body," just as our marriage ceremony speaks of becoming "one flesh." (17)

gods . . . become incarnate and then offer their own bodies as the gift . . . . (58)

Larson casts Whitman in this role, though he acknowledges that the poet will have some trouble fulfilling it:

Rather than being obliterated by this process of exchange, the self ideally incarnates the medium of exchange itself. . . . (40)

Though Whitman's Unionism did not lead him down the road of political compromise, the impulse to articulate an accord whose authority would be irrevocably sealed in the moment of its accomplishment remained essentially the same [as Daniel Webster's]. In his role as Answerer the poet of course intended to make that accomplishment visible by presenting himself as the conjunctive medium for the social discourse. . . . (58)

Whitman's poems, that is, aim to weld us together by themselves incarnating the medium of social exchange rather than simply being messages sent through it; the poet's body, likewise, serves as the divine gift that circulates through the body politic, insuring the solidarity of the group.

We need at the very least to attend carefully to the role the poet accords himself in this fantasy. Being the site or medium of exchange rather than a participant in it, he is himself exempt from the very conjunctive relations he supposedly embodies. The satisfaction we take in Whitman's poet figure may depend at least as much on the exceptional status he enjoys as on the social norm he supposedly secures. We might note as well that the circuit of exchange the poet's presence supposedly incarnates has been redefined in rather remarkable ways. Appearing everywhere at once, the poet does not so much circulate among us as constitute a sort of magical glut that brings exchange itself to an apocalyptic end. The regressive satisfactions afforded by the poet become even clearer if we recall that, according to the sometimes inconsistent topology of *Leaves of Grass*, this figure who flows into us also subsumes us: social space and the exchanges that articulate it are effectively dissolved into the poet's amorphous body, returning us to an archaic realm in which codified transactions would no longer be necessary. To call this a vision of political possibility is to mistake some of the crucial satisfactions it affords.

By contrast, the poet of *Calamus* is no longer intent on being the medium of our union; accepting a more limited role, he reconciles himself to participating in transitive relations rather than figuring them. This will appear to be a retreat only if we insist on reading Whitman's earlier trope of presence exclusively as a political figure, ignoring its psychic implications. In *Calamus* Whitman gives up the self-sufficiency that is a crucial desideratum of the 1855 and 1856 *Leaves of Grass*, entering a circuit of exchange of which he is neither the origin nor the master; it is by assuming a place in this circuit that he receives not only his affectional partners but also his identity. No longer self-sufficient, the poet of *Calamus* is dependent on the sort of intimate, contingent relations that characterize Wordsworth's "Tintern Abbey," relations the first two editions of *Leaves of Grass* effectively foreclose. In *Calamus*, writing is in part the sign of such fragile connections. But the poet's recourse to inscription suggests as well his reliance on a more general circuit of exchange, within which the particular relations into which he enters become possible and take on meaning. This dependence on a general structure obtains despite the opposition *Calamus* sets up between a public heterosexual economy and a secret homosexual one. Like writing, the phallic Calamus root is in Whitman's sequence a sign of this dependence and the lack it installs, which produces desire. In *Calamus* the poet must circulate the phallus instead of claiming to be it. Moreover, the self who takes up his place as an active agent within this economy is himself a product of it: the poet who writes, we shall see, is also written, defined by the passage through him of the phallus he transmits.

1. If the poet's retreat from the panoramic sweep of the first two editions receives explicit comment in *Calamus*, so too does this contrary movement from putative self-sufficiency to involvement with others.[30] Some lines from a draft of "In Paths Untrodden," printed by Fredson Bowers in *Whitman's Manuscripts: Leaves of Grass (1860)*, offer the most concise and explicit formulation of this shift:

Was it I who walked the earth disclaiming all except what I had in myself?
Was it I boasting how complete I was in myself?

O little I counted the comrade indispensable to me!
O how my soul—How the soul of man feeds, rejoices in its lovers, its dear
friends!
And now I care not to walk the earth unless a lover, a dear friend, walk by
my side. (Bowers 68)[31]

"I Saw in Louisiana a Live-Oak Growing" asserts a similar opposition, though the stance the poet renounces there is not associated explicitly with Whitman's own prior poetry:

I saw in Louisiana a live-oak growing,
All alone stood it, and the moss hung down from the branches,
Without any companion it grew there, uttering joyous leaves of dark green,
And its look, rude, unbending, lusty, made me think of myself,
But I wondered how it could utter joyous leaves, standing alone there, with-
out its friend, its lover near—for I knew I could not. (1860 364–65)

Commenting on the opening lines of "Not Heat Flames up and Consumes," Paul Zweig draws out some of the crucial implications of the shift in perspective that remains implicit here:

Whitman had sexualized nature in "Song of Myself," but the eroticism had been solitary; it had been a "religion" of lone ecstasy. Here there is another person; they are two. . . . The voice of the poem, too, is new. The flush of delight is mingled with a suggestion of vulnerability. As a lover, Whitman is not self-contained. He can no longer simply "effuse [his] flesh in eddies, and drift it in lacey jags," like a polymorphously perverse child. He must concentrate on his elusive partner; accept the estrangement of his very self, which now exists far from him, in the guise of a beloved but uncontrollable face, moved by an obscure will. (296; interpolation in original)[32]

In *Calamus* this focus on particular, intimate ties, which are by their nature never assured, emerges quite movingly from the context of Whitman's earlier work. The delicate poignancy of a poem like "When I Heard at the Close of the Day" is especially striking if we recall the performative idiom of prior editions, here conspicuously absent:

When I heard at the close of the day how my name had been received with
plaudits in the capitol, still it was not a happy night for me that followed;
And else, when I caroused, or when my plans were accomplished, still I was
not happy;
But the day when I rose at dawn from the bed of perfect health, refreshed,
singing, inhaling the ripe breath of autumn,
When I saw the full moon in the west grow pale and disappear in the morning
light,

When I wandered alone over the beach, and, undressing, bathed, laughing
with the cool waters, and saw the sun rise,
And when I thought how my dear friend, my lover, was on his way coming,
O then I was happy;
O then each breath tasted sweeter—and all that day my food nourished me
more—And the beautiful day passed well,
And the next came with equal joy—And with the next, at evening, came my
friend;
And that night, while all was still, I heard the waters roll slowly continually
up the shores,
I heard the hissing rustle of the liquid and sands, as directed to me, whisper-
ing, to congratulate me,
For the one I love most lay sleeping by me under the same cover in the cool
night,
In the stillness, in the autumn moonbeams, his face was inclined toward me,
And his arm lay lightly around my breast—And that night I was happy.
    (1860 357–58)

Here performatives are renounced in favor of narrative: the poet evokes
a conspicuously contingent sequence of events. The evident fragility of
these recollected scenes, which lends the poem an elegiac cast, offers a
marked contrast to the sort of magically repeating and perfectly assured
occurrence Whitman's performative utterances characteristically seem to
generate.

As Quentin Anderson notes, in Whitman's work this sort of intimate
narrative is accorded significant power over the self only in *Calamus*.
The involvements these poems detail very largely define who the poet
is.[33] "To a Stranger" explicitly remarks this fatality:

Passing stranger! you do not know how longingly I look upon you,
You must be he I was seeking, or she I was seeking, (It comes to me, as of a
dream,)
[....]
[...] your body has become not yours only, nor left my body mine only.
    (1860 366)

The casualness of fatal encounter here might be regarded either as a
residual, protective distancing or as a sweeping recognition of our susceptibility to others; shaping the poet's very body, this vulnerability
leaves him open in either case to the sort of reciprocal interactions which
the magical announcements of his advent in prior editions serve to
foreclose.

Like the recollected intimacies on which *Calamus* dwells, the future it sometimes anticipates also balks the total control Whitman's earlier manipulation of performative utterance appeared to afford. In the 1855 and 1856 *Leaves of Grass,* the image of presence suggested by Whitman's figure of voice seems itself to produce and govern the future scenes on which it impinges. In *Calamus* the poet is instead characteristically said to write to us. He thus anticipates a future his words influence but do not generate, soliciting relations he cannot simply speak into being. While *Calamus* still makes use of apostrophe, which always effects an equivocal collapse of the moment in which a message is received back into the one in which it was produced, Whitman's foregrounding of writing typically serves to dispel this illusion: "Who is now reading this?" (1860 361). Drawing attention to the poet's inability to specify his future addressee—an incapacity that only faintly haunts apostrophe in prior editions—this written address highlights a contingency Whitman's earlier figure of voice had been enlisted to subdue. If the poet's voice in the first two editions of *Leaves of Grass* seems to be a medium in which we are immersed, the written word of *Calamus* is instead an instrument that reaches toward us across a distance it also registers, drawing attention to a separateness which literal face-to-face encounters might also reveal.

Whitman's characteristic association of the poet with breath, and with a diffuse, elusive touch, thus appears only rarely in *Calamus:* "The old breath of life, ever new, / Here! I pass it by contact to you, America" ("States!" 1860 349).[34] The more typical insistence on textual transmission and its anonymity serves paradoxically to establish not only the contingency but also the particularity of our relations:

> Who is he that would become my follower?
> Who would sign himself a candidate for my affections? Are you he? ("Whoever You Are Holding Me Now in Hand," 1860 345)

> Are you the new person drawn toward me, and asking something significant from me? ("Are You the New Person Drawn toward Me?" 1860 358)

These written addresses suggest that only particular selves can bring to life the relation the poet's questions seek to provoke; awaiting the responses his earlier apostrophes seem to compel, the poet stays open here to plurality and chance.

2. Yet the poet's availability to relations that are particular and contingent draws him into a structure of exchange whose laws are general; in

Calamus Whitman seems to cast his desire out into an organized cultural space in which it might find its place and its fulfillment. *Calamus* enters this arena most explicitly as the poet addresses the future. Underspecifying their addressee, Whitman's written apostrophes draw attention not only to an irreducible multiplicity of individual selves and wills, but also to the wider field within which particulars are arrayed. Each individual "you" who answers the poet's call will in effect step forward from the anonymous, functional category of the second person; marking the gap between these two senses of "you," Whitman's conspicuously tentative written addresses manage to bring both local and global perspectives to our attention. Holding off from the sort of assured zeroing-in that characterizes apostrophe in Whitman's prior editions, the poet's addresses suspend the particular uptake they also invite, poising on the condition of its possibility.

Evoked by the apostrophes cited above, this organized space within which particular relations occur is an explicit concern of the poems in which Whitman transmits a legacy to us. This is so despite his renunciation of ostentatiously public bequests:

> Nor will I be able to leave behind me any wealthy bequest to found a hospital
>   or library,
> Nor reminiscence of any deed of courage, for America,
> Nor literary success, nor intellect—nor book for the book-shelf;
> Only these carols, vibrating through the air, I leave,
> For comrades and lovers. ("No Labor-Saving Machine," 1860 373)[35]

Here the contraction of concern the poet declares is counterbalanced by a subtler expansion implicit in Whitman's apparently intimate concluding phrase: "comrades and lovers" suspends between exclusive and inclusive referents, designating either particular familiars or the general categories to which they belong. Like the pronominal equivocations we attended to above, this ambiguous legacy draws our attention back outward, focusing on the relation between individual intimacies and the communal life that enables them, an ethos the poet's transmission might in turn help to sustain.

Renouncing the nationalism he ascribes to his earlier work, Whitman thus does not simply abandon the public for the private:

> You bards of ages hence! when you refer to me, mind not so much my poems,
> Nor speak of me that I prophesied The States, and led them the way of their
>   glories;

But come, I will take you down underneath this impassive exterior—I will
    tell you what to say of me:
Publish my name and hang up my picture as that of the tenderest lover,
The friend, the lover's portrait, of whom his friend, his lover, was fondest
[. . . .]
Whose happiest days were far away, through fields, in woods, on hills, he
    and another, wandering hand in hand, they twain, apart from other men,
Who oft as he sauntered the streets, curved with his arm the shoulder of his
    friend—while the arm of his friend rested upon him also. ("Recorders
    Ages Hence," 1860, 356–57)

While Whitman closes here by poignantly recalling what feels like a
specially valued intimacy, he is careful to situate this particular tie within
a network of similar relations. The poem indeed convenes a group and
stipulates a commemorative ritual, centering on an icon of the poet.
Repeatedly offering this sort of generalized inheritance in *Calamus,*
Whitman seems less concerned to memorialize a particular relationship
than to transmit the group practices that make it possible and sustain
the community within which it has its meaning.[36]

This generalized transmission can be contrasted to the determinedly
personal mode of inheritance we noted in Wordsworth. It is possible
to regard this difference as a defect: even in *Calamus,* it might be
argued, Whitman cannot quite see the self as fatally shaped by its specific
history.

    One appropriate response to such a criticism can be made in historical
and political terms. As the otherwise various studies by Robert K. Martin, Eve Kosofsky Sedgwick, M. Jimmie Killingsworth, and Charley
Shively have all shown, Whitman not only wrote during the period when
homosexuality was emerging as a cultural category for identity, when
homosexual acts were for the first time taken to define discrete homosexual selves; he was himself crucial to this historic transformation.[37] From
this perspective *Calamus* by no means marks an end to the political
commitments that help structure *Leaves of Grass:* offering itself as a
vehicle for rituals of homosexual self-recognition and self-identification,
the sequence also makes homosexual bonding a model for political
solidarity.[38] While *Calamus* can be said to idealize the demotic potential
of homosexuality, the political implications of the sequence are surely
no less clear and no less practical than those Whitman's earlier trope of
presence is frequently said to possess.[39] If we take seriously the regressive

and primarily autoerotic sexuality which defines this presence who dissolves all structured relations, the political possibility he most nearly figures is utopian anarchism; from this perspective, *Calamus* marks a new willingness on Whitman's part to engage practical politics in a way that makes it central to the imaginative energies that organize *Leaves of Grass*.

The movement in *Calamus* from celebration of individual erotic relations to consideration of the institutional framework that might authorize and sustain them is admittedly sometimes ambivalent:

> I hear it is charged against me that I seek to destroy institutions;
> But really I am neither for nor against institutions,
> (What indeed have I in common with them?—Or what with the destruction of them?)
> Only I will establish in the Mannahatta, and in every city of These States, inland and seaboard,
> And in the fields and woods, and above every keel little or large, that dents the water,
> Without edifices, or rules, or trustees, or any argument,
> The institution of the dear love of comrades. ("I Hear It was Charged against Me," 1860 367–68)

These lines offer an instance of the paradoxical anti-institutional institutionalism Larson finds central to Whitman's work (xviii–xxii). Here, this ambivalent stance might be understood as a particular response to a particular predicament: Whitman is simultaneously seeking to establish a tradition of homosexual ritual and struggling to distinguish it from the entrenched mores and ceremonies of the dominant heterosexual culture. The strain involved in this adversarial stance, and more especially in the attempt to authorize it by romanticizing it, shows up in the oxymoronic notion of an institution devoid of institutional paraphernalia.

Yet *Calamus* as a whole displays far less discomfort with institutions and the rituals that recruit us to them than do the earlier editions of *Leaves of Grass*, in which the institutionalism Larson discerns remains a surreptitious tendency. *Calamus* is indeed committed to spelling out a structure of ritualized relations that bears a striking resemblance to the heterosexual economy from which Whitman is apparently seceding. The poet himself assumes the place of the patriarch, mandating a rite and founding a lineage:

> There shall be from me a new friendship—It shall be called after my name,
> It shall circulate through The States, indifferent of place,

It shall twist and intertwist them through and around each other—Compact
   shall they be, showing new signs,
Affection shall solve every one of the problems of freedom,
Those who love each other shall be invincible,
They shall finally make America completely victorious, in my name.

One from Massachusetts shall be comrade to a Missourian,
One from Maine or Vermont, and a Carolinian and an Oregonese, shall be
   friends triune, more precious to each other than all the riches of the earth.
   ("States!" 1860 349–50)

Whitman's edicts here might well remind us of the provisions that
according to Lévi-Strauss articulate elementary and complex structures
of kinship; the poem goes so far as to offer its own version of the incest
taboo that founds culture, detailing the exogamy this prohibition serves
to institute.[40]

In reading *Calamus*, we can thus legitimately stress either the difference or the resemblance between the dominant heterosexual economy
and the homosexual one Whitman is intent on founding. The important
studies by Martin, Shively, and Killingsworth, which aim to establish the
facilitating role Whitman played at a crucial juncture of homosexual
history and politics, quite appropriately focus on the former. Yet in the
context of Whitman's career, *Calamus* marks not only the poet's coming
out as a homosexual,[41] but also his relinquishing of the archaic stance
that organizes the earlier editions of *Leaves of Grass*. We thus need to
attend not only to Whitman's oppositional politics in *Calamus*, but also
to the coming into culture the sequence facilitates more than resists:
though it may be adversarial and is still surely shaped by the fact of
oppression, the homosexual culture Whitman envisions allows him to
take up his place in the sort of symbolic economy the earlier editions of
Leaves of Grass adamantly reject. Not only the poet's estimate of pre-
existing structures, but also his sense of himself is fundamentally altered
by this shift: in *Calamus* Whitman assumes what Lacan would call his
castration, coming to terms with both the curtailment and the gift this
assumption involves.

Calamus thus shares with "Tintern Abbey" a sense that transmission
is central to who we are: like Wordsworth, the poet of Whitman's
sequence paradoxically seems to come into his own in the moment of
imagining his death and transmitting what will survive it; it is as if

identity itself were a product of the transmissibility the poet activates. Like the poet of "Tintern Abbey," the poet of "Recorders Ages Hence" empties out the present moment in which he addresses us, imaginatively relinquishing his life in order to project the poem forward to a time after his death; he does so not to put on the transfigured body that presides over Whitman's first two editions, but in order to become "the lover's portrait," an icon which succeeding generations can pass on. Like Wordsworth, that is, the poet of *Calamus* turns himself into a sign, giving up living presence for the symbolic bonds that can be sustained beyond its loss. In "Tintern Abbey," we saw, this transformation comes to seem compelling in part because the poet already inhabits a universe of representations or signs; the symbolic status of our objects is likewise a dominant focus of *Calamus*. We further hypothesized that the poet of "Tintern Abbey" must also have assumed the status of a sign himself: he can perform the dramatic self-reduction on which the poem pivots, we suggested, only because it has in a sense already occurred. "Tintern Abbey" does not quite put us in a position to spell out how this transformation happens; as we saw, Wordsworth's determination to treat in intensely personal terms transmission and the symbolic relation it secures may indeed obscure some of what our dependence on a circuit of exchange implies. By contrast, both the generalizing imagination of *Calamus* and its related preoccupation with sexual exchange—with what might be called a homosexual structure of kinship—help to make clear how this accession occurs, and what it means.

The benefits of Whitman's focus in *Calamus* on the general cultural structures that enable particular possibilities are thus not solely pragmatic. If the sequence displays a practical, political concern with how group practices can facilitate and protect individual intimacies, it also suggests that cultural structures subtend particulars in a more radical way, not simply fostering individual behavior but generating the very possibility of its occurrence by forming the subjects who will engage in it. Anachronistically, we might call this attitude structuralist. This admittedly perverse designation at least has the virtue of suggesting with particular sharpness the sort of revolution *Calamus* represents in Whitman's career. In the first two editions of *Leaves of Grass*, we have seen, the proleptic or pre-emptive power of structures that precede the self not only provokes anti-institutional polemics but sometimes occasions outright panic. In *Calamus,* Whitman celebrates structures of exchange that pre-exist and shape us; admitting their power to breach our self-sufficiency, he suggests that they thereby constitute what we properly are.

3. The change represented by this new-found willingness to celebrate symbolic compacts is strikingly suggested in "Roots and Leaves Themselves Alone." There Whitman relinquishes a magical attitude to the word, giving up the self-sufficiency word magic implies. The poet enters a circuit of symbolic exchange, defined by the paradox that his objects can henceforth be possessed only as they are subject to circulation; the objects the poet circulates indeed come into existence by virtue of this process of transmission.

The version of the poem first printed in 1867 gestures at the identification of word and thing that constitutes word magic, a fusion that would assure self-sufficiency by allowing the poet to subsume his objects simply by naming them. Yet the suggestion of fusion is tentative. Whitman's peculiar phrasing indeed seems to call into question the very identity it implies: "Roots and leaves themselves alone are these" (CRE ; V 2:383). If "these" can refer to the words the poet utters, as Whitman's earlier poems would lead us to expect, it might point instead to ordinary roots and leaves, physical objects left outside the poet's text rather than lodged within it as words. The peculiar insistence of "themselves alone" draws our attention to this possibility.

The 1860 text subjects the deictic "these" to stranger disturbances:

Calamus taste,
(For I must change the strain—these are not to be pensive leaves, but leaves
    of joy,)
Roots and leaves unlike any but themselves,
Scents brought to men and women from the wild woods, and from the pond-
    side. (1860 359)

In the second line here, "these" are "leaves," in context quite clearly the leaves of the poet's text. But "Roots and leaves," in the following line, adds a significant complication: Whitman's enumeration is presumably appositive to line two, yet is difficult to understand as a designation for the poet's words; it seems instead to point to natural objects. While this confusion might imply the sort of blurring of object and word with which readers of *Leaves of Grass* are familiar, "unlike any but themselves" seems to insist not on fusion but on difference, a difference made disconcerting by the circumstance that we don't know where we stand in relation to the distinction it implies: is it words or things that are "unlike any but themselves," and which is it we are being offered?

Given this equivocation, the pensiveness the poet aims to put behind him continues to haunt both these lines and the catalogue that succeeds them:

> Roots and leaves unlike any but themselves,
> Scents brought to men and women from the wild woods, and from the pondside,
> Breast-sorrel and pinks of love—fingers that wind around tighter than vines,
> Gushes from the throats of birds, hid in foliage of trees, as the sun is risen,
> Breezes of land and love—Breezes set from living shores out to you on the living sea—to you, O sailors!
> Frost-mellowed berries, and Third Month twigs, offered fresh to young persons wandering out in the fields when the winter breaks up. (1860 359)

The poignancy of this list derives in part from the evanescence of the natural landscapes it renders. But if a sense of nature's mutability suffuses the scenes the poet describes, suggesting incipient loss, the catalogue is also haunted by loss of another sort. If this list names natural objects "unlike any but themselves," then it points to things that remain aloof; the poet's words indicate a reality they cannot produce. If, on the other hand, the objects "unlike any but themselves" are the poet's written "leaves," then we are in the presence of a different category of thing—a verbal, symbolic object that doubles and thereby distances us from the natural reality with which we are eager to conflate it. Like the elegiac landscape descriptions of "Tintern Abbey," these lines in either case commemorate the birth of a human, symbolic universe bought by the fading of the natural world. Part of the delicate beauty of the passage derives from the way nature is itself made to figure this shift: the evanescence and fragility that already characterize the natural scenes the poem evokes, that is, image a relation to the natural that has itself become tenuous.

It is important to note that this catalogue, unlike many of the extended litanies of Whitman's first two editions, is also a ritual of transmission. Offering gifts "to men and women," "to you, O sailors!" and "to young persons wandering out in the fields when the winter breaks up," the poet who names things here is intent on entering a circuit of exchange rather than on achieving the sort of cataclysmic incorporation enacted in the poems of 1855 and 1856. It would be difficult to separate cause from effect here: we would do better to suggest that the poet relinquishes the real for a universe of symbolic objects, and takes up his place in a cultural transmission, in a single gesture.

While the poem's next lines at least partly resolve the ambiguity of the preceding catalogue, suggesting that the objects the poem presents are indeed symbolic, being words rather than natural things, they thus introduce a new complication. The poet insists that the symbolic objects he proffers will thrive only if we tend to and conserve them:

> Love-buds, put before you and within you, whoever you are,
> Buds to be unfolded on the old terms,
> If you bring the warmth of the sun to them, they will open, and bring form, color, perfume, to you,
> If you become the aliment and the wet, they will become flowers, fruits, tall branches and trees. (1860 359)

The transmission these lines depict is admittedly portrayed in sentimental terms. The passage is nonetheless peculiarly moving in the context of Whitman's work: the poet's avowal is also an implicit relinquishing of self-sufficiency, and of the magical power of production suggested by the first two editions of *Leaves of Grass*.

The following line offers a more radical renunciation of this dream of self-containment. It suggests that not simply the perdurance, but also the very existence of the objects the poet transmits depends on us. They exist not as things in themselves, but as elements within a locus of exchange: "They are comprised in you just as much as in themselves— perhaps more than in themselves" (1860 360). These symbolic objects, that is, paradoxically come into being by virtue of the transmission that passes them on: "They are not comprised in one season or succession, but many successions" (1860 360).

The poem's poignancy is thus complex. In a single gesture, Whitman relinquishes word magic and imaginatively enters a cultural circuit in which his objects exist for him only so long as they are exchanged. The conjunctions implied here are central to *Calamus,* and to the shift it marks in Whitman's career. Taking up his place in what amounts to a structure of extended kinship affirmed by bequest, the poet now gives up not only a regressive, fantasmatic relation to things, but also his distance from the social structures that restore our objects to us, but only in mediated and symbolic form, and only as we subject ourselves to the rules of exchange that govern their circulation.

"Roots and Leaves" suggests that this bargain affects us more intimately than we might suppose, governing not simply our transactions with material goods but also the erotic and amorous life we may want to think of as an alternative to its demands. No intimate relation is mentioned in the poem; yet the whole is suffused with tenderness and longing. Whitman's catalogue, moreover, owes its peculiar poignancy to an impulse we commonly associate with love, the impulse to give more than one can, to offer up to the beloved even what one does not have. Noting the muted presence of this ardent aspect, one might conceivably fault the poem for spending borrowed capital: one could argue that "Roots and Leaves" owes its haunting quality to an intimate loss the poet declines to mention, displacing the pain of this event onto the sort of generalized scenario on which the sequence so often focuses. Yet the poem may well derive its power from an insight that is the reverse of this one: desire itself may grow out of the nexus "Roots and Leaves" portrays. A particularly intense experience of love, such as the relation thought to have precipitated *Calamus,* may thus bring the poet to a dramatic realization of where he already is; "Roots and Leaves" seems to mark a recognition of this order.[42] It is at least the case that the poet embedded here in a kind of kinship structure, whose words are no longer magical and whose objects are symbolic, existing in circulation, must of necessity give what he does not have, except as he gives it, and desire from the other what the other does not have and cannot give, except as the poet receives it from him. Naming objects that are and are not present, that do and do not belong to him to dispose, the poet reaches longingly to others. "Roots and Leaves" implicitly grounds desire in a sense of lack, displaying the source of this lack as structural rather than private.

Making this connection clearer, the poem's final line suggests that we have ourselves been formed by the process of circulation into which we then enter as desiring subjects, so that the fading that haunts our objects haunts us as well. Whitman's concluding image is troubling in its own right: "They have come slowly up out of the earth and me, and are to come slowly up out of you" (1860 360). As often in Whitman's work, the topology we are invited to imagine here is confusing. If the poem's prior lines suggest that the objects the poet transmits exist only as products of exchange, and only in transit, here Whitman offers another myth of their genesis, implying that they come from our interiors. The symbolic objects created by exchange thus seem paradoxically to be organic, native growths we individually produce. A closer look, however, suggests that they produce us: coming "slowly up out of the earth and me," they seem to emerge from a depth below individual identity, passing first through the earth and then through the individual, assimilating him or her to their obscure tropism. (A passage from "Scented Herbage of My Breast," we will see further on, makes a similar suggestion more clearly.) While this reversal of priority is not of much help in clarifying the poem's equivocal topology, it does make the import of Whitman's difficult figure more intelligible. Those who take up their places in a circuit of exchange turn out to be hard to distinguish from the objects they transmit. If these are peculiar objects, existing only by virtue of the circuit in which they are circulated, the same can be said of our selves. The fragility that haunts Whitman's catalogue and the objects it evokes but cannot definitively produce would thus haunt the poet himself; the sense of elegy we discerned there mourns not only a relinquished relation to the object world but also an abandoned vision of the self. Yet the poem is not primarily elegiac: in "Roots and Leaves" the poet celebrates an identity he can sustain only by virtue of symbolic transactions, affirming as well the attendant lack of self-completion that precipitates desire and draws him to the circuit in which it moves. What he finds there will draw him into the cycle of exchange more firmly: receiving from the other what he does not have, he might hope to attain the completeness and self-sufficiency that would finally satisfy desire, freeing him from the round in which it moves; yet the object that the other might give is itself symbolic, existing only by virtue of the transactions that pass it on.

As *Calamus* describes it, sexuality acquires its value and engages us with unique intensity by being the crucial locus of this symbolic exchange and the fantasies it provokes. In the homosexual but still patriarchal economy Whitman explores, as in the dominant heterosexual culture he only equivocally leaves behind, the symbolic object one does not have but gives in sexuality is the phallus. It circulates as the absent cause and elusive satisfaction of desire, binding the poet, between origin and end, to a law of exchange which *Calamus* alone, of all Whitman's work, is content not to protest but to celebrate.

4. The relation "Roots and Leaves" suggests between a transmission of symbolic objects and a sexual circulation of selves is presented more clearly in "These I Singing in Spring," which also explores the range of feeling this erotic exchange can provoke.

If "Roots and Leaves" implicitly relinquishes word magic and the autonomy it seems to sustain, "These I Singing in Spring" takes leave of the edenic space to which the dream of autonomy properly belongs:

> These I, singing in spring, collect for lovers,
> (For who but I should understand lovers, and all their sorrow and joy?
> And who but I should be the poet of comrades?)
> Collecting, I traverse the garden, the world—but soon I pass the gates. (1860
>   347)

Entering that other, fallen world beyond the garden, the poet wanders in a space made poignant by contingency. Whitman's ensuing description echoes the lovely scene on which section five of "Song of Myself" comes delicately to rest. "These I Singing in Spring" evokes the pathos of the miniature on which the earlier passage also relies; but the sense of wonder the outsetting bard of "Song of Myself" experiences, as he gazes tenderly on what seems to be his own creation, finding it good, is shaded toward elegy by the act of leave-taking the older poet now describes:

> Now along the pond-side—now wading in a little, fearing not the wet,
> Now by the post-and-rail fences, where the old stones thrown there, picked
>   from the fields, have accumulated,
> Wild-flowers and vines and weeds come up through the stones, and partly
>   cover them—Beyond these I pass. (1860 347)

This leave-taking is no less poignant than the one it follows in quick succession. The poet now abandons a solitude that, despite the faint sign of civilization here, evokes a state of nature and a natural attitude. He finds his place in another scene, to which Whitman lends a peculiar twist:

> Far, far in the forest, before I think where I get,
> Solitary, smelling the earthy smell, stopping now and then in the silence,

Alone I had thought—yet soon a silent troop gathers around me,
Some walk by my side, and some behind, and some embrace my arms or
 neck,
They, the spirits of friends, dead or alive—thicker they come, a great crowd,
 and I in the middle,
Collecting, dispensing, singing in spring, there I wander with them. (1860 347)

What is odd here is the focus on "spirits," together with the stipulation
"dead or alive." We are surely to understand these terms as signs that
the scene is imagined, hence especially poignant because deeply felt; the
poet who leaves all else behind is still stirred by memories of those he
loves. Yet this persistence would have been more striking had the poet
put behind him a clearly populated space, in which he was surrounded
by living lovers or fellow citizens, for a scene of supposed solitude. In
fact, the movement the poem traces is closer to the reverse: passing
beyond a solitude that is first edenic and then natural, the poet finds
himself in a pastoral scene that is also the poem's first communal one,
yet is at the same time a region of ghosts.

It would be pushing things a bit, at this point in the poem, to insist
that what the poet encounters here are thus the signs of lovers, or lovers
as signs. Yet it is signs that he is next said to distribute to them:

Collecting, dispensing, singing in spring, there I wander with them,
Plucking something for tokens—something for these, till I hit upon a name
 —tossing toward whoever is near me,
Here! lilac, with a branch of pine,
Here, out of my pocket, some moss which I pulled off a live-oak in Florida,
 as it hung trailing down,
Here, some pinks and laurel leaves, and a handful of sage. (1860 347–48)

We should of course understand "tokens" as love tokens, "signs" of the
poet's affections; and when we speak of tokens or signs in this sense, we
don't in common parlance mean that they aren't real things. Yet here in
the poem the tokens the poet dispenses are struck with a peculiar latency, seeming to dissolve toward the status of signs in a more rigorous
sense. And it is precisely Whitman's equivocal "spirits" whose proximity
dissolves them. Whether we want to interpret these familiars as ghosts,
or as images the poet's memory conjures up, the poem has in any event
gone out of its way to suggest that they are not flesh-and-blood presences. The surreal comedy that would attend the poet's tossing actual
branches, moss, and leaves at such vaporous forms doesn't seem to be

one the poem is interested in mobilizing. Instead, the "tokens" the poet tosses seem to fade into the ambiguous region between being and non-being, presence and non-presence, which the poet's lovers inhabit: they seem, as it were, to dissolve as they are tossed toward those who have themselves dissolved.

This dissolution would be rather surreal in its own right, were it not for the fact that, in the context of *Calamus,* such latency already haunts the tokens the poet names, by the very fact that he names them: "Here! lilac, with a branch of pine." In *Calamus* the deictic that points at nothing we can see tends to be poignant rather than oracular, enacting that fading of things exacted by a language no longer thought of as magical. Whitman's earlier "spirits of friends" thus give dramatic, apprehensible form to a pervasive falling away from the real which the poem both registers and explores.

In context, this image serves also to suggest that the fading to which selves are subject has something to do with the circulation of erotic signs, and with the extended network of sexual relations the poet's exchange of tokens structures. At this point in the poem, this gift economy and the affectional network into which it draws the poet's ghostly lovers seem primarily beneficent: Whitman bestows his tokens with a prodigality that keeps the poem's elegiac implications in the background. Yet even here there is a sense of impending solemnities: "something for these, till I hit upon a name [....]" It is hard to know just what this phrase means, what the "name" the poet still lacks might be; this very doubt leaves a sort of lacuna in the ceremony of copious bestowing the poet meanwhile performs. This name might be simply the name of the ceremony itself. Or it might be the name of the cultural progenitor who stands behind it, *in whose name* these rites are now performed. It might be a name that, if found, the poet could bestow on his lovers—the name of the missing progenitor himself, perhaps. This ceremony would then be a genealogical one, a rite in which one not only exchanges tokens but also takes up one's place in a structure of kinship; the poet who offers a name would insert us in a symbolic circuit by means of which cultural identity is bestowed. Or again: the name might be the name of a still missing gift, of something else the poet could circulate, in the absence of which he distributes his lesser tokens instead. If we understand "a name" this way, it seems to clinch the sense of latency or fading by which the poet's other tokens are haunted: what the poet would bestow would be not a thing itself, but its linguistic sign. Yet "a name" is a peculiar usage here (we might have expected "a word" instead), and in Whitman's work the name is also a peculiar sort of sign; Whitman's forays into language theory, we saw in chapter 5, often turn on this peculiarity. As Whitman explains it, a name is a word, but a word reserved for a single thing, and thereby wedded to it; the truly proper name, we saw, sustains the dream of a language in which the word does not occult the thing by subsuming it in the symbolic category, but instead lifts it up, in its uniqueness and its presence, into language, and into a social space thereby made visionary.

These possible senses of "a name," contradictory in several respects, express contradictory recognitions and desires by no means peculiar to Whitman. The names bestowed upon us are the marks, not of our sacrosanct individuality, but of its loss. Not truly proper names but designations that inscribe us in structures of kinship, they place us in relation to a progenitor, to the name of the father and his law.[43] Our objects, while their movements and relations are less strictly codified, are struck by a similar latency. Yet there should be, somewhere, a *proper* name, the name of a being or object still proper: someone or something who stabilizes this structure by remaining aloof from the derived and mediated identity it confers, someone or something self-sustaining and self-contained.[44]

Perhaps suggesting this completeness, as well as our own lack of it, in the riddle of "a name," the poem goes on to offer us a more tangible image of such elusive self-containment, the calamus-root on which the next few lines dwell. We can best see what this image implies if we glance first at the symbol that, according to Fredson Bowers, it replaced in the course of Whitman's writing of the *Calamus* cycle: the "live-oak" of "I Saw in Louisiana a Live-Oak Growing," a poem Whitman composed before writing "These I Singing in Spring."[45] One of the lines in the latter poem which we looked at already, in which the poet bestows his tokens, alludes to the earlier image: "Here, out of my pocket, some moss which I pulled off a live-oak in Florida, as it hung trailing down." We noted already that the live-oak comes to symbolize a completeness the poet no longer ascribes to himself, and that his own lack of such self-sufficiency is related intimately to his need for affectional partners. We can add that the live-oak, like the self-sufficient poet on whom Whitman's prior editions center, is described in terms that make it seem conspicuously phallic, and that its phallicism is implicitly associated with the sort of joyously self-contained erotic delight that might now be called *jouissance:*

> I saw in Louisiana a live-oak growing,
> All alone stood it, and the moss hung down from the branches,
> Without any companion it grew there, uttering joyous leaves of dark green,
> And its look, rude, unbending, lusty, made me think of myself,
> But I wondered how it could utter joyous leaves, standing alone there, without its friend, its lover near—for I knew I could not. (1860 364–65)

The poet's response to this difference is to carry away with him a piece of the tree:

> And I broke off a twig with a certain number of leaves upon it, and twined around it a little moss,
> And brought it away—and I have placed it in sight in my room. (1860 365)

This is a complex gesture. If the poet keeps near him something to remind him of a completeness he no longer attributes to himself, this reminder is itself a broken-off part, suggesting as well his own separation and lack. In the context of the *Calamus* sequence, there is further irony in the fact that he designates this twig as a sign: "Yet it remains to me a curious token—" (1860 365). In *Calamus,* our lack of completeness is intimately connected to our entry into a universe of symbolic objects and the circuit in which they are transmitted. What the poet possesses here is not the completeness he cannot regain, but its token—the sign of what we have lost once we take up signs. The phrases immediately following this designation of the twig as a "token" accordingly go on to insist once more on the poet's own lack of the very completeness it symbolizes, a lack associated once more with the poet's erotic life.

In "These I Singing in Spring," the conspicuously phallic calamus-root which substitutes for the live-oak (an operation itself possible only within a universe of signs) is also designated as a token:

> And here what I now draw from the water, wading in the pond-side,
> (O here I last saw him that tenderly loves me—and returns again, never to separate from me,
> And this, O this shall henceforth be the token of comrades—this calamus-root shall,
> Interchange it, youths, with each other! Let none render it back!) (1860 348)

Here Whitman's phallic token is explicitly associated with an operation of erotic exchange. It plays its part in a solemn transmission which the poem's concluding lines explicitly contrast to the prodigality with which the poet's other tokens of love—including not the phallic live-oak twig but only the surrounding moss—continue to be bestowed:

> And twigs of maple, and a bunch of wild orange, and chestnut,
> And stems of currants, and plum-blows, and the aromatic cedar;
> These I, compassed around by a thick cloud of spirits,
> Wandering, point to, or touch as I pass, or throw them loosely from me,
> Indicating to each one what he shall have—giving something to each,
> But what I drew from the water by the pond-side, that I reserve,
> I will give of it—but only to them that love, as I myself am capable of loving.
>   (1860 348)

If we take the phallic calamus-root as a symbolic equivalent for the live-oak, we can suggest that, in the special ceremony the poet institutes here, what is formally interchanged is the sign of a completeness he and his partners lack. They lack it at least in part because of their insertion in the very circuit of symbolic exchange that now proffers them, in the guise of the phallic calamus, a sign of the self-sufficiency they have offered up.

The phallus here signified by the calamus stalk, that is, plays in sexual commerce a role analogous to that reserved for the elusive proper name in the kinship structures with which human sexuality intertwines. If the fantasy of the missing proper name compensates us for the lack of psychic self-completeness exacted not only by our mediated connection to objects but also by a similarly mediated relation to our own identities, the phallus signifies the erotic self-completion or *jouissance* of which our bodies are now likewise bereft. Yet it signifies as well the place of the father, the patriarchal authority that within the symbolic order bars our access to the very *jouissance* for which the phallus stands.

The symbolic exchange of the phallus is thus by no means peculiar to the homosexual rite Whitman mandates here. The phallus is also symbolically transferred in the heterosexual marriage ceremony sanctioned by culture, in the form of the fetishized woman passed between one patriarchal line and another. In its solemnity and its implicit finality, the rite Whitman inaugurates indeed resembles a marriage; it is something very like a homosexual structure of kinship that the ritualized exchange of the symbolic phallus here serves to sustain. "These I Singing in Spring" thus suggests both the lack intrinsic to sexuality once it assumes its role in establishing and maintaining the symbolic relations among persons that found culture, and the symbolic restitution sexuality itself affords. This signifying function of sexual commerce, and the lack or loss of *jouissance* it entails,[46] leaves its mark on all erotic activity, whether explicitly sanctioned and regulated as an act of kinship exchange or surreptitious and apparently exempt from control. Whitman's poem suggests as much: even the seemingly casual erotic relations detailed earlier in the poem and evoked once more toward its close, we saw, are shadowed by the problem of "a name," a ritual and genealogical imperative evidently fulfilled by the ceremonial exchange of the phallus that "These I Singing in Spring" envisions.[47]

If sexuality in Whitman's first two editions oscillates between a regressive fantasy of *jouissance* and a correlative terror of dismemberment, in *Calamus* it is thus instead typically caught up into the realm of masquerade. Heterosexual relations within patriarchy, Jacques Lacan suggests,[48] possess just this character, since they too are structured around a lost object, token of a missing completeness, that can be mimed but never literally produced:

Paradoxical as this formulation might seem, I would say that it is in order to be the phallus, that is to say, the signifier of the desire of the Other, that the woman will reject an essential part of her femininity, notably all its attributes through masquerade. (Lacan, *Feminine Sexuality* 84)[49]

It is not only the woman, Lacan suggests in radicalizing Freud's notions of both fetishism and castration, whose sexuality is defined by lack. The penis is also a fetish, substitute for the lost phallus the man plays at having just as the woman plays at being:

It is for what she is not that she expects to be desired as well as loved. But she finds the signifier of her own desire in the body of the one to whom she addresses her demand for love. Certainly we should not forget that the organ actually invested with this signifying function takes on the value of a fetish. (Lacan, *Feminine Sexuality* 84)

It follows that heterosexuality and homosexuality would be equally caught up in masquerade, while possessing their own particular rituals; Lacan's notion of masquerade is not tied to any fundamental distinction between these orientations as regards castration or the willingness to assume it. This revisionary stance is crucial for appraising *Calamus* in anything like psychoanalytic terms, since Freud characteristically associates homosexuality with a disavowal of (maternal) castration, a scotomizing of which "normal" heterosexuals are supposedly innocent. The first half of this neat distinction is complicated by Freud himself, in his final, unfinished essay "Splitting of the Ego in the Defensive Process": disavowal of castration, Freud argues there, does not preclude recognition of it, the two contrary responses running parallel and serving to split the ego (*Collected Papers* 5:372–75).[50] Acceptance of castration, Lacan's work seems to suggest, may be similarly partial and problematic, running alongside fantasies of restitution pervasive enough to make fetishism of one sort or another, in his account, virtually coextensive with sexuality itself.[51] In *Calamus,* homosexual exchange is thus governed by a fantasmatic structure Lacan regards as normative: "These I Singing in Spring" mandates the ritual transfer of a phallic token which the lover of comrades desires, but characteristically no longer claims as his own.

It would accordingly be a mistake to interpret the poignant gesture with which the poem ends as a sign of disavowal or a claim on the poet's part to be exempt from the symbolic circuit through which the sign of the phallus is restored:

> But what I drew from the water by the pond-side, that I reserve,
> I will give of it—but only to them that love, as I myself am capable of loving.
>   (1860 348)

As these lines make clear, the poet can "reserve" the calamus stalk, but not indefinitely: he concludes by looking forward, with a solemnity which implies that his reticence simply measures the gravity of his gift, to the moment in which he will bestow it. He too possesses the phallic sign of an elusive completeness only as he circulates it, giving it up.[52]

This is admittedly not an attitude toward the phallus and the law of the father *Calamus* uniformly assumes. But if we want to isolate what is peculiar to sexuality as *Calamus* portrays it, we need to abandon the sort of stark distinction between homosexuality and heterosexuality on which Freud's notion of disavowal insists, attending instead to a subtler aspect of erotic exchange ambiguously both fantasmatic and political. The poet who retreats to the margins of pond-sides to stipulate special rituals through which a phallic token will circulate steps outside the structures of kinship and transmission as currently constituted and sanctioned by patriarchal law. While the erotic hide-and-seek that marks Whitman's sequence, lending it a wonderfully flirtatious quality that can be either playful or grave, is surely in part a means of seducing the appropriately inclined reader without offending those differently disposed, it can also be understood as a provocative display put on for the Other, whom the poet ambiguously either woos or flouts.[53] *Calamus* thus continues to register a quotient of ambivalence with regard to the dominant order that is surely in large part a function of sexual politics, but has complex relations nonetheless to the more sweeping suspicion of symbolic compacts central to Whitman's first two editions. As we shall see further on, a related though not identical gesture in "As I Ebb'd with the Ocean of Life," in which the poet tries quite simply to seduce the Other, marks a relation to symbolic exchange and the mediated identity it installs that has become not simply ambivalent but frankly desperate. In *Calamus* too, the poet who solicits a special, imaginary relation to the Other ambivalently seeks both to accommodate himself to the demands of the symbolic order and to win a partial exemption from them.

While this provocative stance suggests an attitude somewhere between the avowals of "These I Singing in Spring" and the archaic ambitions of Whitman's first two editions, *Calamus* sometimes more closely approaches the latter. The poet who aspires to occupy the place of a mythic progenitor who gives the rites of kinship to his tribe seeks a role no self in culture, whether hetero- or homosexual, can assume: not content merely to woo or provoke the Other, he wants, like the hovering presence of 1855 and 1856, to become him. In such moments the adversarial politics of *Calamus* are difficult indeed to separate from more regressive concerns.

Yet in Whitman's sequence the quotients of exhibitionism and megalomania to which we have just been attending seem on the whole far less important than the impulse to imagine a structure of homosexual exchange in which the poet finds his satisfaction as participant rather than eponymous ancestor; it is more nearly true of *Calamus* than of Whitman's other work, though still not entirely so, that the poet assumes the latter role in order to create the scene in which he might play the former one. It is at least the case that *Calamus* performs with remarkable delicacy the difficult task of imagining symbolic rituals that simultaneously shadow and suggest an alternative to the dominant heterosexual economy, envisioning rites in which the poet might be willing and able simply to take up his place.

5. Whitman's celebration of the identity instituted by exchange is clearest in the pieces that depict the poet entering into erotic ritual or assuming his place in a lineage by writing his legacy down. But the costs exacted by subjection to the law of exchange are registered more dramatically in poems that display the poet as himself traversed by inscription. "Scented Herbage of My Breast" presents the poet's own body as a text, a writing he himself encounters as foreign and must struggle to decipher. The poem does not quite depict the literal engraving of body surfaces performed in primitive rituals of scarification. Growing up out of the poet's inner body spaces in the form of leaves, the text the poet ponders instead suggests a tracing of his psychic and somatic terrain by laws whose origin and purpose remain inaccessible or unconscious; the interiority from which this inscription emerges can no longer easily be associated with such notions as essence or self-presence. Such alienation also defines what the poet wants: the writing the poet struggles to read is also the text of his desire; it reveals the otherness of both identity and impulse when these are shaped by a structure that precedes them. Though an organic growth figures this structure and its results in the poem, the clear relation of this "scented herbage" to desire, the association of foliage with the phallic term throughout *Calamus,* and the sequence's pervasive interest in symbolic bequest all allow us to understand the writing that emerges from the poet's interior at least in part as an instance of the cultural inscription that shapes the body and governs erotic life—a tracing, through the self, of the law of the father and the phallus, which writes the poet into the kinship networks *Calamus* depicts.

From its opening, "Scented Herbage" portrays the poet as the conduit of a message that precedes him and will persist beyond his death. The expressive speech that characterizes Whitman's first two editions is accordingly replaced by writing, a writing whose task, moreover, is to transmit or transcribe rather than invent:

> Scented herbage of my breast,
> Leaves from you I yield, I write, to be perused best afterwards,
> Tomb-leaves, body-leaves, growing up above me, above death,

Perennial roots, tall leaves—O the winter shall not freeze you, delicate leaves,
Every year shall you bloom again—Out from where you retired, you shall
     emerge again. (1860 342)

The poet's passive role is stressed here in a number of ways. In the
second of these lines, the text he conveys is depicted as a kind of crop,
an association reinforced by the extended play on "leaves." The poet
himself apparently serves this crop as soil: he is figured as a plot which
will "yield" the leaves we peruse. The notion of surrender which "yield"
also momentarily suggests, though syntactically unsustainable, is likewise appropriate not only to the modest role the poet assigns himself but
also to the sense of violation these opening lines already imply. The
association here of the leaves which emerge from the poet with death is
one to which we can best come back, when we encounter an extended
meditation on it later in the poem. But the related contention that the
poet's text can be "perused best afterwards," in his absence, dramatically displaces his identity from the authoritative, originary position
Whitman accords it in the first two editions of *Leaves of Grass*.

This displacement is insisted on in "Scented Herbage" not simply by
casting the writing poet as mere amanuensis, rather than as the sort of
progenitor of a tribe and a rite who appears, for example, in "These I
Singing in Spring," but also by depicting his body as written, re-shaped
by or into a text. This text by no means reflects the poet's own authorizing presence or intention. While Whitman's prior editions characteristically dissolve text into voice, and voice into the poet's living presence,
"Scented Herbage" suggests an inverse order of operations: here the
"leaves" which are both plant and text emerge from a body they enucleate, breaking down the poet's discrete, autonomous form into what
amount to nutritive elements recycled and assimilated by this alien organism in the process of its growth. Like the Elizabeth Bishop poem
"The Weed" (20–21), which is in many respects a re-writing of it,
"Scented Herbage" lends this process a degree of grotesqueness and a
suggestion of violence that hint at the darker effects of mannerism or
surrealism:

O slender leaves! O blossoms of my blood! I permit you to tell, in your own
     way, of the heart that is under you,
O burning and throbbing—surely all will one day be accomplished;
O I do not know what you mean, there underneath yourselves—you are not
     happiness,

You are often more bitter than I can bear—you burn and sting me. (1860
342)

These lines are disconcerting not simply because a patterned energy
that seems foreign enucleates and reconfigures the poet here, but also
because the source of this process proves impossible to locate. As a
result, both the poet's attempt at prosopopoeia and the comfortingly
anthropomorphic sense of agency it would sustain have trouble attaching themselves to the obscure tropism they seek to bring under control.
Like the slightly fussy, oddly punctilious phrase "I permit you," which
suggests not so much a gracious ceding of authority as an uncomfortable
attempt to insist that one indeed possesses it, the poet's deferential offer
to allow the organism which enucleates him "to tell, in your own way,
of the heart that is under you" provides a moment of nicely understated
black comedy. Not only the speech act the poet pretends to authorize
but also the agency he apostrophizes and invites to perform it fails to
materialize: the supposedly conscious entity the poet tries to address
slides away disconcertingly into ramifying foliage, a tangle of intercon-
necting filiations without discernible origin or end. Whitman's shifter
"you" registers this slide, dissipating the very act of identification it
ought to accomplish or confirm: "O I do not know what you mean,
there underneath yourselves [. . . .]"[54]

Given this slippage and the dissolution of personal agency it suggests,
it is all the more disconcerting that this proliferating structure, at once
plant and text, proves indistinguishable from the poet who struggles to
address it. What has been assimilated to this elusive tropism is indeed
not simply the poet's body but also his desire. Not only do the leaves the
poet at first tries to address emerge from or pass through his heart: "the
heart" is itself made to seem alien by the definite article that introduces
it in lieu of a possessive pronoun (a distancing gesture repeated in
Bishop's text). The leaves the poet addresses are invited to tell of a desire
that has thus implicitly been rendered opaque to the poet himself. This
implication is borne out by the final two lines quoted above, in which
the meaning of the growth that traverses the heart is said both to elude
the poet's understanding and to frustrate rather than afford satisfaction.
The passage's curiously phrased second line leaves it an open question
what other purpose might instead be served: "surely all will one day be
accomplished."

Though the desire figured by these leaves is thus by no means reducible to simple enjoyment, further on in "Scented Herbage" the poet nonetheless implores it to emerge less hesitantly:

Grow up taller, sweet leaves, that I may see! Grow up out of my breast!
Spring away from the concealed heart there!
Do not fold yourselves so in your pink-tinged roots, timid leaves!
Do not remain down there so ashamed, herbage of my breast! (1860 343)

What is moving here is the tenderness with which the poet apostrophizes an eroticism figured as obscure and alien. The "sweet leaves" the poet addresses are objects at once mysterious and auto-erotic; Whitman's address suggests a solicitude directed less at sexual partners than toward his own desire. Mingled with shyness, this solicitude can be understood in part as a response to the culture's proscription of homosexuality. Yet it registers as well the elusiveness of a desire governed by laws not of the poet's own making, laws the *Calamus* sequence as a whole associates not only with the particular predicaments that affect homosexuality but also with the extended structures in which eroticism of whatever sort finds its place.

Accounting at least in part for the opacity of desire, this alienation may also underlie the enigmatic connection "Scented Herbage" makes between desire and death: the *Calamus* sequence suggests that death already inhabits and defines the self who has taken up a place mandated by symbolic laws of exchange. If the poet of *Calamus,* like the poet of "Tintern Abbey," is intent on envisioning his own absence so as to secure the transmission that will make up for it, reducing himself to the portrait or sign as which he will persist, this impulse may thus reflect his sense that this reduction has in effect already occurred.

Like the vegetal imagery with which it intertwines, the death the poet of "Scented Herbage" contemplates can be understood in more than one way. Whitman's extravagantly botanic vehicle surely implies that the link between sex and death is biologically grounded. Yet an extended passage that dilates on this connection first details an alienation of meaning intrinsic to desire, an expropriation the sequence as a whole associates with symbolic mechanisms:

O I do not know what you mean, there underneath yourselves—you are not happiness,

You are often more bitter than I can bear—you burn and sting me,
Yet you are very beautiful to me, you faint-tinged roots—you make me think
   of Death,
Death is beautiful from you—(what indeed is beautiful, except Death and
   Love?)
O I think it is not for life I am chanting here my chant of lovers—I think it
   must be for Death,
For how calm, how solemn it grows, to ascend to the atmosphere of lovers,
Death or life I am then indifferent—my Soul declines to prefer,
I am not sure but the high Soul of lovers welcomes death most;
Indeed, O Death, I think now these leaves mean precisely the same as you
   mean. (1860 342–43)

It might be argued that death itself is responsible for separating desire
from individual, conscious intention, a split Whitman records in the
lines that precede death's explicit appearance here. But death may well
enter the passage as a crucial image for this fading rather than as its
cause. Sexuality, inscribing us in a symbolic order that precedes individual identity and desire, may itself precipitate the psychic fading that
prefigures literal death and henceforth becomes inseparable from our
sense of it.

In the poem's concluding lines, death is accordingly associated not
simply with dissolution, but more insistently with a loss of self-present
meaning. Whitman indeed invokes it as an antithetical corrective not
quite to life, but to "what I was calling life." We can best understand it
as a catachresis of the transparent self-presence that defines life in Whitman's first two editions, a self-presence guaranteed in turn by a notion
of word magic incompatible with the operations of linguistic and erotic
exchange that govern *Calamus:*

Nor will I allow you to balk me any more with what I was calling life,
For now it is conveyed to me that you are the purports essential,
That you hide in these shifting forms of life, for reasons—and that they are
   mainly for you,
That you, beyond them, come forth, to remain, the real reality,
That behind the mask of materials you patiently wait, no matter how long,
That you will one day, perhaps, take control of all,
That you will perhaps dissipate this entire show of appearance,
That may be you are what it is all for—but it does not last so very long,
But you will last very long. (1860 344)

These lines empty out imagery crucial to Whitman's 1855 and 1856
editions. There, we saw, surface forms are characteristically regarded as

representations of a sequestered essence or presence. If the indicative surfaces of things are typically opaque and sometimes downright deceptive, the essences they hide need only be liberated to be comprehended; while surfaces constitute a complicated network of arbitrary signs ultimately associated with the violence and trickery of the cultural order, interiors are self-present, self-sufficient, and self-contained. Voice, we saw, both figures and expresses this pristine interiority. Here in "Scented Herbage," surfaces are still signs; yet they no longer signify transparent self-presence. Instead, life and presence are themselves now masks or disguises: reversing the logic of Whitman's earlier editions, each apparently discrete thing now plays its part as sign of a pervasive scheme that negates its autonomy; what lurks within things is silence rather than voice, and the appearance of this inside would now involve a disappearance or fading of self-presence rather than its triumphant revelation.

We might understand this silence at the heart of things in part as a metaphysical void; in the celebratory context of *Calamus* its implications would be less nihilistic than mystical. Yet the death the poet addresses here also suggests a fading of a different order, one more amply explored in the sequence as a whole: the underlying silence "Scented Herbage" ponders also appears in the sequence as inscription, as the ghostly structure that individuals perpetuate through the sexual and familial configurations they assume, deployed by a law that negates their self-containment and the notion of essence that governs it. We need not deny that the fading the poem meditates can be understood as biological, or metaphysical, to maintain that it is also symbolic. Sexuality, Lacanian analysis suggests, acquires its singular place within culture precisely because of this sort of overdetermined significance:

This is the point of insertion of sexuality into the structure: the loss to which sexuality already testifies as a biological function comes to coincide with the lack inscribed in the signifying chain. (*Feminine Sexuality* 120)[55]

In "Scented Herbage" death can be understood as a name for this double lack.

"Of Him I Love Day and Night" gives these connections among eros, death, and cultural transmission more extravagant scope. By its very strangeness, the poem suggests that the death Whitman meditates in *Calamus* is not solely biological:

Of him I love day and night, I dreamed I heard he was dead,
And I dreamed I went where they had buried him I love—but he was not in
   that place,
And I dreamed I wandered, searching among burial-places, to find him,
And I found that every place was a burial-place,
The houses full of life were equally full of death, (This house is now,)

The streets, the shipping, the places of amusement, the Chicago, Boston,
   Philadelphia, the Mannahatta, were as full of the dead as of the living,

And fuller, O vastly fuller, of the dead than of the living;
—And what I dreamed I will henceforth tell to every person and age,
And I stand henceforth bound to what I dreamed;
And now I am willing to disregard burial-places, and dispense with them,
And if the memorials of the dead were put up indifferently everywhere, even
   in the room where I eat or sleep, I should be satisfied,
And if the corpse of any one I love, or if my own corpse, be duly rendered to
   powder, and poured in the sea, I shall be satisfied,
Or if it be distributed to the winds, I shall be satisfied. (1860 362–63)

Not content to show that we have been preceded by myriad generations now dead, and that our time on earth is ultimately miniscule, the poem's dream vision insists on placing the living among the dead and the dead among the living. In the poet's dream, the one to whom his desire has bound him takes up his place among the dead; and the dead, or the memorials or inscriptions that survive them, have their place in the hearths of the living. The poem indeed suggests that our proper dwelling is a house of the dead, that our most intimate acts occur beneath the gaze of inscriptions written for or by them. Whitman's first two editions vigorously repudiate such intimations, though the presence who presides over these volumes may illustrate the very law he comes to refute. By contrast, "Of Him I Love" is remarkable for the tenderness with which imagery that might have seemed grotesque is set into the cultural land-scape the poem imagines, provoking a solemn recognition that feels liberating rather than macabre.

Rarely rendered in such global terms, this is nonetheless the imaginative space in which the entire sequence is situated. The dream-visions of *Calamus* are characteristically populated by ghostly lovers; they come to define the universe of symbolic exchange *Calamus* adduces. Embracing this ghostliness, *Calamus* calls us to take up willingly the places that are ours.

6. "Full of Life Now," the poem that closes Whitman's sequence, condenses some of the central concerns to which we have been attending. It also both recalls and dramatically revises the paradigmatic encounter of Whitman's 1855 and 1856 editions:

> Full of life, sweet-blooded, compact, visible,
> I, forty years old the Eighty-third Year of The States,
> To one a century hence, or any number of centuries hence,
> To you, yet unborn, these, seeking you.
>
> When you read these, I, that was visible, am become invisible;
> Now it is you, compact, visible, realizing my poems, seeking me,
> Fancying how happy you were, if I could be with you, and become your lover;
> Be it as if I were with you. Be not too certain but I am now with you. (1860 378)

Here several of the facets of exchange which the sequence has explored are combined in a single ritual. Like "Roots and Leaves," the poem centers on an act of transmission in which a symbolic rather than real entity is bequeathed. Like "These I Singing in Spring," it associates such symbolic transactions with eroticism, suggesting more dramatically the fading this connection exacts by assigning to the poet himself the ghostliness the earlier poem attributes to his lovers. "Full of Life Now" indeed goes further, making the poet's seductive gesture equivalent to a last bequest, the circuit of erotic exchange indistinguishable from a circle of inheritors. Whitman thus also enacts a ceremony to which "Recorders Ages Hence" alludes, turning himself by means of his written word into the "lover's portrait" or representation that can be circulated as a type of manly love, a kind of mythic progenitor of the circle of erotic exchange along which he is passed. The poem indeed implies not only that the symbolic phallus whose simulacra are circulated in erotic exchange properly belongs to a mythic progenitor, but also that this progenitor is properly dead: like the phallus, the name of the father which the poet here assumes can be put on only in death; the being whose name secures our sense of a proper place exempt from the circulation of signs can come into being for us only *as* a sign.[56]

In "Full of Life Now" Whitman thus hovers between the two roles in which the series as a whole ambiguously casts him. Seeking us out in a conspicuously symbolic transaction, he makes his way along an erotic circuit, appearing as a participant. Yet in the ritual his text mandates, he also wills himself into the place of the dead father, icon of the lost phallus that might be circulated among us. The poem manages to be both disconcerting and moving by equivocating between these incongruous roles. In "Full of Life Now" the poet both envisions his apotheosis to the throne of the Other and pays his debt to this place, internalizing the death exacted not only by any accession to an eponymous role, but also by participation in the rites that require and memorialize this ritual sacrifice. There is certainly a difference between these guises: the first might conceivably be understood as a compensation Whitman awards himself for enduring the second. Yet both roles acknowledge a death inseparable from the rule of signs, marking it as the poet's proper condition.

Such recognitions are especially poignant because they dramatically revise the trope of living presence that organizes Whitman's first two editions. There the poet's advent augers the death of signs in quite another sense: in the poems of 1855 and 1856, the poet appears to put an end to symbolic transmission and exchange, by-passing inscription and codified bequest and dissolving their hold over us. "Full of Life Now" recalls this magical transaction: the entire poem consists of an apostrophe, evoking the figure of voice Whitmanian address customarily seems to produce. Yet a number of details vitiate this appeal. More like Wordsworth's "Tintern Abbey" than Whitman's "Crossing Brooklyn Ferry," "Full of Life Now" provides a dateline that is conspicuously local and ephemeral: not "sundown" but "the Eighty-third Year of the States." In the third line, "a century hence," and in the fourth, "you, yet unborn," insist on a distance the poem will only tentatively claim to overcome. In the trope of "seeking," the poet offers a figure for desire; in 1855 and 1856, where seeking is finding, desire has collapsed back into magical power and the punctual satisfaction it affords. Here, by contrast, the gap between poet and reader is also stressed by the repeated deictic "these," which puts the material artifact of the text between writer and reader, effectively blocking the poet's magical advent; this gap both awakens and chastens desire, making the poet's overtures seem simultaneously wistful and brave.

In "Full of Life Now" the distance that haunts desire is marked by writing and reading, and is in that sense contingent; yet the *Calamus* sequence as a whole ascribes this gap less to chance than to structural necessity, associating it with a lost object. The second stanza's hopeful-sounding "*now* it is you," which momentarily seems to efface the temporal interval that governs the poem, is accordingly embedded in a passage that insists on it. Here a fading made to seem inevitable structures the encounter between the poet and those his text seeks out; the lines exhibit the apparently inexorable working of a sort of reciprocal-action mechanism, drawing one living being back into ghostliness in exchange for letting another appear:[57]

> When you read these, I, that was visible, am become invisible;
> Now it is you, compact, visible, realizing my poems, seeking me. (1860 378)

Here too, the particulars of this non-encounter, which substitutes a sign for a living presence, are dictated by writing and reading; yet as we have seen, textual transmission emerges as paradigmatic in *Calamus* precisely because it dramatizes a ghostliness that haunts erotic exchange and identity throughout the sequence.

The poem's final lines thus conclude *Calamus* by pondering one of the series' central concerns. Here Whitman insists on the non-coincidence that governs erotic exchange and cultural transmission, as well as on the desire this distance fuels. The penultimate line empties out the magical encounter of 1855 and 1856, making the meeting between poet and audience conspicuously hypothetical: "Fancying how happy you were, if I could be with you, and become your lover." And if, in the final line, Whitman's "now" evokes briefly the powers of performative utterance, as if to raise the poet's actual presence here at the sequence's very end, this gesture is rendered poignant by the equivocating phrase in which it appears (itself set in parentheses after 1871) as well as by the poet's renunciation of the magical powers of the word in what precedes: "Be it as if I were with you. (Be not too certain but I am now with you.)" (V 2:408). Such avowals of unfulfilled and perhaps unfulfillable desire are moving in themselves. But like much of *Calamus*, they acquire their peculiar resonance through contrast to the grand imaginative myth they both allude to and disperse.

"As I Ebb'd with the Ocean of Life"

The ever-hooded, tragic-gestured sea
Was merely a place by which she walked to sing.
Whose spirit is this? we said, because we knew
It was the spirit that we sought and knew
That we should ask this often as she sang.
                —Stevens, "The Idea of Order at Key West," *Collected Poems* 129

I throw myself upon your breast, my father,
I cling to you so that you cannot unloose me,
I hold you so firm, till you answer me something.
                —"As I Ebb'd with the Ocean of Life," 1860 198

"There where it was" ("*Là où c'était*"), I would like it to be understood, "it is my duty
    that I should come to being."
                —Lacan, *Ecrits* 129[58]

If the *Calamus* sequence celebrates poetry as testament, both meditating
on the symbolic bequests that shape and fade us and offering Whitman's
own poems as instances of them, "As I Ebb'd with the Ocean of Life" is
instead a bitter testament to poetry itself. It turns against verse, at least
as Whitman has practiced and understood it, and against the crucial
versions of the self his work has enshrined. Yet the poem's ironies are
strangely divided: Whitman seems to mock not only his myths but also
the self who has failed to realize them; the poem laments the vanishing
of the very powers it bitterly redefines. This ambivalence measures the
intensity of Whitman's investment in the very fictions he here puts
behind him. They proved to be irreplaceable: a poem of leave-taking,
"As I Ebb'd with the Ocean of Life" is also arguably the last great poem
Whitman wrote. While Whitman himself seems to have weathered the
impasse the poem records, he emerged from it a minor poet, his crucial
imaginative sources no longer accessible.

If the skepticism of Whitman's *Sea-Drift* poem is ambivalent, the poet
who judges his enabling myths also being judged by them, the poem's
stance is further complicated by the fact that the visions of identity it
surveys are not only plural but ultimately antithetical. This complexity
is registered most obviously in the variety of specters the poet confronts.
Always equivocal in their import, the metamorphic characters who populate the ongoing psychomachia of *Leaves of Grass* are particularly
elusive in "As I Ebb'd." If "Song of Myself" presents us with "Walt

Whitman," the "self," the "soul," and "the Me myself," Whitman's
1860 *Sea-Drift* poem introduces "the eternal self of me" (metamorphosed by the time of the deathbed edition into "this electric self out of
the pride of which I utter poems"), "the spirit that trails in the lines
underfoot," "the real ME," "this phantom, looking down where we
lead," and "You up there, walking or sitting, / Whoever you are."[59]
These last two characters might in fact be guises assumed not by the
poet but by the father or the Other. That is part of the poem's complex
interrogation of Whitman's myths of self: "As I Ebb'd" explores the
connections between the poet and the various external agencies his
earlier work characteristically seems to dissolve.

Faced with this bewildering array, we need to be on our guard against
over-simplifying; such a crucial icon as "the real ME" possesses a significance that may be ultimately indeterminate. But I want to hazard a
schematic reading of the lines that present the first group of Whitman's
personae, in order to get at a conflict I take to be crucial to the poem.
These figures appear in quick succession:

> I, musing, late in the autumn day, gazing off southward,
> Alone, held by the eternal self of me that threatens to get the better of me,
> and stifle me,
> Was seized by the spirit that trails in the lines underfoot. (1860 195)

Ignoring for a moment the "I" who both registers this vision and
records his part in it, we encounter first a persona who now besets rather
than aids him. The designation of this "self" as "eternal" stipulates an
identity not begotten in time; we can associate this figure with the poet-
hero of Whitman's first two editions, who generates himself as a voice
materializing from the void. This reading is confirmed by the form the
"eternal self" assumes in Whitman's deathbed edition, that of "this
electric self out of the pride of which I utter poems" (V 2:319; CRE
253). This final incarnation is the result of Whitman's persistent tinkering with the line, a gradual modification that suggests not a switch of
characters so much as a clarifying of what Whitman had had in mind
from the first. This "electric self" uttering poems out of his "pride"
surely has less in common with the *Calamus* poet than with the self-
sufficient presence of 1855 and 1856.

If the relation of the "I" to this eternal or electric self by whom he is
held is now estranged or adversarial, so too is his connection with the

even more enigmatic icon by which he is next seized. Before we hazard some guesses concerning this figure's possible affiliations, we can note the bitter irony his appearance in any case marks. Spirit, present in the 1855 and 1856 editions in the form of the poet's own breathing presence, ought not to appear in "lines underfoot," in the detritus Whitman figures as a kind of writing. Here a central trope of Whitman's first two editions is savagely emptied out.

We can thus understand Whitman's second persona in part as a catachresis of his first. If the semantic parallel of "held" and "seized" suggests a relation between these figures that might be one of either similarity or antithesis, the dejecting to which Whitman's image of voice is subjected seems to stress the latter possibility: here the mythic poet of the first two editions squares off against his degraded avatar. As we shall see in a moment, this ironic juxtaposition might mark a distinction between the poet's early achievements and subsequent dereliction. But it can also operate as a bitter deflation of earlier pretensions: "the eternal self," the poem both fears and hopes, may after all be nothing but sheer wind, a figment reducible to the writing that enabled Whitman's fiction of voice—not a self-generating and self-authorizing identity but only the illusion of one.

This reduction seems in part to reflect a natural attitude now devoid of sustaining illusion; here Whitman rejects what might be called the supernatural naturalism of his first two editions. There the poet claims both to restore us to nature and to restore nature to itself, giving voice to the unifying force of *natura naturans* with which his own presence is identified. Here *natura naturans* is instead the ocean, ambiguously either mournful or vengeful, that has cast up an icon of the poet as a fragmentary piece of *natura naturata,* desiccated by its separation from this enigmatic source and left among kindred, equally fragmented forms.

Confronting a natural order now seen as antagonist, the poet indeed turns, further on in "As I Ebb'd," to "my father." It would not be wrong to interpret this figure, in part, as an image of cultural authority. Begging for the embrace of a father from whom he has so far been alienated, the poet pleads with him to translate and render accessible the pre-symbolic murmur of the maternal ocean that has cast him up. It is tempting to read this as a gesture akin to the reconciliations of *Calamus:* abandoning the magical attitude of the first two editions, which both appeal to nature and make it over in the image of the poet's own animating presence, "As I Ebb'd" would embrace the symbolic universe the writer of 1855 and 1856 struggled to subvert.

The poem's allegiances, however, are not so simple. As we shall see, the father for whose intercession the poet pleads also stands between him and another figure of the father, an icon of patriarchal power which the poem depicts as inaccessible and forbidding. The final line in the passage we have been considering—"Was seized by the spirit that trails in the lines underfoot"—seems also to register the cost exacted by a symbolic order Whitman consistently associates with the name of the father. The spirit reduced to writing might well remind us of the poet of *Calamus* traversed by inscription; encountered now among the rows of detritus on the beach, this spirit would lose its proper afflatus by taking up the sort of place in a signifying chain *Calamus* proudly reserves for it. This connection will require demonstrating. But I mean to suggest that "the spirit that trails in the lines underfoot" can be understood not only as a harsh reduction of what may now seem to be the pretensions of Whitman's first two editions, but also as a bitter re-estimation of the symbolic identity celebrated in *Calamus* and the allegiances that have made it what it is.[60] The figuration of "As I Ebb'd" is thus complicated by the fact that the poem simultaneously recalls and darkly revises two contrary myths of the self.

It is made more complex still by the presence of the third figure in the passage quoted above, the "I" confronted by these specters of identity. As the bitter, reductive irony we have noted in Whitman's catachrestic tropes suggests, this "I" now accuses the fictions by which he has hitherto been mesmerized. The insight that enables this critique may well result from the juxtaposition we have been considering, the poet's sustaining myths effectively canceling each other out. Yet here, as throughout "As I Ebb'd," the poet is also accosted and accused by the very visions of identity from which he now feels estranged. His supposed dereliction may also have been brought about by the clash between them. The recognitions of *Calamus* can be said to expose the pretensions of the earlier poetry; yet from a different perspective, the poet himself may have failed the myth of self-sufficient identity by falling into the filiations celebrated in *Calamus*.[61] Conversely, a self still drawn to the archaic satisfactions of the first two editions will have retreated from the commitments of *Calamus;* this can be interpreted either as a recognition that the compensations the 1860 sequence offers are unworthy of the poet, or as a sign of his inability to live with the limitations *Calamus* movingly accepts.

"As I Ebb'd with the Ocean of Life" may mark an impasse in Whitman's career precisely because the author of *Leaves of Grass* was himself caught among these conflicting evaluations and attitudes. If "As I Ebb'd" leaves behind contrary myths of the self which Whitman perhaps no longer saw as viable, and to which he could no longer commit himself, his distance from his antipodal figurations may also have suggested his own unworthiness. The poem, in any event, offers no new vision of identity that might sustain further work on the order of that Whitman here puts behind him. Ambiguously both abject and bitter, the self with whom the poet now finds himself left is indeed a remnant, a fragment cast up by a force either distant or spent.

1. While perhaps reserving its sharpest animus for the patriarchal function celebrated in *Calamus,* Whitman's *Sea-Drift* poem is for the most part more overtly concerned with the myths that organize his first two editions. Dramatically confronting earlier visions of the self in the sort of psychomachia to which we have been attending, "As I Ebb'd" also re-evaluates the relation to objects the poet figure of 1855 and 1856 seemed to make possible. Whitman's *Sea-Drift* poem returns to the catalogue technique enlisted to sustain the poet's incorporative capacities, and to the elemental drama that lent it cosmic proportions, re-casting the latter in such a way as to turn naming itself into an exercise in abjection rather than a display of power.

From its opening, "As I Ebb'd" presents us with a literal landscape that is at once a condensed and symbolically charged version of Whitman's characteristic imaginative topography; the poem is largely organized as an extended catachresis of Whitman's earlier images of flood and voice, still associated with the mother and *natura naturans*. Tramping along the Paumanok beach in a diminished hour and season, "late in the autumn day," the poet turns first to the ocean. Now, however, the natural power of flood has withdrawn, either displeased or spent; not merely the periodic ebbing of flood-tide depicted in "Crossing Brooklyn Ferry," this recession seems cataclysmic. The animating voice of *natura naturans* is likewise remote, and seems angry or exhausted:

As I ebbed with an ebb of the ocean of life,
As I wended the shores I know,

As I walked where the sea-ripples wash you, Paumanok,
Where they rustle up, hoarse and sibilant,
Where the fierce old mother endlessly cries for her castaways. (1860 195)

Nature's speech has become a dirge, a keening, whether mournful or bitter, for a world whose incarnation as discrete, embodied shapes now marks its separation from the very power that created it.

The poet turns next to these abandoned forms. No longer filled and animated by flood, they appear as rows of inert objects deposited by its retreat:

Was seized by the spirit that trails in the lines underfoot,
In the rim, the sediment, that stands for all the water and all the land of the globe.

Fascinated, my eyes, reverting from the south, dropped, to follow those slender winrows,
Chaff, straw, splinters of wood, weeds, and the sea-gluten,
Scum, scales from shining rocks, leaves of self-lettuce, left by the tide. (1860 195–96)

These shapes stretched out in rows possess a kind of emblematic fatality; the poet's fascination here amounts to compulsion, as if his tracing of the wreckage at his feet obeyed a dark enchantment. The scene the poet confronts is indeed the very one his former powers allowed him to transfigure. These separate, desiccated shapes are "husks" rather than "kernels," a row of detritus or *disjecta membra* deposited by the now-remote force which ought to have infused it with life. As we noted, these lifeless rows scanned by the poet's eye are also a kind of writing, a mute and melancholy text left behind by this vanished source: like the created nature in need of redemption in Whitman's first two editions, they are depicted as inert, indicative signs incapable of expressing the life-force that should have animated them. Moreover, the poet "seized by the spirit that trails in the lines underfoot" gleans in these remnants both an ironic emblem of this vanished force and a grim indication of what he himself amounts to once it withdraws. Rather than being a surrogate for flood, he is now simply part of the rejectamenta it tosses up.

The mesmerized litany in the passage we have been considering makes the poet's lapse of power clear. The extraordinary bitterness of this list of desiccations stands out fully only against the background of Whitman's earlier catalogue technique, which seemed to re-animate all it named by gathering it into the poet's imperium. Here this list of *disjecta membra* is instead introduced by the poet's notation that "my eyes [. . .] dropped, to follow those slender winrows." The catalogue thus presents itself not as a re-gathering and a re-animating, but as the following of a receding row, a tracing of traces. Naming is here the self-dispersing repetition of an unredeemed dispersion, the enchanted recitation of a text.

The poem's final section makes this loss of power seem irremediable. The ironies of Whitman's conclusion are mercilessly self-lacerating: there both the poet's presence and his speech are wholly drained of their former resources. The dissolution of the poet's magical presence can be traced in the fate of Whitman's characteristically transfiguring pronoun "we." This "we" appears only late in the central 1856 text "Crossing Brooklyn Ferry," but much of the poem has served to prepare its advent. All Whitman's addresses to his audience create the endlessly emanating presence that comes to fill time and space; time and space, conversely, are folded back in toward the intimate place and occasion the tone of these announcements implies. These transfigurations are not so much negotiated as tenderly confirmed in the pronominal gathering of the poem's eighth section:

> We understand, then, do we not?
> What I promised without mentioning it, have you not accepted? (1856 219)

The transfiguring vision into which the poet folds us here is magnificently self-centering: Whitman's "we" attains its redemptive force from the omnipotent "I" into which it gathers us, yet here names us part of.

This spheral "we," so crucial to Whitman's transfigurings, is grimly unraveled in the conclusion of his *Sea-Drift* poem, as if a pronoun itself might be subjected to catachresis. In lines he added to the poem in 1871, Whitman's "we" has become an incoherent mumble of contiguities:

> We murmur alike reproachfully, rolling our sands and drift, knowing not why. (V 2:320)

Yet in context this revision serves to deflect and soften the impact of the poem's final image, where the spreading out of this "we" into random lines and rows is even more bitterly accomplished. In the line just quoted, the poet in a sense gathers sands and drift to him by addressing them directly—apostrophe typically has this function in Whitman's work. At the poem's end, the protagonist instead addresses a remote and enigmatic "you" who lurks above him in the sky:

> You, up there, walking or sitting,
> Whoever you are—we too lie in drifts at your feet. (1860 199)

No longer addressed but described instead to this "you," the drifts on the beach are not only not redeemed by being named—they are bitterly offered up to dispersion.

The list that precedes these lines, like the short catalogue in the poem's opening section, already enacts this relinquishing: Whitman's most negative catalogue, it is a kind of sundering by naming, a repetition, in a language no longer performative but simply indicative, of a desiccation the word is now powerless to redeem. Significantly, it seems to begin as a gathering, albeit both haunted and wistful—perhaps a catalogue of consolations:

> I gather for myself, and for this phantom, looking down where we lead, and
>   following me and mine. (1860 198)[62]

Perhaps nowhere in Whitman's work is there so wholly bitter a reversal as in what follows. This tentative announcement of possession becomes immediately part of "the blab whose echoes recoil upon me" (1860 197), an epithet applied earlier in the poem to Whitman's past productions. The declaration need only be repeated, that is, to turn into its own bitter parody: "Me and mine!"[63] What follows, cued by a likewise repeated and ironized "we," is like a catalogue with a minus sign in front of it:

> Me and mine!
> We, loose winrows, little corpses,
> Froth, snowy white, and bubbles,
> (See! from my dead lips the ooze exuding at last!
> See—the prismatic colors, glistening and rolling!)
> Tufts of straw, sands, fragments,
> Buoyed hither from many moods, one contradicting another. (1860 199)

Organized as one of Whitman's typical appositive lists, this short catalogue nonetheless wholly desiccates the "we" it enumerates, and thus everything it names, by emptying its contents out into the dispersing, ironized space its opening repetitions establish.

2. Turning against the catalogue technique crucial to Whitman's 1855 and 1856 editions and the claims to incorporative mastery the poet's litanies there sustain, these ironic lists can also be understood as a bitter re-valuation of the universe of symbolic transmission celebrated in *Calamus*. As we shall see in a moment, the emblems strewn on the beach ironically re-figure the circuit of erotic exchange in which the poet of *Calamus* discovers both the source of his desire and his fate.

This skeptical re-examination of *Calamus* pervades "As I Ebb'd." Whitman's brooding over the implications of the earlier sequence is suggested by a plethora of ironic echoes. Thus, for example, the maternal ocean of "As I Ebb'd," to whose animating powers the poet of 1855 and 1856 was to give voice, is depicted in forbidding terms that recall and reverse not only the figuration of Whitman's earlier editions, but also that of *Calamus:*

> As I walked where the sea-ripples wash you, Paumanok,
> Where they rustle up, hoarse and sibilant,
> Where the fierce old mother endlessly cries for her castaways. ("As I Ebb'd,"
>   1860 195)

> Cease not your moaning, you fierce old mother,
> Endlessly cry for your castaways—but fear not, deny not me,
> Rustle not up so hoarse and angry against my feet, as I touch you, or gather
>   from you. ("As I Ebb'd," 1860 198)

This rustling repeats with a difference the sea's sounds in "When I Heard at the Close of Day," a *Calamus* poem Bowers (lxiv) assigns to the period prior to the composition of "As I Ebb'd":

> And that night, while all was still, I heard the waters roll slowly continually
>   up the shores,
> I heard the hissing rustle of the liquid and sands, as directed to me, whisper-
>   ing, to congratulate me,
> For the one I love most lay sleeping by me under the same cover in the cool
>   night,
> In the stillness, in the autumn moonbeams, his face was inclined toward me,
> And his arm lay lightly around my breast—And that night I was happy.
>   (1860 358)

While the American continent, faced with *Calamus,* may be in the awkward position of having to find some other poet to be its singer, the maternal ocean is here evidently in no such predicament and feels no corresponding pique. Yet in "As I Ebb'd," the ocean's rustling suggests estrangement and anger rather than congratulation. The *Calamus* poet who immersed himself in erotic exchange perhaps thereby abandoned the very charge from *natura naturans* he took himself to be still pursuing.

Some lines from the next poem in *Calamus,* "Are You the New Person Drawn toward Me," are also echoed in the above passage from "As I Ebb'd," though less overtly. These lines are ominous in their own right:

> Do you suppose I am trusty and faithful?
> Do you see no further than this façade—this smooth and tolerant manner of me?
> [. . . .]
> O let some past deceived one hiss in your ears, how many have prest on the same as you are pressing now. (1860 358, 359)

The "hiss" of the disabused lover here ironically echoes the lines from "When I Heard at the Close of Day" concerning "the hissing rustle of the liquid and sands": whereas the ocean's hiss congratulates the poet on his erotic good fortune, the lover's hiss condemns him for betraying it. "As I Ebb'd" manages to displace this condemnation rather than simply repeat it. Like the lover of "Are You the New Person Drawn toward Me," the waves that "rustle up, hoarse and sibilant" have been deceived by the poet. Yet given the panoramic vantage of "As I Ebb'd," it would be less a particular erotic deception than the poet's very assumption of a lover's role that violates a prior compact—his commitment to give voice, not to particular affections, but to the single animating force of *natura naturans* that underlies them.

A third echo of *Calamus* is awakened by the enigmatic "real ME," a figure whose complex resonance we will take up a bit further on. This figure accosts the poet

> With peals of distant ironical laughter at every word I have written or shall write,
> Striking me with insults till I fall helpless upon the sand. (1860 197)

These lines are prefaced by a dark admission that immediately precedes the appearance of "the real ME":

> Aware now, that, amid all the blab whose echoes recoil upon me, I have not once had the least idea who or what I am. (1860 197)

That "blab" is at least in part the discourse of *Calamus*. What "the real ME" laughs at recalls and empties out a passionate phrase from "Trickle Drops." There the poet, with an odd mix of anguish and pride, calls upon the "drops" of blood or semen within him to emerge from his body and stain his page, marking it as erotic confession:[64]

> Saturate them with yourself, all ashamed and wet,
> Glow upon all I have written or shall write, bleeding drops. (1860 361)

In "As I Ebb'd," "every word I have written or shall write," including the poetry of erotic revelation to which the phrase alludes, has become simply another evasion of self, falsifying a "real ME" that remains unknown.

Whitman's 1867 re-casting of the insult offered by "the real ME" suggests one possible reason for this implicit judgment that *Calamus* has amounted to self-betrayal:

> With peals of distant ironical laughter at every word I have written,
> Pointing in silence to all these songs, and then to the sand beneath. (V 2: 320)

Here Whitman has "the real ME" equate the poet's prior writing with the sand beneath his feet, and implicitly with the rows of detritus that lie there. While the irony here is complex, one possible way to interpret the gesture "the real ME" performs is as a bitter critique of the aspirations and allegiances of *Calamus*: Whitman's poems are here reduced to the status of inert links in a chain of desiccated signs. We need to note how this image is itself a reductive re-writing of the central figuration of the earlier sequence.

We can best do so by attending to Whitman's obsessive play, in "As I Ebb'd," with the problem of signification. It centers on the poet's examination of the lines of sediment that strew the beach, the first mention of which we should look at again:

> Was seized by the spirit that trails in the lines underfoot,
> In the rim, the sediment, that stands for all the water and all the land of the globe. (1860 195)

As we noted, this image serves simultaneously to empty out the claims of the 1855 and 1856 editions and to re-evaluate the antithetical allegiances of *Calamus*. We can add that both the connection of part to whole and the relation of signifier to signified postulated in Whitman's first two editions are negated here; the universe of symbolic circulation celebrated in *Calamus* is thereby re-created but also darkly re-cast.

Harold Bloom rightly sees the trope of synecdoche in these lines (*A Map of Misreading* 181):[65] epitomizing the abandoned and exhausted world of created nature, Whitman's rim of sediment functions as a symbolic gathering worked by the poet's imagination.[66] Yet the effect of Whitman's figure is peculiar. What Whitman's synecdoche ironically figures or condenses is dispersion itself: these rows stand for the extended, disjunctive metonymy of created nature, of which they are simply a small but similarly dispersed, metonymically organized part.[67] Whitman's synecdochic gathering negates itself in another way as well: the immanence that should characterize romantic synecdoche is emptied out by the implicit comparison to writing. If Whitman's trope condenses an otherwise fragmented created nature back into this single symbol in which it can be rendered present, it also reduces it to the status of a text, an indicative sign which substitutes for an animating essence that has itself withdrawn.

It is partly the pretensions of the 1855 and 1856 editions that are deposed here. Whitman's characteristic catalogue technique operates to fold metonymy back toward metaphor, making all objects types of a presence ultimately identifiable with the poet himself. Some lines further on in "As I Ebb'd" accordingly offer the rim of sediment at the poet's feet as the ironic fulfillment of the project of the "eternal self":

> Paumanok, there and then, as I thought the old thought of likenesses,
> These you presented to me, you fish-shaped island,
> As I wended the shores I know,
> As I walked with that eternal self of me, seeking types. (1860 196)

Given the conspicuous attention "As I Ebb'd" devotes to the poet's tracking of a row of emblems that leads him further and further along the desolate shore, this adversion to a search for "likenesses" or "types" is rather caustic. The husks on the beach are types in a failed typology: devoid of the sort of meaningful pattern or repetition in which figure finds its fulfillment, they instead suggest a merely mechanical principle of succession from one element to the next. If these husks are "likenesses," they are alike precisely in violating the sort of patterning, and the sense of connection to a deep source or central organizing principle, that Whitman's customary catalogue technique serves to adduce.

It is just these qualities that allow the rows on the beach also to be read as an ironic reduction of the symbolic circuit celebrated in *Calamus*. While the catalogues of 1855 and 1856 suggest the gathering of disparate beings back into their single living source, *Calamus* instead traces a movement of exchange not guaranteed by any such ground. In "As I Ebb'd," this perpetual circulation of meaning and value seems to bankrupt rather than sustain the poet defined by it.

In *Calamus,* we saw, the selves who enter a kinship network structured by erotic transmission are in a crucial sense similar to the symbolic objects offered in gift exchange: identity, too, is a product of this circulation rather than a ground for it. The poet of "As I Ebb'd," whose fascinated gaze keeps reverting to the chain of emblems at his feet, and to the "spirit" encountered there, likewise discovers his significance in a chain of emblems among which he is fated to find his place:

I, too, but signify, at the utmost, a little washed-up drift,
A few sands and dead leaves to gather,
Gather, and merge, myself as part of the sands and drift. (1860 196)

Abandoning the dream of self-creation that organizes the 1855 and 1856 editions, these lines also offer an ironic re-estimation of the reconciliations effected in *Calamus*. Having been generated by a source he no longer claims to contain or comprehend, the poet must now glean what he is, rather than celebrating his autonomous selfhood; like the poet of *Calamus,* he must infer his own significance, encountering it not in himself but in his relation to a signifying chain. Yet in "As I Ebb'd," to be defined in this way is to be desiccated rather than fulfilled. What the poet signifies is "washed-up drift": a row of husks devoid of initiative or animation, a series of empty, indicative signs.

Like *Calamus,* "As I Ebb'd" further implies that this loss of self-presence cannot be made good; unlike the earlier sequence, it evaluates this impasse grimly. The poet will encounter, in the lines on the beach, no autonomous meaning or discrete identity that might be extracted from the network of signs he traces: reading what he is in a row of emblems that itself requires reading, he discovers no proper terminus to this chain, and no proper term within it. In the lapse of animating flood or informing spirit—a lapse which the allegiances of *Calamus* might seem to have provoked or invited—objects have not only become signs. These signs can no longer return us to their proper referents or their animating source. Confronting the sediment on the beach, the poet does not read back from *natura naturata* to *natura naturans,* but along a receding row, a metonymic text of objects whose ironic residue of likeness consists in the shared absence of an animating spirit or true signified. These washed-up drifts are all alike and can thus all signify each other, that is, precisely because none of them can point back to the informing energy which their surface forms should rightly manifest. If one shape on the beach signifies a second, the second is not its organic meaning or essence, not its true signified, but merely its equally dessicated neighbor, a signifier whose very poverty allows it to substitute provisionally for the first.[68]

Since it proceeds from no proper origin and arrives at no telos, this signifying movement is endlessly reversible. In a further bitter compounding, Whitman thus inverts the direction of his first reading. Having perused himself and determined that he signifies no more than "a little washed-up drift," he turns further on to the "little shreds" on the beach and discovers instead that they stand for him, and for the shore-world of created selves he addresses:

> We murmur alike reproachfully, rolling our sands and drift, knowing not why,
> These little shreds indeed, standing for you and me and all. (V 2:320)[69]

Brusquely reducing the circulation of signs to a commutable relation that seems to cancel meaning rather than sustain it, Whitman here empties out one of the crucial organizing figures of *Calamus.* Celebrated in the earlier sequence as the origin of such identity as we can possess, and of the erotic and affectional ties that bind us to one another and to the community of which we are part, the signifying chain in "As I Ebb'd" appears instead to decimate us. The reversible movement of signification Whitman grimly depicts here is thus oddly compatible with the breaking of the circle of gift exchange which the lines of sediment trailing off toward the horizon also suggest. In "As I Ebb'd," what is given up to exchange—whether it be the gift, the phallus, or the self—is not rendered back, since the signs through which it might return are now seen as bankrupt, but lost without recompense.

3. Whitman's *Sea-Drift* poem thus mourns the vanishing of the mode of identity celebrated in the 1855 and 1856 *Leaves of Grass,* while no longer finding it tenable; it laments the loss of a self, perhaps always

only figmentary, not dependent on the sort of symbolic transmission *Calamus* celebrates, which "As I Ebb'd" harshly assesses. If the poem worries the question of where and how an identity both sustainable and sustaining got lost, Whitman seems unwilling to assign blame to a single source; "As I Ebb'd" displays his disillusion without assuaging it, giving vent to mutually contradictory and ultimately self-cancelling recriminations. The complex, self-lacerating bitterness that accompanies this irresolution is most dramatically evident in what I earlier called Whitman's psychomachia, in which competing personae challenge one other. Almost all the scenes in this psychic drama concern the poet's fall into signs. But as we shall see, they gradually shift in focus: beginning by pitting enigmatic icons of the poet himself against one another, they end by confronting equivocal figurations of the father. The scenes that make up the poem's psychomachia thus roughly re-trace the trajectory of Whitman's career; they suggest that it has issued onto a dead end. Never resolving the question of whether a reliance on symbolic transmission that now seems disastrous might have been avoided, "As I Ebb'd" leaves the poet caught in an Oedipal configuration from which there seems no longer to be any possible escape.

We have already examined the first of these encounters, in which three equally suspect versions of the poet square off. But we should note one further irony in this scene, since it concerns the relation of voice to writing and probes the source of the poet's reliance on signs. If the "eternal self" gives way to or collapses into "the spirit that trails in the lines underfoot," this debacle may simply make plain what Whitman's figure of self-presence always was. We noted that the "eternal self" confronts the "I" not to inspire but to "stifle" him. This threat may perhaps suggest the intimidating power of an exalted image of identity which the poet can no longer live up to. Yet the particular form this intimidation assumes has a history in Whitman's work: it is characteristically inscription that chokes or stifles voice;[70] here an avatar of Whitman's figure of voice exerts a disastrous effect customarily ascribed to writing, exercising the proleptic power from which it supposedly frees us. Whitman's enigmatic image here implicitly raises the problem of whether this icon of self-presence is not already entangled in the universe of signs—and thus the question of whether this entanglement was avoidable and culpable. It may have been neither: if Whitman's figure of voice was itself a function of writing, it must bear the blame of having seduced the poet with a figmentary prospect. Yet the poem will never satisfy itself that this is so.

The poem's next extended confrontation likewise brings together distinct versions of the poet himself. Here too, the more primordial of these figures of identity seems to accuse the current one of having lapsed from self-sufficient presence into reliance on signs. Yet here again, the poet's apparent accuser might himself be accused—except that in this passage reliance on signs may no longer be figured as culpable. This encounter between the poet and "the real ME" is if anything more enigmatic than the one it succeeds:

O baffled, balked,
Bent to the very earth, here preceding what follows,
Oppressed with myself that I have dared to open my mouth,
Aware now, that, amid all the blab whose echoes recoil upon me, I have not once had the least idea who or what I am,
But that before all my insolent poems the real ME still stands untouched, untold, altogether unreached,
Withdrawn far, mocking me with mock-congratulatory signs and bows,
With peals of distant ironical laughter at every word I have written or shall write,
Striking me with insults till I fall helpless upon the sand. (1860 196–97)

We have already broached one possible interpretation of the gesture performed by "the real ME" here: perhaps equating the poet's writing to mere detritus, "the real ME" may be attributing this presumed degradation to the poet's willingness to regard his own productions as links in a chain of signs. The "blab whose echoes recoil upon me" would on this reading be the discourse of *Calamus*.

Yet "the real ME" itself makes use of signs here; in the context of Whitman's work, the fact that this privileged figure of identity should do so is indeed the greatest irony of the scene. Nor are these the organic signs Whitman's earlier writing invokes to vanquish signs of the wrong kind: "Withdrawn far, mocking me with mock-congratulatory signs and bows," "the real ME" hides behind signifiers that are ironic and indirect rather than transparent and expressive. Perhaps the primordial figure who confronts the poet here is giving him no worse than he deserves: the latter, having been seduced by the symbolic transactions celebrated in *Calamus* into relinquishing an innate, organic identity, would on this reading be confronted by a figure of living presence who ironically veils himself in the very signs for which the poet has foolishly squandered his birthright. Yet the passage may instead suggest that "the real ME," a core of identity that fades before our attempts to track it, is itself a product of signs. We might understand this elusive figure, that is, as a subject in something like Lacan's sense: a precipitate of symbolic operations of exchange rather than an autonomous ego. It would be to the scene of such operations that "the real ME" summons the poet here. Pointing to the sands and rows of signs beneath his feet, this figure would not be dismissing Whitman's songs for having fallen into the condition of writing, but mocking the poet for resisting this reduction; not displaying what the poet has foolishly let himself become, but showing him what he too must be. " 'There where it was,' " as Lacan has it, " . . . 'it is my duty that I should come to being' " (*Ecrits* 129). The "blab whose echoes recoil upon me" would on this reading be not the *Calamus* sequence but the poems of the first two editions, which pit themselves against this recognition and the altered sense of subjectivity it entails.

I mean to insist not on this interpretation but only on its plausibility. Like the nucleus of identity called "the real ME," both the significance of our fall into signs and the question of whether any aspect of the self has escaped it, or might have, remain enigmatic to the very end of "As I Ebb'd."

As the poem progresses, however, the signs under whose sway the poet now finds himself are associated more and more firmly with the law of the father; the problem of identity is thus re-cast in terms of the Oedipal configuration the first two editions of *Leaves of Grass* resist, and from which the poet's self-generating presence was to offer escape. This law is both registered and evaded in the next dramatic encounter in "As I Ebb'd." As "the real ME," arguably the poem's final figure for the sort of aboriginal identity celebrated in "Song of Myself," fades into enigma, Whitman invokes instead a figure of the father, begging for the very filiation his earlier images of identity had served to annul. Here the patriarchal authority implicit in *Calamus* is returned to the intimate personal nexus with which it always intertwines. This stress on intimacy, however, registers tensions that make the passage as profoundly ambivalent as it is deeply affecting:

I throw myself upon your breast, my father,
I cling to you so that you cannot unloose me,
I hold you so firm, till you answer me something.

Kiss me, my father,
Touch me with your lips, as I touch those I love,
Breathe to me, while I hold you close, the secret of the wondrous murmuring
    I envy,
For I fear I shall become crazed, if I cannot emulate it, and utter myself as
    well as it. (1860 198)

We need to acknowledge how moving this is. Here Whitman returns
to a scene and a source from which his poetry has long been in flight. As
Zweig suggests

Whitman calls upon his father, kisses and implores him. From the scene of his
vanished strength, he reaches out, in a brotherhood of failure, to the father he
had buried. . . . here now is his father, come back from the dead, as psycho-
pomp, or spirit guide, a companion of dark moods. The father Whitman had
fled in his 'gigantism' and his lusty assertions catches up with him. . . . Here, his
hurt has enabled him to see his father as if for the first time, and draw from him
a kind of negative strength: the ability to endure and thrive in failure. (309)

Harold Bloom makes larger claims, suggesting that the poet arrives at
a covenant here. Atypically, Bloom argues that poetic loss should thus
be understood as human gain:

As the covenant with Emerson that begat the poetic self ebbs, so the rejected
covenant with the actual father is accepted and made whole. Emersonian Self-
Reliance freed Whitman from the totalizing afflictions of the family romance.
Now the consequences of the poetic analogue of the family romance allow
Whitman a reconciliation he never found while his father was alive. Imaginative
loss quite literally is transformed into experiential gain, in a far more direct way
than Wordsworth or Coleridge could have envisioned. (*A Map of Misreading* 182)

This is not wrong. But in its eagerness to embrace a Whitman who has
become one of us it tends to sentimentalize, missing something important. Like Zweig, Bloom wants to read the scene as a reconciliation. Yet
however moving the passage's avowals are, this imagined encounter is
deeply evasive, and it is partly Whitman's appeal to the personal that
makes it so: this invocation of the father is paradoxically an ambiguous
attempt to revoke the consequences of paternal law.

We can begin to see how this is so by querying Bloom's notion of the
"actual father." Which actual father is it, we need to ask, that Whitman

tries to embrace here? The father as failure, Zweig suggests, consoling
his failed son. This too is right in its way, but likewise slides off the
aspects of this encounter that make it strange. I have in mind especially
the son's plea for a kiss, which ought not to be understood as simply a
paternal benediction: "Kiss me, my father, / Touch me with your lips, as
I touch those I love." It isn't the implicit homosexuality that is strange
here: one doesn't beg one's mother to touch one on the lips "as I touch
those I love" any more than one does one's father. Or rather: it isn't
simply the "actual" mother or father one might interact with in this
way, but a parental figure urged to step out of its sanctioning role. Nor
is it simply the father as failure that needs to be lured to this scene,
which would amount not to a reconciliation so much as a tryst. It is less
the actual or the failed father than a peculiar fantasy of what the father
might be and do, could one appeal to him "personally" and get him to
shuck off his generic function, with which we are presented here. The
encounter for which Whitman pleads is charged with the possibilities of
what one might become, and what one might escape, if one managed to
seduce the father in this way.

Despite the plea for embrace, Whitman's father-figure indeed turns
out to be important here less for any compact the poet might conclude
with him than for his imagined role as facilitator or intercessor. Finally,
as we shall see, it is indeed between the poet and paternal law that the
father is paradoxically asked to intercede. More immediately, the poet
asks the father to restore his relation to the mother, now estranged.

Here, as is often the case with Whitman's evocation of parental
figures, the place assigned to the mother is more traditional than Whitman's declared sexual politics might lead us to expect.[71] The mother
with whom the father is to intercede is still the generic figure associated
with the ocean and *natura naturans;* it is indeed an unmediated, pre-
symbolic connection to both the mother and the word, relations characteristic of what Kristeva calls the semiotic *chora,* that the father is asked
to restore. This can be understood only in part as a continued acceptance
of the paternal metaphor celebrated in *Calamus.* True, the poet pleads
for the paternal intercession he earlier claimed to by-pass. Yet the father
is to be seduced into restoring access to the mother rather than barring
it; the poet's plea both acknowledges the paternal function and seeks to
evade the prohibition that is its consequence. Whitman's concluding
words to the father here confirm that his aim is to escape rather than

embrace the paternal compact: asking not for a name that would embed him in a structure of kinship but for a translation of the mother's murmur and the ability to "emulate it, and utter myself as well as it," the poet pleads for a performative power of self-production that would exempt him from symbolic exchange, as it had the hero of Whitman's 1855 and 1856 editions.

We should note, though, that the power which would allow the poet to escape the rule of the father also exceeds the domain of the mother. Here the poet asks for a word that would allow him, not quite to return to the pre-Oedipal mother, but to recover the self-completion which a blissful fantasy of our relation to her suggests: he wants, not to subject himself to, but instead to "emulate" a maternal power that, when yoked to a patriarchal, positional force likewise both enlisted and subverted, would amount to a capacity for self-creation. What the poet pleads for, that is, is the power of word magic, and what it should sustain is the sort of self-sufficiency the first two editions of *Leaves of Grass* celebrate. There, however, the commerce between this charmed state and the more archaic realm of the *chora* is typically relaxed and assured; in this passage, the poet not only begs the father to restore to him the unmediated presence of the mother's lull and hum, but simultaneously seeks paternal protection against the dangers now glimpsed lurking in the superseded register associated with her, dangers intuited in the mother's angry rustle and fierce moan. A passage that looks at first like a desperate plea for restored relation—already ambiguous since the poet seeks either a compact with the father or a return to the mother—is in fact an ambivalent attempt both to solicit these ties and to keep them at bay. Awkwardly negotiating its way toward the threshold between these parental icons, a site Whitman's first two editions seemed to occupy effortlessly and at will, this scene registers the poet's estrangement from both the maternal realm with which the poet of 1855 and 1856 seemed to be on easy terms and the paternal metaphor celebrated in *Calamus*.

It is the latter by which the closing movements of "As I Ebb'd" are increasingly troubled. The poet's plea for the father's embrace might thus also be understood as an ambivalent attempt to forestall the very reconciliation it seems to invite. This paradox also turns on the intently personal focus of the poet's appeal. Whitman's biographical father, called to in the passage, serves in part as a stand-in for the Other or paternal law, acting as a surrogate the poet might be able to seduce.

Whitman thus seeks to woo back from the place of the father a power that the author of the 1855 and 1856 editions had refused to accord him in the first place; this gesture registers both involvement with and resistance to paternal authority, an ambivalent mix characteristic of neither *Calamus* nor the work that precedes it. The particular form this apparent gesture of reconciliation takes is also intensely ambivalent. Calling the father up out of the earth, Whitman not only tries to commune with his biographical parent, now dead, but also paradoxically hints at autochthonous generation. The poet thus seeks to seduce the father into surrendering a power of self-production, laying claim to a positional force ordinarily wielded, in attenuated form, only within the symbolic structure from which the poet tries to steal it.

The poet's attentions will shortly shift from ground to sky, and to a series of silent but accusatory figures that hover there above him. His appeal to the father might thus also amount to seduction in another sense. In Whitman's characteristically magical transactions with space, to draw the father up out of the ground might amount to drawing this other figure down out of the air. In this sense too, communion with the father might offer the poet access to the Other, enabling him to soften the enigmatic but exacting gaze by which the poem's close is darkened.

As Zweig implies, however, the biographical father Whitman appeals to in these lines makes a rather unlikely avatar of patriarchal authority. We might thus prefer to think of him as a shield against cultural authority rather than an instance of it, a figure who might hide the poet from the Other rather than granting special access to him. It is partly the ambiguous status assigned to the father that makes the passage moving: this seductive evocation mingles anxiety with an intensity of regret virtually unprecedented in Whitman's work.

Whichever role we cast the father in, however, the poet's appeal to him seeks to evade the stark confrontation toward which "As I Ebb'd" inexorably gathers. The impassioned address to the maternal ocean which succeeds this scene already implies the failure of the poet's efforts to evoke the father's sympathy, suggesting a heartbreaking lack of response:

Ebb, ocean of life, (the flow will return,)
Cease not your moaning, you fierce old mother,

Endlessly cry for your castaways—but fear not, deny not me,
Rustle not up so hoarse and angry against my feet, as I touch you, or gather
  from you.

I mean tenderly by you,
I gather for myself, and for this phantom, looking down where we lead, and
  following me and mine. (1860 198)

Though Whitman's tone here seems to hover between desperation and
hope, the passage is most forced when most openly optative—"(the flow
will return,)"—a sign that the relation to the mother the poet pleads for
here has also suffered an estrangement he fears is definitive. This final
address to the mother is indeed already shadowed by an ominous figure
who seems to have the sort of pre-emptive claim on the poet that would
preclude other attachments. Gathering his sediment, or trying to, the
poet is watched by an enigmatic "phantom" in the sky, a spot associated
with paternal agency as early as "Song of Myself" and "Crossing Brooklyn Ferry." This ghostly figure is less person than function, a place in a
structure or an anxious fantasy of it. Here "As I Ebb'd" reluctantly
draws toward the sort of schematic confrontation the preceding appeal
to the poet's own father was in part structured to avoid.

Under the gaze of this phantom, the poet spells out for himself a
humbling of his earlier pretensions already indicated to him in his encounter with "the real ME," a figure of identity likewise lurking above
him and perhaps associated with the fading of self-presence that insertion in a structure of exchange exacts. Here Whitman's declarations
assume an oddly distant perspective, as if the poet's own sense of himself
now passed through the place of the phantom, internalizing its detached,
severe judgment:

Me and mine!
We, loose winrows, little corpses,
Froth, snowy white, and bubbles. (1860 198)

The bitterness here, I suggested earlier on, is extreme; but it soon
grows even harsher. Echoing an earlier passage to which we devoted
considerable attention, the poet who sees himself as one of the "little
corpses" on the beach goes on to make explicit what this death implies
within the universe of Leaves of Grass:

See! from my dead lips the ooze exuding at last!
See—the prismatic colors, glistening and rolling!)
Tufts of straw, sands, fragments. (1860 199)

Splayed out beneath a spectral gaze emanating from the sky, the detritus on the beach now explicitly includes the poet's word. While in the first two editions of *Leaves of Grass* the poet's vatic ambitions often served to raise him up to the place of this gaze himself, here voice oozes from the poet's lips to join the lifeless husks on the sand, dying finally into a writing that emerges grotesquely from the poet's mouth. The poet takes up his place in an endless, remorseless inscription organized for the gaze and for the Other.

The extended passage of which these lines are part robs the poet of his speech in another way as well; less savage, it is more uncanny. As the lines that conclude the poem finally make clear, the poet's long closing apostrophe drifts from one addressee to another:

> We, capricious, brought hither, we know not whence, spread out before You, up there, walking or sitting,
> Whoever you are—we too lie in drifts at your feet. (1860 199)

A passage that begins by apprehensively mentioning a phantom hovering over the poet has by its end turned into an address made to him; Whitman's final appeal to the mother turns with seeming inexorability into the confrontation she might have forestalled. Here at the poem's end it is the sky, the father, and the Other that make inescapable claims on the poet, drawing to themselves the very utterance that should have fended them off.

It is not only the poet's voice and speech but also his identity that has been purloined at the poem's close. This is so despite the fact that the poet himself ends up prostrated beneath the enigmatic icon in the sky. The "You" the poet addresses, lodged in a domain associated with paternal power, seems to have metamorphosed not only from the phantom, but also from "the real ME"; the poet's own elusive identity reappears to confront him from the field of the Other. One need not fix Whitman's eerily metamorphic personae in any final relation. But it seems as if the poet who wanted to draw the father up out of the ground, in order to draw the Other down out of the sky, or to find protection from him, has instead had his own identity rapt up into the air. What the figure lying on the sand divines above him, at least, is a threatening congeries of father, Other, phantom, and his own elusive self, not a presence any longer but a task. It is at once an icon of cultural authority and an alienated identity sequestered by it that gazes down and accuses

the poet, and before which he prostrates himself at the poem's end.[72]
This closing confrontation thus empties out both the figure of voice that
governs Whitman's first two editions, turning self-presence into a remote
icon, and the benign vision of the Other that had permitted the reconciliations of *Calamus*.

Like the poem as a whole, however, this grim catachresis remains
enigmatic in its import. The ending of "As I Ebb'd" has something of
the force of revelation, as if the Other and the self lodged with it had
finally disclosed the forbidding aspects they always possessed. Yet the
sense of muffled outrage here is mingled with a forlorn quality suggestive
instead of abandonment: depicting an estrangement between the poet
and his enabling idols that seems definitive, "As I Ebb'd" poises between
blaming these figures for having been delusive fictions from the first and
trying to come to terms with what may instead be their altered attitude
toward him, their forsaking of a chosen vessel now left empty and bereft.

Like the rest of the poem, the closing lines of "As I Ebb'd" leave
equivocal whether this alternation toward the poet, if that is what it is,
has been caused by a mysterious change in his idols or was provoked by
some failing of the poet himself. The poem that marks an end to the
mythopoeic career of *Leaves of Grass* thus concludes on a note that
mingles bitterness and longing, humility and self-laceration. Whitman's
final line starkly dramatizes not only the changed relation between the
poet and his enabling fictions, but also the sharp ambivalence this estrangement occasions: "Whoever you are—we too lie in drifts at your
feet." Addressing the distant figure to whom his former powers now
belong, the poet seems at once accusatory and abject. His distant and
bitter "Whoever you are" repays the mockery "the real ME" had earlier
directed at the poet; yet the poet then declares his own abasement, in a
phrase that mingles submission with a hint of scorn. The enigmatic
figure in the sky, at once the Other who presides over *Calamus* and the
presence who governs Whitman's first two editions, has now withdrawn,
apparently betraying the poet he should have sustained. Yet the poet
behaves as if the responsibility for this debacle might be his own. Whitman's unreconciled leave-taking thus clings to the very terms it tries to
lay to rest; the poet of "As I Ebb'd" is still in thrall to the myths that
mock him.

If we assume the sort of panoramic perspective the poem's concluding
scenes invite, viewing "As I Ebb'd with the Ocean of Life" as the end of

a long trajectory that begins with "Song of Myself," it is especially the transumptive vision of omnipotent identity to which Whitman bids equivocal farewell here. the tramp recalls the god, and the poem renames the powers of poetry, acutest at their vanishing.

Notes

1. See Erkkila 267–73 for a discussion of Whitman's late work as a partial evasion of post–Civil War political, social, and economic developments.
2. On the poem's avoidance of closure see Dayan 1054–55 and Larson 118–21.
3. See chapter 4, 95–102 and 129–32, above.
4. Dayan discerns a "perpetual, liberated *sparagmos*" (1055) in section fourteen of the poem (1855 36). I take up the passage she discusses, from a different vantage, on 381.
5. For a discussion of these passages, see chapter 4, 149, above.
6. On this sense of the body in Whitman's work see Anderson, *Imperial Self* 102–18, especially 115.
7. On this point see Larson, who notes a tension "Between the everything the self vows to encompass and the nothing it gets reduced to in taking on a discernible shape to confirm that calling . . ." (140). Larson goes on to suggest that "the moment conception is delivered over into visible, realized form is also the moment of overburdening, hypertrophy, and stoppage" (140).
8. One key difference between introjection and fantasmatic incorporation, according to Abraham and Torok, is that the former is mediated by language, whereas the latter forecloses linguistic representation; introjection is thus properly a symbolic operation (see "Introjection—Incorporation" 5–6). Yet the imaginary operations of the Lacanian mirror stage already establish the subject-object division that naming and syntax will formalize. See Lacan, *Ecrits* 2, and Kristeva, *Revolution in Poetic Language* 46.
9. On this mediated or specular origin of one's own stabilized body image, see Lacan, "The mirror stage as formative of the function of the I," *Ecrits* 1–7.
10. On Whitman's genteel, conventional portraiture see Anderson, *Imperial Self* 103.
11. Anderson describes this dialectic of the body in Whitman's work: see *Imperial Self* 139–52.
12. See for example section nineteen of "Song of Myself," lines 372–76 (1855 42).
13. See for example the account of the runaway slave who stops at the poet's house: section ten, lines 183–92 (1855 33–34).

14. See V 1:59 for subsequent versions of this passage. Erkkila provides an illuminating account of the lines that follow those I quote, clearing up some of their obscurities by convincing appeal to Hicksite notions of the incarnation. See *Whitman the Political Poet* 111–12.

15. See Thomas 16–30, for an excellent discussion of how Whitman's portraits of urban life and artisanal activity both reflect and resist the effects of emergent capitalism on city and work-place. See Erkkila, *Whitman the Political Poet* 10–24, for an analysis of Whitman's roots in the artisan republicanism of New York City. Both Thomas and Erkkila draw on Wilentz's monumental *Chants Democratic*; see especially 107–42, on the bastardization of the artisan workshop.

16. Anderson locates a similar quality even in Whitman's portraits of the poet's body; see *Imperial Self* 104.

17. On the "accidental and erratic" quality of the figures in Wordsworth's poems of fancy, see Ferguson 65–66.

18. On the pragmatics and politics of figuration, see the Emersonian title essay of Kenneth Burke's *The Philosophy of Literary Form*, especially 3–8.

19. Inasmuch as Bakhtin allows room for "novelized" poetry—Pushkin's work is his prime example—"poetic style" serves as something of a trope here; but Bakhtin surely isolates a stance toward language intrinsic to the lyric. On novelization in poetry see Bakhtin 287n12; on Pushkin's *Evgenij Onegin* see 322–23.

20. See especially PW 2:562–63.

21. On this aspect of Whitman's idiom see James E. Miller, *Walt Whitman* 136–44; Matthiessen 526–32; and Asselineau 2:225–38.

22. Whitman's idiomatic play here is quite close to Pound's in the latter's free translations of Propertius: compare "I do not decline to be the poet of wickedness also" with "Where bold hands may do violence to my person," or "Who so indecorous as to shed the pure gore of a suitor?!" (*Personae* 212). My discussion of the social implications of Whitman's verbal wit is indebted to James E. Miller: see *Walt Whitman* 138–43.

23. I derive this notion of the function of the sentimental from Lynda Zwinger, *Daughters, Fathers, and the Novel*.

24. Such attempts to make the poem exhibit structural neatness are admittedly not now much in fashion; I follow a number of recent commentators in jettisoning this project.

25. On this paradox see Larson 47.

26. I owe this point to Kenneth Koch, who suggested it in a lecture at Columbia University some years ago; my discussion of this section of "Song of Myself," as well as my analysis of Whitman's idiomatic wit, is indebted to Koch's lectures.

27. We might also recall Hartman's suggestion that apostrophe and the vocative are attenuations of ritual performative power (*Beyond Formalism* 287–88);

section six tempers the more forceful claims of the first five sections of "Song of Myself" in this regard, as in others.

28. This poem appeared only in the 1860 edition; see V 2:378. For this and other *Calamus* poems omitted from the deathbed edition, I have employed the titles given by the editors of the *Variorum* (taken, like the titles Whitman gave the poems he retained, from their opening lines); I have omitted the brackets that surround these titles in the *Variorum*.

29. Further on in *Whitman the Political Poet*, Erkkila qualifies this thesis. While she argues that the earliest-written poems in the sequence, first grouped as "Live-Oak with Moss," constitute a retreat from politics, she suggests that, in the *Calamus* sequence as a whole, homosexual comradeship itself becomes a figure for political possibility. At the same time, she also modifies her view of Whitman's homosexual love poetry as a displacement of political malaise, suggesting that *Calamus* is genuinely motivated by "private homosexual feeling" (179). Erkkila nonetheless suggests either that the politics of *Calamus* marks a retreat, albeit strategic, from the more inclusive democratic commitments of the first two editions, or that the sequence is itself split between exclusive homosexual and inclusive democratic ambitions (152–54, 178–83). I shall be arguing for an obverse interpretation of *Calamus* as a significant expansion of the poet's commitments and an intensification of his engagement with others.

30. Anderson and Zweig both hypothesize that this shift in the poetry parallels a shift in Whitman's life: see Anderson, "Whitman's New Man" 33 and 47, and Zweig 301. While Shively argues that Whitman was already an active homosexual as early as the late 1830s, he suggests an emotional breakthrough similar to the one Anderson and Zweig posit: "While there is considerable evidence of Whitman's homosexual liaisons as early as 1836, there were no lovers until [Fred] Vaughan" (30).

31. I have regularized the text printed by Bowers, eliminating the vertical lines he inserts to indicate the places within a single line of verse where Whitman switched from one line of his notebook to the succeeding one. This manuscript passage has drawn a good deal of attention: see for example Zweig 296–97; Shively (190) restores these lines to the text of "In Paths Untrodden" he chooses to print.

32. Martin (75) anticipates Zweig's argument here, as does Anderson ("Whitman's New Man" 32–33).

33. On Whitman's characteristic aversion to narrative, and on the way *Calamus* departs from this stance, see Anderson, "Whitman's New Man" 24–27 and 32–33.

34. After 1860, "States!" was revised into two separate poems: the *Calamus* poem "For You O Democracy" and the *Drum-Taps* piece "Over the Carnage Rose Prophetic a Voice." Most of the lines I quote, however, appear in neither poem. See V 2:371–75.

35. This designation of the poet's productions as "carols" or songs is less typical

of *Calamus* than of Whitman's earlier work; and even here the poet's songs
are legacies, not emanations of his living presence.

36. Following Bowers's suggestion that the twelve poems which make up the
manuscript sequence "Live-Oak with Moss," the earliest-composed of
the poems later included in *Calamus*, "appear to be highly unified and
to make up an artistically complete story of attachment, crisis, and renunciation" (lxvi), critics have tended to regard Whitman's original focus as
personal and private, and to consider the public-minded aspect of *Calamus*
as the result of a later attempt on Whitman's part to legitimate such
intimate concerns. See for example Kaplan 239, Zweig 301–06, and Erkkila
152–54 and 179–83. But a preoccupation with group mores pervades
Calamus, surfacing repeatedly even in "Live-Oak with Moss": "Recorders
Ages Hence" was part of this early group, as were "This Moment
Yearning and Thoughtful" (1860 367), "What Think You I Take My
Pen in Hand?" (1860 372–73), "I Dream'd in a Dream" (1860 373), and
"To a Western Boy" (1860 377) (Bowers lxiv). James E. Miller treats
the hypothesis of progressive distantiation skeptically (*Critical Guide*
59–60).

37. See especially Martin 51–52 and Killingsworth 97–102. On the historical
production of discourses of homosexuality see Foucault 101.

38. Whitman's judgment is partially seconded by Freud: in his speculations on
the autobiography of Dr. Schreber, *Psycho-Analytic Notes Upon an Autobiographical Account of a Case of Paranoia (Dementia Paradoides)*, Freud
not only argues that sublimated homosexual impulses are a crucial contrib-
utor to "comradeship, to *esprit de corps* and to the love of mankind in
general" but also suggests that "it is precisely manifest homosexuals, and
among them again precisely those that struggle against an indulgence in
sensual acts, who distinguish themselves by taking a particularly active share
in the general interests of humanity. . ." (*Collected Papers* 3:447). *Calamus*
foregoes Freud's qualification.

39. Killingsworth (97–111) suggests that Whitman's "sentimental" treatment
of homosexuality is strategic, though he has in mind not so much the
sequence's political claims as its yoking of homosexual acts with bourgeois
idealizations of male friendship.

40. See *Elementary Structures of Kinship* 478–97 for Lévi-Strauss's crucial
reversal of the apparent cause-effect relation between incest and exogamy:
Lévi-Strauss argues that the incest taboo comes into being in order to insure
exogamy, which itself makes culture possible and gives it its first grammar
of relations.

41. Partly unsuccessful, as it turned out. Erkkila (311) focuses on the attendant
historical irony: while *Children of Adam* was vilified as immoral because of
its portrayal of female sexuality, *Calamus* provoked little disapproval in an
America intent on repressing the very existence of homosexuality. Killingsworth (98–102) sees this oversight as a consequence of Whitman's care-

fully coded rhetoric, designed to speak to the initiated while speaking past those who had no wish to hear.

42. See Shively 36–50 on Whitman's relation to Fred Vaughan, memorialized in *Calamus*.

43. On the impropriety of the so-called proper name, see Derrida, *Grammatology* 107–18. In this critique of *Tristes Tropiques* as throughout his extended reading of Lévi-Strauss, Derrida claims to be drawing out the radical implications of Lévi-Strauss's own insights.

44. According to Derrida the function of the posited "center" of any structure is to stand for this impossible possibility; see "Structure, Sign, and Play" 247–48.

45. "I Saw in Louisiana a Live-Oak Growing" (*Calamus* 20) is one of the original "Live-Oak with Moss" poems (Bowers lxiv); "These I Singing in Spring" (*Calamus* 4) was composed after Whitman completed "Live-Oak with Moss" but before he sent the partial manuscript for the 1860 edition to Rome Brothers (Bowers li). See Bowers lxvii on the relation between live-oak and calamus-root.

46. Lacan suggests that this barring of *jouissance* which defines eroticism once it assumes its signifying function already shadows biological possibility: beyond the pleasure principle, itself organically unsustainable, there is no absolute *jouissance;* see *Ecrits* 319. On the relation between these two sources of lack see *Four Fundamental Concepts* 204–5.

47. Since I have been drawing heavily on Lacan here, it may be useful to adumbrate the pertinent arguments, which center on the psychic consequences of the symbolic kinship structures Lévi-Strauss describes, and of the Oedipal relations which are their remainder within the bourgeois nuclear family.

Like Lévi-Strauss, Lacan situates the requisitioning of the subject to serve as a signifier in kinship structures at a level anterior to our individual assumption of language and the symbolic relations to our objects it installs. There is always, Lacan suggests,

before any formation of the subject, of a subject who thinks, who situates himself in it—the level at which there is counting, things are counted, and in this counting he who counts is already included. It is only later that the subject has to recognize himself as such, recognize himself as he who counts. (*Four Fundamental Concepts* 20)

The kinship structures that take us up to serve as signifiers may indeed be the origin of signification itself:

It is at the level of matrimonial alliance, as opposed to natural generation, to biological lineal descent—at the level therefore of the signifier—that the fundamental exchanges take place and it is there that we find once again that the most elementary structures of social functioning are inscribed in the terms of a combinatory.

The integration of this combinatory into sexual reality raises the question of whether it is not in this way that the signifier came into the world, into the world of man. (*Four Fundamental Concepts* 150–51)

As the *Calamus* sequence will also suggest, the expropriation of identity thereby initiated is registered not only psychically, but also on our very bodies, most graphically in the scarification and tattooing rituals during which the body's surface is quite literally inscribed. As in the variety of less violent and explicit cultural rituals through which the body is structured, what is proscribed in such rites is the erotic self-completion of *jouissance*. As the Lacanian journal *Scilicit* suggests:

in so far as *jouissance* is auto-erotic, there is a limit or bar imposed on it. This is what is meant by saying that the Oedipus complex constitutes *jouissance* as forbidden by relying on paternal law. . . . (*Feminine Sexuality* 117)

Sexuality, most especially but not exclusively in its genital manifestation, must be structured in such a way that the subject will henceforth seek his erotic objects along the possible routes prescribed by kinship structures:

the genital drive is subjected to the circulation of the Oedipus complex, to the elementary and other structures of kinship. (*Four Fundamental Concepts* 189)

Genital mutilation thus becomes the crucial sign of the body's expropriation. Circumcision serves as the ritual, symbolic mark of an expropriation registered at a fantasmatic level by the more drastic trope of castration, the lack of the phallus by which the image of the body is haunted. Symbolizing the law of the father which demands this sacrifice within patriarchy, the phallus comes also to stand for a *jouissance* now rendered unattainable:

Thus the erectile organ comes to symbolize the place of *jouissance,* not in itself, or even in the form of an image, but as a part lacking in the desired [maternal] image. . . . (*Ecrits* 320)

This moment of cut is haunted by the form of a bloody scrap—the pound of flesh that life pays in order to turn it into the signifier of the signifiers, which it is impossible to restore, as such, to the imaginary body; it is the lost phallus of the embalmed Osiris. (*Ecrits* 265)

Not ours, this *jouissance* and the phallus that signifies it must be present somewhere, a kind of compensation for what we have given up:

That there must somewhere be *jouissance* of the Other is the only possible check on the endless circulating of significations. . . . (*Feminine Sexuality* 117)

The passage . . . of the phallic image from one side to the other of the equation, from the imaginary to the symbolic, renders it positive. . . . the symbolic phallus that cannot be negated, the signifier of *jouissance.* (*Ecrits* 320)

The sexual relations structured by this law register both lack and the elusive, strictly unattainable *jouissance* held out as the end of desire.

48. On masquerade and the fetishization of women see also Irigaray, *Speculum* 103, 114–15, and 124; and *This Sex Which Is Not One* 170–91.

49. See also *Ecrits* 207: "women in the real order serve, if they'll forgive me saying so, as objects for the exchanges required by the elementary structures of kinship and which are sometimes perpetuated in the imaginary order, while what is transmitted in a parallel way in the symbolic order is the phallus."

50. On disavowal see Laplanche-Pontalis, *Language of Psychoanalysis* 118–21; on scotomization, see also the entry on the Lacanian concept of foreclosure (166–69).

51. Lacan thus makes room for what might be called male masquerade: "The fact that femininity takes refuge in this mask, because of the *Verdrängung* inherent to the phallic mark of desire, has the strange consequence that, in the human being, virile display itself appears as feminine" (*Feminine Sexuality* 85). On *parade*, Lacan's term for this kind of display, see Heath, especially 55–56.

52. On this point see Larson: "he underscores the truism that for the gift to retain its value it must remain in constant circulation, continuously available for use without being destroyed in its consumption" (165). Larson, however, reads *Calamus* as a lament for, rather than a celebration of, the power of poetry to promote such circulation: "In these songs of 'adhesiveness' . . . one detects a mounting despair over the efficacy of written documents, poetry foremost among them, to bond, mediate, or reconcile" (166).

53. The Lacanian analyst Jean Clavreul offers some observations rather strikingly applicable to this provocative aspect of the poet's speech acts, though he implies a much sharper distinction between "normal" acceptance of castration and "perverse" disavowal than I have been suggesting:

   The fact that these contracts are secret, that their terms and their practices are only known to those involved, does not in the least signify that the third party is absent. On the contrary: it is this absence of the third party, his being left out, that constitutes the *major element* of this strange contract. This third party, who is necessarily present to sign, or better, to countersign, the authenticity of a normal love relation, must here be excluded, or to be more precise, he is present but only insofar as he is blind or an accomplice or impotent. (218–19)

54. Though it intertwines with a moving impulse to confess his homosexuality more overtly, the poet's attempt to speak *for* this patterned energy proves equally comic: beginning histrionically—"Emblematic and capricious blades, I leave you—now you serve me not, / Away! I will say what I have to say, by itself" (1860 343)—it soon entangles itself in the ramifying mystery it claimed to leave behind. The manuscript version printed by Bowers is less bellicose, and more limited in its claims, focusing on confession but not proclaiming the power of unmediated self-expression:

   Do not any longer hide yourselves, you timid leaves,
   Do not remain down there, so ashamed, blossoms of my breast!

> Come I am determined to unbare my breast—I have stifled and choked too long
> I will escape from the costume, the play which was proposed to me
> I will sound myself and love [. . . .] (72)

55. See also *Four Fundamental Concepts* 204–5.

56. On the dead father see Lacan, *Ecrits* 199 and 237; on the relation of the dead father to the fading of the self, see *Ecrits* 300.

57. This mechanism both resembles and effectively reverses prosopopoeia as de Man describes it, since Whitman here dramatizes his own fading and the appearance of his inheritors, rather than the reverse.

58. This is Lacan's translation of and commentary on Freud's dictum, "Wo es war, soll Ich werden," translated in *New Introductory Lectures* as "Where id was, there shall ego be" (71). For Lacan's discussion of the difficulties with the standard French and English renderings of Freud's phrase, see *Ecrits* 128–29. See also *Ecrits* 171: "The end that Freud's discovery proposes for man was defined by him at the apex of his thought in these moving terms: *Wo es war, soll Ich werden*. I must come to the place where that was."

59. Dayan (1056–57) maps Whitman's 1855 vocabulary for identity against his 1860 terms, though her argument differs from mine.

60. "As I Ebb'd with the Ocean of Life" was composed after Whitman mailed the preliminary manuscript of the 1860 edition to Rome Brothers for typesetting; only nine of the forty-five *Calamus* poems were written during this period; see Bowers li.

61. Anderson makes the latter point in his analysis of "As I Ebb'd" ("Whitman's New Man" 32–33).

62. Whitman's syntax is oblique here: I read "we" as "me and mine"; the "phantom" is doing the "looking" and "following."

63. The exclamation point, and with it something of the bitterness of tone, disappears from the first of these lines in 1881. See V 2:321.

64. While not part of "Live-Oak with Moss," "Trickle Drops" pre-dates Whitman's delivery of copy material to Rome Brothers (Bowers li and lxiv).

65. I am indebted as well to Bloom's suggestion that "the entire poem is remarkable as a version of *kenosis*, of Whitman undoing the Whitmanian bardic self of *Song of Myself*" (*A Map of Misreading* 180).

66. On Romantic, and especially Coleridgean, synecdoche, see Hodgson, especially 273–78 and 282–88. Here Whitman empties out the poetics of immanence with which such an understanding of synecdoche intertwines.

67. On metonymy in "As I Ebb'd" see Bloom, *A Map of Misreading* 180; but Bloom sees Whitman's synecdoche as "a restituting representation" (181), whereas I see it as undercut by dispersive metonymy.

68. Saussure (114–22) suggests that just this redefinition moves us beyond essentialism to a proper understanding of the constitutive power of the sign. See also Lacan, *Ecrits* 149–54.

69. I quote the 1871 text, which is more explicit and emphatic in its inclusion

of the poet among the things signified by the "little shreds." In place of the two lines quoted, the 1860 text has simply, "These little shreds shall, indeed, stand for all" (1860 197).

70. See chapter 5, 248, above.
71. See Killingsworth (62–73) and Erkkila (308–16) on Whitman's generally anti-Victorian but decidedly ambivalent treatment of female sexuality and maternity.
72. I follow Anderson in seeing the "You" the poet addresses here as at least in part an image of his own estranged identity ("Whitman's New Man" 47).

8. Vistas

EPICTITUS
(Description of a Wise Man)
[....]
All his desires depend on things within his power.
[....]
He observes himself with the nicety of an enemy or spy, and looks on his own wishes as
betrayers.

—UPP 2:94

the fear of conflicting and irreconcilable interiors, and the lack of a common skeleton,
knitting all close, continually haunts me.

—Democratic Vistas, PW 2:368

It is a truism of Whitman criticism, and a useful one, that after 1860 the
poet of the body gradually gives way to the poet of the soul. As M.
Jimmie Killingsworth notes, taking up a long line of commentary, the
incendiary sexual stance that energizes Whitman's first three editions
metamorphoses into the grimly sublimated eros of *Drum-Taps* and
Memoranda During the War, and then disappears (131–54).[1] C. Carroll
Hollis offers a different account of the change that overtook *Leaves of
Grass* after 1860: Whitman's fascination with performative utterance,
and with poetry as speech act, is replaced by an increasingly disabling
commitment to a poetry of statement; illocutionary acts, in Austin's
terms, give way to locutionary ones (Hollis 88–123).[2] These changes
can be understood as part of a single shift, involving the poet's presence:
the magical body that redefines eros by assuming the contours voice
suggests, incarnating the performative word, scarcely makes an appearance in the poems Whitman wrote after 1860.

The mythology of the body that shapes Whitman's early editions does
resurface sporadically in later work; it appears less often in Whitman's
poems than in his prose, which as Betsy Erkkila has recently argued

increasingly became the focus of Whitman's creative energies (*Whitman the Political Poet* 273, 293). A much-diminished avatar of the poet's pneumatic body turns up in *Specimen Days*.[3] And in *Democratic Vistas*, Whitman broods over the sort of self-divided body that haunts his early editions. Like much of Whitman's work after 1860, the passages in which this fragmented body image appears are concerned quite explicitly with political matters:

Society, in these States, is canker'd, crude, superstitious and rotten [. . . .]

I say we had best look our times and lands searchingly in the face, like a physician diagnosing some deep disease [. . . .] The underlying principles of the States are not honestly believ'd in, (for all this hectic glow, and these melodramatic screamings,) nor is humanity itself believ'd in. What penetrating eye does not everywhere see through the mask? (*Democratic Vistas* PW 2:369)

Here the body clearly becomes what a number of recent commentaries on Whitman's work suggest that it already is in the early editions of *Leaves of Grass*: a trope for the body politic. The "cankered" body was indeed a rather commonplace image, during the period, for social corruption.[4]

It is worth noting, however, that even in the context of *Democratic Vistas* Whitman's figure is by no means a transparent or neutral vehicle. These passages are filled with a strange intensity, lodged precisely in the detail Whitman lavishes on his metaphor. In *Democratic Vistas* this vehicle not quite reducible to its tenor may serve to imply that the massive economic and social transformations currently re-shaping the American republic will have dire consequences for individual selves and bodies. The essay is a trenchant critique of the political repercussions of technological explosion; the dangers by which the body image is plagued, which arise from both unbridled materialism and the alienation of labor that accompanies industrial expansion, are accordingly those of uncontrolled, monstrous growth and grotesque self-division:[5]

It is as if we were somehow being endow'd with a vast and more and more thoroughly-appointed body, and then left with little or no soul. (PW 2:370)

The fear of conflicting and irreconcilable interiors, and the lack of a common skeleton, knitting all close, continually haunts me. (PW 2:368)

The ideological work these passages perform depends partly on this parallel: Whitman enlists our energies to combat the ills of the body politic by awaking primordial anxieties concerning analogous dangers that implicitly threaten our individual bodies.

Yet in Whitman's work the dangers the body politic poses to the body are by no means confined to the damaging effects of the particular economic and social changes lamented in *Democratic Vistas*; nor are they adequately described by the sort of homological relation we have just noted. As we have seen, what provokes anxiety in Whitman's earlier writing is not simply the prospect that social pathology will lead to analogous individual pathology, but the belief that socialization is inherently threatening to identity; if social malfunction destroys our proper autonomy, in *Leaves of Grass* such malfunction emerges as pervasive. In these passages from *Democratic Vistas,* this more inclusive threat posed by social formations is registered only indirectly. Whitman's figure of the body, which is still overdetermined, can also be interpreted according to a peculiar logic of displacement we have already seen at work in his language theory. In *The Primer of Words,* we noted, Whitman can be found obsessively protecting words themselves against the very violence words supposedly do to persons and things; here in *Democratic Vistas* he struggles to defend the body politic against aggressions that social mechanisms themselves are elsewhere said to inflict on the body proper. At this level, Whitman's figure obeys the logic not of homology but of a slippage somewhat harder to track: what looks like analogy turns out to be agon instead. The rapt attention Whitman devotes to his rhetorical figure suggests that the vehicle-tenor relation functions to some degree as a screen: what is in part a trope for the body politic is also a means for continuing to worry the disastrous impact socialization itself has on individuals and their bodies.

In *Democratic Vistas* such rhetorical overdetermination is sporadic rather than sustained; it disturbs but no longer controls the unfolding or the significance of a discourse that is primarily political. We can understand *Democratic Vistas* well enough even if we disregard such complexity and treat Whitman's images of the body simply as the tropes they claim to be. It is precisely to the degree that this sort of allegorizing ceases to be problematic, however, that we have left behind the imaginative universe of the first three editions of *Leaves of Grass*. There the poet's body exists as an entity in its own right; Whitman's overt attempts to allegorize this presence are only occasional. Moreover, to the extent that the body which dominates Whitman's early editions does function as a trope for the social body, it serves less as a mere analogy than as a magically redemptive synecdoche: the transfigured body politic the poet's body implies would be difficult to realize by any means except the idiosyncratic ones that are made to figure it. Yet the effect this image of presence has on our conception of political union and our relation to it is hardly exhausted by even this magical synecdochic role. The latent antagonism between body politic and individual body that we noted in *Democratic Vistas* is both more striking and more important in the early *Leaves of Grass*; the body which supposedly figures social cohesion and consensus may indeed perform the contrary function of making them seem expendable.

Such slippage is crucial to the 1855 and 1856 editions. While my reading of Whitman's image of voice has pretty much bracketed the cultural function of the poet's presence, in order to attend to this figure's peculiar contours and the transfigured mode of identity they imply, I mean my analysis to have bearing on the question of Whitman's ideological role. More particularly, I hope to counter recent suggestions that this role depends primarily on the way the poet's body tropes the body politic, a figurative operation typically explicated by appeal to homology. The complex ideological work Whitman's poetry performs tends to disappear if we take this approach. We can best understand the ambivalent labor the poet's presence performs on behalf of an ideology of consensus by attending not only to the partial congruence but also to the opposition between his body and the polity for which it supposedly stands.

1. Whitman himself sometimes declares that the poet's body serves as a double for the body of the republic, and we can certainly understand part of the cultural function of *Leaves of Grass* by interpreting the connection between poet and nation in the homological terms he proposes.[6] Some of the peculiar traits of the poet's presence—but not all— can be adequately understood as attempts to model particular social values, a mobilization of the body by no means confined to literary representation. A careful look at the dominant preoccupations which members of a culture exhibit concerning their bodies, anthropologist Mary Douglas suggests, can tell us a good deal about the social formation to which they belong. Douglas argues that the body is enlisted as a symbolic site, its functions being regulated so as to model especially

crucial or precarious social values. Following this lead, Betsy Erkkila has begun to perform the sort of detailed analysis of Whitman's portraits of the body that might suggest the particular social values it is meant to incarnate.[7] She attends as well to the fact that social conflicts make the body a contested site in culture, so that images of it can be deployed polemically to suggest the ascendancy of certain cultural values over others, rather than merely to replicate an invariant social structure.[8] Erkkila argues, for example, that the indiscriminate sexual receptivity of the poet's body should be understood as representing a social inclusiveness crucial to America's often ignored or vitiated egalitarian ideals (*Whitman the Political Poet* 102–3).

It is worth pursuing this approach in a bit more detail here, in order to get a feel for both its utility and its limits. The terminology Douglas proposes in *Natural Symbols* might help us specify the social values the poet's body serves in part to exhibit.[9] Douglas distinguishes cultures according to the value they attach to determinants of social structure she terms "group" and "grid." "Group," she notes in explanation of her terms, "is obvious—the experience of a bounded social unit. Grid refers to rules which relate one person to others. . . . [Strong] grid and group may be found together. In this case the quality of relations is ordered and clearly bounded" (viii). Such cultural values will be mapped onto individuals. Discussing the "group" variable, Douglas notes of the individual body:

Interest in its apertures depends on the preoccupation with social exits and entrances, escape routes and invasions. If there is no concern to preserve social boundaries, I would not expect to find concern with bodily boundaries. (*Natural Symbols* 70)

Whitman, of course, is by no means heedless of such boundaries—he is intensely preoccupied with them. But he insists that the surfaces of the poet's body are permeable rather than rigid; this body is indeed almost infinitely receptive, an omnivorous mouth being one of its crucial synecdoches. In this respect it figures one important vision of the body of the republic, the boundaries of which were a national obsession throughout Whitman's life; while Whitman came to have his doubts about some of the implications of Manifest Destiny, he was on the whole an enthusiastic champion of American expansion.[10]

Like the attitudes of many of his contemporaries, Whitman's responses to immigration were more ambivalent. A series of newspaper editorials he wrote in 1842 supposedly helped precipitate the New York No-Popery riot.[11] Yet in the aftermath of the disturbance he had helped cause, Whitman announced a commitment to inclusiveness he afterwards continued to affirm: "We go for the widest liberty—the widest extension of immunities of the people, as well as the blessings of government. Let us receive these foreigners to our shores, and to our good offices" (*Walt Whitman of the New York Aurora* 83).[12] Whitman's omnivorous poet embodies this inclusive sense of American citizenship as well as of American territorial claims.

On the evidence of *Leaves of Grass,* however, the danger against which Whitman had inveighed before the No-Popery riot continued to preoccupy him. He had written in the New York Aurora before the clash:

We have taken high American ground [. . . .] There are a thousand dangerous influences operating among us—influences whose tendency is to assimilate this land in thought, in social customs, and, to a degree, in government, with the moth eaten systems of the old world. Aurora is imbued with a deadly hatred to all these influences; she wages open, heavy, and incessant war against them. (*Walt Whitman of the New York Aurora* 117)

If America was going to be inclusive, the immigrants it admitted thus had to be transformed into American individuals, rather than being allowed to turn America's body into a foreign one: "group," that is, needed to be simultaneously open and cohesive. *Democratic Vistas* suggests that the poet can play a crucial role in developing such new democratic allegiances by encouraging fealty to key national values. In *Leaves of Grass* this shared cultural space depends for its realization on what might be thought of somewhat crudely as the poet's gastric juices: in Whitman's catalogues the poet not only seems to internalize but also to blend us, wearing away enough of our idiosyncrasies to turn us into interfused American selves. These peculiar powers of the poet's body might be understood as attempts to call up analogous resources of the body politic.

This digestive operation has the added advantage of wearing away what Douglas terms "grid." If the somaticized space into which the poet's presence melds us is conspicuously undifferentiated, Douglas notes of such indistinction that at the level of social philosophy this image corresponds to an optimism about the possibility of society remaining undifferentiated: injustice can be rectified merely by purging the system of internal traitors allied with outside enemies. It produces political negativism. (*Natural Symbols* ix)[13]

Here "negativism" means not pessimism but something like the "no government" position important to the American political rhetoric of Whitman's day.[14] The poet's body serves in part to figure the sort of extravagantly undifferentiated polity that seemed all the more valuable to many Americans as the prospects of maintaining any semblance of it dwindled with progressive industrialization, political factionalism, and sectional strife. In the poet's inclusive body not only foreignness but also the invidious social differentiation that threatened to compromise the demotic indistinction of the body politic are dissolved; in *Leaves of Grass* we come to inhabit the socially fluid American space the poet's somatic resources define.

There is something inherently satisfying about such neat ratios. They hold out the promise that whatever seems overbearing or strange about the poet's presence ultimately obeys an over-arching rationale, fitting into a political program neither idiosyncratic nor undemocratic. This pleasing symmetry and the shared cultural values it supposedly illus-trates, however, are by no means the only sources of the poet's appeal. The tenuous quality of the political claims the poet's presence can be taken to figure, and the indispensable role played by the poet's body in displaying them, already strain this proportional logic; other aspects of the poet's presence, we shall see in a moment, flagrantly vio-late it.

We need to note that the homology between the poet's body and the American body politic is performative rather than constative. We have to do, that is, not with an achieved correspondence between hegemonic cultural values and individual bodies, but with the capacity of an idio-syncratic body image, made malleable by individual imagination, to give form to, and thus make compelling, one particular social agenda—an agenda that was in Whitman's day increasingly embattled, though the grammar of *Leaves of Grass* makes its reality not retrospective but present or prospective.[15] The poet's body becomes a talismanic site in which otherwise elusive ideals are incarnated.

If we can interpret the salient characteristics of the poet's presence in part according to a syllogistic logic—the desirable traits of the body politic determining what qualities the poet's presence should possess—we thus need to attend as well to the operation of what might be called a logic of performative metaphor, in which the peculiar qualities of Whitman's vehicle make conceivable the very tenor for which it allegedly stands. The polity the poet's presence implies might therefore be termed utopian, since it exceeds possible as well as actual achievement: both the absolute omnivorousness of the poet's body and its perfect internal indistinction, for example, suggest a body politic that is not merely unrealized but strictly unrealizable. But we should perhaps call the vision the poet's presence figures apocalyptic instead: the poet's body suggests not simply the perfecting but the triumphant self-immolation of social forms, a limit at which polity passes over into something else. As we noted in chapter 7, the presence which both contains and inhabits us suggests not just a perfectly equitable circulation of resources, but a magical glut that would render exchange itself superfluous. Here the social body appears to transcend itself, putting an end to the laws of exchange that according to Lévi-Strauss define it. While the details of Whitman's figuration are certainly peculiar to *Leaves of Grass,* it is by no means unprecedented that an uncanny image of the individual body should figure this apocalypse: what presents itself to us as the triumphant self-transcendence of sociality may necessarily borrow its images from another order of experience, being generated as a displaced version of archaic, fantasmatic material.[16]

If the possible homology between the poet's body and the body politic thus ultimately implies a passage beyond politics, it at least suggests the consummation rather than the subversion of social purposes: exchange, as it were, passes out of existence by assuming a form in which its function is definitively fulfilled. But even this sort of performative homology fails to explain crucial sources of the poet's appeal. Other aspects of the poet's presence, to which we have already attended at length, suggest not the apocalyptic fulfillment of politics but a fantasy of exemption from the very polity the poet supposedly incarnates; these implications arise from the antagonism rather than the possible correspondence between the two terms whose relation we have been tracing.

We need not belabor the ways in which the poet's body renders him immune to the social imperatives he is often said to secure, since they have been a principal focus of this study; but this immunity is crucial

not just to the imaginative universe of *Leaves of Grass* but more especially to the ideological work Whitman's poems perform. We noted that
the figure who supposedly embodies social exchange, as it were becoming the god or the gift the rest of us circulate, has managed to excuse
himself from the rule of exchange he purportedly incarnates. We should
also remember that his fluid body seems to elude the gaze and the law
associated with it, enjoying an archaic indistinction that subverts the
very notion of organized circulation. We cannot adequately understand
these aspects of the poet's presence in terms of the homological model
with which we have been dealing: it will not quite do, for example, to
see these traits as figuring the "no government" position mentioned
earlier, since they permit not a redefinition of social space but an escape
from it.

The appeal of the poet's presence may well depend largely on such
regressive fantasies. But the ideological work this figure performs inheres
more particularly in the way it manages to yoke archaic satisfactions to
social allegiances strictly incompatible with them. The body that incarnates the American polity is also a body whose capacities suggest a
refusal of socialization. A celebration of American community that centers on the ritual manifestation of the poet's presence may thus be
equivocal in its import, since we are likely to be reveling in a fantasized
immunity to the very solidarity we are busy praising. Yet it is just this
equivocation that makes the poet's presence a powerful if peculiar instrument of American consensus: channeled through the body of the
poet, a stratum of fantasies potentially inimical to social bonds is enlisted in a vision of community loosely compatible with a millennial
interpretation of the American errand. Imbuing democratic consensus
with satisfactions it cannot properly provide, the poet's presence paradoxically helps recruit us to a political vision it both figures and exceeds.[17] The ideological work performed by Whitman's image of the
body thus depends less on the homology than on the slippage between
this figure and the body politic for which it is made to stand—or more
precisely, on the way this slippage is both suggested and made to disappear.

2. A similar slippage, likewise illogically enlisted to support the consensus it should call into question, is crucial to the poet's efforts on behalf
of an American ideology of political and social succession. Transmission,

we have seen, is a central concern of *Leaves of Grass*; it was also an obsessive preoccupation of American politics and society, not only in the years leading up to the Revolution but also in its aftermath. The poet's presence both appeals to and transgresses a vision of beneficent transmission precariously maintained by the political and domestic rhetoric of Whitman's period. It thereby implies both the aggressive energies this rhetoric was mobilized to control or occlude and the anxieties that attended them—energies Whitman himself exhibited and anxieties by which he was conspicuously beset. Yet the tensions evoked by this figure serve paradoxically to affirm rather than subvert the idealized model of transmission put forward in Whitman's period, suggesting that even violent social forces and troubling individual desires and fears can be accommodated within a benign image of American succession, since they are already embodied and subsumed in the poet's inclusive and apparently beneficent presence.[18]

In Whitman's poems as in contemporary political discourse, familial relations are a favorite trope for inheritance of whatever sort and a preferred model for conceptualizing it. Whitman's 1855 "I Sing the Body Electric" accordingly counters the extended portraits of socially sanctioned degradation and enslavement it presents with a vision of familial succession as charmed as it is bucolic:

> I knew a man .... he was a common farmer .... he was the father of five
> sons .... and in them were the fathers of sons .... and in them were the
> fathers of sons.
>
> This man was a wonderful vigor and calmness and beauty of person;
> The shape of his head, the richness and breadth of his manners, the pale
> yellow and white of his hair and beard, the immeasurable meaning of his
> black eyes,
> These I used to go and visit him to see .... He was wise also,
> He was six feet tall .... he was over eighty years old .... his sons were
> massive clean bearded tanfaced and handsome,
> They and his daughters loved him .... all who saw him loved him .... they
> did not love him by allowance ... they loved him with personal love.
> (1855 118)

This portrait adheres faithfully to what Jay Fliegelman calls the discourse of sentimental paternity. As Fliegelman shows, in America this discourse played a crucial role in shaping not only familial behavior but also both Revolutionary and post-revolutionary political rhetoric. Assimilating the colonial situation to a filial one, Revolutionists argued that England, by acting like an unnatural, tyrannical parent, had forfeited its claim to American loyalties (Fliegelman 93–106). Based on Lockean premisses as well as Rousseauist variants, the "natural" relation between parent and child appealed to for contrastive force was essentially a sentimental one: "patriarchal family authority was giving way to a new parental ideal characterized by a more affectionate and equalitarian relationship with children" (Fliegelman 1). The topic of inheritance, broadly conceived as the transmission of adult prerogatives from one generation to the next, figured prominently both in what Fliegelman calls an anti-patriarchal familial rhetoric and in the American political discourse it helped shape:

The imposition of a protracted adolescence by one generation upon another was . . . [a] pernicious violation of the laws of nature. Indeed, such an imposition of "perpetual guardianship" was . . . the ultimate tyranny, a blow to the very process of history. . . . (Fliegelman 3)

Having helped children develop their proper powers, the sentimental parent supposedly then got out of their way. Such apparently self-limiting authority would be repaid by filial affection represented as not exacted but freely given (Fliegelman 9–35).

If Revolutionary rhetoric thus impugned English rule by associating it with parental power of the wrong sort, post-revolutionary discourse cast Washington in the role of what Fliegelman calls an anti-patriarchal father, deserving of affectionate, spontaneously granted loyalty (Fliegelman 199, 215). Yet while sentimental portraits of Washington helped instill a culturally important vision of America as a family whose cohesion and continuity depended on freely bestowed affection, the gloss they provided perhaps did not so much alter as occult the power relations endemic to transmission, relations by which American post-revolutionary politics and culture remained deeply troubled.[19] Though this is not the thrust of Fliegelman's account, he notes in conclusion that:

The pantheon of Revolutionary heroes, the godlike founding fathers, intimidated subsequent generations too young to remember the war and yet raised to reverence the nation's saviors. Feelings of filial inferiority contributed to the desire many felt to be free of the demands of filiopietism and to find a stage for their own heroism. (267)

George Forgie describes in starker terms this conflict experienced by America's post-revolutionary generations. Analyzing the eulogies offered in 1826 to Adams and Jefferson, the last of the heroic founders to die, he notes that they

contained a paradoxical double message: on the one hand, the fathers are gone, and a new generation has succeeded them to power; on the other, the fathers are immortal and they will always rule.... some people began to fear that the danger facing the Republic was not that these cords would snap, but that they would be used by the dead to strangle the living. (53)

The rhetoric of sentimental paternity which persisted in the political and familial argumentation of the post-revolutionary period can thus be understood only in part as a sign of continued allegiance to an intrinsically worthy ideal; it was also a kind of screen discourse, serving to fend off more troubling intimations.[20]

These concerned not only the intimidating heroism of the founders, but also the changing status of political and cultural power, and of the patriarchal authority with which it intertwined. As Michael Rogin suggests, America's post-revolutionary generations typically attributed these ominous changes to their own derelictions, preserving a sacrosanct image of the generation of the founding fathers, an image whose contrastive force might have either a regenerative or a paralyzing effect (14–15).[21] This contrast depended for its credibility on another—the supposed distinction between English and American authority examined by Fliegelman. Rogin draws out the problematic nature of this enabling dichotomy:

Republican rhetoric rightly pointed to a reality of English domination. But it also reflected the existence of repressed internal threats to the colonial household. "The innocent Children" (John Adams) were all too fascinated by lust, sadistic power, and conspiracy. They loaded upon parental England a weight of grievance it could not bear. They conjured up monstrous parents to preserve American innocence. (27)

The American social order also generated disharmony.... Revolutionaries blamed monarchical feudalism, hardly an American danger, for social inequality, love of money, and political domination. They averted their eyes from the internecine, personalized factional conflict endemic to the colonies, and from the commodity capitalism beginning to sprout from household soil. (28)

As Rogin notes, those coercive tendencies had been produced by unprecedented economic and social change. Crucial sources of social anxiety in post-revolutionary America thus in one sense had little to do with problems of legal inheritance or transmission. The familial model, especially, might seem to be an inappropriate analogy for these difficulties, since the nascent commodity capitalism that produced dislocation as well as progress at least appeared to loosen family bonds and weaken patriarchal authority. Such changes had already begun to redefine the American family in important ways before the Revolution:

Seventeenth-century American fathers, controlling the disposition of land, kept grown sons under the paternal roof. By the beginning of the eighteenth century sons were marrying younger and settling on their own homesteads. The supply of land and the absence of a deeply rooted, aristocratic family undermined absolute paternal power. (Rogin 20–21)

This shift in familial arrangements was accelerated in the early nineteenth century by urbanization and industrialization. Yet the economic and social changes which in a sense fulfilled what Fliegelman calls an anti-patriarchal revolution hardly produced the liberation that sentimental rhetoric associated with it:

Revolution and rising capitalism weakened the authority of the leading families; ordinary fathers also faced a world in which their households were less central. Desiring advancement and enmeshed with the market, men did not feel as free as their doctrines told them they were. It was as if the ghosts of the royal governors had entered family and society. Americans experienced a mysterious and punitive paternal authority. (Rogin 54)

If Rogin is right, this ghostly persistence of the paternal term suggests that sentimental rhetoric served at least in part to extend patriarchal authority in the face of changing circumstances rather than simply curtail or neutralize it: associated by the sentimental model with supposedly benign supervision rather than direct intervention, the gaze of the fathers might appear to persist everywhere. American society, of course, continued to be patriarchal at the level of the sort of global symbolic operations to which Lévi-Strauss attends, if not at the level of economic functioning analyzed by Rogin. A more immediate source of this persistent association of economically generated anxieties with the paternal term was the deployment of sentimental rhetoric as a means of allaying the fears which industrial rationalization provoked. New institutions of social control were typically justified by appeal to the very domestic sphere and paternal supervision whose literal functions they increasingly supplanted:

An advocate of the new mental hospitals wrote, "The internal arrangements of the Asylum are nearly the same as those of a well-regulated family." . . . But the asylums, David Rothman has shown, were more like armies than families. They classified their inmates, dressed them in uniforms, drilled them, regimented their behavior, and strictly arranged and regulated their time.

The asylums, suggests Rothman, resembled the new factories. And the factories also claimed to act as family surrogates. Textile-mill owners promised the benefits of paternal supervision to the young girls who left their farm families to live and work under closely regimented supervision in the New England mill towns. Like those who promoted asylums, mill-owners appealed to family to legitimize new bureaucratic forms of control.

The Jacksonian era also witnessed the first extended efforts to defend slavery on paternal grounds. (Rogin 274)

This "new paternalism," Rogin notes, performed an important ideological function since it "disguised exploitation" (275). Yet the fears left unassuaged by sentimental rhetoric served paradoxically to make the paternal place an even more heavily freighted one: this rhetoric, after all, linked impersonal economic coercion and diffuse but powerful social control to a patriarchal term made to seem all the more ominous and unassailable because it transcended the power of actual fathers and possessed no tangible human embodiment.

In combination with the mix of jealousy and guilt directed toward the founding fathers, this complex intertwining of institutional and economic coercion with sentimental rhetoric helped assure that generational transmission, figured in familial terms and centering on the patriarchal role, would continue to be a crucial image for American social anxieties. Appeal to the rhetoric of sentimental paternity thus always risked provoking the turmoil it was meant to allay. Yet as Forgie notes, the sentimentalization of the founding fathers nonetheless reached new extremes in the 1850s, perhaps provoked by an increasingly desperate nostalgia:

The celebration of maternal values extended ultimately to the fathers themselves as, in the 1850s particularly, people began to comment on the feminine qualities in their characters. (188)

In the case of Washington, some accounts of the father of his country seemed prepared to transform him into the *mother* of his country. *Putnam's Monthly* suggested in 1854 that Washington's countenance grew more womanly as he grew older. (189)

Leaves of Grass participates in important ways in this rhetorical ground swell. Whitman's portraits of sentimental paternity include not only the sort of bucolic evocation of an anonymous patriarch we looked at earlier, but also scenes drawn from American public life; Whitman shares his period's tendency to make sentimental paternity a model for political authority and its transmission. The portrait of Washington in "The Sleepers" is a conspicuous instance:

> Now of the old war-days . . the defeat at Brooklyn;
> Washington stands inside the lines . . he stands on the entrenched hills amid a crowd of officers,
> His face is cold and damp . . . . he cannot repress the weeping drops . . . . he lifts the glass perpetually to his eyes . . . . the color is blanched from his cheeks,
> He sees the slaughter of the southern braves confided to him by their parents.
>
> The same at last and at last when peace is declared,
> He stands in the room of the old tavern . . . . the wellbeloved soldiers all pass through.
>
> The officers speechless and slow draw near in their turns,
> The chief encircles their necks with his arm and kisses them on the cheek,
> He kisses lightly the wet cheeks one after another . . . . he shakes hands and bids goodbye to the army. (1855 110)

Lincoln implicitly plays a similar role in "When Lilacs Last in the Dooryard Bloom'd." Like the rhetoric of the poem as a whole, a brief evocation of Lincoln near its end is clearly shaped by the tradition Fliegelman describes:

> With the lustrous and drooping star with the countenance full of woe,
> With the holders holding my hand nearing the call of the bird,
> Comrades mine and I in the midst, and their memory ever to keep, for the dead I loved so well,
> For the sweetest, wisest soul of all my days and lands—and this for his dear sake. (V 2:539, CRE 337)[22]

Leaves of Grass is nonetheless troubled by the less happy fantasies Rogin describes: as we saw in earlier chapters, images of sentimental transmission in Whitman's poems both occult and covertly register threats of coercion that Whitman associates with the proleptic authority of the fathers. These threats sometimes emerge more starkly. "The Sleepers," of course, itself provides a notable instance of such fantasies of paternal authority, in a passage we examined in chapter 4: the portrait of Washington offers a sentimental alternative to the vision of the poet as a justified Lucifer oppressed by an omnipotent patriarchal power Whitman presents as openly malign (1855 111).[23] And throughout Whitman's early editions, we have seen, the poet in his finite, unregenerated guise is repeatedly oppressed by a disembodied gaze we should associate with both the depersonalized institutional power Rogin describes and the paternal term with which he links it.

If the sentimental portraits Whitman intercalates in *Leaves of Grass* both encode and assuage these anxieties, offering an ostensibly softened image of paternal authority, the poet's transfigured presence can instead suggest a more radical cure than sentimental rhetoric recommends: he sometimes seems to abrogate the very transmission that occasions the fears sentimentality works to belie. He does so in part by means of his apparent powers of evasion: in his labile, elusive guise, which evokes Kristeva's *chora,* the poet seems to be exempt from the paternal law and the gaze by which he is elsewhere oppressed.

As we noted in chapter 6, however, Whitman is as fascinated by the positional power of the father as he is leery of it. *Leaves of Grass* thus also accords the poet the ability to wield the very force he elsewhere escapes or annuls, and in extremest form: his power of positing, we have seen, is supposedly magical rather than merely conventional. The poet thus effectively returns to the scene of the fathers' act of founding and goes them one better, bringing not just a nation but an entire world into being *ex nihilo;* the belatedness that oppressed Lincoln and Whitman's generation is abruptly overcome.[24] Moreover, the defects lurking in the fathers' act of founding are apparently avoided; but it is difficult to say whether this is due to the purging or the intensifying of the coercive effects of the political and social transmission they inaugurated. On the one hand, the poet who can speak things into being, creating what is natural rather than conventional, would seem to avoid the aggressions by which the patriarchal act of positing is plagued; the poet's self-contained presence seems to figure the unmortgaged identity his founding act should grant others as well. Yet his power can have the obverse effect of seeming to constrain us in perpetuity: in contrast to the self-limiting power which sentimental rhetoric at least overtly recommends, the poet's self-renewing speech acts seem to bind us to a founding moment and a foundational authority we can never escape or outvie. It is hard to know whether to think of this power as liberating us from the demands the fathers place upon us—to subject us, perhaps, to powers of a different sort—or as imposing upon us a more absolute, autocratic version of patriarchal social control.

The point I want to make here is that such possibilities are at odds with the stylized, indirect, and ostensibly self-limiting mode of authority recommended by the sentimental model crucial to the American ideology of transmission. Yet this is a model Whitman himself espouses. The poet, we have seen, is repeatedly imaged in just such sentimental terms:

> I lead no man to a dinner-table or library or exchange,
> But each man and each woman of you I lead upon a knoll,
> My left hand hooks you round the waist,
> My right hand points to landscapes of continents, and a plain public road.
>
> Not I, not any one else can travel that road for you,
> You must travel it for yourself. (1855 80)

The fact that the poet's overt pronouncements in such sentimental scenes hardly offer an adequate account of his transactions with us by no means makes them irrelevant to understanding his cultural role. Like the identification of the poet's body with the body politic, the assimilation of his acts of transmission to the sentimental model enshrined in American political rhetoric performs valuable ideological work precisely because of the contradictions the poet's amorphous, inclusive presence accommodates. Not only making overt the tremendous power still covertly residing in a sentimentalized paternal term, the poet is also not averse to wielding a version of this power that exceeds the stylized proprieties sentimental rhetoric instills. Whether surreptitiously avoiding transmission or redefining it in magical terms, the expansive figure who also appears in a sentimental guise thus serves to shelter under the rubric of benign consensus a number of features properly incompatible with it. To enter the polity which the poet's body and word imply is at one and the same time to escape from a fearful proleptic power; to identify with the agent who wields an overt, extreme, but ambiguous version of it; and to celebrate the supposedly wholly beneficent interpretation of this power which sentimental discourse recommends. We are permitted, in effect, both to exempt ourselves from succession and inheritance and the anxieties they provoke and to indulge in exercising the sort of frankly atavistic patriarchal powers sentimental rhetoric proscribes, while publicly celebrating a political transmission supposedly exempt from all such recalcitrant material.

This accommodation, of course, is quintessentially American. In estimating the cultural function of Whitman's figure of presence, we should thus attend not only to the disturbance of enlightened social norms this figure implies, but also to the normative uses to which such potential resistance is put. If we wish to stress Whitman's Americanness, we should indeed concentrate on this latter function. In Whitman's work archaic imaginative resources very much like the incendiary ones Kristeva describes are paradoxically put to the cultural uses Sacvan Bercovitch details: as in Emerson's work, a potentially anarchic individuality is deployed in such a way as to reinforce a figural American individualism.[25] Though crucial features of Whitman's work might lead us to group him with the revolutionists of poetic language whose practice Kristeva extols, his cultural function might on the whole better be described as a shoring up than as a subversion of ideological consensus.

But we should remember that the offering Whitman makes American culture is as ambiguous as it is ambivalent. The desires *Leaves of Grass* invites us to indulge will always remain irreducible to the social vision to which Whitman yokes them; this potentially disruptive remainder lurks in the very figure of consensus Whitman concocts.

3. The complex, overdetermined etiology of Whitman's figure of presence makes it unsurprising that this should be so. It would clearly be illegitimate to treat biographical material, in the particular form of Whitman's personal anxieties, as the exclusive determinants of the poet's presence. But we can point to such material as one crucial source of *Leaves of Grass;* it is particularly useful to do so in a critical climate inclined to privilege the sort of public concerns that can be adduced in support of the claim that the poet's body figures the body politic. That body also staves off fears and satisfies desires of a more intimate order.

Those fears and desires still crop up in the notebooks Whitman kept after the Civil War, a period during which his published writings were increasingly concerned with public, political matters. A series of entries from Whitman's notebook for the period 1868–1870, for example, concludes with a passage that seems like a belated attempt to resurrect the self-propagating and self-contained poet of the 1855 and 1856 editions, who by the 1860s had ceased to dominate Whitman's poetry:[26]

Outline sketch of a superb calm character

_____

his emotions &c are complete in himself irrespective (indifferent) of whether
   his love, friendship, &c are returned, or not
He grows, blooms, like some perfect tree or flower, in Nature [. . . .]
His analogy the earth complete in itself enfolding in itself all processes of
   growth effusing life and power for hidden purposes. (UPP 2:96)

This looks very much like the sort of presence we might be asked to understand as the embodiment of American polity: he makes no entangling alliances and grows through organic absorption rather than mechanical annexation. Yet Whitman's notebook passage suggests that both this figure's provenance and the purposes it fulfills are rather more intimate. The apparently calm evocation of this superb character modulates abruptly into discourse of a markedly different sort: "Depress the adhesive nature" (UPP 2:96). The shift here is rather startling. Urgently admonitory despite its abstract-sounding phrenological jargon, this phrase offers tough practical advice to someone in desperate straits; it precipitates a rhetorical shift that seems like a bad joke at the expense of Whitman's interrupted revery, abruptly juxtaposing incongruous contexts and self-conceptions. What follows is too earnest to seem anything but sad:

It is in excess—making life a torment

_____

All this diseased, feverish disproportionate *adhesiveness*

_____

Remember Fred Vaughan

_____

Case of Jenny Bullard

_____

Sane Nature fit & full rapport therewith

_____

Merlin strong & wise & beautiful at 100 years old. (UPP 2:96–97)

Wavering and then recovering a bit wanly, Whitman's evocation of the sort of self-sufficient figure which the early editions claim to incarnate frames a passage whose poignancy is rather terrible. The torment condensed, for example, into a few elliptical lines in section six of "Crossing Brooklyn Ferry," describing the poet's "past" experience, here defines a life the author of that earlier poem is still very much in the midst of. Unconcerned with the public possibilities Whitman's superb calm character can serve to embody, these notebook passages reveal instead, with special sharpness, this figure's roots in the more agitated self-conceptions he is meant to eclipse.

The entries that precede Whitman's "outline sketch" identify the immediate source of the torment this ideal figure was invoked, in 1870, to assuage. In this earlier passage, "she" takes the place of a "he" Whitman evidently rubbed out and wrote over; "16" and "164" are ciphers for "P" and "PD," Peter Doyle, the confederate soldier and street-car driver with whom Whitman had fallen in love:

cheating, childish abandonment of myself, fancying what does not really exist in another, but is all the time in myself alone—utterly deluded & cheated by *myself*, & my own weakness—REMEMBER WHERE I AM MOST WEAK, & most lacking. Yet always preserve a kind spirit & demeanor to 16. But PURSUE HER NO MORE. (UPP 2:95)

And a bit further on:

TO GIVE UP ABSOLUTELY & *for good, from this present hour* [all] this FEVERISH, FLUCTUATING, *useless undignified pursuit of 164—too long, much too long)* persevered in,—so humiliating—*It must come at last* & had better come now—*(It cannot possibly be a success)*

LET THERE FROM THIS HOUR BE NO FALTERING, [or] NO GETTING [word erased] *at all henceforth,* (NOT ONCE, *under any circumstances)—avoid seeing her, or meeting her, or any talk or explanations*—or ANY MEETING WHATEVER, FROM *THIS HOUR FORTH, FOR LIFE.* (UPP 2:96)

It used to be the fashion to quote these passages as evidence that Whitman's homosexuality involved him in preponderantly unhappy, even doomed, relationships. I don't mean to put them to such uses here: intent on putting a stop to this sort of appropriation, Charley Shively has taken the simple and effective expedient of quoting another letter Whitman wrote Doyle a short time later, reveling in their intensely shared affection (113–14). These entries do show, however, that in a

moment of personal anxiety and despair Whitman's imagination re-
verted to fantasies centering on a self-sufficient figure, immune to the
torments he himself was in the midst of, who looks very much like the
poet-hero of *Leaves of Grass*—or like a toned-down, slightly tired
avatar of him. This resemblance can remind us that Whitman's self-
generating and self-delighting figure of presence embodies not only national ideals but also some more intimate concerns difficult to reconcile
with them. If he figures consensus, he also incarnates an intransitive self-
containment; it is marshaled against anxieties by no means reducible to
Whitman's political fears.

This same notebook opens with another evocation of such a figure.
We can close with it: not to deny the poet's public, ideological function,
but to help qualify our sense of where it might come from, and what it
might be:

> EPICTITUS
> (Description of a Wise Man)
> [....]
> All his desires depend on things within his power.
> [....]
> He observes himself with the nicety of an enemy or spy, and looks on his own
>   wishes as betrayers. (UPP 2:94)

The poet who embodies American political consensus also recalls us to
an order of experience politics will always be unable to satisfy. *Leaves
of Grass* subdues this tension; but it also awakens it, pointing us back,
or beyond.

Notes

1. Erkkila takes exception to this view, arguing for the continuing insurrectionary implications of homosexuality in *Drum-Taps* (rev. of *Whitman's Poetry
   of the Body* 196). The gradual slippage from "body" to "soul" is discussed
   at length by Asselineau; see especially 2:3–20; see also Edwin Miller 10–18
   and 208–24. Sexuality continues to absorb Whitman in his private life and
   intimate correspondence, as Shively amply documents (63–184); but it is no
   longer the exorbitant, archaic sexuality initiated by the poet's presence.
2. It is true that locution and illocution, for Austin, are by no means mutually
   exclusive; indeed they necessarily co-exist in any utterance: "To perform a
   locutionary act is in general, we may say, also and *eo ipso* to perform an

illocutionary act" (98). But as Hollis shows, Whitman's emphasis in the first three editions of *Leaves of Grass* is on illocutionary force; in later editions this is no longer the case.

3. See for example PW 1:143.

4. Jefferson, for example, employs the figure in *Notes on the State of Virginia:* "It is the manners and spirit of the people which preserve a republic in vigour. . . . A degeneracy in these is a canker which soon eats to the heart of its laws and constitution" (quoted in Erkkila, *Whitman the Political Poet* 26). On Carlyle's use of a similar though not identical rhetoric of pathology, see Kaplan 336.

5. Emerson, of course, employs the fragmenting body as a trope for the industrialized body politic in a well-known passage in "The American Scholar": see 1:53. Berlant (18–19), citing Fanon, suggests that threats to the integrity of the nation-state commonly generate fantasies of psychic and bodily dispersion. See also Smith-Rosenberg 48. Erkkila (104–6) traces a related dynamic in Whitman's work.

6. Such proclamations are especially striking in the 1855 Preface: see for example 1855 7.

7. Erkkila draws on the work of Smith-Rosenberg, herself indebted to Douglas; see *Whitman the Political Poet* 334n12.

8. On this point see also Douglas, *Natural Symbols* 156–67 and Smith-Rosenberg 49.

9. Douglas builds here on her work in *Purity and Danger;* see especially 114–28.

10. On Whitman's responses to Manifest Destiny see Erkkila, *Whitman the Political Poet* 39–40 and Kaplan 128–31. On the oral-incorporative rhetoric that accompanied United States territorial expansion see Rogin 9.

11. On Whitman's role in the No-Popery riot see Kaplan 102–4, Rubin 73–80, Erkkila 28–29, and Pease, *Visionary Compacts* 114. On the role played by nativism in New York City politics in the 1840s, see Wilentz 315–25.

12. On Whitman's championing of open immigration see Erkkila, *Whitman the Political Poet* 34.

13. Douglas is here discussing weak "grid" combined with strong "group": hence the fear of "internal traitors allied with outside enemies." Whitman, by contrast, generally champions a cohesive group whose boundaries are porous. In his poetry, anxious depictions of the outside infiltrating the inside —as, for example, in the "headlands" passage in section 28 of "Song of Myself"—may thus be instances of the antagonism rather than the homology between the body and the body politic: rather than the danger of outsiders invading the social body, that is, such images may instead figure the threat which social sanctions pose to an individual body that ought to have remained immune to them.

14. On the role played by anti-institutionalism and "no government" ideology in ante-bellum America, see Fredrickson 7–10 and Ziff 28–29; on Whit-

man's endorsement of this vision, see Fredrickson 20–21. On his related espousal of artisan-republican anti-monopolist ideology, which tended to view government intervention as a conspiratorial attempt to foster monopoly, and on the way this ideology paradoxically facilitated the very economic concentration it aimed to resist, see Erkkila, *Whitman the Political Poet* 34–38 and Thomas 72–79.

15. On Whitman's projection of an idealized past onto an idealized present and future, see Thomas 2–34.

16. Freud, of course, postulates a similar displacement as the origin of the "oceanic feeling" associated with religious mysticism; see *Civilization and Its Discontents* 11–16. Kristeva suggests, though, that even this bliss is borrowed: she argues that the archaic register of primary narcissism owes its charm to retrospective fantasizing: see *Desire in Language* 63.

17. In this respect the function of *Calamus* is perhaps even more complex. While in the 1855 and 1856 editions the poet's presence figures an individual power and freedom in excess of what even "no government" democracy might tolerate, it can at least be viewed as a hyperbolic version of the sort of political freedom Whitman espoused. *Calamus,* by contrast, embraces a significant curtailment of individual liberty: there Whitman's altered sense of sexuality, his feel for the way kinship structures shape body and consciousness, puts real pressure on the millennialist, revolutionary vision of identity he often champions. Throughout Whitman's career, his politics of the body meshes with his politics of the state only by tolerating a significant amount of slippage and strain.

18. In this respect *Calamus* is less evasive: for the most part, the sequence embraces transmission without clinging to the saving exceptionalism that paradoxically allows the poet-hero of 1855 and 1856 both to exempt himself from paternal law and to impose on others a patriarchal power that retains its archaic privilege. And while patriarchal power is beneficent in *Calamus,* it has not been neutralized as in sentimental rhetoric.

19. Lynda Zwinger argues that this simultaneous mobilization and occulting of patriarchal power is one characteristic cultural task of the sentimental; see for example 93. My treatment of the rhetoric of sentimental paternity is indebted to her account, which is both more wary than Fliegelman's and more attentive to the complex, ambivalent resourcefulness of the sentimental mode.

20. On this feature of sentimental rhetoric see Zwinger, especially 62–64.

21. I mean here both to evoke the tradition of the jeremiad as Sacvan Bercovitch describes it and to suggest, as Rogin and Forgie do, that in the postrevolutionary period the rhetoric of declension could have the effect of stifling social energies rather than renewing them. On the potentially paralyzing effect of American figural rhetoric see also Pease, *Visionary Compacts* 248–56.

22. Whitman's "drooping star" gives the entire scene here a maternal ambiance;

the phrase echoes a more explicit image from "Out of the Cradle Endlessly Rocking": "The yellow half-moon, enlarged, sagging down, drooping, the face of the sea almost touching" (1860 275).

23. See chapter 4, 104–5, above.

24. As Forgie notes, a dark view of his generation's belated relation to the act of founding shapes Lincoln's 1838 Lyceum speech:

> Disagreeing with optimists who spoke of a second age of godlike Washingtons, Lincoln concluded that in present circumstances immortality of the Republic not only made immortality of the self unlikely—it actually precluded it. For how could such a treasure be attained? By participating in the act of founding? The act was done. (65)

25. On Emerson's transformation of a potentially anarchic romantic "individuality" into an American "individualism" compatible with the typology of America's mission, see Bercovitch, "Emerson, Individualism, and the Ambiguities of Dissent." On the related co-optation of dissenting energies effected by an American ideology of consensus, see *American Jeremiad,* especially 132–210, and "The Problem of Ideology in American Literary History," especially 636–48.

26. On the dating of this notebook see UPP 2:94n1.

Works Cited

Aarsleff, Hans. *From Locke to Saussure: Essays on the Study of Language and Intellectual History*. Minneapolis: U of Minnesota P, 1982.

Abraham, Nicolas, and Maria Torok. "Introjection—Incorporation: Mourning or Melancholia." *Psychoanalysis in France*. Ed. S. Lebovici and D. Widlocher. New York: International Universities P, 1980. 3–16.

———. *The Wolf Man's Magic Word: A Cryptonymy*. Trans. Nicholas Rand. Minneapolis: U of Minnesota P, 1986.

Abrams, M. H. *The Mirror and the Lamp: Romantic Theory and the Critical Tradition*. New York: Oxford UP, 1953.

Althusser, Louis. "Ideology and Ideological State Apparatuses (Notes towards an Investigation)." *Lenin and Philosophy and Other Essays*. London: New Left Books, 1971.

Anderson, Quentin. *The Imperial Self: An Essay in American Literary and Cultural History*. 1971. New York: Vintage, 1972.

———. "Property and Vision in Nineteenth-Century America." *Virginia Quarterly* 54 (1978): 385–410.

———. "Whitman's New Man." *Walt Whitman's Autograph Revision of the Analysis of Leaves of Grass (For Dr. R.M. Bucke's Walt Whitman)*. Text notes by Stephen Railton. New York: New York UP, 1974. 11–52.

Ashbery, John. *Self-Portrait in a Convex Mirror*. New York: Viking, 1975.

Aspiz, Harold. *Walt Whitman and the Body Beautiful*. Urbana: U of Illinois P, 1980.

Asselineau, Roger. *The Evolution of Walt Whitman*. 2 vols. Cambridge: Harvard UP, 1960–62.

Augustine. *On Christian Doctrine*. Trans. D. W. Robertson, Jr. New York: Liberal Arts, 1958.

Austin, J. L. *How To Do Things with Words*. Ed. J. O. Urmson and Marina Sbisa. 2nd. ed. Cambridge: Harvard UP, 1975.

Bakhtin, M. M. *The Dialogic Imagination: Four Essays*. Ed. Michael Holquist. Austin: U of Texas P, 1981.

Barrus, Clara. *Whitman and Burroughs: Comrades*. Boston: Houghton Mifflin, 1931.

Bauerlein, Mark. "Whitman's Language of the Self." *American Imago* 44 (1987): 129–48.

Bedient, Calvin. "Orality and Power (Whitman's *Song of Myself)*." *Delta* 16 (1983): 79–94.

Bercovitch, Sacvan. *The American Jeremiad.* Madison: U of Wisconsin P, 1978.

———. "Emerson, Individualism, and the Ambiguities of Dissent." *SAQ* 89 (1990): 623–62.

———. "The Problem of Ideology in American Literary History." *Critical Inquiry* 12 (1986): 631–53.

Berlant, Lauren. "America, Post-Utopia: Body, Landscape, and National Fantasy in Hawthorne's *Native Land.*" *Arizona Quarterly* 44.4 (1989): 14–54.

Bernstein, Charles. *Artifice of Absorption.* Spec. issue of *Paper Air* 4.1 (1987).

Bishop, Elizabeth. *The Complete Poems: 1927–1979.* New York: Farrar, 1983.

Black, Stephen A. *Whitman's Journeys into Chaos: A Psychoanalytic Study of the Poetic Process.* Princeton: Princeton UP, 1975.

Bloom, Harold. "The Internalization of Quest-Romance." *Romanticism and Consciousness: Essays in Criticism.* Ed. Harold Bloom. New York: Norton, 1970. 3–24.

———. *A Map of Misreading.* New York: Oxford UP, 1975.

———. *Poetry and Repression.* New Haven: Yale UP, 1976.

———. *The Visionary Company: A Reading of English Romantic Poetry.* Rev. ed. Ithaca: Cornell UP, 1971.

———. *Wallace Stevens: The Poems of Our Climate.* Ithaca: Cornell UP, 1977.

———. "Whitman's Image of Voice." *Agon: Towards a Theory of Revisionism.* New York: Oxford UP, 1982. 179–99.

Boehme, Jacob. *The Aurora.* Trans. John Sparrow. London: John M. Watkins, James Clarke, 1960.

———. *Mysterium Magnum or An Exposition of the First Book of Moses called Genesis.* Trans. John Sparrow. 2 vols. London: John M. Watkins, 1924.

———. *The Signature of All Things and Other Writings.* [Trans. William Law.] Cambridge: James Clarke, 1969.

Bové, Paul A. *Destructive Poetics: Heidegger and Modern American Poetry.* New York: Columbia UP, 1980.

Bowers, Fredson, ed. *Whitman's Manuscripts: Leaves of Grass (1860): A Parallel Text.* Chicago: U of Chicago P, 1955.

Breitwieser, Mitchell Robert. "Who Speaks in Whitman's Poems?" *The American Renaissance: New Dimensions.* Ed. Harry R. Garvin and Peter C. Carafiol. Lewisburg, Pennsylvania: Bucknell UP, 1983.

Bucke, Richard Maurice. *Walt Whitman.* Philadelphia: David McKay, 1883.

Bunsen, Christian Charles Josias. *Outlines of the Philosophy of Universal History, Applied to Language and Religion.* 2 vols. London: Longman, Brown, Green, and Longmans, 1854.

Burke, Kenneth. *The Philosophy of Literary Form: Studies in Symbolic Action.* 3rd. ed. Berkeley: U of California P, 1973.

———. "Policy Made Personal: Whitman's Verse and Prose—Salient Traits."

Leaves of Grass One Hundred Years After. Ed. Milton Hindus. Stanford: Stanford UP, 1955. 74–108.

Burroughs, John. "The Flight of the Eagle." *Birds and Poets*. Boston: Houghton Mifflin, 1877. 213–63.

———. *Notes on Walt Whitman as Poet and Person*. New York: American News Co., 1867.

———. *Whitman: A Study*. 1896. New York: AMS, 1969.

Byers, Thomas B. *What I Cannot Say: Self, Word, and World in Whitman, Stevens, and Merwin*. Urbana: U of Illinois P, 1989.

Calabrese, Steven Vincent. "Our Muse in a Golden Frame: A Study of Whitman, Money, and Language." Diss. Columbia U, 1979.

Cameron, Sharon. *The Corporeal Self: Allegories of the Body in Melville and Hawthorne*. Baltimore: Johns Hopkins UP, 1981.

———. *Lyric Time: Dickinson and the Limits of Genre*. Baltimore: Johns Hopkins UP, 1979.

Carpenter, Edward. *Days with Walt Whitman, with Some Notes on His Life and Work*. 2nd ed. London: George Allen, 1906.

Cassirer, Ernst. *Language and Myth*. Trans. Susanne K. Langer. 1946. New York: Dover, 1953.

Chase, Cynthia. *Decomposing Figures: Rhetorical Readings in the Romantic Tradition*. Baltimore: Johns Hopkins UP, 1986.

———. " 'Viewless Wings': Keats's 'Ode to a Nightingale.' " *Lyric Poetry: Beyond New Criticism*. Ed. Chaviva Hosek and Patricia Parker. Ithaca: Cornell UP, 1985. 208–25.

Chase, Richard. *Walt Whitman Reconsidered*. New York: William Sloane Associates, 1955.

Clavreul, Jean. "The Perverse Couple." *Returning to Freud: Clinical Psychoanalysis in the School of Lacan*. Ed. and trans. Stuart Schneiderman. New Haven: Yale UP, 1980. 215–33.

Coffman, Stanley K. " 'Crossing Brooklyn Ferry': A Note on the Catalogue Technique in Whitman's Poetry." *Modern Philology* 51 (1954): 225–32.

Collins, Richard. "Whitman's Transcendent Corpus: 'Crossing Brooklyn Ferry' to History." *Calamus* 19 (1980): 24–39.

Culler, Jonathan. "Apostrophe." *The Pursuit of Signs: Semiotics, Literature, Deconstruction*. Ithaca: Cornell UP, 1981. 135–54.

———. "Changes in the Study of the Lyric." *Lyric Poetry: Beyond New Criticism*. Ed. Chaviva Hosek and Patricia Parker. Ithaca: Cornell UP, 1985. 38–54.

Dahlen, Beverly. *A Reading 1–7*. San Francisco: Momo's, 1985.

Daiches, David. "Walt Whitman: Impressionist Prophet." *Leaves of Grass One Hundred Years After*. Ed. Milton Hindus. Stanford: Stanford UP, 1955. 109–22.

Dayan, Joan. "Finding What Will Suffice: John Ashbery's *A Wave*." *MLN* 100 (1985): 1045–79.

504   Works Cited

de Man, Paul. *Allegories of Reading: Figural Language in Rousseau, Nietzsche, Rilke, and Proust.* New Haven: Yale UP, 1979.

————. *Blindness and Insight: Essays in the Rhetoric of Contemporary Criticism.* New York: Oxford UP, 1971.

————. "Lyrical Voice in Contemporary Theory: Riffaterre and Jauss." *Lyric Poetry: Beyond New Criticism.* Ed. Chaviva Hosek and Patricia Parker. Ithaca: Cornell UP, 1985. 55–72.

————. *The Rhetoric of Romanticism.* New York: Columbia UP, 1984.

————. "Time and History in Wordsworth." *Wordsworth and the Production of Poetry.* Ed. Andrzej Warminski and Cynthia Chase. Spec. issue of *Diacritics* 17.4 (1987): 4–17.

Derrida, Jacques. *Dissemination.* Trans. Barbara Johnson. Chicago: U of Chicago P, 1981.

————. "Foreword: *Fors:* The Anglish Words of Nicolas Abraham and Maria Torok." Trans. Barbara Johnson. *The Wolf Man's Magic Word: A Cryptonymy.* By Nicolas Abraham and Maria Torok. Trans. Nicholas Rand. Minneapolis: U of Minnesota P, 1986. xi–xlviii.

————. "Limited Inc." *Glyph* 2 (1977): 162–254.

————. *Margins of Philosophy.* Trans. Alan Bass. Chicago: U of Chicago P, 1982.

————. *Of Grammatology.* Trans. Gayatri Chakravorty Spivak. Baltimore: John Hopkins UP, 1976.

————. "Signature Event Context." *Glyph* 1 (1977): 172–97.

————. *Speech and Phenomena, and Other Essays on Husserl's Theory of Signs.* Trans. David B. Allison. Evanston: Northwestern UP, 1973.

————. "Structure, Sign, and Play in the Discourse of the Human Sciences." *The Structuralist Controversy: The Languages of Criticism and the Sciences of Man.* Ed. Richard Macksey and Eugenio Donato. 1970. Baltimore: Johns Hopkins UP, 1972.

————. *Writing and Difference.* Trans. Alan Bass. Chicago: U of Chicago P, 1978.

De Selincourt, Basil. *Walt Whitman: A Critical Study.* 1914. New York: Russell & Russell, 1965.

Douglas, Mary. *Natural Symbols: Explorations in Cosmology.* 1970. New York: Pantheon, 1982.

————. *Purity and Danger: An Analysis of the Concepts of Pollution and Taboo.* 1966. London: Ark-Routledge, 1984.

Durand, Régis. "The Anxiety of Performance." *New Literary History* 12 (1980): 167–76.

————. "Whitman, le rythme, le sujet de l'écriture." *Delta* 16 (1983): 63–78.

Ellison, Julie. *Emerson's Romantic Style.* Princeton: Princeton UP, 1984.

Emerson, Ralph Waldo. *The Collected Works of Ralph Waldo Emerson.* Ed. Alfred R. Ferguson et al. 10 vols. Cambridge: Belknap-Harvard UP, 1971– .

Erkkila, Betsy. Rev. of *Whitman's Poetry of the Body: Sexuality, Politics, and the Text,* by M. Jimmie Killingsworth. *Walt Whitman Quarterly Review* 7 (1990): 194–96.

———. *Whitman the Political Poet.* New York: Oxford UP, 1989.

Feidelson, Charles, Jr. *Symbolism and American Literature.* Chicago: U of Chicago P, 1953.

Ferguson, Frances. *Wordsworth: Language as Counter-Spirit.* New Haven: Yale UP, 1977.

Fish, Stanley. "With the Compliments of the Author: Reflections on Austin and Derrida." *Critical Inquiry* 8 (1982): 693–721.

Fletcher, Angus. *Allegory: The Theory of a Symbolic Mode.* Ithaca: Cornell UP, 1964.

Fliegelman, Jay. *Prodigals and Pilgrims: The American Revolution against Patriarchal Authority, 1750–1800.* Cambridge: Cambridge UP, 1982.

Forgie, George B. *Patricide in the House Divided: A Psychological Interpretation of Lincoln and His Age.* New York: Norton, 1979.

Foucault, Michel. *The History of Sexuality. Volume I: An Introduction.* Trans. Robert Hurley. 1978. New York: Vintage-Random, 1980.

Fredrickson, George M. *The Inner Civil War: Northern Intellectuals and the Crisis of the Union.* New York: Harper, 1965.

Freud, Sigmund. *Beyond the Pleasure Principle.* Trans. James Strachey. New York: Norton, 1961.

———. *Civilization and Its Discontents.* Trans. James Strachey. New York: Norton, 1961.

———. *Collected Papers.* 5 vols. London: Hogarth, 1924–50.

———. *The Ego and the Id.* Trans. Joan Riviere. Rev. and ed. James Strachey. New York: Norton, 1960.

———. *Introductory Lectures on Psychoanalysis.* Trans. James Strachey. New York: Norton, 1966.

———. *New Introductory Lectures on Psychoanalysis.* Trans. James Strachey. New York: Norton, 1965.

———. *Totem and Taboo.* Trans. James Strachey. New York: Norton, 1950.

Fried, Debra. "Repetition, Refrain, and Epitaph." *ELH* 53 (1986): 615–32.

Fry, Paul H. *The Poet's Calling in the English Ode.* New Haven: Yale UP, 1980.

Gilchrist, Anne. "A Woman's Estimate of Walt Whitman." *In Re Walt Whitman.* Ed. Horace L. Traubel et al. Philadelphia: David McKay, 1893. 41–55.

Graves, Robert. *The Greek Myths.* Rev. ed. 2 vols. Harmondsworth, Eng.: Penguin, 1960.

Gregory, Dorothy Manessi-Tsilibari. *A Quest for Psychosexual Verbal Consciousness: Whitman's Imaginative Involvement with Masculinity and Femininity in the First Two Editions of "Leaves of Grass".* Diss. Columbia U, 1980. Ann Arbor: UMI, 1980. 8222398.

Gross, Kenneth. *Spenserian Poetics: Idolatry, Iconoclasm, and Magic.* Ithaca: Cornell UP, 1985.

Grossman, Allen. "The Poetics of Union in Whitman and Lincoln: An Inquiry toward the Relationship of Art and Policy." *The American Renaissance Reconsidered.* Ed. Walter Benn Michaels and Donald E. Pease. Baltimore: Johns Hopkins UP, 1985. 183–208.

Gura, Philip F. *The Wisdom of Words: Language, Theology, and Literature in the New England Renaissance.* Middletown, Connecticut: Wesleyan UP, 1981.

Hartman, Geoffrey H. *Beyond Formalism: Literary Essays 1958–1970.* New Haven: Yale UP, 1970.

———. *Criticism in the Wilderness: The Study of Literature Today.* New Haven: Yale UP, 1980.

———. *The Fate of Reading and Other Essays.* Chicago: U of Chicago P, 1975.

———. *Saving the Text: Literature/Derrida/Philosophy.* Baltimore: Johns Hopkins UP, 1981.

———. *The Unmediated Vision: An Interpretation of Wordsworth, Hopkins, Rilke, and Valéry.* New Haven: Yale UP, 1954.

———. *The Unremarkable Wordsworth.* Minneapolis: U of Minnesota P, 1987.

———. "Words, Wish, Worth: Wordsworth." *Deconstruction and Criticism.* By Harold Bloom et al. New York: Continuum—Seabury, 1979.

———. *Wordsworth's Poetry, 1787–1814.* New Haven: Yale UP, 1971.

Heath, Stephen. "Joan Riviere and the Masquerade." *Formations of Fantasy.* Ed. Victor Burgin, James Donald, and Cora Kaplan. London: Methuen, 1986. 45–61.

Heidegger, Martin. *Poetry, Language, Thought.* Trans. Albert Hofstadter. New York: Harper Colophon, 1975.

Herder, Johann Gottfried. *Essay on the Origin of Language. On the Origin of Language.* Trans. John H. Moran and Alexander Gode. New York: Frederick Ungar, 1966.

Hertz, Neil. *The End of the Line: Essays on Psychoanalysis and the Sublime.* New York: Columbia UP, 1985.

Hodgson, John A. "Transcendental Tropes: Coleridge's Rhetoric of Allegory and Symbol." *Allegory, Myth, and Symbol.* Ed. Morton W. Bloomfield. Harvard English Studies 9. Cambridge: Harvard UP, 1981.

Hollis, C. Carroll. *Language and Style in Leaves of Grass.* Baton Rouge: Louisiana State UP, 1983.

Humboldt, Wilhelm von. *Humanist without Portfolio: An Anthology of the Writings of Wilhelm von Humboldt.* Trans. Marianne Cowan. Detroit: Wayne State UP, 1963.

———. *Linguistic Variability and Intellectual Development.* Trans. George C. Buck and Frithjof A. Raven. Coral Gables, Florida: U of Miami P, 1971.

Husserl, Edmund. *Ideas.* 2 vols. Trans. J. N. Findlay. London: Routledge Kegan Paul, 1970.

Hutchinson, George B. *The Ecstatic Whitman: Literary Shamanism and the Crisis of the Union.* Columbus: Ohio State UP, 1986.

Hyde, Lewis. *The Gift: Imagination and the Erotic Life of Property.* New York: Vintage-Random, 1983.

Irigaray, Luce. *This Sex Which Is Not One.* Trans. Catherine Porter with Carolyn Burke. Ithaca: Cornell UP, 1985.

———. *Speculum of the Other Woman.* Trans. Gillian C. Gill. Ithaca: Cornell UP, 1985.

Irwin, John. *American Hieroglyphics: The Symbol of the Egyptian Hieroglyphics in the American Renaissance.* New Haven: Yale UP, 1980.

Jacobus, Mary. "Apostrophe and Lyric Voice in *The Prelude.*" *Lyric Poetry: Beyond New Criticism.* Ed. Chaviva Hosek and Patricia Parker. Ithaca: Cornell UP, 1985. 167–81.

Johnson, Barbara. Introduction. *Dissemination.* By Jacques Derrida. Trans. Barbara Johnson. Chicago: U of Chicago P, 1981. vii–xxxiii.

Kaplan, Justin. *Walt Whitman: A Life.* New York: Simon & Schuster, 1980.

Keats, John. *The Poems of John Keats.* Ed. Jack Stillinger. Cambridge: Belknap-Harvard UP, 1978.

Killingsworth, M. Jimmie. *Whitman's Poetry of the Body: Sexuality, Politics, and the Text.* Chapel Hill: U of North Carolina P, 1989.

Kinnaird, John. "*Leaves of Grass* and the American Paradox." *Partisan Review* 25 (1958): 380–405. Rpt., rev. in *Whitman: A Collection of Critical Essays.* Ed. Roy Harvey Pearce. Englewood Cliffs, N.J.: Prentice-Hall, 1962. 24–36.

Kraitsir, Charles. *Glossology: Being a Treatise on the Nature of Language and the Language of Nature.* New York: George P. Putnam, 1852.

Kristeva, Julia. *Desire in Language: A Semiotic Approach to Literature and the Arts.* Trans. Thomas Gora, Alice Jardine, and Leon S. Roudiez. Ed. Leon S. Roudiez. New York: Columbia UP, 1980.

———. *Powers of Horror: An Essay on Abjection.* Trans. Leon S. Roudiez. New York: Columbia UP, 1982.

———. *Revolution in Poetic Language.* Trans. Margaret Waller. New York: Columbia UP, 1984.

Kronick, Joseph G. *American Poetics of History: From Emerson to the Moderns.* Baton Rouge: Louisiana State UP, 1984.

Lacan, Jacques. *Ecrits: A Selection.* Trans. Alan Sheridan. New York: Norton, 1977.

———. *The Four Fundamental Concepts of Psycho-Analysis.* Ed. Jacques-Alain Miller. Trans. Alan Sheridan. New York: Norton, 1978.

Lacan, Jacques, and the *école freudienne. Feminine Sexuality.* Ed. Juliet Mitchell and Jacqueline Rose. Trans. Jacqueline Rose. New York: Norton, 1982.

Laplanche, J., and J.-B. Pontalis. "Fantasy and the Origins of Sexuality." *International Journal of Psycho-Analysis* 49 (1968): 1–18.

———. *The Language of Psycho-Analysis.* Trans. Donald Nicholson-Smith. New York: Norton, 1973.

Larson, Kerry C. *Whitman's Drama of Consensus.* Chicago: U of Chicago P, 1988.

Lawrence, D. H. *Studies in Classic American Literature.* 1923. New York: Viking, 1964.

Lévi-Strauss, Claude. *The Elementary Structures of Kinship (Les Structures éle-mentaires de la Parenté).* Rev. ed. Trans. James Harle Bell, John Richard von Sturmer, and Rodney Needham. Ed. Rodney Needham. Boston: Beacon, 1969.

Lewis, R. W. B. *The American Adam: Innocence, Tragedy, and Tradition in the Nineteenth Century.* Chicago: U of Chicago P, 1955.

MacCannell, Juliet Flower. *Figuring Lacan: Criticism and the Cultural Unconscious.* Lincoln: U of Nebraska P, 1986.

Marki, Ivan. *The Trial of the Poet: An Interpretation of the First Edition of Leaves of Grass.* New York: Columbia UP, 1976.

Martin, Robert K. *The Homosexual Tradition in American Poetry.* Austin: U of Texas P, 1979.

Matthiessen, F. O. *American Renaissance: Art and Expression in the Age of Emerson and Whitman.* New York: Oxford UP, 1941.

Middlebrook, Diane. *Walt Whitman and Wallace Stevens.* Ithaca: Cornell UP, 1976.

Miller, Edwin Haviland. *Walt Whitman's Poetry: A Psychological Journey.* New York: New York UP, 1968.

Miller, James E., Jr. *A Critical Guide to Leaves of Grass.* Chicago: U of Chicago P, 1957.

———. *Walt Whitman.* New York: Twayne, 1962.

Moon, Michael. *Disseminating Whitman: Revision and Corporeality in Leaves of Grass.* Cambridge: Harvard UP, 1991.

Nathanson, Tenney. "Private Language: Ashbery and Wittgenstein." *Raritan* 2.3 (1983): 91–108.

———. "Whitman's Presence: Apostrophe, Voice, and Text in *Leaves of Grass.*" *Deconstruction.* Ed. Suresh Raval. Spec. issue of *Journal of Comparative Literature and Aesthetics* 9 (1986): 141–69.

———. "Whitman's Tropes of Light and Flood: Language and Representation in the Early Editions of *Leaves of Grass.*" *ESQ* 31 (1985): 116–34.

Oegger, G[uillaume]. *The True Messiah; or The Old and New Testaments, examined according to the Principles of the Language of Nature.* [Trans. Elizabeth Peabody.] 1842. *Emerson the Essayist.* Ed. Kenneth Walter Cameron. Hartford: Transcendental Books, 1945. 2:83–99.

Olson, Charles. *Call Me Ishmael.* San Francisco: City Lights, 1947.

Ong, Walter J., S. J. *Interfaces of the Word: Studies in the Evolution of Consciousness and Culture.* Ithaca: Cornell UP, 1977.

———. *The Presence of the Word: Some Prolegomena for Cultural and Religious History.* 1967. New York: Simon and Schuster, 1970.

———. *Rhetoric, Romance, and Technology.* Ithaca: Cornell UP, 1971.

Pears, David. *Ludwig Wittgenstein.* New York: Viking, 1970.

Pease, Donald E. "Blake, Crane, Whitman, and Modernism: A Poetics of Pure Possibility." *PMLA* 96 (1981): 64–85.

———. *Visionary Compacts: American Renaissance Writings in Cultural Context.* Madison: U of Wisconsin P, 1987.

Poirier, Richard. *A World Elsewhere: The Place of Style in American Literature.* London: Oxford UP, 1966.

Pound, Ezra. *Literary Essays of Ezra Pound.* Ed. T. S. Eliot. New York: New Directions, 1935.

———. *Personae: The Collected Shorter Poems of Ezra Pound.* New York: New Directions, 1971.

Reed, Sampson. *Observations on the Growth of the Mind; with Remarks on Some Other Subjects.* 1827. Boston: Otis Clapp, 1838.

———. "Oration on Genius." 1821. *Emerson the Essayist.* Ed. Kenneth Walter Cameron. Hartford: Transcendental Books, 1945. 2:9–12.

Rogin, Michael Paul. *Fathers and Children: Andrew Jackson and the Subjugation of the American Indian.* New York: Knopf, 1975.

Rousseau, Jean-Jacques. *Essay on the Origin of Languages. On the Origin of Language.* Trans. John H. Moran and Alexander Gode. New York: Frederick Ungar, 1966.

Rubin, Joseph Jay. *The Historic Whitman.* University Park, Pa.: Pennsylvania State UP, 1973.

Saussure, Ferdinand de. *Course in General Linguistics.* Ed. Charles Bally et al. Trans. Wade Baskin. 1959. New York: McGraw-Hill, 1966.

Schele de Vere, M[aximilian]. *Outlines of Comparative Philology, with a Sketch of the Languages of Europe, Arranged Upon Philologic Principles; and a Brief History of the Art of Writing.* New York: G. P. Putnam, 1853.

Schleicher, August. *A Compendium of the Comparative Grammar of the Indo-European, Sanskrit, Greek and Latin Languages.* Trans. Herbert Bendall. London: Trübner, 1874.

Schyberg, Frederik. *Walt Whitman.* Trans. Evie Allison Allen. New York: Columbia UP, 1951.

Searle, John R. "Reiterating the Differences: A Reply to Derrida." *Glyph* 1 (1977): 198–209.

———. *Speech Acts: An Essay in the Philosophy of Language.* London: Cambridge UP, 1969.

Sedgwick, Eve Kosofsky. *Between Men: English Literature and Male Homosocial Desire.* New York: Columbia UP, 1985.

Shively, Charley, ed. *Calamus Lovers: Walt Whitman's Working-Class Camerados.* San Francisco: Gay Sunshine, 1987.

Simpson, David. *The Politics of American English.* New York: Oxford UP, 1986.

Slater, Joseph, ed. *The Correspondence of Emerson and Carlyle.* New York: Columbia UP, 1964.

Smith-Rosenberg, Carroll. *Disorderly Conduct: Visions of Gender in Victorian America.* New York: Knopf, 1985.

Stevens, Wallace. *The Collected Poems of Wallace Stevens.* 1954. New York: Vintage-Random, 1982.

———. *Opus Posthumus.* Ed. Samuel French Morse. 1957. New York: Vintage-Random, 1982.

Stovall, Floyd. *The Foreground of Leaves of Grass.* Charlottesville: UP of Virginia, 1974.

Strachey, James. "Appendix B: The Great Reservoir of Libido." *The Ego and the Id.* By Sigmund Freud. New York: Norton, 1960.

Strauch, Carl F. Introduction. *Observations on the Growth of the Mind; with Remarks on Some Other Subjects.* By Sampson Reed. 1838. Gainesville, Florida: Scholars' Facsimiles & Reprints, 1970. v–xvi.

Strom, Susan. " 'Face to Face': Whitman's Biblical Reference in " 'Crossing Brooklyn Ferry.' " *Walt Whitman Review* 24 (1978): 7–16.

Swinton, William. *Rambles among Words: Their Poetry, History and Wisdom.* New York: Charles Scribner, 1859.

Taylor, Benjamin F. *Attractions of Language, or a Popular View of Natural Language, in all its Varied Displays, in the Animate and Inanimate World; and as Corresponding with Instinct, Intelligence and Reason.* 2nd ed. Hamilton, New York: J. & D. Atwood, and S. C. Griggs, 1843.

Thomas, M. Wynn. *The Lunar Light of Whitman's Poetry.* Cambridge: Harvard UP, 1987.

Tocqueville, Alexis de. *Democracy in America.* Trans. Henry Reeve. Rev. Francis Bowen. Ed. Phillips Bradley. 1945. 2 vols. New York: Vintage, 1954.

Torok, Maria. "Maladie du deuil et fantasme du cadavre exquis." *Revue française de psychanalyse* 32 (1968): 715–33.

Traubel, Horace. *With Walt Whitman in Camden.* 6 vols. [Various places: various publishers], 1908–83.

Traubel, Horace L. et al., eds. *In Re Walt Whitman.* Philadelphia: David McKay, 1893.

van Doren, Mark. "Walt Whitman, Stranger." 1942. *The Poetry and Prose of Walt Whitman.* Ed. Louis Untermeyer. New York: Simon & Schuster, 1949. 1150–60.

Warminski, Andrzej. "Facing Language: Wordsworth's First Poetic Spirits." *Wordsworth and the Production of Poetry.* Ed. Andrzej Warminski and Cynthia Chase. Spec. issue of *Diacritics* 17.4 (1987): 4–17.

Warren, James Perrin. "Dating Whitman's Language Studies." *Walt Whitman Quarterly Review* 1.2 (1983): 1–7.

———. " 'The Free Growth of Metrical Laws': Syntactic Parallelism in 'Song of Myself.' " *Style* 18.1 (1984): 27–42.

———. "The 'Real Grammar': Deverbal Style in 'Song of Myself.' " *American Literature* 56 (1984): 1–16.

———. *Walt Whitman's Language Experiment.* University Park: Pennsylvania State UP, 1990.

———. *Walt Whitman's Language and Style.* Diss. Yale U, 1982. Ann Arbor: UMI, 1983. 8310528.

———. "Whitman as Ghostwriter: The Case of *Rambles Among Words.*" *Walt Whitman Quarterly Review* 2.2 (1984): 22–30.

Weiskel, Thomas. *The Romantic Sublime: Studies in the Structure and Psychology of Transcendence.* Baltimore: Johns Hopkins UP, 1976.

Whitman, Walt. "America's Mightiest Inheritance." *New York Dissected: A Sheaf of Recently Discovered Newspaper Articles by the Author of Leaves of Grass.* Ed. Emory Holloway and Ralph Adimari. New York: Rufus Rockwell Wilson, 1936. 51–65.

———. *The Complete Writings of Walt Whitman.* Ed. Richard Maurice Bucke et al. 10 vols. New York: Putnam, 1902.

———. *The Correspondence.* Ed. Edwin Haviland Miller. 6 vols. New York: New York UP, 1961–77.

———. *Daybooks and Notebooks.* Ed. William White. 3 vols. New York: New York UP, 1978.

———. *Leaves of Grass: Comprehensive Reader's Edition.* Ed. Harold W. Blodgett and Sculley Bradley. New York: New York UP, 1965.

———. *Leaves of Grass: Facsimile Edition of the 1860 Text.* Introd. Roy Harvey Pearce. Ithaca: Cornell UP, 1961.

———. *Leaves of Grass: Facsimile of 1856 Edition.* Introd. Gay Wilson Allen. Norwood, Pa.: Norwood Editions, 1976.

———. *Leaves of Grass: The First (1855) Edition.* Ed. Malcolm Cowley. New York: Viking, 1959.

———. *Leaves of Grass: A Textual Variorum of the Printed Poems.* Ed. Sculley Bradley et al. 3 vols. New York: New York UP, 1980.

———. "Leaves of Grass: A Volume of Poems Just Published." *In Re Walt Whitman.* Ed. Horace L. Traubel et al. Philadelphia: David McKay, 1893. 23–26.

———. *Notebooks and Unpublished Prose Manuscripts.* Ed. Edward F. Grier. 6 vols. New York: New York UP, 1984.

———. *The Poetry and Prose of Walt Whitman.* Ed. Louis Untermeyer. New York: Simon & Schuster, 1949.

———. *Prose Works 1892.* 2 vols. Ed. Floyd Stovall. New York: New York UP, 1963–64.

———. *The Uncollected Poetry and Prose of Walt Whitman.* Ed. Emory Holloway. 2 vols. Garden City, N.Y.: Doubleday, Page, 1921.

———. "Walt Whitman and His Poems." *In Re Walt Whitman.* Ed. Horace L. Traubel et al. Philadelphia: David McKay, 1893. 13–21.

———. *Walt Whitman of the New York Aurora, Editor at Twenty-Two: A Collection of Recently Discovered Writings.* Ed. Joseph J. Rubin and Charles H. Brown. 1950. Westport, Conn.: Greenwood, 1972.

Wilentz, Sean. *Chants Democratic: New York City & the Rise of the American Working Class, 1788–1850.* New York: Oxford UP, 1984.

Wittgenstein, Ludwig. *Philosophical Investigations.* Trans. G. E. M. Anscombe. 3rd ed. New York: Macmillan, 1968.

Wordsworth, William. *Essays upon Epitaphs. The Prose Works of William Wordsworth.* Ed. W. J. B. Owen and Jane Worthington Smyser. London: Clarendon-Oxford UP, 1974. 2:43–119.

———. "A Letter to the Bishop of Landaff on the extraordinary avowal of his Political Principles contained in the Appendix to his late Sermon by a Republican." *The Prose Works of William Wordsworth.* Ed. W. J. B. Owen and Jane Worthington Smyser. London: Clarendon-Oxford UP, 1974. 1: 17–66.

———. *The Prelude: A Parallel Text.* Ed. J. C. Maxwell. 1971. New Haven: Yale UP, 1981.

———. *The Poems.* Ed. John O. Hayden. 2 vols. 1977. New Haven: Yale UP, 1981.

Ziff, Larzar. *Literary Democracy: The Declaration of Cultural Independence in America.* New York: Viking, 1981.

Zweig, Paul. *Walt Whitman: The Making of the Poet.* New York: Basic Books, 1984.

Zwinger, Lynda. *Daughters, Fathers, and the Novel: The Sentimental Romance of Heterosexuality.* Madison: U of Wisconsin P, 1991.

Index

Aarsleff, Hans, 188, 197–99, 209–10, 272 n35, 273 n52, 274 n59, 274 nn66, 69
Abjection, 101, 400
Abraham, Nicolas, 143–45, 160 n70, 468 n8
Abrams, M. H., 275 n73
Adamicism, linguistic, 197–200, 224, 388
Adams, John, 488
Addressee, 370, 436; ambiguous status of, 87, 320–23, 414–15; anonymity of, 319–20, 322–23, 328–29, 356–57, 414–15; election of, 320–21; transformed by apostrophe, 321–23. *See also* Audience
Aggression: in apostrophes, 347–59, 364 n57; against dead, 332–34, 339–40; of dead against living, 334–35, 340–42
Althusser, Louis, 278 n97
Anaphora, 141, 142, 287; in catalogues, 37
Anderson, Quentin, 20, 25 nn5, 8, 27 n21, 28 n31, 51, 53 nn2, 4, 54 nn10, 13, 63–64, 71, 82 nn6, 7, 8, 12, 84 n27, 94, 146, 148, 154 nn1, 4, 155 n8, 156 n18, 157 n32, 159 nn49, 55, 160 n71, 163, 269 nn1, 5, 270 nn11, 14, 16, 271 n23, 364 n57, 413, 468 nn6, 10, 11, 469 n16, 470 nn30, 32, 33, 475 n61, 476 n72
Anonymity: of poet's addressee, 319–20, 322–23, 328–29, 356–57, 414–15; in cultural compacts, 324, 330, 356–57
Anti-institutionalism, 184, 290; Whitman's, 417
Anxiety, 283, 292, 464; about body, 369, 478–79; of influence, 23–24; political,

486, 488–90; about transmission, 329–46; Whitman's personal, 494
Apostrophe: aggression in, 330, 347–58, 364 n57; apparent generosity of, 86–87; archaic space shaped by, 2–3, 110–11, 282, 347; as defense, 237; erotic surplus generated by, 321–23; fading provoked by, 308–9, 347–58; in lyric tradition, 10; mystification and demystification in, 279–84, 292; poet's presence faded by, 308–9; poet's presence produced by, 1–4, 6–8, 10–11, 110–13, 114–15, 120–21, 147, 280–81, 305–16, 319–20, 327–29, 356–57; and political praxis, 365 n57; powers of, attenuated, 306–23, 328–29, 402–3, 408–9, 436, 437, 442–43; presence defined by, 1–6, 110–15; priority in, 289–92, 325–28, 348–58; purloined, 466; in romantic rhetoric, 22; as seductive, 320–23; as self-production, 120–21; symbolic authority exercised by, 291–92, 307, 308–9, 347–58; transformations implied by, 321–23; as utopian, 359; and writing, 11–14, 307, 310, 313, 414; and word magic, 9–10, 16, 35, 114–15, 307–8, 310–11, 326, 463
Arbitrary sign. *See* Name: indicative
Archaic body: occulted by signs, 311, 314, 316; poet's, 309, 311
Archaic resonance: of apostrophe, 2–3, 282, 347; of catalogues, 31, 39, 46–48, 344; of image of voice, 124–25, 293, 302, 325; of *Leaves of Grass*, 293, 298, 325, 346, 416–17, 433, 447; of orality, 124; of performative utterance, 6–7; of poet's presence, 1–6, 9–11, 18, 21–22,